ISSUES FOR DEBATE IN AMERICAN PUBLIC POLICY

18TH EDITION

Sara Miller McCune founded SAGE Publishing in 1965 to support the dissemination of usable knowledge and educate a global community. SAGE publishes more than 1000 journals and over 800 new books each year, spanning a wide range of subject areas. Our growing selection of library products includes archives, data, case studies and video. SAGE remains majority owned by our founder and after her lifetime will become owned by a charitable trust that secures the company's continued independence.

Los Angeles | London | New Delhi | Singapore | Washington DC | Melbourne

ISSUES FOR DEBATE IN AMERICAN PUBLIC POLICY

SELECTIONS FROM *CQ RESEARCHER*

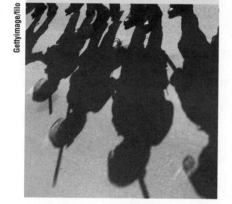

Gettyimage/filo

18TH EDITION

$SAGE | CQPRESS

FOR INFORMATION:

CQ Press
An Imprint of SAGE Publications, Inc.
2455 Teller Road
Thousand Oaks, California 91320
E-mail: order@sagepub.com

SAGE Publications Ltd.
1 Oliver's Yard
55 City Road
London EC1Y 1SP
United Kingdom

SAGE Publications India Pvt. Ltd.
B 1/I 1 Mohan Cooperative Industrial Area
Mathura Road, New Delhi 110 044
India

SAGE Publications Asia-Pacific Pte. Ltd.
3 Church Street
#10-04 Samsung Hub
Singapore 049483

Printed in the United States of America

ISBN 978-1-5063-6880-1

Library of Congress Control Number: 2017932268

Acquisitions Editor: Carrie Brandon
Editorial Assistant: Duncan Marchbank
Production Editor: Kelly DeRosa
Copyeditor: Kim Husband
Typesetter: C&M Digitals (P) Ltd.
Cover Designer: Michael Dubowe
Marketing Manager: Jennifer Jones

17 18 19 20 21 10 9 8 7 6 5 4 3 2 1

Contents

Annotated Contents

ENVIRONMENT

Coal Industry's Future

Most U.S. coal is used to generate electricity, but it gives off carbon dioxide and other pollutants, and the industry is getting crushed as power plants turn to cheap, cleaner natural gas and zero-emissions solar and wind power. Recent environmental regulations of power plant emissions are encouraging the shift. Hundreds of coal-fired power plants have closed since 2010, and U.S. coal production has fallen 40 percent from its 2008 peak. Most American coal-mining companies have sought bankruptcy protection in the past 2 years. Environmentalists want coal-fired electricity plants phased out by 2030, saying they are too costly to operate and too harmful to the environment. But the industry says shutting more coal-fired plants could threaten the reliability of the power grid and that coal-generated electricity is cleaner than decades ago and relatively cheap. Meanwhile, depressed mining communities want increased federal aid to help unemployed miners find new jobs, while industry and coal-mining states are challenging environmental regulations in court.

Managing Western Lands

Armed protesters who occupied Oregon's Malheur National Wildlife Refuge in January 2016 focused national attention on local anger over federal management of public land in Western states. But for several years, a quieter rebellion has occurred in the West, where the federal government owns nearly half the land. In 2012, Utah enacted a law demanding that the federal government relinquish more than 31 million acres of public land in the state, and Arizona's governor vetoed a similar bill. Five Western states have enacted laws to study the issue. Proponents of land transfers say federal mismanagement of public lands contributes to catastrophic wildfires and costs logging, ranching, and mining jobs. But opponents say courts settled the federal land ownership issue long ago and that the federal government does a good job of managing public lands under often-conflicting mandates, such as conserving lands and facilitating resource extraction. Moreover, the opponents say if states controlled federal lands they would increase commercial development or sell land to private interests.

Drinking Water Safety

While water-quality experts deem most of the nation's drinking water safe, the recent crisis over lead-tainted water in Flint, Mich., dramatized the problems that plague communities nationwide: Lead and other toxic substances continue to pose a threat, and government agencies responsible for monitoring water safety sometimes fail to protect the public. Investigations conducted since the Flint crisis came to light last year have found that thousands of water systems nationwide have failed to meet federal safety standards for lead and other harmful substances. Moreover, environmentalists warn that tens of thousands of industrial pollutants and pharmaceutical compounds slip through water-treatment systems without being tested or regulated. The Environmental Protection Agency sets water-safety standards, but the sourcing, treatment, and distribution of water is left to local utilities, some dealing with polluted water sources, old pipes, or shrinking budgets. Cost estimates to fix the aging U.S. water infrastructure include $30 billion to replace lead pipes and $1 trillion to upgrade water mains.

BUSINESS AND ECONOMY
The Gig Economy

Enabled by the digital revolution, employers increasingly are outsourcing work to contractors and self-employed or part-time workers, many working offsite thanks to apps and Wi-Fi. Supporters of the so-called gig economy say it gives workers flexibility and freedom to work anytime and anywhere and allows struggling companies to survive and healthy firms to compete globally. But labor unions say outsourcing exploits workers and undermines the economy by allowing companies to replace full-time employees with lower-paid workers without guaranteed hours, income, or benefits. And millions of laid-off workers must cobble together multiple jobs as independent contractors. On-demand gig workers, such as Uber drivers, are protesting their lack of benefits, while Uber lobbies local and state governments to exempt it from "old economy" wage and labor laws. Recently, however, some employers have begun hiring full-time employees with full benefits again, largely because of the high turnover rates and recruitment costs associated with the gig economy.

Jailing Debtors

The United States outlawed the practice of imprisoning people for failure or inability to pay their debts more than two centuries ago, and several Supreme Court rulings have supported that prohibition. Yet local courts are jailing people for debts stemming from minor infractions such as unpaid parking tickets without regard to their ability to pay. Moreover, to cover rising administrative expenses, many courts are making defendants pay for public defenders, probation supervisors, and jail cells—costs that traditionally have been a state responsibility—and people unable to pay are locked up. Local officials say defendants who use the criminal justice system should shoulder its costs. But the Department of Justice is urging the adoption of a more equitable punishment system, and civil rights advocates charge that jailing debtors criminalizes poverty, disproportionately affects minorities, and leads to a modern form of debtors' prisons. Meanwhile, reformists are advocating an overhaul of the bail system, which can leave people without money behind bars while awaiting trial.

RIGHTS AND LIBERTIES
Populism and Party Politics

Populism—the deep public mistrust of political parties and other so-called "establishment" institutions—is disrupting traditional politics in the United States as well as abroad. Analysts and academics say Donald Trump demonstrated populism's reach by winning the Republican presidential nomination, while Vermont Sen. Bernie

Sanders waged what often was described as a left-wing populist challenge to Hillary Clinton for the Democratic nomination. Populist movements have spread across Europe with the rise of antiestablishment politicians in several countries, underscored by the United Kingdom's June "Brexit" vote to leave the 28-nation European Union. But the meaning of populism has become elastic, as it is applied to a wide range of politicians and movements. Today's populists are amplifying many of the movement's earlier traditions through heavy use of Twitter, Facebook, and other social media to launch venomous "us-versus-them" attacks on opponents. The new media warfare has led some experts to wonder if populism is compatible with what they think should be a sober and deliberative political process.

Campaign Finance

After four decades of court decisions lifting restrictions on campaign spending, Americans are going to the polls this year in the most expensive presidential campaign in U.S. history, financed mainly by a handful of wealthy individuals and business and labor groups. Public outrage over the big spending fuels some of the popularity of GOP billionaire Donald Trump's largely self-financed campaign and that of Democratic Sen. Bernie Sanders of Vermont, who is supported mostly by small individual donors. But money did not help the top spender in the Republican presidential primaries: Former Florida Gov. Jeb Bush abandoned his well-financed candidacy amid weak voter support. Conversely, Sanders ran an unexpectedly strong campaign against deep-pocketed former Secretary of State Hillary Clinton. Stymied by GOP congressional opposition and partisan gridlock on the Federal Election Commission, opponents of big-dollar politics are successfully pushing some states and cities to rein in election spending. But advocates of less regulation say limiting money in politics infringes on free speech.

Racial Profiling

Civil liberties and minority groups are pressuring police departments to eliminate racial and ethnic profiling in pedestrian and traffic stops, while police groups and some experts insist the complaints about the practice are exaggerated. African Americans have long complained of traffic stops seemingly for "driving while black," and many—including President Obama and Oprah Winfrey—said recently they have felt profiled by store clerks for "shopping while black." Hispanics and Muslims also feel singled out as suspected immigration violators or terrorists. Two big law enforcement agencies—the New York City Police Department and the Maricopa County Sheriff's Office, which covers Phoenix—are under court order to eliminate the practice.

SOCIAL POLICY
Social Security

Social Security has guaranteed an income for retirees, their survivors, and people with disabilities for more than 80 years. But the landmark New Deal program is paying out more in benefits than it collects in payroll taxes, and the problem is forecast to get worse. As millions of Baby Boomers—born between 1946 and 1964—retire, the increasing demands on Social Security threaten to overwhelm the system. Some experts say the $2.8 trillion Social Security trust fund will run out of money within a generation without major changes. Among the proposals: raise payroll taxes, reduce benefits, or shift some Social Security money into the stock market. But others reject major reforms and contend that minor adjustments, such as increasing payroll taxes on wealthier workers, would keep the system solvent. Democratic and Republican presidential hopefuls differ sharply over whether to drastically change the system, tweak it, or even expand it to cover more low-income Americans. Even after President Trump's election, the Social Security debate is expected to persist.

Future of the Middle Class

The percentage of middle-income U.S. households has declined significantly in recent years, leading some economists, policy experts, and politicians to argue that the American middle class is in deep trouble—or even disappearing. Globalization, automation, and declining union membership have shrunk the manufacturing workforce—historically a bulwark of the middle class—and an increasing share of the nation's wealth has accrued to the richest Americans. Many experts say achieving middle-class status today is unlikely without a college education and entry into the white-collar work world—a stark turnaround from the booming post–World War II years, when a stable blue-collar job anchored millions of families in a middle-class lifestyle. Still, some experts call fears of a middle-class decline overblown, saying poor Americans who face far tougher conditions are being overlooked. Presidential candidates in both parties responded to middle-class discontent, with Democrats promising to cut college costs and Republicans proposing changes in the tax code.

Student Debt

A majority of college graduates are leaving school owing more than $25,000, and nearly 7 million have defaulted on their student loans. Student debt nationwide totals almost $1.3 trillion—up 350 percent since 2005. Many experts say the rise is due partly to growth in enrollment, expanded eligibility for federal loans, and predatory lending. But others say student debt is growing mainly because of skyrocketing tuition. Officials at public colleges blame tuition hikes on declining state support, which fell by about 20 percent between 2001 and 2015. But critics say colleges are spending too much on administration, expensive intercollegiate athletic programs, and academic programs with weak demand. Others say the easy availability of student loans encourages colleges to raise prices. Student debt became a major issue in the 2016 presidential campaign, with Democratic candidates promoting free college tuition and Republican candidate Donald Trump—now president-elect—proposing an income-based repayment plan and debt forgiveness after 15 years.

HEALTH
Prescription Drug Costs

Recent high-profile Senate hearings have highlighted a phenomenon many Americans know well: the soaring price of prescription drugs, some needed to keep patients alive. New blockbusters routinely cost more than $100,000 for a course of treatment, and similar "me too" drugs for the same conditions later launch at almost identical prices. Drug manufacturers blame the rising cost of research and development, but critics blame excessive profit seeking and exorbitant marketing budgets. Meanwhile, prices for some common,

decades-old generics also are rising as competition in that part of the industry collapses. The price of the antibiotic tetracycline, for example, rose more than 7,500 percent in 2 years. A majority of Americans say keeping drug prices affordable should be the top national health care priority. To help slow the rising costs, states are introducing bills and ballot measures to require drug makers to disclose their actual costs and, in some cases, cap prices.

Opioid Crisis

Overdoses of opioid drugs, including powerful prescription painkillers and heroin, have killed almost 250,000 Americans since 2000, leading many experts to compare the crisis to the HIV and AIDS epidemics. Opioid addiction, once largely an urban minority affliction, has spread to every corner of the United States, hitting young adults and white people especially hard. One study has found that more adults use prescription painkillers than cigarettes, smokeless tobacco, and cigars combined. As opioid abuse grows, propelled in part by a flood of cheap heroin from Mexico, alarmed authorities are trying to figure out how to fight back. In July, President Obama signed a bill encouraging the expansion of treatment programs and the development of alternatives to opioid painkillers. But many experts are divided over how best to help opioid addicts. Some advocate providing them with limited doses to control their addiction, while others say that such an approach would make the crisis worse.

Vaccine Controversies

Two centuries of scientific evidence have proven conclusively that vaccines can prevent deadly diseases, but a small, vocal group of skeptics—aided by high-profile celebrities—continues to fight mandatory immunization, especially of babies and school-age children. More than 90 percent of Americans immunize their children against diseases such as measles, diphtheria, and whooping cough, but the remainder either reject immunization or don't get the vaccinations on schedule. Public health officials say refusing to follow vaccine protocols allows diseases to spread rapidly, as happened in December 2014, when a measles outbreak began at Disneyland and spread to seven states. But opponents of mandatory vaccination contend that the escalating number of vaccines poses safety concerns and that requiring parents to immunize their children impinges on parental rights and personal freedom. The conflict extends beyond school-age children to include mandatory immunization against the influenza virus for health care workers and military requirements that recruits be vaccinated against yellow fever, anthrax, and other dangers.

NATIONAL SECURITY

Closing Guantanamo

President Obama has tried for years to close the U.S. military-run detention facility at Guantanamo Bay, Cuba, and incarcerate terrorism suspects in the United States. Critics of Guantanamo say it serves as a potent propaganda tool for the Islamic State, which makes the prisoners it captures wear orange jumpsuits nearly identical to those worn by Guantanamo inmates. But Republicans and some Democrats have fought to keep the facility open, contending that transferring detainees to U.S. soil would be dangerous. The prison has drawn the opposition of many U.S. allies, who cite allegations of torture there. Democratic presidential nominee Hillary Clinton wants to close the prison, whilst then-Republican nominee President Trump vowed to expand its use. The Obama administration has stopped sending new prisoners to Guantanamo and is steadily reducing the population—now 61 inmates—by transferring detainees to the custody of U.S. allies. National security analysts say the Guantanamo controversy underscores the need to reform how suspects captured in the terrorism fight are tried in court.

Protecting the Power Grid

The United States is spending more on cybersecurity today than ever before but is experiencing a growing number of cyberattacks on the power grid and other targets. A Nebraska-based consortium of small municipal utilities, for example, recently detected nearly 4 million hacking attempts in one 8-week period. The electric grid—a patchwork of more than 300,000 miles of transmission lines and 9,200 generating stations—also is vulnerable to attacks by gun- or bomb-wielding terrorists or saboteurs. Although some security experts say a massive, long-term blackout is unlikely, industry and government officials are working to protect the grid and improve coordination between agencies and utilities. In February, President Obama announced a plan to help government agencies, businesses, and the public prevent and respond to attacks. But securing the grid against attack is difficult, and many analysts say the task is becoming harder as the use of renewable energy and cloud-linked "smart" energy-efficiency technology grows.

Preface

Does populism undermine confidence in government? Is keeping Guantanamo open helping fuel global terrorism? Does income stagnation mean the middle class is in decline? These questions—and many more—are at the heart of American public policy. How can instructors best engage students with these crucial issues? We feel students need objective yet provocative examinations of these issues to understand how they affect citizens today and will for years to come. This annual collection aims to promote in-depth discussion, facilitate further research, and help readers formulate their own positions on crucial issues. Get your students talking both inside and outside the classroom about *Issues for Debate in American Public Policy*.

This 18th edition includes 16 up-to-date reports by *CQ Researcher*, an award-winning weekly policy brief that brings complicated issues down to earth. Each report chronicles and analyzes executive, legislative, and judicial activities at all levels of government. This collection is divided into six diverse policy areas: environment, business and economy, rights and liberties, social policy, health, and national security—to cover a range of issues found in most American government and public policy courses.

CQ RESEARCHER

CQ Researcher was founded in 1923 as *Editorial Research Reports* and was sold primarily to newspapers as a research tool. The magazine was renamed and redesigned in 1991 as *CQ Researcher*. Today, students are its primary audience. While still used by hundreds of journalists and newspapers, many of which reprint portions of the reports, the *Researcher*'s main subscribers are now high school, college and public libraries. In 2002, *Researcher* won the American Bar Association's coveted Silver Gavel award for magazine excellence for a series of nine reports on civil liberties and other legal issues.

Researcher writers—all highly experienced journalists—sometimes compare the experience of writing a *Researcher* report to drafting a college term paper. Indeed, there are many similarities. Each report is as long as many term papers—about 11,000 words—and is written by one person without any significant outside help. One of the key differences is that writers interview leading experts, scholars, and government officials for each issue.

Like students, writers begin the creative process by choosing a topic. Working with the *Researcher*'s editors, the writer identifies a controversial subject that has important public policy implications. After a topic is selected, the writer embarks on 1 to 2 weeks of intense research. Newspaper and magazine articles are clipped or downloaded, books are ordered, and information is gathered from a wide variety of sources, including interest groups, universities, and the government. Once the writers are well informed, they develop a detailed outline and begin the interview process. Each report requires a minimum of 10 to 15 interviews with academics, officials, lobbyists, and people working in the field. Only after all interviews are completed does the writing begin.

CHAPTER FORMAT

Each issue of *CQ Researcher*, and therefore each selection in this book, is structured in the same way. Each begins with an overview, which briefly summarizes the areas that will be explored in greater detail in the rest of the chapter. The next section chronicles important and current debates on the topic under discussion and is structured around a number of key questions, such as "Is the U.S. power grid vulnerable to major attack?" and "Do high development costs justify soaring drug prices?" These questions are usually the subject of much debate among practitioners and scholars in the field. Hence, the answers presented are never conclusive but detail the range of opinion on the topic.

Next, the "Background" section provides a history of the issue being examined. This retrospective covers important legislative measures, executive actions, and court decisions that illustrate how current policy has evolved. Then the "Current Situation" section examines contemporary policy issues, legislation under consideration, and legal action being taken. Each selection concludes with an "Outlook" section, which addresses possible regulation, court rulings, and initiatives from Capitol Hill and the White House over the next 5 to 10 years.

Each report contains features that augment the main text: two to three sidebars that examine issues related to the topic at hand, a pro-versus-con debate between two experts, a chronology of key dates and events, and an annotated bibliography detailing major sources used by the writer.

ACKNOWLEDGMENTS

We wish to thank many people for helping make this collection a reality. Thomas J. Billitteri, managing editor of *CQ Researcher*, gave us his enthusiastic support and cooperation as we developed this 18th edition. He and his talented editors and writers have amassed a first-class library of *Researcher* reports, and we are fortunate to have access to that rich cache. We also thankfully acknowledge the advice and feedback from current readers and are gratified by their satisfaction with the book.

Some readers may be learning about *CQ Researcher* for the first time. We expect that many readers will want regular access to this excellent weekly research tool. For subscription information or a no-obligation free trial of *Researcher*, please contact CQ Press at www.cqpress.com or toll free at 1-866-4CQ-PRESS (1-866-427-7737).

We hope that you will be pleased by the 18th edition of *Issues for Debate in American Public Policy*. We welcome your feedback and suggestions for future editions. Please direct comments to Carrie Brandon, Senior Acquisitions Editor for Public Administration and Public Policy, CQ Press, an imprint of SAGE, 2600 Virginia Avenue, NW, Suite 600, Washington, DC 20037; or send e-mail to *Carrie.Brandon@sagepub.com*.

—*The Editors of CQ Press*

Contributor Bios

Jill U. Adams writes a health column for *The Washington Post* and reports on health, biomedical research, and environmental issues for magazines such as *Audubon*, *Scientific American*, and *Science*. She holds a Ph.D. in pharmacology from Emory University.

Leslie Allen is a Washington, D.C.-based writer who specializes in science, the environment and natural resources. Her articles have appeared in *The New York Times*, *National Geographic*, *The Washington Post Magazine*, *Smithsonian*, and other publications. As a long-time staff writer for *National Geographic*, she reported from five continents. She is also the author of two books and coauthor of two dozen others. Raised in South America, she is a graduate of Bryn Mawr College.

Kevin Begos is a freelance journalist who writes about science, energy, and the environment. He is a contributor to *A Field Guide for Science Writers* and a former Associated Press correspondent, Knight Science Journalism Fellow at MIT, and Environmental Law Fellow at Vermont Law School. His work has appeared in *Scientific American's 60-Second-Science*, *The New York Times*, and many other newspapers.

Christina Hoag is a freelance journalist in Los Angeles. She previously worked for *The Miami Herald* and the Associated Press and was a correspondent in Latin America. She is the coauthor of *Peace in the Hood: Working With Gang Members to End the Violence*.

David Hosansky is a freelance writer in the Denver area. He previously was a senior writer at *CQ Weekly* and the *Florida Times-Union* in Jacksonville, where he was twice nominated for a Pulitzer Prize. His previous *CQ Researcher* reports include "Wind Power" and "Distracted Driving."

Kenneth Jost has written more than 160 reports for *CQ Researcher* since 1991 on topics ranging from legal affairs and social policy to national security and international relations. He is the author of *The Supreme Court Yearbook* and *Supreme Court From A to Z* (both CQ Press). He is an honors graduate of Harvard College and Georgetown Law School, where he teaches media law as an adjunct professor. He also writes the blog Jost on Justice (http://joston justice.blogspot.com). His previous reports include "Police Misconduct" (2012) and "Policing the Police" (2000).

Peter Katel is a *CQ Researcher* contributing writer who previously reported on Haiti and Latin America for *Time* and *Newsweek* and covered the Southwest for newspapers in New Mexico. He has received several journalism awards, including the Bartolomé Mitre Award for coverage of drug trafficking from the Inter-American Press Association. He holds an A.B. in university studies from the University of New Mexico. His recent reports include "Police Tactics" and "Central American Gangs."

Jane Fullerton Lemons is a freelance writer from Northern Virginia with more than 25 years of journalism experience. A former Washington bureau chief for the *Arkansas Democrat- Gazette* and *Farm Journal* magazine, she has covered the White House, Congress, food policy, and health care. She is currently seeking a master's degree in creative nonfiction from Goucher College in Towson, Md.

Barbara Mantel is a freelance writer in New York City. She was a 2012 Kiplinger Fellow and has won several journalism awards, including the National Press Club's Best Consumer Journalism Award and the Front Page Award from the Newswomen's Club of New York for her Nov. 1, 2009, *CQ Global Researcher* report "Terrorism and the Internet." She holds a B.A. in history and economics from the University of Virginia and an M.A. in economics from Northwestern University.

Patrick Marshall, a freelance policy and technology writer in Seattle, is a technology columnist for *The Seattle Times* and *Government Computer News*. He has a bachelor's degree in anthropology from the University of California, Santa Cruz, and a master's degree in international studies from the Fletcher School of Law and Diplomacy at Tufts University.

Eugene L. Meyer, a former *Washington Post* reporter and editor, has contributed reports on media ethics and the rise of citizen journalism to the Center for International Media Assistance. In addition, he has written articles for, among other publications, *The New York Times* and *U.S. News & World Report* and is editor of the quarterly *B'nai B'rith Magazine*. His most recent book, *Chesapeake Country—Second Edition*, was published in March 2015.

Chuck McCutcheon is an assistant managing editor of *CQ Researcher*. He has been a reporter and editor for *Congressional Quarterly* and Newhouse News Service and is coauthor of the 2012 and 2014 editions of *The Almanac of American Politics* and *Dog Whistles, Walk-Backs and Washington Handshakes: Decoding the Jargon, Slang and Bluster of American Political Speech*. He also has written books on climate change and nuclear waste.

Tom Price, a contributing writer for *CQ Researcher*, is a Washington-based freelance journalist whose focus includes politics and government. Previously, he was a correspondent in the Cox Newspapers Washington Bureau and chief politics writer for *The Dayton Daily News* and *The* (Dayton) *Journal Herald*. He is author or coauthor of five books including, with former U.S. Rep. Tony Hall (D-Ohio), *Changing the Face of Hunger: One Man's Story of How Liberals, Conservatives, Democrats, Republicans and People of Faith Are Joining Forces to Help the Hungry, the Poor and the Oppressed*. His previous *CQ Researcher* reports have examined political polarization and social media in campaigns.

Issues for Debate in American Public Policy

18th Edition

Former New York City Mayor Michael Bloomberg has given $50 million to the Sierra Club's Beyond Coal campaign, a movement to eliminate coal-fueled electricity. "You'd think the politicians would at least care about the air they breathe themselves," the media mogul said.

From *CQ Researcher,*
June 17, 2016.

1

Coal Industry's Future

Barbara Mantel

Since 1968, Gail Japp has lived in Gillette, Wyo., the heart of the resource-rich Powder River Basin. "I've seen the oil boom come and go. I've seen good times and bad times, but it's never been this bad," said Japp, one of 235 coal miners laid off by St. Louis-based Peabody Energy in March.[1]

"What in the world am I gonna do? I'm single. I'm 64. I have a mortgage. Am I gonna lose my house?" she asked. Japp can't leave Gillette to find a new job because her 90-year-old father lives there, and she babysits her two grandchildren, she said.[2]

Until a few years ago, energy dollars had made Gillette a boomtown, with high paying jobs and strong economic growth, said City Administrator Carter Napier. "It is an absolute and complete turnaround right now. We have food trucks coming to our community to provide basic supplies for life," he said, as first the oil industry and now coal has contracted.[3]

The vast majority of U.S. coal is used to fuel electric power plants, but greater energy efficiency, competition from cheap — and cleaner — natural gas, falling costs for solar and wind power and new environmental regulations of power plant emissions are crushing the coal industry. Eight years ago, coal generated half of the nation's electricity. Now it generates a third.[4]

Coal-fired power plants are being shuttered, U.S. coal production has fallen 40 percent from its 2008 peak, and in the past two years most U.S. coal mining companies have filed for Chapter 11 bankruptcy protection. Japp's former employer, Peabody Energy, the world's largest private-sector coal company, filed in April.[5]

48 States Cut Coal Use for Power

Between 2007 and 2015, coal consumption fell in every coal-consuming state except Nebraska and Alaska, with the biggest declines in Indiana, Ohio, Pennsylvania and Georgia. Idaho, Vermont and Rhode Island do not use coal to generate power.

Change in Power Sector Coal Demand, 2007-2015, by State

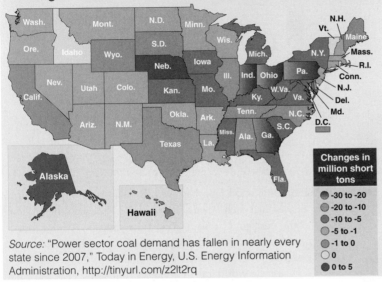

Changes in million short tons
- -30 to -20
- -20 to -10
- -10 to -5
- -5 to -1
- -1 to 0
- 0
- 0 to 5

Source: "Power sector coal demand has fallen in nearly every state since 2007," Today in Energy, U.S. Energy Information Administration, http://tinyurl.com/z2lt2rq

Environmentalists are pushing for the closure of all remaining U.S. coal-fired power plants by 2030, saying they no longer make economic sense and create too much pollution. But mining and power companies warn that shutting more plants could threaten the reliability of the power grid and defend coal-generated electricity as relatively cheap and cleaner than decades ago. Meanwhile, depressed mining communities are demanding federal aid, and industry and coal-mining states are challenging the Obama administration's environmental regulations in court.

"We've got to fight for all we're worth to protect the industry that is the backbone of our state," said John O'Neal, a member of the West Virginia House of Delegates. Coal "is our number one natural resource, and we just can't let that go."[6]

But environmentalists and their supporters say the coal industry is rightfully fading. "You'd think the politicians would at least care about the air they breathe themselves," said media mogul and former New York City Mayor Michael Bloomberg, who has given $50 million to the Beyond Coal campaign of the Sierra Club, an Oakland, Calif.-based environmental organization spearheading a movement to eliminate coal-fueled electricity.[7]

The popular image of a coal miner may be of a soot-covered worker in Appalachia emerging from a deep underground shaft. But these days, only about 25 percent of the nation's coal comes from Appalachia, either from its underground mines or mountaintops that have been blasted away to expose the black rock. Forty percent of the nation's coal now comes from Wyoming, in part because environmental regulations encourage the use of Western low-sulfur coal, found close to the surface and uncovered and removed by large machines.[8]

This shift has taken a decades-long toll on coal jobs in Appalachia. For example, the number of coal-related jobs in Harlan County, Ky., declined from more than 3,000 in 1988 to fewer than 1,000 in 2014, the last year of available government data.[9] Still, 45,000 people worked for coal operators in Appalachia in 2014, compared to fewer than 7,000 in Wyoming. That's because mining the more difficult-to-extract coal in Appalachia is labor intensive.[10]

Now all of coal mining is losing jobs, from Appalachia to Colorado to Wyoming. A total of 68,000 people worked in coal mining in 2015, a drop of 19 percent from the year before, according to the Bureau of Labor Statistics.[11] And other industries have not replaced lost coal jobs. "The community is not only suffering. It's dying," said Harlan County resident and former mining company driver Chester Napier, 75.[12]

Environmentalists support giving federal aid to coal communities, and in November, Hillary Clinton, the presumptive Democratic presidential nominee, announced a $30 billion aid plan.[13] In contrast, Donald Trump, the presumptive Republican nominee, promised to rescind environmental rules and revive the coal sector and its jobs.

"We're going to bring back the coal industry, save the coal industry," Trump said in late May. "I love those people."[14]

But energy analysts say that's probably impossible, given market forces, particularly cheap natural gas, which emits less carbon dioxide than coal. The U.S. Energy Information Administration projects that this year, for the first time, natural gas will generate more of the nation's electricity, at 34 percent, than coal, at less than 31 percent. The shift is happening in part because natural gas prices have been falling since 2009, as energy companies flooded the market with gas extracted through hydraulic fracking from underground shale deposits.[15]

To a lesser extent, coal is also taking a hit from renewable energy. Use of wind and solar power has increased significantly since 2007: They now supply nearly 7 percent of the country's electricity, the result of "federal tax credits, state-level mandates and technology improvements," said government analysts.[16] Those improvements have driven down the cost of wind power per megawatt hour by 61 percent between 2009 and 2015, and the cost of large solar panel arrays fell by 82 percent during the same period.[17]

Meanwhile, the United States has become more energy efficient. The annual demand for electricity has remained flat since 2007, even as the economy, adjusted for inflation, has grown 10 percent.[18]

The Obama administration has issued environmental rules to protect water quality from mining, limit toxic metal emissions from power plants and reduce carbon dioxide pollution. "Over the past eight years and after a huge amount of advocacy, a lot of egregious regulatory loopholes that the coal industry has enjoyed have been closed," says Mary Anne Hitt, director of the Sierra Club's Beyond Coal campaign.

The coal industry sees things differently. "We've been very disadvantaged by this administration's regulatory policies," says Luke Popovich, spokesperson for the Washington-based National Mining Association.

Demand for Coal Falling

The amount of coal used to generate electric power in the United States fell 29 percent, from a high of more than 1 billion tons in 2007 to an estimated 739 million tons in 2015. Coal use is declining because of improved energy efficiency, stricter environmental regulation of coal-fired power plant emissions and falling prices for other fuel sources, such as natural gas, solar and wind power.

Coal Used to Generate U.S. Electricity (in millions of tons)

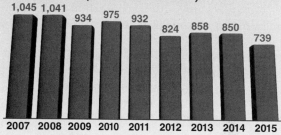

2007	2008	2009	2010	2011	2012	2013	2014	2015
1,045	1,041	934	975	932	824	858	850	739

Sources: "Power sector coal demand has fallen in nearly every state since 2007," Today in Energy, U.S. Energy Information Administration, April 28, 2016, http://tinyurl.com/z2lt2rq; "Coal Consumption by Sector," http://tinyurl.com/zmpktd4

Of all the recent regulations, the Mercury and Air Toxics Standards for Power Plants, promulgated by the Environmental Protection Agency (EPA) in 2012, may have had the biggest impact so far. The standards cut power plant emissions of mercury, arsenic and other toxic pollutants. The EPA gave coal-fired plants and the nation's relatively few oil-fired plants until April 2015 to comply, although some plants got one- or two-year extensions. Many power companies chose to shut down their oldest, smallest and dirtiest coal plants rather than invest in pollution-reducing technology, especially where state regulators did not approve rate increases to cover investment costs. Even some larger plants have been shut.

"It was just not cost effective to retrofit them," says Paul Bailey, head of federal affairs and policy at the Washington-based American Coalition for Clean Coal Electricity, whose members include coal mining, railroad and power companies.

The administration's Clean Power Plan may have an even greater impact on the coal industry. It would require states to devise plans for power companies to significantly reduce emissions of carbon dioxide, the primary greenhouse gas contributing to climate change, starting in 2022. However, the Supreme Court has issued a stay while it's being challenged in court.

To make matters worse, coal mining companies went deep into debt to expand capacity in anticipation of growing offshore demand that never materialized. The United States sells about 10 percent of its coal abroad, mostly to Europe and Asia. But coal exports have dropped precipitously since setting a record in 2012. Overseas demand has slid for some of the same reasons it has in the United States, and a strong dollar has made U.S. coal more expensive compared to coal from Australia, Indonesia, Colombia, Russia and South Africa.[19]

Against this background, here are questions that mining and power companies, coal communities, environmentalists and government officials are debating:

Should all coal-fired power plants eventually close?

Most U.S. coal-fired power plants were built between 1950 and 1990, a period of rapid growth in electricity demand.[20] However, since early 2010, 236 coal plants have either shut down or announced a retirement date, leaving 287 remaining, according to the Sierra Club.[21]

The environmental organization would like to see those plants shuttered, too, creating a coal-free electricity grid by 2030. "We think that's what the climate science calls for, and we think that's a time frame in which we can have plenty of clean alternatives," says the Sierra Club's Hitt.

Climate warming isn't environmentalists' only concern. The EPA says pollution from coal-generated electricity is linked to cancer, respiratory illness, heart attacks and nervous system damage.[22]

But Bailey of the American Coalition for Clean Coal Electricity says most remaining coal-fired power plants now meet the EPA's 2012 standards for air toxics and mercury, a neurotoxin. And they emit much less sulfur dioxide and nitrogen oxides, contributors to soot, smog and acid rain. Congress required that such emissions be reduced when it passed the 1970 Clean Air Act and subsequent amendments.

"A kilowatt hour of electricity generated from the coal fleet today is 92 percent cleaner than it was in the 1970s. People forget that," says Bailey. The power industry has spent more than $100 billion on advanced air pollution controls since 1970, according Bailey's organization.[23]

But none of that makes coal anything close to clean, says Shannon Fisk, an attorney at Earthjustice, an environmental law organization in San Francisco. "The amount of air pollution that's produced by coal plants is still significant," Fisk says. "And they are the largest source of carbon emissions in the country." Fossil fuel-fired electric power plants, primarily coal, are responsible for the greatest share of emissions of the greenhouse gas in the United States, at 37 percent; transportation, at 31 percent, is next, according to government calculations.[24]

But the National Mining Association's Popovich says climate change is a global issue, and taking coal out of the U.S. energy mix isn't going to significantly reduce worldwide carbon emissions. China accounts for half of the world's coal use, followed by the United States and India, which together account for about a fifth according to government data.[25]

"Why don't we [the government] put a comparable effort into the development of technology that makes coal more socially responsible to use," such as ultra-supercritical combustion? asks Popovich. Ultra-supercritical combustion makes burning coal more efficient so it produces about 15 percent less carbon dioxide than the current coal power fleet, says Jeffrey Phillips, head of advanced coal power generation research at the Electric Power Research Institute, a scientific organization whose members include electric utilities and government agencies.

But there are only two ultra-supercritical coal plants in the United States. "Right now in the U.S., natural gas-fired combined cycle power plants can beat any new coal power plant in terms of initial capital cost and ongoing operating cost," says Phillips in an email. And the new state-of-the art coal plants would still emit twice the carbon dioxide as natural gas, he says.

One of the industry's main arguments for keeping coal-fired power plants running is that natural gas prices are unlikely to stay low forever.

"Let's say there are policies put in place that limit fracking so there is less natural gas," says Bailey. (New York state and cities and counties in California, Colorado and elsewhere have banned fracking over concerns that chemicals used in fracking may contaminate groundwater and that fracking can cause earthquakes.[26]) Natural gas prices would climb, and without coal to fall back on, electricity rates would climb as well, he says. A number of other unforeseen developments could also cause natural gas prices to rise, so "we need diverse sources of electricity," he says.

Mark Haggerty, an analyst with the nonpartisan research group, Headwaters Economics, in Bozeman, Mont., says he sympathizes with the need to move to cleaner fuels but says industry has a point. Transitioning to natural gas is a long-term investment, he says. "We will become dependent on natural gas, and its price is volatile, more so than coal."

Fisk says, "Diversity should not be used as an excuse to prop up a fuel source that simply isn't competitive anymore." Power companies want to invest to keep their coal-fired plants operating because the 32 states that regulate electricity generation typically guarantee power companies about a 10 percent return on any regulator-approved capital investment, says Fisk. When that happens, consumers pay more for electricity.

"How much should they be allowed to milk these old plants?" asks Fisk, who, like Sierra Club attorneys, spends a lot of time trying to persuade state regulators to nix capital investments, such as scrubbers to reduce mercury pollution, in aging coal plants. And if plants can't meet pollution standards, they must close. Switching to wind, solar and some natural gas is cheaper for customers, says Fisk.

But Popovich says the economy suffers as coal disappears from the energy mix. Jobs in mining, coal transportation and mining equipment manufacturing pay, on average, more than $80,000 a year, he says. "One employee can support a family on that, particularly in rural areas where coal is mined," Popovich says. "Annual wages . . . in the renewable industry, they're not near what they are in the fossil energy industry."

Environmental groups support a variety of aid proposals in Congress and from President Obama to help communities transition away from coal.

Is the EPA's plan to reduce CO_2 emissions from power plants legal?

Last August, the EPA released the final version of the administration's Clean Power Plan, which sets state-by-state goals for reducing carbon emissions from existing power plants. States have eight years to meet those goals, starting in 2022. If all goes according to

The A & G Coal Corp. dynamites an Appalachian mountaintop in Wise County, Va., in 2012. Today, only about 25 percent of the nation's coal comes from Appalachia. Forty percent now comes from Wyoming, in part because environmental regulations encourage the use of Western low-sulfur coal, found close to the surface.

Photo by Mario Tama/Getty Images

plan, U.S. carbon pollution from the power sector will fall 32 percent below 2005 levels in 2030.[27] (It has already fallen 22 percent since 2005 as coal plants have closed.)[28]

The Clean Power Plan "will give our kids and grandkids the cleaner, safer future they deserve," said EPA Administrator Gina McCarthy.[29]

The plan is central to Obama's international commitment to address global warming. In April, the United States signed the Paris Agreement, a treaty negotiated last December by 195 nations to reduce greenhouse gases in order to keep global warming to no more than 2 degrees Celsius above preindustrial levels.

But a collection of coal companies, coal-burning power companies, industry trade associations and more than two dozen states have challenged the Clean Power Plan in court.

It's a "political power grab of America's power grid to change our country in a diabolical, if not evil, way," said Robert E. Murray, chairman of Murray Energy, the country's largest independent coal producer and a plaintiff in the case.[30] In February, the Supreme Court put the plan on hold, while the U.S. Court of Appeals for the District of Columbia Circuit hears arguments and issues a ruling. No matter how it rules, the case will almost certainly return to the Supreme Court.

"EPA remains fully confident in the legal merits of the Clean Power Plan," an agency spokesperson said in an email statement. But others aren't so sure.

"I think it could go either way," says James Van Nostrand, an environmental law professor at West Virginia University. Although he thinks the Clean Power Plan is within the EPA's statutory authority, foes have raised "some valid legal questions that deserve to be heard in court," he says.

Opponents make two arguments. The first is technical and depends on conflicting language in the Clean Air Act. The EPA is using Section 111(d) of the Clean Air Act as the basis for its authority to issue the Clean Power Plan. But in 1990, the House added language to the Clean Air Act that appears to prevent the agency from regulating a *source category*, such as power plants, under Section 111(d) if that source is already regulated under Section 112. Also in 1990, the Senate added language stating that the EPA cannot regulate *the same pollutant* under the two different sections of the law.

Opponents of the Clean Power Plan prefer the House language, because the EPA already regulates power plants under Section 112 through its four-year-old mercury standards. The EPA likes the Senate language, because the agency has never regulated carbon dioxide emissions from power plants before the Clean Power Plan.

"EPA's interpretation is entitled to deference," says Richard Revesz, a law professor at New York University and director of its Institute for Policy Integrity, a think tank on government decision making.

But Jeffrey Holmstead, an attorney representing operators of coal mines and coal-fired power plants in the case, says even assuming the EPA is correct on this point, the Clean Power Plan faces a bigger problem. The second argument against the plan revolves around how the EPA allows states to cut carbon emissions.

It goes "way, way, way beyond anything the EPA has ever claimed before, and I think goes well beyond what Congress intended under Section 111(d) of the Clean Air Act," says Holmstead.

Under the plan, the EPA gave states three options, to be used as they see fit: require existing coal-fired power plants to become more efficient, which would reduce their carbon emissions; substitute electricity generated from natural gas plants for electricity generated from coal; use zero-emission renewable sources, such as wind and solar, to generate electricity instead of coal.

"The EPA has never, ever in its history asserted that it has authority to require certain plants to be shut down and other types of plants to be built to replace them," says Holmstead. Under Section 111(d) of the Clean Air Act, the EPA has the authority to regulate emissions at a particular plant but not systemwide, he says. So option one is OK, but options two and three are not, he says. And private and government energy analysts agree that states would never achieve the mandated emissions reductions if they limited themselves to option one.

But Revesz says, "They make the claim that it's unprecedented, and that claim is wrong." The EPA has taken a systemwide approach plenty of times, under Section 111(d) and other sections of the Clean Air Act, and previous EPA programs have favored one fuel source over another, he says. For example, in 1995 the EPA allowed municipal waste combustion plants to trade emissions of nitrogen oxides with other plants — a systemwide approach, and the EPA predicted that its 2012 mercury emissions standards would increase natural gas generation at the expense of coal, says Revesz.[31]

If the EPA loses in court, the agency would have to "basically start from scratch," says Holmstead. It would need to limit itself to efficiency improvements at individual power plants, and the required reductions in carbon emissions would have to be smaller, he says.

The Sierra Club's Hitt says even if the Clean Power Plan remains tied up in the courts for a long time, carbon emissions will continue to decline. "Advocacy campaigns and market forces will continue to put pressure on coal, and there's going to be continued new opportunities for clean energy," she says.

Should the government make companies pay more to mine coal on federal lands?

About 40 percent of the nation's coal comes from public lands, mostly in the West and most of that from the Powder River Basin, which straddles Wyoming and Montana and is the largest source of low sulfur, subbituminous coal in the United States. Most of that coal is federally owned and managed by the Interior Department's Bureau of Land Management (BLM), which leases land to coal companies to extract the fuel.[32] The basin's largest mines are in Wyoming.

In January, the Interior Department halted sales of new leases for extracting coal on BLM lands while the department analyzes — for the first time in 30 years — the leasing program's environmental impact and whether taxpayers are getting a fair return.

"There's no question that the costs that coal companies have been paying for coal is extremely low — less than a dollar a ton," said Interior Secretary Sally Jewell. The result has been relatively small payments for coal "that belongs to all Americans," she said.[33]

The coal industry opposes the moratorium and review, which the government estimates will take up to three years. "Obama to Wyoming: 'drop dead,'" is how Travis Deti, assistant director of the Wyoming Mining Association in Cheyenne, characterized the January announcement.[34]

"The moratorium and the programmatic review both lead to a lot of uncertainty in what is already a very difficult market," says Rick Curtsinger, spokesperson for Cloud Peak Energy, based in Gillette. Cloud Peak, along with Peabody Energy and the St. Louis-based Arch Coal, dominate coal mining in the Powder River Basin.

For years, environmental groups, the Government Accountability Office (GAO), which is Congress' investigative arm, and the Interior Department's Office of the Inspector General have complained that the government is not getting as much as it should from its coal leases. Weaknesses in the leasing program "could put the Government at risk of not receiving the full, fair market value for the leases," the Inspector General's office said in a 2013 report.[35]

Environmental groups have been harsher. The federal coal leasing system "in effect" is "a major corporate welfare program," the Washington-based Greenpeace said in a March report.[36]

The leasing program in the Powder River Basin has several moving parts. First, a coal company picks a promising area and applies to the BLM for a license to explore for coal on that tract. If the exploration is successful, the company applies for a lease, estimating the amount and quality of the coal it expects to produce. Based on that information, the BLM computes a fair market value for the lease and holds a lease sale, awarding it to the company with the bid that meets or exceeds that fair market value.

But 90 percent of the lease sales have only one bidder, according to a 2014 GAO investigation. It's expensive to open a mine, and the lone bidder is often a company with adjacent operations.[37] Thus, the BLM's fair market value calculation serves as a kind of substitute for bidding competition. But the agency does not independently verify the information in the lease application, and companies could underestimate the amount of coal available on the land they are seeking to lease.

"Without verification, a company could provide incorrect data to BLM, resulting in BLM's undervaluing the [fair market value] and unknowingly accepting a low bid," said the Interior Department Inspector General's report.[38] The Inspector General's office released a list of

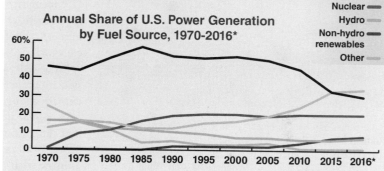

Natural Gas Edging Out Coal as Power Source

Natural gas is forecast to surpass coal this year as the largest fuel source for U.S. power generation. Between 2000 and 2008, coal was significantly less expensive than natural gas. Beginning in 2009, the price difference between coal and natural gas began to shrink as the supply of gas produced from shale formations rose. Use of some renewable energy sources, such as wind and solar, has grown in recent years, while nuclear-powered generation has stayed relatively stable and hydro power has declined.

Coal —
Natural Gas —
Nuclear —
Hydro —
Non-hydro —
renewables
Other —

Annual Share of U.S. Power Generation by Fuel Source, 1970-2016*

60%
50
40
30
20
10
0
*1970 1975 1980 1985 1990 1995 2000 2005 2010 2015 2016**

* Projected.

Source: "Natural gas expected to surpass coal in mix of fuel used for U.S. power generation in 2016," U.S. Energy Information Administration, March 16, 2016, http://tinyurl.com/hoqaghv; the 1950-2015 data are at http://tinyurl.com/h8be395, and the 2016 forecast is at http://tinyurl.com/j9dwlkh

Connie J. Spinardi/Contributor/Getty Images

Solar panels and wind turbines generate energy in the San Gorgonio Pass in Palm Springs, Calif.; the San Jacinto Mountains rise in the background. U.S. coal production has fallen 40 percent since 2008 as power plants turn to cheap, cleaner natural gas and renewable sources.

15 leases in which the amount of coal eventually produced exceeded the company's original coal reserve estimate, sometimes by almost double.[39]

"The industry controls this process," says Joe Smyth, the author of the Greenpeace report and now a researcher at the Climate Investigations Center, a corporate monitoring group in Alexandria, Va.

Once a coal company wins a lease, it makes a onetime lease payment and then pays the BLM an annual royalty on the value of the company's coal sales. The BLM's official royalty rate is a minimum 12.5 percent for surface mining, which is how coal is mined in the Powder River Basin. But the average reported royalty payment in Wyoming has been 12.2 percent because of BLM-approved discounts.[40]

But Haggerty of Headwaters Economics says the effective royalty rate is actually more like 5 percent, because coal is sometimes sold through company-affiliated brokers, complicating the calculation of the value of coal sales. The National Mining Association's Popovich calls Haggerty's 5 percent effective royalty rate figure "ridiculous."

In any case, the Interior Department is considering raising the minimum royalty rate. Haggerty says that's a good idea and urges the federal government to establish a trust that would hold federal coal revenues for the benefit of struggling coal communities across the country.

But mining companies already pay enough, not only in lease payments and royalties but in federal and state taxes and other fees, says Popovich. American taxpayers "are getting a good deal on the prices that we pay," he says.

Greenpeace and others would like to see the federal government go even further and charge mining companies an extra fee related to the social costs of carbon emissions.

"The federal government sells the coal with no consideration that the coal will be burned and contribute to climate change and air pollution, and none of those costs, which are born by society, are reflected in the costs that the industry has to pay for this coal," says Smyth. "That is a massive subsidy." Government economists estimate what's known as "the social cost of carbon," and it can range as high as $105 a metric ton of carbon dioxide currently.[41]

Meanwhile, the Obama administration says the moratorium will not affect production, because companies will continue to mine coal under existing leases.

"Based on current production levels, coal companies now have approximately 20 years of recoverable coal reserves under lease on federal lands," says Amanda DeGroff, an Interior Department spokesperson. The reserves may last even longer if demand for coal continues to decline as the government forecasts, she says.

BACKGROUND
U.S. Coal Discoveries

The nation's coal formed when heat and pressure cooked and compressed the dead remains of trees and plants that lived in swamps 300 million to 400 million years ago. Seawater swamps produced the high-sulfur coal found in the eastern United States. Freshwater swamps produced the low-sulfur coal found mostly in the West.[42]

The amount of pressure and heat determined which of four types of coal would be created. Lignite, a soft, brownish coal found primarily west of the Mississippi River, is about 60 percent carbon. Dull black sub-bituminous coal, found mostly in Montana and Wyoming and other Western states, contains more carbon than lignite and produces more energy when burned. Bituminous coal is the result of even more pressure and heat and is found primarily in the Midwest and along the Appalachian Mountains. Anthracite, the hardest coal and consisting almost entirely of carbon, gives off the most heat when burned. It is found primarily in eastern Pennsylvania.[43]

"America's great bounty of coal was no secret to early settlers," wrote journalist Jeff Goodell in *Big Coal: The Dirty Secret Behind America's Energy Future.* "Unlike petroleum or natural gas, which pools in reservoirs deep underground and migrates through fissures and fractures, coal rises and falls with the folds of the earth in predictable patterns." Oil and gas was not discovered in the United States until the Industrial Revolution was well underway, wrote Goodell, while coal, often breaking the surface, was used by Hopi Indians of the Southwest nearly 1,000 years ago to fire clay pots.[44]

In 1673, the French explorer Louis Joliet and the missionary Jacques Marquette, the first Europeans to explore the Mississippi River, discovered coal seams in river bluffs in what is now Illinois. In the 1750s, a Philadelphia mapmaker surveying the Ohio River Valley reported that coal "may be picked up in the beds of the streams or from the sides of exposed hills."[45]

The coal that impressed the mapmaker "is part of a vast field that stretches along the Appalachians from Pennsylvania to Alabama," wrote Barbara Freese, a former Minnesota assistant attorney general and enforcer of the state's pollution laws. The field is widest, about 190 miles, in western Pennsylvania, near where the Ohio River forks into the Monongahela and the Allegheny. In 1759, the British built Fort Pitt there. By the late 1790s, this small post had been transformed into Pittsburgh, a major manufacturing center, "propelled in no small part by the concentrated energy beneath its hills," Freese said.[46]

By the 1830s, Pittsburgh had become the steam capital of the Western Hemisphere, its factories powered by steam engines running on cheap, local coal. But the resulting black smoke dirtied clothes, homes and skin. One visitor wrote that it formed "a cloud which almost amounts to night and overspreads Pittsburgh with the appearance of gloom and melancholy."[47]

Veteran coal miner Dennis Ferrell monitors conveyer belts at the Sally Ann 1 mine in Welch, W. Va., on Oct. 6, 2015. Environmentalists say coal-fired electricity plants are too costly to operate and too harmful to the environment. But the coal industry says shutting more coal-burning plants could threaten the nation's power grid and that coal-generated electricity is relatively cheap and cleaner than decades ago.

AP Photo/David Goldman

Mine owners had no way to transport coal over the mountains to the Eastern Seaboard, where most of America's population and factories were located. As a result, except for water-powered textile mills, Americans had not invested in large-scale factory production, unlike in coal-rich Britain. "But this was about to change," wrote Freese.[48]

In 1825, the Schuylkill Canal, the nation's first successful commercial canal, opened in Pottsville, Pa., in the eastern part of the state where anthracite coal had been discovered 70 years earlier. Winding mountain paths and treacherous river rapids had made the coal difficult to transport, but canal boats pulled by horse or mule could easily travel the couple of hundred miles to Philadelphia. Navigation companies, mine owners and other investors began building a series of canals, extending eastward through New Jersey and up into New York. Coal canals "quickly paid for themselves as coal use multiplied," Freese said.[49]

But boats were slow, and the canals froze in winter. Soon rail companies were laying track alongside the canals, draining away business. The Philadelphia and Reading Railroad dominated the trade in anthracite, which was well suited for iron production. Cheap coal

CHRONOLOGY

1825-1890 *Coal mines are developed and workers unionize.*

1825 Schuylkill Canal brings coal from Pottsville, Pa., to Philadelphia.

1843 Philadelphia and Reading Railroad competes with the Schuylkill Canal.

1867 Union Pacific Railroad opens Wyoming's Powder River Basin to coal mining; the railroad soon takes control of the territory's coal mines.

1875 Union Pacific Railroad replaces striking miners with Chinese immigrants.

1877 Chesapeake & Ohio Railway transports coal from West Virginia.

1882 Inventor Thomas Edison opens the nation's first coal-fired power plant in lower Manhattan.

1886 West Virginia mine operators import Hungarians to replace strikers.

1890 United Mine Workers of America (UMWA) is formed.

1900-1950 *Coal mining fatalities rise and regulation begins.*

1900 Nearly half a million people work in U.S. mines; 1,489 are killed in mine accidents.

1902 UMWA coal strike in Pennsylvania wins a 10 percent wage increase.

1907 Nearly 700,000 people are employed in U.S. mines; fatalities peak at 3,242.

1910 Congress establishes the Bureau of Mines within the Interior Department to reduce mining accidents.

1921 Striking West Virginia coal miners battle law enforcement; President Warren Harding sends troops and Army bombers and ends strike.

1935 Public Utility Holding Company Act breaks up utility holding companies with regional monopolies.

1938 Fair Labor Standards Act establishes the minimum wage, overtime pay, record keeping and child-labor standards for workers.

1950 Coal accounts for just under half of U.S. electric power generation as natural gas erodes its dominance; 643 of just under a half-million coal miners die in mining accidents.

1970-Present *Congress passes environmental laws; cheap natural gas crushes coal.*

1970 Clean Air Act requires the U.S. Environmental Protection Agency (EPA) to set emissions standards for air pollutants.

1973-1974 OPEC oil embargo causes an energy crisis in the United States.

1977 President Jimmy Carter calls for doubling U.S. coal production to lessen dependence on imported oil. . . . Utility companies build new coal-fired power plants.

1985 Coal-fired power plants generate 57 percent of the nation's electricity.

1990 Clean Air Act amendments establish a cap-and-trade system for emissions of acid rain-causing sulfur dioxide; tighten motor vehicle emission standards; and regulate 189 toxic air pollutants harmful to human health, up from seven.

2010 Explosion at Massey Energy's Upper Big Branch Mine in West Virginia kills 29 coal miners, the deadliest U.S. mining disaster in 40 years.

2012 EPA issues Mercury and Air Toxics Standards.

2015 EPA introduces the Clean Power Plan to reduce carbon emissions at coal-fired power plants; coal states, power companies and coal mine operators sue. . . . Electric utilities are using 29 percent less coal than during coal's high in 2007 and paying 75 percent less for natural gas.

2016 U.S. Supreme Court stays the Clean Power Plan as legal challenges in federal court proceed (February). . . . Since 2010, a total of 236 coal plants have closed or announced a retirement date, leaving 287 remaining. . . . Coal is expected to account for less than a third of U.S. electricity generation, falling behind natural gas for the first time.

and iron "led to the rise of mass production between 1835 and 1855," wrote Freese.[50]

Railroad companies also extended their reach into the bituminous coal country in the Appalachians. In 1877, for example, the Chesapeake & Ohio Railway (C&O) tunneled through the mountains to extend its track from Richmond, Va., to Huntington, W. Va. New C&O rail lines into the remote region allowed mine companies to begin shipping coal to national markets. "The great West Virginia coal rush was on," wrote historian James Green in *The Devil Is Here in These Hills: West Virginia's Coal Miners and Their Battle for Freedom.*[51]

After the Civil War, railroads extended their tracks to the Pacific, bringing settlers west and their crops east.[52] The railroads were instrumental in the development of commercial coal mining in the West.

U.S. government mapping expeditions had discovered coal in what is now western Wyoming in 1843 and in the Powder River Basin in 1859. But commercial coal mining did not begin until the arrival of the Union Pacific Railroad in 1867. The Wyoming Coal and Mining Co. leased land from the Union Pacific and sold the coal it mined to the railroad, whose steam-powered locomotives depended on coal. In the 1870s, the railroad effectively took over the mines, gaining a monopoly in coal production in the territory, according to the Wyoming State Historical Society.[53]

Rise of Unions

The industrialists who owned the coal mines depended on "keeping labor costs down so they could sell their coal at low prices and gain an edge in the national market," wrote Green.[54]

For example, in 1873 the Reading Railroad, which was buying up anthracite coal mines in eastern Pennsylvania, formed a "pool" with other railroads and independent mine owners in the region to fix coal prices and fight unionization, gravely weakening miners' efforts to organize themselves, wrote Freese.[55]

In West Virginia, syndicates of northern industrialists, bankers and investors were building mines and constructing company towns, where miners lived in company-owned housing, worshiped at company-built churches, shopped in company-owned stores and paid in company-issued currency. A mine operator hired and fired at will, and "hit down with a heavy hand on any activity that might menace his business," wrote Green.[56]

Strikes were quickly suppressed, from Appalachia to the West. In 1871, the Wyoming Coal & Mining Co. fired striking miners demanding decent working conditions and better pay and replaced them with Scandinavian immigrants who worked for the cut-rate wage of $2 a day. Four years later, the Union Pacific Railroad replaced striking miners protesting a cut in pay with Chinese immigrant labor, wrote energy analyst Richard Martin in *Coal Wars: The Future of Energy and the Fate of the Planet.*[57] In 1886, West Virginia mine operators imported Hungarian workers to replace striking miners, predominantly African-Americans, at the Pocahontas coal field.[58]

The striking workers were not only demanding more pay but were protesting unsafe working conditions. Mining was dangerous. In Wyoming, more than 300 miners died in mine explosions and fires between 1886 and 1924. Pennsylvania's deeper anthracite mines were even deadlier. Hundreds were killed each year by cave-ins, explosions, gases and floods. "Union representatives took the initiative and spoke up publicly to protest mining disasters, insisting on more compensation for dependents of miners killed," according to the Wyoming State Historical Society. "Labor unions attracted new members by promising to seek greater safety."[59]

In 1890, representatives from local unions met in Columbus, Ohio, and formed the United Mine Workers of America (UMWA), which successfully organized miners across several states, winning the eight-hour workday in the late 1890s. A UMWA strike in Pennsylvania's anthracite mines in 1902 won public sympathy even though it caused a coal shortage in the United States. President Theodore Roosevelt intervened, pressuring the mine-owning railroads to settle. They granted the miners a 10 percent wage increase. The successful strike was a "vivid lesson in how dependent the nation was on coal," Freese said.[60]

But union activists had little luck organizing in West Virginia, where between 1890 and 1912, miners suffered the highest death rate in America. Most miners there were so afraid of their employers that a union organizer said he "could do nothing."[61]

Mining remained dangerous. In that first decade of the new century, coal mine fatalities exceeded 2,000 annually, and in 1910, Congress established the Bureau of Mines within the Department of the Interior to

Struggling Coal Towns Seek a Brighter Future

"This is an effort to supplement the coal jobs we've lost."

Rusty Justice has worked in mining all his life. Now he's a co-owner of one-year-old Bit Source, a website developer in the eastern Kentucky town of Pikeville, deep in the heart of Appalachian coal country. The company's nine employees are laid-off coal miners whom Bit Source has trained to write computer code. When Justice first advertised the positions, nearly 1,000 people applied.[1]

"Our slogan is 'a new day, a new way,'" Justice told NPR in May. "And it's a new day here in Appalachia and we're trying to do things a new way."[2]

But eastern Kentucky must improve its broadband infrastructure for Bit Source to thrive, said company manager John Handshoe. "We're not shipping coal out of here anymore; we're shipping code." The region's internet speeds lag behind those in most cities.[3]

There's no shortage of billion-dollar proposals to help depressed coal mining communities like Pikeville, most of which are located in Appalachia. Presumptive Democratic presidential nominee Hillary Clinton has a plan, members of Congress are sponsoring legislation and private analysts have suggestions.

One plan, although relatively small, is already up and running. Last year, the Obama administration launched the Partnerships for Opportunity and Workforce and Economic Revitalization, known as the POWER Initiative.

"The Obama administration is committed to supporting our workers and communities as they face challenges related to a changing energy landscape in this country," said Jay Williams, assistant secretary of Commerce for economic development, whose department is leading the program. The POWER Initiative pools money from various federal agencies and awards grants to local groups in coal country for workplace and economic development.[4]

Last October it announced 36 awards across 12 states and tribal nations worth a total of nearly $15 million. They include a grant to the state of Kentucky to expand and improve broadband access; a grant to a Kentucky drug abuse program; and a grant to a Kentucky nonprofit to train workers for high tech jobs. In March, the Obama administration announced it would give out another $66 million this fiscal year, with $46 million reserved for Appalachia.[5]

But to some observers, the POWER initiative is small potatoes. "The Obama administration is off to a promising if modest start," said Tom Sanzillo, director of finance at the Cleveland-based Institute for Energy Economics and Financial Analysis, a research group favoring a transition from coal to renewable energy. "More must be done."[6] The administration wants to expand the program to $10 billion, calling it the POWER+ Plan, but that would require congressional approval.[7]

Sanzillo said he would like to see the federal government emulate the Department of Defense's Office of Economic Adjustment, which helps communities transition when a military base closes or a defense contractor scales back. Such a program could include economic assistance to local businesses; money to local governments to cover budget gaps and job training and health benefits for laid-off workers. But perhaps most importantly, local and state governments need to strategize on how best to attract small businesses and big corporations and to capture jobs in the growing wind and solar energy sector, he said.[8]

"Whole new energy markets can be created in most places in the U.S., and a large, existing infrastructure or rural cooperatives and municipal electric systems already have the organization to drive such development," said Sanzillo.[9]

Last November, Clinton committed to making the United States a "clean energy superpower" and proposed a $30 billion aid plan for coal country to ease the transition, similar to what Sanzillo has in mind. It would ensure health and retirement benefits for retired workers of bankrupt coal companies; safeguard local school budgets hit by mine closures; invest in new roads, bridges, water systems, airports

reduce coal mining accidents. However, it had no inspection authority until 1941. Since then, Congress has periodically strengthened its mine safety laws, culminating in the Federal Mine Safety and Health Act of 1977, which expanded the rights of miners and created the Mine Safety and Health Administration within the Department of Labor. Mining fatalities dropped sharply from 272 in 1977 to 86 in 2000.[62]

and transmission lines; expand broadband access; streamline permitting for renewable-energy permits; support research at local universities; provide tax incentives to companies investing in coal communities and provide local grants for job training, health care, housing and the arts.[10]

In Congress, Republican and Democratic lawmakers from Appalachia are supporting the Reclaim Act, which is also part of Obama's proposed POWER+ Plan. It would direct the federal government's $2.8 billion Abandoned Mine Lands fund, used to help clean up abandoned mine sites, to allocate $1 billion to develop reclaimed land to attract new industries.

"We're not giving up on coal," said House Appropriations Committee Chairman Hal Rogers, R-Ky., a sponsor of the bill. "It's going to be around for a good while, although greatly diminished. . . . But this is an effort to supplement — not replace, but supplement — the coal jobs that we've lost."[11]

But the bipartisan bill has opposition. "West Virginians want their good-paying coal jobs, not government bailouts," said Rep. Alex Mooney, R-W. Va.[12] In any case, diversifying coal communities, especially in Appalachia, is going to be extraordinarily difficult, says Mark Haggerty, an analyst with Headwaters Economics, an economic analysis group in Bozeman, Mont.

"These communities are isolated, they only really exist because of extractive industries, and they are not in a position to capture jobs that are being created, such as in finance, health care or technology," he says. "Those jobs are being created in around universities, where there is access to markets, such as an airport, and an educated population. Many of these small communities don't have these things."

— *Barbara Mantel*

After the coal mine he worked at closed, Mark Muncy got a government-backed loan and opened the Riverside Cafe and Bakery in Welch, W. Va.

[1] Erica Peterson, "From Coal To Code: A New Path For Laid-Off Miners In Kentucky," NPR, May 6, 2016, http://tinyurl.com/hjs66po.

[2] *Ibid.*

[3] *Ibid.*

[4] "Senior Administration Officials and KY Governor Steve Beshear Announce the Partnerships for Opportunity and Workforce and Economic Revitalization (POWER) Initiative," press release, U.S. Economic Development Administration, March 27, 2015, http://tinyurl.com/jsly37k.

[5] "Fact Sheet: Administration Announces New Workforce and Economic Revitalization Resources for Communities through POWER Initiative," The White House Office of the Press Secretary, Oct. 15, 2015, http://tinyurl.com/jt27aez; Vicki Rock, "Workshop participants discuss help for coal communities," *The Daily American* (Somerset, Pa.), April 27, 2016, http://tinyurl.com/zxmz4y4.

[6] Tom Sanzillo, "How to Invest in Struggling Coal-Industry Communities? Let Us Count the Ways," Institute for Energy Economics and Financial Analysis, April 6, 2016, http://tinyurl.com/j7n2nst.

[7] "What is the POWER+ Plan?," powerplusplan.org, www.powerplusplan.org/whatispowerplus.

[8] Sanzillo, *op. cit.*

[9] *Ibid.*

[10] "Fact Sheet: Hillary Clinton's Plan for Revitalizing Coal Communities," Hilary for America, November 2015, http://tinyurl.com/gpu8hzh.

[11] Devin Henry, "Coal country rages against fall," *The Hill*, April 25, 2016, http://tinyurl.com/jh3e8lh.

[12] *Ibid.*

Mine owners in the early 20th century suppressed miners' efforts to unionize in West Virginia. After World War I, miners who had fought in Europe during the war returned to West Virginia emboldened to fight for their rights. Wildcat strikes exploded in the state, culminating in a pitched battle in early September 1921. Known as the Battle of Blair Mountain, the clash between an estimated 10,000 armed miners and 3,000 state police, sheriff's

Clean-Coal Technology Alluring But Pricey

"Companies are not going to invest when cheaper options are available."

On a 2010 December morning, workers broke ground at a remote site in Kemper County, Miss., for a power plant billed as a national showcase for clean coal technology.

"The Left said there's no such thing as clean coal — well, this is it!" then-Gov. Haley Barbour, a Republican, declared. The $2.4 billion plant, which was scheduled to open in 2014, "is going to produce reliable power for Mississippi for decades and decades to come," Barbour said.[1]

The state-of-the-art plant would gasify coal, making combustion more efficient and thus producing less carbon dioxide, the primary greenhouse gas. The plant would then capture and compress most of the carbon dioxide produced and sell it to an oil company, which would force it into its wells to extract more crude. Most of the plant's carbon dioxide would never be emitted into the atmosphere.

Five and a half years later, however, the plant remains unfinished, and its price tag has ballooned to $6.6 billion. The facility is generating electricity, but it uses natural gas and won't switch to coal until later this year. The Securities and Exchange Commission (SEC) is investigating whether the owner, Atlanta-based Southern Co., misled the public about how long construction would take, and local businesses are suing the company. They claim they are being harmed by rate hikes to cover cost overruns.[2]

The plant is a "boondoggle," said their attorney, Michael Avenatti. The company said it is cooperating with the SEC and that the ratepayer lawsuit is "without merit."[3]

The Kemper plant demonstrates the difficulties of producing so-called clean coal, which the federal government has promoted over the past 30 years with tax credits, industry grants and research.

Two steps are involved in constructing a clean coal plant: making it burn coal more efficiently; and capturing the carbon dioxide and sequestering it in the ground. Carbon capture and sequestration technology can also be added to an existing, conventional power plant.

Coal can be burned more efficiently if it is first turned into a gas, as at the Kemper plant. But that requires tricky and expensive technology. For example, gasification is responsible for much of Kemper's delays, says Howard Herzog, a senior research engineer at MIT. Only two other U.S. power plants gasify coal, TECO Energy's Polk Power Station in Polk County, Fla., and Duke Energy's Edwardsport Generating Station in Knox County, Ind. But those plants do not capture and sequester carbon dioxide emissions.

Coal power also can be made more efficient through ultra-supercritical pulverized coal combustion, which creates steam in ultra-high-pressure, ultra-high-temperature boilers. Only two such plants operate in the United States, AEP's John W. Turk, Jr. Power Plant in Fulton, Ark., and MidAmerican Energy's Walter Scott, Jr. Energy Center in Council Bluffs, Iowa, and they don't capture carbon dioxide either.

Both technologies allow power plants to use less coal, their primary purpose. But given cheap coal prices, "it has been difficult to justify investing capital to save on fuel

---

deputies and mine guards was the largest civil insurrection in the United States since the Civil War.[63] President Warren Harding imposed martial law and sent in federal troops and Army aircraft, and the strikes failed.[64]

Elected in 1932 during the Great Depression, President Franklin D. Roosevelt signed the Fair Labor Standards Act six years later. The act established the minimum wage, overtime pay, record keeping and child labor standards for government and private sector workers.[65] The president's pro-labor legislation sparked the resurgence of the United Mine Workers of America.

"Following the most successful organizing drive the nation had ever witnessed, the [UMWA] was once again the nation's strongest union," wrote Freese.[66]

Era of Regulation

Roosevelt also overhauled the nation's power sector. Inventor Thomas Edison had flipped the switch on the nation's first coal-fired power plant in lower Manhattan in 1882 to provide nearby residents with electricity to light their homes and businesses. By the time Roosevelt was inaugurated, "largely unregulated private utility holding

costs," says Jeffrey Phillips, head of advanced coal power generation research at the Electric Power Research Institute, whose members include electric utilities and government agencies. In addition, while these kinds of plants reduce carbon emissions by about 15 percent compared to conventional coal plants, they still produce about twice the carbon dioxide of natural gas-fired plants, which are cheaper to build and operate, says Phillips.

Pairing carbon capture and sequestration (CCS) with gasification or ultra-supercritical pulverized coal combustion or bolting the technology onto an existing, conventional plant would be the only ways to significantly reduce a coal plant's carbon dioxide emissions, theoretically by up to 90 percent.[4] "We believe that CCS offers a significant step forward to remove carbon dioxide emissions from modern power plants," says Rick Curtsinger, spokesperson for Cloud Peak Energy, a mining company in Gillette, Wyo. "As more work is done on CCS, as more plants come on line, we believe that the cost will fall."

However, no U.S. power plants currently use carbon capture and sequestration, and only two are in the works: the Kemper plant and a NRG Energy plant near Houston. NRG, which is retrofitting a conventional coal plant, expects it to be operational later this year.[5]

The lack of investment in CCS is easy to explain, says Phillips. "Companies are not going to invest in a more expensive, complicated option when cheaper, less complicated options are available," such as natural gas, although the carbon dioxide reduction would not be as large.

CCS also would burn more coal. "About 25 to 30 percent of the energy produced by the power plant would have to be used in capturing, compressing, transporting and sequestering the carbon dioxide," says Richard Heinberg, a senior fellow-in-residence at the Post Carbon Institute, a climate change think tank in Santa Rosa, Calif. "We would actually have to burn 30 percent more coal to get the same amount of energy."

"You're much better off spending that money developing new, cleaner technologies," such as ways to store the intermittent solar and wind energy, says Shannon Fisk, an attorney at San Francisco-based Earthjustice, an environmental law organization. "And CCS does not fix a lot of the other environmental problems caused by the whole life cycle of coal," such as land and water pollution from mining, says Mary Anne Hitt, director of the Sierra Club's Beyond Coal campaign, which aims to eliminate coal power.

But Herzog says he doesn't expect a breakthrough in energy storage in the next several decades so the country will need more than renewable energy sources to reduce greenhouse gas emissions to near zero. The country will need nuclear power and carbon capture and sequestration; it just won't be paired with coal, he says.

CCS "can be used on natural gas plants, it can be used on biomass," he says. "CCS is more than just coal."

— *Barbara Mantel*

[1] Jennifer Jacob Brown, "Mississippi Power breaks ground on Kemper County IGCC Power Plant," *The Meridian* (Miss.) Star, Dec. 17, 2010, http://tinyurl.com/ hfp2a3r.

[2] Rebecca Smith, "Southern's Clean-Coal Woes Mount," *The Wall Street Journal*, May 14, 2016, http://tinyurl.com/j8dzaq5.

[3] *Ibid.*

[4] "Carbon Dioxide Capture and Sequestration," U.S. Environmental Protection Agency, www3.epa.gov/climatechange/ccs/index.html.

[5] "WA Parish CO2 Capture Project," NRG Energy, http://tinyurl.com/ jfvewe6.

companies, mostly coal-powered, controlled more than 90 percent of the nation's electricity," wrote Martin.[67]

Roosevelt's response was the Public Utility Holding Company Act of 1935, which forced the holding companies to register with the Securities and Exchange Commission, spin off unrelated businesses, simplify their ownership and limit their geographic reach.[68] By 1950, natural gas, and to a lesser extent oil, had made inroads in power generation, accounting for just under a quarter of electricity generation in the United States. Coal accounted for just under half and hydropower the rest.[69]

The most intense period of regulation for coal mining and coal-fired utilities came in the 1970s, at the beginning of the environmental movement. In 1970, dense, visible smog in the nation's cities prompted Congress to pass the Clean Air Act, which set 1975 as the deadline for cleaning up the nation's air. The law required the newly created Environmental Protection Agency to set National Ambient Air Quality Standards, which it did the following year for six pollutants: particulate matter, nitrogen oxides, ozone, lead, carbon monoxide and sulfur dioxide. The greatest source of sulfur dioxide by far were coal-fired power plants, "which doubled their SO2 emissions every decade between 1940 and 1970," according to Freese. States had to devise plans to meet those standards.[70]

The law also required the EPA to set emission standards for hazardous air pollutants, such as heavy metals, that may cause cancer or other serious health effects. Initially, the agency set standards for only seven such pollutants.[71]

At about the same time, international events led to a sustained upswing in coal use and production.

The 1973-74 oil embargo by the Organization of the Petroleum Exporting Countries (OPEC) and the resulting energy crisis triggered long lines at the gas pump, prompting President Jimmy Carter to call for energy independence and an almost doubling of U.S. coal production to help reduce oil imports. In 1975, about 15 percent of electricity was generated using petroleum.[72] Utility companies "embarked on a huge program to build new power plants that burned domestic fuels — mostly coal and uranium," Martin said. By 1985, coal-fired power plants were generating 57 percent of the nation's electricity, and petroleum accounted for just 4 percent.

Regulators approved retail electricity rate hikes to cover the costs of the construction, "leading to a vicious cycle of price increases and overbuilding, and sending several big [privately owned utilities] to the brink of bankruptcy," according to Martin. By the 1990s, the industry had consolidated in a wave of mergers that "created an industry landscape similar to that of the reviled holding companies of the 1920s," wrote Martin.[73]

Congress passed sweeping revisions to the Clean Air Act in 1990 "designed to curb three major threats to the nation's environment and to the health of millions of Americans: acid rain, urban air pollution, and toxic air emissions," according to an EPA overview of the law. Among other things, the amendment capped emissions of sulfur dioxide, a component of acid rain that had been killing aquatic life in the nation's lakes, and allowed power plants to trade SO2 emission allowances to meet the law's requirements. It also tightened emission standards for motor vehicles and raised the number of regulated toxic air pollutants harmful to human health from 7 to 189.[74]

By 2008, coal production reached a peak, and coal plants were generating half of the country's electricity.[75]

But in 2010, an explosion ripped through Massey Energy's Upper Big Branch Mine in West Virginia, killing 29 coal miners, the deadliest U.S. mine disaster in 40 years. Then-CEO Donald Blankenship had "spent much of his time pushing faster, more efficient, and cheaper production," wrote Peter Galuszka in *Thunder on the Mountain: Death at Massey and the Dirty Secrets Behind Big Coal.* Blankenship battled regulators and supported coal-friendly politicians and judges.[76] This April, a federal judge in West Virginia sentenced Blankenship to a year in prison for conspiring to commit mine safety violations before the explosion.[77]

By the time of the explosion, U.S. coal production had begun to slip from its 2008 peak, and coal-fired power was on the decline as cheap natural gas extracted from the nation's shale formations flooded the market.

The EPA's Mercury and Air Toxics Standards also played a role. After the agency proposed the standards in 2011, a coalition of states and trade associations challenged them in court. In 2014, the case came before the U.S. Supreme Court, which said last year that the EPA had failed to properly account for costs. A federal appeals court then allowed the rules to stand while the EPA conducted a formal cost-benefit analysis. Power companies had already spent billions either complying by retrofitting coal-fired plants or shutting them down.

Last year, the EPA issued its Clean Power Plan to reduce carbon dioxide emissions at existing power plants, which is being challenged in court by 27 states, coal companies, owners of coal-fired power plants and trade associations.

CURRENT SITUATION
Regulations Challenged

The EPA is facing a renewed legal challenge to its Mercury and Air Toxics Standards.

In mid-April, the EPA ruled that a cost evaluation did not change the agency's determination that regulating hazardous air pollutant emissions from coal- and oil-fired power plants is "appropriate and necessary." The agency estimated that the rules would cost the industry $9.6 billion a year to implement, compared with up to $90 billion in annual health benefits to the public.[78]

Murray Energy, a major U.S. coal company, promptly challenged the finding in the U.S. Circuit Court of

AT ISSUE

Should the federal moratorium on new coal leases be permanent?

YES   Jeremy Nichols
Climate and Energy Program Director,
WildEarth Guardians

Written for *CQ Researcher*, June 2016

Limiting rises in global temperature means our society must move away from fossil fuels. In fact, studies have confirmed that to safeguard the climate, we must keep virtually all coal reserves in the ground.

Given this, it makes sense for our federal government to lead the way and stop leasing publicly owned coal.

The climate footprint of the federal coal program is enormous. More than 40 percent of all coal produced in the United States comes from publicly owned deposits managed by the Department of the Interior. Most of these deposits lie in the West, a landscape whose rugged beauty symbolizes freedom around the world.

A staggering 11 percent of all U.S. greenhouse gas emissions can be traced to mining and burning of publicly owned coal. This makes the federal coal program — and, by extension, the Interior Department — a root contributor to global warming in the United States.

In early 2016, Interior Secretary Sally Jewell enacted a pause on new leasing. Responding to mounting controversy and the need to modernize the way publicly owned coal is managed, she called for a "time out" to adopt reforms.

The pause makes sense, but the moratorium must become permanent.

Leasing conveys not only a right but also a mandate to mine. Every ton of coal leased to industry guarantees more carbon pollution. In other words, for every ton leased, the U.S. government is sending the message that it's OK to keep investing in coal. To continue this policy would be nothing short of climate denial.

We can't flip a switch and stop all coal burning tomorrow. Yet if we don't take meaningful steps today to wind down our reliance, we'll never fully move on to clean energy.

Industry already has more than a decade of publicly owned coal reserves under lease. A moratorium would ensure an orderly, yet effective, end to the federal coal program. It also would guarantee an end to our government's role in fueling global warming.

The opportunity could not be greater. Leading coal companies such as Peabody Energy and Arch Coal have filed for bankruptcy protection. At the same time, renewable energy is taking hold and becoming more affordable and profitable.

Our future does not lie with coal. It's time to acknowledge this reality and end leasing of our publicly owned coal.

NO   Laura Sheehan
Senior Vice President of Communications,
American Coalition for Clean Coal Electricity

Written for *CQ Researcher*, June 2016

One way to strangle an industry is through more and increasingly onerous government regulations, an approach the Obama administration uses all too frequently in its crusade to eliminate coal-based power from America's energy portfolio. A recent example of this in action is the radical, 2,100 page rewrite of policy governing the mining of coal on federal lands, quietly released in mid-January by the Interior Department's Office of Surface Mining.

Buried within this mountain of paper is a moratorium on leases to mine low-sulfur coal from government owned land. Forty-one percent of the nation's coal comes from federal lands, with a majority, 85 percent, being mined in the Powder River Basin of Wyoming and Montana.

Some want the moratorium to be made permanent, but doing so would be an egregious act of bureaucratic malpractice. These new regulations not only defy dozens of existing laws, they place one of our nation's largest coal reserves off-limits. This is bad news not just for the coal industry but for America's entire economy as it further restricts the way we produce power, forcing an overreliance on more expensive, less reliable energy sources.

We're told that the moratorium would allow additional time to study the environmental considerations of mining this Western coal. The administration's actions thus far, as evidenced by a perpetual juggernaut of regulations from the Mercury Air Toxics Standards, to the Stream Protection Rule and Clean Power Plan, suggest a larger effort designed to cause death by a thousand paper cuts.

The costs of these rules are staggering. The Power Plan alone would cost $30 billion or more per year and raise electricity costs in all of the lower 48 states, with 41 seeing double digit increases. Rate hikes of this nature will be devastating to low- and middle-income families, America's manufacturing base and our economy as a whole.

The temporary freeze on new leases to mine coal on federal lands is a bad idea. Making it permanent is exponentially worse. We can balance environmental concerns with the need for a reliable and clean source of electricity without risking America's economic standing. That balance cannot be achieved, however, when the government is determined to eliminate coal as a power source, regardless of the facts or the havoc it wreaks.

JIM WATSON/AFP/Getty Images

Demonstrators at the White House on Sept. 27, 2010, urge the Obama administration to end mountaintop mining, which environmentalists say pollutes water and causes other environmental problems. The administration's Clean Power Plan would require states to devise plans for power companies to significantly reduce emissions of carbon dioxide, the primary greenhouse gas contributing to climate change, starting in 2022. The plan is on hold pending a legal challenge.

Appeals for the District of Columbia Circuit. "This final 'finding' is flagrantly arbitrary, and fails to comply with the law and with the Supreme Court's mandate," the company said in a statement.[79] The EPA said in an email that it cannot comment on active litigation.

Meanwhile, in mid-June, the Supreme Court refused to hear an appeal from a group of states, led by Michigan, of last year's lower court decision to allow the mercury rules to remain intact.[80]

In May, the D.C. court postponed a hearing before a three-judge panel on the Clean Power Plan lawsuit, originally scheduled for this month, until September before the full bench. "The move to skip the customary three-panel review . . . is almost unheard of and could signal that the judges feel the issues of the case are so significant that they all must weigh in," said Tim Profeta, the founding director of Duke University's Nicholas Institute for Environmental Policy Solutions.[81]

If the court rules in favor of the EPA, the plan will not go into effect until the case is presented to the U.S. Supreme Court, which put the plan on temporary hold in February while the challenge proceeded. If opponents decide not to take the case to the Supreme Court, the plan would take effect.

"But, there is zero chance of that happening," says plaintiff attorney Holmstead. "I think whoever loses in the D.C. Circuit is 100 percent likely to go to the Supreme Court," he says.

Campaign Controversy

As presumptive presidential nominees Clinton and Trump campaign across the country, the depressed coal industry and the loss of jobs in coal mining states has turned out to be a hot topic.

In March, Democratic candidate Clinton stirred up controversy when she told CNN that she wanted to help coal country benefit from the move toward renewable energy "because we're going to put a lot of coal miners and coal companies out of business, right?" After getting slammed, by Trump and others, she later apologized for the wording of her comments, which were part of a longer answer that was hardly mentioned in the attacks: "Now we've got to move away from coal and all the other fossil fuels, but I don't want to move away from the people who did the best they could to produce the energy that we relied on." Several months earlier, Clinton had announced a $30 billion plan with a long list of initiatives, from ensuring health and retirement benefits for coal workers and safeguarding local school funding to building roads and bridges in coal country, expanding broadband access and repurposing mine lands and retired power plant sites.[82]

But Democratic leaders in West Virginia say the out-of-context comment has severely damaged Clinton's chances of winning the general election in the state where in 2008 she won the Democratic primary in a landslide. The airways have been "just pummeled with that [quote], just constant," said former West Virginia Democratic Party Chairman George Carenbauer.[83]

In May, it was Trump's turn. At an oil industry conference in North Dakota, Trump promised to rescind the Clean Power Plan if elected president. "Regulations that shut down hundreds of coal-fired power plants and block the construction of new ones — how stupid is that?" Trump said. Energy analysts and journalists quickly questioned his grasp of the issue.

The next president would not have the authority to unilaterally rescind the plan, according to *The New York Times*, although Trump could affect the outcome of the court challenge to the plan by appointing a conservative to the open position on the U.S. Supreme Court.[84]

Trump promised that his actions would restore coal jobs, but energy analysts questioned his logic. "Most analysts would say that coal is hurting because natural gas prices have collapsed," said Robert McNally, an energy consultant and a senior energy official in the George W. Bush administration. "Donald Trump would have to find a way to raise natural gas prices."[85] But energy markets determine that.

Bankruptcies and Cleanup

Under the Surface Mining Control and Reclamation Act of 1977, coal companies must restore the land they've mined once they stop operations, but the recent wave of bankruptcies is threatening to undermine the process, said Tom Sanzillo and David Schlissel of the Cleveland-based Institute for Energy Economics and Financial Analysis, a research group committed to moving the country away from nonrenewable energy. Coal company collapses "threaten to leave behind a costly legacy that will haunt taxpayers and consumers for years," Sanzillo and Schlissel wrote in an April editorial in *The New York Times.*

Regulators over the years had allowed many large coal companies to "self-bond" to cover cleanup costs rather than purchase outside surety bonds — basically insurance — or put up cash or other collateral. A self-bond is basically a promise, an IOU. As companies work out their finances in bankruptcy courts, the courts may allow cash-strapped companies to earmark amounts that do not cover the full cost of reclamation, Sanzillo and Schlissel said.[86]

For example, bankrupt Alpha Natural Resources anticipates replacing all of its self-bonds in Wyoming with outside insurance or other collateral, but only 60 percent of its self-bonds in West Virginia, according to *The New York Times.*[87]

A few weeks after Sanzillo and Schlissel's article, bankrupt Peabody Energy wrote a letter in response. "Just in the last decade, Peabody has paid many millions of dollars to restore our own mined lands in high-quality fashion, as we should," said Vic Svec, head of global investor relations. "Each year, we restore thousands of acres into hardy and productive rangeland, wildlife habitat, hardwood forests and wetlands."[88]

But it's the future, not the past, that worries outside analysts who question who will have to pay the cost of reclamation going forward. "The states have, I think, a significant risk — the federal government does as well," said coal analyst James Stevenson at the consulting firm IHS, based in Englewood, Colo.[89]

Environmentalists have called on the federal government to reform its regulations that allow coal companies to self-bond. And some companies are voluntarily shifting away from the practice. "We are proactively working to address the ongoing regulatory uncertainties regarding self-bonding programs by seeking to voluntarily transition fully to third-party surety bonds," Heath Hill, Cloud Peak Energy's chief financial officer, told analysts in April.[90] Cloud Peak is the only publicly traded Powder River Basin coal operator to avoid bankruptcy.

OUTLOOK
Smaller, Cleaner, Safer

The coal mining industry will certainly be smaller in 10 years' time, but also more efficient and cleaner, says the National Mining Association's Popovich. "And I see a steady increase in mine safety. We had a record year last year." Eleven people died in coal mine accidents in 2015, the lowest number since the federal Mine Safety and Health Administration was created nearly 40 years ago.[91]

Curtsinger of Cloud Peak Energy says he agrees with government forecasts that coal-fired power plants will still generate about a quarter of the country's electricity if the Clean Power Plan is fully implemented, and more if it is not. And the company's mines are well positioned to supply that demand, he says. "The Powder River Basin, where Cloud Peak's mines are located, produces some of the lowest cost, highest quality coal in the country. It also supplies some of the country's newest power plants," he says.

In April, Cloud Peak reported a $36.4 million first-quarter loss, nearly eight times its losses for the same period a year earlier. The company blamed, in part, one of the mildest winters on record.[92]

Paul Bailey of the American Coalition for Clean Coal Electricity says coal's future largely "depends on who the next president is and what policies they put in place."

It may also depend on the U.S. Supreme Court's decision on the Clean Power Plan, the centerpiece of Obama's strategy to arrest global warming, "If I were betting, I would say that the Supreme Court probably strikes down the Clean Power Plan," says industry attorney Holmstead.

NYU law professor Revesz disagrees. "The best that I can do is predict, based on my understanding of the strength of the arguments. . . . I think the Supreme Court, when it takes this case, will uphold the Clean Power Plan," he says.

The Supreme Court's stay of the Clean Power Plan was a blow to the EPA and the environmental community. The decision was 5-4, and Associate Justice Antonin Scalia was in the majority. But Scalia died in February, and the Republican-controlled Senate has vowed to block President Obama's nominee, Chief Judge Merrick Garland of the U.S. Court of Appeals for the District of Columbia. Thus, the plan's fate will likely be determined by the next president.

But the Sierra Club's Hitt says it won't matter so much who is president or whether the Clean Power Plan is enacted soon. "Our advocacy is largely targeting state and local decision makers of utilities and PCs," says Hitt, referring to public utility/services commissions. "So we have a strategy that is resilient to the political winds no matter which way they blow."

Earthjustice's Fisk predicts zero-emission renewable energy will continue to grow rapidly over the next decade, which, he says, "will be better for the environment and will actually be better for job creation and economic development."

NOTES

1. Leigh Paterson, "Coal Communities Consider Life After Layoffs," *Inside Energy*, April 22, 2016, http://tinyurl.com/zym4aa2.

2. *Ibid.*

3. *Ibid.*

4. Tyler Hodge, "Natural gas expected to surpass coal in mix of fuel used for U.S. power generation in 2016," U.S. Energy Information Administration, March 16, 2016, http://tinyurl.com/hoqaghv.

5. Brian Park, "Power sector coal demand has fallen in nearly every state since 2007," U.S. Energy Information Administration, April 28, 2016, http://tinyurl.com/z2lt2rq; "Weekly Coal Production,"

U.S. Energy Information Administration, April 2008, April 2016, http://tinyurl.com/j9qmoo7; "North American Coal — Lights Go Dark on Coal: Industry in Restructuring," Moody's Investors Service, May 6, 2016, http://tinyurl.com/zuq4b64.

6. Chuck Holton, "Obama's War on Coal Decimating 'America's Powerhouse,'" CBN News, May 9, 2016, http://tinyurl.com/h27yjto.

7. Michael Grunwald, "Inside the War on Coal," *Politico*, May 26, 2015, http://tinyurl.com/nmx57pc.

8. "Rankings: Coal Production, 2014 (thousand short tons)," U.S. Energy Information Administration, http://tinyurl.com/j47wwfm. "Coal Data Browser," U.S. Energy Information Administration, http://tinyurl.com/hztyzuz.

9. Jeff Kelly Lowenstein, "Life After Coal in Harlan County, U.S.A.," *In These Times*, May 23, 2016, http://tinyurl.com/zxgfjo7.

10. "Coal Mining Productivity by State and Mine Type," U.S. Energy Information Administration, March 23, 2016, http://tinyurl.com/zrxmgsk.

11. "(unadj)Employed — Coal Mining," U.S. Bureau of Labor Statistics, http://tinyurl.com/hpgsc2v.

12. Lowenstein, *op. cit.*

13. "Fact Sheet: Hillary Clinton's Plan for Revitalizing Coal Communities," Hillary for America, November 2015, http://tinyurl.com/gpu8hzh.

14. Ashley Parker and Coral Davenport, "Donald Trump's Energy Plan: More Fossil Fuels and Fewer Rules," *The New York Times*, May 26, 2016, http://tinyurl.com/zv9s8jz.

15. "Short-Term Energy Outlook," U.S. Energy Information Administration, May 2016, p. 11, http://tinyurl.com/a8l52do; Tyler Hodge, "Natural gas expected to surpass coal in mix of fuel used for U.S. power generation in 2016," U.S. Energy Information Administration, March 16, 2016, http://tinyurl.com/hoqaghv.

16. Brian Park, "Power sector coal demand has fallen in nearly every state since 2007," U.S. Energy Information Administration, April 28, 2016, http://tinyurl.com/z2lt2rq; "Monthly Energy Review,

Table 7.2b," U.S. Energy Information Administration, p. 110, May 2016, http://tinyurl.com/j4z9h7p.

17. "Lazard's Levelized Cost of Energy Analysis — Version 9.0," Lazard, November 2015, p. 10, http://tinyurl.com/hralhrc.

18. Katherine Tweed, "U.S. Electricity Demand Flat Since 2007," *IEEE Spectrum*, Feb. 6, 2015, http://tinyurl.com/zr2q4wm; "Table 1.1.3. Real Gross Domestic Product, Quantity Indexes," U.S. Bureau of Economic Analysis, http://tinyurl.com/jssfdsx.

19. "U.S. coal exports declined 23% in 2015, as coal imports remained steady," U.S. Energy Information Administration, March 7, 2016, http://tinyurl.com/hn2uppj.

20. "Coal made up more than 80% of retired electricity generating capacity in 2015," U.S. Energy Information Administration, March 8, 2016, http://tinyurl.com/hsks8go.

21. "Victories," Sierra Club's Beyond Coal, http://tinyurl.com/pyh22gp.

22. "Fact Sheet: Final Consideration of Cost in the Appropriate and Necessary Finding for the Mercury and Air Toxics Standards for Power Plants," U.S. Environmental Protection Agency, April 14, 2016, http://tinyurl.com/j69tzb7.

23. "Coal Facts," American Coalition for Clean Coal Electricity, March 2016, p. 3, http://tinyurl.com/jotz7fj.

24. "Overview of Greenhouse Gases," U.S. Environmental Protection Agency, http://tinyurl.com/nuuf3x4; "How much carbon dioxide is produced when different fuels are burned?" U.S. Energy Information Administration, http://tinyurl.com/pwk6uu3.

25. "International Energy Outlook 2016: Chapter 4. Coal," U.S. Energy Information Administration, May 11, 2016, http://tinyurl.com/z5d9kao.

26. For background, see Daniel McGlynn, "Fracking Controversy," *CQ Researcher*, Dec. 16, 2011, pp. 1049-1072.

27. "Obama Administration Takes Historic Action on Climate Change/Clean Power Plan to protect public health, spur clean energy investments and strengthen U.S. leadership," news release, U.S. Environmental Protection Agency, Aug. 3, 2015, http://tinyurl.com/zu2vlvu.

28. "Annual Energy Outlook 2016 Early Release: Annotated Summary of Two Cases," U.S. Energy Information Administration, May 17, 2016, p. 6, http://tinyurl.com/hxwdlqm.

29. "Obama Administration takes historic action on Climate Change/Clean Power Plan to protect public health, spur clean energy investments and strengthen U.S. leadership," *op. cit.*

30. Jad Mouawad, "A Crusader in the Coal Mine, Taking On President Obama," *The New York Times*, April 30, 2016, http://tinyurl.com/gtsv34e.

31. Richard L. Revesz, Denise A. Grab, and Jack Lienke, "Familiar Territory: A Survey of Legal Precedents for the Clean Power Plan," *The Environmental Law Reporter*, March 2016, http://tinyurl.com/zbj3637.

32. For background, see Barbara Mantel, "Managing Western Lands," *CQ Researcher*, April 22, 2016, pp. 361-384. Also see James A. Luppens *et al.*, "Coal Geology and Assessment of Coal Resources and Reserves in the Powder River Basin, Wyoming and Montana," U.S. Geological Survey *Professional Paper 1809*, May 12, 2015, http://tinyurl.com/j7np3g6.

33. Dylan Brown, "Coal: Republicans committed to blocking moratorium," *Environment and Energy Daily*, Feb. 24, 2016, http://tinyurl.com/zugxyek.

34. Stephanie Joyce, "In Latest Move On Climate, Obama Administration Halts Coal Leasing," *Inside Energy*, Jan. 18, 2016, http://tinyurl.com/hmqbwk3.

35. "Coal Management Program, U.S. Department of the Interior," Office of Inspector General, U.S. Department of the Interior, June 2013, p. 1, http://tinyurl.com/z3szhfx.

36. Joe Smyth, "Corporate Welfare for Coal," Greenpeace, March 2016, p. 3, http://tinyurl.com/hjfcv32.

37. "Coal Leasing: BLM Could Enhance Appraisal Process, More Explicitly Consider Coal Exports, and Provide More Public Information," U.S.

Government Accountability Office, December 2013, pp. 16-17, http://tinyurl.com/h8hdvqj.

38. "Coal Management Program, U.S. Department of the Interior," *op. cit.*

39. Smyth, *op. cit.*

40. Mark Haggerty and Julie Haggerty, "An Assessment of U.S. Federal Coal Royalties: Current Royalty Structure, Effective Royalty Rates, and Reform Options," Headwaters Economics, p. 12, http://tinyurl.com/hhd7vfv.

41. "EPA Fact Sheet: Social Cost of Carbon," U.S. Environmental Protection Agency, December 2015, http://tinyurl.com/jf69bcr.

42. "How Fossil Fuels were Formed," U.S. Department of Energy, http://tinyurl.com/d5aujb9.

43. "Coal: Our Most Abundant Fuel," U.S. Department of Energy, http://tinyurl.com/juaddwe; Jeff Goodell, *Big Coal: The Dirty Secret Behind America's Energy Future* (2006), p. 9.

44. "Coal: Our Most Abundant Fuel," *op. cit.*; Goodell, *op. cit.*, p. 11.

45. Goodell, *op. cit.*, p. 11.

46. Barbara Freese, *Coal: A Human History* (2003), pp. 106-108.

47. *Ibid.*, pp. 108-109.

48. *Ibid.*, pp. 106-108.

49. *Ibid.*, pp. 119-120.

50. *Ibid.*, pp. 121-122, 125-126.

51. James Green, *The Devil Is Here in These Hills: West Virginia's Coal Miners and Their Battle for Freedom* (2015), p. 17.

52. Freese, *op. cit.*, p. 127.

53. Chamois L. Andersen, "The Coal Business in Wyoming," The Wyoming State Historical Society, http://tinyurl.com/j692a5g.

54. Green, *op. cit.*, p. 20.

55. Freese, *op. cit.*, pp. 131-132.

56. Green, *op. cit.*, pp. 20-22.

57. Richard Martin, *Coal Wars: The Future of Energy and the Fate of the Planet* (2015), p. 98.

58. Green, *op. cit.*, p. 30.

59. Andersen, *op. cit.*; Freese, *op. cit.*, p. 139.

60. *Ibid.*, Freese, p. 141.

61. Green, *op. cit.*, p. 34.

62. "History of Mine Safety and Health Legislation," U.S. Mine Safety and Health Administration, http://tinyurl.com/gpt3o7r. For background see Daniel McGlynn, "Mine Safety," *CQ Researcher*, June 24, 2011, pp. 553-576; and Pamela M. Prah, "Coal Mining Safety," *CQ Researcher*, March 17, 2006, pp. 241-264.

63. For background, see "Blair Mountain: The History of a Confrontation," Preservation Alliance of West Virginia, http://tinyurl.com/hdv2pml; and "Introduction: The Mine Wars," American Experience, PBS, http://tinyurl.com/jo9ja4w.

64. David Alan Corbin, *Life, Work, and Rebellion in the Coal Fields: The Southern West Virginia Miners, 1880-1922* (1981), pp. 196, 219-224.

65. "1938 President Roosevelt signs the Fair Labor Standards Act," Massachusetts AFL-CIO, http://tinyurl.com/hv5z23n.

66. Freese, *op. cit.*, p. 158.

67. Goodell, *op. cit.*, p. 102; Martin, *op. cit.*, p. 17.

68. *Ibid.* (Martin), p. 21.

69. "Monthly Energy Review, Table 7.2b," U.S. Energy Information Administration, p. 110, May 2016, http://tinyurl.com/j4z9h7p.

70. "EPA Sets National Air Quality Standards," press release, U.S. Environmental Protection Agency, April 30, 1971, http://tinyurl.com/hdx28m5; Freese, *op. cit.*, p. 168.

71. "Summary of the Clean Air Act," U.S. Environmental Protection Agency, http://tinyurl.com/jzsxhju.

72. Jimmy Carter, Speech, April 18, 1977, PBS, http://tinyurl.com/jhfy8sb.

73. Martin, *op. cit.*, p. 22.

74. "1990 Clean Air Act Amendment Summary," U.S. Environmental Protection Agency, http://tinyurl.com/hbepyvw; and http://tinyurl.com/zmaajkx.

75. "Monthly Energy Review, Table 7.2b," U.S. Energy Information Administration, May 2016, p. 110, http://tinyurl.com/j4z9h7p.

76. Peter A. Galuszka, *Thunder on the Mountain: Death at Massey and the Dirty Secrets Behind Big Coal* (2012), p. 7.

77. Tim Murphy, "Notorious Coal Baron Don Blankenship Sentenced To a Year in Prison, *Mother Jones*, April 6, 2016, http://tinyurl.com/hanqrh5.

78. "Supplemental Finding That It Is Appropriate and Necessary To Regulate Hazardous Air Pollutants From Coal- and Oil-Fired Electric Utility Steam Generating Units; Final Rule," *Federal Register*, April 25, 2016, pp. 24420, 24425, http://tinyurl.com/j6kpqq9.

79. Sarah Tincher, "Murray Energy continues fight against EPA's MATS rule with new lawsuit," *The State Journal* (W. Va.), April 25, 2016, http://tinyurl.com/hsbulf9.

80. Lawrence Hurley, "Supreme Court rejects challenge to Obama mercury air pollution rule," Reuters, June 13, 2016, http://tinyurl.com/hymsqkh.

81. Tim Profeta, "Clean Power Plan Court Hearing Delayed to September," *National Geographic*, May 19, 2016, http://tinyurl.com/hpkofo6.

82. "Fact Sheet: Hillary Clinton's Plan for Revitalizing Coal Communities," Hillary for America, November 2015, http://tinyurl.com/gpu8hzh.

83. Daniel Strauss, "Clinton haunted by coal country comment," *Politico*, May 10, 2016, http://tinyurl.com/zg9fqgv.

84. Ashley Parker and Coral Davenport, "Donald Trump's Energy Plan: More Fossil Fuels and Fewer Rules," *The New York Times*, May 26, 2016, http://tinyurl.com/zv9s8jz.

85. *Ibid.*

86. Tom Sanzillo and David Schlissel, "After Bankruptcies, Coal's Dirty Legacy Lives On," *The New York Times*, April 14, 2016, http://tinyurl.com/j62y88n.

87. Michael Corkery, "Regulators Fear $1 Billion Coal Cleanup Bill," *The New York Times*, June 6, 2016, http://tinyurl.com/jl7kdkv.

88. Vic Svec, "Restoring Coal Lands," *The New York Times*, April 29, 2016, http://tinyurl.com/h48jt5h.

89. "Mine environmental risk grows with bankruptcies in big coal," The Associated Press, May 19, 2016, http://tinyurl.com/gmvqyx3.

90. Benjamin Storrow, "Faced with massive cleanup bill, state lowers Peabody Energy self-bonds by $138 million," *Billings Gazette*, April 30, 2016, http://tinyurl.com/hkrxwr8.

91. "Coal Fatalities for 1900 Through 2014," Mine Safety and Health Administration, http://tinyurl.com/gwucxlk; "Mine Safety and Health At a Glance: Coal Mine Safety and Health," Mine Safety and Health Administration, April 1, 2016, http://tinyurl.com/jd34h65.

92. Benjamin Storrow, "Cloud Peak Energy reports $36 million loss," *Billings Gazette*, April 28, 2016, http://tinyurl.com/hqyeoc5.

BIBLIOGRAPHY
Selected Sources
Books

Freese, Barbara, *Coal: A Human History*, Perseus Publishing, 2003.
A former enforcement official of air pollution rules in Minnesota follows the history of U.S. coal from discovery by early settlers through modern-day environmental regulations.

Galuszka, Peter A., *Thunder on the Mountain: Death at Massey and the Dirty Secrets Behind Big Coal*, St. Martin's Press, 2012.
A journalist analyzes events leading up to a deadly 2010 explosion at a Massey Energy coal mine in West Virginia, the worst U.S. mine disaster in 40 years.

Green, James, *The Devil Is Here in These Hills: West Virginia's Coal Miners and Their Battle for Freedom*, Atlantic Monthly Press, 2015.
An emeritus University of Massachusetts, Boston, history professor traces West Virginia coal miners' struggle to unionize at the turn of the 20th century.

Martin, Richard, *Coal Wars: The Future of Energy and the Fate of the Planet*, Palgrave Macmillan, 2015.
An energy analyst describes the recent decline of the coal industry.

Articles

Grunwald, Michael, "Inside the War on Coal," *Politico*, May 26, 2015, http://tinyurl.com/ nmx57pc.
The Sierra Club, with financial support from ex-New York City Mayor Michael Bloomberg, wants coal-fired power plants shut down and lobbies state regulators to reject expensive upgrades to the plants.

Henry, Devin, "Coal country rages against fall," *The Hill*, April 25, 2016, http://tinyurl.com/jh3e8lh.
Depressed coal communities are asking for $1 billion in federal aid.

Joyce, Stephanie, "In Latest Move on Climate, Obama Administration Halts Coal Leasing," *Inside Energy*, Jan. 18, 2016, http://tinyurl.com/grlldhg.
The Department of the Interior freezes new coal leases on federal land while it reviews its coal leasing program and the fees it charges coal mining companies.

Lowenstein, Jeff Kelly, "Life After Coal in Harlan County, U.S.A.," *In These Times*, May 23, 2016, http://tinyurl.com/zxgfjo7.
Residents in a hard-hit Kentucky county talk about job losses in the coal industry.

Mouawad, Jad, "A Crusader in the Coal Mine, Taking On President Obama," *The New York Times*, April 30, 2016, http://tinyurl.com/gtsv34e.
The chairman of Murray Energy, the country's largest private coal company, challenges environmental regulations in court.

Parker, Ashley, and Coral Davenport, "Donald Trump's Energy Plan: More Fossil Fuels and Fewer Rules," *The New York Times*, May 26, 2016, http:// tinyurl.com/zv9s8jz.
Presumptive Republican presidential nominee Donald Trump promises to revive the coal industry by rescinding environmental rules.

Paterson, Leigh, "Coal Communities Consider Life After Layoffs," *Inside Energy*, April 22, 2016, http:// tinyurl.com/h937toa.
Gillette, Wyo., suffers as the coal industry contracts.

Reports and Studies

"Fact Sheet: Final Consideration of Cost in the Appropriate and Necessary Finding for the Mercury and Air Toxics Standards for Power Plants," U.S. Environmental Protection Agency, April 14, 2016, http://tinyurl.com/hghf9dc.
The Environmental Protection Agency (EPA) explains the costs and benefits of its controversial rules to reduce emissions of mercury and other hazardous pollutants.

"International Energy Outlook 2016: Chapter 4. Coal," U.S. Energy Information Administration, May 11, 2016, http://tinyurl.com/z5d9kao.
The federal government issues its forecast for the U.S. energy sector, including coal, for which continued declines in demand are expected.

Park, Brian, "Power sector coal demand has fallen in nearly every state since 2007," U.S. Energy Information Administration, April 28, 2016, http://tinyurl.com/ z2lt2rq.
Coal-fired power plants are generating less of the nation's electricity.

Revesz, Richard L., *et al.*, "Familiar Territory: A Survey of Legal Precedents for the Clean Power Plan," *The Environmental Law Reporter*, March 2016, http://tinyurl.com/zbj3637.
New York University law professors defend the EPA's Clean Power Plan, which industry and state governments are challenging in court.

Smyth, Joe, "Corporate Welfare for Coal," Greenpeace, March 2016, http://tinyurl.com/hjfcv32.
The environmental activist organization argues that the federal government should charge coal companies more for mining federal coal.

For More Information

American Coalition for Clean Coal Electricity, 1152 15th St., N.W., Suite 400, Washington, DC 20005; 202-459-4800; www.americaspower.org. Partnership of mining, railroad and power companies.

Earthjustice, 50 California St., Suite 500, San Francisco, CA 94111; 800-584-6460; www.earthjustice.org. Environmental law organization.

Electric Power Research Institute, 3420 Hillview Ave., Palo Alto, CA 94304; 650-855-2000; www.epri.com. Research group focusing on electricity generation, delivery and use; members include electric utilities and government agencies.

Greenpeace, 702 H St., N.W., Suite 300, Washington, DC 20001; 202-462-1177; www.greenpeace.org. Activist group that exposes environmental problems.

National Mining Association, 101 Constitution Ave., N.W., Suite 500 East, Washington, DC 20001; 202-463-2600; www.nma.org. Trade group that advocates on behalf of U.S. mining companies.

Sierra Club, 2101 Webster St., Suite 1300, Oakland, CA 94612; 415-977-5500; www.sierraclub.org. Grassroots environmental organization.

U.S. Energy Information Administration, 1000 Independence Ave., S.W., Washington, DC 20585; 202-586-8800; www.eia.gov. Collects and analyzes energy information.

U.S. Environmental Protection Agency, 1200 Pennsylvania Ave., N.W., Washington, DC 20460; 202-272-0167; www.epa.gov. Enforces federal laws protecting human health and the environment.

2

Managing Western Lands

Barbara Mantel

The Clearwater River runs through the Nez Perce National Forest in north-central Idaho. Forest managers are working with local environmental, community and industry representatives on a collaborative project to restore the forest ecology. Advocates of collaboration say these kinds of projects are the best way to give voice to local concerns.

From *CQ Researcher,*
April 22, 2016

Armed activists grabbed national attention earlier this year when they occupied the headquarters of the Malheur National Wildlife Refuge in rural southeastern Oregon. The group of about two dozen protesters demanded that two local ranchers imprisoned for arson on public land in the region be freed and that federal lands be turned over to private and local government control.[1]

The federal government is "coming down into the states and taking over the land and the resources, putting the people into duress, putting the people into poverty," said protest leader Ammon Bundy, owner of a truck repair shop in Phoenix.[2]

Bundy is the son of Nevada rancher Cliven Bundy, who rejects federal authority over public lands and has refused for decades to pay federal fees for grazing his cattle there. Federal agents tried to confiscate the cattle in 2014 but backed down in the face of resistance from armed Bundy supporters.[3]

In late January, LaVoy Finicum, a protester at the wildlife refuge, was shot and killed while trying to run a police blockade, according to the FBI. Two weeks later, the last holdouts walked out of the wildlife refuge peacefully. Twenty-five people, including Ammon Bundy, were arrested and pleaded not guilty to charges of impeding federal government employees from performing their duties. Bundy, along with his father, also faces charges related to the earlier skirmish in Nevada.[4]

While these armed confrontations garner national headlines, a quieter rebellion against federal ownership of public lands is going on in Western states. A group of conservatives in Western

Kevin R. Morris/Corbis/VCG via Getty Image

Much of the West Is Federal Land

The federal government owns 27.4 percent of the land in the United States, most of it in Alaska and 11 Western states. Nevada has the highest share — 85 percent — of federal land, followed by Utah, Idaho and Alaska.

Percentage of Land Owned by Federal Government, by State, 2013

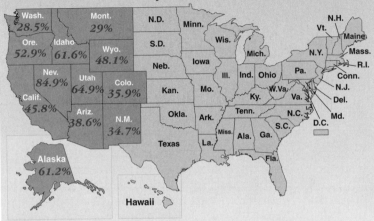

Source: Carol Hardy Vincent, Laura A. Hanson and Jerome P. Bjelopera, "Federal Land Ownership: Overview and Data," Congressional Research Service, Dec. 29, 2014, pp. 4-5, http://tinyurl.com/h6j36rf

shift in Western states in which increasingly urbanized residents want public lands "managed for clean water, for wildlife and for outdoor recreation."

Nevertheless, some Western politicians have introduced state measures to transfer federal land to state ownership or allow greater local management of those lands. In Congress, some Republicans from the West are pushing bills to allow states to take ownership or control of large swaths of national forest and are opposing calls by Native American groups for President Barack Obama to designate nearly 2 million acres in southeastern Utah a national monument.

Presidential hopefuls such as Sen. Ted Cruz, R-Texas, are weighing in. "If you trust me with your vote, I will fight day and night to return full control of Nevada's lands to its rightful owners — its citizens," Cruz said in a television ad before that state's Republican caucus in late February.[6]

congressional delegations, state legislatures, county commissions and rural communities deplores the Bundys' tactics but shares their deep distrust of Washington, which owns nearly half the land in the West. These critics of federal land policy say government agencies disregard local concerns and impose rigid environmental laws and regulations that are decimating the logging, ranching and mining industries and costing jobs. They favor transferring ownership or control of federal lands to the states.

"More than half of my district is under federal management, or lack thereof," U.S. Rep. Greg Walden, R-Ore., said during the first days of the Malheur refuge occupation. Federal officials "have come out with these proposals to close roads into the forests," he continued. "They have ignored public input."[5]

But Steve Pedery, conservation director at Oregon Wild, a Portland-based conservation group, says the land transfer movement ignores broader economic forces, such as global competition and a decades long cultural

But critics of state takeovers of federal land call it a pipe dream based on dubious legal arguments. Meanwhile, both sides argue over the quality of federal management of public lands and the effect state ownership would have on access, development and the environment. Lost in the noise is the growing number of collaborative agreements between communities and federal agencies that are trying to balance the need for jobs and a healthy environment, say supporters of a middle way. (See sidebar, p. 374.)

The sides don't always separate neatly. Some ranchers and rural communities push for state ownership, while others argue for only a greater say. And in Western legislatures, many Democrats oppose a shift in ownership. But environmental groups are united, decrying a transfer of federal lands to states as a gift to the timber and energy industries, and several prominent sportsmen's groups favor the status quo.

"Simply put, state treasuries cannot afford to manage these lands," *Field & Stream* Editorial Director Anthony Licata wrote last year. "These game-rich areas that currently belong to all of us will be developed or sold to large corporations, degrading critical habitat and locking out millions of sportsmen."[7]

The federal government owns about 624 million acres, roughly 27 percent of the United States, spread unequally throughout the country. It owns 46.9 percent of the land in the 11 contiguous Western states and 61.2 percent of Alaska, but just 4 percent across the rest of the continental United States.[8]

The federal government first took possession of land in the 1780s, when several of the original 13 states ceded wilderness between the Appalachian Mountains and the Mississippi River. In the 1800s, it acquired all the land between the Mississippi and the Pacific through purchases, conquests and treaties. Congress initially intended to dispose of these lands to settlers, which was easiest in the flat, fertile plains in the middle of the country but more difficult in the mountainous, often arid West. But as environmental concerns arose in the late 1800s and accelerated in the 1960s, the emphasis shifted to retention.

Four agencies with differing missions administer most federal land. Three of the four — the Bureau of Land Management (BLM), the U.S. Fish and Wildlife Service (FWS) and the National Park Service (NPS) — are overseen by the Department of the Interior. The BLM, the largest holder, must manage its lands for sustained yield and multiple use such as energy development, recreation, grazing, conservation and protection of wild horses and burros.* The NPS must both protect its wildlife habitat and make its lands available to the public for recreation. Removal of any resources, such as timber and oil, is prohibited. FWS lands are managed primarily to conserve and protect plants and animals. The fourth agency, the U.S. Forest Service, which is within the Department of Agriculture, must manage its lands for sustainable yield and multiple use: timber harvesting, recreation, grazing and protection of watersheds and of fish and wildlife habitats.[9]

Proponents of state ownership typically do not want to take over national parks, wilderness or wildlife refuges. Instead they focus on land administered by the BLM and Forest Service.

---

*Sustained yield is the amount of a resource that can be harvested or extracted without causing depletion.

A recent study examined the relationship between federal lands and rural economic growth in the 11 contiguous Western states between 1970 and 2014. The study found that population, employment and personal income grew, on average, faster in non-metro counties with the highest share of federal lands than in non-metro counties with the least amount of federal lands.[10]

The results reflect the changing nature of the rural West, says study author Megan Lawson of Headwaters Economics, an independent, nonpartisan research group in Bozeman, Mont., that focuses on land management. Many communities are diversifying, she says, moving away from commodity-only economies — based on mining, energy or farming — to a more service-based economy, particularly high-wage services. Engineers, architects, accountants, computer scientists and other professionals, attracted to the scenic landscapes, are moving in and are working from home or willing to drive to an office an hour or two away, she says.

A second study commissioned by the state of Utah also found that population, employment and income growth are higher in non-metro Western counties in which the federal government owns a greater share of the land — but only up to a point. Population growth peaked when federal land ownership was 46 percent, job growth when federal ownership was 43 percent and income growth when the federal ownership share was 38 percent.[11]

"You could interpret that to say that there is an ideal amount of federal land ownership in a county," says Therese Grijalva, a study co-author and an economist at Weber State University in Ogden, Utah.

The two studies differed in several ways. Grijalva's group examined counties in nine Western states and over a shorter period of time, from 2000 to 2007. It also limited its study to multiple-use land. But perhaps most important, her group controlled for factors such as wage levels, housing prices, climate and the presence of nearby highways or airports, which could muddy the results. "It's important to control for these factors, otherwise you might be attributing growth to public land when, in fact, growth is attributable to these other things," says Grijalva.

Against this backdrop, here are some of the major issues that elected officials, local communities, environmentalists, industry groups, Native American groups and others are debating:

Alaska Has Biggest Share of Federal Lands

The federal government owns more land in Alaska — more than 100 million acres — than in any other state. Federal ownership is heavily concentrated in the West, with only 4 percent of non-Western states, on average, owned by the federal government.

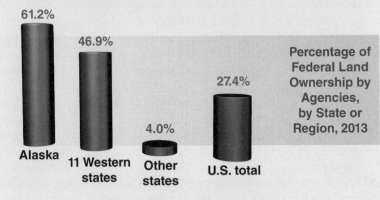

Percentage of Federal Land Ownership by Agencies, by State or Region, 2013

61.2% Alaska
46.9% 11 Western states
4.0% Other states
27.4% U.S. total

Source: Carol Hardy Vincent, Laura A. Hanson and Jerome P. Bjelopera, "Federal Land Ownership: Overview and Data," Congressional Research Service, Dec. 29, 2014, p. 20, http://tinyurl.com/h6j36rf

Does the federal government manage federal lands well?

Proponents of state ownership sharply criticize the government's record on managing federal lands.

"The dysfunction that characterizes so much of the federal government today extends to the public land agencies like the U.S. Forest Service and the Bureau of Land Management," said Robert Nelson, a University of Maryland public policy professor and former Interior Department analyst. Their greatest failure, he said: wildfire prevention.[12]

Today, twice as much U.S. forest acreage burns each year compared with 30 years ago, according to a 2015 Forest Service report, and agency scientists predict that acreage burned "may double again by midcentury."[13] Catastrophic fires endanger wildlife and natural resources, as well as lives and the growing development on lands bordering national forests. Climate change is a big factor, according to the report, but overgrown forests are the main culprit, says Ken Ivory, a Republican member of the Utah House of Representatives and the sponsor of a 2012 state law that demands the transfer of millions of acres of federal lands to Utah.

"We need a return to active management, when timber companies, under conditions and restrictions, would 'weed' the forest," reducing the threat of fire and creating jobs in the process, says Ivory. He blames the decline in logging on federal red tape, environmental regulations and environmental lawsuits.

Economist Holly Fretwell agrees. "Whether it's an actual harvest to provide logs or a harvest to restore an area, reduce fire risk or open up landscape for different types of habitat, just the planning is excessive," says Fretwell, a research fellow at the Property and Environment Research Center, a Bozeman, Mont., think tank that advocates using market principles to manage the environment.

In particular, she cites the National Environmental Policy Act (NEPA), which requires federal agencies — with public input — to prepare environmental impact statements for proposed actions, such as issuing oil well permits or allowing timber sales. However, the 1969 law applies only to federal agencies and lands. So "if we hand our federal lands over to the states and say, 'You're going to abide by your state laws,' that would change things," says Fretwell. "State environmental policy acts are typically similar to NEPA but oftentimes less restrictive."

However, those who oppose such a transfer say NEPA requirements and legal challenges are the price of democracy. "We have multiple people with multiple interests on multiple-use-mandated land, and people are going to disagree and mobilize existing laws," says Phil Brick, director of environmental studies at Whitman College in Walla Walla, Wash.

Besides, challenges don't occur when the Forest Service follows the law and resists timber company pressure to allow logging on wilderness-quality land or in endangered-species habitat, says Pedery of Oregon Wild. Moreover, he says, old logging methods helped to intensify forest fires by cutting down the oldest, largest and most fire-resistant trees.

"Now we're logging smaller, and we're logging more ecologically appropriate trees than 20, 30 years ago," says Pedery, who refutes Ivory's contention that more logging is needed.

Wildfire conditions have been made worse, say many forest ecologists, by climate change, drought and decades of fire suppression, which have allowed fuels to accumulate rather than be burned as part of the natural fire cycle. The forestry experts who co-authored a 2015 *Science* magazine article called for shifting away from current fire-suppression policies in favor of allowing controlled burns "under favorable weather and wind dispersal conditions."[14]

"There is plenty of room for improvement, but there are ways to work within the current system to make that happen," says Brick.

Proponents of state ownership of public lands also complain that regional and national supervisors at federal agencies run roughshod over local concerns. "Their attitude is: 'It's our way or the highway,' " says Denver-based lawyer Constance Brooks, who has represented states in suits against federal agencies. "We're . . . seeing a rolling road-closure system. The feds are putting gates up in some cases and saying you have to get a right-of-way permit, [which] can cost thousands" of dollars. (Utah is suing the federal government for the right to use some 12,000 rural roads on public lands.[15])

Federal budget pressures may be partially to blame. For example, wildfire costs now account for just over half of the Forest Service's budget — up from 16 percent 20 years ago. That has meant cutbacks in vegetation and watershed management, research, facilities maintenance, wildlife and fisheries habitat management and road maintenance.[16]

Despite manpower and funding shortages, however, local Forest Service and BLM managers say they have focused on participating in collaborative agreements between local government officials, industry and environmental groups in order to meet competing needs. (See sidebar, p. 374.) Collaboration means creating a space "where individuals do not have to defend their values and views, where people seek to understand one another and to work together to find solutions," Forest Service chief Thomas Tidwell told an Idaho forestry conference in 2014.[17]

Critics also say the federal agencies are inefficient. "The federal government loses money for almost every activity they do on public lands, with the exception of minerals management," says Fretwell. For instance, the Forest Service and BLM run in the red on the management of timber, recreation and grazing, while states make money on state-owned land, according to an analysis by Fretwell and a colleague. While states and federal agencies charge roughly the same timber fees, states typically charge higher grazing and recreation fees.[18] "We seem to be squandering our resources oftentimes on public lands," says Fretwell.

Federal and state laws and regulations differ in that the federal government must manage its lands for multiple use without necessarily considering the greatest dollar return. But Western states must manage their "trust" lands — provided by the federal government when the states entered the Union — to maximize revenue to support schools and other state institutions.[19]

Thus, comparing federal and state efficiency misses the point, contended Martin Nie, a professor of natural resources policy at the University of Montana. It would be possible to harvest more timber if the national forests were privatized or if their management were exempted from some environmental laws, he said.[20]

"But that is not what the public or Congress has asked from our federal lands," he said.[21]

Do states have a legal right to take ownership of federal lands?

Utah state Rep. Ivory has been urging Western state legislators to follow Utah's lead and demand federal transfer of public lands to state ownership. "The federal government has a constitutional obligation to relinquish the land," says Ivory.

But legal arguments cited by Ivory and others are not sound, according to many experts, including the attorney general of Idaho, where the House of Representatives in March passed a bill providing management guidelines for any federal lands transferred to the state. The attorney general's office said the Idaho bill's main legal argument for claiming federal lands within Idaho's borders "has no support in the law."[22]

The legal debate involves differing interpretations of the U.S. Constitution and the laws Congress passed authorizing Western territories to become states. Those "enabling" acts, along with a 1787 federal ordinance, stipulated that new states entering the union did so on

Andy Nelson/The Register-Guard via AP

A demonstrator in Eugene, Ore., on Jan. 19, 2016, defends federal control of public lands. Many opponents of the occupation at the Malheur National Wildlife Refuge and of the land transfer movement say urbanized residents in the West want public lands managed for outdoor recreation, clean water and wildlife conservation, not resource extraction and development.

equal footing with the original 13 states on all matters of sovereignty. That included the ability to form a government, raise taxes, enforce laws and elect representatives to Congress.

The "equal footing doctrine" meant that new states should have received all the federal lands within their borders because the 13 colonies had taken ownership from the British crown of all public lands within their borders when they became states, argues San Diego-based lawyer John Howard, a member of a consulting team hired by Utah to evaluate legal theories supporting a state takeover of federal lands.[23]

"Utah was admitted as a state, right? But for some reason the [public] land wasn't admitted as Utah's land," says Howard. "Utah should have gotten that land."

But John Ruple, a University of Utah law professor and co-author of a legal analysis of the transfer movement, says Utah and the other Western states did not receive all the federal land within their borders at statehood because nothing in the equal footing doctrine required the federal government to relinquish the land.[24]

"The Supreme Court has said that the equal footing clause is about political rights and sovereignty, and it is not about economic status or condition," says Ruple. "Some states had a lot of federal land, others did not, and they had different economic resources. The equal footing doctrine was never intended to get rid of that diversity." Ruple and many legal experts consider the issue long settled.

Howard counters that the large amount of federal land within Utah's borders impinges on its political sovereignty, preventing it from building roads, settling the land and increasing the number of representatives it sends to Congress. Howard and his fellow consultants have recommended that Utah sue the United States to force a transfer of federal lands.

They are pinning their hopes on Supreme Court Chief Justice John Roberts and his interpretation of states' rights in *Shelby County v. Holder*, a landmark 2013 case concerning the 1965 Voting Rights Act. In the 5-4 decision, the court struck down a provision that determined which states must obtain federal preclearance of changes to their voting laws or practices because of a history of racial discrimination in voting. The majority opinion, delivered by Roberts, said the provision violates the " 'fundamental principle of equal sovereignty' "among states because it distinguishes between states "based on 40-year-old data" about racial discrimiation.[25]

Thus, says Howard, "states are entitled to be treated equally to the other states in all ways," including having control over the public lands within their borders.

Other experts are doubtful. "I'm not sure what Justice Roberts would say about applying the equal sovereignty doctrine to federal lands," says Erin Ryan, a Florida State University environmental law professor. "It seems attractive to those arguing for transfer, but it doesn't come out of solid jurisprudence."

Besides, says Ryan, state enabling acts contained disclaimer clauses, such as one for Colorado that says inhabitants "forever disclaim all right and title" to public lands and that those lands "shall be and remain at the sole and entire disposition of the United States."[26]

Agencies Manage Nearly 624 Million Acres

The five agencies that oversee federal lands administer 623.5 million acres. The U.S. Forest Service — founded in 1905 — is the oldest federal land-management agency, but the Bureau of Land Management (BLM) administers the most land — nearly 250 million acres. The Forest Service and BLM must balance multiple and sometimes conflicting priorities, such as conservation and resource development.

Federal Land-Management Agencies and Their Functions

Name of Agency	Year Created	Amount of Land Administered	Function
U.S. Forest Service (Agriculture Dept.)	1905	192.9 million acres, mostly in the West; manages more than half of all federal lands in the East	Protect lands, wilderness, water flows; provide timber, recreation, livestock grazing, wildlife and fish habitat
National Park Service (Interior Dept.)	1916	79.7 million acres, about 66 percent of it in Alaska	Preserve unique resources while making them available for public recreation
Fish and Wildlife Service* (Interior Dept.)	1940	89.1 million acres, 86 percent of it in Alaska	Conserve plants and animals; uses such as timber, grazing and minerals development are secondary priorities
Bureau of Land Management (Interior Dept.)	1946	247.3 million acres, mostly rangeland; 99.9 percent in 12 Western states, including Alaska	Provide recreation, grazing, timber, conservation and protection of watershed, wildlife and fish habitats
Department of Defense	1947	14.5 million acres, mostly in the West	Support mission-related activities

Created when two federal agencies were consolidated; also administers nearly 210 million acres of marine refuges and national monuments.

Source: Carol Hardy Vincent, Laura A. Hanson and Jerome P. Bjelopera, "Federal Land Ownership: Overview and Data," Congressional Research Service, Dec. 29, 2014, pp. 8-11, http://tinyurl.com/h6j36rf; also see "About the U.S. Fish and Wildlife Service," U.S. Fish and Wildlife Service, www.fws.gov/help/about_us.html

But such disclaimer clauses were inserted to serve a very narrow purpose, said attorney William Perry Pendley, president of Colorado-based Mountain States Legal Foundation, which advocates for property rights and small government. They were designed "to protect the clean title of the United States so that the United States could dispose of or sell public lands," he said.[27]

However, it's not as if the federal government didn't try to dispose of its Western lands, says Ryan, but "nobody wanted it." The federal government made these lands available for development throughout the 19th century, but "it wasn't suitable for farming," she says.

Trumping all, says Ruple, is the Constitution's Property Clause, which states entering the union had to accept as the supreme law of the land. "The Property Clause grants Congress the power to dispose of and make all needful rules and regulations" respecting its lands, says Ruple, "and the Supreme Court has made it clear that 'dispose of' includes the ability to retain lands," even indefinitely.

Howard responds, "Yes, the federal government can do whatever it wants to with land it actually legitimately owns — I'm not going to argue with that — but it doesn't legitimately own this land."

Ruple and Ryan say any lawsuit against the United States would have to overcome very high hurdles and is unlikely to succeed. "But here's the thing about litigation," says Ryan. "It can be a tool to advance public policy." Even if unsuccessful, "it could influence who the next president appoints as secretary of the Interior, or how the department manages its lands. Or it could influence Congress," she says.

Would states develop, sell and reduce public access to federal lands they acquire?

Western states own nearly 40 million acres of state trust lands, managed to maximize revenue, while the Forest Service and the Bureau of Land Management manage more than 300 million acres in the contiguous Western states for multiple use — without regard to profit.[28] If states were to take over that federal land, it's unclear which mandate they would follow.

"It will be managed for multiple uses and sustained yield," and wilderness protection would not be ignored, said Republican state Rep. Mike Noel of Utah, the primary sponsor of a new law outlining how the state would manage federal lands.[29] Under Noel's law multiple use includes grazing, timber production, energy exploration and production, rights-of-way, fish and wildlife development, recreation and wilderness conservation.[30]

That may be true in theory, says law professor Ruple, but "financial realities" would lead states, including Utah, to favor "commodity-producing and other revenue-producing uses," an emphasis many environmental groups oppose. Others, such as Jim Caswell, a BLM director under President George W. Bush, say transferring control to the states "will almost surely result in parcels being auctioned off; states simply can't afford the management costs."[31]

Several studies have estimated state management costs. One study, prepared for the Utah governor's office, predicted that in 2017 it would cost the state $280 million, adjusted for inflation, to manage the more than 31 million acres of federal lands it wants to claim. The largest cost, by far, would be for wildfire prevention and response.[32]

On the other side of the ledger, "revenues produced on public lands are significant," said the report. More than 90 percent come from mineral leases to private companies — mostly from oil and gas royalties, but also from coal. Currently, the federal government shares half of those royalties with the states.[33]

The study says if oil prices averaged $62 a barrel and natural gas averaged $3.30 per thousand cubic-feet, Utah would more than cover its costs, but only if the pace of drilling for new wells increased and the state received all of the royalty payments.[34] But while the U.S. Energy Information Administration is predicting natural gas prices in that range for 2017, crude oil is predicted to hover around $42 a barrel.[35]

In addition, says Ruple, it's unrealistic to expect Utah to be able to keep all the royalty payments. "I can't imagine the federal government would suddenly give up an existing revenue stream," he says. Federal agencies always have been careful to retain most mineral rights when they have given up land in the past, and courts have upheld that arrangement, he says.

In Idaho, which also has a vocal land transfer movement, the mix of commodities is different. There the Forest Service controls most of the federal land, and timber, rather than mineral extraction, is the main source of revenue. A state-commissioned study concluded that Idaho would lose millions of dollars in eight of nine different scenarios if it took control of federal lands. Only under the most optimistic timber harvest assumptions would Idaho make a profit.[36]

But an economic analysis for the Boise-based Idaho Conservation League said a state takeover would be dire under any scenario, with Idaho losing almost $1 billion within five years of a land transfer and more than $2 billion after 20 years. As in Utah, the biggest cost would relate to wildfires.[37]

"Last time I looked, 10 out of the 11 contiguous Western states had some kind of balanced-budget requirement," says Ruple. Thus, the states either would have to pull money from other programs or figure out how to make revenues cover costs on public lands, say analysts.

Utah's Ivory says state control would lead to more logging and the option for more energy development — and that would be a good thing. "We would control our own destiny," says Ivory. And those who worry about large land selloffs are misinformed, he says. Under Utah's 2012 land transfer bill, the state would get only 5 percent of any land sale revenues. "So what incentive is there to sell the land?" says Ivory.

But Jonathan Oppenheimer, the Idaho Conservation League's staff lobbyist, says billions of dollars in accumulating losses would make land sales inevitable in Idaho. Plus, the state does not have a system for managing the hikers, hunters, anglers, off-road vehicle users, snowmobilers, skiers and others who use Forest Service land, he says.

It likely would mean "a reduction of visitations on our public lands," says Oppenheimer. Outdoor recreation generates $6.3 billion in consumer spending a year and more than 76,000 jobs in the state, according to the Outdoor Industry Association, a Boulder, Colo.-based trade group that calls the transfer movement "the public land heist."[38]

BACKGROUND
Amassing Federal Lands

Americans always have fiercely debated the purpose, management and ownership of public lands.

When the 13 colonies declared their independence from Britain in 1776, Massachusetts, Connecticut, New York, Virginia, North Carolina, South Carolina and Georgia claimed huge tracts of land stretching from the East Coast to the Mississippi River. The Articles of Confederation, which gave each state an equal vote in Congress, held in check the political power of these larger states. But they had a significant economic advantage, wrote historian John R. Van Atta in *Securing the West: Politics, Public Lands, and the Fate of the Old Republic, 1785-1850.*[39] Their wilderness could be sold to retire their Revolutionary War debts, to attract settlers or be given to militia members who had been promised land in exchange for fighting the British.

The smaller states, particularly Maryland, argued strenuously that lands between the Appalachian Mountains and the Mississippi should be regarded as the "common property" of the nascent nation. But they could not convince opponents, who, in 1777, defeated a proposal to transfer these lands to congressional control.[40]

But pressure for such a transfer continued to build. Congress desperately needed revenue to finance the Revolutionary War; this land could serve as collateral for loans from abroad and be sold to raise money. Congress also needed land to fulfill its promise of bounties to Continental Army soldiers. Meanwhile, states were struggling to control the "the tide of migrating population, the proliferation of squatter strongholds and the

threats of separatist movements on their frontiers," wrote Van Atta. Transferring the land to Congress would shift this burden.[41] In 1780, New York became the first to cede its westernmost lands to Congress.

The 1783 peace treaty with Britain formally gave the United States all the land east of the Mississippi between Canada and Florida. Over the next seven years, the six remaining states with lands beyond the Appalachians ceded those territories to the federal government, which by 1802 held 237 million acres.[42]

The United States acquired the lands west of the Mississippi through war, treaties and purchases from foreign governments, beginning in 1803 with the Louisiana Purchase from France and culminating with the Alaska Purchase from Russia in 1867. Over the course of nearly 90 years, the federal government had amassed more than 1.8 billion acres, all the while confronting Native American and Mexican claims to the land.[43]

"The often contradictory, poorly enforced, and ill-conceived attempts to broker and implement land purchases, exchanges and treaty agreements between the United States and Native American tribes mark one of the saddest chapters in U.S. history," wrote environmental studies professor Randall K. Wilson in *America's Public Lands: From Yellowstone to Smokey Bear and Beyond.*[44]

Disposing of U.S. Lands

Initially, the federal government was determined to dispose of much of its public land. Since 1781, it has sold or granted nearly 1.3 billion acres to homesteaders, military veterans, private buyers, states, railroad corporations and others, with most of the transfers occurring before 1940.[45]

In the 1780s, Congress' stated policy was that public lands should be "disposed of for the common benefit of the United States" and settled and formed into states which "shall have the same rights of sovereignty, freedom and independence, as the other States."[46] But serious questions loomed, wrote Van Atta, including the rights of indigenous tribes, the method for distributing land to settlers and the conditions for statehood.[47]

In 1785, Congress enacted the first land ordinance law. After purchasing Native American lands, the federal government was required to survey the land, mark it off into townships and subdivide it into 640-acre sections to

CHRONOLOGY

1780-1867 *United States amasses, and disposes of, public lands.*

1780 New York cedes its frontier to the United States; other states follow over the next 10 years.

1785 Land Ordinance Act allows auction of 640-acre parcels of public land to settlers for $1 an acre.

1803 United States purchases Louisiana territory from France and lowers minimum land auction to 160 acres.

1846 Oregon Treaty establishes U.S. control over the current American Northwest.

1848 Mexico cedes the current American Southwest.

1862 Homestead Act allows settlers to claim 160 acres for a small fee.

1867 U.S. acquires Alaska from Russia.

1872-1946 *U.S. starts retaining public lands.*

1872 General Mining Law opens federal lands to mineral exploration. . . . Yellowstone National Park is created.

1891 General Land Reform Act authorizes presidents to create forest reserves.

1906 Antiquities Act allows presidents to declare national monuments.

1929 President Herbert Hoover proposes giving Western states some public lands but states refuse.

1934 Taylor Grazing Act establishes grazing allotments, permits and fees on the open range.

1946 Interior Department's Bureau of Land Management (BLM) is established.

1964-1993 *Environmental laws spark Western rebellions.*

1964 Wilderness Act protects wilderness.

1969 National Environmental Policy Act requires federal agencies, with public input, to prepare environmental impact statements for proposed actions.

1970 Clean Air Act passed. Clean Water Act approved two years later.

1973 Endangered Species Act passed.

1976 Federal Land Policy and Management Act mandates that BLM and Forest Service lands be managed for multiple use.

1979 Nevada Legislature asserts control over BLM lands and sues the federal government; over the next few years, Arizona, New Mexico, Utah and Wyoming enact similar laws.

1980 Alaska National Interest Lands Conservation Act protects 104 million federal acres in Alaska.

1981 Nevada federal court dismisses state's lawsuit; so-called Sagebrush Rebellion of Western states resisting federal ownership of public lands fades.

1993 "Sagebrush Rebellion" resurfaces when Nye County, Nev., bulldozes open roads on federal land.

2012-Present *Land transfer movement revives.*

2012 Utah enacts law demanding hand-over of federal lands; Arizona passes similar law, but Republican Gov. Jan Brewer vetoes it.

2013 Idaho Legislature passes resolution favoring federal transfer of public lands to the state; other states later consider dozens of related bills.

2014 In an armed confrontation, federal agents fail to confiscate Nevada rancher Cliven Bundy's cattle for nonpayment of grazing fees.

2016 In January, armed protesters, including Bundy's son Ammon, begin a six-week occupation at Oregon's Malheur National Wildlife Refuge, demanding disposal of federal lands. One protester is shot and killed by the FBI; the rest eventually surrender. . . . In February, Cliven Bundy is arrested on charges related to the Nevada skirmish. . . . In March, Utah's Legislature appropriates funds for a possible lawsuit against the United States to force the transfer of federal lands.

be auctioned off for a minimum of $1 an acre. Within each township, the federal government reserved one section, and later two sections, to be used to raise funds for local schools.[48]

A second land ordinance in 1787 and the newly drafted U.S. Constitution resolved the conditions for statehood. First, a federally appointed governor would administer a territory; then, as the population grew, he would share authority with a representative assembly. Finally, the territory would achieve statehood on equal footing with the original states.[49] At that point, lands reserved for the support of schools would be transferred to state ownership and become so-called state trust lands. In 1792, Kentucky became the first "western" state to join the union (Vermont, in the East, had become a state a year earlier), followed by Tennessee in 1796 and Ohio in 1803.

After the Louisiana Purchase, Congress extended credit to land buyers and reduced the minimum sale to 160-acre sections. A land rush ensued, and in 1812 Congress established the General Land Office to cope with the huge task of land surveys and sales. But by 1819, the rush had turned to a bust, as farmers flooded markets with agricultural goods, driving down prices.[50]

During the Civil War, Northern politicians in control of Congress lost no time passing the Homestead Act of 1862 to encourage small farms and discourage Southern plantation-style agriculture in the West. Settlers could claim 160 acres of federal land essentially for free, as long as they lived on and improved the land for five years. But settlers often found the best lands in other hands: The federal government had begun to give states and private companies land for building canals and railroads.[51]

Gold and silver rushes in California, Nevada and Colorado prompted Congress to pass the General Mining Law of 1872, still in effect today, stipulating that federal lands would be open to mineral exploration and occupation. Miners could stake a claim for a nominal fee as long as they made $100 worth of improvements each year. Large companies, which could afford machinery needed for drilling deep mines, benefited the most from the law.[52]

In 1877, Congress passed the Desert Lands Act to encourage agriculture in arid regions. It allowed purchases of 640 acres of public land for $1.25 per acre, as long as the owner promised to irrigate the land within

three years. But the law reflected a fundamental misunderstanding of desert ecology and was a "monumental failure" in promoting farming, wrote Wilson.[53]

Meanwhile, homesteaders often needed to graze their sheep and cattle on public lands because the government refused to issue "larger homestead claims that were better suited for the West's arid landscape," wrote Shawn Regan, a research fellow at the Property and Environment Research Center. Homesteaders had no formal rights to, or obligations on, this open range, and overgrazing, erosion and poor livestock conditions resulted, according to Regan.[54]

Retaining Federal Lands

By the time Colorado, the Dakotas, Montana, Washington, Idaho, Wyoming and Utah became states in the last quarter of the 19th century, land speculation, overgrazing, denuded forests and massive wildfires were alarming sportsmen, conservationists, preservationists and government managers. Congress began to shield land from development, setting aside 2.2 million acres in 1872 to create Yellowstone, the country's first national park.

In the late 19th century and early 20th century, Congress set about creating a series of national parks, including Yosemite in California. In 1906, President Theodore Roosevelt, an ardent sportsman and conservationist, signed the Antiquities Act, which granted presidents unprecedented powers "that would forever alter the manner, politics, and scope of land protection in the United States," wrote Wilson. The law made it a federal crime to disturb sites on public lands with historical, cultural and scientific significance, and it allowed presidents to unilaterally declare such sites — potentially covering tens of millions of acres — national monuments.[55] Roosevelt, who created the U.S. Forest Service in 1905, protected approximately 230 million acres of public land, creating 150 national forests, 51 federal bird reserves, four national game preserves, five national parks and 18 national monuments (including the Grand Canyon National Monument).[56]

The General Land Reform Act of 1891 had authorized presidents to create forest reserves from the public domain. About a decade later, Congress put the Agriculture Department's Division of Forestry, soon renamed the Forest Service, in charge. But regulations for mining, timber cutting and pasturing within the

BLM Struggles to Manage Wild Horses

Activists say herds are culled inhumanely to mollify ranchers.

A harshly critical government report last fall confirmed animal rights activists' worst suspicions. Over the three-year period ending in 2012, the Interior Department's Bureau of Land Management (BLM) sold nearly 1,800 wild horses to Colorado rancher Tom Davis, who sent them to Mexican slaughterhouses.[1]

While it is illegal to slaughter horses on U.S. soil, it is not a crime to export them for slaughter elsewhere. Still, it is BLM policy not to sell wild horses to foreign slaughterhouses or to so-called "kill buyers" such as Davis.[2]

"The only thing standing between mustangs and certain doom is the American public, which opposes horse slaughter," said Suzanne Roy, director of the American Wild Horse Preservation Campaign in Hillsborough, N.C.[3]

The BLM estimated that 47,329 wild horses, called mustangs, and 10,821 burros roam agency lands in the West. That's more than twice the number the land can support, according to the agency, which rounds up thousands of animals each year and auctions them off for adoption or pays for their lifelong care at private corrals or pastures. Currently, nearly 47,000 horses and burros are in private facilities.[4]

Davis purchased the wild horses through the adoption program and told investigators that "in selling so many loads of horses, BLM had to know the horses would end up at the slaughterhouse." Moreover, the bureau continued to sell horses to Davis even after learning about his activities, said a report by the Interior Department's Office of Inspector General.[5]

"We take the report's findings really seriously," said Michael Tupper, the adoption program supervisor. The BLM has since instituted a new policy, Tupper said: It only will sell four horses to any buyer within a six-month period.[6]

Ever since Congress passed the Wild Free-Roaming Horses and Burros Act of 1971 to protect and manage these wild animals, animal rights activists and ranchers have faced off over the government program. Activists accuse the government of inhumanely culling the herds to mollify ranchers, whose cattle graze on the same public lands at below-market fees. (Grazing fees on states' lands can be as much as eight times the federal grazing fee.)[7] Ranchers complain the government is not doing enough to rid the range of wild horses and burros that, they say, decimate grass and water.

"I rely on these ranges and have spent thousands of dollars acquiring permits, and I can't afford for the wild horses and burros to put me out of business," said Utah rancher Dustin Huntington at a recent Emery County Commissioners meeting.[8]

But the Washington-based Animal Welfare Institute claims individual herds of wild horses and burros are too small — not too large — and as a result, the animals' "long-term health and genetic viability are seriously imperiled." The group also says densely concentrated livestock are degrading the range conditions rather than the wild horses, and that the BLM does not adequately screen, educate and monitor those adopting the animals.[9]

To counter the various groups' accusations, the BLM maintains a "myths and facts" webpage. It says the agency monitors the genetic health of each herd; that far from doing the bidding of ranchers, it has presided over a 35 percent drop in livestock grazing on its lands since 1971;

nation's forest reserves fed a growing rebellion in the West; ranchers, miners, homesteaders and local politicians began demanding that the reserves be turned over to the states. The rebellion ended when Forest Service chief Gifford Pinchot forcefully told a 1907 public lands convention in Colorado that the government would not back down.[57] By 1909, the Forest Service was managing nearly 200 million acres of forest reserves.[58]

In 1916 Congress created the National Park Service, within the Interior Department, to administer the nation's parks and monuments.

Aside from parks, forests and some wildlife refuges, the federal government held roughly 235 million acres of unregulated land in the American West — often remote, mountainous or parched — that had never been sold and was being treated as "open commons for ranchers, miners

and it has had to reduce wild horse and burro public range-lands by 41 percent since 1971 because of conflicts with other wildlife, lack of water and too-close proximity to state and private lands.[10]

Roundups, adoptions and holding costs account for three-quarters of the BLM's wild horse and burro program's annual expenditures, and critics say that is way too much. Roundups "need to stop," said Scott Beckstead, Oregon director for the Humane Society of the United States. Instead, he said, the BLM should seriously consider fertility control.[11]

The fertility control vaccine works for up to 22 months, but the BLM says locating and tracking individual horses on vast ranges makes delivering the vaccine difficult. However, a 2013 National Academy of Sciences report said "the process is no more disruptive than the current method of population control — gathering and removal — without the further disruption of removing animals."[12]

Activists say they are ready to help. "In Colorado alone, several nonprofit organizations have been working for years to ensure that wild mustangs remain free and safe," said Charlotte Roe, an advocate with the Longhopes Donkey Shelter in Bennett, Colo. Volunteers help the BLM dart mares with the vaccine, said Roe, and these organizations "deserve our strongest support and involvement."[13]

— **Barbara Mantel**

The U.S. Bureau of Land Management rounds up wild horses southwest of Milford, Utah, on July 28, 2014.

[1] John M. Glionna, "1,800 protected wild horses sent to their deaths in Mexican slaughterhouse," *Los Angeles Times*, Oct. 29, 2015, http://tinyurl.com/jnspmrwc.

[2] "Wild Horse and Burro Quick Facts," Bureau of Land Management, April 6, 2016, http://tinyurl.com/7eru694.

[3] Glionna, *op. cit.*

[4] "Wild Horse and Burro Quick Facts," *op. cit.*

[5] Glionna, *op. cit.*

[6] *Ibid.*

[7] Holly Fretwell and Shawn Regan, "Divided Lands: State vs. Federal Management in the West," Property and Environment Research Center, February 2015, p. 15, http://tinyurl.com/zk4u4hw.

[8] "Commission hears concerns on wild horse/burro issue," *Emery County Progress* (Castle Dale, Utah), March 8, 2016, http://tinyurl.com/zo92jxl.

[9] "Myths and Facts About Wild Horses and Burros," Animal Welfare Institute, http://tinyurl.com/zn49lzw.

[10] "Myths and Facts," Bureau of Land Management, April 12, 2016, http://tinyurl.com/jf9w3d2.

[11] Camilla Mortensen, "Oregon Wild Horse Roundup Spurs Debate," *Eugene Weekly* (Ore.), Nov. 19, 2015, http://tinyurl.com/nzczjq5.

[12] "Using Science to Improve the BLM Wild Horse and Burro Program: A Way Forward," The National Academy of Sciences, p. 3 of the Summary, 2013, http://tinyurl.com/hv6hubd.

[13] Charlotte Roe, "Keep wild equines free," *Daily Camera* (Boulder, Colo.), Dec. 5, 2015, http://tinyurl.com/gqpbxd2.

and loggers," wrote geography professor James Skillen in *The Nation's Largest Landlord: The Bureau of Land Management in the American West*. In 1929, President Herbert Hoover wrote to Western governors recommending that these lands be granted to the states, which, Hoover said, had the local knowledge to manage them best.[59]

Hoover eventually offered states only the surface rights, with the federal government retaining rights to underground minerals. Sen. William Borah of Idaho compared the plan to handing states "an orange with the juice sucked out of it." Gov. George Dern of Utah also rejected the proposal, saying: "The States already own . . . millions of acres of this same kind of land, which they can neither sell nor lease, and which is yielding no income. Why should they want more of this precious heritage of desert?"[60]

Collaboratives Aim to Lessen Tensions

Proponents say groups balance environmental, economic interests in public lands.

In Idaho, everyone had ideas about what should be done within the CLearwater Basin, 6 million acres of spectacular mountains, forests and rivers.

Conservationists wanted to protect the complex ecosystem. Hunters and anglers wanted to protect wildlife habitat. The timber industry wanted to protect its logging interests. The booming off-road vehicle community wanted more trails. Area towns wanted jobs. And the Nez-Perce Tribe wanted to foster forest health and protect the basin's ability to support hunting, fishing and gathering, says Jonathan Oppenheimer, staff lobbyist at the Boise-based Idaho Conservation League.

"We've had a number of competing, and sometime complementary interests and concerns," says Oppenheimer. "For a long time, no one had been able to agree, but everyone agreed that it was important to do something."

The solution was to start the 22-member Clearwater Basin Collaborative in 2008.

The effort is part of a two-decade movement by federal agencies, rural communities and other stakeholders to form collaborative agreements to manage public lands, especially forests, where stakeholders work together to balance the need for both jobs and a healthy environment.

"Some people joke that forest collaboration has gone viral," said Emily Jane Davis, a forestry professor at Oregon State University. Oregon has more than two dozen collaborative groups — up from one in 1992. "Each national forest in the state has at least one," she said.[1]

The collaborations refute the argument that states must take ownership of federal lands because federal managers are too remote, says Steve Pedery, conservation director at Oregon Wild, a Portland-based group working to protect the state's waterways and wild, public lands. "I find that argument ridiculous, and it usually comes from people who have never attended a collaborative meeting where local people are actually participating with [government] land managers and making decisions."

But collaborative conservation has divided the environmental community. Some environmental groups say the agreements involve only a limited number of participants, shut out public discussion and promote too much commercial development on public lands.

"They are inherently anti-democratic," says Gary Macfarlane, ecosystem defense director for Friends of the Clearwater, based in Moscow, Idaho. The group works to protect land, wildlife and water in the Clearwater Basin.

At the other end of the spectrum, advocates of greater state control of public lands also are skeptical of collaboratives. "Collaboration can be great, and it can be total failure," says Holly Fretwell, a research fellow at the Property and Environment Research Center, a Bozeman, Mont., think tank advocating market principles for environmental management. It all depends on who is running the group and who is in opposition, she says. "There are some local environmental groups here in Montana that say you should never cut a tree" and that refuse to negotiate.

In 2009, the movement got a boost when Congress passed the Collaborative Forest Landscape Restoration Act, which set aside up to $40 million annually to accept proposals from collaborative groups and to fund up to

---

In the early 1930s, overgrazing and erosion, combined with drought and the economic Depression, led a demoralized livestock industry to reluctantly accept active federal management of open rangelands.[61] The Taylor Grazing Act of 1934 established grazing allotments, permits and fees. A portion of the fees were to be returned to local grazing districts to make rangeland improvements such as fencing and irrigation systems. As a result, the number of livestock and ranchers grazing livestock on public lands significantly decreased, while the remaining ranchers who received permits "realized increased stability in their operations," according to the government.[62]

In 1946, the office that administered grazing regulations was merged with the General Land Office to form the Bureau of Land Management.

Regulation and Rebellion

According to a policy analysis for the state of Utah, "The 1960s and 1970s marked a transition into the modern

10 restoration projects within national forests.[2] Many forests have become overgrown, bug-infested and prone to wildfires as a result of climate change, logging of fire-resistant old-growth trees and a decades-long policy of fire suppression, according to many forest ecologists.

A restoration project for the 1.4-million-acre Selway-Middle Fork ecosystem within the Clearwater Basin was one of the first to be funded. It was the brainchild of the Clearwater Basin Collaborative and local Forest Service managers.

In its first five years, the Selway-Middle Fork restoration project has decommissioned 66 miles of roads to reduce habitat fragmentation and road erosion that can pollute streams; improved 63 miles of stream habitat, 1,915 acres of forest vegetation and 16,000 acres of wildlife habitat; maintained and improved 3,564 miles of trails; reduced hazardous materials, such as small-diameter trees, on 61,241 forest acres that can fuel fires; sold 40,325 cubic feet of timber; and directly created or maintained more than 400 jobs, according to its 2015 progress report.[3]

"I have seen the firsthand benefits to people, water and wildlife that this program is doing, which I hope future generations will be able to share with their own families," said Joyce Dearstyne, executive director of Framing Our Community, a member of the Clearwater Basin Collaborative, based in Elk City, Idaho, which places former timber workers and college students in forest-restoration jobs.[4]

But the Selway-Middle Fork group's biggest project is yet to come. Slated to begin this spring, the collaboration seeks to lower fire hazards, improve habitat and reduce sediment in the water within the 44,000-acre Clear Creek watershed. It will involve the largest timber sale in the collaborative's six-year history.

But it has run into opposition. "Friends of the Clearwater may sue over this sale," says Macfarlane. The logging could significantly degrade water quality and wildlife habitat, he says.

His and other environmental groups have broader objections to collaborative restoration agreements.[5] "So-called collaborative groups cut deals, couched as recommendations, before the required analysis takes place under the National Environmental Policy Act ever begins," says Macfarlane. The law, commonly referred to as NEPA, requires federal agencies, with public input, to prepare environmental impact statements for proposed actions, such as logging.

"When a 'deal' between so-called conservation, government, community and timber industry interests takes place, the NEPA process [that] follows becomes a pro-forma exercise," he says. In addition, all citizens can weigh in during the NEPA process, but "only a few participate in a so-called collaborative process," says Macfarlane.

Oppenheimer says the goal of collaboratives is "not necessarily to provide a solution that is acceptable to everyone, but to appeal to the broad population in the middle: folks who agree that there can be some logging, but at the same time agree that there can be new wilderness designations as well."

— *Barbara Mantel*

---

[1] Andrew Spaeth, "What is a forest collaborative?" Sustainable Northwest, Feb. 18, 2015, http://tinyurl.com/hh3lp46.

[2] "Collaborative Forest Landscape Restoration Program Overview," U.S. Forest Service, http://tinyurl.com/os72obh.

[3] "Selway-Middle Fork Collaborative Forest Landscape Restoration Program: 5 Year Report, 2010-2014," Clearwater Basin Collaborative, February 2015, p. 3, http://tinyurl.com/zowyfmd.

[4] "Idaho: Meet Joyce Dearstyne," The Nature Conservancy, http://tinyurl.com/zkt6qh9.

[5] "Collective Statement on Collaborative Group Trends," Blue Mountains Biodiversity Project, June 2015, http://tinyurl.com/jxfphwh.

---

era of federal land management with the enactment of federal statutes protecting air, water, habitat and wildlife resources and establishing administrative protocols for managing federal lands."[63]

Preservationists were demanding that parts of the public domain be maintained as wilderness where logging, energy development and grazing were prohibited. In response, Congress passed the Wilderness Act of 1964, which set aside millions of acres. Within the next decade, Congress passed several far-reaching laws that affected activities on federal lands, including the:

- National Environmental Policy Act of 1969;
- Clean Air Act of 1970, which regulated air emissions;
- Clean Water Act of 1972, which regulated water pollution and quality standards for surface waters;
- Endangered Species Act of 1973, which protected plants and animals deemed threatened or endangered by extinction.

Then in 1976, Congress passed the Federal Land Policy and Management Act. It legally established the government's policy of favoring land retention over disposal, which had been in place since President Hoover failed to shift public lands to the states 40 years earlier. The act also declared that federal lands be managed for multiple use: not only energy development and extraction, logging and ranching but also environmental, scientific, scenic and historic protection; land preservation; habitat protection; and outdoor recreation.[64]

But the law did not address how the BLM might reconcile all its competing responsibilities. As a result, "public lands politics since 1976 has been a struggle to balance these 'equal' mandates," Skillen said.[65]

In 1979, that struggle erupted into the so-called Sagebrush Rebellion, sparked by the belief that environmental regulations were producing an unacceptable burden, wrote R. McGreggor Cawley in *Federal Land, Western Anger: The Sagebrush Rebellion & Environmental Politics*. That year, the Nevada Legislature passed a bill asserting control over BLM-managed lands inside the state — amounting to roughly 79 percent of the state. Arizona, New Mexico, Utah and Wyoming followed suit, with Wyoming also claiming U.S. Forest Service lands.[66]

In 1982 — two years after Congress had designated 104 million acres of federal land in Alaska as national parks, refuges, monuments, recreational areas, forests and conservation areas — Alaskan voters in a referendum overwhelmingly passed a ballot initiative laying claim to more than half of BLM-administered land in the state.[67] But land transfer bills later were defeated in California, Colorado, Idaho, Montana, Oregon and South Dakota.[68]

Nevada pursued its claim in court, arguing that the Federal Land Policy and Management Act of 1976 was unconstitutional and that the federal government only could hold public lands in temporary trust pending eventual disposal. But a federal court dismissed the case, and other state transfer laws were never enforced.[69]

Bills also were introduced in Congress to provide a mechanism for transferring federal lands to state ownership, but they died in committee. However, "the movement received important support when 1980 presidential candidate Ronald Reagan proclaimed: 'Count me in as a [Sagebrush] rebel!' " wrote Cawley.[70]

Once in office, Reagan's secretary of the Interior, James Watt, argued that arrogant federal managers, rather than federal ownership, were the root of the problem and promised a good-neighbor policy with local communities. But administration economists had persuaded Reagan that the solution was to privatize federal lands. Sagebrush rebels and environmentalists opposed privatization, and the effort stalled. Watt eventually resigned, and by the mid-'80s, "a relative calm had returned to the public land policy arena," wrote Cawley.[71]

The rebellion flared again in the 1990s when Nye County, Nev., used a bulldozer to open closed roads on federal land, and Republican majorities took control of both houses of Congress. Several bills were introduced or circulated for transferring federal lands, but none made it out of committee.[72]

CURRENT SITUATION
Federal Legislation

A small group of Western congressmen once again hopes to drastically alter who controls the nation's public lands.

In February, a subcommittee hearing was held on a bill proposed by Rep. Don Young, R-Alaska, that would allow any state to select and purchase up to 2 million acres of national forest within its borders "to be managed for timber production and other purposes under the law."[73] Also in February, another hearing considered a measure proposed by Rep. Raul Labrador, R-Idaho, that would give states and counties the right to take control, although not ownership, of between 200,000 and 900,000 acres of national forest, with a nationwide cap of 4 million acres. The land would be managed for maximum revenue.[74]

Perhaps the most ambitious legislation originates from Utah's delegation, led by GOP Rep. Rob Bishop, chairman of the House Natural Resources Committee. In January, he and Republican Rep. Jason Chaffetz unveiled a draft of the Utah Public Lands Initiative Act, which would institute a massive land-use plan for eastern Utah. The region encompasses 18 million acres of federal domain, including national parks, such as the iconic Arches National Park, wilderness areas, forests and BLM lands.

The plan, which Bishop called a "grand bargain," was crafted over three years after more than 1,200 meetings

Should Obama designate Bears Ears a national monument?

YES
Regina Lopez-Whiteskunk
Councilwoman, Ute Mountain Ute Tribe

Written for *CQ Researcher*, April 2016

Working with other tribes, the Ute Mountain Ute Tribe is proposing a 1.9 million-acre national monument named for the Bears Ears — two prominent buttes at the heart of an area rich in history, containing more than 100,000 cultural sites sacred to dozens of tribes. Bears Ears, in southeast Utah, should have been protected long ago, yet grave robbing, looting and the destruction of cultural sites continue today.

Our Ute people have lived in the Bears Ears country since time immemorial, long before Utah or the United States existed. We are intrinsically tied to this place; our individual and collective health and prosperity depend upon these lands. Few things are more important to us than the protection we can offer Bears Ears today.

Native Americans from many tribes continue to use Bears Ears as a place for healing, ceremonies and the gathering of medicinal herbs. Our people are surrounded by the spirits of our ancestors and embraced by the ongoing evolution of our culture and traditions. Bears Ears is also a place for teaching children — both Native American children and the world's children — about lasting connections with sacred and storied lands.

Working as part of the Bears Ears Inter-Tribal Coalition — a formal body including the Hopi, Navajo, Uintah and Ouray Ute, Ute Mountain Ute and Zuni tribal governments — we submitted a proposal to protect the Bears Ears in 2015 to Utah Reps. Rob Bishop and Jason Chaffetz and to President Obama.

We requested that Bishop and Chaffetz incorporate our proposal into their draft Utah Public Lands Initiative legislation. Unfortunately, the bill fails to incorporate Native interests and falls far short of what is needed to protect our ancestral lands. This is why we have asked the Obama administration to do what the Utah delegation would not — listen to tribes and to all Americans who want Bears Ears protected.

Our proposal is the first national monument plan submitted by sovereign Native American tribes, and our formal agreement to work together to protect Bears Ears is truly historic. One voice alone can be lost in a canyon, but with many voices we create a song. With the togetherness of our coalition and the support of the National Congress of American Indians and tribal governments and the communities they represent, we sing our collective song and call for the protection of our ancestral lands for today and for future generations.

NO
Bruce Adams
Board of County Commissioners, San Juan County, Utah

Written for *CQ Researcher*, April 2016

The intended purpose of a presidential designation of a national monument through the Antiquities Act is to take action quickly to protect objects and lands and to avoid possible damage to resources. Such a process assumes there are imminent threats to unprotected lands and resources that cannot wait for protective measures to be developed by Congress. This is not the case in southeast Utah, and such a top-down executive process is not warranted.

Proponents of presidential designation of a 1.9 million-acre national monument in southeast Utah often state the need to protect "unprotected" lands from imminent threats. Public lands in southeast Utah are not "unprotected." They are managed under laws, regulations, policies and land-use plans. These plans, developed over a period of years by agencies using staff expertise and input from the public and Native American tribes, prescribe management that ensures the protection of cultural and other sensitive resources and provides for the use and enjoyment of natural resources in accordance with laws and regulations.

All permitted uses on public lands are regulated by law, regulation and policy to minimize surface disturbance, prevent erosion and negative impacts on water quality, avoid damaging cultural resources, wildlife and other sensitive resources and preserve certain landscape vistas and character. Monument designation would not of itself strengthen these laws, regulations or policies.

Presidential designation is not the best or most democratic method of establishing a monument. Such unilateral designation bypasses the congressional deliberation and public participation processes that normally are part of monument or other land-designation processes. Presidential designations often lack local public support, input or planning, which are critical to the successful design and management of any special land designation. Such unilateral designation excludes consideration of other types of designations such as national conservation area, which may be more appropriate.

A better approach for developing land designations is the ground-up process that has been underway in southeast Utah for the past few years. This is the Public Lands Initiative proposed by Reps. Rob Bishop and Jason Chaffetz. San Juan County's proposal for this initiative is based on input from a broad range of county residents and interests including Native American tribes. The proposal includes wilderness as well as national conservation area designations and is a far more democratic approach to this issue.

The two prominent buttes known as Bears Ears in southeast Utah are at the center of a 1.9 million-acre area that contains more than 100,000 cultural sites sacred to many Native American tribes. The tribes have asked President Obama to declare the area a national monument under the Antiquities Act. Local county officials and Utah's congressional delegation oppose such a move.

with elected officials, local citizens, industry representatives, environmentalists and Native American tribes. Seven Utah counties then submitted land use proposals to the congressmen.[75]

The draft legislation's summary says it would, among other things, create 40 wilderness areas and 14 National Conservation Areas on more than 4 million acres of federal land, convey 40,449 acres of federal land to state and local entities and designate energy zones on BLM land, where the "highest and best use" will be expedited energy development.[76]

The draft has gotten mixed reviews. The Denver-based Western Energy Alliance, an oil and gas industry advocacy group, praised its approach to commercial development. "Right now, a company can't even submit a permit to drill until a federal NEPA analysis, is done," says Kathleen Sgamma, the alliance's vice president of government and public affairs. That can take eight years, and then . . . two years more to get the permit." The proposal would cut the environmental review process to as little as 18 months and the permitting process to 60 days, she says.

But the Denver-based Center for Western Priorities, a conservation and advocacy organization, said that timeline "would preclude even the most minimal review of environmental impacts or potential destruction of irreplaceable cultural, historic or natural resources, turning much of Utah into an oil and gas free-for-all."[77]

And the Salt Lake City-based Southern Utah Wilderness Alliance, which works to preserve wilderness, calls Bishop's grand bargain a grand bust. Executive Director Scott Groene says the legislation's additional wilderness numbers are misleading because some of that land already is being managed under wilderness standards. And "the wilderness that it designates will not be true wilderness," he says, because exceptions would allow motorized vehicles and aircraft for wildfire management, continued grazing of livestock and commercial outfitting activities.

Bishop dismissed those objections as "crap."[78]

While the measure would designate about half a million acres as the Bears Ears Conservation Area, the region's Tribal Nations say it should be four times that size to encompass more than 100,000 sacred and archaeological sites. The bill also does not include tribes' request to co-manage the conservation area with the BLM. "We've seen what has happened under BLM management with their limited resources. They have failed to adequately protect these areas," says Mark Maryboy, a board member of Utah Diné Bikéyah, a Salt Lake City-based nonprofit working to protect Navajo lands.

In frustration, the Bears Ears Inter-Tribal Coalition — comprising the Hopi Tribe, Navajo Nation, Ute Indian Tribe, Ute Mountain Ute Tribe and Pueblo of Zuni — has asked President Obama to declare 1.9 million acres as the Bears Ears National Monument. The request is generating heated opposition from San Juan County, Utah, commissioners and Utah's congressional delegation. Obama has not said how he will respond to the request, but Interior Department Secretary Sally Jewell promised Congress that the administration would "engage with local communities" should there be "any efforts to move forward in that region."[79]

Meanwhile, in February Obama used the Antiquities Act to designate three new monuments in the California desert, totaling 1.8 million acres and nearly doubling the amount of public land Obama has protected during his presidency. Last summer, Obama designated more than a million acres in California, Nevada and Texas as national monuments.[80]

State Action

In March, the Utah Legislature set aside $4.5 million to help pay for a potential lawsuit against the federal government over land control.[81]

Four years ago Gov. Gary Herbert, a Republican, signed into law the Transfer of Public Lands Act and Study, which demanded that the federal government hand over to Utah more than 31 million acres of by the end of 2014 or the state would sue. The act excluded national parks, national monuments — except the Grand Staircase-Escalante National Monument-wilderness areas, Department of Defense areas and tribal lands.[82]

"The federal government retaining control of two-thirds of our landmass was never in the bargain when we became a state, and it is indefensible 116 years later," said Herbert.[83] But Interior Secretary Jewell has made it clear the United States will not comply, said department spokeswoman Jessica Kershaw. "It's a waste of time and resources for Utah to debate the state's takeover of public lands," Kershaw said.[84]

More recently, the state has commissioned economic and legal analyses of a land transfer, and although the deadline imposed by the law has passed without a lawsuit being filed, Herbert has said he wouldn't rule one out. In January, legal consultants urged the state to sue but warned that it could cost Utah taxpayers up to $14 million, take years and was far from a sure victory.[85]

Herbert said he would be more enthusiastic about suing if other states joined in and shared the costs; he added that discussions among Western states are underway.[86] (Herbert also supports the Utah Public Lands Initiative Act and said the threat of a lawsuit might lead to favorable federal legislation.)[87]

But it's unclear whether Utah would get much support. "In recent years, at least 10 other states have considered legislation similar to Utah's," according to the National Conference of State Legislatures, a bipartisan organization based in Washington, D.C.[88] Only Arizona passed a bill, also in 2012. But then-Gov. Jan Brewer, a Republican, vetoed it, saying it would create too much uncertainty for individuals with existing leases on federal land. Meanwhile, Arizona, Idaho, Montana, Nevada and Wyoming have enacted laws to study the issue.[89]

Last year, Utah also passed the Catastrophic Wildfire and Public Nuisance Act, which allows local officials to declare a public nuisance on federal land if they believe wildfires risks are due to excessive tree density or if wildfires threaten water quality, air quality, vegetation needed for grazing or the health, welfare and safety of nearby residents. The law allows local authorities to take emergency action if the federal government does not provide an abatement plan within a certain timeframe.[90]

Similar legislation has been introduced in Idaho. But both bills have no enforcement mechanism, and when a county in New Mexico tried to take over management of federal land, a court blocked it. Proponents of the bills have said their point is to embarrass federal agencies into action. Environmental groups have said the bills are aimed at diminishing public support for federal ownership of public lands.[91]

The Idaho "nuisance" bill and several state land-transfer measures closely resemble model legislation from the Arlington, Va.- based American Legislative Exchange Council (ALEC), which advocates free markets, limited federal regulation and states' rights.[92] Executives from energy, pharmaceutical, telecommunications, insurance and other business sectors sit on ALEC's advisory board, and the organization reportedly receives funding from groups controlled by libertarian industrialists David and Charles Koch.[93]

"Utah comes up with these ideas, passes them into law through their Legislature, and through the ALEC network, [legislators] try and pass them in other states," said Greg Zimmerman, the Center for Western Priorities' policy director.[94]

ALEC's model legislation and policies on a wide variety of hot-button issues can be found on its website, which calls them "dynamic and innovative ideas that reduce the cost of everyday life and ensure economic freedom."[95]

OUTLOOK
Bridging Divides

Wide disagreement exists about whether the land transfer movement will gain steam or fizzle out. Legal consultant Howard says it's difficult to predict whether Utah will pursue a lawsuit aimed at forcing the United States to transfer federal lands to state ownership. Utah Attorney General Sean Reyes has the final say, but first the Legislature would have to appropriate the necessary money, he says.

"I am confident that at least three other Western states will join in" if Reyes decides to litigate, says Howard, although he would not disclose particulars.

University of Utah law professor Ruple isn't so sure. "Other states have, thus far, been happy to let Utah lead the charge and incur the expense of litigation," says Ruple, but adds that if Utah were to prevail in court, at least some Western states likely would also sue.

"It is also possible that the movement will fizzle if Republicans win both houses of Congress and the presidency, and if transfer backers conclude that they are more likely to get what they want through friendly federal legislation than litigation," says Ruple.

But Denver land-use lawyer Brooks says she's pessimistic that Washington will be inclined toward more state control. "In 1980, when President [Ronald] Reagan was elected, the federal agencies started listening to local people, and there was an effort or resolve things," says Brooks. "I don't see that happening again."

Brooks says continuing urbanization means the status quo will prevail, which she describes as "a bitter divide between the Western states and the rest of the country, with rural areas increasingly feeling like they have no access to services and no way to pay for those services."

Oregon Wild's Pedery looks at those same demographic trends through a different lens. "Most people, even most Republicans, like their public lands public, open to hunting, fishing, hiking and camping just like they have always been," says Pedery. "So what sounds good to a group of rural ranchers, loggers and oil and gas development types or to folks trying to figure out how to maximize voter turnout in conservative rural areas, doesn't play that well to the general public." He does not expect the transfer movement to succeed.

Brick, the Whitman professor, says the best hope to bridge divides is to expand the number of successful collaborative agreements between local communities and federal agencies. "I think much depends, in my experience of over 20 years looking at these things, on leadership." If communities have good local leadership, paired with good local leadership at federal agencies, then "really amazing things can happen," says Brick.

He points to the corner of northeast Oregon, where a few small communities are working with local environmentalists, county officials and the Forest Service to develop a plan to bring back a lumber mill and 50 of the 300 mill jobs that once existed there. "I think they're going to be able to do it," says Brick.

NOTES

1. Les Zaitz, "Demands by Oregon standoff leaders defy logic and law, authorities say," Oregon Newswire, Jan. 24, 2016, http://tinyurl.com/hfdtt5h.

2. "Ammon Bundy speaks to reporters at wildlife refuge headquarters," *The Oregonian*, Jan. 4, 2016, http://tinyurl.com/zqybvas. Also see Valet Fleet Service, http://tinyurl.com/glsw9qp.

3. "Nevada rancher Cliven Bundy: 'The citizens of America' got my cattle back," CBSNews, April 13, 2014, http://tinyurl.com/ppa7sch.

4. Kirk Johnson, "25 Plead Not Guilty in Standoff at the Oregon Wildlife Refuge," *The New York Times*, Feb. 24, 2016, http://tinyurl.com/hw6ddsg.

5. Jack Healy and Kirk Johnson, "The Larger, But Quieter Than Bundy, Push to Take Over Federal land," *The New York Times*, Jan. 10, 2016, http://tinyurl.com/jxs4trq.

6. "Nevada Land, Ted Cruz Ad" YouTube, http://tinyurl.com/j6exeog.

7. Anthony Licata, "This is Our Land," *Field & Stream*, March 23, 2015, http://tinyurl.com/zhtsuy2.

8. Carol Hardy Vincent *et al.*, "Federal Land Ownership: Overview and Data," Congressional Research Service, Dec. 29, 2014, pp. Summary, 4-5, http://tinyurl.com/gr62wuc.

9. *Ibid.*

10. Megan Lawson, "Federal Lands in the West: Liability or Asset?" Headwaters Economics, February 2016, http://tinyurl.com/gl83ohs.

11. Jan Elise Stambro *et al.*, "An Analysis of a Transfer of Federal Lands to the State of Utah," Table 4.20, 2000-2007 (Model 4A) FEDGEN, Utah Public Lands Policy Coordination Office, November 2014, p. 191, http://tinyurl.com/z78b773.

12. Robert H. Nelson, "Give States Control Over Public Land Out West," *The New York Times*, Jan. 7, 2016, http://tinyurl.com/z9w9kv6.

13. "The Rising Cost of Wildfire Operations: Effects on the Forest Service's Non-Fire Work," Forest Service, U.S. Department of Agriculture, Aug. 4, 2015, p. 2, http://tinyurl.com/za4jn7c.

14. M. P. North *et al.*, "Reform forest fire management," *Science*, Sept. 18, 2015, http://tinyurl.com/z3qulk7.

15. Lindsay Whitehurst, "Utah Supreme Court weighing public lands roads dispute," The Associated Press, April 5, 2016, http://tinyurl.com/zrk2sq4.

16. "The Rising Cost of Wildfire Operations: Effects on the Forest Service's Non-Fire Work," *op. cit.*, pp. 4, 8-13.

17. Thomas Tidwell, "Restoration Partnerships: Idaho Leads the Way," Idaho Forest Restoration Partnership, 4th Annual Winter Conference, Feb. 19, 2014, http://tinyurl.com/zkl99b5.

18. Holly Fretwell and Shawn Regan, "Divided Lands: State vs. Federal Management in the West," PERC, March 2015, pp. 14-22, http://tinyurl.com/jvx57q5.

19. Martin Nie, "Statement of Martin Nie," Montana Legislature, Sept. 11, 2013, pp. 7-8, http://tinyurl.com/znn2jkk.

20. *Ibid.*

21. *Ibid.*

22. Steven W. Strack, "Letter to Rep. Ilana Rubel," Office of the Idaho Attorney General, March 14, 2016, p. 2, http://tinyurl.com/j8mftdj.

23. John W. Howard *et al.*, "Legal Analysis of the Legal Consulting Services Team Prepared for the Utah Commission for the Stewardship of Public Lands," Utah Legislature, Dec. 9, 2015, http://tinyurl.com/z8dxuvp.

24. Robert B. Keiter and John C. Ruple, "A Legal Analysis of the Transfer of Public Lands Movement," University of Utah S. J. Quinney College of Law, Oct. 27, 2014, http://tinyurl.com/hydr3ez.

25. *Shelby County, Alabama, Petitioner v. Eric H. Holder, Jr., Attorney General et al.*, Opinion of the Court, June 25, 2013, www.oyez.org/cases/2012/12-96.

26. Colorado Enabling Act, March 3, 1875, http://tinyurl.com/zmw6psq.

27. William Perry Pendley, "The Federal Government Should Follow the Constitution and Sell Its Western Lands," *National Review*, Jan. 19, 2016, http://tinyurl.com/grbzwz3.

28. Fretwell and Regan, *op. cit.*

29. Lee Davidson, "Bill passes to outline how Utah would manage federal public lands," *The Salt Lake Tribune*, March 12, 2016, http://tinyurl.com/j7u5zrj.

30. "Utah Public Land Management Act, Enrolled Copy," March 28, 2016, p. 7, http://tinyurl.com/z5w67n2.

31. Jim Caswell, "Keep public lands in public hands; Guest Opinion Refuge Dispute," *The Idaho Statesman* (Boise), Jan. 27, 2016, http://tinyurl.com/zklnspm.

32. Stambro *et al.*, *op. cit.*, pp. xxvi-xxvii.

33. *Ibid.*

34. *Ibid.*

35. "Short-term Energy Outlook, Data," U.S. Energy Information Administration, March 8, 2016.

36. "Report: Transferring public lands in Idaho could cost as much as $111 million a year," The Associated Press, Dec. 8, 2014, http://tinyurl.com/gm6c66p.

37. Evan Hjerpe, "Fiscal Impacts to the State of Idaho from HR 22 Implementation," Idaho Conservation League, p. 8, December 2013, http://tinyurl.com/zu4nv6d.

38. "Outdoor Recreation Economy," Outdoor Industry Association, Feb. 13, 2013, http://tinyurl.com/z84qlvh; "For the good of all; Not the profit of a few," Outdoor Industry Association, http://tinyurl.com/jhymaqu.

39. John R. Van Atta, *Securing the West: Politics, Public Lands, and the Fate of the Old Republic, 1785-1850* (2014), pp. 29-30.

40. *Ibid.*

41. *Ibid.*, p. 31.

42. "Public Land Statistics, 2014," Bureau of Land Management, May 2015, p. 3 (Table 1-1), http://tinyurl.com/jp4n4g2.

43. *Ibid.*

44. Randall K. Wilson, *America's Public Lands: From Yellowstone to Smokey Bear and Beyond* (2014), p. 19.

45. "Public Land Statistics, 2014," *op. cit.*; Stambro *et al.*, *op. cit.*

46. Paul W. Gates, History of Public Land Law Development, Public Land Law Review Commission, 1968, p. 51, http://tinyurl.com/hjte2ko.

47. Van Atta, *op. cit.*, p. 32.

48. Wilson, *op. cit.*, p. 25.

49. Kristina Alexander and Ross W. Gorte, "Federal Land Ownership: Constitutional Authority and the History of Acquisition, Disposal, and Retention," Congressional Research Service, Dec. 3, 2007, p. 4, http://tinyurl.com/zl9ns5l.

50. Wilson, *op. cit.*, p. 27.

51. *Ibid.*, pp. 28-30.

52. *Ibid.*, p. 31.

53. *Ibid.*, p. 32.

54. Shawn Regan, "Managing Conflicts Over Western Rangelands," PERC, Jan. 21, 2016, http://tinyurl.com/hyrfwna.

55. Wilson, *op. cit.*, pp. 77-78.

56. "Theodore Roosevelt and Conservation," National Park Service, http://tinyurl.com/hhbe5ys.

57. Michael McCarthy, "The First Sagebrush Rebellion: Forest Reserves and States Rights in Colorado and the West, 1891-1907," in *The Origins of the National Forests: A Centennial Symposium* (1992), http://tinyurl.com/h43l4ft.

58. Stambro *et al.*, *op. cit.*, p. 5.

59. James R. Skillen, *The Nation's Largest Landlord: The Bureau of Land Management in the American West* (2009), p. 5.

60. *Ibid.*, pp. 6-7.

61. Gates, *op. cit.*, p. 610.

62. "History of Public Land Livestock Grazing," Bureau of Land Management, http://tinyurl.com/hwwbkcy.

63. Stambro *et al.*, *op. cit.*, p. 6.

64. Skillen, *op. cit.*, pp. 105-106.

65. *Ibid.*

66. R. McGreggor Cawley, *Federal Land, Western Anger: The Sagebrush Rebellion & Environmental Politics* (1993), p. 2.

67. The landmark Alaska National Interests Lands Conservation Act was the largest land conservation measure ever enacted. For background see "Alaska National Interests Lands Conservation Act: Creation of Wrangell-St. Elias," National Park Service, undated, http://tinyurl.com/h32jpk7.

68. Cawley, *op. cit.*

69. Alexander and Gorte, *op. cit.*, p. 11.

70. Cawley, *op. cit.*, pp. 2-3.

71. *Ibid.*

72. Alexander and Gorte, *op. cit.*, pp. 11-13.

73. "House Panel Reviews Young's Forestry Legislation," Press Release, Rep. Don Young Feb. 25, http://tinyurl.com/z2oouyq.

74. H.R. 2316 — Self-Sufficient Community Lands Act, http://tinyurl.com/jew8lwv.

75. "Utah Public Lands Initiative," www.utahpli.com.

76. "The Public Lands Initiative: Summary and Section-by-Section," Rep. Bob Bishop, http://tinyurl.com/zsvg5de.

77. Aaron Weiss, "Rob Bishop's 'Public Lands Initiative' is an Insidious Attack on Our Public Lands," Center for Western Priorities, Jan. 19, 2016, http://tinyurl.com/zxpaogw.

78. Amy Joi O'Donoghue, "Bishop public lands bill unveiled, eliciting support and criticism," *Deseret Morning News*, Jan. 20, 2016, http://tinyurl.com/z7dju42.

79. Budget Hearing — Department of the Interior: Q&A (video), House Appropriations Committee, March 2, 2016, http://tinyurl.com/gpfq5as.

80. Mark Landler and Julie Turkewitz, "With 3 California Sites, Obama Nearly Doubles Public Land He's Protected," *The New York Times*, Feb. 12, 2016, http://tinyurl.com/js65gmt.

81. Robert Gehrke, "Legislature creates fund for Utah's $14 million public lands lawsuit," *The Salt Lake Tribune*, March 10, 2016, http://tinyurl.com/gr2rs3m.

82. Brian Maffly, "Bills keep pushing federal land transfer," *The Salt Lake Tribune*, Feb. 25, 2013, http://tinyurl.com/zmwae7m; "Transfer of Public Lands Act and Study," Utah's Public Lands Policy Coordinating Office, http://tinyurl.com/gms4n3t.

83. "Governor Herbert, Federal Delegation, and State Legislators Join Together to Demand Transfer of Public Lands to Utah," Utah Governor's Office, March 23, 2012, http://tinyurl.com/jsuftt7.

84. Brian Maffly, "Legal Scholars predict Utah land transfer takes the public out of public lands," *The Salt Lake Tribune*, Feb. 6, 2015, http://tinyurl.com/gs62nc6.

85. "Utah Lawmakers Consider $14 Million Public Lands Lawsuit," The Associated Press, Jan. 29, 2016, http://tinyurl.com/j7n9wnc.

86. *Ibid.*

87. Tripp Baltz, "Utah Governor Backs Lawsuit Over Federal Land Management," Bloomberg BNA, March 11, 2016, http://tinyurl.com/hah9lqp.

88. Kevin Frazzini, "This Land Is Whose Land?" State Legislatures, National Conference of State Legislatures, July-August 2015, http://tinyurl.com/hm6thu4.

89. "Our American Public Lands," Center for Western Priorities, http://tinyurl.com/jvdnfny; internal document, National Conference of State Legislatures, Jan. 6, 2016.

90. "Catastrophic Wildfire and Public Nuisance Amendments," State of Utah, 2015 General Session, http://tinyurl.com/zw6ua9k.

91. Bryan Clark, "Wildfire nuisance bill considered," Post Register — West Yellowstone, Feb. 24, 2016, http://tinyurl.com/gvljo3b.

92. "Archives: Environmental Stewardship/Model Policies," American Legislative Exchange Council, http://tinyurl.com/zz5jvao.

93. "Private Enterprise Advisory Council," American Legislative Exchange Council, www.alec.org/about/leadership; Jamie Corey, "Koch-Funded Special Interest Groups and Utilities Bankrolling ALEC Meeting," The Center for Media and Democracy's PRWatch, Dec. 4, 2015, http://tinyurl.com/jbwfx6a.

94. Lyndsey Gilpin, "How an East Coast think tank is fueling the land transfer movement," *High Country News*, Feb. 26, 2016, http://tinyurl.com/hu3oduo.

95. "About ALEC," American Legislative Exchange Council, www.alec.org/about.

BIBLIOGRAPHY
Selected Sources
Books

Skillen, James R., *The Nation's Largest Landlord: The Bureau of Land Management in the American West,* University Press of Kansas, 2009.
An environmental studies professor at Calvin College in Grand Rapids, Mich., traces the history of the BLM.

Van Atta, John R., *Securing the West: Politics, Public Lands, and the Fate of the Old Republic, 1785-1850,* Johns Hopkins University Press, 2014.
An independent historian examines the nation's accumulation of public lands.

Wilson, Randall K., *America's Public Lands: From Yellowstone to Smokey Bear and Beyond,* Rowman & Littlefield, 2014.
An environmental studies professor at Pennsylvania's Gettysburg College describes challenges facing federal public lands.

Articles

"Utah Lawmakers Consider $14 Million Public Lands Lawsuit," The Associated Press, *The Seattle Times*, Jan. 29, 2016, http://tinyurl.com/j7n9wnc.
A legal consulting team says Utah has strong legal grounds for suing the United States for control of federal lands.

Frazzini, Kevin, "This Land Is Whose Land?" *State Legislatures*, July-August 2015, National Conference of State Legislatures, http://tinyurl.com/hm6thu4.
A movement is growing to force the federal government to relinquish public lands to states.

Gilpin, Lyndsey, "How an East Coast think tank is fueling the land transfer movement," *High Country News*, Feb. 26, 2016, http://tinyurl.com/hu3oduo.
The American Legislative Exchange Council, a free-market think tank, has crafted model state legislation demanding state control of federal public lands.

Glionna, John M., "Protected wild horses slaughtered; BLM sold 1,794 to rancher who sent them to deaths," *Los Angeles Times*, **Oct. 29, 2015, http://tinyurl.com/nspmrwc.**

A government investigation finds that the Bureau of Land Management sold wild horses to a rancher who sent them to Mexican slaughterhouses, violating government policy against killing adopted horses.

Healy, Jack, and Kirk Johnson, "The Larger, but Quieter than Bundy, Push to Take Over Federal Land," *The New York Times*, **Jan. 10, 2016, http://tinyurl.com/jxs4trq.**

Western politicians have introduced dozens of bills addressing federal land transfers.

Maffly, Brian, "Legal Scholars predict Utah land transfer takes the public out of public lands," *The Salt Lake Tribune*, **Feb. 6, 2015, http://tinyurl.com/gs62nc6.**

Legal scholars predict a state takeover of public lands would reduce public access.

Reports & Studies

Fretwell, Holly, and Shawn Regan, "Divided Lands: State vs. Federal Management in the West," Property and Environment Research Center, March 2015, http://tinyurl.com/jvx57q5.

Two economics researchers conclude in a study for a free-market think tank that states manage their public lands more profitably than the federal government.

Hardy Vincent, Carol, *et al.*, "Federal Land Ownership: Overview and Data," Congressional Research Service, Dec. 29, 2014, http://tinyurl.com/gr62wuc.

Congress' research arm finds that federal ownership of public lands varies dramatically by state.

Howard, John W., *et al.*, "Legal Analysis of the Legal Consulting Services Team Prepared for the Utah Commission for the Stewardship of Public Lands," State of Utah, Dec. 9, 2015, http://tinyurl.com/z8dxuvp.

A legal consulting team makes the case for a Utah takeover of federal lands.

Keiter, Robert B., and John C. Ruple, "A Legal Analysis of the Transfer of Public Lands Movement," University of Utah, Oct. 27, 2014, http://tinyurl.com/hydr3ez.

Legal scholars say the federal government is not obligated to transfer lands to states.

Keiter, Robert B., and John C. Ruple, "The Transfer of Public Lands Movement: Taking the 'Public' Out of Public Lands," University of Utah, Jan. 28, 2015, http://tinyurl.com/gwy484s.

Legal scholars say state control of federal lands would reduce public access.

Lawson, Megan, "Federal Lands in the West: Liability or Asset?" Headwaters Economics, February 2016, http://tinyurl.com/gl83ohs.

A study by an economic research firm concludes that greater amounts of federal land in a community are associated with higher economic growth, up to a point.

Stambro, Jan Elise, *et al.*, "An Analysis of a Transfer of Federal Lands to the State of Utah," Utah Public Lands Policy Coordination Office, November 2014, http://tinyurl.com/z78b773.

A study commissioned by an arm of the Utah governor's office says economic growth grows — and then slows — as federal land acreage rises in a community.

For More Information

American Lands Council, 859 W. South Jordan Parkway, Suite 100, South Jordan, UT 84095; 801-252-6622; www.americanlandscouncil.org. Lobbies for transfer of federal public lands to states.

Headwaters Economics, 270 W. Kagy, Suite G, Bozeman, MT 59715; 406-570-8937; headwaterseconomics.org. Researches land management in the West.

Property and Environment Research Center, 2048 Analysis Dr., Suite A, Bozeman, MT 59718; 406-587-9591; www.perc.org. Advocates using property rights and markets to improve the environment.

Southern Utah Wilderness Alliance, 425 East 100 South, Salt Lake City, UT 84111; 801-486-3161; www.suwa.org. Works to permanently protect lands in the Colorado Plateau.

U.S. Bureau of Land Management, 1849 C St., N.W., Washington, DC 20240; 202-208-3801; www.blm.gov. Federal agency that administers more than 245 million acres of land, concentrated in 12 Western states.

U.S. Forest Service, 1400 Independence Ave., S.W., Washington, DC 20250; 800-832-1355; www.fs.fed.us. Federal agency managing 154 national forests and 20 grasslands.

Utah Diné Bikéyah, 352 S. Denver St. #315, Salt Lake City, UT 84101; 385-202-4954; www.utahdinebikeyah.org. Nonprofit working to protect Navajo lands.

Western Energy Alliance, 1775 Sherman St., Suite 2700, Denver, CO 80203; 303-623-0987; westernenergyalliance.org. Represents the Western oil and natural gas industry.

3

Drinking Water Safety

Jill U. Adams

A sign warns bathers about algae infestation at Maumee Bay State Park in Ohio on Aug. 4, 2014. In nearby Toledo, excessive algae in Lake Erie, caused by fertilizer runoff, forced a temporary ban on drinking water. Drinking water contaminants include industrial and pharmaceutical chemicals as well as lead and other toxins.

Aaron P. Bernstein/Getty Images

From *CQ Researcher,*
July 15, 2016.

By the time officials in Flint, Mich., warned residents last October to stop drinking city water because of dangerous lead contamination, it was too late: The lead levels in children's blood had already spiked to harmful levels.[1]

The Centers for Disease Control and Prevention (CDC) found that the risk of excessive blood lead levels among Flint children under age 6 had risen 50 percent during the months the city used improperly treated Flint River water for drinking.[2]

Young children are particularly sensitive to lead exposure: Even small doses can lower IQ and cause lifelong learning disabilities, attention disorders and violent behavior.[3]

Flint's water contamination likely had begun 18 months before residents were notified by local officials, who had learned of the problem in February but waited seven months to tell the public.[4] The problem developed after the city, to save money, stopped buying treated water from Detroit and began drawing water from the polluted Flint River. To kill bacteria, Flint had to treat the river water with more chlorine than usual, which corroded the lead pipes. Three officials — two from the state and one from the city — have been charged with evidence tampering concerning the reporting of Flint's lead levels to the Environmental Protection Agency (EPA).[5]

The Flint crisis prompted reporters, watchdog organizations and public officials to analyze the effectiveness of city, state and federal management of a key public safety sector. But the water-safety situation in other cities is even worse than in Flint, according to two recent investigations. *USA Today* and the Natural Resources

Water Infrastructure Costs Highest in South

The South needs the largest investment — $507 billion — to upgrade its water mains, followed by the West, at $237 billion, according to the American Society of Civil Engineers. Most of the projected costs in those two regions stem from population growth. Cost increases projected in the Midwest and Northeast stem mostly from the need to replace aging pipes.

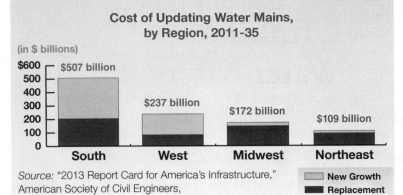

Cost of Updating Water Mains, by Region, 2011-35

(in $ billions)

Source: "2013 Report Card for America's Infrastructure," American Society of Civil Engineers, http://tinyurl.com/jpf9e5s

reform at the Reason Foundation, a free-market think tank in Los Angeles. "And with government ownership, the process is politicized. There's incentive to keep rates low, while the investment needs continue to stack up."

What happened in Flint was "so preventable," says Jeffrey Griffiths, a professor of public health at Tufts University and former chair of the EPA's Drinking Water Committee. He assigns "99.5 percent of the blame to the people who decided to use river water and decided not to use [proper] corrosion control — and lied to the EPA about it."

To keep America's drinking water safe, says Howard Neukrug, who served as CEO of Philadelphia's water utility for 37 years, infrastructure must be upgraded, creative and efficient treatment systems must be established, and scientific research on the health effects of toxic chemicals in drinking water must be beefed up.

Defense Council (NRDC), an environmental advocacy group, found in separate examinations that between 2,000 and 5,000 water systems nationwide — serving up to 18 million people — have failed to meet federal lead safety standards.[6]

"There's no question we have challenges with lead in drinking water across the country [involving] millions of lead service lines in thousands of systems," said Joel Beauvais, deputy assistant administrator for the EPA's Office of Water.[7]

And lead contamination is not the only threat to America's drinking water. Thousands of industrial pollutants and pharmaceutical compounds slip through municipal water treatment, having never been tested or regulated by the EPA. And, while the agency sets federal water safety standards, the sourcing, treatment and distribution of water is left to thousands of local utilities, many of which are dealing with polluted water sources, aging pipes or shrinking budgets. As the Flint crisis revealed, economic distress and poor regulatory oversight can endanger the quality of drinking water in many cities.

"Maintenance is a chronic problem for public water utilities," says Leonard Gilroy, director of government

Many older cities still use lead-containing water pipes because a 1986 ban on leaded water pipes applied only to new construction. Water is lead-free when it leaves municipal treatment plants, which filter and disinfect water, but lead can leach into the water from lead service lines — pipes that connect water mains to individual houses — or sometimes through a building's plumbing. Lead is more likely to leach if pipes are corroded.

While water officials usually know when they have some lead pipes in their systems, they rarely know exactly where the pipes are. Nor do they know how many: Estimates of the number of lead service lines nationwide range from 3 million to 10 million. The American Water Works Association, a Denver-based organization representing water utility professionals, estimates there are 6.1 million, but that is not based on "a hard inventory," said the association's director for government affairs, Tracy Mehan. Using an estimate of $5,000 each, the association said replacement would cost $30 billion.[8]

To control corrosion, water treatment plants add orthophosphate, a chemical that coats the inside of the pipes and prevents leaching. "Corrosion control works, but it's not perfect," says Mae Wu, a senior NRDC attorney. "As long as there are lead service lines, lead will continue to be a problem."

When corrosion control doesn't work, service lines must be replaced, with the cost typically shared with homeowners. Some communities, such as Madison, Wis., have found creative ways to pay for replacing pipes. But most cities must raise water rates, borrow from the state or partner with a private company.

When cities partner with a private firm, the company invests in new infrastructure in exchange for the right to run the system and collect the fees. Privatization agreements can be an economic boon for a struggling municipality, especially if the company pays off the city's debt, but leasing a critical public safety utility such as water treatment to a profit-based system is controversial.[9]

How Lead Gets Into Drinking Water

Drinking water in homes with old water pipes is more likely to contain lead than water in newer homes with lead-free pipes. When drinking water leaves municipal treatment plants, it is lead-free. But it can be contaminated with lead when corrosion-control measures fail to keep lead pipes from leaching lead into drinking water.

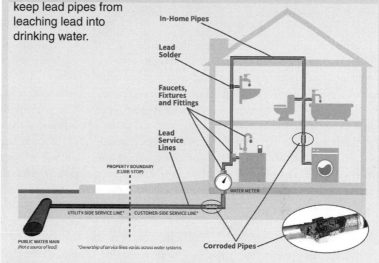

In-Home Pipes

Lead Solder

Faucets, Fixtures and Fittings

Lead Service Lines

PROPERTY BOUNDARY (CURB STOP)

WATER METER

PUBLIC WATER MAIN *(Not a source of lead)*

UTILITY-SIDE SERVICE LINE*   CUSTOMER-SIDE SERVICE LINE*

*Ownership of service lines varies across water systems.

Corroded Pipes

Source: Clean Water Action, 2016, http://tinyurl.com/hvjf2la

Besides lead, other problems plague the nation's 54,000 community drinking water systems. As pipes age, their failure rates rise. About 650 water mains — the large pipes that run under city streets — break down each day, and utilities must replace 4,000 to 5,000 miles of mains per year. The American Society of Civil Engineers in 2013 gave America's drinking water infrastructure a grade of D+ and estimated it would cost $1 trillion over the next 25 years to replace leaking pipes and keep up with growth.[10]

In addition, utilities deal with other contaminants besides lead. Last December, Hoosick Falls, N.Y., warned residents not to drink tap water due to dangerous levels of the industrial pollutant perfluorooctanoic acid, a manmade chemical used in nonstick cookware and stain-resistant carpeting.[11] And in 2014, residents in Charleston, W. Va., and Toledo, Ohio, were told not to drink city water. In Charleston a chemical storage tank had leaked a coal-washing chemical, 4-methylcyclohexane methanol, into the Elk River, the city's water source.[12] In Toledo the culprit was a bacterial toxin,

microcystin, created from excessive algae in Lake Erie, caused by farmland fertilizer that washed into the lake.[13]

Moreover, in regions near oil and gas drilling operations, some residents have complained of drinking water contaminated by hydraulic fracturing, or fracking, in which oil and natural gas are extracted from underground shale by pumping chemically treated water into the rock formations under high pressure. An EPA study in 2015 concluded that the problem is not systemic or widespread.[14] However, a panel of scientists recommended that the EPA review its findings.[15]

Many water treatment plants are not equipped to remove certain pollutants or toxins, and many chemicals found in drinking water are not regulated. The toxins detected in Hoosick Falls and Toledo are unregulated but are candidates for EPA evaluation for potential health effects. The chemical in Charleston is neither regulated nor listed as a potential contaminant.

Under the Safe Drinking Water Act of 1974, the primary federal law governing the quality of the nation's drinking water, the EPA regulates a set of "actionable contaminants," including lead, arsenic, the herbicides atrazine and glyphosate (used in Roundup weed killer) and the microbial pathogens Legionella and giardia.[16] Under the law, the EPA also maintains a list of as-yet unregulated substances, known as contaminants "of concern" — chemicals or toxins found in rivers and lakes that are candidates for EPA analysis to determine unsafe levels.[17]

Suspected contaminants can be added to the list, but too often regulators don't have enough data to act, says Rebecca Klaper, an expert on emerging water contaminants at the University of Wisconsin, Milwaukee. Plus, the EPA review process can take decades to complete, while American industry is creating and using new chemicals at a rapid clip. Regulators have detected widely used pharmaceuticals, pesticides and flame retardants at low levels in many rivers and lakes, says Klaper, but water or wastewater treatment systems fail to capture many of these "emerging" contaminants.

"We need more resources in order to determine the long-term impacts of exposure to small concentrations of chemicals," Klaper says. But "there's no funding for this."

Over the past decade, Congress has cut the EPA's Office of Ground Water and Drinking Water budget by 15 percent and its staff by 10 percent, diminishing its ability to regulate, monitor and enforce drinking water regulations, critics say.[18] Further, the Safe Drinking Water Act is not the only law governing pollutants that could end up in drinking water.[19] The others are:

- The Clean Water Act of 1972 authorizes setting quality standards for lakes and rivers (called "surface waters"), including those used for drinking water, and allows states to prevent factory or farm pollution from being discharged into those waters. 20
- The Toxic Substances Control Act (TSCA) governs the production, use and disposal — potentially into waters used for drinking water — of industrial chemicals.

In a rare bipartisan move in a perennially gridlocked Congress, lawmakers in June adopted the first major overhaul of the TSCA since its enactment 40 years ago.[21]

Some clean-water advocates also want tougher penalties for those who pollute "source water" — any water that flows into a drinking water treatment plant. "You

and I are paying to get stuff out of the water that someone else puts in," says the NRDC's Wu.

As cities, residents, environmentalists, industry officials and lawmakers debate what to do about the nation's aging water systems, here are some of the questions they are asking:

Is America's drinking water safe?

Overall, Americans enjoy some of the world's cleanest, safest tap water, says Neukrug, the former Philadelphia Water CEO who is a senior fellow at the U.S. Water Alliance, a nonprofit organization that promotes sustainable water policy. Nevertheless, every year, unsafe water is found across the country.

"By and large, Americans drink safe water, in that it doesn't make them sick," says Tuft's Griffiths. "That doesn't mean there are not threats."

In addition to the *USA Today* and NRDC findings that thousands of water systems have violated federal lead standards, a recent review of EPA enforcement actions by University of Alabama law professor William Andreen discovered that in 2013 some 10,000 community-level water systems had at least one significant violation of federal drinking water regulations. One-fourth of those violations involved health-based standards, while the rest were monitoring and reporting violations, says Andreen, a former EPA in-house counsel. About 5,000 water systems had been flagged as priorities for enforcement because of serious or repeated violations, Andreen adds.

"It's just a snapshot, from 2013," but it highlights the scope of the problem, he says.

Under the Safe Drinking Water Act, threats to water are managed in three places: at the source of the water, in the water treatment plant and in the underground water distribution system. The law requires states to identify the risk of contamination from water sources — such as reservoirs, rivers or mountain snowmelt. Yet, many communities struggle to control contamination in their source waters. In fact, tributaries or wetlands not covered by clean-water laws serve up to one-third of Americans.[22]

The Obama administration sought to address these gaps in 2015 by issuing the Clean Water Rule, expanding the definition of rivers and wetlands covered by the Clean Water Act. Advocates say the protections were overdue because previous interpretations of protected waters were far too narrow. "We are enormously grateful for the administration's work to develop and defend the Clean Water Rule from attacks that would weaken safeguards for clean water," said NRDC Director Rhea Suh.[23]

But opponents, including farmers and manufacturers, say the rule represents government overreach and that regulations should not cover small wetlands and streams on private property. "We all want clean water," said Sen. Joni Ernst, R-Iowa. "This rule is not about clean water. Rather, it is about how much authority the federal government and unelected bureaucrats should have to regulate what is done on private land."[24]

But environmentalists say the rule doesn't deal with one of the biggest water quality problems: unregulated contaminants. "There's a slew of chemicals present in the water," such as pesticides and pharmaceuticals, Griffiths says, that may well be in trace amounts but may still have human health effects.

The U.S. regulatory system works in a reactionary, after-the-fact way, Griffiths says. "Unless we have evidence of harm, [new chemicals] are OK," he says. In other words, a contaminant that harms human health could get into drinking water and not be identified or managed until government scientists deem the substance harmful. In contrast, he says, European countries operate under the "precautionary principle," in which industry scientists, rather than the government, must prove that a new chemical is safe before it enters the marketplace.[25]

As a result, Griffiths says, "water treatment in America doesn't protect against the new stuff that might get into water." And most water treatment uses century-old technologies: filtration and disinfection.

In addition, water treatment produces its own contaminants. Chlorine or similar disinfectant compounds, while cheap and efficient, also are "associated with a small risk of [bladder] cancer," Griffiths says. Water treatment likely contributes to a few thousand of the 30,000-50,000 cases of bladder cancer each year, but it also protects millions of people from bacterial pathogens, he says. "These are the trade-offs."

Yet no one has analyzed the risks and benefits of many new, unregulated chemicals, says the University of Wisconsin's Klaper.

Bacteria pose another danger. Water can pick up bacteria or other contaminants as they pass through the distribution pipes. "A lot of water pipes are laid next to

A physician draws a child's blood to test for excessive lead levels in Flint, Mich., on Jan. 26, 2016. The risk of lead poisoning among Flint children under age 6 rose 50 percent during the months the city used improperly treated Flint River water for drinking. In young children, even low exposure to lead can lower IQs and cause learning disabilities, attention disorders or violent behavior.

sewer pipes," says the NRDC's Wu. If pipes are leaking, bacterial contamination can enter the clean water supply, she says.

Should the federal government help localities upgrade their water infrastructure?

Upgrading the nation's water systems — a largely underground infrastructure that is out of sight and sometimes out of mind — is an enormous and underappreciated task, said Janet Kavinoky, executive director of transportation and infrastructure at the U.S. Chamber of Commerce.

"People think water should be free," she said. "My response is that, if you're in Washington, D.C., you can go down to the Potomac with your bucket, carry the water home, treat it, and when you're done figure out a way to dispose of it. It's hard to convince people that these things cost money, which is why it's hard to get investment in water infrastructure."[26]

Many cities do not have the money to fix their crumbling water distribution systems. Yet, as the Flint situation shows, skimping on utility costs can be disastrous. A cost-conscious decision "caused millions of dollars [worth] of problems, including health problems," says Tufts professor Griffiths.

Child Lead-Poisoning Rate Plummets

The percentage of children, ages 1 through 5, with lead poisoning has fallen steeply in recent years, from nearly 8 percent in 1997 to 0.5 percent in 2014, the most recent year for which data are available. A child with at least 10 micrograms of lead per deciliter of blood is considered to have lead poisoning, which can lower IQs and cause attention disorders, violent or other antisocial behavior or delinquency.

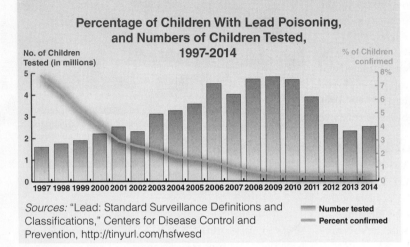

Percentage of Children With Lead Poisoning, and Numbers of Children Tested, 1997-2014

Sources: "Lead: Standard Surveillance Definitions and Classifications," Centers for Disease Control and Prevention, http://tinyurl.com/hsfwesd

Number tested
Percent confirmed

But what if a municipality can't pay for needed improvements? asks Lynn Broaddus, a nonresident senior fellow at the Brookings Institution, a centrist think tank in Washington. When a town's population drops, as in Flint, so do city tax revenues. Then "it becomes a social justice issue," she says.

For instance, small water utilities — those with fewer than 3,300 customers — that cannot afford upgrades are frequently cited for violations. "They can't afford the fix," says the University of Alabama's Andreen, and then "they can't afford the penalty."

And the cost of water treatment varies by community. Some places, such as Los Angeles and San Francisco, get much of their water from national parks in the Sierra Nevada Mountains.[27] "It's low-cost water with no industry around it," says Griffiths, so it doesn't need much treatment. "One could say they're stealing it from the public."

Other communities, such as Orange County, Calif., and desert communities in the Southwest, recycle their sewer water.[28] And some customers are paying more for

intensive water treatment. Water bills in Washington, D.C., have doubled in the past 10 years because treating the polluted Potomac River water requires more treatment than in cities that get water from a protected reservoir, says the NRDC's Wu.

The federal government has helped finance water infrastructure in the past, notes Neukrug, of the U.S. Water Alliance. Construction grants for sewage treatment plants and other infrastructure initially were made available under the 1972 Clean Water Act. "It changed the game and it made our rivers and streams much cleaner," he says. "Now that funding is gone."

The federal government maintains a loan program, called the Drinking Water State Revolving Fund, for states to provide loans to cities needing to upgrade water systems. But many experts feel the program is underfunded.

"Typically, the federal government appropriates $800 million to $850 million per year," Andreen says. In 2009, that amount was bumped up to $2 billion as part of President Obama's economic stimulus package, adopted in response to the recession that began in 2007. "That was probably a very wise expenditure, but it didn't continue at that level," he says.

Over the past two decades, $20 billion has gone into the state revolving funds — one-fifth of the estimated $1 trillion experts say is needed for maintenance and upgrades of drinking water infrastructure. But the amount the federal government spends on mass transit and roads dwarfs spending on water utilities. Of 2014 federal infrastructure spending, 48 percent went to highways and 16 percent to mass transit and rails, but only 5 percent to water utilities, according the Congressional Budget Office.[29]

The NRDC's Wu argues that funding infrastructure projects not only prevents crises but also creates jobs, a key goal of Obama's stimulus package. However, not everyone agrees federal funding is a good idea.

"The federal government does a lousy job of funding local issues," says Chris Edwards, director of tax policy studies at the Cato Institute, a libertarian think tank that advocates less regulation. Instead, he says, "state and local governments can issue debt. It's the best way to fund long-term investments such as infrastructure."

A water infrastructure financing portfolio should include raising water rates, writes Gregory Baird, an infrastructure asset management expert. "Everyone dislikes the need for higher rates, but there are things that are feared more than a rate battle — sinkholes and the loss of water services, contamination and public health issues, unplanned rate shocks and moratoriums on growth and development."[30]

"Rate payers have the primary responsibility and bear most of the cost," says Mehan, of the American Water Works Association. "Our rates [for drinking water] are half those in Northern Europe and far less than typical cellphone data plans, cable television or electric bills." Moreover, he says, "The federal government has its own fiscal issues. Its ability is limited."

Public-private partnerships are another option. "This has been done for highways, such as the Capital Beltway in Virginia," Edwards says. "A company added four lanes for a 15-mile stretch and gets to collect the tolls for a set period of time. Anything with a user charge can be privatized — or made half private. A local government might need $1 billion to upgrade. A private company funds this and gets a 50-year lease on the system. They get a return from rate-payers over time."

About 2,000 municipalities have entered public-private partnerships to upgrade their water systems.[31] Critics, such as Food and Water Watch, an organization that promotes safe and sustainable food and water supplies, say private partners will not put public health and safety above profit. Indeed, the group found that between 2007 and 2011, about 16 percent of privately held water systems reverted to public ownership, with quality a top complaint. And rates typically rise with privatization, which can reflect truer market value but can also have a disproportionately negative effect on low-income customers.[32]

Edwards argues that when a resource is provided too cheaply, it leads to wastefulness: People use more than they need and don't bother investing in the resource's future. "Water should be in the marketplace at market price," he says. "It ensures efficiency."

As for Mehan's comparison of water privatization to highways or cable TV, safe drinking water seems different, say advocates such as Public Citizen, because society considers it a need — a basic human right.[33]

But Edwards says that for low-income families who cannot afford higher water rates, "it's better to give them cash, through the Earned Income Tax Credit, for instance. But don't distort the water market."

Does the Safe Drinking Water Act effectively protect the public?

The 1974 Safe Drinking Water Act authorized the EPA to establish quality standards for clean drinking water and ensure that local utilities' disinfection and filtering methods met those standards.

Neukrug, the former Philadelphia Water CEO, says the act and the Clean Water Act "are 1970s designs [that] did an incredible job." But today's water environment "needs new rules," he says.

Congress has amended the Safe Drinking Water Act twice. In 1986, it banned the use of lead in water pipes and fittings in new houses and buildings. In 1996, lawmakers expanded the EPA's regulatory responsibilities to include protecting the quality of entire water systems, including rivers and lakes, that supply drinking water. The amendments also required utilities to better inform customers about problems and established the "contaminant candidate" list, or "chemicals of concern" found in water that may need to be regulated.[34]

Environmentalists say these amendments, while good, are not enough. What's more, they say, enforcement is slow or sometimes weak.

For example, progress in identifying dangerous new chemicals has been slow, critics say. Five years ago, for example, the EPA determined that perchlorate, used in rocket propellants, fireworks and matches, "has an adverse health impact, especially in fetuses, and that millions of Americans are exposed to it," NRDC's Wu says. EPA officials "haven't proposed a standard yet. They've blown through their deadline. And that's just one chemical."

Despite having promised to publish a proposed rule on perchlorate in 2013, the agency is seeking scientific experts to convene a panel to determine at what level perchlorate should be regulated.[35]

Jay L. Clendenin/Los Angeles Times via Getty Images

A geyser erupts from a broken water main in Los Angeles on July 29, 2014. The costs of upgrading the nation's aging water-distribution system include $30 billion to replace all lead service lines, $500 billion to repair leaking water mains and another $500 billion to meet growth demands over the next 25 years.

"There are 85,000 chemicals in use in the U.S., many of them in high volume," says Laura Orlando, executive director of the Resource Institute for Low Entropy Systems, a nonprofit in Boston that advocates for sustainable protection of public health and the environment. "How do we address that?" she asks. "Are they in source water? How much can we demand of industry to stop using them? These are political questions."

Given all the new chemicals introduced since the Safe Drinking Water Act was written, or even since it was last amended, the law's "framework is not protective," she says.

For instance, she says, under the act, the EPA in 1991 established the Lead and Copper Rule, which required utilities to test for those metals in tap water. If levels exceeded maximum standards, utilities were required to fix the problem. However, NRDC researchers recently found that 5,000 water systems had violations or enforcement actions related to the rule, including poor testing methods, failure to report contamination and inappropriate corrosion control. And Flint was not on the list of violators: Michigan state officials had not officially reported the too-high lead contamination to the EPA.[36]

Moreover, newspaper investigations have found many cities test for lead using procedures that do not detect problems. In Chicago, for instance, tap water testing is often done in the homes of the water utility staff and rarely in areas where recent water main work, known to increase the risk of lead contamination, has occurred.[37]

Such practices worry public health advocates. "Often, utilities test the same homes over and over," says Tom Neltner, director of Environmental Defense Fund (EDF) chemicals policies. "If you don't know where your lead service lines are, you could be testing in the wrong houses."

Chicago's water utility said the procedures comply with EPA regulations and that the utility's management of the city's pipes is above reproach. Testing staff homes allows consistency in monitoring lead contamination, the department said, adding, "Chicago's corrosion control has been so successful that the U.S. EPA has placed the city on a reduced monitoring program."[38]

An investigation by the British newspaper *The Guardian* found that some U.S. cities, such as Detroit and Philadelphia, frequently use testing methods that underestimate the extent of lead contamination.[39]

Tufts' Griffiths says that under the Safe Drinking Water Act's framework, the federal government sets drinking water standards but state governments usually have oversight. "The state makes official reports about this stuff," he says. "The EPA gets access [to reports] but cannot do anything without an invitation from the state," unless egregious violations occur, such as in Flint.

The University of Alabama's Andreen complains that "federal enforcement is not exercised very often." Even when a literal reading of the safe water act seems to provide a means for the EPA to swoop in when violations are sustained or serious, he says, the current practice is far more deferential to states' primacy. "I think the EPA should be the gorilla in the closet that helps states be on their toes."

Some have suggested that rather than amending the act, updating the Lead and Copper Rule could fix the lead problem. In 2015 an EPA advisory group recommended amending the rule to make replacement of lead service lines a priority over continuing to manage lead levels through corrosion control.

In most cities, "we only replace lead service lines when something else fails," says Neltner, who served on the advisory group. Thus, when a water main breaks, utilities might take advantage of a dug-up street to replace adjacent lead service lines. But the working group found that approach unacceptable because systems fail unpredictably. "Removing them is worth doing," Neltner says. "Not just in emergency situations. It's a long-term view."

But critics say if the EPA were to prioritize replacement over corrosion control, it would be prohibitively expensive for some local governments. "It's appropriate for the federal government to set standards, as long as their doing so doesn't end up being an unfunded mandate," says Adrian Moore, vice president of policy at the free-market Reason Foundation think tank.

The EPA is not bound to follow the advisory group's advice, but its recommendations have been endorsed by many water-related groups and associations, such as the American Water Works Association, the largest organization of water utilities and water professionals.

Tuft's Griffiths would like to see utilities improve their treatment processes. "If I were the czar, I would do water treatment more comprehensively" by requiring activated charcoal and reverse osmosis, he says. Charcoal "absorbs trace chemicals and is not that expensive," he says, while reverse osmosis involves "a membrane filter that complex chemicals and metals don't get through." But reverse osmosis is "expensive because it's energy intense," he says.

BACKGROUND
Public Waterworks

In 312 B.C., Rome built the first stone aqueduct to carry large volumes of clean water to the city's bathhouses. Over the next 500 years, at least 10 other aqueducts were built, some up to 50 miles long, providing more than 30 million gallons of fresh water daily to the city for fountains, gardens and drinking water. Water in public basins was free, but those who piped it into their houses or baths paid a tax.[40]

Rome's water system set a precedent for public drinking water through the ages: It was "a public good provided by right though imperial beneficence on the one hand, and as a private good for domestic consumption, on the other," wrote author James Salzman.[41]

In colonial America, Dutch settlers collected rainwater in cisterns and shallow wells in New York City because the rivers around Manhattan were too salty.

Later, the British dug deeper wells, but they soon became polluted. Enterprising businessmen began delivering clean water from distant springs or water pumps.[42]

Around the time of the Revolutionary War other American cities recognized the need for safe drinking water when a yellow fever epidemic — actually caused by mosquitoes but blamed at the time on foul water — prompted action. By 1801, Philadelphia had completed a public water system that included two pumping stations to pull water from the Schuylkill River.[43]

Protecting Water

Many early civilizations created rules and rituals for keeping drinking water supplies safe from contamination, including collecting and disposing of human waste away from water sources. But as cities became more crowded, waste and water often comingled, causing repeated disease outbreaks.

London was a prime example, with open sewers lining streets and an extremely polluted River Thames.[44] The city's 1854 cholera epidemic initially was blamed on foul air. But physician John Snow proved that the disease's rapid but localized spread occurred around a particular public water pump.

"Snow's findings supported the germ theory, as did the later realization that the mother of an infant suffering from cholera had disposed of the child's soiled diaper in a cesspit directly adjacent the Broad Street Pump just days before the cholera outbreak," wrote Salzman.[45]

In the United States, Chicago's public works system in the early 1900s kept water and waste separate. It drew water from Lake Michigan for drinking and piped sewage into the Mississippi River via a canal. Typhoid fever rates went down in Chicago, but downriver in St. Louis disease rates rose. Missouri sued Illinois but, with no clear proof that Chicago's waste was the cause, lost the case.

Even with protected water sources, humans used various methods — straining, siphoning, aerating and distilling — to further clean their drinking water. Boiling water was not generally used until the germ theory of disease was discovered in the 19th century. Growing cities often used sand filtration; Glasgow, Scotland, installed sand filtration in 1827. Some American cities, however, resisted filtration, fearing it would give their water a bad reputation: If it has to be cleaned, it must be bad water, they reasoned.[46]

C H R O N O L O G Y

1800s *Cities begin addressing need for clean drinking water. Physicians begin linking lead in water to certain health conditions.*

1801 Philadelphia completes a public water system with two pumping stations and a reservoir.

1827 Glasgow, Scotland, installs a sand-filtration system in its water plant.

1837 New York City begins damming the Croton River to supply water for the city.

1854 A London cholera epidemic kills 616; British doctor John Snow proves the disease is water-borne.

1851 A New York City doctor traces four cases of lead poisoning to tap water.

1855 Philadelphia purchases land along the Schuylkill River to buffer its clean water supply from pollution.

1889 A British doctor attributes miscarriages and infertility to lead in drinking water, but his reports are generally dismissed.

1890 Massachusetts Board of Health recommends against lead water pipes.

1900s *Chlorine disinfection programs are established, and Congress passes landmark legislation to ensure clean drinking water.*

1900 Chicago begins using different water bodies for its water intake and sewage output, leading to a decrease in typhoid fever but an outbreak of disease further downriver.

1902 Middelkerke, Belgium, installs first known chlorine disinfection system.

1908 Jersey City, N.J., becomes first U.S. city to use chlorine.

1930s Lead pipes begin losing their appeal, although some cities — including Boston, Milwaukee, Philadelphia, Denver and Chicago — continue to install them.

1950 Philadelphia begins building the first of three sewage-treatment plants and a sewer system to alleviate industrial and domestic waste pollution.

1960s Scientists develop a test to detect lead in human blood and begin monitoring exposure and setting safety thresholds for workers.

1970s-1990s *Federal government takes action on clean water.*

1970s U.S. public health officials estimate that 250,000 children are affected by lead poisoning each year.

1970 Environmental Protection Agency (EPA) established.

1972 Congress passes Clean Water Act.

1974 Congress passes Safe Drinking Water Act to protect drinking water supplies.

1978 U.S. Consumer Product Safety Commission bans lead from most consumer paint.

1986 Amendment to Safe Water Drinking Act bans lead pipes in buildings served by a public water system.

1991 Lead and Copper Rule sets permissible levels for drinking water.

2000s *Cities struggle with water contamination.*

2001 Washington, D.C., water is found to have high lead levels.

2014 To save money, Flint, Mich., begins using Flint River for drinking water, without using appropriate pipe-corrosion controls.

2015 Flint officials urge residents to stop drinking tap water after testing shows high lead levels. . . . Congress enacts law to allow greater funding flexibility for public utilities that accept federal water infrastructure grants.

2016 Congress adopts landmark overhaul of the Toxic Substances Control Act, requiring more information on health risks from chemicals found in drinking water. . . . Studies show thousands of cities' water systems have lead problems as bad as Flint's.

Jersey City, N.J., in 1908 became the first American city to use chlorine treatment. The method quickly caught on because it was inexpensive, effective and relatively simple to implement. By 1941, 85 percent of the country's water treatment systems were using chlorine.[47]

Chlorine instilled faith in municipal drinking water as outbreaks of water-borne diseases practically vanished. "It has been claimed that chlorination of drinking water saved more lives than any other technological advance in the history of public health," Salzman wrote.[48]

Lead Pipes and Health

In ancient times, water pipes were constructed from stone, hollow logs and clay. Later, concrete, iron, steel, copper and lead were used.

In 1767, a British doctor connected the malady known as Devonshire colic to lead. He described a "sharp onset and recurrent spasms in which the patient writhes in pain, retracts his legs spasmodically to his abdomen, groans, clenches his hands, grits his teeth, with beads of sweat on his brow." The doctor theorized that lead weights used to crush apples for cider contaminated the cider.[49]

In the 1800s, several individuals in the United States and Europe suspected lead-tainted water was damaging health. A New York City doctor in 1851 traced four cases of lead poisoning to tap water. In 1889, a British doctor attributed several miscarriages and cases of infertility to lead in drinking water, but his reports were generally dismissed.[50]

Lead remained a preferred material for water pipes, primarily because it was pliable, less prone to corrosion than other materials and durable: A 1917 report comparing pipe materials found that lead pipes lasted an average of 35 years (and up to 100 years), whereas those made from steel lasted, on average, for 16 years, galvanized iron 20 years and pipes lined with cement, 28 years.[51] Long-lived material is preferred for underground pipes because of the difficulty of accessing them for repair or replacement. By the early1900s most large cities used lead piping.

Gradually, however, science began to link lead exposure to a variety of ailments — anemia, palsy, joint pain, encephalopathy, blindness and colic. Women working in industries that used lead knew that it caused miscarriages; in fact, the substance was often used to perform illegal abortions.[52] As early as 1890 the Massachusetts State Board of Health recommended that lead piping be abandoned because of health risks. New Hampshire took up a similar cause shortly after that.[53] Efforts also emerged to prevent workplace exposure to lead, especially for those using white lead paint — either painting with it or scrubbing a painted surface clean.[54]

By about 1930 lead pipes began losing their appeal, although some cities — including Boston, Milwaukee, Philadelphia, Denver and Chicago — continued to install them.[55]

In the late 1960s, scientists developed a blood test to detect lead exposure. At the time, an adult level below 60-80 micrograms per deciliter of blood was considered safe. For many years, 10 micrograms was considered the threshold level for safety.[56] But the CDC, which periodically reassesses the safety level, lowered it to 5 micrograms per deciliter in 2012.[57]

In the 1970s, U.S. public health officials estimated that 250,000 children developed lead poisoning each year, and campaigns aimed to increase blood monitoring and reduce exposure, mostly from lead paint in old houses.[58] In addition, the federal government began phasing out leaded gasoline in the 1970s. Unleaded gasoline became the law of the land in 1996.

In 1986, Congress banned further installation of lead water lines when it amended the Safe Drinking Water Act.[59]

Water Safety Laws

Starting in the 1970s, the newly created Environmental Protection Agency began enforcing new laws on water pollution, including the Clean Water Act of 1972, which regulated pollution discharges into rivers and lakes that serve as sources of drinking water. It also funded the construction of sewage treatment plants.

As concern over polluted waters grew, so did worries about the health effects of chemicals found in drinking water. A U.S. Public Health Service survey of water systems in 1969 had found that only 60 percent of the systems delivered water that met existing safety standards, set by the service. The survey also found deficiencies in water treatment facilities and distribution pipes that led to cloudiness and poor pressure, in addition to contamination.[60]

In 1974 Congress passed the Safe Drinking Water Act, which focused on ensuring the safety of America's drinking water, as opposed to controlling pollution in

Lead's Childhood Legacy:
A Lifetime of Problems

"The kids will not be as smart and will make less money in their working life."

The tiny town of Sebring, Ohio, issued a water advisory this past January after learning that routine testing had found excessive lead in tap water samples. Schools in the town, population about 4,400, were closed, and children and pregnant women were told not to drink the water.[1]

The following week, the Ohio Department of Health found elevated blood lead levels in five Sebring children, three of whom lived on the same street.[2]

In Pennsylvania, several cities this year have reported higher rates of lead poisoning among children than occurred in Flint, the Michigan city notorious for its ongoing lead contamination crisis. Flint's average exposure rate was 3.2 percent of children tested, and its highest rate was 6.3 percent. Seventeen Pennsylvania cities had rates higher than 10 percent, based on 2014 data from the state's health department.[3]

About 500,000 American children aged 1 through 5 have excessive lead levels in their blood, according to the Centers for Disease Control and Prevention (CDC). While that may sound high, the figure is actually considered a great public health success. The percentage of youngsters in that age range with excessive lead levels fell from nearly 8 percent in 1997 to 0.5 percent in 2014, the most recent year for which data is available.[4]

And yet, no amount of lead is safe. Even small exposures — from soil, paint chips or contaminated water — accumulate in the bones and organs, potentially damaging the brain, heart and kidneys. Exposure can lower children's IQs and cause behavioral problems, especially in adolescence, such as attention-deficit/hyperactivity disorders (ADHD), antisocial or violent behavior and delinquency.[5]

The effects of lead poisoning are most devastating in young children because their bodies are smaller and their brains still developing. Yet exposure is usually highest in young children, especially toddlers, who tend to put foreign matter like soil or paint flakes into their mouths, or infants who ingest formula made with lead-tainted tap water.

No quick treatment is available for children with excessive blood lead levels. At very high levels, above 45 micrograms per deciliter, lead can be pulled out of the blood by administering drugs called chelating agents, but such therapies can be dangerous for a child.[6]

wetlands, lakes and rivers, as covered by the Clean Water Act. The drinking water act authorized the EPA to set standards for harmful contaminants in drinking water and established a federal grant program to help water systems modernize equipment.

Amendments to the Safe Drinking Water Act in 1986 required the EPA to set maximum levels for 83 contaminants, including microbial pathogens and chemicals, and banned lead piping for new construction. Under the law, the EPA in 1991 issued its Lead and Copper Rule, which required cities to take remedial action if 15 parts per billion of lead were detected in more than 10 percent of the taps sampled.

In 1996, lawmakers again amended the act, authorizing the EPA to protect the quality of water in rivers and lakes if they were the source of drinking water and to establish a list of candidate chemicals found in water that were suspected of harming health and potentially needed to be regulated.[61] It was a list from which to work out future regulations and standards for drinking water. The amendments also required water utilities to report to customers on water quality and established a revolving fund to provide grants to states for upgrading water systems.

In 1976, Congress passed the Toxic Substances Control Act, which authorized the EPA to regulate the production, importation, use and disposal of chemicals to protect the environment from new and potentially toxic chemicals. While the Clean Water Act had protected against pollutants in rivers and lakes and the Safe Water Drinking Act focused on keeping pollutants out

"A child during chelation needs close monitoring to make sure their kidneys are able to handle the lead burden as it's being metabolized in the body, make sure their liver is OK, make sure their white blood cell count is OK," says nurse practitioner Barbara Moore, who runs the lead clinic at Mount Washington Pediatric Hospital in Baltimore.

However, research has shown that chelation doesn't work for those with lower blood lead levels. Good nutrition — diets rich in iron, calcium and vitamin C — can help, as can early-childhood education and regular visits to a pediatrician to monitor for emerging health problems.[7]

Harvard University neurologist David Bellinger has examined studies of American children to assess how damage to IQ caused by lead exposure compares with damage from other childhood stressors, such as preterm birth, Type 1 diabetes and iron deficiency. He found that lead was second only to preterm birth in affecting childhood IQ.[8]

Flint's children were exposed to lead in their drinking water for 18 months after city officials decided to save money by switching to the Flint River as a source of drinking water, which caused the lead contamination. That decision will affect Flint's children throughout their lives, says Jeff Griffiths, a professor of public health and community medicine at Tufts University and former chair of the EPA's Drinking Water Committee.

"The kids will not be as smart, will get less schooling, will make less money in their working life," he says. "And they'll need medical services. The cost of the screw-up is borne by the public."

But Tom Neltner, chemicals policy director at the Environmental Defense Fund, an environmental advocacy group, says, "Don't write these kids off." Even though they are at risk for behavioral problems, he says, "You can offset the damage, but it takes a lot of effort."

— *Jill U. Adams*

---

[1] "Sebring's water system has high levels of lead," CantonRep.com, Jan. 22, 2016, http://tinyurl.com/h6gdewh.

[2] Mark Gillispie and John Seewer, "High lead levels in 5 kids in town with tainted water," The Associated Press, Jan. 27, 2016, http://tinyurl.com/z2g37ra.

[3] Sarah Frostenson, "18 cities in Pennsylvania reported higher levels of lead exposure than Flint," *Vox*, Feb. 3, 2016, http://tinyurl.com/hj8ecd2.

[4] "Lead," Centers for Disease Control and Prevention, www.cdc.gov/nceh/lead/.

[5] T. I. Lidsky and J. S. Schneider, "Lead neurotoxicity in children: basic mechanisms and clinical correlates," *Brain*, Jan. 1, 2003, http://tinyurl.com/hu54pp9.

[6] April Fulton, "Flushing Out Lead, Metals With Chelation Therapy," NPR, Jan. 3, 2011, http://tinyurl.com/2at7ohm.

[7] Lizzie Wade, "Flint's High Lead Levels Have Doctors Struggling For Answers," *Wired*, Jan. 14, 2016, http://tinyurl.com/z3uy9kk.

[8] David C. Bellinger, "A Strategy for Comparing the Contributions of Environmental Chemicals and Other Risk Factors to Neurodevelopment of Children," *Environmental Health Perspectives*, Dec. 19, 2011, http://ehp.niehs.nih.gov/1104170/.

---

of municipal drinking water sources, the toxic control act aimed to protect against harmful substances before they become widespread environmental pollutants.

Controlling chemicals under the act differed from how drugs and pesticides were regulated, in that chemical manufacturers did not have to show their products were safe. They needed only to notify the EPA that they have a new compound. The burden of proving harm fell on the federal agency. For years, critics had seen this provision as a major weakness, because the EPA was unable to keep up with testing existing and new chemicals for potential safety problems. A widely cited 2006 Government Accountability Office report found that 30 years after the law was enacted, only 200 of the 62,000 chemicals listed under the act had been tested.[62]

While complaints about the Toxic Substances Control Act's weaknesses continued, calls for updating the Clean Water Act emerged in 2015, when the Obama administration sought to clarify — and expand — the types of water sources protected under the act to any water that served as a source for public drinking water. The new Clean Water Rule would bring an additional 2 million miles of streams and 20 million acres of wetlands under the EPA's protective purview.

The Clean Water Rule also stirred controversy. Industry, farmers, small-business groups and real estate developers claimed the rule interfered in private landowners' rights. Congress sought to block the rule, but President Obama vetoed the resolution Congress used to try to block it. Now federal courts will decide the matter.[63]

Thousands of Cities Face Water-Quality Problems

Poor communities with slim budgets are hardest hit.

When Madison, Wis., found lead concentrations in its water to be dangerously high in the early 1990s, the city took a radical approach to solving the problem: It spent $20 million to replace all the lead pipes in town, even paying part of the cost to replace pipes buried in homeowners' front yards.[1]

But as the state capital and home of the University of Wisconsin's main campus, Madison is more affluent than many localities around the country. Some communities such as Bayonne, N.J., and St. Joseph, La. — both afflicted with water system woes — face sometimes overwhelming circumstances to provide basic services.

As many municipalities struggle to maintain, repair and upgrade water facilities, some experts say it's a social justice issue. "It is the nonwhite suburbs that are the poorest places in metro America, with the smallest tax bases," said Myron Orfield, director of the Institute on Metropolitan Opportunity at the University of Minnesota Law School. "There are thousands of them, and they are all going to have Flint problems."[2]

The city of Flint, Mich., is now notorious for its poorly managed public water system, in which a decision to save money ended up corroding old pipes and contaminating the water of thousands of homes with lead.

For Madison, replacing the 2,500 pipes owned by the utility was the easy part. Getting water customers to replace their 5,500 lead service lines was tougher. But it had to be done, experts said, because partial pipe replacement can worsen lead contamination: Metal fragments inside service pipes can dislodge during replacement work, according to the utility's water quality manager, Joe Grande.[3]

In Madison, however, financing the massive project was relatively manageable. The water utility paid for half the $1,400 cost, on average, for replacing each homeowners' pipes, and the city offered loans for the remainder, which could be paid back via higher property taxes.[4]

Over a decade, 8,000 lead pipes were replaced by copper ones.[5] Madison raised some of the money by renting space on city water tanks and towers to cell phone companies to install their antennas.[6]

"It costs the same in Madison to replace the pipes as it does in Flint," says Lynn Broaddus, nonresident senior fellow with the Brookings Institution. "It certainly helped that Madison is a relatively affluent city with a median household income of $50,000. Homeowners could afford to pay their share."

Most water utilities, when faced with lead-tainted water, adjust their corrosion control methods. For Madison, the chemical treatment approach — adding orthophosphate to the water to prevent lead from leaching out of the pipes — posed another problem. The city's sewage treatment plant was under state orders to remove phosphates from city water to keep the chemicals out of the region's lakes. Phosphates trigger algae blooms, which befoul lakes.[7] So, while chemically treating the water would have been cheaper and easier, it would have made sewage treatment more expensive because the phosphate would have to be removed.

Madison's systems approach to water treatment — looking at drinking water, waste water and storm water as interconnected parts of a greater whole — is advocated by experts such as Howard Neukrug, a senior fellow at U.S. Water Alliance, an organization that promotes sustainable water systems. In most cities, these parts are managed and regulated separately. "It's critically important to not look at one thing at a time, but at the overall system," Neukrug says.

Madison is a success story. But, says Broaddus, "they made their decision when the rules [about using phosphates] were changing. For communities who have put in the capital investment for an orthophosphate treatment program, well, what are they going to do now?"

Poor communities face high hurdles. In St. Joseph, a town of about 1,200 in northeastern Louisiana, residents are worried about tap water filled with rust sediment, frequent service stoppage and frequent advisories to boil their drinking water because of bacterial contamination. The town's tiny $1.5 million budget leaves little or no money to fix frequent breaks in the 1930s-era water mains. The state allocated $6 million for water infrastructure repairs three years ago, but it won't release the funds until the town submits a financial audit, which was due in 2013, but the town has had difficulty securing an audit firm.[8]

Meanwhile, the water distribution system continues to deteriorate and about half of the treated water leaks into the ground. "This is typical of communities probably all over the U.S., especially poor communities," said Davis Cole, a civil engineer working to redesign St. Joseph's system.[9]

Bayonne, a city of about 66,000 east of Newark, tried another route to solve its perennial drinking water and wastewater problems. The aging water system already had been prone to operating problems and often ran afoul of environmental regulations even before it was hit hard in 2012 by Hurricane Sandy, which devastated the local energy grid.

Once the hurricane crisis was over, the Bayonne Municipal Utilities Authority started looking for solutions in earnest. The city's high debt level made borrowing expensive, so it chose a path that 2,000 other water utilities in the United States have taken: They entered a partnership with a private company.[10]

The private firm made an initial payment to help the city pay off much of its debt, and pledged $157 million to upgrade both the drinking water and wastewater utilities. Water rates initially jumped by 8.5 percent and three years later by another 4 percent, which likely would have happened anyway, according to the public half of the partnership.

One analysis estimated that the city will save $35 million over the 40-year contract.[11]

"Public-private partnerships are the ideal solution for the fiscal problems plaguing many American cities," wrote energy and infrastructure lawyer Kent Rowey, in a *New York Times* opinion column.[12]

— *Jill Adams*

Chemical storage tanks sit beside the Elk River in Charleston, W. Va. In 2014 a tank leaked a coal-washing chemical that is neither regulated nor listed as a contaminant into the river, the city's water source.

[2] Quoted in Jake Blumgart, "The Next Flint," *Slate*, Jan. 28, 2106, http://tinyurl.com/gnln2xx.

[3] Fears and Dennis, *op. cit.*

[4] Adam Rodewald, "Lead pipe replacement: Who pays for it?" *Green Bay Press Gazette*, March 25, 2016, http://tinyurl.com/hj49aea.

[5] Fears and Dennis, *op. cit.*

[6] Maya Dukmasova, "To remove lead pipes, Chicago can learn from Madison's example," *The Chicago Reporter*, May 2, 2016, http://tinyurl.com/zvtfkw2.

[7] *Ibid.*

[8] Lauren Zanolli, "Water woes: Tap runs brown in Louisiana's impoverished northeast," Al Jazeera, Feb. 7, 2016, http://tinyurl.com/h4m5yfj.

[9] Quoted in *ibid.*

[10] Mindy Fettermen, "As Water Infrastructure Crumbles, Many Cities Seek Private Help," *Stateline*, March 30, 2016, http://tinyurl.com/jgxeqs6; "A Tale of Two Public-Private Partnership Cities," *Knowledge*, June 10, 2015, http://tinyurl.com/ortsldg.

[11] *Ibid.*

[12] Kent Rowey, "Public-Private Partnerships Could be Lifelines for Cities," *The New York Times*, July 15, 2013, http://tinyurl.com/hyfurpw.

[1] Darryl Fears and Brady Dennis, "One city's solution to drinking water contamination? Get rid of every lead pipe," *The Washington Post*, May 10, 2016, http://tinyurl.com/zncxk6k.

CURRENT SITUATION
Flint Fallout

In early June, the EPA warned city officials that Flint faced new risks to its drinking water because of the arrival of summer. In warm weather, bacteria that cause Legionnaire's disease can grow, and the bacteria has been detected in Flint, especially if chlorine is not kept consistently at appropriate levels throughout the water distribution system. Correct pH levels, a measure of acidity, must be maintained throughout the system so corrosion control can be effective, the EPA has warned.[64]

Officials recently told Flint residents, who have been using bottled water since October, that the city's tap water was safe to wash with and to drink, if filtered first. Obama drank a glass of Flint tap water during a May visit to the city.[65] But customers still report problems, such as burning sensations and rashes, even from very short showers.[66]

Meanwhile, a pilot program to replace lead service lines in the city has been completed on 30 of an estimated 10,000 sites. But costs have averaged $7,500 per line, almost double initial estimates. The city has received $2 million from the state of Michigan, and on June 29, Gov. Rick Snyder signed a state budget bill with $240 million in funds for the Flint water crisis.[67] The city also is slated to get another $128 million in federal funds if approved in the pending congressional budget deal.[68]

Three government workers in April — a Flint employee and two state employees assigned to monitor water quality — face criminal charges for the city's water debacle, including misconduct and tampering with evidence. Michigan Attorney General Bill Schuette said, "These charges are only the beginning. There will be more to come — that I can guarantee you."[69]

More fallout is highly likely, experts say. Some 8,000 Flint children under age 6 have been exposed to dangerous levels of lead for extended periods, a public health disaster that will require extra health care support for families and additional educational support for schools.[70]

The debacle in Flint has prompted the rest of the country to look for lead-tainted water. Parents across the country are pressuring school districts to check for lead in the drinking water at their children's schools. "Before Flint, we'd get a call maybe once a month from a school,"

Utility workers in Syracuse, N.Y., repair a broken water main on Sept. 21, 2015. The Environmental Protection Agency sets national water-safety standards, but the sourcing, treatment and distribution of water is left to local utilities, some dealing with polluted water sources, aging pipes or shrinking budgets.

said Robert Barrett, the chief operating officer for Aqua Pro-Tech Laboratories, an environmental testing lab in New Jersey. "Now it's daily."[71]

In Portland, Oregon's largest public school district, parents demanded that the superintendent resign after officials failed to promptly notify parents that high lead levels had been detected in school water. In New Jersey, after dozens of schools were found to have lead-tainted water, Republican Gov. Chris Christie ordered that every school in the state test for lead. Schools that get their water from public water utilities — about 90 percent of the nation's schools — are not required to test regularly for lead.

"Every parent assumes that someone must have taken care of this problem decades ago," said Virginia Tech engineering professor Marc Edwards, who documented the first high lead reading in a Flint resident's home. "They're always shocked to discover that it hasn't been fixed."[72]

Even Congress is not immune. In late June, drinking water in the Cannon House Office Building was found to violate EPA lead standards. Rep. Dennis Ross, R-Fla., expressed outrage, especially on behalf of pregnant staffers working in the building. "Even more distressing is the fact the signs posted due to this matter simply state 'out of order,' with no explanation whatsoever, rather than informing the public as to the reason," he said.[73]

AP Photo/Mike Groll

AT ISSUE

Is the federal government doing enough to keep America's drinking water safe?

YES
Adrian Moore
Vice President, Reason Foundation

Written for *CQ Researcher*, July 2016

The federal government is doing enough. It sets minimum water-quality standards and should play a role in independently monitoring state and local government compliance with standards.

But the call for more federal funding is wrongheaded. Water infrastructure is entirely local in nature, and problems with safe drinking water are almost entirely local in nature. People in Maryland don't benefit from Flint, Mich., improving its water infrastructure, so they shouldn't be asked to pay for it. The same goes for localities all over the nation.

When Congress starts funding local projects, several bad things happen. First, Congress can't target money to where it is most needed. Instead, every member thinks his district should get a fair share of the funds, and the most powerful members can earmark big chunks of funds for their districts. Second, even if Congress does allocate funds based on need, that approach simply rewards jurisdictions that failed to invest in their own infrastructure, paid for by taxpayers whose jurisdictions did make adequate local investments. Finally, the prospect of free federal money is a powerful disincentive for local governments to adequately spend their own resources on water infrastructure. It is much more appealing to lobby for federal funding than to pay for a project out of the local budget.

We have seen all three of these problems play out over and over with federal infrastructure funding programs.

Many, many local governments are responsibly managing their water infrastructure all on their own. Rather than ask for a federal handout, other local governments should emulate them. The responsible localities allocate property taxes, impact fees or other revenues to build new capacity as needed. They build into water rates the real costs of maintenance and include a capital fee to build up a fund to replace major facilities that reach the end of their lifespan. When there is a need for spending on water infrastructure, they move that to the top of the budget list, ahead of many "nice to have" spending items. Thousands of local governments use public-private partnerships to keep costs down and improve performance, or even rely on regulated private water utilities to provide safe drinking water.

The responsible path is for local water users to pay for the infrastructure they use, not to ask people far across the nation to fund it for them.

NO
Tom Neltner
Chemicals Policy Director, Environmental Defense Fund

Written for *CQ Researcher*, July 2016

Americans expect safe, affordable drinking water delivered to their homes on demand. But our water infrastructure suffers from an out-of-sight, out-of-mind problem. We build it, but we all too often fail to maintain it. At every level of government, we need smarter investment, stricter oversight, regular coordination and more public transparency to ensure safe drinking water.

According to the Environmental Protection Agency's 2011 Drinking Water Infrastructure Needs Survey, the nation's aging water infrastructure needs about $400 billion in capital improvements over the next 20 years. That is 12 times more money than the federal government has invested in water infrastructure since it created the Drinking Water State Revolving Loan Fund in 1997.

While the burden for these upgrades ultimately rests with the local utility and its customers, Congress needs to do more. This is particularly important in places where customers likely are unable to cover the costs of infrastructure loans. Congress, the Obama administration, states and municipalities must work together to create funding alternatives to help these communities make the necessary improvements and have the technical, managerial and financial capacity to run the systems effectively.

State oversight agencies that must ensure the work is done right are understaffed. In 2013, the Association of State Drinking Water Administrators estimated that states have an average of 3,100 people inspecting its water utilities. That's 1,300 fewer people than are needed to provide basic oversight. With some 150,000 public water suppliers operating across the country, increasing state staffing will prove a costly, if essential, safeguard.

Water officials and utilities need a reliable federal partner, too. The Environmental Protection Agency must provide more guidance to its state and local partners. And its approach of regulating chemicals on an individual basis cannot keep pace with the thousands of commercial chemicals potentially entering our drinking water. As a result, too many water systems are ill-prepared to address emerging problems.

Finally, we need an honest, open dialogue regarding the state of our nation's water infrastructure. Infrastructure improvements have been postponed, operating budgets cut and staff sizes reduced, at the risk of safe drinking water. Only by working together, committing to investing additional capital, updating old policies and practices and improving technical and operating procedures can we keep America's drinking water safe.

Staffers have access to free bottles of water in the Cannon House Office Building in Washington, D.C., on July 7, 2016, where drinking water fountains are "out of order" due to excessive levels of lead.

Mark Wilson/Getty Images

The *USA Today* and NRDC investigations of EPA records found lead contamination of the drinking water in thousands of communities in every state. Among other findings, the NRDC said 1,000 water systems serving 4 million people had excessive lead levels.[74] *USA Today* reporters found that only about 10 percent of the 8,225 schools and day care centers with their own small water systems are required to test for lead. Of those that do test, 350 detected unsafe lead levels in the past three years.[75]

An investigation by the Vox online media website found that children in at least 18 Pennsylvania cities, including Philadelphia, Allentown and Harrisburg, were found to have significant lead exposure — as high as or higher than in Flint. But it is unknown whether the culprit is tainted water or lead paint.[76]

The latest tainted water discoveries add to a long list of lead-contaminated drinking water incidents: Washington, D.C., in the early 2000s; Columbia, S.C., in 2005; Durham and Greenville, N.C., in 2006; Brick Township, N.J., in 2011; Jackson, Miss., last July; and Sebring, Ohio, last August.[77]

Legal Actions

Several lawsuits have been filed to try to force improvements in the regulation, monitoring and treatment of America's drinking water.

One — filed in January by the NRDC, the American Civil Liberties Union of Michigan, Concerned Pastors for Social Action and Flint resident Melissa Mays — seeks federal intervention to fix Flint's water situation, including the replacement of all lead service lines.

"The water in Flint is still not safe to drink because city and state officials are violating the federal law that protects drinking water," said Dimple Chaudhary, a senior NRDC attorney. "We are asking a federal court to step in because the people of Flint simply cannot rely on the same government agencies that oversaw the destruction of its infrastructure and contamination of its water to address this crisis."[78]

In February, three Chicago residents sued that city, charging that for years it failed to warn residents about lead in their drinking water — especially when construction work to fix and replace water mains was in progress — as documented in a 2013 EPA study.[79] The residents are asking the court to order the city to replace lead water pipes.

"We believe the city of Chicago knew well the risks and dangers of toxic lead contamination associated with these construction projects but chose to turn a blind eye to its own, allowing this mounting problem to become a widespread public health issue across the city of Chicago," said Steve Berman, the attorney for the plaintiffs.[80]

The NRDC sued the EPA in February, demanding action on setting a standard for perchlorate in drinking water.[81]

Congressional Action

On June 22, Obama signed into law the Lautenberg Chemical Safety Act, a massive overhaul of the 40-year-old Toxic Substances Control Act and the first major environmental legislation enacted in more than 20 years.

The law enhances the EPA's authority to regulate new chemicals found in everything from consumer products to industrial manufacturing. It requires the agency, for the first time, to test all chemicals before they go on the market and to prioritize those chemical studies based on their health hazard and their "proximity to drinking water sources." The additional information about dangerous chemicals can provide scientific evidence needed to prompt standard-setting under the Safe Drinking Water Act as well. The new chemical bill had opponents, mostly from industry groups that fear increased costs, but was passed with bipartisan support in Congress and with the support of chemistry groups such as the American Chemistry Council.[82]

Meanwhile, congressional Democrats have introduced several bills aimed at helping to fix the drinking water problem. In the House, Rep. John Conyers, D-Mich., proposed a dedicated fund to upgrade the nation's water infrastructure. In the Senate, Democrats Dick Durbin of Illinois and Ben Cardin of Maryland introduced legislation to require expanded testing and reporting for lead through an updated Lead and Copper Rule.[83]

Sen. Cory Booker and Rep. Donald Payne Jr., both New Jersey Democrats, introduced a bill to require public utilities to test drinking water in schools as part of their lead testing programs and to notify parents within two days when levels are too high. Sen. Chuck Schumer, D-N.Y., and Rep. Bill Pascrell, D-N.J., introduced measures to establish a grant program to pay for lead testing at schools and day care centers.[84]

So far, only Democrats are supporting the proposals. In New Jersey, Republican Gov. Christie — in addition to ordering mandatory testing for lead contamination in all public schools in the state — plans to lower the state's threshold blood-lead level that warrants medical attention.[85]

Republicans were the primary sponsors of a provision, adopted by Congress last December, to allow cities that receive federal stimulus funds under the Water Infrastructure Finance and Innovation Act (WIFIA) to supplement that money with tax-exempt bonds.[86] "It's creative financing that allows municipalities to get more bang for their buck," says Mehan, of the American Water Works Association, which strongly supported the bill.

After praising Congress for freeing the federal infrastructure funds to address America's "enormous water infrastructure challenge," water association CEO David LaFrance said, "We now urge Congress to move swiftly to appropriate the necessary funds for WIFIA to do its important work."[87]

Obama has requested an additional $20 million and 12 staff members to expand the water infrastructure funds program and $2 billion for the two state revolving funds, which are federal low-interest loan programs to help fund water infrastructure upgrades.[88]

OUTLOOK
Water and Politics

The fall presidential election could set the tone for new drinking water policy.

Presumptive GOP nominee Donald J. Trump has called the Flint water crisis a "total breakdown in government" caused by "gross incompetence" and "another example of bad government." In an interview with a Grand Rapids TV station on the morning of the Michigan presidential primary, Trump said, "There were a lot of mistakes made here from the city and the state and probably even the federal government. If I were president, I would be there to help."[89]

Trump also has said repeatedly that he would abolish the EPA, in favor of letting states manage environmental issues. "Environmental protection — we waste all of this money," he said in a February debate. "We're going to bring that back to the states."[90]

Meanwhile, presumptive Democratic nominee Hillary Clinton, who has visited Flint residents and city officials, has promised to eliminate lead as a public health threat in the next five years. She plans to create a presidential commission to recommend solutions, and she has pledged to deliver $5 billion toward lead abatement from all sources, including those most likely to affect children: water and paint.[91]

The Flint crisis and subsequent investigations of lead-tainted drinking water have generated plenty of hand-wringing, legal action and condemnation of water mismanagement, but long-term change is uncertain.

Several challenges remain. The EPA estimates that $384 billion is needed through 2030 to maintain and upgrade water distribution pipes and water treatment plants. Replacing lead service lines would be costly, but the only way to solve the problem once and for all. "There's a huge problem with political will," said Tufts professor Griffiths. "We have neglected our own infrastructure."[92]

Crises often spur change, but the water association's Mehan says education also is key, because few members of the public appreciate "the sheer technical expertise, the complexity and the staggering cost involved in the collecting, treating, delivering and recycling or disposing of water." Water professionals are realizing that they must be more than good engineers, he says. "They've got to be good at strategic communication, they've got to educate the public about the expertise and the costs behind safe drinking water."

While new contaminants will continue to be a challenge, the overhauled Toxic Substances Control Act promises to complement the Safe Drinking Water Act by assessing the health hazards of new chemicals entering the market. That will enable drinking water officials to set standards for more potentially harmful contaminants. "I've been working on this for 15 years," said Richard Denison, a senior scientist at the Environmental Defense Fund. "It fixes every major problem with the current law."[93]

If upheld by the courts, the Clean Water Rule will help EPA regulate polluters and industrial and agricultural practices that threaten the purity of drinking water sources. Obama advocated for the rule when he vetoed congressional action to overturn it. "Too many of our waters have been left vulnerable," Obama said. "Pollution from upstream sources ends up in the rivers, lakes, reservoirs and coastal waters near which most Americans live and on which they depend for their drinking water, recreation and economic development."[94]

Climate change also threatens drinking water. More frequent droughts, especially in the water-scarce Southwest, pose challenges not only to water supplies but also to keeping them clean and safe. Lower water levels can mean higher concentrations of contaminants. And extreme weather, predicted to increase in frequency and intensity due to climate change, can overload storm-water systems, a common path for water contamination.[95]

Americans are accustomed to turning on their taps and getting safe drinking water. Indeed, says Lynn Thorp of Clean Water Action, "every drop of water that comes out of your tap is an engineering marvel."

But maintaining that level of safety will require that citizens prioritize water safety, says Neukrug, of the U.S. Water Alliance. "Our water is safer than at any time in history anywhere in the world," he says "And then there are Flint, Toledo and West Virginia." Safe water is "too important of an issue not to solve," he says.

NOTES

1. Todd Spangler, "CDC confirms kids' blood-lead levels went up in Flint," *Detroit Free Press*, June 24, 2016, http://tinyurl.com/j3hmqk8.

2. *Ibid.*

3. "Lead poisoning and health fact sheet," World Health Organization, updated July 2016, http://tinyurl.com/oppuccq.

4. Monica Davey, "Flint Officials Are No Longer Saying the Water Is Fine," *The New York Times*, Oct. 7, 2015, http://tinyurl.com/pfvkbr8. Todd Spangler and Paul Egan, "E-mails: EPA indecision led to inaction in Flint crisis," *Detroit Free Press*, May 13, 2016, http://tinyurl.com/hbr32e9.

5. Monica Davey and Richard Pérez-Peña, "Flint Water Crisis Yields First Criminal Charges," *The New York Times*, April 20, 2016, http://tinyurl.com/jdstndw.

6. Alison Young and Mark Nichols, "Beyond Flint: Excessive lead levels found in almost 2,000 water systems across all 50 states," *USA Today*, March 11, 2016, http://tinyurl.com/jfv7vlh. Also see "What's in Your Water?" Natural Resources Defense Council, June 6, 2016, http://tinyurl.com/zj4zkoc.

7. Young and Nichols, *ibid.*

8. John Wisely and Todd Spangler, "Where are the lead pipes? In many cities, we just don't know," *Detroit Free Press*, Feb. 28, 2016, http://tinyurl.com/hvlfk2b. "Replacing all lead water pipes could cost $30 billion," *Water Tech Online*, March 11, 2016, http://tinyurl.com/zdg7kpg.

9. Rachel Dovey, "4 Things to Know Before Your Water Is Privatized," *Next City*, Jan. 7, 2015, http://tinyurl.com/jeus9on.

10. "Buried No Longer: Confronting America's Water Infrastructure Challenge," American Water Works Association, 2011, http://tinyurl.com/bou9svq.

11. Jesse McKinley and Vivian Yee, "Water Pollution in Hoosick Falls Prompts Action by New York State," *The New York Times*, Jan. 27, 2016, http://tinyurl.com/jshursx.

12. Tim Friend, "Water in America: Is It Safe to Drink?" *National Geographic News*, Feb. 17, 2014, http://tinyurl.com/po9nakt.

13. Codi Kozacek, "Toledo Issues Emergency 'Do Not Drink Water' Warning to Residents," Circle of Blue, Aug. 2, 2014, http://tinyurl.com/gq38vbk.

14. Kate Sheppard, "EPA Finds Some Cases Of Water Contamination Related To Fracking, But Says It's Not Widespread," *The Huffington Post*, June 4, 2015, http://tinyurl.com/ofn6qs4.

15. Jon Hurdle, "EPA science panel, in new draft, repeats concerns about fracking report," NPR, Feb. 17, 2016, http://tinyurl.com/jk8rra4.

16. "Table of Regulated Drinking Water Contaminants," Environmental Protection Agency, http://tinyurl.com/gvgnd6q.

17. "Draft Candidate Contaminant List 4," Environmental Protection Agency, http://tinyurl.com/hxsmkfd.

18. Michael Wines and John Schwartz, "Unsafe Lead Levels in Tap Water Not Limited to Flint," *The New York Times*, Feb. 8, 2016, http://tinyurl.com/hmff3rz.

19. "Understanding the Safe Drinking Water Act," Environmental Protection Agency, June 2004, http://tinyurl.com/jgnsuvw.

20. "A Brief History of the Clean Water Act," PBS, undated, http://tinyurl.com/mumj8lz.

21. Juliet Eilperin and Darryl Fears, "Congress is overhauling an outdated law that affects nearly every product you own," *The Washington Post*, May 19, 2016, http://tinyurl.com/zwlu78f.

22. Wines and Schwartz, *op. cit.*

23. Robert Pore, "Obama vetoes resolution of disapproval of WOTUS," AgNet, Jan. 20, 2016, http://tinyurl.com/htp997j.

24. Gregory Korte, "Obama vetoes attempt to kill clean water rule," *USA Today*, Jan. 19, 2016, http://tinyurl.com/h72hgz8.

25. For background, see Jennifer Weeks, "Regulating Toxic Chemicals," *CQ Researcher*, July 18, 2014, pp. 601-624.

26. "America's Neglected Water Systems Face a Reckoning," Knowledge@Wharton, June 10, 2015, http://tinyurl.com/jlqe6m7.

27. Charles Duhigg, "That Tap Water Is Legal but May Be Unhealthy," *The New York Times*, Dec. 16, 2009, http://tinyurl.com/japxfz6.

28. John Schwartz, "Water Flowing From Toilet to Tap May Be Hard to Swallow," *The New York Times*, May 8, 2015, http://tinyurl.com/pmqcaey.

29. Danny Vinik, "Is Washington creating more Flints?" *Politico*, May 25, 2016, http://tinyurl.com/hbykm6m; "Public Spending on Transportation and Water Infrastructure, 1956-2014," Congressional Budget Office, March 2015, http://tinyurl.com/hlqr47v.

30. Gregory Baird, "A game plan for aging water infrastructure," *Journal AWWA*, April 2010, http://tinyurl.com/gs83s2u.

31. Mindy Fetterman, "As Water Infrastructure Crumbles, Many Cities Seek Private Help," *Stateline*, March 30, 2016, http://tinyurl.com/jgxeqs6.

32. Dovey, *op. cit.*; "Top 10 Reasons to Oppose Water Privatization," Public Citizen, undated, http://tinyurl.com/ztzlxbz.

33. "Top 10 Reasons to Oppose Water Privatization," *ibid.*

34. "Safe Water Drinking Act," Environmental Protection Agency, https://www.epa.gov/sdwa.

35. "Perchlorate," Environmental Protection Agency, http://tinyurl.com/h33kl9a. Also see "Perchlorate in Drinking Water Raises Health Concerns," *Scientific American*, Dec. 21, 2012, http://tinyurl.com/j6uqvq9.

36. "What's in Your Water?" *op. cit.*; Davey and Pérez-Peña, *op. cit.*

37. Michael Hawthorne and Jennifer Smith Richards, "Chicago often tests water for lead in homes where risk is low," *Chicago Tribune*, Feb. 26, 2016, http://tinyurl.com/zpfboou.

38. *Ibid.*

39. Oliver Milman, "US authorities distorting test to downplay lead content of water," *The Guardian*, Jan. 22, 2016, http://tinyurl.com/gkqtsl9.

40. James Salzman, *Drinking Water* (2012), pp. 53-54.

41. *Ibid.*, pp. 57-60.

42. *Ibid.*

43. Michael Wang, "Cool, Clear Water: The Fairmount Water Works," Pennsylvania State University Libraries, Fall 2010, http://tinyurl.com/hg2lkat.

44. Salzman, *op. cit.*, pp. 85-87.

45. *Ibid.*, p. 98.

46. *Ibid.*

47. *Ibid.*, pp. 99-100.

48. *Ibid.*

49. Sven Hernberg, "Lead Poisoning in a Historical Perspective," *American Journal of Industrial Medicine*, 2000, http://tinyurl.com/z8quoav.

50. Werner Troesken, *The Great Lead Water Pipe Disaster* (2006), pp. 7, 62-63.

51. *Ibid.*, pp. 151-152.

52. Hernberg, *op. cit.*

53. Troesken, *op. cit.*, p. 202. Also see Hernberg, *op. cit.*

54. Hernberg, *ibid.*

55. Richard Rabin, "The Lead Industry and Lead Water Pipes: A Modest Campaign," *American Journal of Public Health*, September 2008, http://tinyurl.com/h89spn7.

56. Hernberg, *op. cit.*

57. "What do parents need to know to protect their children?" Centers for Disease Control and Prevention, March 15, 2016, http://tinyurl.com/j8dlhod.

58. *Ibid.*; Hernbug, *op. cit.*

59. "EPA Takes Final Step in Phaseout of Leaded Gasoline," press release, Environmental Protection Agency, Jan. 29, 1996, http://tinyurl.com/zo3bd59.

60. "25 Years of the Safe Drinking Water Act: History and Trends," Environmental Protection Agency, 1999, http://tinyurl.com/he5svso.

61. "Safe Water Drinking Act," Environmental Protection Agency, https://www.epa.gov/sdwa.

62. "Chemical Regulation: Actions Are Needed to Improve the Effectiveness of EPA's Chemical Review Program," Government Accountability Office, Aug. 2, 2006, http://tinyurl.com/hjjyc4b.

63. Robert Pore, "Obama vetoes resolution of disapproval of WOTUS," *The Grand Island Independent*, Jan. 20, 2016, http://tinyurl.com/he76o69; Todd Neeley, "WOTUS Conflict," DTN/The Progressive Farmer, June 27, 2016, http://tinyurl.com/jffgv8b.

64. Amanda Emery, "EPA concerned about 'urgent' situation with chlorine levels in Flint water," MLive, June 4, 2016, http://tinyurl.com/grz6vgy.

65. Gregory Korte, "Obama drinks Flint water as he urges children be tested for lead," *USA Today*, May 4, 2016, http://tinyurl.com/huxhrv3.

66. T. J. Raphael, "After months, the Flint water situation is finally getting a little bit better," PRI, June 3, 2016, http://tinyurl.com/zlu9cfa.

67. David Eggert, "Michigan Governor Signs Budget With $165M More for Flint," The Associated Press, June 29, 2016, http://tinyurl.com/j8xwtyq.

68. Matthew Dolan, "Replacing Flint's lead pipes is double the estimate," *Detroit Free Press*, May 28, 2016, http://tinyurl.com/z53zrq2.

69. Davey and Pérez-Peña, *op. cit.*

70. Abby Goodnough, "Flint Weighs Scope of Harm to Children Caused by Lead in Water," *The New York Times*, Jan. 29, 2016, http://tinyurl.com/zfs5zdk.

71. Brady Dennis, "Schools often lag on lead testing," *The Washington Post*, July 5, 2016, http://tinyurl.com/heh8kv8.

72. *Ibid.*

73. Quoted in Warren Rojas, "Water in House Office Building Too Dangerous to Drink," *Roll Call*, June 29, 2016, http://tinyurl.com/h2vf4ew.

74. Brady Dennis, "More than 5,300 U.S. water systems violated lead-testing rules last year," *The Washington Post*, June 28, 2016, http://tinyurl.com/h7zsgxt.

75. Laura Ungar, "Lead taints drinking water in hundreds of schools, day cares across USA," *USA Today*, March 17, 2016, http://tinyurl.com/hlw7lyg.

76. Sarah Frostenson, "18 cities in Pennsylvania reported higher levels of lead exposure than Flint," *Vox*, Feb. 3, 2016, http://tinyurl.com/hj8ecd2.

77. Wines and Schwartz, *op. cit.*

78. "Groups File Federal Lawsuit to Secure Safe Drinking Water in Flint," press release, American Civil Liberties Union of Michigan, Jan. 27, 2016, http://tinyurl.com/jgzcg2x.

79. Michael Hawthorne, "Lawsuit seeks removal of lead pipes in Chicago," *Chicago Tribune*, Feb. 18, 2016, http://tinyurl.com/hx4ke2q.

80. *Ibid.*

81. "NRDC Sues EPA to Force it to Limit Toxic Chemical in Drinking Water," press release, Natural Resources Defense Council, Feb. 18. 2016, http://tinyurl.com/hod88lo.

82. Eilperin and Fears, *op. cit.*; Richard Denison, "Why passage of the Lautenberg Act is a really big deal," Environmental Defense Fund, June 10, 2016, http://tinyurl.com/h6gk8xg.

83. Laura Ungar, "With nation at risk, lawmakers target lead in drinking water," *USA Today*, April 14, 2016, http://tinyurl.com/zm2l8ue; Dolan, *op. cit.*

84. Helena Bottemiller Evich, "Avoiding the next Flint: Testing school water," *Politico*, April 22, 2016, http://tinyurl.com/j7mmbtf.

85. David Giambusso, "Christie to require lead testing in all public schools," *Politico*, May 2, 2016, http://tinyurl.com/jf9ch92.

86. "AWWA celebrates Congressional fix to WIFIA," issue statement, American Water Works Association, undated, http://tinyurl.com/9wzc23j.

87. *Ibid.*

88. "EPA's FY 2017 Budget Request Increases Support for Communities to Deliver Core Environmental and Health Protection," press release, Environmental Protection Agency, Feb. 9, 2016, http://tinyurl.com/zzkbwnp.

89. "Trump on FOX 17: Flint caused by 'gross incompetence,' mass shootings a mental health issue," Fox17 News, March 8, 2016, http://tinyurl.com/jelr4ak.

90. Oliver Milman, "Republican candidates' calls to scrap EPA met with skepticism by experts," *The Guardian*, Feb. 26, 2016, http://tinyurl.com/zowabrr.

91. Natasha Geiling, "Hillary Clinton Just Released A Plan To Target This Often-Ignored Environmental Issue," ThinkProgress, April 13, 2016, http://tinyurl.com/gw8pmrr.

92. Wisely and Spangler, *op. cit.*; Wines and Schwartz, *op. cit.*

93. Quoted in Eilperin and Fears, *op. cit.*

94. Quoted in Korte, *op. cit.*, "Obama vetoes attempt to kill clean water rule," *op. cit.*

95. "Adaptation Strategies Guide for Water Utilities," Environmental Protection Agency, February 2015, http://tinyurl.com/hyfkybz.

BIBLIOGRAPHY

Selected Sources

Books

Salzman, James, *Drinking Water*, Overlook Duckworth, 2012.
A Duke University law professor follows water from source to tap, creating a popular history of the resource through the prism of a single commodity.

Troesken, Werner, *The Great Lead Water Pipe Disaster*, MIT Press, 2006.
A University of Pittsburgh history professor argues that lead pipes are a long-running environmental and public health catastrophe.

Wilson, H. W., *The Transformation of American Cities*, Grey House Publishing, 2015.
A publisher of reference books issues a compilation of newspaper articles on how U.S. cities are surmounting shortcomings with water infrastructure and other problems.

Articles

Friend, Tim, "Water in America: Is It Safe to Drink?" *National Geographic News*, Feb. 17, 2014, http://tinyurl.com/po9nakt.
A journalist looks at whether a chemical spill in West Virginia that sickened residents reveals broader holes in the safety net for unregulated pollutants in drinking water.

Hernberg, Sven, "in Lead Poisoning a Historical Perspective," *American Journal of Industrial Medicine*, 2000, http://tinyurl.com/z8quoav.
A Finnish research physician documents lead exposure incidents and knowledge about lead's toxicity throughout history.

McKinley, Jesse, and Vivian Yee, "Water Pollution in Hoosick Falls Prompts Action by New York State,"

The New York Times, Jan. 27, 2016, http://tinyurl
.com/jshursx.
A small village in New York scrambles to understand the
risks posed by a monitored but unregulated drinking-
water contaminant.

Schwartz, John, "Water Flowing From Toilet to Tap
May Be Hard to Swallow," *The New York Times*, May
9, 2015, http://tinyurl.com/pmqcaey.
A science journalist take a close look at recycling wastewater into drinking water, a method becoming more
common in the drought-stricken Southwest.

Vink, Danny, "Is Washington creating more Flints?"
Politico, May 25, 2016, http://tinyurl.com/hbykm6m.
A journalist analyzes the government's response and fail-
ures to the threats posed to safe drinking water.

Wines, Michael, and John Schwartz, "Unsafe Lead
Levels in Tap Water Not Limited to Flint," *The New
York Times*, Feb. 9, 2016, http://tinyurl.com/hmff3rz.
Two reporters examine lead and other contaminants in
drinking water in communities across America.

Wisely, John, and Todd Spangler, "Where are the lead
pipes? In many cities, we just don't know," *Detroit
Free Press*, Feb. 28, 2016, http://tinyurl.com/hvlfk2b.
Two reporters write that hundreds of American cities
cannot locate their lead service lines, which means regular water testing may miss some homes.

Young, Alison, and Mark Nichols, "Beyond Flint:
Excessive lead levels found in almost 2,000 water systems across all 50 states," *USA Today*, March 11,
2016, http://tinyurl.com/jfv7vlh.
Two investigative journalists identify almost 2,000 water
systems in all 50 states where recent testing has shown
high levels of lead contamination.

Reports and Studies

"2013 Report Card for America's Infrastructure,"
American Society of Civil Engineers, 2013, http://
tinyurl.com/c6rxtef.
An engineers' organization gives the United States a
D-plus grade on drinking water quality as part of its
comprehensive assessment of the nation's roads, bridges,
pipelines and other infrastructure.

"The State of Public Water in the United States,"
Food and Water Watch, February 2016, http://tinyurl
.com/h4dcnht.
An environmental advocacy group analyzes forces that
keep water utilities in the public sector.

"What's in Your Water?" Natural Resources Defense
Council, June 6, 2016, http://tinyurl.com/zj4zkoc.
Researchers from the environmental advocacy group dug
through the Environmental Protection Agency's 2015
records and found 5,000 water systems, serving 18 million Americans, with violations or enforcement actions
relating to the agency's rule governing lead and copper
contaminants in water.

Curtis, Tom, "Water Infrastructure: The Last and
Next 100 years," *Journal AWWA*, August 2014,
http://tinyurl.com/hhzh6fp.
A water expert details the history of water infrastructure
in the U.S. and looks ahead to the challenge of keeping
water operations effective.

Varghese, Shiney, "Privatizing U.S. Water," The
Institute for Agriculture and Trade Policy, July 2007,
http://tinyurl.com/zjcvr35.
The report surveys privatized water utilities in the United
States and analyzes the political and economic context in
which privatization occurs.

For More Information

American Society of Civil Engineers, 1801 Alexander Bell Drive, Reston, VA 20191; 800-548-2723; www.asce.org. Publishes report cards on water and other aspects of U.S. infrastructure.

American Water Works Association, 6666 W. Quincy Ave., Denver, CO 80235; 303-794-7711; www.awwa.org. Membership association of water utility professionals.

Cato Institute, 1000 Massachusetts Ave., N.W., Washington, DC 20001; 202-842-0200; www.cato.org. Libertarian think tank advocating greater private oversight of drinking water.

Clean Water Action, 1444 I St., N.W., Suite 400, Washington, DC 20005; 202-895-0420; www.cleanwateraction.org. Environmental advocacy group focused on clean water.

Environmental Defense Fund, 275 Park Ave., South, New York, NY 10010; 800-684-3322; https://www.edf.org. Environmental group calling for greater oversight of drinking water.

Natural Resources Defense Council, 20 West 20th St., 11th Floor, New York, NY 10011; 212-727-2700; https://www.nrdc.org. Environmental group that has filed lawsuits seeking to improve drinking water safety.

Reason Foundation, 5737 Mesmer Ave., Los Angeles, CA 90230; 310-395-2245; http://reason.org. Conservative, free-market think tank advocating less direct federal investment in drinking water.

U.S. Environmental Protection Agency, 1200 Pennsylvania Ave., N.W., Mail Code 4606M, Washington, DC 20460; 202-272-0167; https://www.epa.gov/ground-water-and-drinking-water. Federal agency responsible for drinking water standards and regulations.

U.S. Water Alliance, 1816 Jefferson Place, N.W., Washington, DC 20036; 202-533-1810; http://uswateralliance.org/. Nonprofit group that seeks to improving water-system policies.

4

The Gig Economy

Eugene L. Meyer

New York City taxi drivers on Sept. 16, 2015, protest what they call weak regulation of ride-hailing services, which they say gives companies like Uber and Lyft an unfair competitive advantage. Ride-sharing companies want local and state officials to exempt them from "old economy" wage and labor laws, but many of their drivers are demanding benefits and worker-protection laws.

From *CQ Researcher,*
March 18, 2016.

D avid Gandy is an apostle of the "gig economy," the brave new work world in which people take temporary jobs or work for themselves. He sees this growing sector of the economy as a godsend because of the freedom it affords self-starters like him.

"It's good all around," says the 48-year-old Florida native, who has moved from city to city and job to job as an Uber driver, a corporate event producer, a caterer, a lighting designer and a disc jockey. He's worked in Chicago and Washington and plans to move soon to the San Francisco area.

"As America coins itself as the land of entrepreneurship, this is where a lot of the benefits that may not be known to a lot of people will come to the surface and be utilized," Gandy says. In fact, he says, the gig economy will boost entrepreneurs and eventually "break the backs . . . of these big-box chains and corporate overlords."

But for others, part-time gigs are not a choice but a painful necessity. Diane Gowder of San Pedro, Calif., used to be a manager for a market research firm with a good salary, benefits, paid time off and a retirement account. But she lost her job in 2005 when her firm downsized and has been scrambling ever since.[1]

Despite sending out hundreds of résumés, she said, she hasn't found full-time work. She cites her age as the reason. "At 55, I was either overqualified or they thought I wanted too much money — even though we hadn't even discussed money," Gowder said.

Unable to land anything steady, Gowder became an independently employed eyewear sales representative. "It was a huge

Contractors Are Biggest Freelance Segment

More than a third of freelance workers were independent contractors, or freelancers without a single employer who work project to project, according to a study of 2014-15 employment trends. More than one-fourth were "diversified workers," earning small shares of income from a mix of traditional employers and freelance assignments, and about the same share were moonlighters who performed freelance work in addition to their full-time primary jobs.

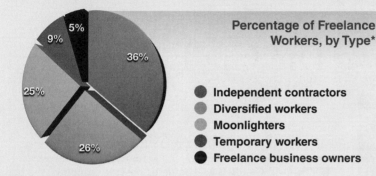

Percentage of Freelance Workers, by Type*

- Independent contractors
- Diversified workers
- Moonlighters
- Temporary workers
- Freelance business owners

* Percentages do not add to 100 due to rounding.

Source: "Freelancing in America: 2015," Freelancers Union, Upwork and Edelman Berland, September 2015, p. 6, http://tinyurl.com/hjlhkfx

switch," she said, because she received no health insurance and had to cover her own expenses. "I didn't have a steady income. It was up. It was down."[2]

Welcome to the gig economy, in which individuals take on transient work — sometimes voluntarily, sometimes not. Gig workers run the gamut from laid-off factory workers offering dog-walking services to artists delivering food for online companies to pay the rent. Economists and others refer to them as, among other things, freelancers, part-timers, moonlighters, the self-employed, "perma-temps" and independent contractors.

To its critics, the gig economy is exploiting workers and undermining the national economy by allowing companies to replace full-time employees with cheaper part-timers who do not get guaranteed hours, income or benefits. But to its defenders, the gig economy is a savior that, besides offering workers flexibility and freedom, allows struggling companies to survive and healthier firms to remain nimble in a competitive economy.

Experts differ on the size of the gig economy in part because of limited recent data and varying job

definitions. The federal government put "contingent" employees at 7.9 percent of the workforce in 2010, or a total of 12.2 million, according to an April 2015 study by the U.S. Government Accountability Office.[3] Economists Seth D. Harris of Cornell and Alan B. Krueger of Princeton estimated there were between 600,000 and 1.9 million workers providing services through an on-demand company or an online enterprise that offers convenient access to goods or services. They say such workers represent a small — up to just over 1 percent — but growing percentage of the population.[4]

In a 2015 survey, the nonprofit Freelancers Union, which advocates for independent workers, asserted that nearly 54 million people — one-third of the nation's labor pool — do at least some freelance work.[5] The survey broadly defined "freelancers" to include traditional project-by-project independent contractors, moonlighters, temporary workers with a single employer and freelancers who also own a small business.

"Freelancing is the new normal," write Sara Horowitz, the organization's founder and executive director, and a colleague, summarizing a survey showing freelancers are integral to the new economy.[6]

"Increasingly," writes Steven Hill, a senior fellow at New America, a left-leaning public policy think tank in Washington, "we are going to find that more and more workers exist simultaneously in multiple worker categories — a worker, for example, who has a regular part-time job (W-2, but with little safety net), and supplements that with being an Uber driver and/or Instacart [food] deliverer (1099 worker, still no safety net), as well as other mini-gigs and nano-gigs, and perhaps a second part-time job (temp, freelancer, etc.). Many workers already have multiple employers — sometimes within a single day!

"How will that look in the labor statistics?" Hill asks. "Will we be able to count this complexity, using current methods?"[7]

While experts disagree over the size and makeup of the gig economy, many economists, union leaders and others do agree that the 20th-century model of long-term employment with one company is largely history and that, in this new world, the risks — and costs — previously borne by employers largely have shifted to workers.

Highlighting this change, President Obama told Congress in his 2016 State of the Union speech in January: "Of course, a great education isn't all we need in this new economy. We also need benefits and protections that provide a basic measure of security. After all, it's not much of a stretch to say that some of the only people in America who are going to work the same job, in the same place, with a health and retirement package, for 30 years, are sitting in this chamber."[8]

In fact, some temporary workers do qualify for limited benefits, particularly those hired through job agencies. Snelling Staffing Services, which provides employees to companies in the clerical, light industrial and medical fields, says some contracting firms offer a 401(k) retirement plan to workers after 30 days on the job as well as holiday pay and medical, dental, vision and life insurance.[9]

Boosters tout the benefits to both workers and businesses of freelancing in a gig economy, often calling it a new digital-driven industrial revolution. Mobility is the biggest benefit, many say, because work done via the Internet can be done anywhere with a Wi-Fi connection. "Mobility is our reality, and this enabling technology" means employees are no longer tethered to a physical office, says Microsoft, the multinational software technology company.[10]

According to Boise, Idaho-based TSheets, which helps firms track payroll, the gig economy "simply means more options and a broader horizon for employees. . . . Gone are the days when 'self-employed' was a thinly veiled term for unemployment. Increasingly, freelance work and self-employment are associated with greater freedom, flexibility, options, new possibilities and

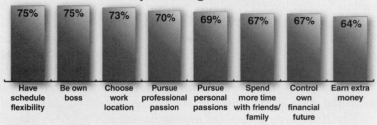

Flexibility Attracts Most Freelancers

Schedule flexibility and the opportunity to manage oneself were primary motivators for three in four full-time freelancers, according to a study by market research firm Edelman Berland. Freelancers also cited being able to choose a work location and to pursue professional and personal passions as top reasons for freelancing.

Motivations for Full-Time U.S. Freelancers, July 2014-August 2015

Have schedule flexibility	Be own boss	Choose work location	Pursue professional passion	Pursue personal passions	Spend more time with friends/ family	Control own financial future	Earn extra money
75%	75%	73%	70%	69%	67%	67%	64%

Source: "Freelancing in America: 2015, Results Deck," Freelancers Union, Upwork and Edelman Berland, September 2015, slide 14,http://tinyurl.com/hdqmdqo

a safety cushion."[11] While recognizing the downside of "fewer protections" for workers, TSheets concludes that the benefits far outweigh the risks.

Others, however, view the gig economy as just a new version of 19th-century piecework, a system that exploited workers and led them to form labor unions. The "new" model is really a throwback "from a much older concept," in which "instead of working in a factory for a wage or a salary, workers sewed or assembled goods at home and were paid by the finished item rather than for their time," writes Laura Clawson, labor editor of *Daily Kos*, a liberal weblog, quoting journalist Sarah Jaffe. "This 'revolutionary' work built out of Silicon Valley convenience is not really about technological innovation — it's just the next step in a decades-old trend of fragmenting jobs, isolating workers and driving down wages."[12]

Other critics say the gig economy arose largely from the ashes of the 2007-09 recession, when companies replaced full-time and hourly work with on-demand employment beyond the traditional temp agency or union hall hiring environment. This greater use of part-timers, as well as the outsourcing of jobs overseas, is contributing to the shrinking of the middle class and wage stagnation, they say.[13]

For instance, a 2014 Federal Reserve Bank of Chicago paper found "a strong association" between slow real wage growth "and marginally attached workers, particularly those working part time involuntarily for economic reasons."[14]

Countervailing trends appear to be at work, however. Some employers are moving away from part-time workers in favor of using full-time employees. Hello Alfred, a New York City company that provides a range of personal butler-type services to clients, pays employees $18 an hour, plus benefits, to those working at least 30 hours weekly. Company officials say full-time workers are better able to build a sense of community and customer loyalty.[15]

Munchery, an on-demand company that prepares and delivers food in San Francisco, Los Angeles, Seattle and New York, formerly classified its drivers as independent contractors, with no overtime, unemployment insurance, workers' compensation or other benefits. But in 2013, it reclassified them as employees to stanch turnover and ensure a steady workforce.[16]

And with unemployment falling and the labor market seemingly tightening, some employers, notably Walmart, are raising the wages of full-time employees to stem turnover and reduce hiring and training costs.[17]

As workers, businesses, economists and others debate the gig economy, here are some of the questions under discussion:

Is the gig economy good for workers?

After the 2007-09 recession, the stars seemed aligned, or crossed, depending on one's job needs. Unemployment peaked at 10.1 percent, not counting so-called "discouraged" workers who had given up looking for work. Layoffs were rife, and job prospects were grim for many people, including new college graduates.

On the other hand, the resulting gig economy seemed like a great opportunity for those needing work. As technical consultants, freelance writers, dog walkers or temp workers stocking warehouse shelves or answering phones, they could earn cash and perhaps develop entrepreneurial skills while enjoying flexible hours and more freedom than a traditional 9-to-5 office job offered.

"Today, consulting or freelancing for five businesses at the same time is a badge of honor," writes Micha Kaufman, a writer about the gig economy, entrepreneurs

and the future of work and the CEO and co-founder of Fiverr, an online marketplace for on-demand workers and persons needing services.[18] "It shows how valuable an individual is. Many companies now look to these 'ultimate professionals' to solve problems their full-time teams can't. Or they save money by hiring 'top-tier experts' only for particular projects."

While recognizing the challenges, Horowitz of the Freelancers Union notes in her book, *The Freelancer's Bible*, that "freelancing is a fluid work medium that rewards nimbleness and flexibility. When it's working well, there's no better feeling." It's all about opportunity — and of security and sustainability (savings on clothes and meals, for example), leverage (freelancers banding together) and camaraderie in having a community, she writes.[19]

Gig proponent Gandy, too, cites the benefits of independent work. "A lot of traditional benefits we get [from companies] in a lot of ways are holding us back" by stifling the entrepreneurial impulse. But with tax breaks and write-offs offered to business entities such as sole proprietorships and limited liability corporations, he says, "I like the prospect of what's going on."

A study for Uber, the ride-hailing service, also supports the sunnier view of the gig economy. Based on December 2014 online interviews of 601 drivers in 20 markets, the study concluded that 78 percent were satisfied with their experience, 71 percent reported earning more than they did before signing up with Uber and 61 percent felt more financially secure than before. Three-quarters said they went to work for Uber to "earn more income to better support myself or my family," and 63 percent did so "to have more flexibility in my schedule and balance work with my life and family." Their average pay was $19 an hour.[20]

In addition, being so-called 1099 workers (for the IRS wage statements they receive from clients during tax season) enables the savvy self-employed to deduct their business expenses.

However, not everyone views the 1099 lifestyle as a plus.

"This trend [of on-demand work] shifts all economic risks onto workers," former U.S. Labor Secretary Robert Reich wrote in his blog. "A downturn in demand, or sudden change in consumer needs or a personal injury or sickness can make it impossible to pay the bills. It eliminates labor protections such as the minimum wage, worker safety, family and medical leave and overtime. And it ends employer-financed insurance — Social Security, workers' compensation, unemployment benefits and employer-provided health insurance."[21]

Britta Lunden knows from personal experience the perils of the gig economy. After graduating from the University of Texas in 2013, she headed to Hollywood with dreams of working her way up in the film industry. Instead, she has gone from gig to gig, toiling in a series of temp jobs, including a stint at a digital-media company that, she says, included "no benefits, no health insurance, no paid time off, no vacation," despite her putting in 40-hour weeks.

The job-hopping, Lunden says, has taken a toll. "You don't know at any point if you'll have another gig," she says. "I feel like I'm constantly looking two weeks out." And, she says, a lot of her friends who are working in the gig economy — driving Uber cars or delivering food or other items for Postmates, a network of couriers — "would take a full-time job if they could get one. But they are hard to come by."

Georgia native Jenna Payne, 31, also has bounced from job to gig to gig since moving to New York City in 2003. She began as an executive assistant with benefits at a law firm, then left for a temporary job that she thought was full-time. She also worked as an executive assistant through a temp agency. "I ended up barely getting unemployment benefits," she says. During this time, she took a couple of film workshops and produced some short films, using Kickstarter, a crowdfunding platform, and her credit cards to finance the effort. She also waited tables.

Payne worked briefly in Florida, then moved back to New York and, finally, to Los Angeles in 2010 as an independent contractor working in films, "living paycheck to paycheck and supporting myself with credit when I needed to." Now, at last, she has a regular job for a small film production company, and she just received her W-2 for 2015, along with four 1099s from other gigs. But neither she nor her employer is able to provide for her retirement or health insurance.

"Worker well-being is often ignored in discussions that emphasize productivity, profitability, economic growth and similar concerns," wrote Jeffrey Pfeffer, a professor of organizational behavior at Stanford University's Graduate School of Business.[22] Indeed, the

Rapper Michael Olmos makes short videos at his home studio in Alhambra, Calif., for clients using rapping puppets. When his business began to grow, he hired additional workers through Fiverr, an online marketplace for on-demand workers that lets freelancers bid on jobs.

Gary Friedman/Los Angeles Times via Getty Images

leader of the world's estimated 1.2 billion Roman Catholics, Pope Francis, says global capitalism's failure to create fairness and dignified livelihoods for the poor is the primary economic challenge of this era.[23]

Is the gig economy good for companies?

The increasing use of temporary or part-time workers, independent contractors, freelancers and consultants has been a boon to corporate bottom lines, allowing employers to cut costs and boost profits, say supporters. Shedding employees, they say, has made for stronger and more nimble companies, relieving them of the responsibility for providing a range of benefits, some mandated by law, others by tradition.

"Companies typically pay part-time employees an hourly wage and can schedule them for whatever number of hours the company desires," says the website Small Business.[24]

The reported benefits extend far beyond U.S. shores. "There is a huge army of well qualified people out there who would be prepared to work, and to work hard, if they could only work on a flexible part-time basis," says Duport, a British firm that advises businesses on such matters.[25] "In fact, it is not uncommon for part-time workers to do as much in their shorter day or week than a full-time worker on the same staff."

Emile Wamsteker/Bloomberg via Getty Images

To cut costs, the pharmaceutical giant Merck sold a plant in Pennsylvania to a company that fired the 400-person workforce and then rehired them all as independent contractors. Merck then contracted with the company to continue making antibiotics, "using the exact same employees," according to an account of the transaction. Above, a Merck facility in Summit, N.J.

In the traditional model that prevailed into the middle-to-late 20th century, employers guaranteed pensions, paid all or most health insurance premiums and absorbed the costs of paid vacations, holidays and overtime pay. In addition, employers and employees split the contributions for Social Security and Medicare, which the self-employed must cover entirely.

In the gig economy, however, companies benefit from flexibility in hiring because they no longer have to keep full-time workers on the payroll for entire production cycles when demand for workers may fall. According to a U.S. Bureau of Labor Statistics report, workweek cuts are companies' "initial response to sagging product demand" during a recession.[26]

And sometimes, it's just plain cheaper to replace regular employees with contract workers. Merck, the pharmaceutical giant, sold its factory in Philadelphia to a company that got rid of the entire 400-person workforce and then hired them back as independent contractors. Merck "then contracted with the company to carry on making antibiotics . . . using the exact same employees," according to an account of the transaction.[27]

Similarly, LP&G, a public relations firm in Tucson, Ariz., let go 88 percent of its staff and then brought them back as freelancers working out of their homes, with no benefits.[28]

Other examples abound. In a California survey of 300,000 contractors, two-thirds said they had no "direct employees," so labor-related costs — such as payroll taxes or workers' compensation insurance — were reduced by 30 percent.[29]

Such cost-cutting permits companies to satisfy shareholders and boost stock values and executive compensation, but it forces many displaced workers to join the on-demand gig economy.

Yet, for many companies, the gig economy comes at a cost, including loss of institutional knowledge, high turnover, lack of loyalty and greater hiring and retraining costs.

Some online startups have abandoned the independent gig worker for the more traditional employer-employee relationship, to avoid problems stemming from high turnover and rehiring and retraining costs.

Other on-demand companies, such as San Francisco-based Instacart, are adopting a blended model. The online food delivery service determined its exclusive use of independent contractors was resulting in poorer service. In 2015, after three years in business, it joined with supermarkets to embed full-time employees in stores to do the shopping while the contractors made deliveries.

"We've seen a cadre of workers who are better, have fewer issues than we used to see before in terms of missed items, bad produce," said Nikhil Shanbhag, an Instacart vice president. "They are getting more and more efficient."[30]

Similarly, DoorDash, another food-delivery startup powered by a digital app, faced high turnover among its drivers because they were independent contractors who often adhered to their own schedules. As a result, the firm has had to spend some $200 per worker in recruitment and referral bonuses to keep drivers.[31]

Yet another company, the butler service Hello Alfred, has on-demand employees who, if they work more than 30 hours a week, receive benefits. "Turnover in this kind of industry is very high," says Marcela Sapone, CEO and co-founder. "There should not be a disconnect between the success of a company and the success of its workers. We believe treating our employees as our primary customer is how we can best satisfy our end users. It can become difficult to achieve this with the 1099 classification, because it inherently distances the worker from the company."[32]

Ultimately, for both workers and management, the gig economy is a mixed bag. Further complicating the picture is the growing use of automation.

As artificial intelligence advances and robots become increasingly sophisticated, more corporations see automation as a way to save money, according to some experts. Unlike humans, robots don't need days off or health insurance; nor do they get tired. But they do need maintenance and large upfront investments.[33]

If carried to its logical conclusion, automation would make the gig economy seem like a quaint relic of a gentler time, when self-employed independent contractors could at least make a buck or two as they hustled from task to task in the on-demand gig economy.

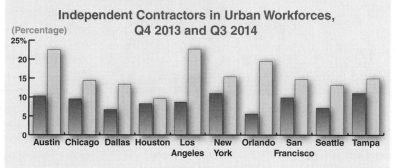

Contractor Workforce Soars

Independent contractors made up a growing share of the workforce in 10 major cities between late 2013 and mid-2014, according to research by Gusto, a cloud-based platform for payroll, benefits and human resources. The share of contractors — those earning at least $600 and filing a Form 1099 with the IRS — more than doubled in Austin, Dallas, Los Angeles and Orlando.

Independent Contractors in Urban Workforces, Q4 2013 and Q3 2014

Source: Joshua Reeves, "The Rise of the 1099 Economy [Infographic]," Gusto.com, Dec. 11, 2014, http://tinyurl.com/gq9qloj.

Uber CEO and co-founder Travis Kalanick has already endorsed the need to develop driverless cars, which would reduce the number or even eliminate Uber drivers. "Are we going to be part of the future?" he asked. "Or are we going to resist the future, like that taxi industry before us? For us, we're a tech company, so we've said, let's be part of that. It's a super exciting place to be."[34]

Should the definition of independent contractor be changed?

The growth of the gig economy in recent years has prompted calls by some economists, academics and freelance advocates for a new definition for independent contractors, one that accommodates the less regulated business models exemplified by Uber, Lyft, Etsy — the peer-to-peer commerce website — and a host of other on-demand companies.

At the same time, union officials and other pro-worker groups insist the issue is not one of definition but of enforcing existing laws and regulations to force companies to adhere to traditional values of equity and fairness in the workplace. The most egregious violation, critics say, occurs when a company misclassifies an individual as an independent contractor even though the company

determines hours, pay and conditions of employment — the legal criteria for classifying someone as an employee rather than a contractor — in order to avoid paying benefits to the worker.

At the root of these questions is the extent to which these on-demand, digitally based businesses should be regulated in an economy that depends on the availability of self-employed contractors so companies can reduce labor costs.

Some economists propose what they describe as a "middle way." Notably, economists Harris and Krueger argued in a December 2015 report for the Brookings Institution's Hamilton Project, "New and emerging work relationships arising in the 'online gig economy' do not fit easily into the existing legal definitions of 'employee' and 'independent contractor' status." They call for "a new legal category, which we call 'independent workers,' for those who occupy the gray area between employees and independent contractors."[35]

Harris and Krueger see independent workers more as independent businesses than employees, although the companies, which they call "intermediaries," exert some control by setting fees and "firing" workers. The economists suggest that independent workers receive some but not all benefits accorded to traditional employees. These

Daniel Acker/Bloomberg via Getty Images

An employee prepares for Black Friday at a Walmart in Chicago on Nov. 25, 2015. Even with the gig economy growing, some employers — faced with a tightening job market — are moving away from outsourcing work and back to using full-time employees. Walmart has raised the wages of full-time employees to stem turnover and reduce hiring and training costs.

would include "the freedom to organize [with other independent workers] and collectively bargain, civil rights protections, tax withholding, and employer contributions for payroll taxes."[36]

Other experts call for "portable benefits," an extension of a practice long common in the union trades. Gig economy critic Hill suggests creating Individual Security Accounts (ISA), into which every business hiring an independent worker would pay. The worker then would use the ISA "to buy that safety net," he says.

Others argue that no new definition of independent contractor is needed and that traditional regulations should not apply because rules stifle profit and quality of services. "After all, profit is a much more powerful driver for quality than regulatory compliance," argues Aran Sundararajan, a professor at New York University's Stern School of Business, in an essay in *Wired.com*. "Many of today's regulations were right for their time, and contributed to the safe and efficient growth of services over the last century. But emerging digital institutions have already started to make them obsolete."[37]

The use of perma-temps has led to a spate of union grievances and lawsuits — and settlements in which companies have reclassified individuals and paid out millions of dollars in settlements.

In 2000, Microsoft agreed to a landmark $97 million settlement in a class-action lawsuit brought by perma-temp workers who contended they were illegally denied benefits. Many had been hired through "temp" agencies but had worked at Microsoft for more than two years.[38]

Perma-temp work accounted for 3.4 million jobs in 2013, or about 2.3 percent of the national total; between 2008 and 2012, these jobs increased by 41 percent.[39] Looking at it on a weekly basis, temp job growth has far outpaced overall employment growth rates since the recession, rising from a weekly average of 2.2 million jobs in 2009 to 3.2 million in 2014, according to the American Staffing Association.[40]

This increasing use of temporary workers has led to a call for more stringent protections. From California to Illinois and Massachusetts, legislatures have passed bills to enforce labor laws on both staffing agencies and their client companies.[41]

But temporary workers hired through staffing agencies tend to have "a core safety net" that includes some legal protections, such as anti-discrimination laws, which contractors and freelancers do not, says Hill of New America.

Misclassification of employees as independent contractors — not a redefinition — is the primary problem, argues the National Employment Law Project, a progressive think tank, because it "exacts an enormous toll on workers, law-abiding employers and our economy." For instance, the group pointed out, when competitors misclassify workers, it "hurts law-abiding employers who play by the rules but are under-bid and out-competed."[42]

The Economic Policy Institute, a pro-labor think tank in Washington, questions the notion that the number of self-employed in the gig economy is growing. Moreover, the institute's diagnosis and prescriptions are more expansive, calling for full employment and enforcement of consumer, tax and labor laws.

"The problems are far larger and long-standing than the gig economy," Lawrence Mishel, the institute's president, said in a paper last October.[43]

BACKGROUND
Gig's Roots

When it comes to work, there is not much new under the sun, only different iterations of how labor, commerce and compensation are structured. Throughout history, society has reorganized or "reinvented" work according to available technologies and economic models.

Even the word "freelance" harkens back to another time. "Free lance was coined during the Industrial Revolution of late eighteenth- and nineteenth-century England, when factories and machines were changing how people lived and worked," writes Horowitz of the Freelancers Union. She notes that Sir Walter Scott first used the term in his 1820 novel *Ivanhoe*: "I offered [King] Richard the services of my Free Lances," Scott wrote, referring to knights not bound to any feudal lord who would offer their services for a fee.[44]

Use of the word "gig" also is not new, though it long had a strictly musical connotation. According to jazz historian Robert S. Gold, the word may have originated from the Old French word gigue, "a lively dance form of Italian origin. . . . According to jazzman Eubie Blake, bandleader James Reese Europe used the term in its jazz sense as early as c. 1905." Gig is also defined as a "single engagement" and as "a non-jazz job reluctantly taken by a jazzman for purely monetary reasons."[45]

Linguist Geoff Nunberg cited "gig" as his word of the year for 2015. "It's the last chapter in the life of a little word that has tracked the rise and fall of the great American job," he said in a commentary on NPR.[46]

To some, today's gig economy jobs bring to mind pre-Industrial Revolution piecework, when workers were paid on a piece-by-piece basis. Then the 19th-century Industrial Revolution led to creation of large corporations and a Gilded Age for the titans of industry. Work was plentiful and labor was cheap, allowing industrialists to increase working hours while keeping wages low.

Horrendous working conditions and poor pay led to the formation in 1886 of the American Federation of Labor (AFL), which organized unions of craft workers to bargain collectively. AFL leader Samuel Gompers was no radical — he championed capitalism, purposely excluded low-skilled workers from his organizing efforts and did not engage in political campaigns for dramatic change. But he helped get the union movement off the ground. By the turn of the century, more than 500,000 tradesmen would be members.[47]

During the last two decades of the 19th century, workers rebelled against what they regarded as unfair labor practices and inadequate pay, conducting more than 20,000 strikes.[48] Some were marked by violent

Shipping containers are loaded onto driverless trucks during tests at California's Long Beach Container Terminal. The automated cargo-handling system is scheduled to go into use this year. As artificial intelligence advances and robots become increasingly sophisticated, more corporations see automation as a way to save money, potentially eliminating employees and forcing more workers into the gig economy. Uber CEO and co-founder Travis Kalanick, for one, supports the development of driverless cars, which would reduce the number or even eliminate Uber drivers.

confrontations between management and labor, most notably the Homestead Strike of 1892, when thousands of armed steelworkers clashed with 300 company-hired security personnel in Homestead, Pa.[49] The confrontation dealt a setback to the national labor movement.

The Progressive Era (1890s-1920s) led to reforms in working conditions and legislation to curb corporate monopolies' powers over prices and wages. Unsafe and hazardous working conditions were a major focus of reformers' efforts.

In 1911, at a conference on industrial safety, U.S. Secretary of Commerce and Labor Charles Nagel said, "It takes the government to establish the rules of the game" to ensure fairness and to protect workers. The Triangle Shirtwaist fire on March 25, 1911, in which 146 women, mostly Italian and Jewish immigrants, perished because they could not escape their locked Manhattan clothing factory, dramatized the risks of unregulated industry.[50]

Observing the fire from a nearby park, President Franklin D. Roosevelt's future secretary of Labor, Frances Perkins, the first female Cabinet member, became convinced that "something must be done," she later recalled. "We've got to turn this into some kind of

CHRONOLOGY

1880s-1913 *The union movement emerges.*

1886 American Federation of Labor is formed.

1892 Violent steelworkers strike in Homestead, Pa., deals blow to labor movement.

1913 Henry Ford introduces the auto assembly line.

1929-1939 *Unemployment soars during the Great Depression.*

1933 Unemployment peaks at 25 percent.

1935 National Labor Relations Act recognizes workers' right to unionize and bans child labor. . . . Social Security Act is passed. . . . Committee for Industrial Organization (CIO) is formed.

1936-37 Autoworkers demanding union representation begin strike at General Motors plant in Flint, Mich., transforming United Auto Workers into a major union.

1945-1970 *Postwar boom creates large middle class, with employers providing long-term employment and health and pension benefits.*

1947 Taft-Hartley Act restricts union activity.

1952 President Harry S. Truman seizes control of the steel industry to avoid a steelworkers' strike.

1954 Union membership peaks at 34.8 percent of nonfarm U.S. workers.

1955 CIO and American Federation of Labor merge to form AFL-CIO, representing some 15.5 million workers.

1980s *U.S. economy sputters and recovers.*

1980 To tame inflation, Federal Reserve Board raises interest rates to 20 percent, helping trigger a severe recession; unemployment peaks at 10.8 percent in December 1982.

1987 Wall Street crash hits stock prices and corporate profits, but gains from subsequent rebound lead companies to be judged by their quarterly bottom lines. To cut costs, businesses replaced traditional pensions while increasingly shifting health insurance costs to workers.

1990-2009 *Companies accelerate outsourcing of work to contractors or foreign plants and increase hiring of part-time or temporary workers.*

1995 Freelancers Union established in New York City.

1995-2000 Boom in digital commerce causes technology-dominated Nasdaq stock exchange to soar before the tech market goes bust, causing numerous companies to close.

2007 Zimride (later renamed Lyft) offers on-demand rides with drivers who own their cars and bear gas and other expenses.

2007-09 Steep recession spurs layoffs and downsizing at many large corporations, forcing formerly full-time workers to enter the "gig economy" in search of short-term jobs.

2009 UberCab, which connects customers and drivers through a cellphone app, is established in San Francisco.

2010-Present *New online platforms connect workers to on-demand jobs.*

2010 Fiverr website allows freelancers to bid on jobs starting at $5 a task.

2014 California Uber drivers sue to be reclassified as employees with unemployment and other benefits. . . . Affordable Care Act allows self-employed workers to purchase health insurance on exchanges.

2015 Seattle City Council allows Uber and Lyft drivers to unionize, setting national precedent. . . . Drivers of luxury Uber cars in Dallas successfully force the company to retract its demand that they accept the lower-fee Uber X customers. . . . California judge grants Uber drivers class-action status, allowing their claims to be decided in a single case.

victory, some kind of constructive action." She and others lobbied successfully for the adoption of new workplace safety standards in New York state.[51]

Technological innovations during this period also brought changes that would dramatically alter the workplace and society. One of the most important was Henry Ford's introduction in 1913 of the moving assembly line at his Highland Park, Mich., automobile plant. This revolutionary innovation cut the time needed to produce one car from 12 hours to about 90 minutes and also made the automobile more affordable.[52]

Ford went further, returning some of his profits to employees in the form of the $5 workday, which the company's website describes as "a significant wage at the time, to enable his employees to buy the vehicles they built. The move created loyalty among Ford workers and is credited with giving rise to a new middle class of consumers unencumbered by geography, free to travel the open roads, to live where they please and chase the American dream."[53]

Boom, Bust

After World War I, the Roaring '20s lifted the national economy, resulting in low unemployment and expansive growth. The economy seemed so strong that President Calvin Coolidge famously said, "The chief business of the American people is business." But the good times did not last.

In October 1929, the stock market crashed. By 1932, stocks had lost 80 percent of their pre-crash value; a year later, a staggering 25 percent of the nation's workforce was unemployed, as businesses failed and banks closed.

Jobless World War I veterans, seeking accelerated payment of a bonus they were scheduled to receive in 1945, marched on Washington in 1932. There they were routed, their shanty town on the Anacostia River flats burned down by Army troops under the command of Douglas MacArthur, who achieved fame in World War II as a general in the Pacific theater.

The Great Depression gave rise to a gig economy of sorts, as hobos climbed onto railroad boxcars and traveled from place to place in search of work.

The severe economic conditions prompted eight militant unions to break away from the AFL in 1935 to form the organization that would later become the Congress of Industrial Organizations (CIO); the two federations would merge again two decades later. Autoworkers at the Flint, Mich., plant of General Motors staged a sit-down strike, setting a precedent for peaceful civil disobedience in labor disputes and, later, in the civil rights movement.

The Depression gave rise to President Roosevelt's New Deal programs and laws intended to provide a safety net for workers. Foremost among them were the National Labor Relations Act, which guaranteed the right of workers to bargain collectively, and the Social Security Act, intended to provide a modest retirement annuity to retired workers, funded by employers and employees through a payroll tax. Both were enacted in 1935.

The onset of World War II ended the Depression and brought a boom in defense spending, as the nation's corporations retooled their factories to support the war effort with the production of armaments, ships and planes. With 12 million Americans serving in the military, civilian labor shortages led to widespread employment of women for the first time in what had been traditionally men's factory jobs.

With peace in 1945 came the so-called peacetime dividend: Pent-up consumer demand fueled construction of new homes for returning GIs and the production of cars, televisions and other consumer goods. Veterans attended college in large numbers for free on the GI Bill. Women receded from the workforce, but unemployment was low and wages were rising.

At the same time, the union movement suffered a setback in 1947 with passage of the Taft-Hartley Act, which strengthened the hand of management in collective bargaining. President Harry S. Truman chose not to invoke the law in 1952, when, under an executive order, he seized control of the steel industry to avoid a steelworkers' strike he deemed detrimental to national security while Americans were at war in Korea.[54]

During this time a robust middle class expanded, which helped keep the national economy rolling along into the 1960s. Commonly, employers provided a safety net of pensions and health insurance for long-term employees, many of whom spent an entire career at a single company. But the huge costs of the Vietnam War and President Lyndon B. Johnson's "Great Society" social programs ignited inflation and helped lead to economic turmoil in the 1970s.

Co-working Spaces Catching On

Shared offices seek to end gig workers' isolation.

White-collar "gig" workers, toiling away in a cramped back bedroom or at a crumb-dusted table at the local Starbucks, need be lonely no longer.

They now can rent a "co-working" space where they'll find, at the minimum, a seat at a shared table, a cubby or locker, Wi-Fi, a small kitchen, fresh coffee, conference room and a business address that can transform a self-employed worker into what is, to outward appearances, a real player in the business world.

Some 800 locations provided short-term co-working spaces nationwide in 2015, up from only 40 in 2008, according to deskmag, an online industry magazine.[1]

And the phenomenon is global, with about 7,800 co-working locations worldwide in 2015, up 36 percent from the previous year, deskmag said. "The co-working movement is undeniably here to stay," the publication said.[2]

"The recession obviously helped it go up the stairway, but it's not the sole factor," says Raymond Rahbar, founder and CEO of Make Offices, which started in 2012 in Arlington, Va., and provides work spaces at five Washington, D.C.-area locations. He cites other factors, such as the outsourcing of work and reduced office-space needs in the digital age.

"Nowadays, almost everybody emails documents, reads on a laptop, and there is not as much need for a computer printout. Every industry in the world has adapted to a smaller, virtual way to do work," Rahbar says.

Moreover, he says, rising rents and budget constraints have forced companies to shed real estate. "Companies like ours can make up the void," Rahbar says.

Monthly rent at Make Offices ranges from $75 for a "virtual" office, which includes a mailing address, mail collection and access to social networking events, to $250 and up for a "bullpen" desk, and $550 and up for a fully furnished separate office. Its month-to-month leases appeal to self-employed people and others whose revenues are uncertain.

Rahbar's firm, recently rebranded from Uber Offices (no relation to the ride-hailing service), plans to open two more D.C. locations in 2016. It also has expanded to Chicago and Philadelphia.

Creative Colony, a 1,720-square-foot open office in a 1960s high-rise in Silver Spring, Md., adjoining

To break the back of inflation, the Federal Reserve Board raised interest rates to as high as 20 percent, which helped trigger a severe recession in 1981 and '82. Once again, unemployed workers hit the road in search of jobs; camps of the destitute sprang up, mostly out of sight — from the outer suburbs of Washington, D.C., to the outskirts of Forks, Wash., a lumber town fallen on hard times.

This period also saw the rise of temporary employment agencies that provided on-demand workers to companies with short-term or occasional needs. Some firms used perma-temps, a practice unions protested, since these workers lacked protections and benefits. Their use also undercut the security of full-time workers.

A 1987 stock market crash may have been a harbinger of harder times to come, but its impact was only short-term. During the stock market frenzy that took hold after the crash, large private corporations went public, and profits that formerly rewarded employees and paid for expansions were diverted to buying back stock to raise corporations' market price.

During the extended postwar period that lasted into the 1980s, writes Jerry Davis, a professor of management and sociology at the University of Michigan, "American corporations became model long-term employers," serving "a critical function in providing pathways to economic security and mobility. . . . A corporate job was a good job, with a chance to move up in the world."[55] But the pathway came to a crossroads as the 20th century neared its end.

In the 1990s, investors increasingly judged companies by their quarterly performance, pressuring executives to further slash costs. Workers bore the brunt of this, as companies replaced traditional pensions with "defined" benefits with 401K plans, in which workers'

Washington, tends to attract what manager Megan Tyson King calls "niche creative professionals" who find working from home too isolating. Monthly rates range from $55 to $495, depending on the length of a lease and what's included.[3]

Its members include graphic designers, writers, photographers, business consultants and filmmakers. And 24/7 access means "you can work Christmas Day or at 2 in the morning," she says. Creative Colony's amenities include a social calendar filled with events and a mock phone booth for private calls.

Melissa K. Smith is renting space in Make Office's bullpen. The 36-year-old is CEO of Phoenix Filming, a startup company she co-founded last year that deploys drones to make aerial videos. She says she likes "the exposure to different companies at different levels of startup, the daily interaction with people, the great networking." She has 10 independent contractors scattered around the country working for her remotely.

Smith is hoping for a separate office at Make Offices, but more than 500 people are on a waiting list at the company's various sites, according to Rahbar.

Creative Colony, a much smaller operation with about 39 "members," has no waiting list, but word has gotten around. The company has had inquiries from other states on its expansion plans, but right now its focus is local, according to King.

BRENDAN SMIALOWSKI/AFP/Getty Images

The Cove co-working space in Washington, D.C., is part of a growing network of shared office environments spawned by the gig economy.

As for the future of co-working, Rahbar says, "Everything has a ceiling, but that ceiling is a faraway place right now."

— *Eugene L. Meyer*

[1] "A Snapshot of Coworking in America," Modworks Coworking, April 30, 2015, http://tinyurl.com/jce9gmh.

[2] "First Results of the New Global Coworking Survey," deskmag, Nov. 20, 2015, http://tinyurl.com/htm27kc.

[3] Creative Colony, http://tinyurl.com/gqrxrzr.

make pretax contributions to a retirement fund that the employer invests at the employees' direction. Employers also shifted more and more health insurance costs to workers as premiums rose.

Path to Gig Economy

Another tectonic shift occurred in 1991, when the Internet, previously available only for academia and government under the control of the National Science Foundation, was opened to individuals and businesses.[56]

The Internet "makes it much easier to find and outsource the many business tasks you need to complete," according to Conversational Receptionists, a North American firm that provides receptionist services. "Often, when you outsource, you will pay for the work instead of paying by the hour or a full-time salary for an employee to provide the work."[57]

An explosion of digital commerce led to the "dotcom" boom, with a proliferation of startup companies and high-flying investors seeking to profit from the new technology. The boom, during which the technology-dominated Nasdaq stock exchange index soared from 1,000 to 5,000 in five years, went bust in 2000, but its effect on all but a small class of high-risk investors was muted. Cellular phones, meanwhile, began morphing into "smart" phones, capable of running applications that allowed users on the go to conduct business transactions over the Internet.

Otherwise, the economy that had prospered during the Clinton administration in the 1990s continued to do so under President George W. Bush — until December 2007.

What then-Federal Reserve Chairman Alan Greenspan would call "irrational exuberance" in both the stock and real estate markets deflated badly. The resulting mortgage

Freelancers Union Fights for the Self-Employed

Founder advocates a "new mutualism" between workers and communities.

The Freelancers Union isn't really a union. It doesn't bargain collectively for members and it collects no dues. Instead, its 288,000 members get access to a vast network of self-employed individuals similarly trying to survive in the new, on-demand "gig" economy. Anyone working full or part time for themselves can join the organization, whose mission is to ensure that freelancers get a fair deal from their clients. It also markets and sells health, life, disability and dental insurance to members.

Other features of union membership include interest groups known as "hives," which bring together like-minded individuals, and "Spark" meetings in 18 states. Both are heavily geared to helping members hone their professional and marketing skills.

The founder and executive director of the Brooklyn, N.Y.-based organization is Sara Horowitz, a graduate of the Cornell University School of Industrial and Labor Relations and SUNY Buffalo Law School. In the early 1990s, Horowitz was under the impression she had a regular job in a law firm, only to discover she was an independent contractor without benefits.[1] "It really got me to see what was happening in the world of work, and that work was profoundly changing," she says.

A New Yorker from a family with strong union ties, Horowitz founded the Freelancers Union under the name Working Today in 1995.[2] The group, renamed in 2003, rose in prominence after Horowitz received a MacArthur Foundation "genius grant" in 1999 and hired the BerlinRosen public relations firm, whose efforts helped land her on *Business Week*'s 2011 list of "America's Top Social Entrepreneurs."

Under Horowitz's leadership, the union has grown into a nonprofit with $22.6 million in assets and $8.7 million in revenue in 2013, the most recent year for which its financial records are publicly available.[3] Its revenue comes largely from commissions on premiums that its members pay on group health insurance policies. The commissions help support the union's operations and expenses.

With Horowitz as its most public face, the Freelancers Union today is a major player in discussions about the gig economy, and she is in demand as a panelist and speaker. She has advocated what she calls a "new mutualism," in which, absent more traditional work arrangements, consumers and freelancers create an economic model that works for all. "I want to start having groups come together to solve problems," Horowitz says. In her 2012 book, *The Freelancer's Bible*, she explained, "We're returning to a pre-industrial model of human-scaled, self-caring communities that were the norm in the United States for generations — but with a new awareness that our solutions must be cost-effective in the short term and sustainable in the long term, with technology accelerating the pace, breadth and depth of our contact."[4]

When she speaks or writes about the gig economy, her tone tends to be boosterish regarding the prospects for success. "As a freelancer, you're a master of new beginnings," she writes.[5] Further, the cover of her book promises "Everything you need to know to have the career of your dreams — on your terms." This promise has drawn some criticism from some who say it doesn't present the full picture.

"She's taken on the tough job of advocating for freelancers [that] no one else was doing," says Steven Hill, a fellow at the left-leaning New America think tank. "But she needs to be part of this fight for jobs, better education and not just accepting the status quo that you're all going to become freelancers. She's totally not preparing these young people for

and financial crisis brought corporate mergers, investment house bankruptcies and bank closures and bailouts. Millions of homeowners' mortgages were foreclosed; home values that had risen sharply during the bubble fell

sharply. Families lost their homes and jobs, and their retirement savings evaporated. Unemployment reached 10.6 percent in May 2009 — a level rarely seen since the Great Depression.

what they're facing," such as long periods without income, the constant need to market and an inability to qualify for such benefits as unemployment insurance and worker's compensation. A lot of what she says, he adds, "sounds like Silicon Valley happy talk." Horowitz, in her book, also addresses the many challenges that freelancers face.

On the political front, however, the Freelancers Union successfully lobbied New York City in 2009 to roll back its 4 percent tax on unincorporated businesses for those earning less than $100,000. Through its "Freelancing Isn't Free" campaign, the union is fighting for legislation to protect freelancers from late or unpaid fees owed them.[6] Horowitz also has advocated a business-funded account to purchase benefits that would follow freelancers from job to job, assuring them some level of security.

The Freelancers Union "has been a pretty important voice in this space for quite some time," says Rebecca Smith, deputy director of the nonprofit National Employment Law Project, which advocates for workers. "They have concentrated a lot of their work on delivering benefits to freelancers."

The group's most ambitious undertaking has been in health insurance. For a time, the Freelancers Union ran two medical clinics in the city. In 2008, it created the Freelancers Insurance Co., but it closed in 2014 after the Affordable Care Act (ACA) went into effect. For members who do not qualify for subsidies under the ACA, it continues to provide other insurance options in New York City through Empire BlueCross BlueShield and CareConnect. It also helped three independent health co-ops elsewhere obtain $341 million in low- and no-interest federal loans.[7]

In defining its constituency, the Freelancers Union casts a wide net. Its 2015 study counted 54 million freelancers nationwide — one-third of the nation's labor force. But that number includes full-time employees who also do some freelancing.[8]

"The fact is," says Horowitz, "that when workers enter the workforce now, at some point in their lives they are going to be working freelance."

— *Eugene L. Meyer*

NICHOLAS KAMM/AFP/Getty Images

Freelancers Union founder and CEO Sara Horowitz appears at a town hall meeting at the White House on Oct. 7, 2015. She started the group to help independent workers get fair treatment from employers.

---

[1] Freelancers Union, http://tinyurl.com/gl3ruyb.

[2] "Sara Horowitz," Freelancers Union, http://tinyurl.com/hduag6h.

[3] Form 990, Guidestar, 2013, p. 25, http://tinyurl.com/hbzgqps.

[4] Sara Horowitz, with Toni Sciarra Poynter, *The Freelancer's Bible* (2012), p. 301.

[5] *Ibid.*, p. 464.

[6] According to the Freelancers Union, 71 percent of freelancers will experience late or nonpayment for work during their career. The bill, introduced Dec. 7, 2015, can be found at http://tinyurl.com/jqs4cqq.

[7] "CO-OP FAQs," Freelancers Union, http://tinyurl.com/zmg4e2y.

[8] "Freelancing in America: 2015," Freelancers Union and Upwork, 2015, http://tinyurl.com/hjlhkfx.

In 2009, even as many Americans were struggling to get back on their feet and find permanent employment, there was an explosion of digitally based companies — such as Uber, Etsy, TaskRabbit and Airbnb — that use the Internet, smartphones and algorithms to connect providers and consumers. Some hailed their rise as the new "sharing economy," promising more freedom and flexibility for workers eager to become entrepreneurs.

"Listen to the optimists, and the Great Recession and its aftermath sounds like a great opportunity," writes Scott Timberg in his 2015 book, *Culture Crash*.[58]

One survey of 10 major urban areas found the number of workers receiving IRS Form 1099 as independent contractors steadily rose from 2013 to 2014, suggesting a growing trend.[59] But others questioned what they called the "race to the bottom" business model that produces workers without guaranteed hours, income or benefits.[60]

Yet, advances in artificial intelligence and algorithms could enable robots to replace workers. Automation has already dispensed with the need for many secretaries, bank tellers and autoworkers.

Some analysts have forecasted a new industrial revolution of "autonomous innovation," in which humans would become superfluous for many if not most of the tasks they formerly performed.[61]

CURRENT SITUATION

The Economy

On the surface, the jobs picture appears positive. The unemployment rate has dropped from 10.6 percent in May 2009 to less than 5 percent in January 2016.[62]

But U.S. Sen. Bernie Sanders of Vermont, running for the Democratic presidential nomination, told a crowd in Portland, Maine, last summer that the actual unemployment rate was 10.5 percent, double the then-official rate of 5.3 percent.[63] Sanders arrived at this figure by including those who have given up looking for work and those working part time.

"We continue to have a very weak labor market," says Dean Baker, co-founder and co-director of the Center for Economic and Policy Research, a left-leaning Washington, D.C., think tank. "Really, by every measure, we're very, very far from being recovered. It speaks to the fact so many people are willing to take part-time jobs, casual work, because they don't have the option to get a full-time paying job."

The numbers appear to bear him out. According to the American Staffing Association, although many jobs have been regained since the 18-month recession and the unemployment rate has dropped, "the percentage of people participating in the labor force has dropped to the lowest level in four decades," to 62.6 percent in June-August 2015 — down from a peak of 67.3 percent in April 2000 and on a par with the 62.4 percent seen in October 1977.

Currently, the association says, "There are nearly 6 million open jobs, and more than 8 million people out of work — contributing to the longer than anticipated recovery cycle."[64] The nonpartisan Congressional Budget Office attributes the falling labor force participation rate largely to the slow recovery that led many workers to become discouraged and stop looking for work.[65]

Yet, muddying the picture, some employers say the job market has tightened so much that they are raising wages and hiring more workers. "The economy is as strong as it has ever been here," said Dave Rozenboom, president of First Premier Bank in Sioux Falls, S.D. "It's a very tight labor market, and we continue to hire."[66]

The Lawmakers

City councils and state legislatures are haltingly confronting issues raised by the gig economy.

Ride-hailing companies such as Uber and Lyft have been lobbying hard and largely successfully for laws and ordinances to allow them to operate without the stringent regulations applied to traditional taxicabs. Uber has been one of the most active, hiring at least 161 people and multiple lobbying firms to influence legislation.[67]

The full-court press mounted by Uber — recently valued at $61.5 billion — has defeated proposed regulations in state after state and city after city, allowing it to operate largely unregulated or self-regulated. When San Antonio leaders rejected Uber's demands last year, the company ceased service there. But months later, after the city modified its requirements, Uber returned.[68]

In general, the newly adopted laws and ordinances allow ride-hailing and other services to operate legally without providing redress for complaints by drivers or other gig economy workers that are being misclassified as independent contractors.

In 2014, Colorado became the first state to enact a legal framework authorizing "transportation network companies" such as Uber and Lyft to operate, but under only limited regulation.[69]

Last May, after Kansas enacted stringent insurance requirements and background checks for ride-hailing drivers, Uber announced it was ending operations there; the company resumed service after the state passed a compromise bill.[70] On May 29, Nevada imposed a 3 percent tax on fares for ride-hailing services.

There have also been hurdles. In June 2015, the Office of the California Labor Commissioner ruled that an Uber driver should have been classified as an employee rather than an independent contractor, and Uber was ordered to pay her $4,152 for driving-related business expenses, plus interest.[71] On June 18, Lyft agreed to pay New York state $300,000 to settle claims that it violated state and municipal laws.

In December 2015, Seattle became the first city in the country to give drivers for ride-hailing firms the ability to unionize.[72] Uber and Lyft argued that the ordinance violated federal labor and antitrust laws. After its passage, Uber said it retained the right to challenge the law but also suggested ways to insure the fairness of any union election.[73]

In New York City, the Freelancers Union successfully lobbied the municipal government to eliminate a 4 percent tax on unincorporated businesses for drivers and other undependent workers earning less than $100,000. The group is also waging a "Freelancing Isn't Free" campaign, for legislation to protect freelancers from late or nonpayment of wages, by requiring full payment within 30 days of completion of services and penalizing companies that fail to comply.[74]

What, if anything, will be done at the federal level is an open question. Income inequality and the gig economy have become subjects in the 2016 presidential race. Then-Republican presidential contender Jeb Bush made a point of using Uber to demonstrate his support for the new employment model. Democratic presidential candidate and U.S. Sen. Bernie Sanders said he has "serious problems" with "unregulated" on-demand companies like Uber.[75] At the same time, Democratic candidate Hillary Clinton raised questions of equity and workers' rights inherent in the gig economy.

Obama's budget submitted to Congress in February contained no bold proposals along the lines of the sweeping labor law reforms proposed by Sanders.[76] Instead, Obama proposed improving access to 401(k) retirement plans, expanding Social Security benefits and supplementing incomes of workers who take lower-paying jobs after becoming unemployed. However, these proposals do not address the problems of self-employed, on-demand workers.

Earnest Williams turned to collecting scrap metal after losing his job in Washington, D.C. Laid-off gig economy workers may have plenty of company in the coming years, according to a study at Oxford University. It predicted that "47 percent of total U.S. employment is in the high-risk category" of being automated, possibly within two decades, mostly in low-skill, low-wage jobs.

Jared Bernstein, a former economic adviser to Vice President Joseph R. Biden, said administration officials "have not viewed it as their job to try to change the underlying shifts in [job] risks." Rather, according to *The New York Times*, these limited proposals were "a concession that the major macroeconomic trends of the past two generations — particularly the loss of benefits that once went with formal employment relationships — are largely irreversible."[77]

The Courts

While legislatures have been slow or have refused to act on complaints about the gig economy, the courts, especially on the West Coast, are hearing challenges from workers. They are questioning the companies' position that those who use their digital platforms to provide services are not employees entitled to unemployment compensation, back pay and other benefits normally accorded to employees.

Lawsuits, most notably against Uber and other ride-hailing services, question the classification of drivers as independent contractors when the companies determine the fares and schedules.

Is the "gig economy" here to stay?

YES

Steven Hill
Senior Fellow, New America; author, Raw Deal: How the 'Uber Economy' and Runaway Capitalism Are Screwing American Workers

Written for *CQ Researcher*, March 2016

The "gig economy" is here to stay, but its impacts can be hard to measure. Our understanding of these trends is bedeviled by a fierce numbers game. The Pricewaterhouse Coopers consulting company recently estimated that the gig economy's global revenues could increase from roughly $15 billion today to around $335 billion by 2025. And in April 2015, the U.S. Government Accountability Office said "the size of the contingent workforce can range from less than 5 percent to more than a third of the total employed labor force." The Bureau of Labor Statistics has found little increase in the size of the contingent workforce, but Harvard economist Larry Katz cites evidence that the bureau's estimate is "missing a large part of the gig economy." So, different methodologies are producing different conclusions.

Yet it is clear that the old New Deal economy and its safety net are crumbling for millions of U.S. workers, both those in the traditional economy and those trying to succeed in the gig economy. The competitive advantages for a business using such non-regular workers can be substantial: Labor costs can be reduced by 30 percent or more if a company does not have to pay workers benefits.

Even many regularly employed, part-time workers are being subjected by employers to various tactics aimed at reducing labor costs and increasing flexibility. One — known as "just-in-time scheduling" — means that part-timers are basically on-call, subject to job insecurity, low pay and little-to-no safety net.

Given that reality, worker categories should not be defined too rigidly because there is a lot of overlap in terms of working conditions. We are going to find that more and more workers exist simultaneously in multiple worker categories — regular part-timers with a weak safety net who supplement those jobs with various gigs: for instance, being an Uber driver and/or Instacart grocery deliverer, still with no safety net, plus taking on other mini-gigs and perhaps a second part-time job. They might even work in the "gray economy" doing under-the-table work off the books. We have to begin thinking of "work" for more and more workers as existing along a spectrum of different types of employment situations.

How will all of this look in the labor statistics? Will we be able to count this complexity, using current methods? We desperately need to figure out better methodologies, because these new ways of work are not going away.

NO

Dean Baker
Co-Director, Center for Economic and Policy Research

Written for *CQ Researcher*, March 2016

The "gig economy" is one of the many trendy revolutions capturing the news media's attention. But some simple realities apply to the gig economy, buried in a great deal of hype.

"Gig economy" work is the same sort of casual labor that has always existed. It's a variation on the day-labor centers where workers go in the morning in the hope of finding work for all or part of a day. The only difference is that the gig economy operates over the Internet and involves workers in a wider range of occupations, some relatively skilled. However, just as some day-labor companies hope to profit by evading regulations and cheating workers, many gig economy companies hope to legally skirt labor laws that apply to other employers.

The survival of gig economy companies depends on the overall state of the economy. It is no accident that the gig economy exploded following the recent steep recession. More than eight years after the onset of the recession, the economy is still down more than 3 million jobs from trend levels.

If we pursue policies designed to weaken the labor market, such as higher interest rates from the Federal Reserve Board, we likely will continue to see large numbers of workers desperate for employment from Uber, TaskRabbit and other gig economy companies. In a bad economy, irregular work is better than no work.

The survival of the gig economy also depends on whether governments will apply labor laws to gig economy companies. There is no reason Uber should be exempt from minimum-wage laws, overtime regulations and workers' compensation coverage. If the company's claim is true — that compliance is too difficult to figure out — then companies that are more adept with technology will outcompete Uber. But if gig economy companies are exempt from rules that apply to their competitors, gig companies will be allowed to thrive in a very weak labor market.

Of course, there is a place for the type of casual labor that fills gig economy advocates' stories. There are people who would like to earn some extra money in their spare time. If gig economy companies can provide more opportunities for such work, that would be great. But there is no reason this cannot be done in a way that complies with existing labor laws.

A class-action suit in California, filed on behalf of Uber drivers, argues that they are employees because: "They are required to follow a litany of detailed requirements imposed on them by Uber, and they are graded, and subject to termination, based on their failure to adhere to these requirements. . . . However, based on their misclassification as independent contractors, Uber drivers are required to bear many of the expenses of their employment, including expenses for their vehicles, gas, and other expenses. California law requires employers to reimburse employees for such expenses, which are for the benefit of the employer and are necessary for the employees to perform their jobs." A trial is scheduled to begin on June 20.[78]

Shannon Liss-Riordan of Boston has become the go-to lawyer challenging the on-demand economy, including in the California suit against Uber. She has also filed lawsuits against Lyft, DoorDash, GrubHub and Washio, an on-demand laundry service, alleging they illegally exercise control akin to employers without extending benefits.[79]

"The Gig Economy Won't Last Because It's Being Sued to Death" is the headline on a *Fast Company* article. "This rising legal retribution is a huge threat to the gig economy," the author writes. "Lose this workforce structure — either by a wave of class-action lawsuits, intervention by regulators, or through the collective action of disgruntled workers — and you lose the gig economy."[80]

Some gig workers, absent action by courts or legislatures, are taking matters into their own hands. When Uber told Dallas-area drivers for the high-end car service UberBlack that they must also carry passengers hailing its lower-cost UberX service, the drivers rebelled. After a three-day standoff at Uber's downtown headquarters, the company allowed them to opt out.

"We started realizing we're not contractors; we're more like employees," UberBlack driver Berhane Alemayoh said. "They tell us what kind of car to drive. They kick you out if a customer accused you of not having a clean car. They started to tighten the rope. Gradually, we can't breathe anymore."[81]

OUTLOOK
Uncertain Times
Initial exuberance and hype over the gig economy have given way to more critical and complex evaluations, as advocates for workers make their case in the courts and legislatures that such work can be exploitive. The outlook, according to experts, is mixed and uncertain.

"The last five years have been like the Wild West for the gig economy," says Horowitz of the Freelancers Union. "In 10 years, we're going to see short-term gigs become the norm, and policymakers, business executives and labor leaders are going to start planning critical infrastructure around this new economy."

Says Rebecca Smith, deputy director of the National Employment Law Project: "It's anyone's guess whether the companies, and many others like them that misclassify workers as independent contractors, will convince policymakers and enforcement agencies to affirmatively exempt them and/or turn away from enforcement. Or that workers will figure out ways to organize and demand the policy changes that will make gig jobs good jobs. We will all have to stay tuned."

The outlook also hinges on whether the overall economy creates more full-time jobs with benefits or whether firms continue to hire contractors to do work formerly done by employees.

"There is a limit to how much the gig economy can expand, especially if the economy is relatively healthy so that employers have to compete to find workers," says Baker of the Center for Economic and Policy Research.

Harris and Krueger of Brookings' Hamilton Project, who are former top Obama administration officials, have suggested "a new legal classification" for independent workers that would provide more rights and protections without threatening "online-intermediate work." Whether or not they work through an "online intermediary," these independent workers would receive some of the benefits accorded employees, "including the freedom to organize and collectively bargain, civil rights protections, tax withholding, and employer contributions for payroll taxes."[82]

One proposal being discussed is to have companies pay into a fund that would provide "portable" benefits as workers go from job to job, much as trade unionists have done for decades.

"The real question," says Horowitz, "is what will be the evolving role of government during this period? Will it become less involved and let the market and workers fend for themselves, or will it nurture worker-oriented groups that have a job in delivering a new social safety net for this new way of working?"

Technological advances in robotics are also likely to have a major impact on the gig economy, and the world of work in general.

"It might seem like science fiction, but robots are taking over," writes a blogger on WTF? (What's the Future of Work?). "Robots in different forms are currently performing tasks as varied as keeping watch, building websites, cleaning and chatting with customers."[83]

This "digital transformation of the world" is being welcomed by both executives and citizens, according to the 2016 GE Global Innovation Barometer, with 68 percent of executives and 64 percent of citizens optimistic about the "innovation revolution," including automation. Under the category of "minds and machines working together," only 17 percent of executives and 15 percent of citizens fear "any negative impact on employment as a result of the digital revolution."[84]

However, a 2013 study at Oxford University predicted that "47 percent of total U.S. employment is in the high-risk category" of being automated, possibly within two decades.[85] Most are low-skill and low-wage jobs, the authors write, and, as technology "races ahead," these displaced workers will migrate to jobs "non-susceptible to computerization — i.e., tasks requiring creative and social intelligence. For workers to win the race, however, they will have to acquire creative and social skills."

"Yet," writes Fiverr's Kaufman, "there are glimmers of hope. Slowly but surely, a revolution is taking shape — an entirely different kind of economy. . . . It could be the force that saves the American worker. . . . [A]s the global economy continues to be disrupted by technology and other massive change, the Gig Economy will itself become an engine of economic and social transformation. And workers everywhere will have something to celebrate again."[86]

NOTES

1. Brian Watt, "Aging workforce finds flexibility but not piece of mind in growing 'gig economy,'" 89.3KPCC, Feb. 1, 2016, http://tinyurl.com/z498cxq.

2. *Ibid.*

3. "Contingent Work Force: Size, Characteristics, Earnings, and Benefits," U.S. Government Accountability Office, April 20, 2015, http://tinyurl.com/jsdb7zd.

4. Seth D. Harris and Alan B. Krueger, "A Proposal for Modernizing Labor Laws for 21st Century Work: The 'Independent Worker,'" Brookings Institution, December 2015, pp. 13-14, http://tinyurl.com/jrahgum.

5. "Freelancing in America: 2015," Freelancers Union & Upwork, 2015, http://tinyurl.com/hjlhkfx.

6. Sara Horowitz and Fabio Rosati, "53 million Americans are freelancing, new survey finds," Freelancers Union, — Sept. 4, 2014, http://tinyurl.com/h3jnosr.

7. Steven Hill, "How Big Is the Gig Economy?" *The Huffington Post*, Sept. 16, 2016, http://tinyurl.com/j595rxc.

8. "President Obama's 2016 State of the Union Address," White House, Jan. 12, 2016, http://tinyurl.com/juatdhn.

9. "Debunking the Top Five Myths of Temporary Work," *The Candidate Connection* blog, Snelling, Oct. 2, 2012, http://tinyurl.com/gn5og4l.

10. "The Mobile Workforce: More productive, efficient, and healthy," Microsoft, Nov. 12, 2013, http://tinyurl.com/hhw2rrj.

11. "What Is the Gig Economy — and How Does It Impact Employees?" T Sheets, undated, http://tinyurl.com/zyaehf2.

12. Laura Clawson, "This week in the war on workers: The new piecework economy," *The Daily Kos*, July 26, 2014, http://tinyurl.com/jlepru5.

13. See Steven Greenhouse, "Our Economic Pickle," *The New York Times*, Jan. 12, 2013, http://tinyurl.com/jm5ebv7.

14. Daniel Aaronson and Andrew Jordan, "Understanding the relationship between real wage growth and labor market conditions," Federal Reserve Bank of Chicago, October 2014, http://tinyurl.com/h8xreoj.

15. Oscar Perry Abello, "This 'Gig Economy' Firm Prefers to Have Employees, Not Contractors," *Next City*, Aug. 5, 2015, http://tinyurl.com/h2urjjr.

16. Noam Scheiber, "A Middle Ground Between Contract Worker and Employee," *The New York Times*, Dec. 10, 2015, http://tinyurl.com/hbz3ce2.

17. Sarach Nassauer, "Wal-Mart Broadens Pay Increase," *The Wall Street Journal*, Jan. 23, 2016, p. B1.

18. Micha Kaufman, "The Gig Economy: The Force That Could Save the American Worker?" *Wired*, September 2013, http://tinyurl.com/jp5qbg7.

19. Sara Horowitz, *The Freelancer's Bible* (2015), pp. 2, 10-11.

20. "Uber: The Driver Roadmap" Benenson Strategy Group, January 2015, http://tinyurl.com/gkrjmt8.

21. Robert Reich, "Why the Sharing Economy is Harming Workers — and What Must Be Done," RobertReich.org, Nov. 27, 2015, http://tinyurl.com/jle9e9n.

22. Jeffrey Pfeffer, "The Case Against the Gig Economy," *Fortune*, July 30, 2015, http://tinyurl.com/jqa6sd7.

23. Jim Yardley and Binyamin Appelbaum, "In Fiery Speeches, Pope Francis Excoriates Global Capitalism," *The New York Times*, July 11, 2015, http://tinyurl.com/q6rsfm5.

24. Neil Kokemuller and Demand Media, "Advantages & Disadvantages of a Part-Time Employees," Chron.com undated, http://tinyurl.com/6nexl6w.

25. "What are the benefits of employing part-time workers?" *duport*, April 2006, http://tinyurl.com/zrw4wj9.

26. Philip L Rones, "Response to Recession: Reduce Hours or Jobs?" *Monthly Labor Review*, October 1981, http://tinyurl.com/j7tasjt.

27. Claire Gordon, "How Employers Can Legally Strip Your Job of Benefits," AOL Jobs, April 27, 2012, http://tinyurl.com/hvy9m7m.

28. Brian Pedersen, "Employees Turned into Contract Workers at Tucson PR Firm," *Arizona Daily Star*, March 18, 2009, http://tinyurl.com/zm99hoa.

29. James Surowiecki, "The Underground Recovery," *The New Yorker*, April 29, 2013, http://tinyurl.com/jhx8fms.

30. Scheiber, "A Middle Ground Between Contractor Worker and Employee," *op. cit.*

31. Mike Isaac, "Delivery Startups Face Road Bumps in Quest to Capture Untapped Market," *The New York Times*, Feb. 12, 2016, http://tinyurl.com/hbybahz.

32. Abello, *op. cit.*

33. For more information, see Patrick Marshall, "Robotics and the Economy," *CQ Researcher*, Sept. 25, 2015, pp. 793-816.

34. Jillian D'Onfro, "Travis Kalanick says Uber needs self-driving cars to avoid ending up like the taxi industry," *Business Insider*, Oct. 21, 2015, http://tinyurl.com/pz5fg9h.

35. Harris and Krueger, *op. cit.*, p. 5.

36. *Ibid.*, p. 2.

37. Arun Sundararajan," Why the Government Doesn't Need to Regulate the Sharing Economy," *Wired*, Oct. 22, 2012, http://tinyurl.com/h2lgd62.

38. Steven Greenhouse, "Temp Workers at Microsoft Win Lawsuit," *The New York Times*, Dec. 13, 2000, http://tinyurl.com/b4sg25b.

39. Marc Lifsher, "Rising use of 'perma-temp' workers is stirring up a legislative fight," *Los Angeles Times*, May 7, 2014, http://tinyurl.com/l5qqgy3.

40. Cynthia Poole, "Steady Growth Continues: Staffing and Recruiting Industry Outpaces the Economy and the Labor Market," American Staffing Association, September 2015, http://tinyurl.com/go6vaz4.

41. Richard J. Reibsteine *et al.*, "The 2015 White Paper on Independent Contractor Misclassification: How Companies Can Minimize the Risk," Pepper Hamilton LLP, April 27, 2015, http://tinyurl.com/h5y68fp (See: V. Legislative Initiatives).

42. "Independent Contractor Misclassification Imposes Huge Costs on Workers and Federal and State Treasuries," National Employment Law Project, July 2015, http://tinyurl.com/zw3hnpn.

43. Lawrence Mishel, "Gigs and robots, oh my!" *Yumpu*, Oct. 29, 2015, http://tinyurl.com/hmf8xc3.

44. Horowitz, *op. cit.*, p. 8.

45. Robert S. Gould, *A Jazz Lexicon* (1964), pp. 123-124.

46. Geoff Nunberg, "Goodbye Jobs, Hello 'Gigs': How One Word Sums Up A New Economic Reality," NPR, Jan. 11, 2016, http://tinyurl.com/hxkv8yo.

47. "AFL-CIO: A Brief History," The Social Welfare History Project, http://tinyurl.com/hemrb8a.

48. "American Federation of Labor," USHistory.org, http://tinyurl.com/8xy8rex.

49. For background, see "The Homestead Strike," The American Experience, PBS, http://tinyurl.com/atcns. Also see "Homestead Strike," History.com, http://tinyurl.com/ccmlska.

50. "Remembering the 1911 Triangle Factory Fire," Cornell University, http://tinyurl.com/z3roruk.

51. "The Worst Day I Ever Saw," U.S. Occupational Safety and Health Administration, http://tinyurl.com/zgp7zpw.

52. "100 Years of the Moving Assembly Line," Ford, http://tinyurl.com/hphfu32.

53. *Ibid.*

54. "Executive Order 10340: Directing the Secretary of Commerce to Take Possession of and Operate the Plants and Facilities of Certain Steel Companies," The American Presidency Project, April 8, 1952, http://tinyurl.com/hzpmxde.

55. Jerry Davis, "Capital markets and job creation in the 21st century," Center for Effective Public Management at Brookings Institution, December 2015, p. 2, http://tinyurl.com/go6rm68.

56. The National Science Foundation, the primary governing authority over the Internet, did not officially lift its ban on commercial activity until 1995. See Kevin Kelly, "We Are the Web," *Wired*, August 2005, http://tinyurl.com/p2zdsbw.

57. "Why Does Outsourcing Work in Today's World?" Conversational Receptionists, http://tinyurl.com/guyjgvs.

58. Scott Timberg, *Culture Crash: The Killing of the Creative Class* (2015), p. 73. Chapter 3, pp. 73-83, "Of Permatemps and Content Serfs" specifically addresses the challenges facing "all citizens of Freelance Nation."

59. Joshua Reeves, "The Rise of the 1099 Economy [Infographic]," *Gusto.com*, Dec. 11, 2014, http://tinyurl.com/gq9qloj.

60. Dartagnan, "The Sharing Economy is Just Another Race to the Bottom," *Daily Kos*, July 26, 2015, http://tinyurl.com/zubo6h3,

61. Klaus Schwab, "The Fourth Industrial Revolution: What It means, How to Respond," World Economic Forum, Jan. 14, 2016, http://tinyurl.com/hmllz82. Also see "The Collaborative Economy Sets the Stage for Autonomous Innovation," Crowd Companies, undated, http://tinyurl.com/jauzv2v.

62. For peak unemployment, see Andrew Sum *et al.*, "The Great Recession of 2007-2009: Its Post-World War II Record Impacts on Rising Unemployment and Underutilization Problems Among U.S. Workers," Center for Labor Market Studies, June 2009, http://tinyurl.com/hdmtewe. For January 2016 unemployment, see Nelson D. Schwartz, "Wages Rise as U.S. Unemployment Rate Falls Below 5%," *The New York Times*, Feb. 5, 2016, http://tinyurl.com/jsow293.

63. Chuck Ross, "Bernie Sanders Says 'Real' Unemployment Rate Is Actually 10.5 Percent, DOUBLE The Official Rate," *The Daily Caller*, with video, July 6, 2015, http://tinyurl.com/jv3c3gp.

64. Poole, *op. cit.*

65. "The Slow Recovery of the Labor Market," Congressional Budget Office, February 2014, p. 2, http://tinyurl.com/h5mh5vc.

66. Schwartz, *op. cit.*

67. Rosalind S. Helderman, "Uber pressures regulators by mobilizing riders and hiring vast lobbying network," *The Washington Post*, Dec. 13, 2014, http://tinyurl.com/zud4n3z.

68. Alison Griswold, "Uber's Siege on San Antonio," *Slate*, Oct. 16, 2015, http://tinyurl.com/oyq8n2h.

69. Andy Vyong, "Colorado likely first to legislatively authorize ride-share services," *The Denver Post*, April 29, 2014, http://tinyurl.com/zfumg26.

70. Bryan Lowry, "Uber is back in Kansas after Gov. Sam Brownback signs bill into law," *The Kansas City Star*, May 22, 2015, http://tinyurl.com/zfxke55.

71. Megan Geuss, "Uber drivers are employees, California Labor Commission ruling suggests," *ArsTechnica*, June 17, 2015, http://tinyurl.com/htmrzee.

72. Daniel Beekman, "Seattle first U.S. city to give Uber, other contract drivers power to unionize," *The Seattle Times*, Dec 14, 2015, http://tinyurl.com/h5b3jpt.

73. Taylor Soper, "Uber asks City of Seattle to follow 4 'key principles' when crafting driver union law," *Geekwire*, Feb. 29, 2016, http://tinyurl.com/zs5ou3y.

74. According to the Freelancers Union, 71 percent of freelancers will experience late or non-payment for work during their career. The bill, introduced Dec. 7, 2015, can be found at http://tinyurl.com/jqs4cqq.

75. David McCabe, "Sanders has 'serious problems' with Uber," *The Hill*, Aug. 6, 2015, http://tinyurl.com/hgl7qxm.

76. Ned Resnikoff, "Bernie Sanders proposes sweeping labor law reforms," Aljazeera America, Oct. 6, 2015, http://tinyurl.com/oyh2ru4.

77. Noam Scheiber, "Budget Seeks to Ease Economic Fears for U.S. Workers," *The New York Times*, Feb. 9, 2016, http://tinyurl.com/hf2jhql.

78. Uberlawsuit.com contains links to complaint against Uber. See p. 5 of *Douglas O'Connor, Thomas Colopy, Matthew Manahan, and Elie Gurfinkel v. Uber Technologies, Inc.*, http://tinyurl.com/hwy6ldj.

79. Tracey Lien, "Meet the Attorney Suing Uber, Lyft, GrubbHub and a dozen California Tech Firms," *Los Angeles Times*, Jan. 24, 2016, http://tinyurl.com/h6srv62.

80. Sarah Kessler, "The Gig Economy Won't Last Because It's Being Sued To Death," *Fast Company*, Feb. 17, 2015, http://tinyurl.com/m2b9pop.

81. Noam Scheiber, "Uber Drivers and Others in the Gig Economy Take a Stand," *The New York Times*, Feb. 2, 2016, http://tinyurl.com/zkqps7p.

82. Harris and Krueger, *op. cit.*

83. "This is Your Life in 10 Years Time," What's the Future of Work? (WTF?), Nov. 24, 2015, http://tinyurl.com/zb8k695.

84. "GE Global Innovation Barometer," *GE Reports*, Jan. 19, 2016, http://tinyurl.com/hur2moj.

85. Carl Benedikt Frey and Michael A. Osborne, "The Future of Employment: How Susceptible Are Jobs to Computerisation?" University of Oxford, Sept. 17, 2013, http://tinyurl.com/oj67kae.

86. Kaufman, *op. cit.*

BIBLIOGRAPHY

Selected Sources

Books

Chase, Robin, *Peers Inc: How People and Platforms Are Inventing the Collaborative Economy and Reinventing Capitalism*, Public Affairs, 2015.

The co-founder of Zipcar offers an expansive vision of the collaborative economy.

Hill, Steven, *Raw Deal: How the "Uber Economy" and Runaway Capitalism Are Screwing American Workers*, St. Martin's Press, 2015.

A senior fellow with the New America think tank calls the so-called sharing economy the "latest economic fraud" spurred by Silicon Valley technology.

Horowitz, Sara, with Toni Sciarra Poynter, *The Freelancer's Bible: Everything You Need to Know to Have the Career of Your Dreams — On Your Terms*, Workman Publishing, 2012.

The founder of the Freelancers Union offers a prescription for economic survival in a dramatically changed economic landscape and suggests legislative changes to protect freelance workers.

Schor, Juliet B., *True Wealth: How and Why Millions of Americans Are Creating a Time-Rich, Ecologically-Light, Small-Scale, High-Satisfaction Economy*, Penguin Press, 2011.

A professor of sociology at Boston College offers an upbeat, early assessment of workers diverging from the "work-and-spend cycle" to a world of "time, creativity, information and community."

Weil, David, *The Fissured Workplace: Why Work Became So Bad for So Many*, Harvard University Press, 2014.

A Boston University economics professor provides an historic overview of the reasons for changes in corporate strategies that resulted in greater outsourcing of work.

Articles

Crichton, Danny, "Technology can reduce wage theft while making work more flexible," *National Review*, Feb. 23, 2015, http://tinyurl.com/jo27px8.

A doctoral student in labor economics says widespread wage theft — the failure of employers to pay workers what they are entitled to — can be addressed by reforming labor laws to reflect the new on-demand economy.

Greenhouse, Steven, "Uber: On the Road to Nowhere," *The American Prospect*, Winter 2016, http://tinyurl.com/p4qny6g.

A former *New York Times* labor reporter and current visiting researcher at the Russell Sage Foundation argues that the gig economy is shortchanging workers.

Hiltzik, Michael, "How the Uberization of work is rooted in the cult of 'shareholder value,' " *Los Angeles Times*, Jan. 5, 2016, http://tinyurl.com/zuk68ns.
A columnist challenges the notion of large corporations as "job creators," asserting that full-time job security has fallen victim to a bottom-line mentality.

Kaufman, Micha, "The Gig Economy: The Force That Could Save the American Worker?" *Wired*, 2013, http://tinyurl.com/jp5qbg7.
The co-founder and CEO of Fiverr, an online marketplace, argues that the gig economy will help workers by encouraging creativity and initiative.

Kreider, Benjamin, "Risk Shift and the Gig Economy," Economic Policy Institute, Aug. 4, 2015, http://tinyurl.com/z2ts2mg.
A writer for a think tank affiliated with labor unions explores how the on-demand economy has shifted economic risk from management to workers.

Schieber, Noam, "Solo Workers Unite to Tame Their Gig Jobs," *The New York Times*, Feb. 3, 2016, http://tinyurl.com/hmmzn3c.
Independent workers in the gig economy increasingly are joining to protest what they regard as inadequate compensation and unjust controls over the terms of their app-based services.

Reports and Studies

"Contingent Work Force: Size, Characteristics, Earnings and Benefits," U.S. Government Accountability Office, April 2015, http://tinyurl.com/jq3sta2.
Congress' investigative arm analyzes the size and state of the contingent workforce.

Davis, Jerry, "Capital markets and job creation in the 21st century," Brookings Institution, December 2015, http://tinyurl.com/jdmpmlr.
A professor of management at the University of Michigan argues that the rise of the gig economy is directly tied to corporate changes that policymakers must recognize in order to foster job creation.

Harris, Seth D., and Alan B. Krueger, "A Proposal for Modernizing Labor Laws for Twenty-First-Century Work," The Hamilton Project, December 2015, http://tinyurl.com/ht56lhm.
A professor of labor relations at Cornell University (Harris) and a professor of economics at Princeton University (Krueger) propose ways for independent workers to retain rights and benefits.

For More Information

AFL-CIO, 815 16th St., N.W., Washington, DC 20006; 888-373-6497; www.aflcio.org. Largest federation of unions in the United States; advocates on behalf of workers.

Brookings Institution, 1775 Massachusetts Ave., N.W., Washington, DC 20036; 202-797-6000; www.brookings.edu. Center-left think tank whose wide-ranging mission includes fostering the economic and social welfare of all Americans.

Center for Economic and Policy Research, 1611 Connecticut Ave., N.W., Suite 400, Washington, DC 20009; 202-293-5380; https://cepr.net. Left-leaning think tank that promotes democratic debate on the most important economic and social issues affecting people's lives.

Economic Policy Institute, 1333 H St., N.W., Suite 300, East Tower, Washington, DC 20005-4707; 202-775-8810; www.epi.org. Liberal think tank that focuses on the needs of low- and middle-income workers.

Freelancers Union, 408 Jay St., Brooklyn, NY 11201-5150; 718-532-1515; www.freelancersunion.org. Advocates for the self-employed and provides networking opportunities for its nearly 300,000 members; also markets health, life and disability insurance policies.

National Employment Law Project, 1601 I St., N.W., Washington, DC 20006; 202-887-8202; www.nelp.org. An advocacy organization for low- and minimum-wage workers.

R Street Institute, 1050 17th St., N.W., #1150, Washington, DC 20036; 202-525-5717; www.rstreet.org. A conservative, coalition-building think tank dedicated to free market solutions.

5

Jailing Debtors

Christina Hoag

Mayor James Knowles of Ferguson, Mo., speaks to the media after a Department of Justice report detailed how the city's police department and municipal court targeted African-Americans with large fines and traffic tickets to raise revenue for the city. The Justice Department investigated the city following the fatal shooting of Michael Brown, a black teenager, by a white police officer, and subsequent riots.

From *CQ Researcher*,
September 16, 2016.

Michael Thomas/Getty Images

Stephen Papa paid a heavy price for drunkenly climbing onto the roof of a building in Grand Rapids, Mich. An Iraq War veteran who was living on friends' couches at the time, Papa was arrested and ordered to pay $2,600 in fines for trespassing, court costs and restitution.

At a court hearing a month later to pay the first installment of $50, he had just $25. But he told the judge, he had a new job that paid $12 an hour at a steel plant. The judge said he should have tried harder to come up with the $50 and sentenced him to 22 days in jail.

"I tried telling the judge, throwing me in jail is going to do you no good," Papa said. "You're not going to get your fines like you want, and I'm going to lose my job, and you're really not going to get your fines if I don't have a job. . . . It just baffled me."

When he got out of jail, he had indeed lost his job. He found another, as a security guard, but it paid $4 an hour less.[1]

In what civil rights advocates say is a modern-day "debtors' prison" system, poor people nationwide are being jailed over non-payment of fines and fees stemming from minor offenses such as traffic violations and misdemeanors and then are often charged interest and additional fees to cover their time in jail. The situation creates a mounting pile of debt, and some offenders lose their jobs for missing work while jailed, spiraling deeper into poverty. Civil rights activists say the practice, which disproportionately affects minorities, is effectively creating a two-tier system of justice — one for those who can afford fines and fees and one for those who cannot. "People are being jailed for their poverty," says

Court Revenues Fall in Ferguson

Revenue from court fines and forfeitures dropped by half in Ferguson, Mo., after a 2015 federal probe found that the city was using law enforcement to raise money to fund its court system and that the practice disproportionately targeted African-Americans. Racial tension had erupted in Ferguson after the 2014 shooting of unarmed black teenager Michael Brown by a white police officer.

Ferguson Fine/Forfeiture Revenues

Source: "2015 Comprehensive Annual Financial Report," City of Ferguson, December 2015, p. 70, http://tinyurl.com/hfamddh

Nusrat Choudhury, a staff attorney for the Racial Justice Program of the American Civil Liberties Union (ACLU). "They are being criminalized for being poor."

But many local judges and officials say fines hold people accountable for their transgressions. If scofflaws do not obey court orders to pay, judges must impose a harsher punishment, such as jail, they say.

In addition, these judges and officials say, in an era of tax-cutting and tight budgets the fines and fees are needed to cover the growing cost of administering local criminal justice systems. The higher costs are the result of get-tough-on-crime policies adopted in the 1980s that lengthened prison sentences for certain felonies and treated minor offenses more harshly. Annual criminal justice expenses jumped 70 percent from 1993 to 2012, to more than $270 billion, according to a 2016 White House report, and the incarcerated population rose 220 percent — to 2.2 million — between 1980 and 2014.[2]

"Legislatures have not funded criminal justice systems to the extent needed to handle the huge increase in the number of people cycling in and out of the justice system," says Lauren-Brooke Eisen, a senior counsel at the Brennan Center for Justice in New York City, which studies the legal aspects of public policy.

To remedy the situation, many jurisdictions have passed the increased costs — for everything from courthouse overhead to jail operations to public defender salaries — on to the offenders by increasing fines and tacking on late fees and user fees. The practice is widespread: In 2014, 44 states charged offenders for probation and parole supervision, up from 26 in 1990.[3] Since 1996, Florida has added 20 new categories of justice system fees.[4]

For municipal governments, making offenders pay is both economic and politically palatable. Some officials say those who commit crimes should pay for them. "The only reason that the court is in operation and doing business at that point in time is because that defendant has come in and is a user of those services," said Mike Day, administrator of the Allegan County Circuit Court in Michigan. "They don't necessarily see themselves as a customer because, obviously, they're not choosing to be there. But in reality they are."[5]

Such policies disproportionately affect the poor and minorities, who are the majority of people involved in the criminal justice system, says Todd Clear, a criminal justice professor at Rutgers University in New Jersey. While blacks and Hispanics account for only 30 percent of the population, they constitute more than 50 percent of the incarcerated population, and 80 percent of felony defendants are indigent.[6]

"It's a distortion of justice," Clear says. "The criminal justice system isn't just for offenders. We all rely on it as a fair system." Moreover, defendants who later are found innocent may lose their jobs due to time lost while in jail, and — depending on the jurisdiction — some may be charged for room and board while they were in jail awaiting trial.

In 2015, the U.S. Department of Justice highlighted the use of fines and fees to generate municipal revenue when it investigated Ferguson, Mo., following riots over the fatal shooting of Michael Brown, a black teenager, by a white police officer the previous August. The 105-page report detailed how Ferguson officials imposed large fines and traffic tickets, and targeted black residents.[7] It cited the case of a woman who was fined $151 for a parking violation in 2007. After becoming homeless, she missed several court hearings, and her fines grew. She was arrested twice for failing to show up for court hearings and spent six days in jail. By December 2014, she had paid a total of $550 and still owed $541 for that single parking ticket received seven years earlier.[8]

Attorneys for civil rights groups maintain these policies are illegal and have successfully sued numerous cities and counties, arguing that jailing poor people for failing to pay fines violates their 14th Amendment right to equal protection under the law. The attorneys also cite case law: Three Supreme Court decisions, the most recent in 1983, said people cannot be jailed because of an inability to pay, and that courts must determine a person's capacity to pay before imposing a fine, the ACLU's Choudhury says. However, people can be jailed if they have the means to pay but refuse to do so, the justices said.[9]

Judges say it can be difficult to determine whether a defendant is truly destitute. Superior Court Judge Robert Swisher in Benton County, Wash., said he makes judgments based on how people present themselves in court. "They come in wearing expensive jackets or maybe a thousand dollars' worth of tattoos on their arms, and they say, 'I'm just living on handouts.' " If defendants say the jacket or tattoos were a gift, he said, he tells them they should have asked for the cash to pay their court fees instead.[10]

Bail reform has emerged as a related issue. Often, poor people awaiting trial cannot afford to post even small amounts of bail, an amount of money held in abeyance by the court to ensure the defendant shows up for court, says Cherise Fanno Burdeen, CEO of the Pretrial Justice Institute, a Maryland-based nonprofit that advocates eliminating the bail system. As a result, people are being held in jail for minor offenses because of their inability to pay, she says. According to one study, more than 450,000 people being held in the nation's jails are awaiting trial.[11]

But the bail-bond industry says that on the whole, the system works, which is why it has been used for

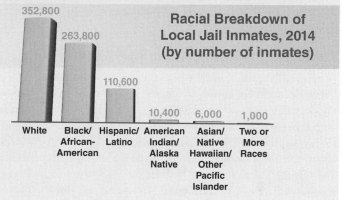

Inmate Count Disproportionately Minority

Minorities accounted for about 40 percent of the U.S. population but made up 53 percent of local jail inmates in 2014, the most recent count. Experts say bail policies often disproportionately affect minorities and the poor.

Racial Breakdown of Local Jail Inmates, 2014 (by number of inmates)

Race	Inmates
White	352,800
Black/African-American	263,800
Hispanic/Latino	110,600
American Indian/Alaska Native	10,400
Asian/Native Hawaiian/Other Pacific Islander	6,000
Two or More Races	1,000

Source: "Jail Inmates at Midyear 2014," Bureau of Justice Statistics, p. 3, June 2015, http://tinyurl.com/jjvsbuy

centuries. "We can't throw out the whole bail system," says Jeffrey Clayton, policy director for the American Bail Coalition, an industry advocacy group based in Greenville, S.C.

A Texas case in July 2015 highlighted how the bail system can affect poor people. Sandra Bland, a 28-year-old black woman arrested following an altercation with a police officer during a traffic stop, spent three days in a Texas jail after she could not raise the $515 for a bail bond. She was found hanging in her cell, her death ruled a suicide.[12]

Earlier this year, the Justice Department sent a nine-page memo to federal, state and local courts reminding them about the Supreme Court rulings that jailing people for inability to pay is unconstitutional.[13] The memo said judges must consider a person's ability to pay before setting fines and bail amounts. Activists say the federal government's interest bodes well for policy change, although the Justice Department cannot monitor compliance in every court.

"It's a huge step forward," says Choudhury.

Counties and cities have instituted judicial system reforms in several states — including Washington, Colorado, Louisiana and Alabama — following lawsuits by civil rights groups. In Colorado and Missouri, for instance, legislatures are vigorously debating whether to limit fines and fees. Bills to reform the cash bail system are pending in Congress, while some states are implementing pretrial supervision programs aimed at replacing bail.

As local officials, legislators and civil rights advocates debate the issue, here are some of the questions they are considering:

Should people be jailed for failing to pay fines?

When police pulled over Ashlee Lucero in Mountain View, Colo., in September 2014, she was cited for having defective tires and fined $80.

But that wasn't all she owed. A judge also ordered her to pay $130 in court costs and service fees. Unable to afford the total amount, Lucero made a $55 payment and was told to pay the rest by February. In December, she was summoned to court again but figured she didn't have to go because she already had a court date for payment. The following month, she was arrested for contempt of traffic court and spent a night in jail. A year later, she was still paying off her court debt.[14]

Advocates for the poor say stories like Lucero's are common across the country: Poor people end up in jail because they cannot afford to pay fines. Many judges say they allow poorer people to pay fines in installments, but if defendants do not obey, judges have little choice but to impose a harsher punishment, which usually means jail.

"If I've got someone standing in front of me for something that's labeled a misdemeanor, and they've failed to follow through with court orders on that, am I supposed to tell the rest of the world, the rest of the law-abiding citizens, that they're chumps and fools for having respected the law and respected the court's orders?" asked Michigan Chief Judge Raymond Voet of Ionia County District Court.[15]

In Colorado, Presiding Judge Richard Weinberg of the Aurora Municipal Court told legislators a proposed ban on jailing the indigent "allows any person to ignore their responsibility for their criminal acts" and discriminates against people who do pay.[16]

But civil rights groups say courts ignoring Supreme Court rulings that it is unconstitutional to jail people because of an inability to pay. But Eisen of the Brennan Center points out that determining financial status usually requires extra hearings, which pose an additional burden on already overloaded court dockets and public defenders. "In practicality, that doesn't happen," she says.

Some judges also fail to consider that jail is expensive, she and others say. Housing an inmate typically costs $60 to $80 per day, and numerous jurisdictions try to pass that cost on to offenders as daily "room and board" fees, adding to their debt, Eisen says. On top of that, jailed offenders often lose their jobs since they cannot work, which can spiral into loss of housing, child custody and other penalties, she adds. As a result, people who are truly destitute end up paying far more than people who can afford to pay, says Chris Albin-Lackey, a senior researcher at Human Rights Watch, a human rights nonprofit based in New York.

But judges say they do not jail people lightly. In Kansas City, Mo., for instance, Municipal Court Presiding Judge Anne J. LaBella said, "We do not jail people for money. Kansas City spends more than $1 million annually on indigent legal defense and $90,000 to provide free community service for the indigent. We are a national model for Drug, Mental Health and Veteran's Treatment Courts, which focus on treatment and rehabilitation rather than incarceration."[17]

Incarceration is necessary when people fail to pay their fines even after being put on "probation" and allowed to pay fines in installments, she said. "Without any possibility of jail time, probation is impossible," she stated.[18]

> "If they don't want to pay a fee, don't commit a crime. Why should taxpayers of the state of Michigan have to foot the entire bill of the court system?"
>
> — *Mike Day,*
> *Administrator,*
> *Allegan County Circuit Court, Allegan, Mich.*

Critics, including some county sheriffs, question whether failing to pay a fine merits a jail sentence. "These inmates really don't belong there because their offenses are not that serious," said Peg Ackerman, a lobbyist for the County Sheriffs of Colorado, a sheriffs' association.[19]

Civil rights advocates say courts could lower or waive fines or impose community service, but such programs cost money and do not produce revenue, so courts may feel pressured to impose fines. "There's a very real economic difficulty in funding courts," says Albin-Lackey. Fines are "a politically expedient solution."

Some jurisdictions have devised alternative penalties that legal experts say are equally discriminatory against poor people.

For instance, Benton County, Wash., allowed offenders to choose between paying off their debt by performing manual labor in a work crew for $70 a day in credits or by serving jail time for $50 a day in credit. "Our function is to modify behavior, and currently we view this policy as a means of doing that," said District Judge Robert Ingvalson.[20] After the ACLU sued, charging that the system discriminated against poor people, the county ended the practice in June.[21]

Virginia uses another alternative method — suspending driver's licenses of those who fail to pay court fines. Some 940,000 Virginians have had their licenses suspended even though their offenses often are unrelated to traffic violations, according to a lawsuit filed against the state in July by the Legal Aid Justice Center.[22] Critics of the policy say a suspended license can prevent people from getting to work, reducing their chances of paying off the fines. It also can lead to people driving with a suspended license to avoid losing their jobs, which can result in jail time if caught, the suit said.

Should offenders be charged for use of the criminal justice system?

When Fred Cunningham pleaded guilty to a prescription drug fraud charge in Michigan, he was sentenced to a year in prison and ordered to pay $1,000 in court costs: $500 for his public defender and $500 for the operational costs of running the Allegan County courthouse, including salaries, utilities and even the county employees' fitness center.[23]

With the ACLU's help, Cunningham challenged the court costs, and the Michigan Supreme Court eventually ruled that such fees were not authorized under state law. Cunningham's victory was short-lived, however. The state Legislature, pressed by local governments, adopted a law authorizing counties to recoup costs by charging fees to offenders.[24]

Similarly, offenders nationwide are being charged to utilize the criminal justice system. In addition to room and board for jail cells, defendants are paying fees for things such as drug testing and the rental of electronic ankle bracelets. "It's become a very popular mechanism for funding courts and other programs," says Micah West, a staff attorney with the Southern Poverty Law Center, a civil rights organization based in Montgomery, Ala. "Fines are punishment, but fees are just about revenue generation."

Local officials say the fees are needed to pay for administering criminal justice and that those who use the system should shoulder that expense, just as is done for other legal services, such as recording a deed or filing a lawsuit.

"If they don't want to pay a fee, don't commit a crime," said Day, the Michigan court administrator whose county collected $315,000 in fees from 2014 to 2015. "Why should taxpayers of the state of Michigan have to foot the entire bill of the court system?"[25]

Government experts say such reasoning is flawed on several levels. Not all people charged with a crime are later found guilty, they point out, yet the innocent often end up paying such fees. And criminal justice is a general government responsibility, such as public education, that should be borne by all because it benefits society as a whole, says John D. Donahue, a senior lecturer in public policy at Harvard University's John F. Kennedy School of Government. "It's a collective undertaking. It's not like delivering water or sewage services," he says.

In April, Alameda County, Calif., which includes Oakland, became the state's first county to stop charging fees to juvenile offenders' families, a practice that had put 2,900 families in debt. The fees, some of which totaled thousands of dollars and netted the county $168,000 last year, included $25.29 per night in Juvenile Hall, $15 per day for electronic ankle monitoring, $90 a month for probation supervision and $250 for a probation investigation, among others.[26]

Mark Reis/The Gazette via AP

Mark Silverstein, legal director of the American Civil Liberties Union of Colorado, announces a settlement with Colorado Springs over what an ACLU suit called its "debtors' prison practices." The city agreed to compensate dozens of people jailed because they couldn't pay fines for minor offenses like panhandling and jaywalking. A 1971 Supreme Court ruling banned such sentences, but they still persist in some city-level courts, he says.

"The families we work with are some of the poorest in the county, and yet they were asked to foot the bill for the juvenile justice system," said Kate Weisburd, youth defender clinic director at the East Bay Community Law Center. "It undermines family stability at a time when stability is needed most."[27]

Some of the most problematic practices arising from fees have resulted from the use of private companies to supervise offenders who are put on so-called probation while paying off court fines, analysts say. The companies, which do not charge the counties for the service, make money by charging offenders a fee.

In Clanton, Ala., offenders under supervision typically were required to pay a $10 setup fee and then $140 per month, $100 of which went toward their fine. The rest went to the company, Judicial Corrections Services.[28] When people fell behind on their payments, the company continued to collect its own fee, thus increasing the amount of the debt while lengthening the offender's probationary term because the money he was paying did not go toward paying the fine. Offenders were threatened with jail if they did not pay.

The Southern Poverty Law Center sued Clanton and Judicial Corrections Services, alleging that the company was "extorting" supervisees. In a settlement, Clanton

canceled the contract. Another 54 municipalities and counties across the state also canceled their contracts after the Southern Poverty Law Center sent them a letter warning them the company's practices were illegal.[29]

Private companies often fail to properly monitor their supervisees, says Dolan of the Institute for Policy Studies. "It's in their interest to keep you caught in the system," she says.

Still, private probation companies remain attractive to counties because debt collection is expensive, Albin-Lackey of Human Rights Watch says. Two Florida counties, in fact, canceled their own debt collection efforts after determining the net gain wasn't worth the expense: Leon County voided 8,000 outstanding arrest warrants and Orange County canceled outstanding nonpayment warrants for homeless people.[30]

Some courts, however, send people to jail for nonpayment. In Bogalusa, La., Rozzie Scott went to jail because he could not pay $50 for an "extension fee" after telling Judge Robert Black he couldn't pay $450 in fines and court costs for shoplifting $5 worth of food.[31] After the Southern Poverty Law Center sued the court on the grounds that Scott's right to equal protection was being violated, Black stopped the practice. However, he said, the fees had defrayed the costs of holding extra court hearings when people returned to court to request a deadline extension on their court fines. The fees had covered a 20- to 30-percent budget shortfall in the court's operating costs.

Moreover, Black said, "It is the court's understanding that the collection of these or similar costs is utilized by other courts in Louisiana."[32]

Should inability to pay bail lead to pretrial detention?

Tyrone Tomlin was faced with a choice after a judge set his bail at $1,500 on a misdemeanor charge of possessing drug paraphernalia — a straw that a clerk had handed him when he bought a soda. Tomlin, who had had numerous previous drug convictions, was arrested after police saw him on a New York City street with friends and suspected them of using drugs — plastic straws being commonly used to package heroin.

Because he couldn't afford bail, Tomlin had to choose between pleading guilty and serving a 30-day sentence or maintaining his innocence and going to jail until his case was resolved. Tomlin pleaded not guilty and was sent to New York's Rikers Island, where he was beaten by other inmates while awaiting trial. At a court hearing three weeks later his case was dismissed after the straw tested negative for drug residue.

He had spent three weeks in jail, endured a beating and lost income for nothing. "I'm not no prince but I got a raw deal," Tomlin said.[33]

About 60 percent of the nation's 644,500 jail inmates are being held while awaiting trial.[34] After arrest, defendants go before a judge to have charges against them formally presented, to state whether they are guilty or not and to determine whether they should be jailed pending resolution of their case. The judge decides whether they can go free after posting bail, or on their own recognizance, meaning they simply promise to show up for court. While some pretrial detainees — typically those charged with severe crimes or deemed likely to flee — are denied bail, the majority are granted bail. If they cannot afford to post bail, they must stay in jail.

If the defendants eventually are acquitted, they may or may not have to pay for their room and board while they were in jail awaiting trial, depending on the practices of the jurisdiction, experts say.

Under the bail system, defendants can either pay the bail themselves or engage a bail bond agent by paying 10 percent of the bail amount, while the bondsman guarantees the rest. If the defendant flees, the bail agent pays the balance. If the defendant returns to court, the agent keeps the defendant's 10 percent as his agent fee. Defendants who later are found not guilty do not get their 10 percent back.

Activists say the money bail system is unfair to the poor and needs to be reformed: While both are presumed innocent, wealthier people can buy their freedom pending trial, whereas poor people cannot. Indigent people charged with petty, nonviolent offenses are particularly affected, the activists say, because they cannot come up with even the paltry amounts to get bailed out of jail.

"Is this jaywalker a menace to society? These aren't people who are flight risks, yet they are locked up because

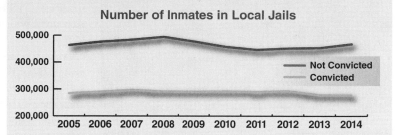

Most Jail Inmates Not Convicted

About 60 percent of the nation's local jail population is made up of inmates who have not been convicted of a crime. Some can't afford to post bail so they are detained while awaiting a hearing or trial.

Number of Inmates in Local Jails

Source: "Jail Inmates at Midyear 2014," Bureau of Justice Statistics, p. 3, June 2015, http://tinyurl.com/jjvsbuy

they can't afford bail," says Karen Dolan, a fellow at the Institute for Policy Studies, a progressive think tank in Washington, D.C.

The bail bond industry opposes one alternative recommended by reformers: replacing the bail system with pretrial supervision programs, which assign risk scores to defendants based on their criminal history and other factors and require defendants to check in with authorities periodically, depending on their score.

Cash bonds are necessary, the industry contends, to ensure that defendants return to court. "Bail works," says the American Bail Coalition's Clayton.

He cites a 2004 study in the *University of Chicago Journal of Law and Economics*, which found that defendants released on bond are 28 percent less likely to fail to appear than those released on their own recognizance. And if defendants fail to appear, they are 53 percent less likely to remain at large for extended periods.

Defendants can ask a judge to reduce bail if they feel the amount is unreasonable, and bail makes the defendant feel emotionally beholden to show up because family and friends usually pay the bond, Clayton notes. "In the vast, vast majority of cases, defendants don't post their own bail," he says.

But the bail system creates some insidious consequences for the poor, reformists say. When people cannot make bail, says Fanno Burdeen of the Pretrial Justice Institute, they are more inclined to take a prosecutor's deal to plead guilty in return for probation or a limited

KENA BETANCUR/AFP/Getty Images

A demonstrator carries a photograph of Sandra Bland during a memorial in New York City on Aug. 9, 2015, for Michael Brown, the Ferguson, Mo., teenager shot and killed by a policeman. Bland was arrested following an altercation with a police officer in Texas during a traffic stop and was jailed after she could not pay the $515 bail. She hanged herself in her cell three days later.

jail term, thus giving themselves unwarranted criminal records simply because they cannot pay fines or court costs, which can be as little as $100.

In Tomlin's case, he was never able to make bail on any of his 41 arrests on misdemeanor charges. For two-thirds of the charges, he took plea deals either at arraignment to avoid going to jail or within two weeks in order to get out of jail.[35]

Pretrial detention reforms are underway in several jurisdictions, including establishment of community bail funds that post bail for poor people, provided by non-profit organizations and private donors. The Brooklyn, N.Y., Community Bail Fund reported a 97 percent court attendance rate for clients, 62 percent of whom had their charges dismissed. By contrast, 90 percent of those who don't make bail in New York City plead guilty.[36]

Other jurisdictions, including some New York City boroughs and the state of New Jersey, are enacting pretrial supervision programs, says Greg Berman, executive director of the Center for Court Innovation in New York, which is running a pretrial program.

The programs are expensive, however. New Jersey's program will cost about $50 million a year, largely for extra staff to monitor defendants, although officials expect that lower jail costs will offset the cost.[37]

Clayton notes that bail bond agents essentially do the same job of keeping track of defendants, especially ones deemed at high risk for committing crimes or fleeing, at no charge to taxpayers.

Both jail and pretrial supervision are costly, said Charlotte McPherson, manager of Pretrial Services for Kentucky, which replaced bail with pretrial supervision four years ago. Some of the supervision expense is passed on to defendants: High-risk defendants, for instance, must pay for their own drug testing and ankle bracelets while under supervision, costs that sometimes exceed what they would have paid in bail, she noted.[38]

Clayton says the industry recognizes that some genuinely destitute defendants deserve bail. He favors developing a system in which the courts contribute a portion of high bail amounts to a bail fund for the poor. But, he notes, the nation's 15,000 bail agents play a vital role to ensure that defendants face justice as well as pursuing fugitives and monitoring people who are at a high risk of committing more crimes while free on bail.

"Allowing violent persons to walk out of jail on low bonds or on a simple promise to return for their court dates is dangerous," he says.

BACKGROUND
Early History

Debtors have been subject to cruel treatment throughout history. Debt slavery, for instance, in which those owing money became slaves to their creditors, who could sell them to recoup their debt, existed as far back as 3000 B.C.[39] The earliest written Roman laws — the Twelve Tables, dating to the 5th century B.C. — codified the practice of nexum, or debt bondage, in which borrowers volunteered themselves as collateral for loans, effectively ending debt slavery. If borrowers defaulted, they worked off the debt.[40]

Nexum caused great social and political turmoil, however, because the contract heavily favored the creditor, often requiring the debt to be paid up to nine times over, resulting in a lifetime of hardship and penury for the debtor.[41] By the 4th century B.C., Rome had outlawed debt bondage in favor of a system of using property as loan security, although debt bondage in different forms continued elsewhere for centuries.[42]

In the Middle Ages, Europe began incarcerating people until their debts were paid, which resulted in long, indefinite sentences, as well as asset seizures. A creditor could obtain a court judgment, allowing bailiffs to go to the debtor's home and remove property. The system led to widespread abuse because bailiffs would confiscate more than was necessary to pay the debt and often took items for themselves or demanded deeds to the property.[43]

In 1542, under King Henry VIII, England's first bankruptcy law allowed merchants and traders to seize debtors' assets. The king's daughter, Elizabeth, who became queen in 1558, adopted a law in 1570 that served as the precursor to bankruptcy laws adopted in the 19th century. It stipulated that creditors could seize assets, sell them and divide the proceeds among themselves. It also allowed for debtors' ears to be cut off.[44]

Imprisonment, however, became the primary way to deal with debtors. By the 18th century, defaulters constituted the bulk of the incarcerated population, with several prisons designated solely for the bankrupt. In 1776, English and Welsh prisons housed 2,437 debtors. Often when a primary wage-earner was imprisoned, his family fell into poverty and was forced into prison as well. Each debtor imprisoned in 1776 had an average of two dependents, usually a wife and child, incarcerated with him.[45]

Debtors were not all working-class people. Some in the middle or upper classes ended up in prison after living beyond their means. They included such luminaries as Daniel Defoe, author of *Robinson Crusoe*, artist William Hogarth and John Dickens, the father of novelist Charles Dickens.[46]

Charles had been forced to leave school at age 12 to work in a boot-black factory to help support his parents and their four youngest children, all living in prison due to his father's debts. The experience ignited Dickens' lifelong compassion for the poor, and he later set one of his books, *Little Dorrit* (1857), in London's Marshalsea Prison for Debt, where his family had been inmates.[47]

Delinquent payers in England could also be sentenced to live "within the extent of the rules" or "in the verge of the court," which meant they could be arrested if they stepped outside a prescribed area except on Sundays. In Henry Fielding's 1751 novel *Amelia*, a footman tells Capt. Booth that his wife fell gravely ill while in a shop. When Booth rushes to the shop, just outside the verge, he's promptly arrested.[48]

Residents of Worsham, Va., who didn't pay their taxes might find themselves in the old debtors' prison, built in 1787. Colonial America followed the English practice of imprisoning people for owing minute amounts. Defaulters included such illustrious names as Robert Morris, who helped finance the American Revolution and signed the Declaration of Independence.

The only way out of debtors' prison was to pay off the debt, often with the help of family or friends, or to reach an agreement with the creditor. People could remain in prison for years, often over trivial amounts. Debts could also accrue during incarceration. The prisons, which were privately run, charged for room and board. For inmates who still had access to money or who had wealthy benefactors, living conditions were passable — they were allowed visitors and could buy better food and drink, and could even pay to live outside the prison, but nearby.

But the indigent had to beg for alms from passersby through windows and grates, or they simply starved. After a 1729-30 parliamentary investigation of prison conditions for poor inmates, several wardens were prosecuted for murder.[49]

U.S. Debt Law

In the wake of the parliamentary investigation, James Oglethorpe, a British philanthropist and member of Parliament, in 1732 came up with a special purpose for settling Georgia, the last of Britain's 13 colonies in North America. He proposed that debtors in London's overcrowded jails be shipped to the settlement for a fresh start. However, in an era when debt was considered a moral weakness, the plan met resistance in

Education Images/UIG via Getty Images

Parliament, and when the first batch of 114 colonists was dispatched in 1732, they were not debtors but "the deserving poor" — hard workers who deserved a helping hand — whose mission was to manufacture goods to export to England.[50]

However, Colonial America followed the English practice of imprisoning people for owing minute amounts. Defaulters included such illustrious names as Robert Morris, who helped finance the American Revolution and signed the Declaration of Independence.[51]

Debt threatened to undermine the stability of the newly formed United States when in 1786, during a time of economic turmoil, farmers from Massachusetts to South Carolina rebelled against attempts by officials to collect debts and unpaid taxes. By 1787, militias had put down the uprisings, known as Shays' Rebellion after Daniel Shays, a Continental Army captain turned farmer. Congress then voted to cut taxes and issued a moratorium on debt collection.[52]

In 1830, the Prison Discipline Society of Boston reported that 30 people were imprisoned in Philadelphia for owing less than $1, equivalent to about $25 today, while one-third of the jail's 817 debtors owed $5 or less.[53] With opposition to imprisonment and calls for debt law reform mounting, the U.S. government in 1833 eliminated federal debtors' prisons, and most states followed suit in the 1830s and 1840s. England, meanwhile, abolished debtors' prisons in 1869.[54]

Accompanying these moves was a shift in how the law treated debt. Instead of viewing debt as a crime, laws began to view bankruptcy as a way to keep creditors at bay while allowing a person to recover from debt. In 1841, the first law was enacted to permit voluntary bankruptcy, which became a central feature of all subsequent bankruptcy laws. But the law was widely regarded as a failure because creditors struggled to recoup debts, and it was repealed in 1843.[55]

Following the Civil War, which left the South in financial ruin, a new federal bankruptcy law in 1867 allowed for both voluntary and involuntary bankruptcy declarations by companies and individuals.[56] But a decade later it, too, was repealed after pressure from creditors, who complained it incurred too many fees and produced small dividends and long delays.[57]

Bankruptcy laws got a fresh look after the Panic of 1893, sparked by the failure of a major railway company,

the Reading Railroad. The stock market plunged, hundreds of banks closed as people withdrew savings, thousands of businesses collapsed and unemployment reached 4 million.[58]

In the aftermath, Congress adopted the Bankruptcy Act of 1898, which became the template for 20th-century bankruptcy laws. The law stipulated that a court-appointed trustee would oversee each bankruptcy. However, the process was cumbersome, with trustees required to file multiple lawsuits in different courts and await their adjudication before finalizing a single liquidation or reorganization.[59]

Modern Bankruptcy

After a flurry of amendments to bankruptcy laws, the next major overhaul came in 1938, in response to the Great Depression, which began when the overheated stock market crashed in October 1929, wiping out millions of investments. By 1933, nearly half of the nation's banks had collapsed and more than 13 million people were unemployed — 25 percent of the workforce.[60]

The Chandler Act divided bankruptcies into "chapters" covering different types of defaults, including real property and corporate reorganizations, laying the groundwork for current bankruptcy law.[61]

Congress adopted the next major bankruptcy reform in 1978 after nearly a decade of study. It was unique in legal history in that it did not come about in response to an economic crisis. In addition to streamlining bankruptcy administration, the law aimed to allow the debtor to shed all debt, except for child support and alimony, by filing for bankruptcy. This change led to a huge increase in filings by individuals in subsequent years.[62]

The law also authorized states to opt out of federal exemptions in favor of their own. This led to several states, most notably Florida, becoming "debtors' paradises." Under Florida law, creditors cannot seize a debtor's primary home, regardless of the value of the property, which can include up to 160 acres. Nor can creditors confiscate financial assets, including wages deposited in bank accounts, annuities, pension plans, individual retirement accounts, life insurance policies or profit-sharing proceeds.[63] Creditors can go after cars, boats, jewelry and other personal property, however. Many wealthy individuals have taken advantage of

CHRONOLOGY

Ancient History-1820s *Debtors' prisons are widespread.*

Roman Empire Creditors are allowed to enslave defaulting debtors; later, those who have worked off their debt are freed.

Middle Ages European laws allow creditors to seize property to pay a debt.

1798 Declaration of Independence signer Robert Morris, known as the "Financier of the American Revolution," enters Philadelphia's Prune Street Debtors' Prison; he is released in 1801.

1808 Revolutionary War Gen. Henry Lee III, father of Confederate Army Gen. Robert E. Lee, writes *Memoirs of the War in the Southern Department of the United States* during his year in a debtors' prison.

1824 Famed English novelist Charles Dickens goes to work in a factory at age 12 after his parents are jailed for debts to a baker. He later sets his novel *Little Dorrit* in a debtors' prison.

1833-1898 *U.S. outlaws federal debtors' prisons.*

1833 The United States eliminates debtors' prisons under federal law. Many states follow suit.

1898 Congress passes first modern bankruptcy law, giving companies protection from creditors.

1900s *Bankruptcy laws provide relief to debtors and set creditor guidelines.*

1938 Amid the Great Depression, Congress passes the Bankruptcy Act, expanding debtors' use of voluntary declarations of bankruptcy.

1970 U.S. Supreme Court rules that extending a prison term because a person is too poor to pay fines violates the 14th Amendment's right to equal protection.

1971 Supreme Court declares it unconstitutional to convert a fine into a jail term because the defendant cannot pay.

1978 In a sweeping overhaul, Congress passes Bankruptcy Reform Act, creating bankruptcy courts and different types of bankruptcy.

1983 Supreme Court rules that the 14th Amendment bars courts from revoking probation for the failure to pay a fine without ascertaining a person's ability to pay.

1990s-Present *As incarceration rates and court costs rise, jailing people for unpaid fines surges.*

1997 Former football star O.J. Simpson, who was acquitted of killing his wife Nicole Brown Simpson and her friend Ron Goldman in a sensational 1995 trial, moves to Florida after a civil jury awards $33.5 million to the Brown and Goldman families in a wrongful-death suit stemming from the case; under state bankruptcy laws, many of his assets are protected from seizure.

2005 Congress limits individual bankruptcy to once every eight years to rein in debtors taking advantage of earlier changes designed to help them.

2009 After receiving complaints, the American Civil Liberties Union (ACLU) starts investigating the practice of jailing people who cannot afford to pay fines.

2010 Judicial Correction Services, a for-profit probation service company, makes **Inc.** magazine's list of "fastest-growing private companies in America" for the third year in a row.

2015 The Bowdon, Ga., Municipal Court closes for a month after a judge is found to be threatening defendants with jail for traffic violations if they do not pay fines; it reopens with lower fines and a community service alternative to jail.

2016 National court organizations establish a task force to investigate court fines and fees (February). . . . ACLU wins a settlement in Colorado Springs, Colo., to stop city from jailing people for failure to pay fines (May). . . . Benton County, Wash., agrees to overhaul its system of mandating jail or manual labor for people who cannot afford fines (June).

Luxury Lockups Welcome Nonviolent Inmates

"We cater to good people who make bad choices."

Personal TVs, phones and mini-refrigerators may be standard at many hotels, but some Southern California jails also provide them as amenities — for a price.

In a twist on the practice of jails charging inmates for room and board, about a dozen suburban police departments in Los Angeles and Orange counties offer "pay to stay" programs where nonviolent offenders can pay fees ranging from $85 to $150 a day to serve their sentences in relative comfort instead of enduring noisy, overcrowded and sometimes violent jails run by Los Angeles County.

Municipal officials say the programs help offset the costs of public safety. The city of Glendale, on the outskirts of Los Angeles, took $63,377 in 2014 from 268 inmates who each paid $85 a day.[1] Offenders "should pay their own way. I don't feel that burden should be placed on the taxpayers," Jail Administrator Juan Lopez said.[2]

But critics of such programs denounce them as "jail for the rich," and argue that while they are legal, they unfairly treat people based on their economic status. "What a slap in the face for the concept of equal justice for all," said Peter Eliasberg, legal director for the American Civil Liberties Union of Southern California. "If it's a public service, that should be offered to everyone, regardless of their ability to pay."[3]

Pay-to-stay programs appear limited to Southern California, where they have existed since the 1990s, with their prime customers being celebrities seeking to avoid the Los Angeles County jails. Inmates must have a judge's approval to enter the programs, and they do not have to live in the small municipality where the lockups, usually far more comfortable than the LA county jails, are located. For instance, in 1998, actor Christian Slater served 59 days of a 90-day sentence in a facility in La Verne, in the hinterlands of Los Angeles County, for battery and drug violations. And rapper and music producer Dr. Dre, whose real name is Andre Young, served five months in the Pasadena lockup on a 1994 probation violation after pleading no contest to DUI. Similarly, actors Kiefer Sutherland and Gary Collins served out their DUI sentences in Glendale in 2007 and 2008, respectively.[4]

Seal Beach, a seaside city in Orange County, reaps about $500,000 a year from a 30-bed detention facility that opened in 2013.[5] It even ran a newspaper advertisement to drum up customers for the premium plan, which costs $100 a night, with work release $20 a day extra: "Why spend your jail sentence of 365 days or less at county? We offer the following amenities: Work Release/Flat Screen TVs/Computer/Media RM/Clean Facility/New Beds," said the facility's ad in *LA Weekly*.[6]

Seal Beach charges $150 for the first night, $100 for each night thereafter and $20 a day extra for work release.[7]

Other departments tout smaller pay-to-stay programs on their websites. The Burbank Police Department offers its "relatively small, clean, new and local jail" for $100 a night and boasts a photo of a spotless cell corridor. To qualify, inmates must test negative for TB and have medical insurance.[8] Conditions in the pay-to-stay jails resemble a modest motel with basic furnishings.

Some Southern California residents even choose to serve sentences imposed in other states in California so they can be closer to home. Police departments typically restrict participants to first-time offenders convicted of nonviolent

Florida's generous laws to live comfortably in beachfront mansions despite owing millions of dollars to out-of-state creditors.[64]

In 2005, Congress passed the Bankruptcy Abuse Prevention and Consumer Protection Act, largely due to concern over the abuse of bankruptcy filings to avoid paying debt and lobbying by the credit card industry.

The new law raised the bar on individual bankruptcy filings by mandating that wealthier people file for Chapter 13 reorganization and pay off debts over a five-year period, and made all household income subject to confiscation by creditors, not just that of the indebted party. The debtor also must complete a personal financial management course.[65]

and minor crimes. Other occupants are people, including law enforcement informants, whose safety may be threatened in the county jail.

The programs have encountered problems through the years. Seal Beach closed its jail for eight months in 2007 and 2008 after three employees of the private company that ran the facility, Texas-based Corrections Systems, were charged with stealing a Sony PlayStation from an inmate and another was charged with conspiring with a former inmate to kill a Newport Beach couple and steal their yacht.[9]

Some crime victims argue that deluxe detention does not sufficiently punish criminals. Chiho Hayakawa, whose daughter died in a 2010 drunk-driving crash, said she was shocked to learn that the man responsible served his two-year jail sentence in a cell that cost him $72,000, and said he had paid his way out of a harsher punishment.[10]

Police emphasize that while inmates may receive certain privileges, such as being able to bring and store food from home in refrigerators and watch satellite TV from couches in lounge areas, they are still in jail. Inmates sleep in locked cells, their movements in the jail are restricted and lights are out at 10 p.m.

"We cater to good people who make bad choices," said Seal Beach Detention Center Sgt. Steve Bowles.[11]

— *Christina Hoag*

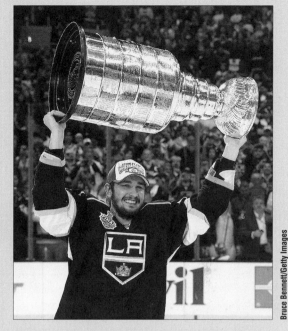

Slava Voynov of the Los Angeles Kings spent time in Seal Beach's luxury "pay-to-stay" detention center after pleading no contest to a misdemeanor domestic violence charge.

[1] Veronica Rocha, "Glendale jail finds many inmates willing to pay its $85-a-day rate," *Los Angeles Times*, April 7, 2013, http://tinyurl.com/z45ym4l.

[2] *Ibid.*

[3] Mary Harris and Hetty Chang, "Pay-to-Stay Jail Programs Offer Upgraded Cells For a Price," NBC Los Angeles, May 1, 2015, http://tinyurl.com/oa2nxvk.

[4] Matt Clarke, "Celebrity Justice: Prison Lifestyles of the Rich and Famous," *Prison Legal News*, July 15, 2010, http://tinyurl.com/hfr5t4a.

[5] Chris Peters, "Report: Kings D Slava Voynov serving time in 'pay-to-stay' jail," CBS Sports, July 29, 2015, http://tinyurl.com/z6pn4bk.

[6] Ron Rohky, "Inmates Can Pay for Luxury Cells in Seal Beach Jail," NBC Los Angeles, Aug. 1 2013, http://tinyurl.com/hvukujo.

[7] Alyssa Duranty, "Would you pay to stay here? For some who can shell out, jail comes with satellite TV, a gym, yoga," *The Orange County Register*, March 12, 2015, http://tinyurl.com/jh6vvbo.

[8] "Pay to Stay Program," Burbank Police, undated, http://tinyurl.com/zux9kyt.

[9] Scott Martindale, "Seal Beach Jail Shut Down," *The Orange County Register*, June 2, 2007, http://tinyurl.com/hqmbx5q; Jorge Barrientos, "Seal Beach Jail re-opens after 8-month shutdown," *The Orange County Register*, Feb. 28, 2008, http://tinyurl.com/jns84h8.

[10] Harris and Chang, *op. cit.*

[11] Alyssa Duranty, "Would you pay to stay here? For some who can shell out, jail comes with satellite TV, a gym, yoga," *The Orange County Register*, May 2, 2015, http://tinyurl.com/jh6vvbo.

Criminal Justice Debt

While bankruptcy laws governed the discharge of commercial debt, another type of debt emerged in the latter half of the 20th century called criminal justice debt, or legal financial obligations resulting from the failure to pay fines levied as punishment for crimes and related court costs.

In 1965 California was one of the first states to impose legal financial obligations by ordering defendants to reimburse victims for losses they suffered due to crime.[66] Subsequently, two cases from Illinois and Texas involving people jailed because they could not pay fines and court costs ended up in the U.S. Supreme Court. In 1970 and 1971, the justices ruled that a maximum

Community Courts Offer Services to Offenders

"This is a more rational, humane and effective response."

Every Monday, a mission of justice takes its place among the bibliophiles at the Spokane, Wash., Public Library. A conference room becomes a courtroom with a table, flanked by a couple of flags, serving as the judge's bench. In an adjoining room, defendants awaiting hearings can sign up for drug counseling, help finding housing and other social services, and get a free lunch.[1]

The program is a so-called community court, designed to handle nonviolent misdemeanors — such as vandalism, trespassing, failure to pay a debt or public intoxication — by holding offenders accountable through community service in lieu of fines or jail sentences. At the same time, the court offers aid to reduce the likelihood of recidivism.

"It's awesome. It's been a blessing for me," said Aubrey Schults of Spokane, who was referred to community court after being jailed on failure-to-appear warrants stemming from a charge of not paying a $10 taxi fare. Through community court, she received housing, was eligible to have missing teeth replaced and avoided a 60-day jail term by completing drug and mental health treatment.[2]

"There's a tendency for judges to resort to short-term jail or fines for minor offending," says Greg Berman, director of the Center for Court Innovation, a New York City-based nonprofit at the forefront of the community court movement. "This is a more rational, humane and effective response."

Community courts, which started in New York City in 1993, have gained traction in recent years as cities have sought to find cheaper alternatives to overcrowded jails and relieve clogged court systems.[3] Such alternatives often rely on the theory of "restorative justice," a nonpunitive system that promotes conciliation and mediation over harsh punishment.[4]

Ten cities — including Chicago, Cleveland, Dallas, Honolulu and Las Vegas — each received a $200,000 grant this year from the U.S. Department of Justice's Bureau of Justice Assistance to start or expand community court programs.[5]

Judges have long had the option of using community service for low-level lawbreaking, but courts have underutilized it because it can prove problematic for some offenders due to child care needs, transportation costs and lost wages, notes Nusrat Choudhury, a staff attorney with the American Civil Liberties Union's Racial Justice Program. "It can become long and onerous."

Community service programs also cost money to run and — unlike fines — do not generate revenue, says Chris Albin-Lackey, a senior researcher with

prison term could not be extended because the defendant had not paid court costs or fines. The justices also said judges cannot jail indigents in lieu of paying fines but that they can devise alternative punishment. In both cases, the court concluded that the states had violated the 14th Amendment guarantee of equal protection under the law.[67]

In 1983, the U.S. Supreme Court expanded its rulings on debt penalization. In *Bearden v. Georgia*, the justices ruled that revoking probation to send an indigent person to jail for failure to pay fines also violated the 14th Amendment. The court said judges must determine whether the nonpayment was "willful" by considering the defendant's ability to pay. The ruling left it up to the lower courts to decide how to determine the ability to pay.[68]

The decision came just as the states and Congress were adopting get-tough-on-crime policies in response to soaring drug trafficking and use. The crackdown, in turn, raised the costs of running increasingly burdened courthouses, jails, prisons and probation and parole programs. From 1980 to 2010, criminal justice costs skyrocketed from $6 billion to $67 billion, according to the U.S. Bureau of Justice.[69]

Human Rights Watch in New York City. "There's also the issue of how do you credit the value of someone's time," he says.

Often the community service assignment has nothing to do with the offense, and offenders are required to start service 30 days from sentencing — conditions critics say lessen the impact of accountability.

Community courts seek to make community service more meaningful as a punishment, Berman says, with judges trying to link the offense and the assignment: For example, if someone urinates in a public park, he or she is ordered to pick up litter in the park where the offense occurred. Offenders also must start the service within 24 hours of a judge's order. The idea is to emphasize the link between the transgression and the penalty, as well as the sense of collective benefit, Berman notes.

"It's about treating the offenders as a member of the community, not as an outcast," he says.

Community courts have proven particularly successful in processing cases speedily, getting people to complete their sentences and helping localities clean up problem-plagued areas. In the five years after New York City's Midtown Community Court opened, 75 percent of defendants completed their sentences, compared with 50 percent for traditional court, and the Midtown neighborhood saw 24 percent fewer arrests for illegal street peddling and 56 percent fewer prostitution arrests.[6]

But community courts have been less successful in reducing recidivism rates, which are either equal to or slightly less than in traditional courts, according to a 2011 Center for Court Innovation study.[7] Even so, proponents say, community courts help hold people accountable for their transgressions while not sticking them with criminal records for petty offenses. In San Diego, a community court program allows offenders to clear their record if they complete two days of community service and pay a $120 administrative fee.[8]

One program participant, Leonel Lopez, spent two days planting trees to clear his arrest for public intoxication, for which he otherwise would have had to pay a hefty fine and been stuck with a criminal record.

"This is the better path to take," he said.[9]

— Christina Hoag

[1] Shawn Vestal, "Spokane Community Court offers chronic offenders another chance," *The Spokesman*, March 23, 2014, http://tinyurl.com/zl7vym7.

[2] *Ibid.*

[3] "Community Courts," Center for Court Innovation, undated, http://tinyurl.com/zrpmhak.

[4] See Christina L. Lyons, "Restorative Justice," *CQ Researcher*, Feb. 5, 2016, pp. 121-144.

[5] "Bureau of Justice Assistance Awards $2 Million to Implement and Enhance Community Courts," U.S. Dept. of Justice, April 13, 2016, http://tinyurl.com/hmrm7ln.

[6] Brian Gilbert and Katy Welter, "Community Courts in Cook County," Chicago Appleseed Fund for Justice, February 2013, http://tinyurl.com/jusrs7w.

[7] *Ibid.*

[8] David Garrick, "'Community court' expanding," *The San Diego Union-Tribune*, April 15, 2015, http://tinyurl.com/hcdcdmz.

[9] *Ibid.*

Faced with rising costs, cities started turning to offenders to pay for administering the justice system by raising fees and fines and broadening the scope of such fees to include a variety of services previously funded by the state. In 1984, Michigan passed the nation's first law allowing inmates to be charged for incarceration costs, and by 1990, offender fees were paying more than 50 percent of the costs of Texas' probation agencies.[70]

In 1991, 25 percent of prison inmates said they owed court-imposed costs, restitution to victims, fines and fees, according to a U.S. Department of Justice survey. In 2004, when the last such survey was taken, 66 percent of inmates owed the system money.[71]

The practice continued to grow and expanded sharply after the 2007-09 recession, triggered by a housing crisis caused by widespread mortgage defaults. Local tax revenues plunged, leaving governments more strapped for cash than ever. After governments began cutting funds for judicial administration, cities and counties started raising fees and fines on defendants, including for room and board in jails and public defender services.

"The rise seems to correspond with a decrease in funding since the economic recession," says the ACLU's Choudhury.

The practice ran amok in some cities.

In 2015, in the wake of the riots the previous summer in Ferguson, Mo., the U.S. Department of Justice released a scathing report detailing how the city targeted its citizens for tickets so it could levy fines and fees to fund its budget, and how local judges threatened people with jail if they did not pay up. In 2013, the Ferguson Municipal Court issued 32,975 arrest warrants for non-violent offenses, mostly driving infractions, in a city of 21,000 people.[72] In one case, a police officer wrote 14 tickets stemming from a single traffic stop.[73] Ferguson also showed how fees and fines affect races disproportionately. The city's population is 67 percent African-American, but 86 percent of drivers pulled over by police in 2013 were black.[74]

The report sparked public outrage and increased attention on how widespread practices had become across the country. Civil rights organizations have filed numerous lawsuits and succeeded in overturning the practices in some jurisdictions, but some states, including Michigan, have passed laws permitting them.

CURRENT SITUATION
Reform Gains Steam

Instead of making headlines for jailing indigent people for failing to pay court fines and fees, Biloxi, Miss., wants to be known as a groundbreaker for its procedures for handling poor offenders, laid out in March to settle an ACLU lawsuit.[75]

"As soon as the suit was filed we . . . said, 'Let's take this as an opportunity to do the right thing, work together on model procedures,' " said Biloxi City Attorney Gerald Blessey. "We get this worked out and other cities can use it."[76] The city has agreed to hold ability-to-pay hearings; provide a public defender for poor defendants, who will receive a card notifying them of options such as community service; and discontinue the use of private probation companies and additional fees for payment plans.[77]

Municipal courts elsewhere also are changing their practices as a result of civil rights lawsuits. In May, Colorado Springs, Colo., agreed — as part of damages in

connection with an ACLU suit — to stop jailing poor people for unpaid fines, and said it would pay $125 for each day spent in jail by about 800 people, who were found by an ACLU investigation to be too poor to pay their fines.[78]

In response to another ACLU suit and one filed by defense attorney, Troy Hendricks of DeKalb County, Ga., in January abolished its Recorder's Court, which meted out excessive traffic fines and fees and jailed people for nonpayment. Now offenders have six weeks to pay off fines, which have been lowered, and can work off fines through community service at a rate of $8 an hour. The county also discontinued its use of private probation companies.[79]

"When lawsuits are filed, judges are backing off," says West of the Southern Poverty Law Center. "It is so unconstitutional, and the case law is pretty clear."

The Justice Department is raising awareness about the unconstitutionality of jailing people for inability to pay. Such practices "can cast doubt on the impartiality of the tribunal and erode trust between local governments and their constituents," said the memo to the nation's presiding judges, sent from the department's Civil Rights Division.[80] The department also held a two-day symposium on fines, fees and bail in December.

Meanwhile, two national court organizations — the Conference of Chief Justices, comprising top judges from each state, and the Conference of State Court Administrators, which represents court management — formed a panel in February to investigate the issue and recommend solutions.[81] The National Task Force on Fines, Fees and Bail Practices began meeting in March.[82]

Still, the question of how to pay for reforms remains a key issue, as does determining what constitutes appropriate punishment. Thus, wide-scale change faces an uphill struggle. In Biloxi, the new procedures, which include hiring a full-time public defender to represent the indigent in ability-to-pay hearings and a court clerk to collect fines, will cost an estimated $350,000 annually.[83] Georgia's DeKalb County (Decatur and part of Atlanta) will lose about $7 million a year after lowering fines and abolishing fees.[84]

In several state legislatures, local officials are contesting various bills that seek to restrict fines, fees and

Should municipal courts face limits on fines and fees?

YES
Eric Schmitt
Missouri State Senator, Republican Nominee for Missouri Treasurer

Written for *CQ Researcher*, September 2016

NO
Meghan Dollar
Legislative and Policy Advocate, Colorado Municipal League

Written for *CQ Researcher*, September 2016

For years, anger and distrust have percolated across many Missouri communities, some of which led to the unrest that erupted two years ago in Ferguson. One of the root causes is that many municipal governments no longer exist to serve their citizens. They instead view residents only as ATMs to fund boondoggles. Officials also have abused police forces by forcing them to write specific numbers of traffic tickets and meet quotas for fines to generate revenue.

To protect Missourians from municipal government abuses, I've advanced historic social justice reforms by changing the way local governments interact with citizens. In 2015, I led the effort in passing Senate Bill 5, which limits the amount of revenue cities can raise from traffic-ticket fines. Many cities in St. Louis County were funding more than half of their annual budgets with ticket money. These "taxation by citation" schemes disproportionately hurt poor residents.

Our reform also requires municipal courts to maintain certain procedures, in which the main goal is to eliminate debtors' prisons and give residents a sense of accountability from the courts. Municipal courts no longer can jail people for minor traffic violations and must offer alternative-payment plans and community service options.

Unconscionably, some local bureaucrats are challenging Senate Bill 5 to keep their taxation-by-citation schemes alive. Moreover, these officials are using tax dollars generated from these schemes to pay their legal bills. I'm hopeful that the Missouri Supreme Court will uphold our reform.

This year, I sponsored Senate Bill 572, which further reforms municipal court operations, updates standards and outlines municipal disincorporation procedures should they become necessary. To ensure that bureaucrats are not using voluminous ordinance books to find new ways to take money from residents, we added other ordinance violations to the discussion.

We also passed Senate Bill 765 prohibiting abusive traffic ticket quotas. The mayor of Edmundson became the unwitting poster bureaucrat for our reform: He brazenly "suggested" in a letter to officers that they write more tickets to raise revenue for the city and preserve their salaries. The letter was enclosed with their paychecks.

All of these reforms will help restore trust between residents and local governments and law enforcement. We must continue to build trust. These social justice reforms are helping to jumpstart that process.

In Colorado, legislation was enacted recently that eliminates a municipal court's ability to jail someone for failing to appear in court to pay a fine or tell a judge why he or she cannot pay. The Colorado Municipal League opposed this legislation on behalf of the 175 cities with municipal courts. Our biggest concern was that the legislation perpetuates a false premise that municipal courts jail the poor without taking into account someone's ability to pay a fine.

Municipal judges have no interest in jailing the poor and disadvantaged when the appropriate sentence is a fine or a deferred sentence for first-time offenders. In fact, municipal judges encourage defendants to set up payment plans, take time to find employment, get necessary treatment or do what needs to be done to overcome the obstacles to payment. If a person cannot pay, courts regularly give alternative sentences such as community service.

Now that this legislation has become law, municipal courts are prohibited from issuing warrants when defendants fail to appear in court for a hearing on their ability to pay an outstanding judgment. Therefore, the law makes municipal court fines unenforceable. Municipalities are concerned that defendants will pay fines only if they voluntarily appear at their hearings.

Under the new law, the only remedy allowed for a court to compel payment is the contempt-of-court process. The Municipal League and its members have concerns about this, mainly because it assumes that courts want to impose a jail sentence for failure to pay a fine.

Before this legislation, the contempt procedure was little used because in cases where defendants have the ability to pay, the courts wanted to compel payment rather than go through a procedure that allows jail time. Our municipal courts believe that a potential 90-day sentence is inappropriate in cases where the offense is minor or a person has no criminal history.

Municipal courts vacated thousands of arrest warrants in response to the new law. The Colorado Municipal League and our members do not expect this to be the last salvo launched at municipal courts. Organizations such as the American Civil Liberties Union may still initiate new legislation to reduce fines and perhaps eliminate jail altogether. But we will continue to vigorously oppose state intrusions into the lawful operations of municipal courts.

Ilya S. Savenok/Getty Images

Reality TV star Beth Chapman, president of the Professional Bail Agents Association, canceled her popular CMT television show about chasing bail jumpers so she could devote more time to fighting what she calls "social justice lackeys," whose efforts to change the bail system are designed, she contends, "to make it easier for the bad guys to get out of jail."

jail sentences because their municipalities would lose revenue. In Missouri, 12 cities sued the state over a 2015 court-reform law, which stemmed from the Ferguson riots that exposed city officials' discriminatory ticketing and fining practices. The law had capped the amount of revenue St. Louis County municipalities can receive from fines and fees at 12.5 percent of their annual budgets and other municipalities, 20 percent.[85]

One of the plaintiffs, Mayor Viola Murphy of Cool Valley, said municipal revenue plunged after the law was enacted, and the town did not have enough money to apply for a matching grant for new sidewalks.[86] The cities won in March, when a Cole County Circuit judge struck down part of the law, ruling that it violated local control rules.[87] State Attorney General Chris Koster vowed to appeal the decision.[88]

Civil rights advocates say the financial ramifications of reform are proving to be a huge hurdle around the country. "So many local courts rely on fines and fees," says Dolan of the Institute for Policy Studies. "We've seen such a reluctance to give it up."

Restricting municipal courts from imposing jail time on scofflaws — indigent or otherwise — is still under debate. Some say ignoring a court summons must have consequences.

"If you get a speeding ticket or whatever, a minor infraction, and you don't appear in court, there doesn't appear to me to be any penalty for that, so why would you ever appear in court?" asked Missouri Republican state Sen. Jay Wasson.[89]

Bail Reform

As with fines and fees, bail reform is gathering steam through lawsuits.

Since January 2015, Equal Justice Under Law, a Washington, D.C.-based organization that advocates pretrial supervision over cash bail, has filed 17 lawsuits to restrict money bail in cities in eight states. The group has recently taken on large jurisdictions: It sued San Francisco last October and Harris County, Texas, which includes Houston, in May.[90]

Harris County has already begun making changes, including revamping a risk assessment test that determines whether defendants are likely to commit a crime if released. It also has hired seven additional pretrial supervisors to oversee released defendants and is implementing a pilot program to provide attorneys for defendants at bail hearings.[91]

The onslaught of lawsuits has galvanized the commercial bail industry. In January, the president of the Professional Bail Agents Association, reality TV star Beth Chapman, created media buzz when she showed up at a court hearing on an Equal Justice Under Law lawsuit against San Francisco.[92] Chapman this year canceled her popular CMT television show "Dog and Beth: On the Hunt," which features her husband, son and herself pursuing bail jumpers, so she could devote more time to fighting "social justice lackeys," whose "only goal," she said, "is to make it easier for the bad guys to get out of jail."[93]

The California Bail Agents Association has intervened in the San Francisco case, while the American Bail Coalition has retained national litigation lawyers to help counter the suits, according to a statement.[94] Meanwhile, Democratic California state Assemblyman Rob Bonta said he plans to introduce a bill to reform the state's cash bail system in December.[95]

However, industry leaders note, no federal court has ruled yet on reformists' key legal argument that bail is unconstitutional. That may come soon: The city of Calhoun, Ga., has appealed to the 11th Circuit Court of Appeals a lower-court ruling upholding the argument that money bail violates the 14th Amendment.[96]

Fanno Burdeen of the PreTrial Justice Institute says despite the industry's efforts public sentiment against money bail is growing, with New Jersey joining Kentucky, Oregon, Illinois, Wisconsin and Washington, D.C., in abolishing cash bail. "We're reaching a tipping point," she says.

Reforms to both bail and fee assessments are pending in Congress, but their progress has been limited due to lobbying by the bail industry and the lack of bipartisan support. In January, Rep. Mark Takano, a California Democrat, introduced the End to Debtors' Prisons Act of 2016, which would cut off federal justice grants to jurisdictions that contract with private probation companies. The bill has five Democratic co-sponsors but no Republicans have signed on.[97]

The following month, another California Democrat, Rep. Ted W. Lieu, introduced the No Money Bail Act of 2016, which would prohibit cash bail in the federal court system and make states ineligible for Justice Department grants if they are still using cash bail three years after the law is enacted.[98] The American Bail Coalition, which has been lobbying against the bill, says the measure has stalled in the House Judiciary Committee.[99]

OUTLOOK
'Real Opportunity'

Activists agree that getting communities to stop using fees and fines to generate revenue will hinge on getting states to properly fund local criminal justice systems. And that, in turn, will necessitate a turnaround in public and legislative opinion.

"It's a political problem that will require a political solution," says Albin-Lackey of Human Rights Watch. "As long as you have governments that are not willing to raise money from taxation, you'll have fines and fees."

But the ongoing debate on the larger issues of fairness in sentencing practices, mass incarceration and general criminal justice administration bodes well for reforming the fees and fines system, he adds. "It's a moment of real opportunity," Albin-Lackey says. "There's a real focus on these issues."

Civil rights and legal advocacy organizations say they plan to continue suing jurisdictions in hopes that other places will reform practices voluntarily to avoid costly lawsuits and negative publicity. "Nobody wants to be known as making money off poor people," says Eisen of the Brennan Center.

Successful reforms being implemented by jurisdictions such as Biloxi will serve as models, they say. "Lawsuits are triggering comprehensive reform," says the ACLU's Choudhury.

Some activists say they are encouraged that the Obama Justice Department has taken a leadership role on the issue, and that court administrators have formed a task force to study practices. The activists note, however, that while both entities can make recommendations, neither has enforcement power over states. The department's key role is to educate local officials and judges who may be unaware of the constitutional issues and legal precedents surrounding debt imprisonment, experts say, which could spur voluntary reforms.

"Everyone wants to do the right thing," says Eisen.

However, some say it could take another Supreme Court ruling — perhaps outlawing fees for criminal justice services such as jail cells and the like — to force more-recalcitrant governments to change practices. The populist argument that offenders should fund the criminal justice system because they are the ones who use it is persuasive for many taxpayers and legislators.

Moreover, the people most affected by criminal justice debt tend to be those disenfranchised by the system at-large with few resources to contest sentences. The poor also lack access to policymakers.

"The people most afflicted by unfair laws, fees and fines are mostly poor, white and black . . . and have no political clout," says Jamie Fellner, a senior adviser at Human Rights Watch. Thus, many jurisdictions are reluctant to give up a ready and politically expedient source of revenue, experts note.

Without significant reform, however, advocates warn that the U.S. criminal justice system is increasingly turning into a two-tier system — one for those with means and one without.

"Wealth determines whether you go free or not," says Fellner.

NOTES

1. Joseph Shapiro, "Supreme Court Ruling Not Enough to Prevent Debtors' Prisons," NPR, May 21, 2014, http://tinyurl.com/l478dol.

2. "Economic Perspectives on Incarceration and the Criminal Justice System," Executive Office of the President of the United States, April 2016, p. 7, http://tinyurl.com/ze3cq5f.

3. Joseph Shapiro, "As Court Fees Rise, The Poor Are Paying The Price," NPR, May 19, 2014, http://tinyurl.com/ll7wk4p.

4. "Fines, Fees and Bail," Council of Economic Advisors Issue Brief, December 2015, p. 3, http://tinyurl.com/h7hahpe.

5. Shapiro, "As Court Fees Rise," *op. cit.*

6. "Economic Perspectives on Incarceration," *op. cit.*

7. "Investigation of the Ferguson Police Department," Civil Rights Division, U.S. Department of Justice, March 5, 2016, http://tinyurl.com/jpk4bjb.

8. *Ibid.*, p. 4.

9. *Williams v. Illinois*, 399 (U.S.) 235 (1970), http://tinyurl.com/gr8owma; *Tate v. Short* 401 (U.S.) 395 (1971), http://tinyurl.com/j5223d7; *Bearden v. Georgia*, 461 U.S., 660 (1983), http://tinyurl.com/hvfx9nc.

10. Shapiro, "Supreme Court Ruling Not Enough To Prevent Debtors Prisons," *op. cit.*

11. Bernadette Rabuy and Daniel Kopf, "Detaining the Poor," *Prison Policy*, May 10, 2016, http://tinyurl.com/zwzxspz.

12. Clifford Ward, "Failure to be bonded out led Sandra Bland to suicide, jail officials allege," *Chicago Tribune*, Nov. 12, 2015, http://tinyurl.com/zugrau8.

13. Vanita Gupta and Lisa Foster, "Dear Colleague Letter," U.S. Department of Justice, March 14, 2016, http://tinyurl.com/z2pyslc.

14. Katie Wilcox, "A Handful of Colorado Towns Rely Heavily on Money from Traffic Tickets," Rocky Mountain PBS News, April 29, 2015, http://tinyurl.com/gu7bhh9.

15. Shapiro, "Supreme Court Ruling Not Enough to Prevent Debtors' Prisons," *op. cit.*

16. Christopher N. Osher, "Colorado lawmakers look to close debtors' prison loophole," *The Denver Post*, April 26, 2016, http://tinyurl.com/jnkxsop.

17. Anne LaBella, "Municipal-court bill would bring more problems than solutions," *Springfield News-Leader*, March 16, 2016, http://tinyurl.com/hskkbhq.

18. *Ibid.*

19. Yesenia Robles, "Bill to prohibit jail time for not paying court fines moves forward," *The Denver Post*, April 16, 2014, http://tinyurl.com/h5pdc4v.

20. Tyler Richardson, "ACLU sues Benton County over jail sentences for unpaid court fees," *Tri-City Herald*, Oct. 6, 2015, http://tinyurl.com/zual2py.

21. Gene Johnson, "County settles over jailing people who can't pay court fines," The Associated Press, June 1, 2016, http://tinyurl.com/ho367sm.

22. Justin Wm. Moyer, "Virginia suspends driver's licenses in 'unconstitutional scheme,' class action says," *The Washington Post*, July 12, 2016, http://tinyurl.com/heccefv.

23. Ed White, "Supreme Court to hear dispute over Allegan court costs," *Holland Sentinel*, March 30, 2014, http://tinyurl.com/h7amn5n.

24. Ed White, "Should convicts be forced to pay court operating costs?" *Detroit Free Press*, Dec. 26, 2015, http://tinyurl.com/hlq4u72.

25. *Ibid.*

26. "Alameda County Halts Juvenile Probation Fees," East Bay Community Law Center, April 7, 2016, http://tinyurl.com/j5bev7k.

27. *Ibid.*

28. "Cities across Alabama cancel contracts with private probation company sued by SPLC," NBC News, Aug. 13, 2015, http://tinyurl.com/jxa7eru.

29. *Ibid.*

30. "Fines, Fees and Bail," Council of Economic Advisors Issue Brief, December 2015, p. 6, http://tinyurl.com/h7hahpe.

31. "Southern Poverty Law Center sues Bogalusa city judge," *Bogalusa Daily News*, June 22, 2016, http://tinyurl.com/z3f7vs5.

32. Jesse Wright, "Black makes changes to court procedure in response to SPLC suit," *Bogalusa Daily News*, June 29, 2016, http://tinyurl.com/gs6jj3g.

33. Nick Pinto, "The Bail Trap," *The New York Times Magazine*, Aug. 13, 2015, http://tinyurl.com/ncwcjwf.

34. "Jail Inmates at Midyear 2014," Bureau of Justice Statistics, June 2015, p. 3, http://tinyurl.com/jivbuy.

35. Pinto, *op. cit.*

36. "Community Bail Funds Reclaim Bail Decision Power," Pretrial Justice Institute, Jan. 19, 2016, http://tinyurl.com/j9eo6r8.

37. John DeRosier, "How much will bail reform cost N.J. taxpayers?" *Atlantic City Press*, July 16, 2016, http://tinyurl.com/zxouwx3.

38. Charlotte McPherson, "Pretrial Supervision, Like Detention, Should Be Carefully Limited," Pretrial Justice Institute, July 19, 2016, http://tinyurl.com/hcmvuz9.

39. "The History of Debt Collection," *The Advocate*, July 2015, http://tinyurl.com/hhklnds.

40. Junius P. Rodriguez, "The Historical Encyclopedia of World Slavery, Vol. 1; Vol. 7," ABC-CLIO, 1997, p. 408, http://tinyurl.com/hfgn83p.

41. "The History of Debt Collection," *op. cit.*

42. Rodriguez, *op. cit.*

43. "The History of Debt Collection," *op. cit.*

44. James P. Caher, John M. Caher, "Personal Bankruptcy for Dummies," John H. Wiley & Sons, 2011, p. 11, http://tinyurl.com/hmyaqs3.

45. Paul Knepper and Anja Johansen, eds., *Oxford Handbook of the History of Crime and Criminal Justice* (2016), p. 665.

46. Jason Zweig, "Are Debtors' Prisons Coming Back?" *The Wall Street Journal*, Aug. 28, 2012, http://tinyurl.com/z8w5cbl.

47. "Dickens, Debt and the Marshalsea Prison," History in an Hour, Feb. 7, 2012, http://tinyurl.com/zmjat8y.

48. Zweig, *op. cit.*

49. Jonny Wilkes, "In a nutshell: Debtors' Prisons," *History Extra*, Feb. 10, 2015, http://tinyurl.com/gn6u4p3.

50. Edward J. Cashin, "Trustee Georgia 1732-1752," *Georgia Encyclopedia*, Sept. 2, 2015, http://tinyurl.com/hqqnheg.

51. *Ibid.*

52. Eric Foner and John A. Garraty, eds., "Shays' Rebellion," *The Reader's Companion to American History*, 1991, History.com, http://tinyurl.com/zr7jdg9.

53. Zweig, *op. cit.*

54. Charles Jordan Tabb, "History of Bankruptcy Laws in the United States," University of Illinois College of Law, p. 16, http://tinyurl.com/j2uwqxu.

55. *Ibid.*, p. 18.

56. Tabb, *op. cit.*

57. *Ibid.*

58. "Panic of 1893," United States History, undated, http://tinyurl.com/mq9gbdr.

59. "Bankruptcy Jurisdiction in the Federal Courts," Federal Judicial Center, undated, http://tinyurl.com/jjkgkdx.

60. "The Great Depression," History.com, undated, http://tinyurl.com/d9r5vsf; "Unemployment Statistics during the Great Depression," United States History, undated, http://tinyurl.com/3pr3bg2.

61. Tabb, *op. cit.*, pp. 29-30.

62. *Ibid.*, pp. 35-36.

63. William G. Morris, "It's the Law: Florida Is A Debtor's Haven," Law Offices of William G. Morris, P.A., Nov. 7, 2012, http://tinyurl.com/zhvc2yq.

64. Larry Rohter, "Rich Debtors Finding Shelter Under a Populist Florida Law," *The New York Times*, July 25, 1993, http://tinyurl.com/zd2xygp.

65. Jeanne Sahadi, "President signs bankruptcy bill," CNN, April 20, 2005, http://tinyurl.com/zfrvzwu.

66. Shapiro, "As Court Fees Rise," *op. cit.*

67. Eli Hager, "Debtors' Prisons: Then & Now: FAQ," The Marshall Project, Feb. 24, 2015, http://tinyurl.com/zfodsfq.

68. Hager, *op. cit.*

69. Shapiro, *op. cit.*

70. *Ibid.*

71. *Ibid.*

72. Joseph Shapiro, "In Ferguson, Fines And Fees Fuel Anger," NPR, Aug. 25, 2014, http://tinyurl.com/mk2zpns.

73. Michael Martinez, Alexandra Meeks and Ed Lavandera, "Policing for Profit: How Ferguson's Fines Violated Rights of African-Americans," CNN.com, March 6, 2015, http://tinyurl.com/gsogeds.

74. Shapiro, "In Ferguson, Fines And Fees Fuel Anger," *op. cit.*

75. Caray Grace, "Residents weigh in on settlement reforms," WLOX-TV, March 6, 2015, http://tinyurl.com/hege572.

76. *Ibid.*

77. "Biloxi And ACLU Settle Lawsuit Over Jailing Indigent People," American Civil Liberties Union, March 15, 2016, http://tinyurl.com/hqnkdbt.

78. Joseph Shapiro, "Colorado Springs Will Stop Jailing People Too Poor To Pay Court Fines," NPR, May 5, 2016, http://tinyurl.com/zj4q36h.

79. Mark Niesse, "DeKalb traffic fines decline after court abolished," *Atlanta Journal-Constitution*, Jan. 15, 2016, http://tinyurl.com/jffxdjq.

80. Gupta and Foster, *op. cit.*

81. "Top national state court leadership associations launch National Task Force on Fines, Fees and Bail Practices," National Center for State Courts, Feb. 3, 2016, http://tinyurl.com/jnrx9o5.

82. "Task Force Meets to Identify Challenges, Solutions on Fines, Fees and Bail Practices," National Center for State Courts, March 14, 2016, http://tinyurl.com/guhocbt.

83. Grace, *op. cit.*

84. Niesse, *op. cit.*

85. Jeremy Kohler, "Cities Sue to Block Missouri's Ferguson-Inspired Court Reforms," Tribune News Service, Nov. 23, 2015, http://tinyurl.com/hgzgsvd.

86. *Ibid.*

87. "Supporters of SB 5 plot course after court ruling," *Missouri Times*, March 29, 2016, http://tinyurl.com/hkhc84t.

88. *Ibid.*

89. Marshall Griffin, "Missouri legislature sends municipal court changes to the governor," St. Louis Public Radio, May 7, 2015, http://tinyurl.com/jnavq7n.

90. Megan Flynn, "Group Sues Harris County Over Bail System That Keeps People in Jail Just Because They're Poor," *Houston Press*, May 20, 2016, http://tinyurl.com/hljpofz.

91. *Ibid.*

92. Sukey Lewis, "$2 Billion Bail Bond Industry Threatened by Lawsuit Against San Francisco," KQED News, May 20, 2016, http://tinyurl.com/zwsf2ok.

93. Clayton Wakida, " 'Dog,' Beth Chapman leave CMT to focus on bail reform," WKITV-TV, Feb. 2, 2016, http://tinyurl.com/jjc4q5m.

94. "American Bail Coalition takes an active role in San Francisco and beyond defending the American Bail System & Surety Bail against baseless attacks," *Premiere Bail Bonds*, Jan. 6, 2016, http://tinyurl.com/juzo8tb.

95. Jazmine Ulloa, "Lawmakers discuss reform for California's bail system," *Los Angeles Times*, July 26, 2016, http://tinyurl.com/gtw7xxn.

96. "Fundamental Cracks in the Foundation," American Bail Coalition, June 13, 2016, http://tinyurl.com/h2so6zc.

97. "Rep. Mark Takano Introduces Legislation to Address Injustice in For-Profit Probation Industry," Office of Mark Takano, Jan. 11, 2016, http://tinyurl.com/jl8uekr.

98. "Fact Sheet No Money Bail Act of 2016," U.S. House of Representatives, http://tinyurl.com/zrfo8uh.

99. "Fundamental Cracks in Foundation," *op. cit.*

BIBLIOGRAPHY

Selected Sources

Books

Bayley, Frederic William Naylor, *Scenes and Stories, By a Clergyman in Debt*, Palala Press, 2016.
An English clergyman describes his confinement for debt in a workhouse. Originally published in 1835, this reissued work is considered a classic for its firsthand historical depiction of a debtor's struggles.

Desmond, Matthew, *Evicted: Poverty and Profit in the American City*, Crown, 2016.
A Harvard University sociologist and MacArthur Foundation "genius" grant recipient delves into the forces that keep people poor in urban America and describes how unforeseen expenses such as fines can trap people in an endless cycle of poverty.

Harris, Alexes, *A Pound of Flesh: Monetary Solutions as Permanent Punishment for Poor People*, Russell Sage Foundation, 2015.
A University of Washington sociologist analyzes the rise of monetary sanctions in the criminal justice system and shows how they marginalize the poor, perpetuating racial and economic inequality.

Articles

Anderson, Rick, "Debtors prison a thing of the past? Some places in America still lock up the poor," *Los Angeles Times*, June 8, 2016, http://tinyurl.com/h4y3d2r.
A reporter looks at recent court battles that have ended "pay or stay" practices in numerous cities that jailed poor people for minor offenses because they could not pay fines.

Balko, Radley, "A debtors' prison in Mississippi," *The Washington Post*, Oct. 21, 2015, http://tinyurl.com/grc5654.
A journalist chronicles how the nation's poorest municipalities and counties are the most aggressive in fining residents and increasing poverty in those places.

Benns, Whitney, and Blake Strode, "Debtors' Prison in 21st Century America," *The Atlantic*, Feb. 23, 2016, http://tinyurl.com/gs83pfc.
A reporter (Benns) and a lawyer detail how imprisoning people for debt disproportionately affects poor African-Americans in St. Louis.

Labella, Anne J., "Municipal-court bill would bring more problems than solutions," *Springfield News-Leader*, March 16, 2016, http://tinyurl.com/h3b4j4h.
A Kansas City, Mo., municipal judge opposes a state law that would curtail municipal courts' power to impose fines and issue arrest warrants.

Pinto, Nick, "The Bail Trap," *The New York Times Magazine*, Aug. 13, 2015, http://tinyurl.com/ncwcjwf.
A reporter examines the bail system and how poor defendants' inability to afford bail worsens their situations.

Shapiro, Joseph, "Guilty and Charged," NPR, May 18, 20, 21, 24, 2014, http://tinyurl.com/pj3d24w.
A series of reports in a reporter's yearlong investigation reveals the wide use of court fees charged to criminal defendants, creating a system that targets the poor.

Stillman, Sarah, "Get Out of Jail, Inc.," *The New Yorker*, June 23, 2014, http://tinyurl.com/mrprsva.
A magazine writer examines how the private probation industry profits by keeping people in debt.

Reports and Studies

Albin-Lackey, Chris, "Profiting from Probation: America's 'Offender-Funded' Probation Industry," Human Rights Watch, February 2014, http://tinyurl.com/hnyxhnq.
An international human rights organization describes patterns of abuse and financial hardship inflicted by the "offender-funded" model of privatized probation used in more than 1,000 U.S. courts.

Dolan, Karen, with Jodi L. Carr, "The Poor Get Prison: The Alarming Spread of the Criminalization of Poverty," Institute for Policy Studies, March 2015, http://tinyurl.com/hu7yz4x.
Researchers at a progressive Washington, D.C., think tank discuss how the poor fall into a vicious circle of unpayable fines, fees and interest.

Eisen, Lauren-Brooke, "Charging Inmates Perpetuates Mass Incarceration," New York University School of Law, Brennan Center for Justice, May 21, 2015, http://tinyurl.com/h6yezwj.
A lawyer with a social justice legal center details how charging criminal defendants fees to use the public court system perpetuates racial disparities and incarceration of the poor.

Sobol, Neil L., "Charging the Poor: Criminal Justice Debt & Modern-Day Debtors' Prisons," *Maryland Law Review*, 2016, http://tinyurl.com/jsy3mv3.
A law professor at Texas A&M University proposes alternatives to federal and state laws surrounding the imprisoning of people over debt and fining them for using the criminal court system.

For More Information

American Bail Coalition, 220 N. Main St., Suite 500, Greenville, SC 29601; 855-718-3006; www.americanbail coalition.org. Trade association representing bail bond companies.

American Civil Liberties Union, 125 Broad St., 18th Floor, New York, NY 10004; 212-549-2500; www.aclu.org. Defends individuals' legal rights and freedoms.

American Probation and Parole Association, 1776 Avenue of the States, Lexington, KY 40511; 859-244-8203; www .appa-net.org. Industry association for agencies involved in probation and parole programs.

Brennan Center for Justice, New York University School of Law, 161 Avenue of the Americas, 12th Floor, New York, NY 10013; 646-292-8310; www.brennancenter. org. Nonpartisan institute that seeks to improve judicial fairness.

Human Rights Watch, 350 Fifth Ave., 34th floor, New York, NY 10118; 212-290-4700; www.hrw.org. Nonprofit that monitors human rights in 90 countries.

Institute for Policy Studies, 1301 Connecticut Ave., N.W., Suite 600, Washington, DC 20036; 202-234-9382; www .ips-dc.org. Researches social justice issues.

National Center for State Courts, 300 Newport Ave., Williamsburg, VA 23185; 800-616-6164; www.ncsc.org. Nonprofit focusing on judicial administration issues.

Pretrial Justice Institute, 7361 Calhoun Place, Suite 215, Rockville, MD 20855; 240-477-7152, www.pretrial.org. Nonprofit organization that advocates for safe, fair and effective pretrial policies and practices.

Southern Poverty Law Center, 400 Washington St., Montgomery, AL 36104; 334-956-8200; www.splcenter.org. Nonprofit dedicated to fighting bigotry and social injustice.

6

Populism and Party Politics

Chuck McCutcheon

Donald Trump, campaigning in Macon, Ga., last Nov. 25, demonstrated the reach of populist disgust with traditional politicians, some analysts say, by defeating more than a dozen more experienced rivals to win the GOP presidential nomination. Populist movements also have spread across Europe with the rise of anti-establishment politicians in several countries, punctuated by the United Kingdom's "Brexit" vote in June to leave the European Union.

From *CQ Researcher,*
September 9, 2016.

New Yorker Karen Bruno liked what she heard from Donald Trump. So the self-described evangelical Christian showed up at the Republican presidential candidate's Trump Plaza headquarters to volunteer for his campaign.

"The more he riles up the establishment, the better I like it," Bruno told a TV station. "I think the establishment is in cahoots to bring this country down. . . . I don't know what they're doing."[1]

Bruno's comments reflect what the media and academic researchers describe as populism, in which citizens rise up in frustration and anger against what they see as an entrenched "establishment" of "elites" in government, industry and other institutions that ignores their concerns.

John Baick, a professor of history at Western New England University in Springfield, Mass., defines populism as "a large group of people united in the suspicion that someone, some group — 'elites' is their shorthand — is controlling things to their detriment." Bart Bonikowski, a professor of sociology at Harvard University, says populists "invariably portray the people as the rightful sources of power" and often favor the use of "direct democracy," such as ballot initiatives that let voters bypass legislators to making laws.

Political analysts and academics say Trump demonstrated the reach of populism by defeating more than a dozen more experienced rivals to win the GOP nomination, revealing deep-seated voter disgust with traditional politicians. Former presidential candidate Bernie Sanders tapped into similar voter anger on the left in his unsuccessful battle with Hillary Clinton for the

Manufacturing Jobs on Steep Decline

The United States has lost more than 5 million manufacturing jobs since 2000, a decline that has helped fuel a rise in populist anger, particularly toward undocumented immigrant workers, who Republican presidential nominee Donald Trump says have taken American jobs. He also blames the loss on trade pacts such as the 1994 North American Free Trade Agreement, which lifted trade barriers among the United States, Mexico and Canada.

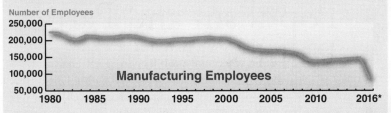

Number of Employees

Manufacturing Employees

* Data through July 2016

Source: "Employment, Hours, and Earnings from the Current Employment Statistics survey (National)," Bureau of Labor Statistics, July 2016, http://tinyurl.com/mgomng9

In the United States, populism has existed in various forms for two centuries. Today's populism, experts say, differs from earlier versions in how politicians such as Trump and Sanders have amplified some of its traditions — particularly appealing to a sense of "us against them" — by relying heavily on Twitter, Facebook and other forms of social media and using combative rhetoric that has drawn extensive coverage from traditional news media. As a result, they have not needed to rely on political parties or large corporate campaign contributions to pay for advertising.

"Media can no longer be treated as a side issue when it comes to understanding contemporary populism," Benjamin Moffitt, a research fellow in political science at Sweden's University of Stockholm, said in his new book, *The Global Rise of Populism*. "Media touches upon almost all aspects of modern life . . . [and] populism is particularly attuned to the contours of the contemporary mediatized landscape."[6]

The pervasiveness of social media "has changed populism as it has changed social movements in general," agrees Nancy Wadsworth, a University of Denver professor of political science. "It's provided a whole new set of resources for connectivity that are way more accessible than they used to be."

The populist-driven antagonism and hostility pervading social and news media are coarsening American culture, many experts say. Populist leaders often play on people's fear and anger by demonizing their opponents and creating and perpetuating a sense of crisis, they say.[7] Wadsworth calls this "toxic populism."

"Populism is more an emotion than it is an ideology. And that emotion is anger," said Michael Kimmel, a professor of sociology at New York's Stony Brook University and author of *Angry White Men: American Masculinity at the End of an Era*.[8]

But populism also can take a less-noxious form as a purely political style. So-called establishment politicians often make populist-sounding remarks to broaden

Democratic nomination. So-called populist movements also have spread across Europe with the rise of anti-establishment politicians in several countries and the United Kingdom's "Brexit" vote in June to leave the 28-nation European Union.[2]

But the meaning of populism has become increasingly elastic. It has been invoked to describe politicians who seek to unite disparate groups as well as those who pit one group against another. And it is applied as a catchall in various contexts beyond politics, including business (the ride-hailing service Uber) and music (country artists and rock groups such as Pearl Jam that want promoters to lower ticket prices for the groups' concerts).[3]

Populism today also characterizes almost any impassioned grassroots movement, ranging from the limited-government, anti-tax tea party that rose up against President Barack Obama to the left-wing Occupy Wall Street groups challenging the financial industry to the Black Lives Matter protests of police shootings of African-Americans.[4]

"It is broadly used in scholarly, media and public affairs circles despite the fact that it has no widely accepted theoretical meaning," said Diego von Vacano, a professor of political science at Texas A&M University.[5]

their appeal. In 2000, Democratic Vice President Al Gore campaigned for the presidency by declaring of Republicans, "They're for the powerful; we're for the people."[9]

Similarly, Clinton, who has drawn criticism on the left for accepting large campaign donations from Wall Street and other corporations, has lambasted "special interests" that prevent citizens from making bigger financial gains. "The economy is rigged in favor of those at the top," she said.[10] The media also have applied the "populist" label to Clinton for her promises to tax multimillionaires and U.S. companies that attempt to relocate overseas.[11]

And some establishment Republicans who ran against Trump, including former Florida Gov. Jeb Bush, also castigated lobbyists and others in ways the media characterized as populist.[12]

Political scientists say populism often flourishes when wealth is concentrated at the top of society, as it is today.[13] Previous populist movements forced a realignment of political parties, with major shifts of voters from one party to the other. Some experts say that already has occurred: Most socially conservative Democrats already have switched to the Republican Party, while few socially liberal, well-off Republicans are left to move to the Democratic camp.

"The party coalitions are pretty well defined," said Michael Lind, a co-founder of New America, a center-left think tank in Washington. "The civil wars within the parties [are] about defining the party platforms more than the party coalitions."[14]

The left- and right-wing versions of American populism have different orientations. Left-leaning populists seek to check the power of banks and big business. To that end, about 800 activists representing several left-wing organizations held a "Populism2015" conference last year in Washington to discuss how their groups can coordinate through social media and other means to blunt the influence of corporations seeking to limit the reach of government.

"As progressives reclaiming the mantle of 'populism,' our alliance is tapping a deep American tradition," said Isaiah J. Poole, one of the organizers, who is editor of OurFuture.org, a liberal website for the Campaign for America's Future. "We see the government as an instrument for the public good."[15]

Populists on the political right, meanwhile, direct their frustration at the government, arguing it favors undeserving groups over ordinary Americans — often minorities or foreigners, but also, like populists on the left, lobbyists and big business. They also blame GOP leaders for failing to stop Obama from being elected and re-elected.

Trump shares similarities with past populist presidential candidates, say experts studying populism, including: Alabama Gov. George Wallace, an outspoken segregationist who ran as an independent in 1968; conservative political commentator Patrick Buchanan, who sought the GOP nomination in 1992 and 1996 (and waged a third-party candidacy in 2000) pledging to curb immigration and free trade; and business tycoon H. Ross Perot, who ran as an independent in 1992 calling for drastic cuts in Washington spending and lobbying.

Some of Trump's critics, such as Avik Roy, an aide to several former GOP presidential candidates, said Trump's success shows his supporters are driven by "white nationalism," or deep resentment of other races and cultures.[16] But Trump supporters themselves say they care more about his articulation of their anger at being left behind economically and socially than about inflammatory statements for which he has drawn criticism.

"I live in Trump's America, where working-class whites are dying from despair. . . . They're angry at Washington and Wall Street, at big corporations and big government," said Michael Cooper Jr., a lawyer in North Wilkesboro, N.C., where manufacturing jobs have plummeted over the last two decades. "When you're earning $32,000 a year and haven't had a decent vacation in over a decade . . . you just want to win again, whoever the victim, whatever the price."[17]

Not all observers consider Trump a populist, citing his proposed breaks for upper-income Americans.[18] They also say he appears more interested in promoting himself than in representing a broad swath of voters.

"Trump is more anti-establishment than he is pro-people, as he is mainly pro-Trump," said Cas Mudde, a University of Georgia professor of international affairs.[19]

On the other hand, Sanders' campaign is widely seen as within the traditions of left-wing populism. A self-described "democratic socialist," the Vermont senator called for a political "revolution" aimed at ending what

Americans' Confidence in Institutions Falls

Fewer than a third of Americans have strong confidence in the nation's major political, financial, religious and news media institutions. The low level is reflected in populist support for anti-establishment candidates such as Republican presidential nominee Donald Trump and Democrat Bernie Sanders, who lost his party's bid for the nomination to Hillary Clinton. Both Trump and Sanders have sharply criticized mainline institutions — the news media by Trump, and banks by Sanders.

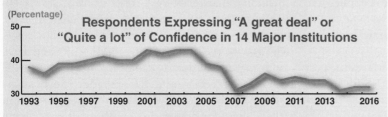

(Percentage)

Respondents Expressing "A great deal" or "Quite a lot" of Confidence in 14 Major Institutions

Source: "Average Confidence Rating for All Institutions, 1993-2016," Gallup, June 13, 2016, http://tinyurl.com/hd3afho

he described as both major political parties' unhealthy reliance on large campaign donors.

Sanders backer Zack Smith of New Hampshire cited Sanders' challenge to the banking industry to reduce consumer transaction fees on debit cards. "It's the average person's issues he brings up," Smith said.[20]

Gun rights long have been a populist issue on the right, while recent mass shootings have helped to spur left-wing grassroots efforts to address gun control. Petition drives in California, Nevada, Maine and Washington state led to the placement of gun-control measures on November ballots.[21]

As politicians, academics and commentators debate populism and its role in the presidential election, here are some questions being debated:

Does populism undermine confidence in government?

Critics of populism say its reflexive mistrust of the Democratic and Republican parties erodes confidence in government institutions and the political process. They say populists reject the necessary checks and balances of government in favor of unquestioned executive power while also rejecting their opponents' legitimacy. "Anyone with a different view speaks for 'special interests,' i.e., the elite," said the University of Georgia's Mudde.[22]

But supporters of populism counter that it has opened the political system to new people and ideas.

Americans have become less attached to the two major political parties in recent years, with the percentage of people identifying as independents rising, according to the Pew Research Center, a nonpartisan polling and research institution in Washington.[23] Meanwhile, the parties have grown more partisan: Pew found that "Republicans and Democrats now have more negative views of the opposing party than at any point in nearly a quarter century."[24]

That situation, many political analysts say, has created an opening for widespread rejection of both parties. "Politics is polarized, and a full-throated, angry populism seems to be burning all of the oxygen in the 2016 race," wrote William Daley, a former Obama chief of staff who is now on the board at the centrist think tank Third Way.[25]

Experts describe the tea party movement, a loose confederation of conservative groups calling for strict adherence to their interpretation of the Constitution, as a form of populism directed at challenging Obama.[26] Historian Robert Kagan, an adviser to Republican and Democratic politicians, said Obama's critics sought to persuade voters during his presidency "that government, institutions, political traditions, party leadership and even parties themselves were things to be overthrown, evaded, ignored, insulted [and] laughed at."[27]

Many observers across the political spectrum say Trump's fiery populist appeals to blue-collar whites pose risks for the Republican Party, which has been seeking to recruit more Latinos and other ethnic and minority groups as the country grows more diverse.[28]

However, some political observers say voters' disdain for the Democratic Party also has stoked populism. Arthur Brooks, president of the American Enterprise Institute, a conservative think tank in Washington, said some Democrats saw Sanders' "far-left populism" as "a pirate ship" seeking to overtake and impose its views on the rest of the party.[29]

Some populists promote conspiracy theories that critics of populism say delegitimize non-populist politicians and institutions. Before he ran for president, Trump claimed Obama was born in Kenya and implied he is a Muslim, and recently he predicted that the fall election "is going to be rigged."[30] Meanwhile, supporters of Sanders accused Clinton's campaign of manipulating election results in several primaries.[31]

In addition, critics of populism say it oversimplifies complicated issues, such as the North American Free Trade Agreement (NAFTA), a joint agreement among the United States, Mexico and Canada that was negotiated by President George H. W. Bush and signed into law by President Bill Clinton in 1993. Trump's and Sanders' arguments that NAFTA and similar pacts caused massive losses of American manufacturing jobs are too simplistic, the critics say. And eliminating those trade deals, NAFTA supporters say, would cause long-term economic harm without restoring good-paying blue-collar jobs. In fact, studies indicate that many of those jobs were lost due to modernization, automation and outsourcing to lower-wage countries both with and without free-trade agreements.[32]

"Populism appeals because it promises simple solutions to complex problems," said a report by two economists at the New York City-based Council on Foreign Relations, a centrist think tank studying international issues.[33]

Outside the United States, some establishment politicians say populism's impatience with the political process is at odds with how democracy works.

"Building prosperity requires caution and patience. It requires time," said Fernando Henrique Cardoso, Brazil's president from 1995 to 2003. "Populism is a shortcut that doesn't work."[34]

Cardoso is a frequent critic of the Workers' Party, a leftist populist movement whose former president, former Brazilian President Dilma Rousseff, and other leaders have become caught in widespread corruption scandals.[35] Brazil's Senate voted in August to impeach and remove Rousseff from office.[36]

But others say populism can invigorate political engagement by inviting participation from people who otherwise shun politics. "It can make politics more accessible, comprehensible and popular," the University of Stockholm's Moffitt said.[37]

Some Trump supporters say they admire his bluntness, in contrast to what they see from establishment politicians. "He talks like me," said Rozilda Greene, a 65-year-old Floridian. "If I have the truth to tell, I tell it."[38]

J. D. Vance, an investment executive in San Francisco and author of the new book *Hillbilly Elegy*, a memoir of growing up in Appalachia, said the white working-class voters who back Trump have forced better-off Americans to take their concerns more seriously. When he won Nevada's GOP primary in February, Trump cited his overwhelming popularity among those without college degrees and said, "I love the poorly educated."[39]

"The two political parties have offered essentially nothing to these people for a few decades," Vance said. "From the left, they get some smug condescension, an exasperation that the white working class votes against their economic interests because of social issues. . . . From the right, they've gotten the basic Republican policy platform of tax cuts, free trade, deregulation, and paeans to the noble businessman and economic growth."[40]

Meanwhile, Sanders' candidacy stirred interest among younger voters who applauded his attacks on the party establishment. The 75 million Americans in their teens, 20s and early 30s, known as Millennials, are the country's single biggest generation, and both Democrats and Republicans are eager to gain their long-term support.[41]

Advocates of populism say heightened participation has nudged the parties toward reflecting the broader public's wishes. They point to Sanders' influence on Hillary Clinton on trade: Clinton had said in 2012 that the Trans-Pacific Partnership — an agreement fostering trade among the United States and 11 other countries bordering the Pacific Ocean — "sets the gold standard in trade agreements." But after Sanders criticized the pact during the Democratic primaries, she came out against it.[42]

Sanders' policy director, Warren Gunnels, also cited the inclusion of some of the senator's priorities in the Democratic platforms adopted. The platform, a non-binding outline of a party's agenda, included Sanders' calls to reform Wall Street and raise the minimum wage to $15 an hour.[43]

Is globalization driving populism?

In seeking to explain populism's ascension, commentators have described it as a rebellion led by the economic losers of globalization — the push for free

Democratic presidential candidate Hillary Clinton greets supporters in Cleveland on Aug. 17. Clinton has sounded populist notes in her campaign, lambasting "special interests" that prevent citizens from making bigger financial gains. The media have applied the populist label to Clinton for her promises to tax multimillionaires and U.S. companies that attempt to relocate overseas.

movement of goods, people and technology across international borders.

Since the end of World War II, many governments have sought to reduce or eliminate trade barriers. Globalization of trade intensified after 2001, when China joined the World Trade Organization, which sets standards for international trade.

Proponents of globalization envisioned it as a solution to deep-seated poverty and unemployment in many developing countries.[44] But the loosening of trade restrictions occurred just as revolutionary new technologies began to eliminate many jobs in developed economies, and the rise of the internet made other jobs exportable to lower-wage countries. As a result, some commentators argue, the drive to globalize free trade unintentionally delivered considerable wealth and power to a small elite while reducing the number of high-paying jobs available to lower-skilled workers.

"Most people don't understand what NAFTA did, or what the TPP is or how trade bills work," says the University of Denver's Wadsworth. "But they are getting the sense that corporate power seems to have superseded political power nationally and globally. I think Sanders tried to provide a narrative that explains and articulates that" in his criticisms of the proposed Pacific trade pact.

In 1960, about one in four Americans worked in manufacturing; less than one in 10 do today. Since 2000, the United States has lost 5 million jobs in that sector, many to China.[45] Trump won the GOP primaries in 89 of the 100 U.S. counties most affected by trade with China, according to *The Wall Street Journal*.[46]

But despite Sanders' anti-free trade positions, fears about globalization do not appear to motivate left-leaning populists. A June poll by the Chicago Council on Global Affairs, a think tank, found that 75 percent of Sanders' self-identified supporters agreed with the statement, "Globalization is mostly good for the United States." That figure was just 1 percentage point below the share of Clinton's supporters expressing the same sentiment.[47]

Others say populism is driven less by the economic consequences of globalization than by the racial and cultural anxieties stoked by immigration. Trump has vowed to build a wall on the border with Mexico and at least temporarily bar Muslim immigrants from entering the country. After the son of Afghan immigrants killed 49 people at the Orlando, Fla., nightclub Pulse in June, Trump expanded his proposed ban to include migrants from any region with "a proven history of terrorism" against the United States or its allies.[48] Trump also has called for "extreme vetting" of would-be immigrants to determine if they reflect U.S. values.[49]

Meanwhile, some experts say the U.K. "Brexit" vote was a consequence of what many Britons see as excessive immigration. Legal annual immigration into that country is 10 times what it was in 1993, and pro-Brexit forces argued many of those immigrants have taken jobs from British natives.[50]

"Immigration is probably the number one issue driving the rise of political populism around the world, whether it's the Brexit vote . . . or the rise of Donald Trump, the Republican presidential nominee," wrote Greg Ip, *The Wall Street Journal*'s chief economics correspondent. "The backlash against immigration is less about jobs and wages — it's more about a sense of national identity and control over national borders,"[51]

Jonathan Rothwell, a researcher for the Gallup polling organization, studied the demographics of Trump's support and found cultural mistrust of other races and ethnicities to be the biggest factor, saying those viewing Trump most favorably are "disproportionately living in racially and culturally isolated ZIP codes . . . with little exposure to blacks, Asians and Hispanics."[52]

Likewise, populism's appeal in Europe appears to stem more from cultural factors than economic ones, according to a new study by Harvard and University of Michigan researchers. In addition to Brexit, they cited hostile anti-immigrant rhetoric and anxiety over recent terrorist attacks. Populism's spread in Europe, they said, "is largely due to ideological appeals to traditional values, which are concentrated among the older generation, men, the religious, ethnic majorities, and less-educated sectors of society."[53]

Daniel Gros, director of the Centre for European Policy Studies, a think tank in Brussels, Belgium, examined education and employment statistics in Europe and found that people with a college degree are more likely to get jobs and earn more than those without one. But, he said, the number of jobs requiring high levels of education has not grown in Europe in recent years, nor has the difference in unemployment rates between the highly educated and the less educated.

"But if these factors account for the rise of populism, they must have somehow intensified in the last few years, with low-skill workers' circumstances and prospects deteriorating faster vis-à-vis their high-skill counterparts," he said. "And that simply is not the case, especially in Europe."[54]

Is U.S. populism identical to Europe's?

The rise of populist movements in the United States and Europe has led many scholars, commentators and journalists to connect the two. They say populist leaders in both places have capitalized on deepening mistrust of politicians and parties.

Americans and Europeans "are more dissatisfied with mainstream politicians and parties than they have been in living memory," said Duncan McDonnell, a professor of government and international relations at Australia's Griffith University and co-author of the 2015 book *Populists in Power*. "People go looking for other alternatives, and the one thing about populists is that they still promise people that voting can actually change something — that democracy can be saved somehow."[55]

Analysts say that attitude particularly appeals to voters on the political right, who are more skeptical of government than Democrats and who see themselves losing influence.

Constanze Stelzenmüller, a senior fellow on foreign policy at the Brookings Institution, a centrist think tank in Washington, cited several recent U.S. books and articles "about the fraying economic and social conditions which offer a potent explanation for the current dark mood of much of the American electorate. Yet 'Europe' could be substituted for 'America' in many of these studies with equal plausibility."[56]

The result, Stelzenmüller and others say, is the tendency among right-wing populists such as the Netherland's Geert Wilders, Austria's Norbert Hofer and France's Marine Le Pen to make claims similar to Trump's that increased immigration is a leading cause of their country's problems, especially crime and terrorism. Although those populists say recent terrorist attacks in Europe reinforce their concerns, critics accuse them of xenophobia, an irrational dislike or fear of foreigners.

Ongoing anti-government mistrust took hold during the global economic recession between 2007 and 2009. As the tea party movement was gaining influence in the United States, separate public pushes for secession flourished in parts of Belgium, Italy, Scotland and Spain.[57]

Some analysts described June's Brexit vote as an echo of Trump's rise. Padraig Reidy, editor of the London news and cultural magazine *Little Atoms*, wrote: "The American political establishment should take note of what has happened — what was inconceivable for Britain just a few months ago has suddenly become reality."[58]

But other experts say the U.S. and European versions of populism are more different than alike. Europe's is based more on a distrust of the EU imposing regulations on member countries than opposition to trade agreements, said Thomas Greven, a professor of political science at Germany's Free University of Berlin.[59]

Jacqueline Gehring, an assistant professor of political science at Pennsylvania's Allegheny College, said Britain "has been ambivalent about the European Union" since it was founded in the 1950s and Britain initially chose not to become a member. The Brexit vote, she added, reflected "a failure of political leadership" from then-Prime Minister David Cameron, who was criticized for failing to foresee pro-Brexit sentiment and who resigned after the referendum, which he had advocated.

"Brexit may have been pushed somewhat by recently increasing xenophobia or populism," Gehring said, "but it is not its primary motivator."[60]

The University of Georgia's Mudde also said populists in Europe and North America see immigration differently. He said Trump — unlike those on Europe's right wing — distinguishes between legal and illegal immigration, blaming the latter for what he said are the United States' problems, and "does not attack the status of the U.S. as a multicultural immigration country."[61]

Others who study populism say the different political structures of the United States and many European countries shape populism in those places. Many European nations have parliamentary systems in which a coalition of parties can form a majority, enabling populist parties to share power. Unlike the United States, where third parties still lag far behind the Republican and Democratic parties, those countries have many national parties; France, for example, has more than a dozen.[62]

"The European context looks very different" from the United States, says Joe Lowndes, a University of Oregon professor of political science. "You have actual populist parties over there and a parliamentary system."

Gros of the Centre for European Policy Studies said left-wing populism has prevailed across southern Europe as a result of the debt crisis that has afflicted Europe since 2009 and that resulted from the global recession.[63] Meanwhile, the United States' economy has rebounded in the last few years.

In the aftermath of the global recession, several EU countries — Greece, Portugal, Ireland, Spain and Cyprus — were unable to repay or refinance their government debt or to bail out overly indebted banks under their national supervision.[64]

BACKGROUND

'Passions, Not Reason'

Without using the word "populism," ancient philosophers such as Plato and Aristotle had reservations about democracy because of their concerns that angry segments of the public could rise up and undermine it.[65]

James Madison, one of the authors of the U.S. Constitution, said his biggest fear of the new United States was that "the passions . . . not the reason, of the public would sit in judgment." If that happened, the future president wrote in his famous *Federalist No. 10* essay in 1787, "the influence of factious leaders may kindle a flame."[66]

Historians say the rise of Democrat Andrew Jackson kindled the populist flame in the 1820s. The former military hero won the popular vote in 1824 but lost to John Quincy Adams. He defeated Adams four years later in what often is described as one of the nastiest campaigns in history. In 1832 Jackson said some congressional proposals, such as using federal money to support road and canal construction, proved that "many of our rich men have not been content with equal protection and equal benefits, but have besought us to make them richer by act of Congress."[67]

The economic slump that followed the Civil War (1861-65) and the start in the late 1800s of the so-called Gilded Age, in which the gap separating the rich and poor grew wider, also spurred populist developments. During the Greenback Movement, which began in 1868, farmers and others sought to prevent a drop in crop prices by maintaining or increasing the amount of paper money being circulated.[68] The Granger Movement of the 1870s featured a coalition of mostly Midwestern farmers fighting railroads' monopoly on transporting grain.[69]

Those alliances gave way in 1890 to the Populist (or People's) Party, a third party championing former Minnesota Rep. Ignatius Donnelly's belief that "public good is paramount to private interests."[70] Its interests overlapped with the Progressive Movement of the 1890s, which also grew out of dissatisfaction with government and the power of corporate monopolies. Progressives, however, argued for less-sweeping change; for example, they opposed the Populists' belief that government should directly control or own railroads.[71]

In 1892, the Populist Party nominated James B. Weaver of Iowa for president and demanded a graduated income tax, with the wealthy taxed at higher rates than those with lower incomes. But Weaver won in just four states, and Democrat Grover Cleveland was elected.[72]

In the next presidential election, a divided group of Populists endorsed Democrat William Jennings Bryan, one of the 19th century's most famous orators, while selecting their own vice presidential nominee.[73] Bryan staunchly opposed the gold standard, which limited the money supply but eased trade with other nations whose currency also was based on gold. He captivated voters with the famous edict, "You shall not crucify mankind on a cross of gold," but lost the election to Republican William McKinley.[74]

Another influential populist thinker of the era was Henry George, whose 1879 book *Progress and Poverty* sold 3 million copies to become the all-time best-selling book on economic theory to that point. George called for abolishing all taxes except for a single tax on land; he argued it would make land widely available to those who would use the property instead of keeping it in the hands of the wealthy. He also campaigned for the right of voters to cast secret ballots, making them less susceptible to intimidation.[75]

The Populists remained politically active until 1908, when the party combined with the Democratic Party.[76] But its beliefs have remained influential.

"Sanders could practically have run on the Populist Party platform of 1892," said Michael Magliari, a professor of history at California State University, Chico, saying Sanders' call to let people cash checks and open savings accounts at post offices was taken directly from the earlier group's plan.[77]

Polarizing Figures

During the first half of the 20th century, outspoken populist leaders became prominent, including "the radio priest," Father Charles Coughlin. He broadcast scathing attacks alleging Jewish bankers controlled the money supply and dismissed Democratic President Franklin D. Roosevelt's New Deal — a wide-ranging series of government programs aimed at lifting the country out of the Great Depression — as a tool of banking interests.[78]

Another flamboyant populist was Huey Long, a Democratic governor and U.S. senator from Louisiana. Long denounced the wealthy and in 1934 proposed creating a "Share Our Wealth Society" whose slogan was "Every man a king." He called for the government to prevent families from owning fortunes larger than $5 million to $8 million (about $90 million to $144 million today, adjusted for inflation), with the proceeds used to provide every family in the country with an annual income.

Long drew an impassioned following, but Roosevelt and other critics dubbed him a dangerous demagogue.[79] Long was assassinated in 1935 but had an enduring influence in Louisiana, where he spearheaded

an aggressive program of building and improving roads and bridges and providing free school lunches and textbooks to poor students.[80]

The 1950s saw the rise of Wisconsin Republican Sen. Joseph McCarthy, another famously polarizing figure. In seeking to expose communists and other left-wing "loyalty risks" in the U.S. government, McCarthy tried "to mobilize an anti-elite sentiment," said Daniel Bell, a Harvard professor of sociology. The Senate voted in 1954 to formally condemn McCarthy for what senators called his "inexcusable" and "vulgar" accusations. Historians say the vote greatly diminished the influence of McCarthy, who died three years later.[81]

Alabama's Wallace also used populism to divide rather than unite, historians say. He concluded his 1963 inaugural speech for governor with the infamous line, "Segregation now, segregation tomorrow, segregation forever." After surviving an assassination attempt, he issued public apologies later in his career for his earlier statements while improving health care and education for blacks as well as whites.[82]

During the 1950s and '60s, Columbia University's Richard Hofstadter became known as one of the 20th century's most influential historians. In such books as *Anti-Intellectualism in American Life* (1963) and *The Paranoid Style in American Politics* (1965), Hofstadter argued that Jacksonian-era populist sentiments had recurred throughout U.S. history, resulting in a prejudice against intellectuals as representatives of an elite that could not be trusted.[83]

Left-wing populism gained followers in the 1970s. Oklahoma Democratic Sen. Fred Harris ran for president in 1972 with the slogan "a new populism," decrying liberal "elitism" while calling for a broader distribution of wealth. After failing to win the nomination, he mounted another failed effort four years later.[84]

Also in 1972, left-wing journalists Jack Newfield and Jeff Greenfield, in *A Populist Manifesto*, sought to mobilize workers, young people and minorities around the belief that "some institutions and people have too much money and power, most people have too little, and the first priority of politics must be to redress that imbalance."[85]

Later in the 1970s, political referendums and state ballot initiatives began attracting attention. The initiative process, which began in South Dakota in 1898, enables citizens to vote on proposed statutes or constitutional amendments at the polls. State legislatures can place initiatives on the ballot, but the initiatives often are generated by petition drives.[86]

California's Proposition 13 in 1978 was the era's best-known initiatives. Conservative activists proposed it in a response to rising home values that caused property taxes to skyrocket. The initiative limited annual property taxes to 1 percent of a property's assessed value and required a two-thirds majority for any state or local tax increase. Though it achieved its goal of reducing taxes, critics said it triggered drastic cuts in public spending that hurt the quality of schools and public services.[87]

California later adopted other controversial ballot initiatives. Proposition 187 in 1994 made immigrants who were in the United States illegally ineligible for public benefits (although it has never been enforced); Proposition 209 in 1996 banned affirmative action at state institutions; and Proposition 227 in 1998 restricted bilingual education in public schools. In a 2005 study, three political scientists said those measures shifted the state's politics toward the Democratic Party by alienating Latinos — who had been drifting toward the GOP — as well as many white voters.[88]

In 1984 a new Populist Party — no connection to the original — started to run far-right candidates in the presidential elections, including former Ku Klux Klan leader David Duke of Louisiana, in 1988. It failed to win any converts beyond a tiny band of extremists.[89]

Buchanan, the political commentator who first ran for president in 1992, also drew upon mistrust of elites. But he promoted an "America First" foreign policy that went against prevailing GOP sentiment by rejecting many international alliances. He also harshly criticized Wall Street and called illegal immigration "the greatest invasion [of the United States] in history."[90]

Texas entrepreneur Perot, meanwhile, reserved his harshest criticisms for lobbyists, political action committees (PACs) and the politicians allied with them. He said they had formed "a political nobility that is immune to the people's will" and called for term limits for members of Congress, a balanced budget amendment and placement of proposed laws on a national ballot for voters to decide.[91]

Neither Buchanan nor Perot attracted widespread support. Although Perot drew 19 percent of the vote, he did not win a plurality of the votes in any states and no Electoral College votes.[92] Consumer activist Ralph Nader, who built a passionate following in the 1960s with his attacks on corporations, also ran in 2000 as the Green Party's candidate. Some political experts say Nader received enough votes in Florida to cost Gore the state and hand the election to George W. Bush.[93]

Tea Party Politics

In the 2008 U.S. presidential election, GOP nominee John McCain, an Arizona senator, bypassed several experienced establishment politicians and selected first-term Alaska Gov. Sarah Palin as his running mate. Palin drew the populist tag for portraying herself as a "hockey mom" who condemned Democratic elites.[94]

The tea party movement arose shortly after McCain's loss to Obama, helping the Republican Party make substantial gains in the 2014 midterm elections. But it targeted some Republicans as well. Tea party-backed college professor Dave Brat startled the political world by toppling House Majority Leader Eric Cantor of Virginia in a June 2014 GOP primary. Brat had blasted Cantor for being too cozy with Wall Street and business leaders.[95]

The tea party was not hostile to all government programs. A Harvard study said resistance to Obama's Affordable Care Act health care overhaul "coexists with considerable acceptance, even warmth, toward longstanding federal social programs like Social Security and Medicare, to which tea partiers feel legitimately entitled. Opposition is concentrated on resentment of perceived federal government 'handouts' to 'undeserving' groups, the definition of which seems heavily influenced by racial and ethnic stereotypes."[96]

In running for president, Trump received Palin's endorsement and became "the leader the tea party never had," according to Griffith University's McDonnell.[97] However, Trump's embrace of some government programs led some tea party members to prefer Texas Sen. Ted Cruz, who in the GOP primaries campaigned as a purer example of conservative principles.[98] Cruz, however, could not beat Trump in many Eastern and Midwestern states, where blue-collar workers embraced Trump's "Make America Great Again" slogan.[99]

Trump's blaming of all politicians — not just Democrats — for what he called their inability to solve problems irked many Republicans, especially the GOP

CHRONOLOGY

1820s-1910s *Early populists back the interests of farmers and laborers.*

1828 Democrat Andrew Jackson, whom historians consider a leading figure in American populism, wins the presidency.

1891 The Populist (or People's) Party is founded, merging the interests of farmers and laborers. A year later, populist prebasidential candidate James Weaver of Iowa loses to incumbent Democratic President Grover Cleveland.

1896 Populists endorse Democrat William Jennings Bryan for president; he loses to Republican William McKinley.

1908 Populists cease to be politically active, combining with the Democratic Party.

1920s-1960s *Controversial populist politicians emerge.*

1926 Father Charles Coughlin, a Roman Catholic priest, begins anti-semitic attacks on banks and other institutions.

1928 Democrat Huey Long is elected Louisiana governor and denounces the wealthy and banks, calling for redistribution of wealth.

1962 Democrat George Wallace is elected Alabama governor on a populist, pro-segregation platform.

1965 Historian Richard Hofstadter argues that populist sentiments of Jackson's era had recurred throughout U.S. history.

1970s-1990s *Populist initiatives on taxes, immigration gain support.*

1972 Oklahoma Sen. Fred Harris unsuccessfully seeks the Democratic presidential nomination with the slogan "a new populism," denouncing liberal "elitism."

1978 California voters approve Proposition 13, which slashed property taxes.

1992 Republican Patrick Buchanan and independent H. Ross Perot wage unsuccessful populist campaigns for president.

1994 California voters approve Proposition 187, which prevents undocumented immigrants from receiving education, health care or other public services.

1996 Buchanan and Perot again run unsuccessfully for president.

2000s *Populist candidates gain national stage.*

2002 Far-right French presidential candidate Jean-Marie Le Pen defeats socialist Prime Minister Lionel Jospin in the first round of voting.

2008 Republican presidential candidate John McCain of Arizona selects as his vice presidential running mate Alaska Gov. Sarah Palin, who denounces Democratic elites.

2009 Tea party movement arises to challenge President Obama.

2011 Occupy Wall Street movement attacks the power of the financial industry.

2013 The Black Lives Matter movement forms to protest police racism and violence against African-Americans.

2014 Tea party-backed college professor Dave Brat topples House Majority Leader Eric Cantor of Virginia in GOP primary. . . . Tea party candidates help Republicans make substantial gains in November elections.

2015 Republican Donald Trump launches presidential campaign on a "Make America Great Again" populist platform. . . . Independent Sen. Bernie Sanders announces he will run for president as a Democrat.

2016 Trump wins the GOP nomination but alienates Republicans with incendiary rhetoric . . . . Sanders loses in Democratic primaries to Hillary Clinton but endorses her. . . . United Kingdom votes to withdraw from European Union . . . . North Dakota voters reject a controversial law that would have relaxed a ban on corporate farms.

Europe a Hothouse for Populist Leaders

On the right and left, populism is sprouting across the continent.

Populism has long found the soils of Europe a fertile place to grow, thanks to a history of tensions with immigrants and a multiparty system that breeds anti-establishment views.

Experts say economic and cultural concerns have fueled populism's growth. The decline of manufacturing jobs and influx of immigrants have helped to stoke populism on the right, while suspicions about government power and institutions such as the European Union have boosted it on the left.

For populists, these developments have been translating into gains at the polls. In a new study, political scientists Ronald Inglehart of the University of Michigan and Pippa Norris of Harvard University found that the average share of the vote for populist parties in European elections has nearly tripled since the 1960s, from 5 percent to 13.2 percent.

During those five and a half decades, the share of seats in legislative bodies held by politicians considered to be populists more than tripled, from just below 4 percent to nearly 13 percent, according to Inglehart and Norris.[1]

Here are some of the most prominent right-wing and left-wing Europeans who are widely described in media and academic circles as populists:

Austria: Norbert Hofer

Hofer, 45, is the leader of Austria's Freedom Party, which Ruth Wodak, an emeritus professor of linguistics and English language at England's Lancaster University and author of a recent book on populism, described as "a far-right populist party claiming that its intention is to protect Austrian culture and national identity."[2]

Hofer lost the presidential election in April, but his party appealed the result and a court invalidated it, citing sloppiness in ballot handling. Another election is scheduled for October.[3]

The presidency is largely ceremonial, but Hofer has promised to seek to fire the coalition government in charge if it fails to control immigration more strictly. His party also has vowed speedier deportations of undocumented immigrants and increased surveillance of mosques and Muslim schools.[4]

France: Marine Le Pen

Le Pen, 48, is the daughter of Jean-Marie Le Pen, the founder of the conservative National Front party who was widely criticized for his anti-Semitism and racism. She took over as its leader in 2011.

The Washington Post described Marine Le Pen as "Europe's pioneer in attempting to cast the populist far right in a more respectable light."[5] Unlike her father, she has acknowledged and condemned the Holocaust but continued his call for drastically limiting legal immigration. She has demanded that legal immigrants who have been unemployed for six months return to their country of origin, regardless of how long they have lived in France.

Le Pen unsuccessfully ran for president in 2012 and is expected to run again in 2017. She said she would hold a referendum on her country's membership in the EU within six months.[6]

Greece: Alexis Tsipras

Tsipras, 42, is the leader of Syriza, which academics and media outlets say is a left-wing populist party. He was elected Greece's prime minister last year on a surge of public hostility to stringent austerity measures that the government had imposed after the country plunged into financial crisis.[7]

Under his leadership, Greek lawmakers in May approved some tax hikes and other, lesser austerity measures that Tsipras said were aimed at eventually making the country less reliant on aid from other European nations.[8]

Like other populist leaders, Tsipras has made frequent use of social media, putting out regular YouTube videos and frequent tweets in which he has argued that the people's will is more important than the wishes of government officials.[9]

Netherlands: Geert Wilders

Wilders, 52, is the founder and leader of the Dutch Party for Freedom, which Wodak said practices an "ethno-nationalist" populism pushing a strong national identity.[10]

Wilders is among the most controversial politicians in Europe, having said the Quran is a "fascist book" that should be banned alongside *Mein Kampf*, in which Adolf Hitler outlined his plans for Nazi Germany.[11] He has been among the loudest in condemning Muslim immigration to his country.[12]

Wilders said he would call for a referendum on Dutch membership in the EU if he is elected as prime minister in March.[13]

Spain: Pablo Iglesias

Iglesias, 37, is secretary-general of Podemos ("We Can"), which academics and media describe as a left-wing populist party. It formed in 2014 and merged in May with several minor parties to become Unidos Podemos ("United We Can"). But the party failed in June's elections to replace the center-left Socialist Party as leader of the country's political left.[14]

Iglesias is a former political science lecturer in Madrid and former member of the European Parliament. He entered politics after taking part in protests against globalization.

He said he and other protesters "understood that a big part of the important decisions weren't being taken by democratically elected governments, but rather, institutions that weren't chosen by anyone, like the International Monetary Fund (IMF) or the World Bank."[15]

United Kingdom: Nigel Farage

Farage, 52, served from 2006 to 2009 and from 2010 until July as the leader of the UK Independence Party, which many describe as a "Euroskeptic" populist party that is suspicious of alliances with other European nations.[16]

He was a prominent leader of the pro-Brexit movement along with Boris Johnson, the former mayor of London who is now the UK's secretary of state for foreign and commonwealth affairs. Farage said in August that he would consider returning to lead the party if Brexit is not implemented to his satisfaction.[17] He traveled to the United States to campaign for Donald Trump and said of Trump's supporters, "They are the same people who made Brexit happen."[18]

— *Chuck McCutcheon*

Geert Wilders, founder of the ultra-nationalist Dutch Party for Freedom, is among the most controversial politicians in Europe. He has called the Quran a fascist book that should be banned.

[6] Cecile Alduy, "The Devil's Daughter," *The Atlantic*, October 2013, http://tinyurl.com/jt6ng59; Elisabeth Zerofsky, "Marine Le Pen Prepares for a 'Frexit,' " *The New Yorker*, June 29, 2016, http://tinyurl.com/zeqmh3f.

[7] Jeff Wallenfeldt, "Alexis Tsipras," *Encyclopaedia Brittanica*, http://tinyurl.com/z8xqnlb.

[8] Niki Kitsantonis, "Greek Lawmakers Narrowly Approve Austerity Legislation," *The New York Times*, May 22, 2016, http://tinyurl.com/gksbujf.

[9] David Auerbach, "The Digital Demogogue," *Slate*, July 2, 2015, http://tinyurl.com/omqe2gp.

[10] Wodak, *op. cit.*, p. 206.

[11] Bruno Waterfield, "Ban Koran Like Mein Kampf, Says Dutch MP," *The Telegraph* (U.K.), Aug. 9, 2007, http://tinyurl.com/jsqsvbs.

[12] Faiola, *op. cit.*

[13] "Dutch anti-immigration leader Wilders calls for Dutch referendum on EU membership," Reuters, June 24, 2016, http://tinyurl.com/ht5u9m3.

[14] Jon Stone, "Spanish leftists Podemos boosted by new electoral alliance," *Newsweek*, May 16, 2015, http://tinyurl.com/j4agzjd; Tobias Buck, "Spain's Podemos mourns losses at 2016 election," *Financial Times*, June 28, 2016, http://tinyurl.com/jfdzb8n.

[15] Zoe Williams, "P?odemos ?leader ?Pablo Iglesias on why he's like Jeremy Corbyn: 'He brings ideas that can solve problems,' " *The Guardian* (U.K.), Dec. 15, 2015, http://tinyurl.com/nk6l5k6.

[16] Wodak, *op. cit.*, p. 207.

[17] Arj Singh and Georgia Diebelius, "Nigel Farage reveals he would consider returning as Ukip leader 'if Brexit is not delivered," *The Mirror* (U.K.), Aug. 14, 2016, http://tinyurl.com/jqkn9ax.

[18] David Wright, "Brexit leader Nigel Farage calls Trump 'the new Ronald Reagan,' " CNN.com, Aug. 29, 2016, http://tinyurl.com/h62bgf8.

[1] Ronald F. Inglehart and Pippa Norris, "Trump, Brexit and the Rise of Populism: Economic Have-Nots and Cultural Backlash," Kennedy School of Government, Harvard University, July 29, 2016, http://tinyurl.com/heh5aqz.

[2] Ruth Wodak, *The Politics of Fear: What Right-Wing Populist Discourses Mean* (2015), p. 191.

[3] Josh Lowe, "Far Right Takes Lead in Austria Presidential Election Re-Run," *Newsweek*, Aug. 2, 2016, http://tinyurl.com/gtjrhkb.

[4] Anthony Faiola, "Meet the Donald Trumps of Europe," *The Washington Post*, May 19, 2016, http://tinyurl.com/hv8e6z5.

[5] *Ibid.*

Are Populism and Social Media Compatible?

Some worry speed and venom can outstrip sober deliberation.

When Donald Trump tweets a populist-oriented attack, as he's done regularly throughout the presidential race, TV networks and other media often waste no time reporting on it.

"I do a tweet on something," Trump boasts, "something not even significant, and they break into their news within seconds."[1]

Trump's use of Twitter shows how it and other social media sites, such as Facebook and Instagram, thrive on the ability of politicians instantly to reach a wide audience — a perfect complement to populist rhetoric, which thrives on striking an emotional us-versus-them chord with the public.

But many experts say those features can overshadow or conflict with what they view as the sober and deliberative process of traditional politics.

Populists long have deployed the media to their advantage, going back to the People's (Populist) Party publishing its own crusading newspapers in the 1890s.[2] But Trump and unsuccessful Democratic presidential candidate Bernie Sanders have employed social media both to send messages to voters and, in newer fashion, to foster a two-way dialogue with them.

Trump and Sanders "are using social media like you or I would use social media," said Matt Lira, a Republican digital strategist. "They're using it as a platform to genuinely engage their supporters."[3]

Such populist-driven uses of social media can have positive results, such as rapidly spreading news about rallies or instantly obtaining hundreds of thousands of petition signatures, said Jill Lepore, a Harvard University professor of history and a writer for *The New Yorker*. But she cited negative consequences as well, including "the atomizing of the electorate," or making voters more individualistic and less concerned about others' well-being by encouraging them to act quickly rather than thoughtfully.

"There's a point at which political communication speeds past the last stop where democratic deliberation, the genuine consent of the governed, is possible," Lepore said. "An instant poll, of the sort that pops up on your screen while you're attempting to read debate coverage, encourages snap and solitary judgment, the very opposite of what's necessary for the exercise of good citizenship."[4]

At the same time, some in politics express concern that social media is reinforcing populist outrage at the establishment and diminishing civility among politicians, campaign workers and the public.

"I have a lot of friends working for various campaigns right now," said Republican strategist Matt Rhoades, who managed Mitt Romney's presidential campaign in 2012. "They hate each other. We have candidates running for the highest office in the United States trolling each other on social media. That's what social media also has given us."[5]

Concerns about social media's effect on political discourse are not limited to the United States. Srgjan Ivanovik, a journalist in Macedonia, said social media has increased politicians' tendency to manipulate opinion by telling the public what it wants to hear without regard for the truth.

establishment, which he described as too beholden to what he said were the party's narrow interests.

During the primaries, Trump did not have to rely on the Republican Party or raise and spend significant sums of campaign money because of his celebrity and ability to command significant media attention. One study in March 2016 estimated that he had received the equivalent of nearly $2 billion in coverage through newspapers, television and other journalistic outlets. That was 21/2 times more than Clinton, and many times greater than any of his Republican rivals.[100] At

the same time, Trump made frequent use of Twitter, often lashing out at opponents.

"Inside the political power structure, Trump has no power," said Nicco Mele, director of Harvard's Shorenstein Center on Media, Politics and Public Policy. "And so he is very effective at forcing himself into it through a combination of Twitter and earned media," or news articles and TV broadcasts.[101]

Sanders, as a member of Congress, was known for criticizing so-called "corporate welfare" — government benefits, such as special provisions in the tax code,

"Leaders have learned a lesson from the internet," Ivanovik said. "Our interest in their campaigns is more like [reality TV's] 'The X Factor' or 'Choose Your Idol' shows than a real political platform with adequate programs, solutions and answers. In response, our leaders simply became populist. They answer what the majority wants to hear."[6]

Ruth Wodak, an emeritus professor of linguistics and English language at England's Lancaster University, said a populist "media-democracy" in Europe and elsewhere has produced a climate "in which the individual, media-savvy performance of politics seems to become more important than the political process." Thus, she said, "politics is reduced to a few slogans thought to be comprehensible to the public at large."[7]

British multimillionaire Arron Banks, the largest financial donor to this summer's "Brexit" referendum in which the United Kingdom voted to leave the European Union, said populist strategists for the leave-the-EU effort used Facebook and other social media to make stark emotional warnings about the dangers of immigration.

By comparison, Banks said, proponents of remaining in the EU "featured fact, fact, fact, fact, fact. It just doesn't work. You have got to connect with people emotionally."[8]

Banks' comments drew a rebuke from Katharine Viner, editor-in-chief of Britain's *Guardian* and a Brexit opponent. "When 'facts don't work' and voters don't trust the media, everyone believes in their own 'truth' — and the results, as we have just seen [with Brexit], can be devastating," Viner wrote. "When the prevailing mood is anti-elite and anti-authority, trust in big institutions, including the media, begins to crumble."[9]

But Scott Adams, creator of the cartoon "Dilbert," said social media can curb some of the excesses of populism. Adams, who regularly blogs about current events, cited the fistfights and other disturbances that arose at several rallies for Trump earlier this year.

"The fear is that the small scuffles will escalate to something terrible," Adams wrote. "But social media solves that. Every person at a Trump rally knows the world is watching. And it isn't just big media that is watching. Every phone in every pocket is a direct link to the world. And Trump supporters know their candidate would be done if a big riot broke out."[10]

— Chuck McCutcheon

[1] Jim Rutenberg, "The Mutual Dependence of Donald Trump and the News Media," *The New York Times*, March 20 2016, http://tinyurl.com/jg4wv9u.

[2] "Kansas populist newspapers," Kansas Historical Society, http://tinyurl.com/h8mgpsn; "People's Party," Texas State Historical Association, http://tinyurl.com/huyc8hm.

[3] Issie Lapowsky, "Trump Isn't the First Tech-Propelled Populist. But This Time It's Different," *Wired*, May 13, 2016, http://tinyurl.com/hqj372p.

[4] Jill Lepore, "The Party Crashers," *The New Yorker*, Feb. 22, 2016, http://tinyurl.com/h2onlbj.

[5] James Irwin, "America Rising Founder: Social Media Fuels Populism," *GW Today*, Feb. 19, 2016, http://tinyurl.com/z8kfgs2.

[6] Srgjan Ivanovik, "Social Media is Making Politicians More Populist Than Ever!" The Good Men Project, Sept. 24, 2014, http://tinyurl.com/jk2gzr5.

[7] Ruth Wodak, *The Politics of Fear: What Right-Wing Populist Discourses Mean* (2015), p. 11.

[8] Robert Booth, Alan Travis and Amelia Gentleman, "Leave donor plans new party to replace Ukip — possibly without Farage in charge," *The Guardian* (U.K.), June 29, 2016, http://tinyurl.com/has69a3.

[9] Katharine Viner, "How technology disrupted the truth," *The Guardian* (U.K.), July 12, 2016, http://tinyurl.com/jecdlaq.

[10] Scott Adams, "Social media is the new government," Scott Adams' Blog, March 21, 2016, http://tinyurl.com/hecmcam.

provided to businesses. In the wake of the housing crisis that started in 2007-08, public resentment toward financial companies gave rise to the Occupy Wall Street movement, which Sanders endorsed.[102]

Many Democrats also supported Occupy Wall Street. Yet some, unlike Sanders, accepted campaign donations from Wall Street companies and their employees that were targets of the Occupy movement. In running against Clinton, Sanders made an issue of how much she received from the banking industry — more than $1.6 million as of August 2016, according to the nonpartisan watchdog Center for Responsive Politics.[103] Sanders refused to ally himself with "super PACs," a type of independent expenditure committee that can raise and spend unlimited amounts of money on political causes or candidates.[104]

Liberals also admired another economic populist, Elizabeth Warren, who decried Wall Street's influence. A Harvard Law School professor, she won election as a Democrat to a U.S. Senate seat in Massachusetts in 2012. She said that when she was growing up in Oklahoma, the United States was "a country of expanding opportunities. . . . Now we talk much more about protecting those who have already made it."[105]

Sanders, who became a Democrat to run for president, frequently feuded with the party's leaders and made economic issues the central focus of his campaign. That emphasis dismayed the populist Black Lives Matter movement, which urged the senator to highlight perceived abuses of African-Americans at the hands of law enforcement.

Clinton, meanwhile, met with Black Lives Matter leaders for almost a year in an attempt to win their endorsement. Although the main group did not comply, a group of mothers of Black Lives leaders did endorse her.[106]

CURRENT SITUATION

Political Races

Since winning the GOP nomination, Trump has continued to feud with establishment Republicans who say his populist appeals have damaged his chances of winning over undecided voters.

Some prominent Republicans have accused Trump of unpresidential conduct and said they will not vote for him.[107] And 50 foreign policy and national security officials who served under several Republican presidents said in an August letter that Trump would be "the most reckless president in history."[108] Also that month, Evan McMullin, a former House Republican aide and CIA officer, launched a long-shot independent bid on a stop-Trump platform.[109]

Trump said in early August that some of his supporters have urged him to lower his antagonistic tone to help him win a broader audience. But he said he is uncertain about doing so. "I am now listening to people that are telling me to be easier, nicer, be softer. And you know, that's OK, and I'm doing that," he told *Time* magazine. "Personally, I don't know if that's what the country wants."[110]

Polls taken after the July Democratic and Republican conventions showed that Trump broadened his support among blue-collar white voters, but not among other demographics. David Wasserman, an analyst for *FiveThirtyEight.com*, a website on polling and demographics, noted that the non-white share of eligible voters has risen since 2012, meaning Trump will have to gain "truly historic levels of support and turnout among working-class whites" while avoiding an erosion of support among other groups.[111]

Despite the widespread dislike for Trump among Democrats, not all of Sanders' supporters have immediately backed Clinton. Some are expected to vote for the Green Party's Jill Stein or Libertarian Party candidate Gary Johnson. But it remains unclear whether Stein or Johnson will appear on the November ballot in every state: As of early September, Johnson was not on the ballot in Rhode Island, while Stein was not on ballots in eight.[112]

Polls in early August showed that if Clinton runs against Trump without a third-party candidate on the ballot, as many as 91 percent of Sanders' backers would vote for her. But if those voters have the option of supporting a candidate other than her or Trump, that percentage drops considerably.[113]

In addition to the presidential campaign, several congressional races feature candidates who are described as populists. They include:

- Democrat Zephyr Teachout, who is running for a House seat in south-eastern New York state to replace retiring GOP Rep. Chris Gibson. A law professor and Sanders supporter, Teachout ran unsuccessfully in the 2014 primary against Gov. Andrew Cuomo. "I like breaking up big banks, and I want to take on big cable," Teachout said, referring to large cable companies she contends are overcharging consumers.[114]
- Democrat Russ Feingold, who is running against Wisconsin Republican Sen. Ron Johnson after being unseated by Johnson in 2010. Feingold has criticized trade deals and government aid to corporations as well as the 2010 Dodd-Frank law overhauling the financial industry, saying it was too lenient.[115]
- Republican Mark Assini, who is in a rematch against veteran Democratic Rep. Louise Slaughter for a seat representing the Rochester, N.Y., area after narrowly losing to Slaughter two years ago. Assini has echoed Trump in decrying "bad trade deals" as well as calling for a crackdown on undocumented immigrants who commit crimes.[116]

Ballot Initiatives

One sign of the strength of modern populism, experts say, is the growth in the number of citizen-driven ballot initiatives appearing on state ballots across the country this fall.

As of early September, 75 petition-driven initiatives will be on the November ballot in various states — more than double the 35 in 2014 and more than in both 2010 and 2012, according to the political website Ballotpedia, which tracks such developments. That growth has come even as the total number of ballot measures — which includes state lawmakers' decisions to put issues to a public vote — has fallen in recent years.

Low turnout in recent elections that has made it easier for advocates of an issue to collect enough signatures to force an initiative vote. In all but three states — North Dakota, Idaho and Nebraska — the number of signatures required for an initiative to be included on a ballot is based on a percentage of votes cast in a previous election.[117]

This year's initiatives cover an assortment of controversial issues, including requiring background checks for all gun purchases in Nevada, closing what gun-control advocates say are legal loopholes permitting unmonitored sales at gun shows and other venues.[118] Voters in Maine and Washington state successfully petitioned for initiatives that would raise the minimum wage in those states.[119]

In North Dakota, opponents of a controversial law that relaxed a ban on corporate-owned farms gathered enough signatures to place a referendum to overturn the law on the ballot in June. The referendum passed by a 3-to-1 margin and was seen as a rebuke to large corporations that have replaced family farms in much of rural America.[120]

Such companies "could buy up all the land, and it means nothing to them," said Laurie Wagner, a Wing, N.D., farmer who sought to overturn the state law. "They could make it impossible for people like us to compete."[121]

International Populism

The U.K.'s Brexit vote has sparked debate in Europe about the broad-ranging implications of populism. Some

Jie Zhao/Corbis via Getty Image

The "us-versus-them" attitude inherent in populism includes criticism of increased economic competition brought about by globalization. Donald Trump won the GOP presidential primaries in 89 of the 100 U.S. counties most affected by trade with China. Since 2000, the United States has lost 5 million manufacturing jobs, many to China. Above, women staff a textile factory in Huaibei, in eastern China.

of those who opposed the move are concerned it could have further negative impacts if the country does not address the concerns that led to its adoption.

"I have feared for many years that large-scale immigration to the U.K. would produce a harmful populist response," said Adair Turner, chairman of the Institute for New Economic Thinking, a New York City think tank. "Global elites must now learn and act upon the crucial lesson of Brexit. Contrary to glib assumptions, globalization of capital, trade, and migration flows is not good for everyone."[122]

Analysts said the vote also could inspire other European nations to hold similar votes to leave the EU. France, the Netherlands, Austria, Finland and Hungary are seen as the most likely candidates.[123] Meanwhile, anti-Brexit supporters in Scotland, which rejected seceding from the U.K. in 2014, have discussed holding another secession vote that would enable Scotland to remain in the EU.[124]

In Latin America, Brazil and other countries are dealing with the fallout from the waning popularity of left-wing populist parties. In Argentina, business-friendly centrist Mauricio Macri became president last December, succeeding Cristina Fernández de Kirchner, whose populist rule was blamed for a sharp economic downturn.[125]

Is Donald Trump a populist?

YES

Ronald Inglehart
Political Science Professor, University of Michigan;
Pippa Norris
Political Science Professor, Harvard University Excerpted from paper presented at American Political Science Association conference, September 2016

Donald Trump's populism is rooted in claims that he is an outsider to D.C. politics, a self-made billionaire leading an insurgency movement on behalf of ordinary Americans disgusted with the corrupt establishment, incompetent politicians, dishonest Wall Street speculators, arrogant intellectuals and politically correct liberals.

The CNN exit polls across all of the 2016 GOP primaries and caucuses from Iowa onwards revealed that the education gap in support for Trump was substantial; on average, only one quarter of postgraduates voted for Trump compared with almost half (45 percent) of those with high school education or less. Despite being located on opposite sides of the aisle, Trump's rhetoric taps into some of the same populist anti-elite anger articulated by Bernie Sanders when attacking big corporations, big donors and big banks.

But Trump and Sanders are far from unique. There are historical precedents in America exemplified by former Louisiana Gov. Huey Long's "Share Our Wealth" movement and former Alabama Gov. George Wallace's white backlash. And Trump's angry nativist rhetoric and nationalistic appeal fits the wave of populist leaders whose support has been swelling in many Western democracies. During the last two decades, in many countries, parties led by populist authoritarian leaders have grown in popularity, gaining legislative seats, reaching ministerial office and holding the balance of power.

Populist movements, leaders, and parties provide a mechanism for channeling active resistance. Hence Trump's slogan "Make America Great Again" — and his rejection of "political correctness" — appeals nostalgically to a mythical "golden past," especially for older white men, when American society was less diverse, U.S. leadership was unrivaled among Western powers during the Cold War era, threats of terrorism pre-9/11 were in distant lands but not at home, and conventional sex roles for women and men reflected patrimonial power relationships within the family and workforce.

Similar messages can be heard echoed in the rhetoric of France's Marine Le Pen, the Netherlands' Geert Wilders and other populist leaders. This nostalgia is most likely to appeal to older citizens who have seen changes erode their cultural predominance and threaten their core social values, potentially provoking a response expressing anger, resentment and political disaffection.

NO

David McLennan
Visiting Political Science Professor, Meredith College

Written for *CQ Researcher*, September 2016

During his presidential campaign, Donald Trump has often been labeled a populist. Although Trump appeals to many in the country who are angry with the political establishment, a closer look shows that he is more of a demagogue than a populist.

At first glance, Trump fits the traditional definition of "populist" regarding social issues and economic policies. Stylistically, populists rail against corrupt institutions like government and business that hurt the average person. Populists often state that solutions to problems are easy to implement, once the political system is changed and the corruption removed. Sound familiar?

The classic populist in American political history was William Jennings Bryan (1860-1925), the three-time Democratic nominee for president, who was known as "The Great Commoner." He attacked the Eastern elite and their support of the gold standard and brought many populists into the Democratic Party. As an orator, Bryan spoke with empathy for the common people, but even when attacking the elites, he showed no ill will toward those who supported the gold standard or other policies.

Bryan's economic, foreign and social policy positions reflected traditional populism. His economic messages often focused on ways to improve the lives of common people, in which he supported a minimum wage, standard workweeks and inspections of food, sanitation and housing conditions.

Although Trump rails against the elites on Wall Street and in Washington and he is popular with a large segment of the working class, he fails to compare to Bryan in the talking points we've heard in his countless rallies to date.

It doesn't help that Trump's policies are constantly evolving and revolving. His positions on immigration and trade restrictions are clearly populist, but large tax cuts for the wealthy and business are not. On foreign policy, his muddled positions on military intervention in the Middle East or Europe are more idiosyncratic than philosophical. It is on social issues, however, that Trump seems more opportunistic than populist. Until his involvement in presidential politics, Trump's positions on abortion or guns were more progressive than many in his current political base.

Rhetorically, Trump sounds like a populist when he attacks the political system or political elites, but his ad hominem attacks on individuals and groups do not fit the approach taken by Bryan. Because Trump scapegoats many ethnic and religious groups, he seems more of a demagogue than a true populist.

OUTLOOK

'Here to Stay'

The dominance of social media and frustration with political parties and other institutions will continue to propel populism, according to many experts, who say Trump and Sanders have tapped an anti-establishment mood that will not disappear soon.

"Trump forces, having entered the arena, aren't likely to simply exit quietly," said Gerald Seib, the *Wall Street Journal*'s Washington bureau chief. "If Mr. Trump wins, they will be empowered. If their standard-bearer fails, Republicans will have to learn to deal with an unhappy, establishment-hating army within. Eventually, Democrats may have to as well."[126]

Meanwhile, many experts say the issues that Sanders' campaign raised — such as free tuition at public colleges — will sustain left-wing populism, even if Sanders' supporters help to elect Clinton in November. "Those ideas, once they're introduced a legitimized way, are hard to tamp down," the University of Oregon's Lowndes says.

In a new book, *Populism's Power: Radical Grassroots Democracy in America*, Wellesley College professor of political science Laura Grattan said the left-wing populism of grassroots groups "can replace the traditional institutions that have failed citizens," pointing to "decimated social services, overcrowded and abandoned schools, shrinking access to higher education" and numerous other problems.

"When people in America face a heightened sense of insecurity, it is more difficult than ever to see political solutions to our problems," she said.[127]

Robert Reich, an economist and liberal activist who served as secretary of Labor under Bill Clinton, predicted that an anti-establishment "People's Party" made up of disaffected Democrats as well as some Republicans could take root as soon as 2020.[128]

But Lee Drutman, a senior fellow at the New America think tank, said the Democratic Party can incorporate populism. He predicted that over the next decade, Republicans will face a split between their populist and business-establishment wings, with the populists prevailing. Meanwhile, he said, Democrats will attract support from the business establishment while taking in the concerns of Sanders' largely city-based voters.

"Eventually, the Democrats will become the party of urban cosmopolitan business liberalism, and the Republicans will become the party of suburban and rural nationalist populism," Drutman said.[129]

Bonikowski, the Harvard sociologist, says the rightwing populism of Trump's campaign likely will encourage future candidates to run similar races playing on fears about immigration and a suspicion of other ethnic groups. "What were once private conversations around the dinner table are now okay in the public sphere — which is unusual," he says. "Even if Trump loses, the genie's out of the box."

The University of Stockholm's Moffitt predicted that in the United States and elsewhere, the lines separating populists and non-populists increasingly will diminish, as politicians of all leanings continue to seek ways to command followings through the news media and social media.

"We will see populist figures become increasingly brought into the 'mainstream' fold, while ostensibly 'mainstream' politicians will likely crib from the populist playbook," Moffitt said. "In other words, populism is here to stay."[130]

NOTES

1. "What Do Voters Think of Donald Trump?" *Manitowoc Herald Times Reporter*, Jan. 25, 2016, http://tinyurl.com/h54wyae.

2. Eduardo Porter, "In 'Brexit' and Trump, a Populist Farewell to Laissez-Faire Capitalism," *The New York Times*, June 28, 2016, http://tinyurl.com/zhahcho.

3. Scott Kirsner, "Test-riding Uber, the populist car service you summon with a mobile app," *Boston.com*, Oct. 18, 2011, http://tinyurl.com/zz4v8nd; Aaron A. Fox, *Real Country: Music and Language in Working-Class Culture* (2004), http://tinyurl.com/hrvh2ps; and Jay Cridlin, "Pearl Jam at 25: Back on the road, and bound for the Rock and Roll Hall of Fame," *Tampa Bay Times*, April 7, 2016, http://tinyurl.com/hwwvsta.

4. E. J. Dionne, "The Tea Party: Populism of the Privileged," *The Washington Post*, April 19, 2010, http://tinyurl.com/y83s9kq; Joe Lowndes and Dorian Warren, "Occupy Wall Street: A Twenty-First Century Populist Movement?" *Dissent*,

Oct. 21, 2011, http://tinyurl.com/h7ydw76; and Robert Borosage, "Embracing the New Populist Moment," Campaign for America's Future, July 19, 2016, http://tinyurl.com/hphkdup.

5. Diego von Vacano, "Hugo Chavez and the Death of Populism," Monkey Cage blog, March 6, 2013, http://tinyurl.com/j6bouk5.

6. Benjamin Moffitt, *The Global Rise of Populism* (2016), p. 160.

7. *Ibid.*, pp. 44-46. See also Tom Price, "Polarization in America," *CQ Researcher*, Feb. 24, 2014, pp. 193-216.

8. Michael Kimmel, *Angry White Men: American Masculinity at the End of an Era* (2013), http://tinyurl.com/zusrkoo.

9. David Goldstein, "Gore's refrain: 'They're for powerful; we're for people,' " *Deseret News*, Aug. 5, 2000, http://tinyurl.com/jfpk9bg.

10. Jennifer Epstein and Margaret Talev, "Clinton Adopts Sanders' Rhetoric of 'Rigged' Economy in Debate," Bloomberg, Feb. 11, 2016, http://tinyurl.com/hdx8paa.

11. Sheelah Kolkhatkar, "How Hillary Clinton Became a Better Economic Populist Than Donald Trump," *The New Yorker*, Aug. 12, 2016, http://tinyurl.com/hgddmga.

12. Paul Waldman, "Jeb Bush says he's going to tackle special interests in Washington. Don't believe him," *The Week*, July 7, 2015, http://tinyurl.com/zez4ueh.

13. See Sarah Glazer, "Wealth and Inequality," *CQ Researcher*, April 18, 2014, pp. 337-360.

14. Mara Liasson, "How This Election's Populist Politics Are Bigger Than Trump And Sanders," NPR, April 25, 2016, http://tinyurl.com/zo5zsk2.

15. Isaiah J. Poole, "Reclaiming Populism: Progressive Movement Is Alive and Well in the 21st Century," *AlterNet*, April 29, 2015, http://tinyurl.com/m39pbzm.

16. Zack Beauchamp, "A Republican intellectual explains why the Republican Party is going to die," *Vox.com*, July 25, 2016, http://tinyurl.com/hkr7s79.

17. Michael Cooper Jr., "A Message From Trump's America," *U.S. News & World Report*, March 9, 2016, http://tinyurl.com/znmrjkc.

18. Patricia Cohen, "What Trump and the GOP Can Agree On: Tax Cuts for the Rich," *The New York Times*, July 10, 2016, http://tinyurl.com/zsmj8aa; Robert W. Wood, "Clinton Vows Estate Tax Hikes, While Trump Vows Repeal," *Forbes*, Aug. 9, 2016, http://tinyurl.com/gnq8k2c.

19. Farai Chideya, "What Can Europe's Far Right Tell Us About Trump's Rise?" *FiveThirtyEight.com*, May 18, 2016, http://tinyurl.com/j4p3pcb.

20. Andy Kroll, "The Bernie Revolution: What's so appealing about a grumpy 74-year-old?" Yahoo! News, Dec. 3, 2015, http://tinyurl.com/jpkad3p.

21. Kira Lerner, "Gun Control Will Be On The Ballot In 4 Big States This November," ThinkProgress, Aug. 16, 2016, http://tinyurl.com/j42wvf4. See also Tamara Lytle, "Gun Control," *CQ Researcher*, July 25, 2016.

22. Cas Mudde, "The problem with populism," *The Guardian* (U.K.), Feb. 17, 2015, http://tinyurl.com/jfjfeqv.

23. "Trends in Party Identification, 1939-2014," Pew Research Center, April 7, 2015, http://tinyurl.com/q4emnog.

24. Carroll Doherty and Jocelyn Kiley, "Key facts about partisanship and political animosity in America," Pew Research Center, June 22, 2016, http://tinyurl.com/zvmdudk.

25. William M. Daley, Jonathan Cowan and Lanae Erickson Hatalsky, "Why Bernie Sanders Can't Win," *Politico*, Dec. 8, 2015, http://tinyurl.com/hk6ssx2.

26. See Peter Katel, "Tea Party Movement," *CQ Researcher*, March 19, 2010, pp. 241-264.

27. Robert Kagan, "Trump is the GOP's Frankenstein monster. Now he's strong enough to destroy the party," *The Washington Post*, Feb. 25, 2016, http://tinyurl.com/h2e7gsy.

28. See Chuck McCutcheon, "Future of the GOP," *CQ Researcher*, Oct. 24, 2014, pp. 889-912.

29. Arthur C. Brooks and Gail Collins, "The Democrats Nailed It. Does It Matter?" *The New York Times*, July 29, 2016, http://tinyurl.com/zu8nsw8.

30. Reid J. Epstein, "Donald Trump: 'I'm Afraid the Election Is Going to Be Rigged,' " *The Wall Street*

Journal, Aug. 1, 2016, http://tinyurl.com/zswbbon. Chris Moody and Kristen Holmes, "Donald Trump's history of suggesting Obama is a Muslim," CNN, Sept. 18, 2015, http://tinyurl.com/nkdxdhj.

31. Monica Bauer, "Berning up the Internet: Conspiracy Theories Poison the Well," *The Huffington Post*, April 21, 2016, http://tinyurl.com/ztwgcau.

32. "The Rage Against Trade," *The New York Times*, Aug. 6, 2016, http://tinyurl.com/hyc9guu. For background see Brian Beary, "U.S. Trade Policy," *CQ Researcher*, Sept. 13, 2013, pp. 765-788.

33. Robert Kahn and Steve A. Tananbaum, "Global Economics Monthly, December 2015," Council on Foreign Relations, Dec. 7, 2015, http://tinyurl.com/js25ufg.

34. "Populism and Globalization Don't Mix," *New Perspectives Quarterly*, Spring 2006, http://tinyurl.com/z793m9f.

35. Andrew Jacobs, "Brazil Workers' Party, Leaders 'Intoxicated' By Power, Falls From Grace," *The New York Times*, May 12, 2016, http://tinyurl.com/how87cf.

36. Jonathan Watts, "Brazil's Dilma Rousseff impeached by senate in crushing defeat," *The Guardian* (U.K.), Sept. 1, 2016, http://tinyurl.com/j223ejg.

37. Benjamin Moffitt, "Populism and democracy: friend or foe? Rising stars deepen dilemma," *The Conversation*, April 23, 2015, http://tinyurl.com/j3woayz.

38. Frank Cerabino, "From well-heeled to Publix retirees, Palm Beach County shows for Trump," *Palm Beach Post*, March 15, 2016, http://tinyurl.com/jbyc45n.

39. Rod Dreher, "Trump: Tribune of Poor White People," *The American Conservative*, July 22, 2016, http://tinyurl.com/hq6ynhp. Josh Hafner, "Donald Trump loves the 'poorly educated' — and they love him," *USA Today*, Feb. 24, 2016, http://tinyurl.com/hqk4774.

40. *Ibid.*, Dreher.

41. See Chuck McCutcheon, "Young Voters," *CQ Researcher*, Oct. 2, 2015, pp. 817-840.

42. Timothy B. Lee, "Why Hillary Clinton's Flip-Flopping on Trade May Not Matter," *Vox*, July 29, 2016, http://tinyurl.com/j7gyvqf.

43. Jamelle Bouie, "What Bernie Sanders Won," Slate, July 11, 2016, http://tinyurl.com/jyzrxjv.

44. Mike Collins, "The Pros and Cons of Globalization," *Forbes*, May 6, 2015, http://tinyurl.com/h7n4r9s.

45. Heather Long, "U.S. Has Lost 5 Million Manufacturing Jobs Since 2000," CNN, March 29, 2016, http://tinyurl.com/j3yfzlu.

46. Bob Davis and Jon Hilsenrath, "How the China Shock, Deep and Swift, Spurred the Rise of Trump," *The Wall Street Journal*, Aug. 11, 2016, http://tinyurl.com/j27es4y.

47. Dina Smeltz, Karl Friedhoff and Craig Kafura, "Core Sanders Supporters' Economic Pessimism Sets Them Apart From Clinton Supporters," Chicago Council on Global Affairs, July 25, 2016, http://tinyurl.com/z2yu85j.

48. For background see Christina L. Lyons, "Immigration," *CQ Researcher*, July 28, 2016.

49. Lauren Said-Moorhouse and Ryan Browne, "Donald Trump wants 'extreme vetting' of immigrants. What is the US doing now?" CNN.com, Aug. 16, 2016, http://tinyurl.com/zgfo5n6.

50. Kim Hjelmgaard and Gregg Zoroya, "Exploding UK immigration helped drive 'Brexit' vote," *USA Today*, June 28, 2016, http://tinyurl.com/h8a8vpg.

51. "What Is Fueling Global Anti-Immigrant Populism?" *The Wall Street Journal* video, June 29, 2016, http://tinyurl.com/jywa2g3.

52. Jonathan T. Rothwell, "Explaining Nationalist Political Views: The Case of Donald Trump," Gallup, Aug. 11, 2016, http://tinyurl.com/z4j745z.

53. Ronald Inglehart and Pippa Norris, "Trump, Brexit, and the Rise of Populism: Economic Have-Nots and Cultural Backlash," Harvard University, Kennedy School of Government, August 2016, http://tinyurl.com/jd5u9pe.

54. Daniel Gros, "Is Globalization Really Fueling Populism?" Project Syndicate, May 6, 2016, http://tinyurl.com/hgwbe2y.

55. Orlando Crowcroft, "Generation Trump: How Donald Trump became the populist leader the Tea Party never had," *International Business Times*, May 30, 2016, http://tinyurl.com/grcjecf.

56. Constanze Stelzenmüller, "A Donald for all of us — how right-wing populism is upending politics on both sides of the Atlantic," Brookings Institution, March 11, 2016, http://tinyurl.com/zvyrt27.

57. Barbie Latza Nadeau, "Europe's Secession Panic," *The Daily Beast*, Sept. 18, 2014, http://tinyurl.com/my7wdmp.

58. Padraig Reidy, "Yes, It Can Happen — Populist Conservatives Led UK Out of the European Union," BillMoyers.com, June 24, 2016, http://tinyurl.com/zjrjh69.

59. Thomas Greven, "The Rise of Right-Wing Populism in Europe and the United States: A Comparative Perspective," Friedrich-Ebert Siftung (Germany), May 2016, http://tinyurl.com/zoca6qj.

60. Jacqueline S. Gehring, "Sorry Donald, Brexit is not about you (or the United States)," Western Political Science Association, New West blog, June 24, 2016, http://tinyurl.com/hmxwf6n.

61. Cas Mudde, "The Trump phenomenon and the European populist radical right," *The Washington Post*, Aug. 26, 2015, http://tinyurl.com/h5fwxth.

62. "France," Parties and Elections in Europe, http://tinyurl.com/q2lvzjg.

63. See Sarah Glazer, "Future of the Euro," *CQ Researcher*, May 17, 2011, pp. 237-262.

64. Gros, *op. cit.* See also Brian Beary, "European Unrest," *CQ Researcher*, Jan. 9, 2015, pp. 25-48.

65. Roger Pilon, "Populism: Good and Bad," Cato Institute, Jan. 25, 2010, http://tinyurl.com/j59el34.

66. Henry Olsen, "Populism, American Style," *National Affairs*, Summer 2010, http://tinyurl.com/zqa94vh.

67. *Ibid.*

68. "Greenback movement," *Encyclopaedia Britannica*, http://tinyurl.com/grpzo6v.

69. "Granger movement," *Encyclopaedia Britannica*, http://tinyurl.com/guestr3.

70. *Political Parties in America* (2001), p. 69.

71. Pilon, *op. cit.*; "From Populism to the Progressive Era, 1900-1912," http://tinyurl.com/z4hsdp2.

72. *Political Parties in America, op. cit.*, p. 70.

73. "The Populist Party," Vassar College 1896 history website, http://tinyurl.com/5ddyft.

74. "William Jennings Bryan," History.com, http://tinyurl.com/j7yp4de. "Bryan's 'Cross of Gold' Speech: Mesmerizing the Masses," History Matters.com, http://tinyurl.com/lxftvy.

75. M. Mason Gaffney, "Henry George 100 Years Later: The Great Reconciler," MasonGaffney.org, 1997, http://tinyurl.com/zmlsm9r; Jill Lepore, "Forget 9-9-9. Here's a Simple Plan: 1," *The New York Times*, Oct. 15, 2011, http://tinyurl.com/hkrsl3v.

76. Political Parties in America, *op. cit.*, p. 70.

77. Matthew Artz, "Trump, Sanders following in California populists' footsteps," *San Jose Mercury News*, March 19, 2016, http://tinyurl.com/h3uv9oy.

78. "The Radio Priest," George Mason University Roy Rosenzweig Center for History and New Media, http://tinyurl.com/zd3zo6y. See also "New Deal Aims at the Constitution," *Editorial Research Reports* (*CQ Researcher*), Nov. 27, 1936.

79. "Share Our Wealth," HueyLong.com, http://tinyurl.com/ajsvsw.

80. Matt Farah, John H. Lawrence and Amanda McFillen, "From Winnfield to Washington: The Life and Career of Huey P. Long," Historic New Orleans Collection, 2015, http://tinyurl.com/zdw7kpw. Huey Long — Every Man a King," PBS.org, http://tinyurl.com/hff9hqg.

81. "Joseph R. McCarthy," History.com, http://tinyurl.com/o724hco; Daniel Bell, "McCarthy and Populism," *Commentary*, May 1, 1983, http://tinyurl.com/j47pajv.

82. "George C. Wallace," Biography.com, http://tinyurl.com/haqljf7.

83. "Richard Hofstadter," *Encylopaedia Britannica*, http://tinyurl.com/z9wzokq; David Greenberg, "Richard Hofstadter's Tradition," *The Atlantic*, November 1998, http://tinyurl.com/gpy9esm.

84. Tom Hayden, "Fred Harris: A Populist With a Prayer," *Rolling Stone*, May 8, 1975, http://tinyurl.com/jnrvzys.

85. Peter Barnes, "A Populist Manifesto," *The New Republic*, April 29, 1972, http://tinyurl.com/he4tu5g.

86. "Initiative, Referendum and Recall," National Conference of State Legislatures, Sept. 20, 2012, http://tinyurl.com/ndznq67.

87. Kevin O'Leary, "How California's Fiscal Woes Began: A Crisis 30 Years in the Making," *Time*, July 1, 2009, http://tinyurl.com/zy9rbop.

88. Shaun Bowler, Stephen P. Nicholson and Gary M. Segura, "Earthquakes and Aftershocks: Race, Direct Democracy and Partisan Change," *American Journal of Political Science*, January 2006, http://tinyurl.com/hhlggl7.

89. Stephen E. Atkins, *Encyclopedia of Right-Wing Extremism in Modern American History* (2011), p. 226, http://tinyurl.com/z5cfm74.

90. "Pat Buchanan on the Issues," OnTheIssues.org, http://tinyurl.com/hruuvln; Steven Stark, "Right-Wing Populist," *The Atlantic*, February 1996, http://tinyurl.com/h4udtwm.

91. Sean Wilentz, "Pox Populi," *The New Republic*, Aug. 9, 1993, http://tinyurl.com/z7yuecy; John Dickerson, "Donald Trump Isn't Another Ross Perot," *Slate*, Sept. 9, 2015, http://tinyurl.com/pwaz84g.

92. Josh Katz, "Can Gary Johnson, the Libertarian Nominee, Swing the Election?" *The New York Times*, Aug. 4, 2016, http://tinyurl.com/hdxvx9d.

93. Bill Scher, "Nader Elected Bush: Why We Shouldn't Forget," *RealClearPolitics*, May 31, 2016, http://tinyurl.com/gpnfntw.

94. Richard E. Cohen with James A. Barnes *et al.*, *The Almanac of American Politics 2016* (2015), p. 89.

95. Geoffrey Kabaservice, "Dave Brat and the Rise of Right-Wing Populism," *Politico Magazine*, June 12, 2014, http://tinyurl.com/gqylgnc.

96. Vanessa Williamson, Theda Skocpol and John Coggin, "The Tea Party and the Remaking of American Conservativism," *American Political Science Association Perspectives on Politics 9*, March 2011, http://tinyurl.com/nl2wl36, pp. 25-43.

97. Crowcroft, *op. cit.*

98. Gerald F. Seib, "The Tea Party Eyes Donald Trump — Warily," *The Wall Street Journal*, May 16, 2016, http://tinyurl.com/jqpec38.

99. Ronald Brownstein, "Trump's Path Runs Through the Rust Belt," *The Atlantic*, March 29, 2016, http://tinyurl.com/zpcj5ws.

100. Nicholas Confessore and Karen Yourish, "$2 Billion Worth of Free Media for Trump," *The New York Times*, March 15, 2016, http://tinyurl.com/jgo7tkq.

101. Issie Lapowsky, "Trump Isn't the First Tech-Propelled Populist. But This Time's Different," *Wired*, May 13, 2016, http://tinyurl.com/hqj372p.

102. See Peter Katel, " 'Occupy' Movement," *CQ Researcher*, Jan. 13, 2012, pp. 25-52.

103. "Commercial Banks," Center for Responsive Politics, http://tinyurl.com/jnw24j8.

104. Michelle Ye Hee Lee, "Sanders's claim that he 'does not have a super PAC,' " *The Washington Post*, Feb. 11, 2016, http://tinyurl.com/z64ddba; Tom Price, "Campaign Finance," *CQ Researcher*, May 6, 2016, pp. 409-432.

105. Cohen with Barnes, *op. cit.*, p. 884.

106. Kerry Picket, "Clinton Chooses Black Lives Matter Over Law Enforcement," *Daily Caller*, Aug. 6, 2016, http://tinyurl.com/hyw7qwx.

107. Meghan Keneally, "Donald Trump Facing Increasing Resistance From Within Own Party," ABC News.com, Aug. 9, 2016, http://tinyurl.com/hgz84um.

108. Eric Bradner, Elise Labott and Dana Bash, "50 GOP national security experts oppose Trump," CNN.com, Aug. 8, 2016, http://tinyurl.com/jdtr76e.

109. Andrew Prokop, "Evan McMullin: a former GOP staffer is now running for president on an anti-Trump platform," *Vox.com*, Aug. 8, 2016, http://tinyurl.com/zklblss.

110. Alex Altman, Phillip Elliott and Zeke J. Miller, "Inside Donald Trump's Meltdown," *Time*, Aug. 22, 2016, http://tinyurl.com/zt8ngqj.

111. David Wasserman, " 'Missing' White Voters Might Help Trump, But Less So Where He Needs It," *FiveThirtyEight.com*, June 2, 2016, http://tinyurl.com/zc6mlf5.

112. "Help Us Put Jill Stein on the Ballot in Every State," Jill Stein for President website, http://tinyurl.com/zar8akm; "2016 Presidential Access Ballot Map," Libertarian Party, http://tinyurl.com/hbey84u.

113. Harry Enten, "About A Third Of Bernie Sanders's Supporters Still Aren't Backing Hillary Clinton," *FiveThirtyEight.com*, Aug. 8, 2016, http://tinyurl.com/ztu6f7a.

114. Mike Vilensky, "Zephyr Teachout, Who Took on Cuomo, Faces Her Own Populist Rival," *The Wall Street Journal*, June 5, 2016, http://tinyurl.com/h4fvkyr.

115. Russell Berman, "Russ Feingold Wants a Rematch," *The Atlantic*, May 15, 2015, http://tinyurl.com/zagwu27.

116. "Issues," Mark Assini for Congress, http://tinyurl.com/zgpymdk; Siobhan Hughes, "Where Donald Trump Resonates, He is Embraced Down-Ballot," *The Wall Street Journal*, April 13, 2016, http://tinyurl.com/h8cdwna.

117. "2016 Ballot Measures," Ballotpedia.org, http://tinyurl.com/jf5aj2d.

118. "Nevada Background Checks for Gun Purchases Initiative, Question 1 (2016)," Ballotpedia.org, http://tinyurl.com/j5e96jb.

119. "Maine Minimum Wage Increase Initiative, Question 4 (2016)," Ballotpedia.org, http://tinyurl.com/jknsqwv; "Washington Minimum Wage Increase, Initiative 1433 (2016)," Ballotpedia.org, http://tinyurl.com/zc9y632.

120. "North Dakota Corporate Dairy and Swine Farming Referendum, Referred Measure 1 (June 2016)," Ballotpedia.org, http://tinyurl.com/h8wvjau.

121. Julie Bosman, "North Dakotans Reconsider a Corporate Farming Ban, and Their Virtues," *The New York Times*, June 12, 2014, http://tinyurl.com/juayylh.

122. Adair Turner, "Post-Brexit populism will not be thwarted by ignoring migration," *Australian Financial Review*, July 12, 2016, http://tinyurl.com/hufa2je.

123. Jonathan Owen, "End of the EU? Germany warns FIVE more countries could leave Europe after Brexit," *Express.com* (U.K.), June 26, 2016, http://tinyurl.com/zys2n92.

124. Michael Pearson, "Scotland likely to seek independence after EU vote, first minister says," CNN.com, June 26, 2016, http://tinyurl.com/zx4h5dz.

125. "The end of populism," *The Economist*, Nov. 28, 2015, http://tinyurl.com/jntgafr.

126. Gerald F. Seib, "Separating Donald Trump from Trumpism," *The Wall Street Journal*, Aug. 8, 2016, http://tinyurl.com/zs22j24.

127. Laura Grattan, *Populism's Power: Radical Grassroots Democracy in America* (2016), pp. 4-5.

128. Robert Reich, "Robert Reich Sees the Future: Why America's Two-Party System May Collapse," Alternet.org, March 22, 2016, http://tinyurl.com/zoj3dww.

129. Lee Drutman, "Donald Trump's candidacy is going to realign the political parties," *Vox.com*, March 1, 2016, http://tinyurl.com/jxzk8xc.

130. Moffitt, *op. cit.*, p. 160.

BIBLIOGRAPHY

Selected Sources

Books

Albertazzi, Daniele, and Duncan McDonnell, *Populists in Power*, Taylor & Francis, 2015.
Professors of politics at England's University of Birmingham (Albertazzi) and Australia's Griffith University (McDonnell) consider whether2 populist parties can govern successfully by examining populism in Italy and Switzerland.

Grattan, Laura, Populism's Power: Radical Grassroots Democracy in America, Oxford University Press, 2016.
A Wellesley College professor of political science argues that left-wing populist movements can improve U.S. democracy.

Moffitt, Benjamin, The Global Rise of Populism: Performance, Political Style, and Representation, Stanford University Press, 2016.

A research fellow in political science at Sweden's University of Stockholm explores how media are influencing contemporary populism.

Wodak, Ruth, The Politics of Fear: What Right-Wing Populist Discourses Mean, SAGE, 2015.
A professor of discourse studies at England's Lancaster University explains how global right-wing populists are bringing what she says are extremist views into the political mainstream.

Articles

Faiola, Anthony, "Meet the Donald Trumps of Europe," *The Washington Post*, May 19, 2016, http://tinyurl.com/hv8e6z5.
A journalist looks at right-wing populist leaders in Europe who often are compared to Donald Trump.

Ip, Greg, "Rise of Populist Right Doesn't Signal Demise of Globalization," *The Wall Street Journal*, June 8, 2016, http://tinyurl.com/gq8henb.
The newspaper's chief economics correspondent contends that immigration, rather than globalization, is fueling populism in Europe and the United States.

Jacobs, Andrew, "Brazil Workers' Party, Leaders 'Intoxicated' by Power, Falls From Grace," *The New York Times*, May 12, 2016, http://tinyurl.com/how87cf.
A reporter outlines the downfall of a left-wing populist party in Brazil whose leaders could not overcome deep economic problems and corruption.

Kolhatkar, Sheelah, "How Hillary Clinton Became a Better Economic Populist Than Donald Trump," *The New Yorker*, Aug. 12, 2016, http://tinyurl.com/hgddmga.
A journalist argues the Democratic presidential nominee is embracing economic populism.

Lapowsky, Issie, "Trump Isn't The First Tech-Propelled Populist. But This Time's Different," *Wired*, May 13, 2015, http://tinyurl.com/hqj372p.
A journalist says Donald Trump's and Bernie Sanders' use of social media differs sharply from earlier populists' use of communication tools.

Lehmann, Chris, "Donald Trump and the Long Tradition of American Populism," *Newsweek*, Aug. 22, 2015, http://tinyurl.com/ztdydmj.
A journalist compares Donald Trump to earlier populist leaders, finding similarities in their grievances against elites.

Liasson, Mara, "How This Election's Populist Politics Are Bigger Than Trump And Sanders," NPR, April 25, 2016, http://tinyurl.com/zo5zsk2.
Experts predict that Trump's and Sanders' versions of populism will extend beyond 2016.

Mudde, Cas, "The problem with populism," *The Guardian* (U.K.), Feb. 17, 2015, http://tinyurl.com/jfjfeqv.
A University of Georgia professor of international affairs explains the various types of populism.

Poole, Isaiah J., "Reclaiming Populism: Progressive Movement Is Alive and Well in the 21st Century," *AlterNet*, April 29, 2015, http://tinyurl.com/m39pbzm.
A left-wing activist says progressive groups are seeking to use populism to counter corporations' influence on government.

Reports and Studies

Alvares, Claudia, and Peter Dahlgren, "Populism, extremism and media: Mapping an uncertain terrain," *European Journal of Communication*, February 2016, http://tinyurl.com/zxm7rmb.
Communications researchers at Portugal's Lusófona University (Alvares) and Sweden's Lund University (Dahlgren) explore how the media are influencing populism in Europe.

Bonikowski, Bart, and Noam Gidron, "The Populist Style in American Politics: Presidential Campaign Discourse, 1952–1996," Social Forces, 2015, http://tinyurl.com/goo4vzm.
Harvard professors of sociology (Bonikowski) and government (Gidron) find frequent use of populist themes in presidential speeches during the latter half of the 20th century.

Inglehart, Ronald, and Pippa Norris, "Trump, Brexit, and the Rise of Populism: Economic Have-Nots and Cultural Backlash," Kennedy School of Government, Harvard University, August 2016, http://tinyurl.com/jd5u9pe.
Professors of political science at the University of Michigan (Inglehart) and Harvard (Norris) examine the factors responsible for the rise of populist parties in Europe

For More Information

American Enterprise Institute, 1150 17th St., N.W., Washington, DC 20036; 202-862-5800; www.aei.org. Conservative think tank analyzing populism and other political trends.

Campaign for America's Future, 1825 K St., N.W., Washington, DC 20006; 202-955-5665; https://ourfuture .org. Liberal political advocacy organization studying left-wing populism.

Centre for European Policy Studies, 1 Place du Congres, 1000 Brussels, Belgium; +32 (0) 2 229 39 11; www.ceps .eu. Think tank studying populism and other developments in Europe.

Donald J. Trump for President, 725 Fifth Ave., New York, NY 10022; 646-736-1779; www.donaldjtrump.com. Campaign offices and website.

FiveThirtyEight.com, 147 Columbus Ave., 4th floor, New York, NY 10023; www.fivethirtyeight.com. Website founded by statistician Nate Silver that examines how populism shapes political campaigns.

Hillary for America, P.O. Box 5256, New York, NY 10185; 646-854-1432; www.hillaryclinton.com. Campaign offices and website.

Our Revolution, 603 2nd St., N.E., Washington, DC 20002; https://ourrevolution.com. Political group begun by Sen. Bernie Sanders to further his populist goals.

Pew Research Center, 1615 L St., N.W., Suite 700, Washington, DC 20036; 202-419-4300; www.pewresearch .org. Nonpartisan think tank providing information on issues, attitudes and trends shaping the United States.

Weatherhead Center for International Affairs, Harvard University, 737 Cambridge St., Cambridge, MA 02138; 617-495-4420; http://wcfia.harvard.edu. Research center whose interests include studying international populism.

7

Campaign Finance

Tom Price

Billionaire businessman Donald Trump, the presumptive GOP presidential nominee, arrives in Laredo, Texas, during a trip to the U.S.-Mexican border on July 23, 2015. Grassroots anger over big money in politics has helped fuel support for Trump, whose campaign is largely self-financed, and Democratic Sen. Bernie Sanders of Vermont, whose $182 million war chest mainly has come from small, individual contributions.

From *CQ Researcher*,
May 6, 2016.

During the run-up to the 2016 political campaigns last August, five Republican presidential candidates along with several governors, senators and U.S. representatives gathered at the St. Regis Monarch Beach, a luxury resort along the Southern California coast.

They were attending one of the twice-yearly conferences organized by conservative multibillionaire industrialists Charles and David Koch, who invite several hundred wealthy compatriots to discuss how to remake America according to conservative or libertarian beliefs.

Conversations in posh settings are just part of their efforts to influence voters and public affairs. The brothers' far-flung network of affiliated organizations seeks to change federal, state and local policies, such as repealing the Affordable Care Act (ACA), cutting business regulations and reducing business subsidies. It includes a data-mining operation and cadres of organizers seeking to replicate political parties' grassroots operations.

Also part of the Koch operation are organizations that provide scholarships, medical checkups and tax-preparation services to various demographic groups, such as Latinos, along with warnings about the dangers of the ACA and the minimum wage.

All told, the Koch brothers and their wealthy associates plan to spend nearly $900 million — later reduced to $750 million — during the 2016 election cycle. Using what *The Washington Post* described as "a labyrinth of tax-exempt groups and limited-liability companies," the Kochs can keep much of the source of that money secret. And they are just one example of how the very

Conservatives Outspending Liberals in 2016 Races

The Republican Party and other conservative groups have spent more than $300 million so far in 2016 on candidates for Congress and the presidency — nearly nine times as much as the Democratic Party and other liberal groups. Conservatives also outspent liberals in the three previous federal election cycles. Spending by both sides reached record levels in 2012, the year of the first presidential election after a controversial Supreme Court ruling allowing unlimited campaign spending by private groups.

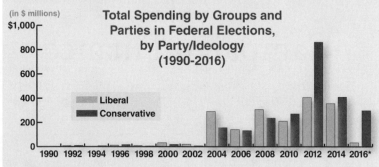

Total Spending by Groups and Parties in Federal Elections, by Party/Ideology (1990-2016)

(in $ millions)

Liberal
Conservative

* Through May 4, 2016

Source: "Total Outside Spending by Election Cycle, All Groups," Center for Responsive Politics, http://tinyurl.com/gofkzck

rich — both conservatives and liberals — are helping to make this the most expensive campaign season in history. Spending to influence the presidential and congressional elections could reach $10 billion.[1]

From early 2015 through April 29 of this year, 2,272 super PACs — political action committees that can raise and spend unlimited amounts of money supplied largely by corporations, unions, associations and wealthy individuals — reported raising $707 million and spending $304 million, mostly on the presidential race.[2] That's nearly three-quarters of the $828 million raised by super PACs during the entire 2012 campaign.[3]

Right To Rise USA, which spent $81 million supporting former Florida GOP Gov. Jeb Bush, so far has raised the most among super PACs, $121 million.[4] Two-fifths of super PAC contributions came from just 50 organizations and wealthy families. Most — 36 — gave to GOP organizations.[5]

While most big donors have supported conservative causes, wealthy liberals contribute as well, though much less overall. Since 2005, for example, the 100 members

of Democracy Alliance have raised and contributed more than $500 million to left-leaning think tanks, research organizations and political support groups.[6]

The cost of campaigning has soared since the Supreme Court began lifting restrictions on contributions and expenditures in the 1970s, raising fears that American democracy could be threatened by the outsized influence of a few wealthy donors.

Supporters of reform are pushing for stricter federal, state and local regulations, but opponents seek to reduce or even eliminate spending restrictions.

While this year's big spending on losing candidates Bush and Sen. Marco Rubio of Florida appears to negate the idea that money controls elections, grassroots anger over big money in politics is helping to feed activism coalescing around non-mainstream candidates Republican Donald Trump, a billionaire whose campaign is largely self-financed, and Democratic Sen. Bernie Sanders of Vermont, two-thirds of whose $182 million war chest has come from small, individual contributions.[7]

Public outrage about excessive political spending is reflected in "the surprising support for Senator Sanders, who has made it a central part of his campaign, and when Trump says he can't be bought," said Wendell Potter, co-author of the 2016 book *Nation on the Take: How Big Money Corrupts Our Democracy and What We Can Do About It.*[8]

Helping to fuel the flood of campaign spending are GOP opposition to campaign restrictions, a Federal Election Commission (FEC) paralyzed by partisan gridlock and a decades-long erosion of regulation by Supreme Court rulings. Those rulings include:

- *Buckley v. Valeo* (1976), in which the court said the First Amendment's protection of free speech prevents Congress from limiting spending by candidates and independent groups.

- *Citizens United v. Federal Election Commission* (2010), which allowed campaign spending by corporations (which had been banished from federal elections since 1907) and unions (whose federal spending had been banned in 1943). Also in 2010, a federal appeals court tossed out limits on how much can be contributed to independent political organizations, opening the door to establishment of super PACs.

- *McCutcheon v. FEC* (2014), in which the high court removed limits on the total amount a person can contribute to all federal candidates, parties and political action committees in each two-year election cycle.[9]

Regulatory rulings by the FEC and the Internal Revenue Service (IRS) also allowed some so-called social welfare organizations to spend without revealing the sources of their funds, enabling what has become known as the rise of anonymous or "dark money."

The dismantling of political spending limits means that today's elections get much more fuel from billionaires, multimillionaires and corporate and union treasuries. Nearly half the money raised for the presidential campaign during the first half of 2015 came from just 158 families and the companies they own or run.[10] During the 2014 cycle, 100 individuals spent more on elections than the 4.75 million Americans who contributed $200 or less.[11]

The super-rich also can finance their own campaigns. By April 21, for instance, Trump had contributed or lent $36 million to his campaign committee, which also received more than $12 million in individual contributions from small and large donors.[12]

Multibillionaire media mogul and former New York City Mayor Michael Bloomberg contemplated running for president as an independent before opting out in March. He had spent $261 million to win three mayoral terms, beginning in 2001.[13]

Those who oppose campaign finance reform say fears that big money can sway elections are overblown, noting that Trump appears to have won the GOP race with a low-budget campaign and that Sanders early in the race mounted an unexpectedly strong challenge to former Secretary of State Hillary Clinton despite her much larger war chest.[14]

Moreover, critics of limiting spending say small donors are starting to supplant wealthy ones in importance. "It's becoming more possible to raise money more quickly . . . by appealing to the general public" instead of wealthy donors, says David Keating, president of the Center for Competitive Politics in Alexandria, Va., which advocates less regulation of campaign finance. And big contributors can "max out" their ability to donate, he adds, while a candidate can repeatedly ask for more small donations.

But supporters of finance limits say while money may not guarantee election outcomes, it can unfairly influence post-election government decisions because legislators are especially sensitive to policies championed by wealthy donors. Research shows that rich contributors exert more influence over elected officials' decisions, essentially overriding the concept of one person, one vote, says Richard Hasen, a professor of law and political science at the University of California, Irvine, School of Law, and author of the 2016 book *Plutocrats United: Campaign Money, the Supreme Court, and the Distortion of American Elections.*

Eugene Volokh, a UCLA law professor who opposes spending restrictions, says Hasen's interest in political equality doesn't "justify restricting speech."

Numerous surveys show most Americans agree with the reformers, however. In a *New York Times*/CBS News poll last year, for instance, three-quarters of respondents favored limiting contributions and independent-group spending and requiring disclosure of all political donations.[15] In other surveys, three-quarters or more said the rich should not have more influence than others and that the *Citizens United* ruling should be overturned.[16]

With Republicans controlling Congress and the makeup of the Supreme Court in flux, reformers have turned to state and local governments. Legislation and voter initiatives have established public financing of campaigns, stiffer transparency requirements and other election changes. But regulation opponents have changed some state laws in their favor, as well.

The 2016 elections could have a huge impact on the future of campaign finance, legal observers say. Reform could hinge on which party controls state and federal legislatures and executive offices. And the February death of conservative Supreme Court Justice Antonin Scalia — coupled with Senate Republicans' intention to prevent

Conservative Super PACs Lead 2016 Spending

The three highest-spending super PACs — Right to Rise USA, Conservative Solutions PAC and America Leads — in the 2016 election cycle have supported Republican candidates who dropped their campaigns because of weak voter support. Nine of the 10 top-spending super PACs have spent a total of nearly $225 million backing conservative candidates or causes. Priorities USA Action, the only liberal super PAC among the top 10, has spent $5.7 million supporting Democrat Hillary Clinton.

Top-Spending Super PACs for 2016 Presidential Candidates, in $ millions*

Name	Ideology	Amount	Supports/Opposes
Right To Rise USA	Conservative	$81.2	Supported Jeb Bush
Conservative Solutions PAC	Conservative	$55.6	Supported Marco Rubio
America Leads	Conservative	$18.5	Supported Chris Christie
Our Principles PAC	Conservative	$17.4	Opposes Donald Trump
Great America PAC	Conservative	$13.1	Supports Donald Trump
Club for Growth Action	Conservative	$11.5	None
New Day For America	Conservative	$10.9	Supported John Kasich
Keep the Promise I	Conservative	$9.4	Supported Ted Cruz
Stand For Truth	Conservative	$9.0	Supported Ted Cruz
Priorities USA Action	Liberal	$5.7	Supports Hillary Clinton

Through May 4, 2016

Source: "2016 Outside Spending, by Super PAC," Center for Responsive Politics, http://tinyurl.com/mfczjv5

President Obama from filling that vacancy — could mean the next president will determine the future of campaign regulation.[17]

As political spending soars to record levels, here are some questions that politicians, activists, scholars and rank-and-file citizens are debating:

Does big money in politics subvert democracy?

During the first quarter of the current presidential race — from the beginning to the middle of last year — more campaign donations came from three Manhattan ZIP codes than from every ZIP code in the country with a majority of African-American residents, combined.[18] Even among the wealthy, big political donors are in the minority, according to a PNC Bank study, which found that only 30 percent of millionaires contributed to a political party or candidate during the 2014 election cycle, and just 9 percent gave more than $1,000.[19]

"The system is not an oligopoly of the top 1 percent or even the top .01 percent," said Richard Painter, a University of Minnesota Law School professor and former ethics adviser to Republican President George W. Bush. "It is far worse than that."[20]

That extreme imbalance subverts democracy because "when the money comes from too few donors that have too much influence, that creates a distortion of our political process," Hasen, the California law professor, says. The wealthy should not have a "much greater chance than an average voter of having their preferred policies enacted into law," he has said. The "main problem with money in U.S. politics is the translation of vastly unequal economic power into unequal political power."[21]

Some recent research appears to support Hasen's contention. In 2013, graduate students David Broockman of Berkeley and Joshua Kalla of Yale had 2,000 individuals request meetings with 191 U.S. representatives. Half identified themselves in the emails as "local constituents," while half described themselves as "local campaign donors." The self-described "donors" were five times more likely to score meetings with either the member or the member's chief of staff.[22]

Sen. Lindsey Graham of South Carolina, an advocate of campaign-finance limits, also worries about unequal access. "What I worry about is that we are turning campaigns over to about 100 people in this country, and they are going to be able to advocate their cause at the expense of your cause," he told New Hampshire voters during his failed run for the GOP presidential nomination last year.[23] Eventually, he continued, "we're gonna destroy American politics with so much money in the political process 'cause they're going to turn you off to wanting to vote."[24]

Voter apathy already may be happening, according to the Center for Responsive Politics, a nonpartisan organization that tracks political money. During the 2014 congressional elections, more money was spent on campaigns than ever before in an off-year campaign but turnout was the lowest since World War II, the center reported.[25]

But Keating of the Center for Competitive Politics cites a study by Louisiana State University political science professor Robert Hogan that suggests high spending increases turnout — at least in state legislative elections. Hogan concluded in 2012 that "higher levels of campaign spending" increased voter participation in legislative contests that he studied in 20 states during two election cycles.[26]

Keating argues that high spending only allows the donors to buy more speech, providing more information to voters, so "there's more debate about campaigns and elections, and that usually seems to be a good thing."

UCLA's Volokh says that throughout American history, some people — such as celebrities and newspaper owners — have had more influence than others. "Imagine if someone said, 'Let's ban newspapers from spending more than $1,000 editorializing for or against a candidate," he says. "We would say that's clearly unconstitutional. Corporations that own newspapers have the right to speak. Corporations that don't own newspapers have the same right to speak."

Celebrity can be more valuable than money, Keating says, citing Trump's success while spending far less than some GOP candidates who dropped out. "A big part of politics is having people know who you are," he says.

Trump has been famous for decades, having published a best-selling memoir, *The Art of the Deal*, in 1987, and starring in his popular television show, "The Apprentice," which first aired in 2004. During his campaign, the news media have been drawn to Trump's highly controversial statements and devoted much more coverage to him than to his opponents, which has diminished his need for campaign cash.[27]

MediaQuant, an Oregon-based company that analyzes the commercial value of news coverage, calculated that by the end of February 2016, the Trump campaign's coverage was worth nearly $2 billion — more than twice Clinton's $746 million worth of coverage, the second-most valuable.[28]

Billionaire hedge fund founder Tom Steyer of San Francisco has spent $13 million so far in this election cycle pushing for liberal causes, particularly action against climate change. He spent more than $70 million on congressional races during the 2014 cycle, making him the biggest spender in that election.

In fact, Trump's coverage has "basically thrown all these arguments [about the dangers of high spending] out the window," says Lisa Rickard, executive vice president of the U.S. Chamber of Commerce and president of the chamber's Institute for Legal Reform.

"Almost everywhere you look," said *National Review* Senior Editor Jonah Goldberg, who opposes Trump, "the super-rich are being stymied by democracy."[29]

Steven Law, president and CEO of the conservative super PAC American Crossroads, said Super PACs are only "the amplification system, so . . . if the music is lousy, it doesn't matter if you turn it up. It's still going to not sound all that convincing."[30]

However, reformers say that while money may not sway a presidential election, it can influence less momentous ones. "The smaller the office — a state legislative office or a city or county office — the more a large amount of money is likely to have a big influence," Hasen says, because such races get far less news coverage.

Should corporations be required to report all their political spending?

So-called dark money — political spending by groups not required to reveal their donors — has soared from $5 million during the 2006 election cycle to more than $174 million in the 2014 elections, according to the

Bo Rader/Wichita Eagle/MCT via Getty Images

Conservative billionaire Charles Koch, above, CEO of Koch Industries, his brother David and their wealthy associates said they plan to spend $750 million — down from an earlier $900 million — to influence voters and public policy during the 2016 election cycle. Charles Koch favors keeping the names of political donors secret because disclosure could invite retaliation against them. Already, he said, "We get death threats, threats to blow up our facilities, kill our people."

Center for Responsive Politics. The more expensive 2012 elections drew more than $300 million in dark money.[31]

Large dark contributions are expected again this year, but it takes watchdog groups some time to estimate spending that isn't clearly reported.

With the Supreme Court overturning many limits on campaign spending, reformers have begun demanding that spending be made public. They are pressing corporations to disclose their spending voluntarily, asking the Securities and Exchange Commission (SEC) — which regulates the securities industry, including stock markets and the periodic reports filed by publicly traded companies — to require disclosure of political activities and urging President Obama to order disclosure by government contractors. Some federal and state lawmakers have proposed legislation to require reporting, and a growing number of corporations are voluntarily revealing their political activities.

Opponents of reporting requirements argue that some anonymous spending is necessary to protect the spenders from retaliation. Some opponents contend that disclosure proponents focus on corporations — rather than unions and other groups — because their real goal is to drive businesses completely out of politics.

It is impossible to know how much dark money is contributed. But often it is given to politically active organizations that must report what they spend.

Douglas Pinkham, president of the Public Affairs Council, a Washington-based association of lobbyists and other public-affairs professionals, says big businesses probably do not supply much dark money because "if found out, it looks like [they are] trying to hide something."

Many big corporations do, however, make dues and other payments to business organizations such as the American Petroleum Institute or the U.S. Chamber of Commerce, which participate in politics and do not have to disclose their sources of income. And corporations overall are on track to give a record amount to super PACs, according to a March *Washington Post* analysis. As of Jan. 31, 680 companies had already contributed nearly $68 million to super PACs during the current election cycle, The *Post* reported. Super PACS received $86 million throughout the full 2012 cycle.[32]

Lee Drutman, a senior fellow at New America, a centrist Washington think tank, agreed with Pinkham that "if you scour the names of super-PAC contributors, with only a few minor exceptions, you don't see the big blue-chip corporations." But with the growth of dark-money organizations, he argued, "it will become easier for big corporations to give more without worrying about publicity. Arguably, this is already starting to happen."

Hasen, the California law professor, says "anybody who's a major player in spending money to elect candidates should have to disclose that publicly."

Political spending can create business risks that shareholders should know about, says Bruce Freed, president of the Center for Political Accountability, which presses businesses to disclose their political actions. "If you lived through Watergate, Watergate shows you what happens when there is secrecy," says Freed, referring to the 1970s scandal in which a break-in at the Democratic National Committee headquarters in Washington, D.C., culminated, two years later, in the resignation of Republican President Richard M. Nixon.

Secrecy also poses a national-security risk, according to the University of Minnesota's Painter, a conservative advocate for finance reform. Lack of disclosure means foreign companies could pour money into campaigns and "help choose our government," he said. While foreign contributions are illegal, he argued that the ban is "as easy to evade as underage drinking laws on college campuses."[33]

Quoting unnamed White House officials, *The New York Times* reported in January that President Obama was seriously considering issuing an executive order to require government contractors to report their political spending. Public Citizen, the liberal activist group, told the newspaper that 70 of the 100 largest U.S. companies would be covered under the order.[34]

According to a study released last month by Maplight, a nonpartisan research organization that tracks money's influence on politics, during the last decade major government contractors have received $1,171 in federal money for every $1 invested in lobbying and political action committee contributions.[35]

Opponents of total disclosure, such as the U.S. Chamber of Commerce, note that almost all campaign-related spending already is reported — nearly 97 percent during the 2014 election cycle. The chamber, which reports its political spending but not its donors, spent $35.5 million during that cycle, more than any other politically active nonprofit, according to the Center for Responsive Politics.[36]

"It doesn't make any sense to report all donors to organizations that spend less than a majority of their budget for political expenditures," the Center for Competitive Politics' Keating says. "You would have donors exposed who gave money with no intention or realization that their money would be used for political purposes." Similarly, he says, requiring only government contractors'

Majority Opposes *Citizens United* Ruling

Four in five American adults say the U.S. Supreme Court's 2010 ruling in *Citizens United v. FEC* — which allowed unlimited campaign spending by corporations, unions and other organizations — should be overturned. Fewer than a fifth support the ruling.

Percentages* of U.S. Adults who Say the Supreme Court's 2010 *Citizens United v. FEC* ruling . . .

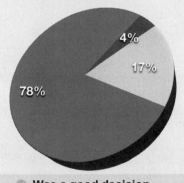

4%

17%

78%

● **Was a good decision**
● **Should be overturned**
● **Not sure**

* *Do not total 100% due to rounding.*

Source: Greg Stohr, "Bloomberg Poll: Americans Want Supreme Court to Turn Off Political Spending Spigot," *Bloomberg Politics*, Sept. 28, 2015, http://tinyurl .com/pn395v9

disclosures would make contracting appear politicized.

Disclosure advocates' real goal is to make businesses afraid to participate in politics, say the chamber's Rickard and others on the political right. "This is about separating corporations from their trade associations and their ability to make their case on issues," says Justin Hakes, senior communications director for the chamber's Institute for Legal Reform. Disclosure advocates "want to know who's giving money to whom. Then they can go and put pressure on those companies to either stop [political] spending or put on restrictions."

Charles Koch said disclosure would endanger donors by inviting retaliation against them. Already, he said, "We get death threats, threats to blow up our facilities, kill our people. We get [the cyber-hacking group] Anonymous and other groups trying to crash our IT systems. So long as we're in a society like that, where the president attacks us and we get threats from people in Congress, and this is pushed out and becomes part of the culture — that we are evil, so we need to be destroyed, or killed — then why force people to disclose?"[37]

Political scientists Bertram Levine of Rutgers and Michael Johnston of Colgate University suggested requiring that all donations be anonymous, so politicians would not know who gave them money. Under such a system, incumbents "could not 'thank' their benefactors with policy 'favors,' nor could they extract contributions through intimidation," Levine and Johnston wrote.

They proposed distributing contributions through the FEC, which would fine or jail contributors who revealed their donations.[38] Yale Law School professors Ian Ayres and Bruce Ackerman made a similar proposal in their 2002 book, *Voting with Dollars.* But, Levine and Johnston wrote, "sadly, the Ackerman-Ayers system has not taken root."

Should public funds help finance congressional, state and local campaigns?

To counter the influence of big campaign donors, some reformers want to extend public financing — which is available for presidential campaigns — to congressional, state and local elections.

Under the presidential system, taxpayers can direct $3 of their federal taxes each year to help pay for presidential campaigns. In the primaries and caucuses, the federal funds match candidates' small donations. The total amount available in each primary or caucus depends on the size of the state holding the election. In the general election, major party candidates receive equal amounts, and recipients cannot raise additional funds.

Recently, major candidates have turned down the public funding so they could raise and spend substantially more with private donations. Obama and Republican nominee Mitt Romney together raised more than $2 billion from private donors in 2012, and this year's candidates may break that record.

Opponents of public financing say it's not a legitimate use of tax revenues and note that the presidential system has collapsed. But reformers are making headway at the state and local levels. And Democratic presidential

Guide to Campaign Finance Terms

501(c)(3)	Charitable, educational, religious or scientific nonprofit group that can engage in limited lobbying but cannot participate in partisan political activity; not required to disclose donors
501(c)(4)	Social-welfare group that must operate primarily to further the common good and general welfare of the community and spend more than half of its money for non-political purposes; not required to disclose donors
501(c)(5)	Labor union or agricultural group that must operate primarily to serve members but may engage in lobbying and political activities; not required to disclose donors
501(c)(6)	Business league, real estate or trade board or similar group that may engage in lobbying and political activities; not required to disclose donors
527 Group	Advocacy group that raises money for political activities; political parties or political action committees (PACs) in this category must disclose donors and donations
Citizens United v. FEC	Supreme Court decision in 2010 that allowed corporations, unions and other groups to spend unlimited amounts to support or oppose candidates
Dark money	Money spent by political nonprofits from undisclosed donors
Federal Election Commission	Six-member regulatory agency created by Congress to enforce campaign finance laws; membership split along partisan lines
PAC	Political action committee — private entity that raises and donates limited amounts to candidates or parties; individuals can contribute up to $5,000 to PACs, while PACs can donate up to $5,000 to candidates and $15,000 to parties
Super PAC	PAC that can raise unlimited amounts from companies, nonprofits, unions or individuals and spend unlimited amounts on campaigns as long as it does not donate directly to candidates
Soft money	Money given to political parties rather than specific candidates; not subject to contribution limits
Straw donor	Campaign donor who illegally contributes to a campaign on behalf of another person
Taxpayer check-off	Option allowing tax filers to donate $3 of their federal income tax to the public Presidential Election Campaign Fund.

Sources: Center for Responsive Politics; Bill Mears, "Where the money is: A campaign spending primer," CNN, Jan. 23, 2012; *United States of America v. Pierce O'Donnell*; Federal Election Commission; Internal Revenue Service

candidates Clinton and Sanders support public financing for congressional elections, although federal action is unlikely while Republicans control Congress.

"Our vision for American democracy should be a nation in which all people, regardless of their income, can participate in the political process, can run for office without begging for contributions from the wealthy and the powerful," Sanders said.[39] Sanders cosponsored the Fair Elections Now proposal, which would give U.S. Senate candidates $6 in federal funds for every dollar they raise in small contributions and would provide a 50 percent tax credit on the first $50 in annual campaign donations.[40]

Clinton would tap federal funds to match small donations in presidential and congressional races. Bills also have been introduced to fund House races.

Meanwhile, 13 states provide public funds for at least some statewide offices in exchange for recipients agreeing to contribution and spending limits.[41] A growing number of cities also are adopting public financing programs. Legislators have approved some of the reforms, while some were approved via referendums.

New York City, for example, provides $6 in city funds for each of the first $175 given to a city candidate.[42] Virginia taxpayers can take a tax credit for the first $25 given to state and local candidates. Oregonians get up to $50 in credits for local, state and federal contributions and can take a tax deduction for larger donations. Arkansas, Ohio and Minnesota allow credits or deductions for small contributions.[43] Connecticut candidates get state funding if they receive a large number of small donations.[44] Tallahassee, Fla., provides some funds to city candidates.[45]

Maryland offers state funding in the general election to gubernatorial candidates who agree not to raise and spend private funds. Republican Larry Hogan accepted the $2.6 million available in 2014 and defeated Democrat Anthony Brown, who declined public funds and quadrupled Hogan's spending.[46]

Seattle voters last year approved giving each registered voter $100 to donate to candidates in city elections. The money can be given only to candidates who agree to abide by spending and contribution limits and who participate in at least three debates.[47]

Yale's Ackerman and Ayres, who advocated anonymous political giving in 2002, now want to take the "Seattle idea" national. They propose giving every registered voter $50 in federal funds during presidential-election years — and a smaller amount in other years — to be used as contributions to candidates who agree to spending limits. The professors said this would balance the impact of big contributors by generating $6.5 billion, about the same as all candidates and independent groups spent on the 2012 federal elections.[48]

Ackerman says he and Ayres also encourage more state and local reforms, noting that Seattle-like proposals will be on ballots in South Dakota and Washington state in November.

Represent.Us, a nonpartisan movement pushing for anti-corruption laws in cities and states across the country, has proposed giving each registered voter a $100 tax rebate to donate to federal candidates and political committees. Candidates would be limited to accepting money from three sources: tax rebates, individual contributions up to $500 per election and committees funded solely by tax rebates and $500 contributions.[49]

Take Back Our Republic, a conservative group that advocates reform, suggests allowing taxpayers to direct $100 of their taxes to candidates each year.[50]

Three Democratic members of Congress — Reps. Tom Rice of North Carolina and Chris Van Hollen of Maryland, as well as Sen. Tom Udall of New Mexico — have introduced legislation to revitalize the presidential funding system by providing substantially more funding to address candidates' perceptions that they must spend more than is offered under the current public financing system. Their proposal would remove the current system's spending limits, provide six federal dollars for each dollar raised in small donations, and raise the taxpayer checkoff from the current $3 to $20.

Despite the reforms that have been enacted for state and local elections, however, public financing faces strong opposition.

Fifty-six percent of those surveyed in a November Associated Press poll said they opposed the idea, and just 25 percent said public financing of campaigns is very effective or extremely effective.[51] Meanwhile, fewer taxpayers are contributing to the current presidential finance system: Only 6 percent of 2012 tax returns opted to allow some of their taxes to fund the system, down from 27.5 percent in 1976.[52]

Keating complains that public finance legislation sometimes comes with spending caps and that it can be difficult to "ensure money isn't stolen from the government." In 2013, for instance, two campaign workers for then-New York City Comptroller John Liu, a Democrat, were convicted of fabricating donors to draw more public funding into Liu's campaign.[53]

Others say public campaign financing diverts resources from more important purposes. New York Republican Dean Skelos, the state Senate majority leader, said, "With our state's limited resources, does anyone really believe we should make it easier for politicians to run for re-election at the expense of funding our schools, fixing our roads and restoring the governor's cuts to programs that affect the developmentally disabled?"[54]

The University of Minnesota's Painter argued, however, that a "tax rebate for democracy," such as the Take Back Our Republic proposal, would send billions of dollars in small donations to candidates "who would no longer depend on a tiny sliver of the population for the money they need to get elected."[55]

BACKGROUND

Curbing Political Money

Americans have worried about the effects of money on politics and government since the early years of the republic. While the partisan divide currently has most Democrats supporting restrictions and most Republicans opposed, those positions have not been consistent.[56]

In the 18th century, George Washington and other candidates distributed whiskey to get votes.[57] Andrew Jackson, in 1828, became the first presidential candidate to spend a substantial amount of money — $1 million — on an organized campaign.[58]

Jackson launched — and his successors maintained — the "spoils system," funding their political activities by assessing government employees' paychecks. In the first campaign-finance regulation, Congress in 1867 banned such assessments on workers at Washington's Navy Yard. In 1876, Congress blocked such assessments from any federal worker. The Civil Service System was created in 1883 to insulate federal employees from politics.

Politicians then sought other sources of campaign funds, primarily business interests. Just before the 1884 election, GOP presidential nominee James Blaine was observed attending a fundraising dinner at the posh Delmonico's Steakhouse in New York City with 200 of the richest Americans. Some analysts said the subsequent public uproar over the gathering contributed to Blaine's loss to Democrat Grover Cleveland.[59]

In the late 19th and early 20th centuries, Mark Hanna, a wealthy Ohio businessman, was a United States senator and chairman of the Republican National Committee. But he is best known as perhaps the earliest big-time political fundraiser who famously declared: "There are two things that are important in politics. The first is money, and I can't remember the second." Hanna helped raise millions of dollars for each of fellow Ohioan William McKinley's two winning presidential campaigns in 1896 and 1900.

Vice President Theodore Roosevelt, who became president after McKinley's assassination in 1901, was embarrassed by corporate contributions to his 1904 campaign and in 1905 proposed banning corporate cash from federal elections. Such legislation passed in 1907, promoted by what has been called the first campaign-reform organization, the National Publicity Law Organization.

Roosevelt also suggested that Congress fund federal elections, arguing that "the need for collecting large campaign funds would vanish if Congress provided an appropriation for the proper and legitimate expenses of each of the great national parties."[60]

Congress did not agree. Instead, it passed the Federal Corrupt Practices Act of 1910, which mandated post-election disclosure in House races of fundraising and spending by political party committees operating across state lines. The law was strengthened the next year to cover Senate elections, require pre-election disclosure by candidates as well as parties and restrict contributions to $5,000 for House and $10,000 for Senate candidates. Legislation in 1925 required quarterly reports every year from all organizations that gave to elected officials.

Labor unions — which, unlike corporations, were not banned from political spending in the 1907 law — became important sources of money for Democrats during Franklin D. Roosevelt's presidency in the 1930s. But in 1943, Republicans and conservative Southern Democrats united to outlaw union contributions in federal elections.

Unions responded by establishing the first political action committees, using members' donations to finance

CHRONOLOGY

1876-1883 *Campaign finance reform era begins.*

1876 Congress prohibits soliciting political contributions from federal workers.

1883 Federal Civil Service Act ends "spoils system," which tied federal employment to campaign contributions.

1896-1907 *Businesses dominate campaign fundraising.*

1896 Wealthy businessman Mark Hanna breaks fundraising records by collecting millions of dollars for fellow Ohio Republican William McKinley, who wins presidential election.

1907 Congress bans corporate contributions to federal candidates.

1911-1974 *Congress gradually reins in campaign spending.*

1911 Congress orders disclosure of contributions and spending in Congressional races.

1943 Congress outlaws union contributions to federal candidates.

1972 Federal Election Campaign Act upholds ban on direct contributions by corporations and unions, but allows them to set up separate political action committees (PACs).

1974 Watergate scandal leads Congress to impose stricter limits on political contributions and spending and to establish public financing of presidential campaigns.

1976-Present *Courts reshape campaign laws.*

1976 In *Buckley v. Valeo*, Supreme Court strikes down limits on candidate and independent spending as a First Amendment violation.

1978 Supreme Court overturns state laws against corporate spending on state ballot issues.

2000 Republican George W. Bush becomes first major presidential candidate to turn down public financing in race for nomination.

2002 McCain-Feingold law restricts spending and requires disclosure on some broadcast ads.

2008 Supreme Court invalidates McCain-Feingold law's "millionaire's amendment," which had eliminated contribution limits for candidates running against opponents who spend large amounts of their own money. . . . Democrat Barack Obama refuses public financing.

2010 In *Citizens United v. FEC* ruling, Supreme Court says corporations and unions can spend unlimited amounts to support or oppose candidates if the organizations act independently of the candidates and their parties. . . . Federal appeals court rules organizations and individuals can make unlimited contributions to independent PACs.

2012 Obama and GOP nominee Mitt Romney turn down all public funding in federal election cycle, which becomes most expensive in history.

2014 Supreme Court strikes down limit on how much an individual can contribute in a federal campaign cycle.

2015 Conservative multibillionaire industrialists Charles and David Koch reveal that they and wealthy associates plan to spend $750 million to promote libertarian and conservative positions during the 2016 election cycle. . . . Seattle voters approve public financing of city campaigns, joining other state and local governments enacting reforms while Congress and the Federal Election Commission are deadlocked. . . . Supreme Court upholds Florida law prohibiting judicial candidates from soliciting contributions.

2016 All major presidential candidates refuse public campaign funds. . . . Highest-spending Republicans trail in delegate count behind wealthy businessman Donald Trump, who runs a relatively inexpensive campaign. . . . Spending on federal races runs ahead of record 2012 pace. . . . February death of conservative Supreme Court Associate Justice Antonin Scalia means the next president could flip the court toward supporting regulation.

More Firms Lifting Veil on Political Activities

Advocacy group finds transparency on the rise.

As debates rage over whether corporations should be required to disclose their political spending, a growing number of companies have chosen to voluntarily tell the public about their political activities.

The Center for Political Accountability, a Washington-based advocacy group that pushes for corporate disclosure, in 2011 created a way to measure transparency in conjunction with the Carol and Lawrence Zicklin Center for Business Ethics Research at the University of Pennsylvania's Wharton School. Of 83 companies rated on transparency since the Index of Corporate Political Disclosure and Accountability first was published, the average score increased to 71.3 out of 100 last year, from 42.5 in 2011.

The index now covers all but three of the firms on the Standard & Poor's 500 stock market listing of major public companies. The average score of those 497 companies was 39.8. The center's index measures how well companies disclose independent political expenditures and corporate contributions to candidates, parties, political committees and super PACs as well as donations to trade associations and nonprofit organizations that may not identify donors.

Also covered by the index are activities of employee-funded political action committees and political spending of corporate funds. The index also reflects whether the companies publish their policies on when and where they spend political money.

Although much of this information must be reported to the Federal Election Commission or state agencies, the center wants it disclosed in one place so shareholders and the public can find it more easily.

Disclosure is increasing, says Bruce Freed, the center's president, because "companies recognize there is a premium placed on transparency. Companies do it with supply-chain management, diversity [and] executive compensation. Political exposure is part of that broad transparency spectrum."

Peer pressure also plays a role, center Associate Director Marian Currinder says. "The index comes out and the CEO hears about it and becomes angry that they had no policy on this," she says. "They're worried that it makes them look bad, makes them look like they're hiding something."

In addition, Freed says, companies find it easier to respond to requests for political contributions if they've published a formal policy. "It creates uniformity and depersonalizes any decision they make."

Political transparency is part of "a solid foundation of good corporate governance" that "significantly contributes to our company's ability to compete effectively," Prudential Financial Vice President Margaret Foran said.[1]

Disclosure by Microsoft Corp., which received a nearly perfect score, is "rooted in our longstanding and very strong commitment to good corporate governance," says Dan Bross, senior director of corporate citizenship.[2]

political activities that couldn't be funded from union treasuries. Later, in the 1960s, corporations and trade associations began to establish their own PACs.

Dark Money

The Treasury Department set the stage for dark money in 1959 when it defined nonprofit "social welfare" organizations, known as 501(c)(4) groups after the section of tax legislation that created them. Under a 1913 law, Congress had exempted from taxes "civic leagues or organizations not organized for profit but operated exclusively for the promotion of social welfare." Such organizations did not have to disclose their donors.

The 1959 rule said 501(c)(4) organizations must work "primarily" (not exclusively) on social welfare. Later, "primarily" came to be understood as more than half, measured by the organization's use of funds.

Today, social-welfare groups often spend up to 50 percent of their funds on politics. And many get away with spending most of their money on political activities because of lax enforcement by the IRS and FEC, according to organizations that track campaign

Microsoft contributes corporate funds to candidates when it is legal and through its employee- and shareholder-financed political action committee. It also spends corporate money on lobbying. Microsoft does not contribute to so-called super PACs, which can raise and spend unlimited amounts of money. It also avoids contributing "dark money" by reporting payments to trade associations that are spent for political purposes, when Microsoft's total payment to an association hits $25,000.

"We wanted to make sure that our spending decisions were driven and guided by our policies, as opposed to giving money to an independent organization that may in some instances spend the money in a way that is not aligned with our views," Bross says of the decision not to give to super PACs. "We have in some instances made it clear that some trade associations do not speak for us on certain issues" and that those associations "shouldn't be spending [Microsoft] money on a particular issue."

Three companies scored 97.1 on the center's index in 2015 — real estate and railway giant CSX Corp., oil and gas driller Noble Energy Inc., and Becton, Dickinson and Co., a medical-devices manufacturer. Another 20 companies scored above 90, including Intel Corp., Monsanto Co., UPS Inc. and Prudential.[3]

Despite rising average scores on the index, most companies fall short of full disclosure. Just 28 percent fully disclose contributions to candidates, parties and political committees. And just 11 percent fully report donations to "social welfare" organizations, which are not required to disclose their donors. A majority of the companies publish a detailed explanation of their contribution policies, and another one-third publish abbreviated explanations.[4]

The center found last year that 30 companies — including Kimberly-Clark and IBM — did not have political action committees and spent little or no corporate cash on elections. Seventeen — including Hershey Co. and Sherman-Williams Co. — made contributions only through their PACs. Nine — including Colgate-Palmolive Co. and investment firm Goldman Sachs — did not spend corporate funds and asked their trade associations not to use their payments for political purposes.[5]

The center also works with shareholders who pressure corporations to disclose political activities, and it has negotiated disclosure agreements with more than 140 companies on the S&P 500. The organization encounters more resistance to disclosure from trade associations than from companies, Freed says.

"You can't be against transparency in this day and age," says Douglas Pinkham, president of the Washington-based Public Affairs Council, an international association of lobbyists and other public-affairs professionals "A lot is driven by employees who want the company to be more open. A policy of openness can build trust among employees and customers at a time when most people are cynical about politics."

— Tom Price

---

[1] "The 2015 CPA-Zicklin Index of Corporate Political Disclosure and Accountability," Center for Political Accountability, http://tinyurl.com/h77yzfs.

[2] See the Microsoft Transparency Hub's political page, http://tinyurl.com/jrqtvpx.

[3] "The 2015 CPA-Zicklin Index of Corporate Political Disclosure and Accountability," *op. cit.*

[4] *Ibid.*

[5] *Ibid.*

---

spending. The Center for Responsive Politics identified 24 groups that broke the 50-percent cap between 2008 and 2013.[61]

In 1971 Congress adopted the Federal Election Campaign Act, which limited spending and contributions and required more comprehensive and frequent reports on spending and fundraising. The act preserved the ban on business and union campaign spending but allowed them to use their funds to administer their political action committees. That helped to kick off rapid PAC growth, from about 1,000 PACs contributing

$12.5 million in 1974 to more than 4,000 PACs contributing $105 million in 1986.[62]

Congress took more aggressive action in 1974 after the Nixon administration's Watergate scandal, which included secret political fundraising, improper spending and other illegal attempts to influence the 1972 election. The scandal took its name from Washington's Watergate building, where burglars employed by Nixon's re-election committee were caught trying to tap phones and steal documents from the Democratic National Committee's office.

Pet Causes Spur Wealthy to Open Their Wallets

From Israel to climate change, policy issues drive political giving.

The multibillionaires drawing so much flak for their political spending this year are sometimes motivated by issues, sometimes by self-interest and sometimes by a happy marriage of the two.

Witness Sheldon Adelson and his wife, Miriam: They judge candidates primarily by their support of Israel, although a secondary issue is opposition to Internet gambling, which could cut into the profits of his casinos.[1] Each April, GOP politicians gather at the annual Republican Jewish Coalition conference held at Adelson's Venetian casino and hotel in Las Vegas — a ritual that has become known as the "Adelson Primary."

"Israel is at the core of everything he does," said Fred Zeidman, a friend of Adelson and the former chairman of the U.S. Holocaust Memorial Museum in Washington. Adelson grew up poor in Boston and made large donations to Democrats until 1996, when he sensed the Democrats "becoming less passionate about Israel," said Michael Leven, former president of the Adelson-owned Las Vegas Sands Corp.

The Adelsons have kept their powder dry so far in this campaign season, but they gave almost $93 million to conservative organizations during the 2012 election cycle — more than three times greater than the second-largest donor.[2] Adelson has said that he could back Donald Trump if the developer wins the GOP nomination.[3] But, as the presidential campaign was just gearing up two years ago, Adelson confidantes said he was looking for a mainstream winner. "He doesn't want a crazy extremist to be the nominee," the late Victor Chaltiel, an Adelson friend who sat on the Sands board, said in 2014.[4]

Adelson — whose wealth has been estimated by *Forbes* magazine at $32 billion — owns two Maybach limousines, which can cost more than a half million dollars each, and two Boeing 747 jumbo jets.[5] He also makes substantial contributions to Jewish and Israeli charities.[6]

Most megadonors support Republican candidates and conservative causes. But wealthy liberals also invest millions in politics. Tom Steyer, who made more than $1 billion as a hedge-fund owner and manager, has spent $13 million in this election cycle pushing for action against climate change.[7]

That puts him second in the ranks of donors in this campaign cycle, trailing only Robert Mercer, a hedge-fund manager and computer scientist who has given $16.7 million to conservatives, according to the Center for Responsive Politics, which tracks campaign spending. Investor George Soros ranks tenth, with $8 million spent, mostly in support of Democratic presidential candidate Hillary Clinton. James and Marilyn Simons, whose fortune also comes from hedge funds, rank seventh, having contributed more than $9 million, almost all to Clinton and liberal causes.[8]

Steyer says his commitment to the environment — especially fighting climate change — grew in part from a sense of guilt about fossil-fuel investments made by Farallon Capital Management, the San Francisco-based hedge fund he founded in 1986.

"I left the firm and committed myself to addressing global climate change because — based on the scientific evidence — I could not reconcile my personal values with managing a fund that by mandate is invested in all sectors of the global economy, including fossil fuels," he said. "But the more I learned about the energy and climate problems we currently face, the more I realized I had to change my life. . . . I believe it is truly the most pressing issue we face."[9]

Steyer sold his ownership share of Farallon in late 2012 and finished withdrawing his investments there in 2014.

In 2010, he gave $5 million to help defeat a ballot measure that would have weakened California's motor-vehicle emissions standards. He then put $30 million into a successful ballot initiative that raised corporate taxes and increased spending on clean-energy projects.[10] He created NextGen Climate, his super PAC, in 2013.[11] He spent more than $70 million — mostly through NextGen — on congressional races, making him the biggest spender in the 2014 election cycle.[12] He and his wife, Kat Taylor, also founded Beneficial State Bank in Oakland in 2007, which loans money to people and small businesses who otherwise couldn't get them.[13]

Some Republicans have called Steyer a hypocrite for railing against fossil fuels after building part of his fortune on them. But Bill McKibben, a founder of the environmental advocacy group 350.org, said: "This is precisely what we want people to do: sell investments in fossil fuels and get to work solving the problem of climate change."[14]

The Ricketts family, which owns the Chicago Cubs baseball team, supports Republicans, with one notable exception. Patriarch Joe Ricketts, founder of the discount brokerage TD Ameritrade, and his wife, Marlene, rank No. 11 on the list of largest donors, having given $7.5 million to conservative groups so far this cycle.[15] He is a former Democrat whose biggest concerns are curbing government spending and reducing the national debt.

The couple gave $5 million last year to Unintimidated, the super PAC backing Wisconsin Gov. Scott Walker for the GOP presidential nomination, but got much of it back when Walker dropped out of the race in the fall.[16]

One of their sons, Todd, was Walker's fundraising co-chair and runs the family's super PAC, Ending Spending, which promotes cuts in government expenditures. Another son, Pete, won a self-funded campaign for governor of Nebraska in 2014, running as a Republican. But their daughter, Laura, is a gay-rights activist who donates to Democratic candidates and organizations and raised hundreds of thousands of dollars for President Obama's 2012 reelection campaign.[17]

— *Tom Price*

Casino operator Sheldon Adelson and his wife Miriam donate to candidates based on their support for Israel. The couple gave nearly $93 million to conservative organizations during the 2012 election cycle, more than triple the second-largest donor.

[1] Molly Ball, "The Sheldon Adelson Suck-Up Fest," *The Atlantic*, April 2, 2014, http://tinyurl.com/hq9az3a; "In Pictures: Outrageous Executive Perks: Sheldon Adelson," *Forbes*, May 5, 2010, http://tinyurl.com/zqjcxzw.

[2] "2012 Top Donors to Outside Spending Groups," Center for Responsive Politics, http://tinyurl.com/zup9qqn.

[3] Jonathan Mahler, "Trump Courting Jewish Voters Wary of His Agenda and Bluster," *The New York Times*, March 21, 2016, http://tinyurl.com/j5rxy2n.

[4] Matea Gold and Philip Rucker, "Billionaire mogul Sheldon Adelson looks for mainstream Republican who can win in 2016," *The Washington Post*, March 25, 2014, http://tinyurl.com/koboxqj.

[5] Ball, *op. cit.*; Howard Stutz, "Adelson slips one spot on the Forbes list," *Las Vegas Review-Journal*, Sept. 29, 2014, http://tinyurl.com/h4enb4k. Also see "In Pictures. . .," *op. cit.*

[6] Marc Fisher, "Sheldon Adelson: Casino magnate, mega-donor is a man of many motives," *The Washington Post*, Oct. 23, 2012, http://tinyurl.com/923xxep.

[7] "2016 Top Donors to Outside Spending Groups," Center for Responsive Politics, http://tinyurl.com/3ufhfoa.

[8] *Ibid.*

[9] Tom Steyer, "How Climate Change Changed Me," *Politico*, July 14, 2014, http://tinyurl.com/zx2bzok.

[10] Fredreka Schouten, "A Billionaire's Green Mission," *USA Today*, Oct. 14, 2014, http://tinyurl.com/jlf88z4.

[11] "Tom Steyer Founder," NextGen Climate, http://tinyurl.com/j2nahou.

[12] Richard Valdmanis, "This Billionaire Environmental Activist Hasn't Picked A Democrat To Back Yet Steyer is one of the party's biggest donors," *The Huffington Post*, Jan. 20, 2016, http://tinyurl.com/h9psrxb

[13] "Tom Steyer Founder," NextGen Climate, http://tinyurl.com/j2nahou.

[14] Michael Barbaro and Coral Davenport, "Aims of Donor Are Shadowed by Past in Coal," *The New York Times*, July 4, 2014, http://tinyurl.com/ngwon7l.

[15] "2016 Top Donors to Outside Spending Groups," *op. cit.*; "Ricketts, John Joe: Donor Detail," Center for Responsive Politics, http://tinyurl.com/hqsmxu2.

[16] Robert Costa, "Ricketts family gives more than $5 million to Walker super PAC," *The Washington Post*, July 30, 2015, http://tinyurl.com/hmx5we3; Jennifer Reingold, "Ricketts: The new billionaire political activist," *Fortune*, Sept. 21, 2012, http://tinyurl.com/hj8z78g; Clare O'Connor, "Meet the Billionaire Ricketts Family: Dad Plans Anti-Obama Attack While Gay Daughter Fundraises For Prez," *Forbes*, May 17, 2012, http://tinyurl.com/goghkt3.

[17] *Ibid.*

The legislation established more-comprehensive contribution and spending limits, established public financing of presidential campaigns and created the FEC to administer the law. Taxpayers could check a box on their federal tax returns directing a portion of their taxes to the presidential election fund.

Public funding seemed to work well for about six elections, but George W. Bush in 2000 became the first major candidate to reject the money in his race for the GOP nomination. Because accepting public funds limited total spending, Bush concluded that he could raise more than the government would give him.

In 2004, Democrats John Kerry and Howard Dean joined Bush in that decision. Four years later, Barack Obama rejected public financing in both the nominating contest and the general election. In 2012, both Obama and GOP nominee Mitt Romney turned down all public funding, as have the leading candidates in the 2016 cycle.[63]

Dismantling Restrictions

The courts have dealt deep blows to the reformers' accomplishments.

In *Buckley v. Valeo*, the Supreme Court in 1976 struck down limits on candidate and independent spending as an infringement on free speech. The challenge to the law was initiated by James Buckley, a Conservative Party senator from New York and brother of conservative writer William F. Buckley Jr. The first-named defendant was Senate secretary and FEC commissioner Francis Valeo. During oral arguments, Justice Potter Stewart famously declared that "money is speech, and speech is money."[64]

The decision began a series of court-ordered dismantlings of campaign restrictions, which continued into 2014. In 1978, for instance, the Supreme Court struck down state laws against corporate spending on state ballot issues. In 1986, in *FEC v. Massachusetts Citizens for Life*, the court ruled that nonprofit corporations can donate to candidates as long as the corporations do not receive contributions from for-profit corporations or unions.[65]

Reformers turned to Congress again in 2002 with the McCain-Feingold Act, named for its chief Senate sponsors, Arizona Republican John McCain and Wisconsin Democrat Russ Feingold. The bill outlawed so-called "soft money" — contributions to political parties above federal limits but allowed because they did not directly support a candidate. The money was supposed to be used for "party-building" activities, such as voter registration and get-out-the-vote drives. Both parties had spent hundreds of millions of soft money dollars on ads that often urged voters to contact a candidate to praise or criticize votes on the issues, which critics said was thinly disguised support or opposition.

The law restricted and required disclosure of spending on broadcast ads that mention a candidate near an election. It also required candidates to appear in ads to say they approved the message and indexed contribution limits to inflation.

In 2007 the Supreme Court said in the *Wisconsin Right to Life v. FEC* case that corporations and unions could use their own money to run ads near elections as long as those ads were not the "functional equivalent" of advocacy for a candidate. Once again, organizations bought ads that implied candidate support or opposition without explicitly saying so.

The next year, the high court overturned the "millionaire's amendment," a provision in the McCain-Feingold law designed to level the playing field for candidates running against wealthy opponents who self-funded expensive campaigns. The court earlier had allowed limits on campaign contributions to stand but said candidates could spend unlimited amounts of their own money on their campaigns. The millionaire's amendment lifted contribution restrictions for candidates opposing someone who spent more than $350,000 of his own money in a House race and a varying amount for Senate races. The court said lifting the cap for opponents of wealthy candidates "impermissibly burdens" the right of a wealthy candidate to spend more money.

Then in 2010 the Supreme Court — in one of its most controversial rulings — overturned restrictions on corporate and union political spending. In *Citizens United v. FEC*, the court said business corporations, unions and some other incorporated organizations could spend unlimited amounts of money to support or oppose candidates, as long as the organizations acted independently of the candidates and their parties.

Writing for the five-justice majority, Justice Anthony Kennedy said "government may not suppress political speech on the basis of the speaker's corporate identity." But Justice John Paul Stevens, writing for the dissenting justices, predicted the ruling would result in "corporate domination" of campaigns.

Kennedy argued that high corporate spending would not corrupt elections, because disclosure requirements and the Internet would enable citizens to know what the organizations were spending and who was benefitting. But subsequent court rulings and regulatory action — or inaction — have enabled much spending to occur in secret.

Later that year, in *SpeechNow v. FEC*, the U.S. Court of Appeals for the District of Columbia ruled that organizations and individuals can donate unlimited amounts to PACs that spend independently of candidates and parties.

In the 2014 *McCutcheon v. FEC* case, the high court welcomed more high campaign spending by striking down the limit on how much an individual could contribute to all federal candidates and organizations in a campaign cycle. Shaun McCutcheon, the wealthy CEO of an Alabama electrical engineering company, challenged the $123,000 limit in 2013. Fewer than 650 people hit that ceiling during the 2012 cycle.

As a result of the court ruling, a wealthy donor now can spend up to $1.3 million on federal elections every two years by giving a maximum of $2,600 in each congressional race plus $32,400 to a political party.[66] The 2012 federal elections the first with a presidential campaign after the *Citizens' United* decision — were the most expensive in history, with more than $6 billion spent by all players, including more than $300 million in dark money. Some predict that overall spending in the current cycle could reach as much as $10 billion.[67]

The power of money also was demonstrated at the state level in Illinois, where an executive described as the state's richest man organized support for a Republican multimillionaire who captured the governor's mansion while Democrats won control of the legislature and voters backed ballot issues supported by liberal interest groups. Kenneth Griffin, a billionaire hedge-fund founder, recruited other wealthy individuals to finance the campaign of Bruce Rauner, who reportedly is worth more than $500 million. Griffin donated $5.5 million to Rauner's campaign and lent Rauner his private plane for use in the campaign.[68]

Rauner also spent millions of his own money. His spending triggered Illinois' version of the millionaire's amendment, which differed in a key provision from the federal provision struck down by the Supreme Court.

While the federal law had raised contribution limits for candidates running against high-spending opponents, the Illinois law removed all contribution restrictions. Ironically, that meant that Rauner's wealthy supporters could donate millions more to his campaign.[69]

The Supreme Court did let one campaign finance restriction stand last year — a Florida law forbidding judicial candidates from personally soliciting contributions.[70]

CURRENT SITUATION
Super PACs

Flush with cash, super PACs are taking on tasks traditionally done by candidates' campaign organizations. It's part of an effort to work as closely as possible with the candidates without violating the ban on coordinating activities. It also is a response to the high cost of TV advertising and the realization that the tens of millions of super PAC dollars spent on Jeb Bush's ads did not prevent his campaign's collapse.

The super PAC Keep the Promise I had people on the ground working for former Republican presidential candidate Ted Cruz, a Texas senator, in key primary states, for example. And Correct the Record, a super PAC supporting Clinton, has been working directly with her campaign to produce Internet communications after the FEC ruled that free online content is exempt from regulation.[71]

Super PACs and other political organizations also are perfecting methods of hiding the sources of some of their funds. Limited liability corporations — LLCs — have joined nonprofit "social welfare" groups as vehicles for channeling dark money. LLCs often are incorporated without disclosing the sources of their income. Some appear to have been established solely to help a candidate.

Decor Services LLC, for example, was incorporated in Delaware in January. Two weeks later it gave $250,000 to a super PAC supporting New Jersey Republican Gov. Chris Christie, who has since dropped out of the presidential race. In February, it made an identical donation to a super PAC backing former GOP candidate Rubio. Children of Israel LLC, which listed "donations" as its type of business when it incorporated last year in California, gave $400,000 to super PACs supporting Cruz and former GOP Arkansas governor Mike Huckabee, both of whom have since dropped out.[72]

LLCs have become more active in this campaign "with no disclosure of the human or humans behind these contributions," according to Paul S. Ryan, deputy executive director of the Campaign Legal Center, a non-profit organization that focuses on protecting the right to vote and restricting money's influence in politics.[73]

Investigation of LLCs has been blocked by partisan gridlock at the Federal Election Commission, he said. Established in 1974 to administer election law, the six-member commission cannot have more than three members of the same political party. In recent years, commissioners have consistently divided along party lines and been unable to act on major issues.

For instance, the FEC recently deadlocked over whether to investigate W Spann LLC, which gave $1 million to Restore Our Future, a super PAC supporting Romney, during the four months that Spann existed in 2011. A Romney business associate acknowledged establishing the corporation to make the contribution, an action Ryan said seems to violate a law against giving in another person's name.[74]

"Unless the FEC is reconstituted with commissioners willing to do their job," Ryan said, anonymous donors "will continue to get away with laundering their money into federal elections."

State and Local Actions

Several states and cities have adopted reforms for state and local elections, even as other states have loosened regulations on political spending.

All states require candidates to report contributions and expenditures, but the regulations for group and individual contributors vary. For example, 14 states require large contributions to be disclosed within 24 hours. Almost all states require political committees to report. Most states also mandate disclosure of independent expenditures by individuals, corporations and other organizations, depending on the amount of the spending.[75] In Alaska, California, Colorado, Montana and North Carolina, independent groups must identify their top sources of income when they buy political ads.[76]

Maryland state Sen. Jamie Raskin, who recently won the Democratic nomination to run for the U.S. House, has introduced a bill to make Maryland-registered corporations obtain shareholder approval for political spending — a provision he acknowledges is aimed at banning corporate spending. "The majority of shares of *Fortune* 500 firms are owned by institutional investors, such as retirement and pension funds, mutual funds, insurance companies, universities, foundations, charities and other nonprofits," and they are not allowed to engage in partisan political activity, said Raskin, an American University law professor.[77]

Take Back Our Republic, the conservative reform group, would raise the federal reporting threshold in order to encourage more small contributions. The current limit could discourage political contributions out of fear that "a person's contributions may become public," the organization said. "Just as voting is secret, so small contributions should be secret to avoid the potential of retaliation by employers, unions, or others."[78]

Meanwhile, Keating, of the Center for Competitive Politics, wants to "get rid of as much [campaign regulation] as possible." He would eliminate contribution limits and raise the federal reporting threshold for individual contributions to at least $1,000. "The individual threshold has been $200 since 1979," he says, "and that's too low."

Some states are loosening campaign spending limits. In December, Wisconsin's Republican governor and GOP-controlled Legislature rolled back campaign spending regulations by allowing corporations to contribute to political parties and legislative campaign committees, doubling the contribution limit for individuals and allowing candidates to coordinate with advocacy groups.[79]

In Arizona, the Republican-led Legislature eased campaign regulations in March by:

- Removing reporting requirements and limits on what individuals can spend raising funds for a candidate,
- Lifting disclosure requirements for social welfare groups, even if the IRS has not yet acted on their registration,
- Allowing candidates to transfer campaign funds to other campaigns, and
- Allowing groups to spend unlimited, undisclosed amounts, including corporate funds, to try to influence legislation.[80]

Keating says his organization opposes regulations because "we think the First Amendment means what it says: Congress shall make no law abridging the freedom

Does big money in politics subvert democracy?

YES
Richard Hasen
Professor Of Law And Political Science, University Of California, Irvine; Author Of Plutocrats United: Campaign Money, The Supreme Court, And The Distortion Of American Elections

Written for *CQ Researcher*, May 2016

The new era of big money in politics is very troubling — but not for the reasons that many reformers think. In recent years, it has become ever easier for wealthy individuals and entities to spend money on elections. Much of this happened because of the Supreme Court's 2010 decision in *Citizens United v. Federal Election Commission*, which allowed corporations to spend unlimited sums independent of candidates on election ads. After this case and other developments came super PACs, groups that collect unlimited contributions from others to engage in this kind of spending. We also have seen other groups doing the same thing, but allowing contributors to remain anonymous.

The amounts the wealthy are spending are staggering. Casino magnate Sheldon Adelson and his wife contributed between $98 million and $150 million in the 2012 elections, and environmentalist Tom Steyer contributed about $74 million in the 2014 elections. The Koch brothers' network of about 400 people has pledged to spend just under $900 million — later reduced to $750 million — to influence public policy and voters in the 2016 elections. And this is just the money we know about.

The problem with this big money is not bribery. Nor is it elections going to the biggest spender. Failed Republican presidential candidate Jeb Bush is just the latest illustration of the principle that even with a lot of spending, the public won't get behind a candidate that it does not otherwise support.

Instead, the key problem is that those who contribute and spend big money in elections have much greater influence over who is elected and what policies are pursued than everyone else. Bush got multiple chances to make his case for election and to be taken seriously, not because many voters backed him but because a handful of extremely wealthy people supported him.

Big money not only makes it more likely that a candidate will be taken seriously; it also gives contributors access to make a case. Studies show that the wealthy are much more likely to see their preferences enacted into law than everyone else. And the views of the super-wealthy tend to be different than those of the rest of us.

In the end, the fundamental problem with the wealthy influencing our elections is that we allow those with great economic power to translate it into political power. That is anti-democratic.

NO
David Keating
President, Center for Competitive Politics

Written for *CQ Researcher*, May 2016

In 1968, a few wealthy liberals backed Eugene McCarthy's presidential campaign against fellow Democrat Lyndon Johnson. Back then, supporters could donate any amount, so a handful gave today's equivalent of millions of dollars. Did this "subvert" democracy? Of course not; it enhanced it.

McCarthy, a U.S. senator from Minnesota, drove Johnson from the race, and in doing so changed the politics of the Vietnam War. Today, while contributions to candidates are capped at $2,700 per election, all Americans can pool their funds through independent super PACs without limit and speak to other Americans. Such speech is vital. As McCarthy observed, "There is clear historical evidence that large contributors have been highly important in supporting controversial and maverick political movements."

No amount of spending will win an election if voters don't like a candidate or his ideas. Just ask Jeb Bush.

Individuals who give significant sums to political groups do so because they believe in the causes or candidates those groups support. Ample academic research demonstrates that donors give to candidates who share their beliefs — not the other way around. Tom Steyer supports candidates who already favor action on climate change, and Sheldon Adelson supports candidates who already support Israel.

Campaign spending has other benefits as well. Higher spending leads to better-informed voters and higher turnout. Limiting spending prevents candidates from performing many of the basic tasks of campaigning and reduces independent voices to a whisper. Both outcomes afford incumbents a huge advantage.

Restricting campaign spending also gives a further advantage to media companies, which are currently exempt from speech regulations. It also helps those with household names such as Republican Donald Trump, who has received nearly $2 billion in "free" media, according to a recent analysis.

Even if limiting campaign spending and speech was a good idea in theory, the rules would be enforced by government officials, the last persons who should have such power.

Consider these thoughts from former Supreme Court Justice Louis D. Brandeis: "Those who won our independence believed . . . that freedom to think as you will and to speak as you think are means indispensable to the discovery and spread of political truth; that without free speech and assembly discussion would be futile; that with them, discussion affords ordinarily adequate protection against the dissemination of noxious doctrine."

of speech," an argument that California law professor Hasen called "simply an incorrect reading of First Amendment doctrine and practice." The Constitution does not require "literally no regulation ever of speech, expression, or the spending of money on speech [or] expression," he said.[81]

Congress Stalls

In what amounts to a symbolic gesture, given GOP control of Congress, more than 100 Democrats in the House have co-sponsored legislation to increase public disclosure of political spending by corporations, unions and other organizations. Such entities would be required to report political spending to shareholders, members or donors and require that political advertisements identify the organizations purchasing those ads and the large donors who helped pay for them.[82]

Democrats Clinton and Sanders support amending the Constitution to invalidate Supreme Court decisions that have eviscerated campaign finance laws. Most proposed amendments would deny First Amendment protections to corporations, but some go even further.

Democratic Rep. Richard Nolan of Minnesota has introduced a constitutional amendment that would restrict free-speech protections to "natural persons only," allowing corporate speech to be regulated. It also would direct federal, state and local governments to regulate campaign spending so that "no person gains, as a result of that person's money, substantially more access or ability to influence" elections. And it would require disclosure of contributions and expenditures and block courts from interpreting campaign spending as constitutionally protected speech.[83]

Hasen, the author of *Plutocrats United*, says amending the Constitution is "the wrong way to go" because it would require approval by two-thirds of each congressional chamber and ratification by three-fourths of the state legislatures.

GOP presidential candidate Trump says the campaign finance system is corrupt and brags that as a businessman he used political contributions to buy influence with government officials. He supports disclosure of political donations and criticized the Supreme Court's *Citizens United* decision allowing corporations, unions and other incorporated organizations to make unlimited independent political expenditures.[84]

Cruz says limiting campaign contributions is an attack on freedom.[85]

OUTLOOK
Supreme Court Is Key

In an interview before Justice Scalia's death in February, California law professor Hasen said the Supreme Court would have to change before campaign finance reform could occur at the federal level. "It would be foolish to push spending limits now, because the courts would strike them down as unconstitutional," he said.

Now, with the possibility that a Democratic president could appoint a liberal as Scalia's replacement, Hasen says, "the court definitely could swing from 5-4 against regulation to 5-4 in favor, and *Citizens United* could be one of the first cases on the chopping block."

Lee Epstein, a professor of law and political science at Washington University in St. Louis, agrees. Epstein listed several Supreme Court decisions that would be overturned with a new liberal justice, particularly those dealing with race, gun control and campaign finance. "Some would go quickly, like *Citizens United*, and some would go slower. But they'll go," Epstein said.[86]

Those projections demonstrate the importance of this year's presidential election to the future of campaign finance.

Reformers had assumed they would have to focus on state and local campaigns, and they still may. Even if Democrats hold the White House and retake the Senate, Republicans remain heavily favored to maintain control of the House, which would keep reforms stalled in Congress.

"When the time comes to place ideas before a new progressive Supreme Court, we have to begin with legislative proposals on the state and local levels," Hasen says. Such proposals, he adds, need to be in states that allow ballot initiatives in order "to get around legislatures that might be reluctant to mess with the rules" that got them elected.

As Represent.Us Director Silver says: "We're not trying to pass national legislation, because Washington, D.C., is where good ideas go to die. We won't bring them to Washington until we have critical mass across the country."

The status of the deadlocked FEC is another crucial factor. Silver, Hasen and John Pudner, executive director of Take Back Our Republic, say the FEC can't be effective with six commissioners — three from each party — who divide along party lines.

"We've got to figure out a way to have someone non-partisan appointed to break ties," Pudner says.

Silver suggests an odd number of commissioners and "a different way to appoint commissioners so it's less political." Perhaps, he says, a judge or nonpartisan government official who does not serve at a president's discretion could make one appointment. Or, Hasen says, the commission could be converted into an administration, led by a single administrator who would implement the law.

Because of the failures of big-spending presidential candidates this year, the Public Affairs Council's Pinkham says, "We're realizing [elections are] not all about money." That view could make Americans less likely to think reform is necessary, he says. It also could "make it less likely that big companies will support super PACs in the future."

Hasen questions whether Trump's candidacy will have much influence on future campaigns because he's unique. But Pinkham and Pudner say they expect candidates to follow his emphasis on attracting free news coverage rather than purchasing advertising, especially as people become less inclined to watch TV commercials.

"They're all taking notes," Pudner says of campaign consultants. "They are always looking at what's working."

NOTES

1. "The truth behind fake political ads," CBS News, Jan. 31, 2016, http://tinyurl.com/hev8l6s. Also see Matea Gold, "Koch-backed political network, built to shield donors, raised $400 million in 2012 elections," *The Washington Post*, Jan. 5, 2014, http://tinyurl.com/pl65soc. Also see Matea Gold, "Charles Koch downgrades his political network's projected 2016 spending from $889 million to $750 million," *The Washington Post*, Oct. 21, 2015, http://tinyurl.com/jbvp4cn.

2. "Super PACs," Center for Responsive Politics, accessed April 29, 2016, http://tinyurl.com/gwazfke.

3. Matea Gold and Anu Narayanswamy, "The new Gilded Age: Close to half of all super-PAC money comes from 50 donors," *The Washington Post*, April 15, 2016, http://tinyurl.com/hugosjn.

4. "Super PACs," Center for Responsive Politics, March 21, 2016, http://tinyurl.com/jppx5jw.

5. Gold and Narayanswamy, *op. cit.*

6. Matea Gold, "Joe Biden and Elizabeth Warren set to address gathering of wealthy liberal donors," *The Washington Post*, Nov. 12, 2014, http://tinyurl.com/gudpr59.

7. "Donald R. Trump: Candidate Summary, 2016 Cycle," Center for Responsive Politics, http://tinyurl.com/hs8wjcp. Also see "Bernie Sanders (D): Candidate Summary, 2016 Cycle," Center for Responsive Politics, http://tinyurl.com/zkeguy2.

8. Jayne O'Donnell, "More than 900 'Democracy Spring' protesters arrested in D.C. — so far," *USA Today*, April 18, 2016, http://tinyurl.com/hlwpag4.

9. Kenneth Jost, "Campaign Finance Debates," *CQ Researcher*, May 28, 2010, pp. 457-480; "McCutcheon, *et al.* v. FEC Case Summary," Federal Election Commission, http://tinyurl.com/pyjcc2h.

10. Nicholas Confessore, Sarah Cohen and Karen Yourish, "Just 158 families have provided nearly half of the early money for efforts to capture the White House," *The New York Times*, Oct. 10, 2015, http://tinyurl.com/pmhwvjn.

11. "The Growing Shadow of Political Money," *The New York Times*, Jan. 24, 2015, http://tinyurl.com/jyvdhko.

12. "Donald Trump: Candidate Summary, 2016 Cycle," *op. cit.*

13. Celeste Katz, "Mayor Bloomberg spent $102M on campaign to win third term — or $175 per vote," *New York Daily News*, Nov. 27, 2009, http://tinyurl.com/zet52oy.

14. "2016 Presidential Race," Center for Responsive Politics, accessed on March 7, 2016, http://tinyurl.com/j38o8o7.

15. "Americans' Views on Money in Politics," *The New York Times*, June 5, 2015, http://tinyurl.com/nh4g83n.

16. "Americans Want Supreme Court to Turn Off Political Spigot," *Bloomberg Politics*, Sept. 28, 2015, http://tinyurl.com/pn395v9; David Donnelly,

"Campaign finance reform must be addressed," *Las Vegas Review-Journal*, Oct. 12, 2015, http://tinyurl.com/hunrf94.

17. Richard L. Hasen, "How Scalia's Death Could Shake Up Campaign Finance," *Politico*, Feb. 14, 2016, http://tinyurl.com/hqxhrhd.

18. Adam Smith, "The Top Money-in-Politics Stories of 2015," *Every Voice*, Dec. 30, 2015, http://tinyurl.com/zalxb9o.

19. "Disclosure levels," Take Back Our Republic, http://tinyurl.com/jkqecgz.

20. *Ibid.*

21. Richard Hasen, *Plutocrats United: Campaign Money, the Supreme Court, and the Distortion of American Elections* (2016). Also see Greg Sargent, "How to rid politics of its pollution by wealthy donors?" *The Washington Post*, Jan. 8, 2016, http://tinyurl.com/zm4apmo.

22. Glen Martin, "Will High Court be Swayed by Research Findings? Not Likely, Says Legal Scholar," *California*, March 27, 2014, http://tinyurl.com/jrcv6ux.

23. "Lindsey Graham Says We Need an Amendment to Fix Money in Politics," Across the Aisle, Aug. 27, 2015, http://tinyurl.com/jk43kqy.

24. *Ibid.*

25. "Are Lessons from the 2014 Election Forgotten as the 2016 Campaigns Begin?" Center for Responsive Politics, summer 2015, http://tinyurl.com/jdahcbb.

26. Robert E. Hogan, "Campaign Spending and Voter Participation in State Legislative Elections," *Social Science Quarterly*, September 2013, http://tinyurl.com/hh8onv5.

27. Philip Bump, "How the Internet has democratized democracy, to Bernie Sanders's benefit," *The Washington Post*, Feb. 18, 2016, http://tinyurl.com/jjnrvjj.

28. Nicholas Confessore and Karen Yourish, "Measuring Donald Trump's Mammoth Advantage in Free Media," *The New York Times*, March 15, 2016, http://tinyurl.com/jcgsmcg.

29. Jonah Goldberg, "The Bogeymen of the 'Billionaire Class," *National Review*, Jan. 15, 2016, http://tinyurl.com/j98tr4t.

30. "Conservative Super PAC's Ads Take Aim At Hillary Clinton," NPR, Feb. 26, 2016, http://tinyurl.com/hdbrptr.

31. "Are Lessons from the 2014 Election Forgotten as the 2016 Campaigns Begin?" *op. cit.*

32. Matea Gold and Anu Narayanswamy, "How 'ghost corporations' are funding the 2016 election," *The Washington Post*, March 18, 2016, http://tinyurl.com/h576g55.

33. Richard W. Painter, "The Conservative Case for Campaign-Finance Reform," *The New York Times*, Feb. 3, 2016, http://tinyurl.com/zpdt3p4.

34. Julie Hirschfeld Davis, "President Obama May Require Federal Contractors to List Campaign Gifts," *The New York Times*, Jan. 19, 2016, http://tinyurl.com/h9jcjoh.

35. "For Top Federal Contractors, Investments in Lobbying, PACs Yield Big Returns," press release, Maplight, April 28, 2016, http://tinyurl.com/z9bhyv6.

36. "Political Nonprofits: Top Election Spenders," Center for Responsive Politics, http://tinyurl.com/hhkzwf6.

37. Gold, *op. cit.*

38. Bertram J. Levine and Michael Johnston, "Making campaign contributions anonymous," *The Washington Post*, Sept. 4, 2014, http://tinyurl.com/hoa57o6.

39. Bernie Sanders, "Getting Big Money Out of Politics and Restoring Democracy," Bernie Sanders campaign website, http://tinyurl.com/jd3zjlw.

40. "S.1538 — Fair Elections Now Act," http://tinyurl.com/hxoaehb. Also see http://tinyurl.com/j4b3fw9.

41. "Overview of State Laws on Public Financing," National Conference of State Legislatures, http://tinyurl.com/oy8eb69.

42. "Hillary Clinton's pragmatic campaign-finance plan," *The Washington Post*, Sept. 8, 2015, http://tinyurl.com/jptaj9e.

43. Harold Meyerson, "A campaign finance idea whose time has come," *The Washington Post*, March 25, 2015, http://tinyurl.com/hjtvdvh; "Taxes and Political Contributions," Take Back Our Republic, http://tinyurl.com/jkqecgz.

44. "Principles of Reform," Every Voice Center, http://tinyurl.com/j6adulq.

45. Paul Blumenthal, "Maine, Seattle Pave Next Path For Campaign Finance Reform," *The Huffington Post*, Nov. 4, 2015, http://tinyurl.com/hmahf48.

46. John Wagner, "Republican Larry Hogan to use public funds in campaign for governor of Maryland," *The Washington Post*, July 9, 2014, http://tinyurl.com/gpdpkce; Erin Cox and Michael Dresser, "Hogan defeats Brown," *The Baltimore Sun*, Nov. 5, 2014, http://tinyurl.com/j2fwesf.

47. "In Seattle, a Campaign Finance Plan that Voters Control" *The New York Times*, Nov. 7, 2015, http://tinyurl.com/j346nw6.

48. Bruce Ackerman and Ian Ayres, " 'Democracy dollars' can give every voter a real voice in American politics," *The Washington Post*, Nov. 5, 2015, http://tinyurl.com/jbvwh96.

49. "The American Anti-Corruption Act Full Provisions," Represent.Us, http://tinyurl.com/hujtwge.

50. "Taxes and Political Contributions," Take Back Our Republic, http://tinyurl.com/jkqecgz.

51. Emily Swanson and Julie Bykowicz, "AP-NORC Poll: Americans not fans of public financing," The Associated Press, Dec. 8, 2015, http://tinyurl.com/gpb9z95.

52. R. Sam Garrett, "Public Financing of Presidential Campaigns: Overview and Analysis," Congressional Research Service, Jan. 29, 2014, http://tinyurl.com/j9m3m5d.

53. Dan Janison, "Albany push-pull on public financing," *Newsday*, May 6, 2013, p. 12.

54. Dean Skelos, "A Recipe For Political Corruption," *The* [Albany, N.Y.] *Times-Union*, May 12, 2013, http://tinyurl.com/juadzt6.

55. Richard W. Painter, "The Conservative Case for Campaign-Finance Reform," *The New York Times*, Feb. 3, 2016, http://tinyurl.com/zpdt3p4.

56. Unless otherwise noted, this historical section draws on the following sources: "Money-in-Politics Timeline," Center for Responsive Politics, http://tinyurl.com/zsw9kku; Jost, *op. cit.*; Christina L. Lyons, "Nonprofit Groups and Partisan Politics" *CQ Researcher*, Nov. 14, 2014, pp. 961-984.

57. "Fundraising a foreign idea to Founding Fathers," Center for Responsive Politics, http://tinyurl.com/hxsxkj9.

58. Lindsay Renick Mayer, "Fundraising Wasn't for the Forefathers," Center for Responsive Politics, Feb. 22, 2007, http://tinyurl.com/jxaw2jb.

59. Paul Starr, "How Gilded Ages End," *The American Prospect*, April 29, 2015, http://tinyurl.com/zf9runj.

60. Meyerson, *op. cit.*

61. Will Tucker, "Two dozen dark money groups have busted 50 percent cap on politics at least once," Center for Responsive Politics, Dec. 9, 2015, http://tinyurl.com/zgxpw9p.

62. Jost, *op. cit.*

63. Kathy Kiely, "Public campaign funding is so broken that candidates turned down $292 million in free money," *The Washington Post*, Feb. 9, 2016, http://tinyurl.com/h2q5ak5.

64. Floyd Abrams, "Buckley After 40 Years," Forum on Communications Law 21st Annual Conference, Feb. 4-6, 2016, http://tinyurl.com/zb4l8fg.

65. *FEC v. Massachusetts Citizens for Life, Inc.* (1986), No. 85-701, http://tinyurl.com/j2ubmnz.

66. Paul Blumenthal, "McCutcheon v. FEC: Supreme Court Skeptical Of Campaign Contribution Limits," *The Huffington Post*, Oct. 8, 2013, http://tinyurl.com/lgccozh; Matea Gold and Tom Hamburger, "Political parties go after million-dollar donors in wake of looser rules," *The Washington Post*, Sept. 19, 2015, http://tinyurl.com/q99jytc.

67. "The truth behind fake political ads," *op. cit.*

68. Nicholas Confessore, "Rich Governor and Allies Tilt Illinois's Future," *The New York Times*, Nov. 30, 2015, http://tinyurl.com/pgkyftr.

69. *Ibid.*

70. Nina Totenberg, "Ruling: Judicial Candidates Can't Personally Solicit Campaign Funds," NPR, April 30, 2015, http://tinyurl.com/hvrbt82.

71. Matea Gold, Anu Narayanswamy and Tom Hamburger, "Donations, big and small, continue to pour into 2016 race," *The Washington Post*, Feb. 1, 2016, http://tinyurl.com/z3q8q2a.

72. Matea Gold, "More mystery corporate donations flow to presidential super PACs," *The Washington Post*, March 22, 2016, http://tinyurl.com/hljyjd3.

73. Matea Gold, "The FEC just made it easier for super PAC donors to hide their identities," *The Washington Post*, March 7, 2016, http://tinyurl.com/jj248sd.

74. *Ibid.*

75. "Disclosure and Reporting Requirements," National Conference of State Legislatures, July 17, 2015, http://tinyurl.com/h7jywop.

76. "Sunlight State By State After *Citizens United*," Corporate Reform Coalition, June 2012, http://tinyurl.com/6sx3jg6.

77. Jamie B. Raskin, "A shareholder solution to 'Citizens United,'" *The Washington Post*, Oct. 3, 2014, http://tinyurl.com/hwgbmsv.

78. "Disclosure levels," Take Back Our Republic, http://tinyurl.com/jkqecgz.

79. Mark Sommerhauser, "Scott Walker signs bills dismantling GAB, overhauling campaign finance law," *Wisconsin State Journal*, Dec. 16, 2015, http://tinyurl.com/gw2vyc7.

80. Howard Fischer, "Bill overhauling campaign finance laws heads to Arizona governor," *Arizona Daily Star*, March 29, 2016, http://tinyurl.com/hn4pgsc.

81. Sargent, *op. cit.*

82. H.R.430 — DISCLOSE 2015 Act, http://tinyurl.com/hpr6ard.

83. "H.J.Res.48 — Proposing an amendment to the Constitution of the United States providing that the rights extended by the Constitution are the rights of natural persons only," http://tinyurl.com/zywj8mp.

84. Chuck Ross, "Trump: 'I Love The Idea Of Campaign Finance Reform,'" *The Daily Caller*, Aug. 14, 2015, http://tinyurl.com/z7pzona.

85. David A. Graham, "GOP Candidates Discover the Problems With Money in Politics," *The Atlantic*, April 20, 2015, http://tinyurl.com/j9kxcan.

86. Adam Liptak, "Supreme Court Appointment Could Reshape American Life," *The New York Times*, Feb. 18, 2016, http://tinyurl.com/h56w4rq.

BIBLIOGRAPHY
Selected Sources
Books

Boatright, Robert G., ed., *The Deregulatory Moment? A Comparative Perspective on Changing Campaign Finance Laws*, University of Michigan Press, 2015.
Political scientists from seven Western countries contribute essays on what they describe as the erosion of regulation in the United States and what it portends for other democracies.

Hasen, Richard L., *Plutocrats United: Campaign Money, the Supreme Court, and the Distortion of American Elections*, Yale University Press, 2016.
A professor of law and political science at the University of California, Irvine, argues that campaign finance restrictions are constitutional, likening these curbs to libel and child-pornography laws that restrict free speech.

Mayer, Jane, *Dark Money: The Hidden History of the Billionaires Behind the Rise of the Radical Right*, Doubleday, 2016.
A staff writer for *The New Yorker* investigates multibillionaire brothers Charles and David Koch and their political network.

Teachout, Zephyr, *Corruption in America: From Benjamin Franklin's Snuff Box to Citizens United*, Harvard University Press, 2014.
A Fordham University law professor, who is running for a U.S. House seat in New York, offers an overview of America's changing understanding of corruption and a critique of Supreme Court reasoning that has loosened campaign-finance regulation.

Articles

Carney, Eliza Newlin, "Political Money: New Best-Selling Book Genre?" *The American Prospect*, Jan. 28, 2016, http://tinyurl.com/gw34zum.
A senior editor at the liberal magazine reviews several books about campaign finance.

Confessore, Nicholas, and Karen Yourish, "Measuring Donald Trump's Mammoth Advantage in Free Media," *The New York Times*, March 15, 2016, http://tinyurl.com/jcgsmcg.

A company analyzes the commercial value of news coverage and explains how Donald Trump became the Republican front-runner despite spending less than opponents.

Estroff, Alex, "In Defense of Citizens United: The Misplaced Anger of the American People and How They Are Battling the Problem of Money in Politics," *Georgia Political Review*, March 14, 2016, http://tinyurl.com/hmyt8rl.
A writer for a University of Georgia publication focusing on politics says concerns over the *Citizens United* decision are unsubstantiated.

Levine, Bertram J., and Michael Johnston, "Making campaign contributions anonymous," *The Washington Post*, Sept. 4, 2014, http://tinyurl.com/hoa57o6.
Two political scientists argue that money's influence on public officials is best combated by secrecy rather than greater disclosure.

Painter, Richard W., "The Conservative Case for Campaign-Finance Reform," *The New York Times*, Feb. 3, 2016, http://tinyurl.com/zpdt3p4.
A University of Minnesota law professor and former ethics adviser to President George W. Bush says Republicans should back campaign finance reforms because big money in politics has created big government.

Stohr, Greg, "Bloomberg Poll: Americans Want Supreme Court to Turn Off Political Spending Spigot," *Bloomberg Politics*, Sept. 28, 2015, http://tinyurl.com/pn395v9.
A poll finds most Americans — including 80 percent of Republicans — support reversing the Supreme Court's 2010 *Citizens United* ruling.

Reports and Studies

"The 2015 CPA-Zicklin Index of Corporate Political Disclosure and Accountability," Center for Political Accountability, Oct. 8, 2015, http://tinyurl.com/h77yzfs.
The Center for Political Accountability surveys the Standard & Poor's 500 index of top companies in leading industries to determine whether the firms are disclosing their political activities.

Garrett, R. Sam, "Public Financing of Presidential Campaigns: Overview and Analysis," Congressional Research Service, Jan. 29, 2014, http://tinyurl.com/jz6pyae.
A government specialist at Congress' research agency reviews the history and current status of public financing.

La Raja, Raymond J., and Jonathan Rauch, "The state of state parties — and how strengthening them can improve our politics," Brookings Institution, March 2016, http://tinyurl.com/jkfyx6w.
A political scientist at the University of Massachusetts, Amherst (La Raja) and a senior fellow in governance studies at Brookings (Rauch) survey parties in the states and find that changes in campaign regulations have weakened them.

Malbin, Michael J., "Citizen Funding for Elections," Campaign Finance Institute, 2015, http://tinyurl.com/zd3emcb.
The executive director of a Washington-based think tank reviews efforts to increase the importance of small donors in political campaigns, such as through tax credits or government subsidies of contributions.

For More Information

Brookings Institution, 1775 Massachusetts Ave., N.W., Washington, DC 20036; 202-797-6000, www .brookings.edu. Think tank studying politics and elections.

Campaign Finance Institute, 1775 I St., N.W., Suite 1150, Washington, DC 20006; 202-969-8890; www.cfinst.org. Nonpartisan think tank that researches and issues reports on campaign finance.

Campaign Legal Center, 1411 K St., N.W., Washington, DC 20005; 202-736-2200; www.campaignlegalcenter.org. Nonprofit law organization that opposes voting restrictions and "elections dominated by wealth."

Center for Competitive Politics, 124 West St. South, Suite 201, Alexandria, VA 22314; 703-894-6800; www.campaignfreedom.org. Advocacy group that favors repeal of campaign-finance regulations.

Center for Political Accountability, 1233 20th St., N.W., Suite 205, Washington, DC 20036; 202-464-1570; http://politicalaccountability.net. Advocacy group that presses corporations to disclose all their political spending.

Center for Responsive Politics, 1101 14th St., N.W., Suite 1030, Washington, DC 20005; 202-857-0044; www.open secrets.org. Nonpartisan research organization that tracks and publishes reports on contributions and expenditures.

Take Back Our Republic, 246 E. Glenn Ave., Auburn, AL 36830; 334-329-7258; www.takeback.org. Conservative advocacy group that supports regulation of campaign finance.

8

Racial Profiling

Kenneth Jost

Demonstrators in Los Angeles on July 16, 2013, protest the acquittal of white neighborhood watch volunteer George Zimmerman in the shooting death of Trayvon Martin, an unarmed black Florida 17-year-old. The verdict touched off a nationwide debate on racial profiling, which minority groups say is widespread.

S an Francisco's police department had been under intense scrutiny for several months before a police sergeant shot and killed an unarmed African-American woman on the morning of May 19 as she drove away in what the sergeant suspected was a stolen vehicle. Within hours of Jessica Williams's death, Mayor Ed Lee fired Greg Suhr as chief of the 2,000-member force and replaced him on an interim basis with a veteran black deputy, Toney Chaplin.[1]

Suhr, who is white, was Lee's choice for the post in 2011 and had vowed as recently as two days earlier to stay in the post. For months, Suhr had been defending the force and his leadership in the face of public protests, media headlines, and a Justice Department investigation over accusations of racial bigotry among the rank and file and racial profiling in traffic stops.[*]

The shakeup in San Francisco comes at a tumultuous time for police departments all around the county after issues of racial profiling and excessive force have spawned a nationwide protest movement under the name "Black Lives Matter." Suhr is the fourth police chief to lose his job within the previous 14 months in the wake of deaths of unarmed African Americans that resulted from encounters with police.[2]

In San Francisco and each of the other cities—Chicago, Baltimore, and Ferguson, Mo.—the fatalities touched off street

From *CQ Researcher*, November 22, 2013; updated May 2016

---

* The widely used term "racial profiling" in this report encompasses the targeting of an individual based on either race or ethnicity.

Majority of States Address Racial Profiling

At least 30 states have passed laws addressing racial profiling, according to the National Conference of State Legislatures. The laws vary widely. About half explicitly prohibit profiling. Others require law enforcement agencies to compile data on the race and ethnicity of drivers and pedestrians stopped by police and to develop policies and train officers on how to avoid profiling.

States with Racial Profiling Laws

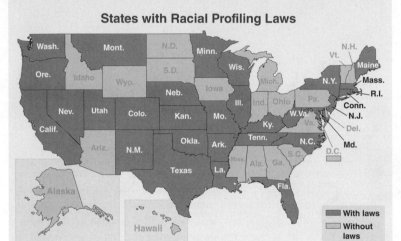

Sources: National Conference of State Legislatures, from unpublished compilation provided on request; Alejandro del Carmen, *Racial Profiling in America* (2008)

protests that underscored deep distrust between predominantly white police forces and in particular the cities' African-American communities. In San Francisco, as in the other cities, observers see the changes at the top as essential steps in efforts to restore confidence.

"Politically, it was necessary," John J. Pitney Jr., a political science professor at Claremont McKenna College in Pomona, Calif., told *The San Francisco Chronicle.* "The experience of other cities strongly suggests that without a firing, the political pressure would become daunting. The mayor also undoubtedly considered the possibility of civil unrest, and that creates enormous problems of its own."[3]

Just 1 month earlier, an investigation by the *Chronicle* reported damaging evidence of racial profiling by San Francisco police in traffic stops—parallel to findings of racial profiling by police in many other U.S. municipalities. The newspaper's examination of traffic stops from 2013 through 2015 found that African-American and

Latino drivers were stopped at much higher rates than white or Asian drivers but that searches of African Americans and Latinos were much less likely to uncover evidence of crime than comparable searches of white or Asian drivers. "A lower hit rate for ethnic minorities is a red flag for bias," Lorie Fridell, an associate professor of criminology at the University of South Florida, told the *Chronicle.*[4]

Racial profiling is not only unfair to the individuals stopped but also unhealthy for police–community relations, experts say. "If the people you serve think you are going about it illegitimately, then there are going to be problems," says Jim Bueermann, president of the Police Foundation, a Washington-based think tank, and a former police chief in Redlands, Calif.

Anecdotal and statistical evidence indicating that police disproportionately stop and ticket African-American motorists compared to white drivers helped popularize the cynical phrase "driving while black." More substantively, that evidence has figured in court cases and legislation requiring law enforcement agencies to collect racial and ethnic data on traffic stops to identify possible racial profiling.

Public opinion polls indicate a widening gap of distrust between minority groups and police. In a survey in summer 2015, the Gallup organization found that 73 percent of African Americans say that blacks are treated less fairly by police than whites are treated. The same figure was found in 2007, the highest level recorded in 20 years of asking that question. Only 34 percent of whites hold that view.[5]

Traditional civil rights groups representing African Americans and Latinos agree that racial profiling is widespread among U.S. law enforcement agencies. "Absolutely," says Hilary Shelton, director of the Washington office of the NAACP, the century-old civil rights organization. "We're still getting reports and complaints of racial profiling still being quite prevalent."

Are Blacks Treated Less Fairly by Police than Whites?

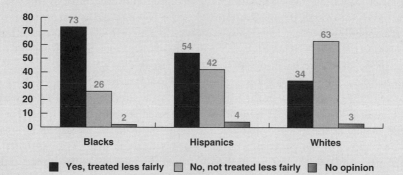

■ Yes, treated less fairly ■ No, not treated less fairly ■ No opinion

Note: Respondents were asked the following question: "*Just your impression, are blacks in your community treated less fairly than whites in the following situations? How about in dealing with the police, such as traffic incidents?*"

Source: Data from "Race Relations," Gallup Poll, June 15-July 10, 2015, http://www.gallup.com/poll/1687/race-relations.aspx

Profiling of Latinos also has become "quite extensive," according to Thomas Saenz, president of the Mexican American Legal Defense and Educational Fund (MALDEF), especially now that police in some jurisdictions have been asked to engage in immigration enforcement. "They are forced to rely on stereotypes," Saenz explains, "and stereotypes in immigration particularly rest on ethnicity and race."

In New York City, a federal judge ordered extensive changes to the city's "stop-and-frisk" policy in minority neighborhoods under the then-police commissioner in August 2013 after concluding the policies amounted to "indirect racial profiling." The newly installed mayor, Bill de Blasio, agreed to settle the suit early in 2014, but a report filed in federal court in February indicates that the new commissioner, William Bratton, is having difficulty getting rank-and-file officers to comply with the restrictions. Meanwhile, Bratton's predecessor, Raymond Kelly, is blaming an increase in homicides in the city on the sharp decline in stop-and-frisk activity.[6]

In a second closely watched profiling case, the tough-talking sheriff Joe Arpaio in Maricopa County, Ariz., is facing sanctions after being found in contempt of court

in May. In a 162-page opinion issued on May 13, 2016, U.S. District Court Judge Murray Snow found Arpaio and three of his top aides guilty of "persistent disregard" for the court's orders prohibiting immigration patrols and requiring better training on constitutional rules for traffic stops. Arpaio, who has served as sheriff in Arizona's most populous county since 1993, faces possible penalties following a May 31 hearing before Snow.[7]

The extent of racial profiling—indeed, its very existence—is a subject of debate and inevitable uncertainty. In the New York stop-and-frisk case, the plaintiffs' evidence before Judge Shira Scheindlin—who retired from the bench in May—showed that 53 percent of those stopped were African Americans and 32 percent Hispanics. Those figures were higher than their respective proportions in the city's overall population—26 percent for African Americans and 29 percent for Hispanics—but then-mayor Michael Bloomberg and then police commissioner Kelly insisted the apparent discrepancy reflects the demographics of criminal offenders.

Heather Mac Donald, a senior fellow at the conservative Manhattan Institute think tank who has followed the racial profiling controversy for more than a decade, agrees with the former New York City officials in disputing the commonly used method for detecting racial profiling. "Police actions continue to be measured against population ratios instead of crime ratios," Mac Donald says. "The relevant measure is not overall population ratios but where crime is happening and where officers are most likely to be encountering criminal force."

Brian Withrow, a professor of criminal justice at Texas State University in San Marcos who was a Texas state trooper from 1981 to 1993, says research on the issue is inconclusive despite continuing studies. "There hasn't been any substantial change in the research that would enable us to measure whether or not police officers are targeting African Americans or other minorities for stops," Withrow says. "The problem is as it always has been: an inability to measure the population of people subject to being stopped."

But David Harris, a professor at the University of Pittsburgh Law School and a leading critic of racial profiling since the late 1990s, says studies in New York, Philadelphia, and other cities "show very clearly that police cannot explain the racially disproportionate use of stop and frisk by any other factor." He says force is also used disproportionately against African Americans and Latinos. "There's bias involved—implicit, conscious or not," he says.

In San Francisco, Williams, age 29, was shot and killed in the predominantly African-American Bayview community in the third police shooting death since December. Mario Woods, an African American, age 26, was shot by police 21 times on Dec. 2, also in the Bayview area, after he refused officers' demand to drop a knife. Luis Gongora, a homeless Latino, age 45, was shot and killed on April 7 in the city's gentrifying Mission District after allegedly lunging at officers with a knife.[8]

The seeming nationwide spate of police killings has roiled large cities such as Chicago, Cleveland, and New York and smaller cities such as Ferguson and North Charleston, S.C. The shooting death of the young African American Michael Brown in Ferguson on Aug. 9, 2014, transformed the long-simmering debate over racial profiling into an intense debate about police use of force by birthing the now-familiar phrase "Black Lives Matter."

Despite the focus of this nonhierarchical movement, the *Washington Post*'s comprehensive database of police killings in the United States indicates that half of the victims in 2015 were white, one fourth were black, and about one sixth were Hispanic. The *Post* reported, however, most of those killed after brandishing a weapon or threatening someone were white while a disproportionate number killed after less threatening behavior—three out of five—were black or Hispanic.[9]

Prompted by the events in Ferguson and other cities, the Police Executive Research Forum is calling for increased training about deescalation, crisis intervention, and electronic weapon control to minimize loss of civilian life or risks to officers' lives. The report, issued in March, credits police with "a step forward," however, by recognizing "the existence of racially biased policing and the serious threat it represents to building strong relationships between police and the communities they serve."[10]

Many of the deaths resulted in criminal investigations and a few in criminal charges, but convictions have been relatively few. Some cases, however, have resulted in financial settlements to victims' families. As legal proceedings, official investigations, public protests, and news coverage continue, here are some of the questions being debated:

Are racial and ethnic profiling prevalent in U.S. law enforcement today?

As chief of police in the predominantly white northern New Jersey suburb of Wyckoff, Benjamin Fox told officers by memo that profiling, "racial or otherwise," has a place in law enforcement "if used fairly." The 40-year law enforcement veteran added that "black gang members from Teaneck commit burglaries in Wyckoff. That's why we check out suspicious black people in white neighborhoods."

Fox's memo, written in December 2014, surfaced in March after having been sent anonymously to the New Jersey affiliate of the American Civil Liberties Union (ACLU). The township committee responded on May 3 by voting to suspend Fox even with investigations underway by the Bergen County prosecutor and state attorney general's office.[11]

New Jersey is no stranger to racial profiling controversies. The state attorney general's office formally acknowledged that state troopers had a policy of targeting black

Fatal Force: Police Killings in 2015

The *Washington Post* gathered information for a continuously updated data base on police killings in the United States and analyzed the killings by the race, age and gender of the victims and other circumstances, such as signs of mental illness, presence of weapons, and threat level. For 2015, almost exactly half of the 990 victims were white, slightly over one-fourth were black, and somewhat more than one-sixth were Hispanic. Nearly 80 percent of the victims had a deadly weapon and nearly 75 percent were attacking police before being killed.

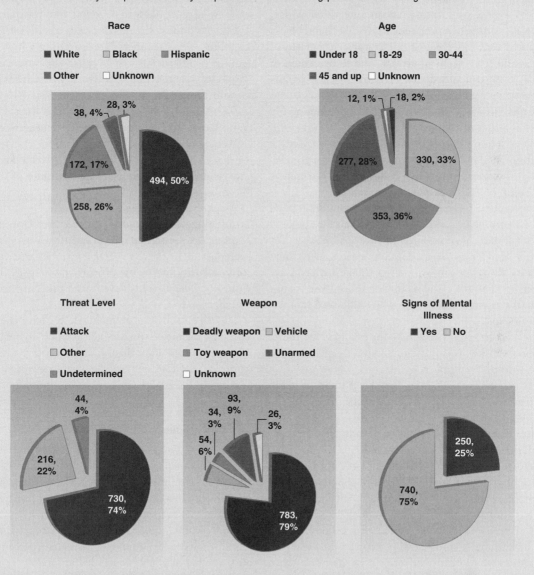

Source: Data from Fatal Force: A *Washington Post* database, https://www.washingtonpost.com/graphics/national/police-shootings/

motorists in the 1990s following a study by a leading researcher on the issue. John Lamberth, a social psychologist turned private consultant who had formerly chaired the Department of Psychology at Temple University in Philadelphia, had produced a similar study earlier in the 1990s that also suggested racial profiling by state troopers in Maryland.[12]

The death of Michael Brown in Ferguson, a St. Louis suburb with a population about one third white, prompted a Justice Department study that found blacks accounted for 85 percent of traffic stops, 90 percent of tickets, and 93 percent of arrests. The study, issued in March 2015, concluded that Ferguson's police department routinely violated the rights of black residents.[13]

In New Jersey, a similar study of the predominantly white township of Bloomfield found that 78 percent of people answering tickets in municipal court were black or Latino. The police department disputed the conclusions of the study, which was conducted by researchers from Seton Hall Law School in Newark.[14]

Researchers agree that census data—commonly used for comparisons in news coverage—should not be used as a benchmark to compare police stops by race. "It's free, easy, and it's the lowest common denominator," says Geoffrey Alpert, a professor of criminal justice at the University of South Carolina in Columbia. "And it's not worth its weight in anything in major cities and complex environments."

Creating the right baseline—for example, for traffic studies—can be "very difficult," Alpert explains. "We know who they pull over, we know to whom they give tickets, we know how long they keep them, but the problem is we don't know who the average driver is," he says. Alpert oversaw a study in Florida's Miami-Dade County that found what he termed "adverse results" at two of the eight intersections covered.

Withrow, the Texas State professor, notes as one methodological problem that it is often unclear whether police know the race of a driver before making a stop. Current studies, he says, attempt to look "more insightfully" at police conduct after motorists are pulled over. "We believe that a study of what happens during a stop provides much more insight into the mindset of a police officer," he explains.

In Texas, a newspaper investigation of traffic stops by state troopers found—as in San Francisco—that minority drivers were more likely than whites to be searched after being pulled over. Hispanics were 33 percent more likely to be searched than white drivers, according to the examination of 5 years' worth of stops by reporters for the *Austin American-Statesman*. A North Carolina newspaper's examination of traffic stops by 24 local police and sheriff's offices similarly found black male drivers more likely to be searched than white drivers even though whites were more likely to be found with contraband.[15]

Experts found the results of both investigations troubling. Texas troopers "are searching a higher percentage of Hispanics just because they appear to be Hispanic," Charles Epp, a University of Kansas professor and the author of *Pulled Over: How Police Stops Define Race and Citizenship*, told the Austin paper. Frank Baumgartner, a political science professor at the University of North Carolina in Chapel Hill, said the results of the investigation by the *News Record* in Greensboro were "an unwelcome reminder of the realities of race in America."

Alejandro del Carmen, chair of the Department of Criminology and Criminal Justice at the University of Texas at Arlington and a frequent instructor at police academies in Texas, says aggregate studies are useful but fail to identify individual officers who engage in racial profiling. Overall, he believes racial profiling exists but is exaggerated.

"Racial profiling as a whole doesn't have the prevalence that the media would lead the public to believe, but it happens more often than the folks on the other spectrum say," del Carmen says. "Racism continues to be a problem in the law enforcement community."

Do aggressive stop-and-frisk tactics help reduce crime?

New York City police officers are stopping far fewer pedestrians for pat-down frisks under Mayor de Blasio and police commissioner Bratton than under the city's previous administration or before a federal court decision setting guidelines for the stops. Police stops numbered around 24,000 in 2015, according to a court-appointed monitor for the department—less than 3 percent of the peak number of 685,274 recorded in 2011.[16]

The number had risen roughly seven-fold over a 10-year period under the city's previous mayor, Bloomberg, and police commissioner Kelly but had started to fall before they left office and has declined further under the new administration. As he was about to leave office, Kelly predicted that violent crime would go up in the city because of the judge's order to revamp stop-and-frisk policies. Overall, however, major crime is down in the city, with a 5.8 percent decline during de Blasio's first 2 years in office despite a 5 percent increase in homicides in 2015 from the previous year.[17]

In her order, Scheindlin directed that officers record the basis for any stop, prohibited the consideration of race or ethnicity as a reason for a stop, and required the department to institute the use of body cameras to record police encounters. In his report to the judge now handling the case, Analisa Torres, the court-appointed monitor Peter Zimroth, a lawyer with a prominent New York firm, described compliance as a work in progress, with new training and monitoring under way. Zimroth described the efforts to guard against racial profiling as "complicated," with no decision yet on "yardsticks" to measure compliance.

The increased attention to police use of force is feeding fears of what law enforcement–minded observers are calling a "Ferguson effect" in deterring police from some proactive enforcement. The claimed phenomenon is sharply disputed but is drawing more attention, with the latest statistics showing an increase in homicides in about half of the nation's biggest 50 cities. "Something is happening," FBI director James Comey remarked after seeing the statistics in mid-May. Comey had earlier pointed to a possible "Ferguson effect" on police but avoided the term in his more recent remarks.[18]

The homicide statistics are far from uniform across the country. Chicago, Los Angeles, Dallas, and Las Vegas all recorded increases in the first 3 months of 2016 on top of increases in the previous year. Many other cities reported declines, however, including New York. The number of homicides in New York City fell to 68 in the first 3 months of 2016 compared to 85 for the same period the previous year—a 20 percent drop.[19]

Mac Donald, the Manhattan Institute expert, views the statistics as confirming the so-called Ferguson effect. "What we are seeing in cities with a high black population is a very worrisome depolicing effect," Mac Donald says. "Officers are doing less of the active policing. As a result, crime is going through the roof in urban areas."

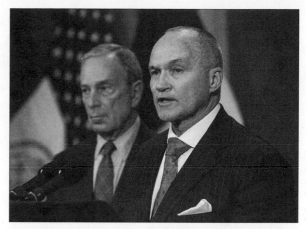

Andrew Burton/Getty Images

On August 12, 2013, New York City Mayor Michael Bloomberg, left, and Police Commissioner Raymond W. Kelly responded to a blockbuster ruling by U.S. District Judge Shira Scheindlin that the city's aggressive stop-and-frisk policy violated the constitutional rights of minorities. The case was later settled under Mayor Bill de Blasio, and in 2015, police stops dropped to less than 3 percent of the peak number from 2011.

In a detailed analysis of 2015 statistics, however, the Brennan Center for Law and Justice at New York University Law Center found no overall increase in crime nationwide, even compared to the historically low levels in recent years. The analysis, released in April, reports that crime in the 30 largest cities was almost unchanged, with drops in two thirds of the cities offset by a sharp increase in one city: Los Angeles.

The study acknowledged a 13 percent increase in homicides in the 30 cities but minimized the change by noting the relatively small number of homicides overall. "Murder rates today are roughly the same as they were in 2012," the report adds. "In fact, they are slightly lower."[20]

Mac Donald credits the previous aggressive stop-and-frisk policies in New York City with contributing to the steady decline in crime during the 1990s. She argues the enforcement strategy benefited minority neighborhoods. "Police should be fighting crime," she says. "The most important thing is to bring safety to law-abiding residents of poor neighborhoods."

Other experts voiced doubts. "The objective of stop and frisk is to put a lot of police officers in high-crime areas to increase deterrence," says Withrow, the Texas State professor. "There are other ways to do that than stop-and-frisk searches."

Blacks, Hispanics More Likely to Be Stopped

Of the approximately 1.6 million pedestrians stopped and questioned by New York City police officers during the period 2010-2012, more than half were African-American and nearly one in three were Hispanic. The statistics were compiled on behalf of the plaintiffs in the federal lawsuit *Floyd v. City of New York.*

Race or Ethnicity of Persons Stopped by NYPD, 2010-2012

- African-Americans
- Hispanics
- Whites
- Other/unknown

7%
9%
52%
32%

Source: "Second Supplemental Report of Jeffrey Fagan, Ph.D.," *Floyd v. City of New York*, p. 11, http://ccrjustice.org/files/FaganSecond Supplemental Report.pdf. Data for 2012 cover period only through June.

Harris, the University of Pittsburgh professor, says the previous policies in New York were deliberately aimed at increasing the numbers. "The effect on driving crime down has been achieved, and what you're doing is overenforcing," he says. "And that tends to drive a wedge between the police and the people you're serving."

The warnings about a change in tactics have not materialized, Harris adds. "Blood is not running in the streets," he says. "We're still at historically low levels of crime."

Should courts take a leading role in combating police racial and ethnic profiling?

The Arizona lawman who bills himself as the nation's "toughest sheriff" has been in federal court for the past 8 years answering charges of racially profiling Latino drivers in his zeal to combat illegal immigration. Already under a court order to halt the practice, Joe Arpaio is now facing severe penalties after the federal judge overseeing the case found him in contempt for "persistent disregard" of the court's rulings.

U.S. District Court Judge Murray Snow issued a 162-page ruling on May 13 finding Arpaio and two of his top aides in civil contempt for violating the broad remedial order he issued in October 2013. Arpaio's lawyers disagreed with the ruling, but a lawyer for the American

Civil Liberties Union of Arizona—which brought the suit along with the Mexican American Legal Defense and Education Fund—praised the judge's action. "It's a damning finding—that they intentionally and repeatedly flouted the court's orders," said ACLU lawyer Cecilia Wang.[21]

Courts have played a leading role in combating racial profiling by police for more than two decades. Two of the earliest cases, in Maryland and New Jersey, resulted in ongoing federal court supervision of state police departments after the states agreed to changes to prevent the practice.[22] By contrast, New York City officials under Bloomberg and Kelly fought tooth and nail against accusations of racial profiling in stop-and-frisk policies until a new mayor, de Blasio, settled the case and worked with his police commissioner, Bratton, to comply with a judge's order to revamp the policies.

Racial profiling critics say the courts' role in combating the practice is useful and necessary. "That's what courts are set out to do, to determine whether police are acting within constitutional bounds," says Dennis Parker, national director of the ACLU's Racial Justice Program. Alejandro del Carmen, chair of the Department of Criminology and Criminal Justice at the University of Texas at Arlington, agrees. "Courts have the obligation and the moral and legal duty to intervene and to dissect, analyze, and respond to concerns that the community may have with respect to racial profiling," del Carmen says.

Mac Donald—who criticized the New Jersey settlement in her book *Are Cops Racist?*—disagrees with the common technique of ongoing supervision by court-appointed monitors as "a tragic waste of resources." She also views the advancing practice of body-worn cameras as a waste. "I'm just not certain they would resolve the issues that are allegedly at stake here," she says. And she complains that Scheindlin, the former judge in the New York case, was guilty of "egregious calumnies" against the New York force in her decision.

Even while supporting the courts' role on the issues, some racial profiling critics say remedies may be more effective if crafted by law enforcement agencies themselves. "Courts have an important role to play, but they cannot be the sole enforcer of constitutional obligations to avoid racial discrimination," says Thomas Saenz, president of MALDEF. "It's important to have administrative processes short of going to court," he says, including an adequate opportunity to file complaints.

Harris, the University of Pittsburgh professor, says police react negatively to court supervision. "It's perceived as a judge who knows nothing, who's never done anything on the street, telling a police department what to do," he says.

"What I would like to see is the change coming primarily from law enforcement itself, from mayors and city governments, from state legislatures," Harris continues. "They are best positioned to know what's going on on the ground around them. They are in the best position to make changes that are likely to be accepted in the departments affected. That's where reform would be best hatched. And many police departments do things like that."

Jim Bueermann, president of the Police Foundation, a Washington-based research organization, and a retired police chief from Redlands, Calif., agrees on the limits of court-ordered changes. "You don't easily change a police department culture with a judicial ruling," Bueermann says. "Judges who think they're going to change a police department culture should spend time riding around in a police car, sitting down with officers in the station."

"Courts serve a very important role in controlling the power of the state, including the police department," says Withrow, the Texas State professor. "Courts play an essential role in improving policing. It doesn't seem like an improvement to cops, but in the long run it almost always results in improvement of policing."

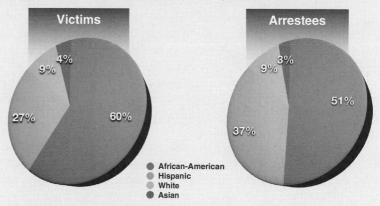

Most Victims, Arrestees Are Minorities

African-Americans and Hispanics were victims in nearly 90 percent of the murders or non-negligent manslaughters in New York City in 2012, according to the NYPD.

Murder Victims and Arrestees in New York City, by Race, Ethnicity, 2012

Victims: 60% / 27% / 9% / 4%
Arrestees: 51% / 37% / 9% / 3%

● African-American
● Hispanic
● White
● Asian

Source: "Crime and Enforcement Activity in New York, Jan. 1-Dec. 31, 2012," New York Police Department, www.nyc.gov/html/nypd/downloads/pdf/analysis_and_planning/2012_year_end_enforcement_report.pdf

BACKGROUND
"A Difficult History"

The term "racial profiling" is of recent coinage, but bias-based policing in the United States dates as far back as the revolutionary era, with the religious profiling of Quakers seen as disloyal to the cause of independence. African Americans have been subject to racial profiling from the days of slavery through the so-called Jim Crow era and up to modern times. Mexicans and other Latinos have been singled out for rough treatment by law enforcement since the time of Texas's independence. And immigration laws dating from the late 19th century amounted to racial or ethnic profiling against, among others, Asians and southern and eastern Europeans. "It's a very difficult history," says del Carmen, the University of Texas professor.[24]

The Continental Congress ordered the arrest and imprisonment of dozens of Pennsylvania Quakers suspected of disloyalty to the revolutionary cause in August 1777, according to an account by Emory University law professor Morgan Cloud.[25] No evidence was offered, no hearings were held, and some of those arrested were exiled to imprisonment in Virginia. The captives were released by April 1778, in part, Cloud says, because of objections to the procedures not only from their families but also from some political leaders.

African Americans comprised around one sixth of the country's population in the pre–Civil War era, the vast majority of them held in slavery, mainly but not exclusively in the South. Those who escaped— "runaway" slaves, as they were called—could be captured by private slave hunters under the Fugitive Slave Act, a 1793 law (strengthened in 1850) that offered few procedural protections. Free blacks had no immunity from capture, as dramatized in the movie *12 Years a Slave*; courts generally recognized a presumption that a black person was a slave.

The end of slavery merely transformed the legally and socially enforced profiling of African Americans. The racial segregation laws of the Jim Crow era reflected the prevailing assumption that blacks were different from— and inferior to—whites. African Americans suspected or accused of committing crimes could be subjected to abusive treatment by police or sheriffs' officers and to patently unjust proceedings in court. Worse was the threat of racially profiled vigilante justice: More than 3,400 African Americans were lynched from the 1880s to 1950, according to a compilation by the Tuskegee Institute, the historically black college in Tuskegee, Ala. (renamed Tuskegee University in 1983).[26]

Mexicans and Mexican Americans were also the victims of ethnic profiling from the time of Texas's independence from Mexico and its subsequent annexation by the United States. The Texas Rangers, founded in 1845 and the nation's first statewide police organization, was known, according to the University of Texas's del Carmen, for "brutal acts against Comanche tribes and thousands of Mexicans."[27] Mexican Americans in Texas and the Southwest were subjected to the same kind of residential and educational segregation as African Americans elsewhere. And in the 1930s, as many as 2 million people of Mexican descent were forced or pressured to leave the United States.

Federal immigration laws dating from the late 19th century reflected ethnic profiling at the national level. The first of the laws, passed in 1875, barred entry to "undesirables," who included Asians brought to the United States for forced labor or prostitution. Seven years later, the Chinese Exclusion Act prohibited all immigration of Chinese laborers. In the ensuing decades, immigration officers enforced admission requirements, such as literacy tests, in ways that favored northern and western Europeans, del Carmen explains. The quota system enacted in the 1920s wrote those preferences into law.

The most notorious episode of ethnic profiling occurred during World War II, with the internment of more than an estimated 110,000 persons of Japanese descent, most of them U.S. citizens. President Franklin D. Roosevelt authorized the internment in an executive order issued on Feb. 19, 1942, two and a half months after Japan attacked Pearl Harbor, based on warnings from the military that the Japanese represented a national security threat. Today, those warnings are widely viewed as unfounded, the internment in ramshackle concentration camps in remote areas as shameful, and the Supreme Court decision, *Korematsu v. United States* (1944), upholding the action as disgraceful.

Still, the court's decision in *Korematsu* established the principle that race-based restrictions in the law are "immediately suspect." Courts "must subject [such restrictions] to the most rigid scrutiny," Justice Hugo L. Black wrote for the 6–3 majority. "Pressing necessity may sometimes justify the existence of such restrictions," he continued. "Racial antagonism never can."[28] That principle laid the basis for courts, legislatures, and law enforcement agencies later in the 20th century to give greater scrutiny to racial and ethnic profiling.

An "Indefensible" Practice

Racial and ethnic profiling emerged as an important issue late in the 20th century because of a confluence of factors. The civil rights revolution embodied the demand of African Americans for equal treatment under the law, including by police. The rapid increase in the Latino population, especially from the 1980s, prompted analogous demands from Latino advocacy groups to eliminate discriminatory treatment. And the criminal law revolution wrought by the Supreme Court under Chief Justice Earl Warren subjected local and state law enforcement to greater scrutiny to comply with constitutional norms. Meanwhile, public concern about crime and, in particular, about illegal drugs led police and law

C H R O N O L O G Y

1960s-1970s *Civil rights movement targets racial inequality; Supreme Court forces changes in criminal justice systems.*

1968 The National Advisory Commission on Civil Disorders (Kerner Commission), charged with examining the causes of urban riots, urges more sensitive, diverse police forces (Feb. 29). . . . Supreme Court approves limited "stop-and-frisk" authority (Terry v. Ohio, June 10).

1970s FBI develops "profiles" of airplane hijackers, serial killers.

1975, 1976 Supreme Court limits use of race or ethnicity in roving Border Patrol stops but allows it at border checkpoints.

1980s-1990s *Racial profiling emerges as issue.*

1989 Supreme Court approves use of drug courier profiles (April 3).

1995 Maryland State Police agree to prohibit stops based on racial drug courier profiles (Jan. 4).

1996 Supreme Court allows traffic stops even if real purpose is drug enforcement (June 10).

1999 N.J. attorney general finds racial profiling by state troopers despite official policies prohibiting it (April 20); Justice Department appoints monitor. . . . President Bill Clinton orders law enforcement agencies to compile race, ethnicity data to guard against profiling (June 10).

2000-Present *Racial profiling litigation increases; states pass laws addressing issue.*

2001 President George W. Bush promises to help end racial profiling (Feb. 27). . . . Al Qaeda hijackers attack United States (Sept. 11); Muslims, Arabs rounded up in immigration sweeps, singled out in airport security checks, face widespread public suspicion.

2003 Bush administration bans racial, ethnic profiling in all federal law enforcement agencies but allows exception for national security–related investigations (June 17). . . . New York City settles racial profiling suit (*Daniels v. City of New York*) (Sept. 18); settlement approved by District Judge Shira Scheindlin (Dec. 12).

2008 Center for Constitutional Rights files new stop-and-frisk suit against New York Police Department (NYPD) (*Floyd v. City of New York*), claiming violations of 2003 settlement in the Daniels case (Jan. 31); new suit is assigned to Scheindlin as "related" case.

2009 Obama becomes first African-American president (Jan. 20); Eric Holder becomes first black attorney general.

2012 White community-watch volunteer George Zimmerman kills unarmed black teenager Trayvon Martin in Sanford, Fla., touching off a nationwide debate on racial profiling (Feb. 26); Zimmerman, charged with second-degree murder, is later acquitted. . . . Muslim plaintiffs file federal suit to halt NYPD surveillance of mosques, Muslim neighborhoods (June 6) . . . . Federal judge dismisses FBI suit over informant's surveillance of mosques in Southern California (Aug. 14).

2013 Federal judge finds Maricopa County Sheriff Joe Arpaio guilty of ethnic profiling of Latinos (May 24); orders appointment of monitor, other steps. . . . Scheindlin finds NYPD guilty of racial profiling, Fourth Amendment violations in stop-and-frisk policies; orders appointment of monitor, test of body-worn cameras (Aug. 12). . . .Bill de Blasio, opponent of stop-and-frisk policies, elected New York City mayor (Nov. 5).

2014 De Blasio agrees to settle stop-and-frisk suit (Jan. 30); . . . Eric Garner, African-American street peddler, dies from NYPD officer chokehold (July 17). . . . Michael Brown, unarmed black teen, shot and killed by white officer in Ferguson, MO. (Aug. 9) . . . Tamir Rice fatally shot by Cleveland police officer while playing with toy gun (Nov. 22). . . . St. Louis County grand jury declines to indict officer Darren Wilson in Brown's death (Nov. 24).

2015 Freddie Gray dies of injuries sustained in Baltimore police custody (April 19); six officers face charges. . . . North Charleston, S.C., officer Michael Slager indicted for murder in shooting of Walter Scott after traffic stop (June 8).

2016 Arpaio held in contempt of court (May 13) . . .

Muslims Challenge 'Religious Profiling'

"We should not be singled out simply because of religion."

Sarah Abdurrahman was in a festive mood as she returned to the United States with friends and family earlier this year after attending a friend's wedding in Canada.

But the good feelings died at the border as she and her traveling party, all U.S. citizens and all Muslims, suffered what the radio journalist later described as a painful and humiliating 6-hour ordeal at the hands of U.S. Customs and Border Patrol (CPB) agents.

Abdurrahman, an assistant producer with the NPR program "On the Media," said the agents detained the traveling party without explanation, refused to identify themselves, and questioned at least one of the travelers, Abdurrahman's husband, about his religious practices. She described the experience—and her fruitless efforts to get an explanation afterward—in a 20-minute report on the program.[1]

The episode typifies the seeming religious profiling that advocates for the United States' 6 million Muslims say has been common since al Qaeda's September 2011 attacks on the United States. Because of terrorism-inspired scrutiny at the federal, state, and local levels, many Muslims today worry that they may be monitored, interrogated, detained, or even arrested for no reason other than religion, according to officials with the San Francisco group Muslim Advocates.

"We're not saying mosques or Muslims should be off limits," explains Glenn Katon, the group's legal director.

"It's that mosques should not be singled out, Muslims should not be singled out simply because of religion."

The complaints extend beyond individual anecdotes such as Abdurrahman's. Muslims are currently challenging in court broad surveillance programs maintained by the New York Police Department (NYPD) and by the FBI in Southern California. Both law enforcement agencies are accused of infringing on religious liberties by infiltrating mosques without adequate justification. But so far, none of the law enforcement practices has been ruled improper.

In California, Craig Monteilh posed as a Muslim convert under an assumed name for more than a year as a paid FBI informant, using audio and video recording devices to gather information. The American Civil Liberties Union (ACLU) of Southern California and the Council on American-Islamic Relations (CAIR) filed a civil rights suit against the FBI on behalf of Muslim community members in Orange County in regard to Monteilh's acknowledged infiltration of approximately 10 Southern California mosques. The government claimed the "state secrets" privilege in refusing to disclose details of Monteilh's surveillance in so-called Operation Flex. In August 2012, U.S. District Judge Cormac Carney dismissed the government as a defendant but allowed the suits against individual FBI agents and officials to proceed. ACLU lawyers appealed the decision; the appeal was argued before the Ninth U.S. Circuit Court of Appeals in December 2015.[2]

---

enforcement agencies to adopt tactics often disproportionately aimed at African Americans and Latinos—sometimes consciously.[29]

The Warren Court's major criminal law decisions—such as the *Miranda* ruling on police interrogation guidelines—benefited white and minority suspects and defendants alike. Despite criticism for supposedly "handcuffing" police, the Warren Court also gave police an important tool in its 1968 *Terry* decision upholding—with only one dissenting vote—the stop-and-frisk procedure. The court noted complaints of "harassment" by African Americans, however, in stressing the need to limit

the procedure to "the legitimate investigative sphere." Meanwhile, the so-called Kerner Commission, appointed by President Lyndon B. Johnson in response to urban riots of the mid-'60s, had issued a comprehensive report in 1968 recommending, among other steps, the hiring of more diverse and more sensitive police forces.[30]

The Supreme Court's initial encounter with the profiling issue came in a pair of immigration-related cases in the mid-1970s. In the first, the court in 1975 ruled that a roving Border Patrol car could not stop a vehicle solely because the driver or passengers appeared to be of Mexican ancestry. Appearance was a "relevant factor,"

In New York, the NYPD faced three separate suits challenging its surveillance of mosques and Muslims as Fourth Amendment violations both in New York and across the state line in New Jersey. Lawyers for the New York–based Center for Constitutional Rights and the Muslim Advocates filed the first of the suits in federal district court in New Jersey in June 2012; the ACLU, along with the New York Civil Liberties Union (NYCLU) and a police accountability project at the City University of New York Law School, filed a comparable suit in federal district court in Brooklyn in June. The city settled the lawsuits in January 2016 by agreeing to appoint an independent civilian to monitor the police department's counterterrorism activities.[3]

In a third case, lawyers from the NYCLU charged the police with violating their own court-approved guidelines for initiating surveillance of political or religious organizations. The guidelines date back to a court-approved settlement of antispying litigation in the 1970s, but the NYPD got the rules eased in 2003 after claiming they hampered counterterrorism work.[4]

Separately, the ACLU sued the FBI under the Freedom of Information Act to try to obtain the agency's guidelines for counterterrorism investigations. In a ruling on Oct. 23, 2013, the federal appeals court in Philadelphia upheld the FBI's decision to limit disclosure of the requested documents because it would reveal investigative techniques.[5]

Abdurrahman was also stymied in her efforts to determine why her traveling party was detained when they reentered the United States earlier this year. On the radio program, Abdurrahman said she filed a complaint about the incident with the Department of Homeland Security's Office of Civil Rights and Civil Liberties. The office rejected the complaint, she said, but the reasons for upholding the agents' actions were redacted in the notice of the decision.

The program quoted Munia Jabbar, an attorney with CAIR, that Muslims are often asked "really invasive" questions about religious practices when reentering the United States. She says the questioning, as Abdurrahman's husband described, is improper. "You're singling people out because of their religion and then subjecting them to longer detentions and to humiliating questioning about stuff that they're allowed to do legally," she says.

Abdurrahman says the episode left her shaken. "I came out of the experience wondering what our rights are," she said.

— Kenneth Jost

[1] See "My Detainment Story: Or How I learned to Stop Feeling Safe in My Own Country and Hate the Border Agents," NPR, Sept. 20, 2013, www.wnyc.org/radio/#/ondemand/319368. For print coverage, see Harrison Jacobs, "American Muslim Reporter Describes 'Dehumanizing' Treatment at US Border," *Business Insider*, www.businessinsider.com/sarah-aburrahman-detained-at-us-border-2013-9.

[2] See Maura Dolan, "Is FBI liable in Muslim spying?," Los Angeles Times, Dec. 21, 2015, p. A1.

[3] See Matt Apuzzo and Al Baker, "Sued Over Spying, New York Police Get Oversight," The New York Times, Jan. 8, 2016, p. A1.

[4] The case is Handschu v. Special Services Division, www.nyclu.org/case/handschu-v-special-services-division-challenging-nypd-surveillance-practices-targeting-politica.

[5] ACLU v. FBI, 12-4345 (3d Cir., Oct. 23, 2013), www2.ca3.uscourts.gov/opinarch/124345p.pdf; for coverage, see Jason Grant, "ACLU denied access to FBI files on profiling," The Star-Ledger (Newark, N.J.), Oct. 24, 2013, p. 11.

Justice Lewis F. Powell Jr. wrote, but not enough to "justify stopping all Mexican Americans to ask if they are aliens." A year later, however, the court ruled that agents at a border checkpoint could select motorists for secondary inspection based solely on apparent Mexican ancestry.[31]

The formal art of "profiling" began in the 1970s, as police and the FBI tried to identify characteristics to spot in potential serial killers or airline hijackers. From those rare offenses, the practice expanded to the so-called war on drugs, with the federal Drug Enforcement Administration's (DEA) development of a drug courier profile in the 1980s. The DEA never published the profile, but evidence in some cases showed that profiles sometimes specifically referred to African Americans or Hispanics. In any event, the open-ended characteristics gave agents broad discretion in selecting individuals to stop. The Supreme Court green-lighted the use of such profiles in a 1989 decision stemming from the search of a deplaning passenger at the Honolulu airport. By a 7–2 vote, the court found the combination of six listed factors justified the stop and search; the dissenters countered that none of the factors specifically pointed to criminal activity.[32]

"Black Lives Matter": A Growing Movement

Deaths in police encounters fuel protests

The death of an unarmed black teenager at the hands of a white police officer in the St. Louis suburb of Ferguson, Mo., gave birth to a diffuse protest movement that took the name "Black Lives Matter." Michael Brown's death came with racial tensions already somewhat high because of the chokehold death of an African-American man in a police encounter less than a month earlier in New York City.

With no formal hierarchy or designated leaders, the movement grew in media visibility and political impact with a succession of highly publicized deaths of African Americans in police encounters. Here in chronological order are brief summaries of some of those incidents1:

Eric Garner, 43, died on July 17, 2014, on New York City's Staten Island after an NYPD officer who suspected him of selling untaxed cigarettes placed him in a prohibited chokehold for 15 to 19 seconds. Garner was heard on a video recorded on a passerby's cell phone to say, "I can't breathe." Officer Daniel Pantaleo and other officers did not attempt to administer CPR as they waited for 7 minutes for an ambulance to arrive; Garner died an hour after arriving in hospital. A state grand jury declined to indict Pantaleo.

Michael Brown, age 18, was shot and killed by Officer Darren Wilson on Aug. 9, 2014, in the racially mixed suburb of Ferguson under circumstances that remain sharply disputed even after a state grand jury declined on Nov. 24 to indict Wilson in the episode. In Wilson's version, he recognized Brown as a suspect in a robbery at a nearby pharmacy, struggled with the teenager as he was seated in his patrol car, and then, out of the car, shot as Brown was headed toward him menacingly. Brown's companion related that Brown had his hands up in the air before the fatal shot was fired.

The death sparked unrest over a period of days, with a militarized response from authorities that fueled further protests. The U.S. Justice Department also declined to prosecute Wilson but issued a damning report in March 2015 accusing the city's police of a "pattern and practice" of racial profiling of African Americans. Police Chief Thomas Jackson resigned within a week. The Brown family's wrongful death suit is rescheduled for May 2017.

Laquan McDonald, age 17, died after having been shot 16 times late on the evening of Oct. 20, 2014, by Chicago police officer Jason Van Dyke as he and others responded to a report of a man armed with a knife breaking into vehicles in a truck yard. McDonald, who had a record of juvenile arrests, allegedly refused the officers' demands to drop his knife. Cook County state's attorney Anita Alvarez released video of the incident a year later, on Nov. 24, 2015, only under a court order in a freedom-of-information suit by journalists; the video

---

Through the 1990s, evidence mounted that African Americans were far and away the majority of motorists stopped in drug-related enforcement. A suit in Maryland by Robert Wilkins, an African-American lawyer, was the first to uncover hard evidence of targeting of African Americans, as recounted by Harris, the University of Pittsburgh professor. A state police "Criminal Intelligence Report," disclosed during the suit and dated only days before Wilkins was stopped, included an explicit profile targeting African Americans.

The data gathering that resulted from the settlement of Wilkins's suit showed that 72 percent of those stopped in Maryland were African Americans. The litigation and newspaper investigations in New Jersey produced similar evidence that the vast majority of motorists stopped on the state's turnpikes were African Americans.

Despite such evidence, the Supreme Court declined in 1996 to question the use of traffic stops as a pretext for drug enforcement. The decisions stemmed from the convictions of two African Americans who had been found with drugs after police officers patrolling a "high-drug" area in Washington, D.C., stopped them ostensibly because of a taillight violation. Unanimously, the court said the officers' "ulterior motives" did not matter as long as they had probable cause for the stop.[33]

President Bill Clinton cited the evidence of racial profiling in traffic stops, however, when he ordered federal law enforcement agencies in June 1999 to

appeared to contradict the police accounts in some respects. Mayor Rahm Emanuel fired Chicago police superintendent Garry McCarthy a week later. Van Dyke is under indictment in state court for murder. The city paid McDonald's family $5 million to settle a civil suit. Alvarez was defeated in a Democratic Party primary on March 15, 2016, in her bid for a third term.

Tamir Rice, age 12, was shot and killed during daytime hours on Nov. 22, 2014, as two Cleveland police officers responded to a report of a young boy wielding a gun in a playground; the officers were not told that the caller had said that the supposed weapon was "probably fake," as in fact it was. Officer Timothy Loehmann opened fire on Rice almost immediately after arriving on the scene, purportedly because he saw Rice reaching inside his waistband as though for a weapon. Loehmann had joined the force 8 months earlier following five months with the police department in nearby Independence, Ohio. A Cuyahoga County grand jury declined to indict either of the officers, but Loehmann resigned from the force. On April 25, 2016, the Rice's family wrongful-death claim against the two officers and the city of Cleveland was settled with the city agreeing to pay Tamir Rice's family $6 million.

Walter Scott was a 50-year-old forklift operator and former Coast Guardsman who was shot and killed on April 4, 2015, as he fled from North Charleston, S.C., police officer Michael Slager following a traffic stop for a nonfunctioning brake light. Scott, who was unarmed, had outstanding warrants for failing to pay child support. Slager, then 33, a 5-year veteran of the North Charleston force, was indicted in state court for murder on

June 8, just 2 months later, and for a federal civil rights violation on May 11, 2016.

Freddie Gray, 25, died on April 19, 2015, of spinal cord injuries sustained a week earlier as he was being transported to Baltimore County jail following his arrest for possession of an allegedly illegal switchblade. Gray had served time in prison for a drug offense and was due in court in late April on a new drug charge. The death sparked riots in the city. Six officers face charges stemming from the arrest and subsequent death; the charges are variously based on an allegedly illegal arrest and alleged neglect in securing Gray in the van or summoning medical assistance. Mayor Stephanie Rawlings-Blake fired police chief Anthony Batts on July 8.

Officer Caesar Goodson faces the most serious charge, second-degree murder, along with other charges; three others are charged with involuntary manslaughter and other offenses: Lt. Brian Rice, Sgt. Alicia White, and Officer William Porter. Two others were charged with assault, misconduct, and false imprisonment: officers Edward Nero and William Porter. Porter's trial ended with a hung jury on Dec. 16, 2015, and he is scheduled to be retried. Nero was acquitted in a bench trial on May 23. Three of the defendants are white: Miller, Nero, and Rice; Goodson, Porter, and White are black. The city reached a $6.4 million settlement with Gray's family without admitting wrongdoing.

—Kenneth Jost

[1] Summaries drawn from well-documented Wikipedia entries.

begin collecting data on the race or ethnicity of individuals they question, search, or arrest.[34] The Justice Department was to use the data to determine whether federal officers were engaging in racial profiling and, if so, what should be done to stop the practice. Clinton said he hoped state and local law enforcement agencies would adopt similar steps to try to eliminate what he called a "morally indefensible" practice. Racial profiling, he said, "is wrong, it is destructive, and it must stop."

"Deliberate Indifference"?

The issue of racial and ethnic profiling gained new importance after the Sept. 11 terrorist attacks on the

United States in 2001 as Muslims and people of Arab or South Asian background came under heightened attention—and suspicion—from law enforcement and the general public. Meanwhile, critics of racial profiling of African Americans and Latinos continued efforts in court and legislative bodies to combat the practice and drew important support from the Obama administration's stepped-up scrutiny of local police forces. And two incidents made racial profiling issues front-page news: the arrest of the prominent African-American scholar Henry Louis Gates Jr. at the door of his Cambridge, Mass., home in 2009 and the killing of Trayvon Martin, an unarmed black teenager, by a white community-watch volunteer in a gated community in Florida in 2012.

Just 1 month after taking office, President George W. Bush followed Clinton's example by promising in his State of the Union address on Feb. 27, 2001, that his administration would work to end racial profiling. Attorney General John Ashcroft echoed Bush's promise, describing the practice as "unconstitutional."[35] After 9/11, however, the government evidently focused attention on Muslims, Arab nationals, and Arab Americans in investigating possible links to al Qaeda—the group responsible for the Sept. 11 attacks—within the United States. Immigration authorities rounded up hundreds of Middle Easterners.

Despite official denials, airport screeners appeared to be giving special attention to Muslims and Arabs; and some prominent commentators—including the Manhattan Institute's Mac Donald—forthrightly defended profiling as common-sense law enforcement.[36] When the Bush administration issued racial profiling guidelines in June 2003, it included an exception for national security–related investigations.[37] A decade later, Arab-American and Muslim groups continue to complain of heightened and unwarranted scrutiny from law enforcement—including a controversial special counterterrorism unit within the NYPD.

The New York City force had come under intense scrutiny for alleged racial profiling beginning in February 1999 with the shooting death of a Guinean immigrant, Amadou Diallo, at his front door in an ethnically diverse Bronx neighborhood. Plainclothes officers in the department's Street Crime Unit thought Diallo matched the description of a suspected rapist; when Diallo reached for his wallet as identification, the officers mistook it as a weapon and fired 41 rounds, killing him. The incident sparked raucous demonstrations and an unsuccessful prosecution of the four officers in a trial moved to Albany, N.Y., because of pretrial publicity.

The episode also led to a lawsuit by the Center for Constitutional Rights, accusing the NYPD of racial profiling and unlawful stop-and-frisk practices. The suit cited, among other evidence, a report by the New York attorney general's office that showed Street Crime Unit officers stopped 16 African Americans for every arrest made. After lengthy discovery, the city disbanded the Street Crime Unit and, in September 2003, agreed to settle the suit—called *Daniels v. City of New York*—by promising to institute policies aimed at eliminating

racial profiling. District Judge Scheindlin approved the settlement in December.[38]

Obama's election as the nation's first African-American president 5 years later was seen by some as marking a new era in race relations, but the Gates episode only 6 months after Obama's inauguration underlined the continuing points of contention between law enforcement and black Americans. Gates was charged with disorderly conduct on July 16, 2009, after a white Cambridge, Mass., police officer mistook him for a possible burglar. The charges were later dropped, and Obama hosted Gates and the officer for a so-called beer summit at the White House on July 30 to smooth things over.[39]

The killing of Martin by the white community-watch volunteer, George Zimmerman, on Feb. 26, 2012, touched off a more protracted nationwide debate over possible racial profiling. Zimmerman, concerned about a rash of home burglaries in the largely white gated community in Sanford, Fla., tailed Martin as the unarmed teenager was returning to his father's home and fatally wounded him during a scuffle.

Zimmerman was charged with second-degree murder and acquitted on July 13, 2013, under Florida's controversial so-called Stand Your Ground law, which eases rules for self-defense in criminal trials. The verdict prompted widespread protests by African Americans.[40]

Meanwhile, NYPD's stop-and-frisk litigation had resumed in 2008 after the Center for Constitutional Rights accused the city of failing to comply with the 2003 settlement. Judge Scheindlin assumed jurisdiction over the new case, *Floyd*, since it was related to the *Daniels* case that she had previously tried. The assignment would underlie later complaints of bias by the city and others, including the Manhattan Institute's Mac Donald, and the appeals court's subsequent decision to order the case reassigned. The trial in the new case began on March 18 and closed 2 months later on May 20 after sharp arguments over the implications of opposing statistical studies and testimony from police officials.

Scheindlin issued her ruling on Aug. 12. Out of the 4.4 million stops logged by police, Scheindlin found that at least 200,000—about 5 percent—were unconstitutional and that the actual figure was probably higher. She went on to find that blacks and Hispanics were more likely to be stopped than whites after controlling for other variables, that blacks were more likely to be arrested, and that blacks and Hispanics were more likely to be subjected to use of force. In all, Scheindlin concluded the data showed "deliberate indifference" on the city's part toward constitutional rights—a necessary finding to establish liability under federal civil rights law. Bloomberg appealed, but the city's newly elected mayor, de Blasio, agreed to settle the case shortly after taking office in January 2014.

Over the next 2 years, the issue of racial profiling became more urgent and more divisive because of a handful of highly publicized killings of African Americans under disputed circumstances.

CURRENT SITUATION
Pressure for Change

Police agencies across the country are under pressure to improve relations with minority communities, address crime-breeding conditions in impoverished neighborhoods, and re-examine policies and practices on the use of force.

The Obama administration and leading police professional associations are taking steps to improve the gathering and reporting of racial data on police stops and arrests. Police departments in 50 big to midsized cities have joined in an administration initiative launched in May 2015 to set up a publicly accessible database on such practices as uses of force, police pedestrian and vehicle stops, and officer-involved shootings.

Police Foundation president Bueermann says the data will allow the public to "make their own analysis and make their own conclusion about whether police are biased in their actions." The foundation manages the portal for the site.[23]

The so-called Police Data Initiative came as part of a broad report by an Obama administration task force on policing created in December 2014. Among other steps recommended in the task force's report, the administration is providing guidance for departments to institute the use of body-worn cameras to record encounters with civilians. In announcing release of the report, Obama also said that the administration was banning the transfer of military-style equipment to local police departments—the kind of equipment that had stoked discontent when deployed in quelling disorder in Ferguson following the Michael Brown shooting.[24]

Separately, a leading police research group is urging police departments to train officers in steps to deescalate encounters with civilians in order to minimize use of deadly force when the officers or bystanders are not themselves threatened. The 136-page report by the Police Executive Research Forum, issued in March, stresses that officer-involved shootings comprise "an infinitesimal fraction of the millions of interactions" between police and public but warns that "even one bad encounter" can damage community trust.[25]

The report largely absolves officers of blames in "most" of what it calls the "controversial" episodes. "[T]he officers should not be faulted," the report says, in bold-faced type, "because their actions reflected the training they received." But the report also says that in the significant fraction of encounters that involve either mental illness or unarmed civilians, there is "significant potential for de-escalation and resolving encounters by means other than the use of deadly force."

Shelton, with the NAACP's Washington office, agrees on the need to reexamine use-of-force policies. "In some cases, the structure for the acceptable use of deadly force is not nearly comprehensive enough," he says. "It is not clear when it is truly necessary to use deadly force."

In cities with changes in police leadership, officials are promising changes in police practices and policies as well. In Ferguson, a new police chief greeted officers with a stern warning against misconduct at his swearing-in ceremony on May 9.

Delrish Moss, an African American chosen from among four finalists after having served as spokesman for the Miami Police Department, threatened officers with being "removed or further prosecuted" if they performed their jobs "with malice." Moss recalled that he had had unpleasant encounters with police as a youth, including one incident in which an officer used a racial slur. As chief, Moss takes on responsibility for implementing reforms agreed to with the Justice Department in March that include better training and record keeping to monitor racial profiling.[26]

In Baltimore, the new police commissioner, Kevin Davis, is promising to cooperate with recommendations from a Justice Department probe of the department initiated in June 2015. Davis, a veteran white officer who served as deputy under the ousted African-American police commissioner Anthony Batts, says he expects the

Is racial profiling by police a serious problem in the United States?

YES
Dennis Parker
Director, Racial Justice Program,
American Civil Liberties Union

Written for *CQ Researcher*, November 2013

In their 2009 report, "The Persistence of Racial and Ethnic Profiling: A Follow-Up Report to the U.N. Committee on the Elimination of Racial Discrimination," the American Civil Liberties Union and the Rights Working Group concluded that despite "overwhelming evidence of its existence, often supported by official data, racial profiling continues to be a prevalent and egregious form of discrimination in the United States."

Time has not altered that conclusion. Numerous studies, data collection and individual anecdotes confirm that law enforcement agents continue to rely on race, color or national or ethnic origin as a basis for subjecting people to criminal investigations.

The cost of this reliance on race or ethnicity as a supposed indicator of likely criminal activity is high for individuals and society. Examples of the practice abound. After analyzing hundreds of thousands of police stops, a federal judge concluded that African-Americans and Latinos in New York City were far more likely than whites to be stopped by police when there was no reasonable suspicion of criminal activity and were less likely than whites to be found in possession of illegal items. Meanwhile, a federal court in Arizona found the Maricopa County Sheriff's Office relied on ethnicity in enforcing immigration laws in a way that was clearly unconstitutional. In both cases, the courts were so concerned about future violations that they ordered the use of impartial monitors to track compliance with remedies intended to stop the illegal practices.

Reliance on racial profiling is not limited to local law enforcement. Six states have adopted immigration enforcement laws that invite the profiling of Latinos. The federal government routinely relies on programs and practices that delegate immigration enforcement authority to state and local agencies, resulting in the unfair targeting of Latino, Arab, South Asian and Muslim people in the name of immigration control and national security.

Despite overwhelming evidence that racial profiling persists, the End Racial Profiling Act continues to languish in Congress. Until appropriate action is taken to address discriminatory profiling, people will continue to be subjected to the humiliation of repeated, unwarranted and intrusive stops and investigations, depriving them of their individual rights and undermining support for our criminal justice system.

The idea of basing law enforcement on actions rather than on race, ethnicity or religion is long overdue.

NO
Heather Mac Donald
Fellow, Manhattan Institute

Written for *CQ Researcher*, November 2013

There is no credible evidence that racial profiling is a serious problem among police forces. Studies that purport to show the contrary inevitably assume that police activity should match population ratios, rather than crime ratios. But urban policing today is driven by crime data: Officers are deployed to where city residents are most victimized by violence. Given the racial disparities in crime commission, the police cannot provide protection to neighborhoods that most need it without generating racially disproportionate enforcement numbers.

In New York City, for example, the per capita shooting rate in predominantly black Brownsville, Brooklyn, is 81 times higher than in Bay Ridge, Brooklyn, which is largely white and Asian. That disparity reflects Brownsville's gang saturation, which affects policing in myriad ways. Police presence will be much higher in gang-infested neighborhoods, and officers deployed there will try to disrupt gang activity with all available lawful tools, including the stopping and questioning of individuals suspected of criminal activity. Each shooting will trigger an intense police response, as officers seek to avert a retaliatory gang hit. Given the difference in shooting rates, it is no surprise that Brownsville's per capita police stop rate is 15 times higher than Bay Ridge's. If it were not, the police would not be targeting their resources equitably, according to need. Yet some advocates cite such stop disparities as prima facie proof of profiling.

Community requests for protection are the other determinant of police tactics. Last fall, I spoke with an elderly cancer amputee in the South Bronx. She was terrified to go down to her lobby to get her mail because of the youths hanging out there, smoking marijuana. Only when the police had been by to conduct trespass stops would she venture out: "When you see the police, everything's A-OK," she said. Police cannot respond to such requests for public order without producing racially disparate enforcement data that can be used against them in the next racial profiling lawsuit.

Young, black males are murdered at 10 times the rate of whites and Hispanics combined, usually killed by other minority males. The New York Police Department has brought the homicide victimization rate among the city's minorities down nearly 80 percent, yet young, black men are still 36 times more likely to be murdered than young, white males. Proactive policing is the best protection poor, minority neighborhoods have against violence and fear.

DOJ report to focus on discretionary arrests, stop-and-frisk encounters, and discipline investigations. "I welcome it," Davis said of the DOJ investigation in a remark to a reporter for the *Baltimore Sun* in December. "It puts us in the position to hit the ground running."[27]

In Chicago, Emanuel replaced the white police superintendent Garry McCarthy with a veteran black officer, Kevin Davis, who grew up in Chicago's infamous Cabrini-Green public housing project. Among initial steps, Emanuel instituted a new policy of transparency on police–civilian encounters by ordering the release of videos, reports, and other materials from about 100 police incidents, including officer-involved shootings. Meanwhile, Johnson responded to the city's $2 million whistleblower suit by two police officers by promising to make it easier for officers to report misconduct against colleagues.[28]

In San Francisco, Mayor Lee says there should be "consequences" for the police sergeant in Williams' death because the shooting went against department policy that generally prohibits shooting at a vehicle except in limited circumstances. Lee's remark came in a meeting with the *San Francisco Chronicle* editorial board on May 26, the day before Sgt. Justin Erb, a 15-year veteran of the force, was identified as having fired the fatal shot.[29]

Mixed Results for Prosecutors

Prosecutors are having relatively little success in bringing criminal charges against police in many of the recent high-profile officer-involved deaths, although some officers have been fired, suspended, or otherwise disciplined.

The mixed results for prosecutors are illustrated by the recent same-day announcements in two fatal shootings by police with charges brought in the killing of a stranded motorist in Florida but no charges against two officers for the death of a Minneapolis man under disputed circumstances.

Nouman Raja, a former Palm Beach Gardens officer, was charged on June 1 with manslaughter and attempted murder in the death of Corey Jones, an African-American musician, who was shot dead after Raja spotted him on the side of a roadway in the early morning hours of Oct. 18, 2015. Jones had called for roadside assistance after his car stalled, but Raja, in plainclothes, stopped to investigate and, after a brief conversation recorded on Jones's cell phone, fired six shots, one of them fatal.

Raja claimed that Jones, who had a gun and a legal permit to carry it, came at him with the weapon pointed. But Jones's body was found 64 feet away from his car and 40 feet away from his weapon, thus appearing to contradict Raja's version of events. Despite the charges, legal observers cautioned that the prosecution faces significant obstacles.[30]

In the Minneapolis case, the Justice Department announced on June 1 that no federal charges would be brought against officers Dustin Schwarze or Mark Ringgenberg for the fatal shooting of Jamar Clark on Nov. 15, 2015, as the white officers responded to a report of a disturbance at a party. Schwarze claimed that he fired the fatal shot after Clark, who was African American, attempted to grab his gun. The Hennepin County state's attorney had previously found no basis for state criminal charges.[31]

Paul Butler, an outspoken African-American professor at Georgetown Law School in Washington, says prosecutions of police officers in episodes such as these often fail because of the broad discretion police enjoy under Supreme Court precedents. "Even when blacks are selectively targeted by police," Butler says, "it is often not against the law."

Despite the varying circumstances, the NAACP's Shelton agrees that the most controversial episodes have all had "elements of racial profiling." In the Baltimore case, for example, "the question is why Freddie Gray was singled out in the first place," he says.

Historically, police officers are prosecuted only rarely for fatal shootings, and relatively few of those result in convictions, according to the *Washington Post*'s analysis of police use of deadly force from 2005 through the first few months of 2015. The *Post* counted 54 prosecutions in the previous 10 years, with 21 cases ending in acquittals or dismissals, 14 in convictions or other dispositions, and 19 cases then pending.[32]

Prosecutors have come up short so far in trials stemming from Gray's death even though six officers are facing charges. Officer Edward Nero was acquitted of assault and false imprisonment on May 23 in a bench trial before Circuit Judge Barry Williams. Nero and fellow officer Garret Miller were charged with assault on the basis of Gray's allegedly illegal arrest; Miller's case is still pending. Earlier, a jury failed on Dec. 16, 2015, to reach a verdict on involuntary manslaughter and other charges against officer William Porter, accused of failing to secure Gray in the police van and to summon medical help when needed. Williams declared a mistrial and scheduled a retrial to begin on June 13.[33]

Officer Caesar Goodson, the driver of the van, faces the most serious charges, second-degree murder and other counts, in the case; his trial was scheduled to begin on June 6. Two other officers, Lt. Brian Rice and Sgt. Alicia White, are awaiting trial on involuntary manslaughter and other counts. Despite the lack of convictions, Shelton has no criticism of the way the case is being handled. "It's being done very methodically and very thoughtfully," he says.[34]

Two of the highest-profile episodes ended with no criminal charges after state grand juries declined to return indictments against the officers involved. In Ferguson, a St. Louis grand jury declined on Nov. 24, 2014, to bring any charges against Ferguson officer Darren Wilson in Michael Brown's death 2 months earlier; Wilson resigned from the force the next week, blaming threats on his life. In Cleveland, a Cuyahoga County grand jury declined on Dec. 28, 2015, to bring charges against officers Timothy Loehmann or Frank Garmback for the fatal shooting of the boy Tamir Rice in November 2014. Loehmann and Garmback are facing administrative reviews, but prosecutor Timothy McGinty defended their actions in deciding not to seek an indictment.[35]

Among the most controversial cases, two officers are awaiting trials for fatal shootings in North Charleston, S.C., and Chicago. In Chicago, officer Jason Van Dyke was suspended from the force after his indictment in November 2015 for the shooting death of the teenager Laquan McDonald; no trial date has been set. In North Charleston, former officer Michael Slager is awaiting a state court trial on Oct. 31 for murder in the death of Walter Scott in April 2015; Slager was fired from the force, indicted on the state charge in June 2015, and then indicted on May 11 on federal civil rights and obstruction of justice counts.[36]

OUTLOOK
Regaining Trust?

When he created the White House task force on policing late in 2014, President Obama stressed the need for public confidence that law enforcement was being administered fairly for each and every community and demographic group. "When any part of the American family does not feel like it is being treated fairly," Obama said, "that's a problem for all of us."[37]

The distrust felt among many in the street turns back on police officers themselves. In the Police Executive Research Forum report on use of force, executive director Wexler writes of what he calls "upheaval" within the policing profession. "Officers who in the past exuded great pride in wearing the badge," Wexler writes, "now feel underappreciated by some members of the public, who seem to question their every move and motive."[38]

Four police chiefs lost their jobs within the past 2 years as a result of confidence gaps with the African-American communities in their cities that were exposed and widened by fatal encounters with civilians under questionable circumstances. In a report issued in April 2015, the police research group called for "honest conversations about race within the police department and with the public." The report goes on to call for devising enforcement strategies in consultation with affected communities and to criticize stop-and-frisk policies that emphasize the number instead of the quality of the stops.[39]

Mac Donald, the Manhattan Institute expert, complains that the issue of police shootings has been "distorted" by comparing the percentage of black victims with the total population instead of criminal offenders. "Any police killing of an unarmed civilian is a stomach-churning tragedy that police have to do all they can to prevent," she says. But the percentage of black victims—25 percent, according to the *Washington Post*'s compilation for 2015— is actually lower than would be projected from the racial breakdown of criminal offenders.

Epp, the University of Kansas expert, credits the Obama task force with "an interesting mix of reform proposals" that "if seriously adopted, would go some distance in addressing the problems of policing today." But he faults the report for treating racial profiling as a problem of individual officers more than one of policy. Butler, the Georgetown law professor, similarly views racial profiling as the result of policies known in police jargon as "order maintenance"—typically deployed in minority neighborhoods.

Withrow, the Texas State professor, expects to see significant changes in police department policies toward minority communities in the coming years. "We're going to see a concerted effort by police departments to engage minority communities in a substantial way," he says.

Police departments will step outside traditional policing and become more prominent social actors in the community, Withrow predicts. "They will really attempt to go out and build communities," he continues. "They will do much more than just answer service calls. That is well outside the traditional policing role, but I think that's what we're going to see."

Bueermann, the Police Foundation president, agrees that police departments will be more responsive to community views than in the past. "There is an increasing voice in America about certain policing activities, and I think there is an increasing sensitivity on the part of many police departments, of thoughtful, progressive leaders listening to what these people say and trying to make significant organizational changes," he says.

Policing as we have known it has not worked for everybody in this country," Bueermann adds, "and it needs to."

NOTES

1. Kevin Schultz, Vivian Ho, and Kimberly Veklerov, "S.F. police chief out," *The San Francisco Chronicle*, May 20, 2016, p. A1. Background also drawn from Joaquin Palomino and Bill Van Niekerken, "Timeline of Police Chief Greg Suhr's troubled tenure," ibid., p. A8.

2. See Julia Carrie Wong, "San Francisco police chief resigns in wake of shootings and scandals," *The Guardian*, May 19, 2016, www.theguardian.com/us-news/2016/may/19/san-francisco-police-greg-suhr-resigns-fatal-shooting-scandal?CMP=share_btn_tw.

3. Quoted in Emily Green, "Inevitable action: Lee had to replace chief to focus on reforms, analysts say," *The San Francisco Chronicle*, May 21, 2016, p. A1.

4. See Joaquin Palomino, "Racial disparities in SF traffic searches raise concerns of bias," *The San Francisco Chronicle*, April 10, 2016, p. A1.

5. Gallup Organization, Race Relations, www.gallup.com/poll/1687/race-relations.aspx (accessed June 2016).

6. See Al Baker, "City Police Still Struggle to Follow Stop-and-Frisk Rules, Report Says," *The New York Times*, Feb. 17, 2016, p. A17; J. David Goodman, "Bratton Battles His Predecessor on Crime Tally," ibid., Dec. 30, 2015, p. A1.

7. See Walter Berry and Jacques Billeaud, "Sheriff Joe Arpaio of Arizona found in contempt of court," The Associated Press, May 14, 2016.

8. Joaquin Palomino and Bill Van Niekerken, "Timeline of Police Chief Greg Suhr's troubled tenure," *The San Francisco Chronicle*, May 20, 2016, p. A8.

9. See Kimberly Kindy, Marc Fisher, Julie Tate, and Todd Lindeman, "A Year of Reckoning: Police Fatally Shoot Nearly 1,000 in 2015," *The Washington Post*, Dec. 26, 2015, www.washingtonpost.com/sf/investigative/2015/12/26/a-year-of-reckoning-police-fatally-shoot-nearly-1000/. The graphic includes a link to an earlier, related story: Sandhya Somashekhar, Wesley Lowery, Keith L. Alexander, Kimberly Kindy, and Julie Tate, "Black and Unarmed," *The Washington Post*, Aug. 8, 2015, http://www.washingtonpost.com/sf/national/2015/08/08/black-and-unarmed/.

10. Police Executive Research Forum, "Guiding Principles on Use of Force," March 2016, http://www.policeforum.org/assets/guidingprinciples1.pdf, pp. 9, 117. See Chuck Wexler and Scott Thomson, "Making Policing Safer for Everyone," *The New York Times*, March 2, 2016, p. A29. Wexler is executive director of the forum; Thomson, president of the forum, is chief of the Camden County Police Department in New Jersey.

11. See Steve Janoski, "Wyckoff Suspends Police Chief," *The Record* (Bergen County, N.J.), May 4, 2016, p. L01; Salvador Rizzo, "Tough Battle to Eliminate Profiling," ibid., March 27, 2016, p. A1.

12. See David A. Harris, *Profiles in Injustice: Why Racial Profiling Cannot Work* (2002), pp. 53–60 (New Jersey), pp. 60–64 (Maryland).

13. See Matt Apuzzo, "Ferguson Police Routinely Violate Rights of Blacks, Justice Dept. Finds," *The New York Times*, March 3, 2015, www.nytimes

.com/2015/03/04/us/justice-department-finds-pattern-of-police-bias-and-excessive-force-in-ferguson.html?_r=0.

14. See Jessica Mazzola, "ACLU Demands N.J. Police Track Racial Data," *The Star-Ledger* (Newark, N.J.), April 14, 2016, p. 28.

15. See Eric Dexheimer, Jeremy Schwartz, and Christian McDonald, "Data: DPS searches Hispanics more often," Austin American-Statesman, Dec. 6, 2015, p. A1; See Margaret Moffett, "Data show black males more likely to be searched during traffic stops throughout North Carolina," *News and Record* (Greensboro, N.C.), Nov. 22, 2015.

16. See Monitor's Second Report, Feb. 16, 2016, p. 3, http://nypdmonitor.org/resourcesreports/monitor-reports/. For coverage, see Al Baker, "City Police Still Struggle to Follow Stop-and-Frisk Rules, Report Says," *The New York Times*, Feb. 17, 2016, p. A17.

17. See Pervaiz Shallwani and Mark Morales, "NYC Officials Tout New Low in Crime, but Homicide, Rape, Robbery Rose," *The Wall Street Journal*, Jan. 4, 2016, http://www.wsj.com/articles/nyc-officials-tout-new-low-in-crime-but-homicide-rape-robbery-rose-1451959203; J. David Goodman, "Bratton Battles His Predecessor on Crime Tally," *The New York Times*, Dec. 30, 2015, p. A1; "New York Policing, by the Numbers," *The New York Times*, Dec. 28, 2015, p. A18 (editorial).

18. See Mark Berman, "Homicides are up again this year in more than two dozen major U.S. cities," *Washington Post* Blogs, May 14, 2016, www.washingtonpost.com/news/post-nation/wp/2016/05/14/we-have-a-problem-homicides-are-up-again-this-year-in-more-than-two-dozen-major-u-s-cities/.

19. See Mark Berman, "Police agencies say homicides are up this year in major cities," *The Washington Post*, May 16, 2016, p. A4; Eric Lichtblau and Monica Davey, "New Data on Homicide Rates Rekindles a Debate," *The New York Times*, May 14, 2016, p A11.

20. Ames Grawert and James Cullen, "Crime in 2015: A Final Analysis," April 20, 2016, https://www.brennancenter.org/sites/default/files/analysis/Crime_in_2015_A_Final_Analysis.pdf.

21. Quoted in Megan Cassidy, "Arpaio held in contempt," *The Arizona Republic* (Phoenix), May 14, 2016, p. A5. The ACLU of Arizona has a summary of the history of the case, *Ortega-Melendres v. Arpaio*, on its web site and a link to the judge's decision: http://www.acluaz.org/sites/default/files/documents/Melendres%20Contempt%20Order%205_13_2016.pdf.

22. See Paul W. Valentine, "Md. Settles Lawsuit Over Racial Profiles," *The Washington Post*, Jan. 5, 1995, p. B1; David Kocieniewski, "U.S. Will Monitor New Jersey Police on Race Profiling," *The New York Times*, Dec. 22, 1999, p. B1.

23. See Public Safety Open Data Portal, http://public-safetydataportal.org/.

24. See Final Report of the President's Task Force on 21st Century Policing, May 2015, www.cops.usdoj.gov/pdf/taskforce/taskforce_finalreport.pdf. For news coverage, see Julie Hirschfeld Davis and Michael D. Shear, "Obama Puts Focus on Police Success in Struggling City in New Jersey," *The New York Times*, May 19, 2015, p. A11; David Nakamura and Wesley Lowery, "U.S. to ban transfer of some military gear to local police," *The Washington Post*, May 19, 2015, p. A4.

25. Police Executive Research Forum, "Guiding Principles on Use of Force," March 2016, www.policeforum.org/assets/guidingprinciples1.pdf.

26. See Stephen Deere, "New Ferguson chief has no 'magic pill' for curing city's problems,": *St. Louis Post-Dispatch*, May 10, 2016, p. A1; U.S. Dep't of Justice, "Justice Department and City of Ferguson, Missouri, Resolve Lawsuit with Agreement to Reform Ferguson Police Department and Municipal Court to Ensure Constitutional Policing," March 17, 2016, www.justice.gov/opa/pr/justice-department-and-city-ferguson-missouri-resolve-lawsuit-agreement-reform-ferguson.

27. Mark Puente, "Davis stands firm for change: City's police chief begins reforms as he awaits results of Justice Dept. probe," *The Baltimore Sun*, Dec. 6, 2015, p. 1A.

28. See Jeremy Gorner, "City to release materials from police shootings," *Chicago Tribune*, May 29, 2016,

p. C14; Jeremy Gorner, "Top cop decries violence, broken justice system," ibid., June 1, 2016, p. C4.

29. See Lizzie Johnson, "S.F. sergeant who killed woman IDd," *The San Francisco Chronicle*, May 28, 2016, p. C1; Vivian Ho, "Lee wants action on police shooting, ibid., May 27, 2016, p. D1.

30. See Daphne Duret and Lawrence Mower, "State attorney charges ex-Gardens cop after grand jury finds fault," *Palm Beach Post*, June 2, 2016, p. 1A; Terry Spencer and Curt Anderson, "Convicting officer in Florida slaying may prove difficult," The Associated Press, June 2, 2016.

31. See Matt Furber and Richard Pérez-Peña, "No Federal Charges for Minneapolis Officers in Fatal Shooting of Black Man," *The New York Times*, June 2, 2016, p. A10.

32. "Police Officers Prosecuted for Use of Deadly Force," *The Washington Post*, April 11, 2015, https://www.washingtonpost.com/graphics/investigations/police-shootings/. The graphic includes a link to related story.

33. See Jean Marbella and Colin Campbell, "Response measured to Nero verdict," *The Baltimore Sun*, May 24, 2016, p. A5; Justin Fenton, "Porter's retrial set for June 13," ibid., Dec. 22, 2015, p. 1A.

34. For other analysis, see Ian Duncan, "Experts say first verdict does not doom cases against five others," *The Baltimore Sun*, May 24, 2016, p. A1.

35. See David Hunn, "No charges for Wilson," *St. Louis Post-Dispatch*, Nov. 25, 2014, p. A1; Cory Shaffer, "No charges for officers," *Plain Dealer* (Cleveland), Dec. 29, 2015, p. A1.

36. See Christy Gutowski, "Backers dispute portrayal of Van Dyke as 'monster,'" *Chicago Tribune*, May 15, 2016, p. C1; John Monk, "Ex-North Charleston officer's indictment: Justice or scapegoating?," *The State* (Columbia, S.C.), May 11, 2016.

37. Quoted in "Task Force," op. cit., p. ??.

38. "Use of Force," op. cit., p. 4.

39. Police Executive Research Forum, "Constitutional Policing as a Cornerstone of Community Policing, April 2015, pp. 5, 14, http://ric-zai-inc.com/Publications/cops-p324-pub.pdf.

BIBLIOGRAPHY
Books

Del Carmen, Alejandro, *Racial Profiling in America*, Pearson/Prentice Hall, 2008.
The chairman of the Department of Criminology and Criminal Justice at the University of Texas-Arlington examines the historical and contemporary perspectives on racial and ethnic profiling in the United States. Includes chapter notes.

Epp, Charles S., Steven Maynard-Moody, and Donald P. Haider-Markel, *Pulled Over: How Police Stops Define Race and Citizenship*, University of Chicago Press, 2014.
Three professors at the University of Kansas in Lawrence present results of research finding that black motorists are five times more likely to be subjected to "investigatory" traffic stops than white drivers. Includes detailed tables, notes. Epp and Maynard-Moody are professors in the School of Public Affairs and Administration; Haider-Markel is a professor of political science.

Glover, Karen S., *Racial Profiling: Research, Racism, and Resistance*, Rowan & Littlefield, 2009.
An assistant professor in the Department of Sociology, Criminology and Justice Studies at California State University–San Marcos examines racial profiling from the perspective of critical race theory through interviews with minority-group subjects who had been stopped by police officers. Includes chapter notes.

Harris, David A., *Profiles in Injustice: Why Racial Profiling Cannot Work*, New Press, 2002.
A professor at the University of Pittsburgh School of Law, who was one of the first to comprehensively cover racial profiling, provides examples and continues with critical arguments on the purported justifications of the practice, as well as its costs and recommendations for reforms. The paperback edition issued in 2003 includes a chapter on post-9/11 ethnic profiling. Includes detailed notes.

Mac Donald, Heather, *Are Cops Racist? How the War Against Police Harms Black Americans*, Ivan R. Dee, 2002 [ebook issued 2010].
A senior fellow at the Manhattan Institute, a conservative think tank, argues in a collection of magazine-length pieces that police do not engage in racial profiling and

that the controversy hurts black Americans by impeding policing in minority neighborhoods.

Rice, Stephen K., and Michael D. White (eds.), *Race, Ethnicity, and Policing: New and Essential Readings*, **New York University Press, 2010.**

The 22 separate essays on racial and ethnic profiling are divided into four parts: context, methods, research, and future. Rice is an associate professor in the Department of Criminal Justice, Seattle University; White is an associate professor at Arizona State University School of Criminology and Criminal Justice.

Articles

Harris, David A., "Picture This: Body-Worn Video Devices (Head Cams) as Tools for Ensuring Fourth Amendment Compliance by Police," *Texas Tech Law Review*, **Vol. 43, No. 1 (2010), pp. 357–372, http://tex astechlawreview.org/wp-content/uploads/Picture_ This_Body_Worn_Video_Devices_Head_Cams_As_ Tools_For_Ensuring_Fourth_Amendment_ Compliance_By_Police.pdf.**

A University of Pittsburgh law professor proposes making video and audio recording of search-and-seizure incidents, as is done already in several cities, a routine police practice.

Williams, Rich, "Under Review: Policing in America," *State Legislatures Magazine*, **December 2015, www .ncsl.org/research/civil-and-criminal-justice/ policing-under-review.aspx.**

The article in the monthly magazine of the National Conference of State Legislatures details work by state lawmakers to address issues of racial profiling and use of force by law enforcement agencies.

Withrow, Brian L., and Jeffrey D. Dailey, "Racial Profiling and the Law," in Craig Hemmens (ed.), *Current Legal Issues in Criminal Justice* **(Oxford University Press, 2014).**

The 11,000-word chapter gives a comprehensive, up-to-date account of law and litigation over racial profiling from the 1960s to the present. Withrow, a former Texas state trooper, is a professor of criminal justice at Texas State University in San Marcos; Dailey is an assistant professor of homeland and border security at Angelo State University in San Angelo.

Reports and Studies

"Racial Profiling and the Use of Suspect Classifications in Law Enforcement Policy," Judiciary Subcommittee on the Constitution, Civil Rights, and Civil Liberties, U.S. House of Representatives, June 17, 2010, serial no. 111-131, http://judiciary.house.gov/hearings/ hear_100617_1.html.

The hearing included testimony and statements from six witnesses, including representatives of the American Civil Liberties Union, Sikh Coalition, and Muslim Advocates. The committee website includes video and print transcript.

On the Web

"Fatal Force," a Washington Post database, https:// www.washingtonpost.com/graphics/national/police-shootings-2016/.

The newspaper gathered information on 990 police killings in 2015 and 390 through the first 5 months of 2016, with detailed statistical analyses: an invaluable resource.

For More Information

American Civil Liberties Union, 125 Broad St., New York, NY 10004; 212-549-2500; www.aclu.org. Monitors and sometimes brings lawsuits in cases involving racial profiling, use of force and other police-practices issues.

Fraternal Order of Police, Grand Lodge, 1410 Donelson Pike, A-17, Nashville, TN 37217; 615-399-0900; www.grandlodgefop.org. Largest membership organization representing rank-and-file law enforcement officers.

International Association of Chiefs of Police, 515 North Washington St., Alexandria, VA 22314; 703-836-6767; www.theiacp.org. Represents operating chief executives of international, federal, state and local law enforcement agencies of all sizes.

Major Cities Chiefs Police Association, https://major citieschiefs.com/about.php. Represents chiefs from 63 large American city or county police organizations.

Mexican American Legal Defense and Educational Fund, 634 S. Spring St., Los Angeles, CA; 213-629-2512; www.maldef.org. A leading civil rights organization for Latinos.

Muslim Advocates, 315 Montgomery St., 8th floor, San Francisco, CA 94104; 415-692-1484; www.muslimadvocates.org. Civil rights organization for Muslims, Arab and South Asian Americans.

NAACP, 4805 Mt. Hope Dr., Baltimore MD 21215; 410-580-5777; www.naacp.org. Century-old civil rights organization for African-Americans.

National Sheriffs' Association, 1450 Duke St., Alexandria, VA 22314; 1-800-424-7827; www.sheriffs.org. Represents and assists sheriffs' offices nationwide through education, training and information resources.

Police Foundation, 1201 Connecticut Ave., N.W., Washington, DC 20036-2636; 202-833-1460; www.policefoundation.org. Established by the Ford Foundation in 1970; sponsors research to support innovation and improvement in policing.

9

Social Security

David Hosansky

Washington state logger Tom Edwards, who has had trouble finding steady work, worries about his eventual retirement benefits because Social Security payments are based on work history. As millions of Baby Boomers like Edwards retire, the demands on Social Security could overwhelm the system. Some experts recommend raising the retirement age, but manual laborers like Edwards may not be able to spend additional years on the job.

From *CQ Researcher,*
June 3, 2016.

AP Photo/Ted S. Warren

Wilma Bogar, 77, doesn't know what she would do without Social Security.

Her house outside Bozeman, Mont., is paid off, but she still has everyday expenses such as food and utilities, as well as trips to Denver to see her daughters. Between a pair of small pensions and her $1,869 monthly payment from Social Security, she is able to enjoy a quiet retirement.

"It's a very big help," she says of Social Security. "Once you pay your insurance and electric bill, [expenses] mount up, that's for sure. Without the Social Security, it would be a tighter pinch."

Bogar is one of more than 60 million Americans, including 49 million retirees and survivors of former recipients, who rely on Social Security payments every month.[1] The popular program, which turned 80 last year, is achieving what its creators intended back in the Depression: provide a modest monthly payment to the nation's seniors so they need not worry about becoming destitute. Social Security also issues cash payments to the permanently disabled and to minor children of deceased workers.

With most companies doing away with pensions and workers still recovering from the 2007-09 recession that devastated retirement savings, some experts say Social Security is more important than ever.

"Social Security is really the backbone of our retirement system," says Alicia Munnell, director of the Center for Retirement Research at Boston College. "It's shielded from market changes, it's shielded from inflation, and it comes out as an annuity. It's the major source of retirement income in our country, and it works."

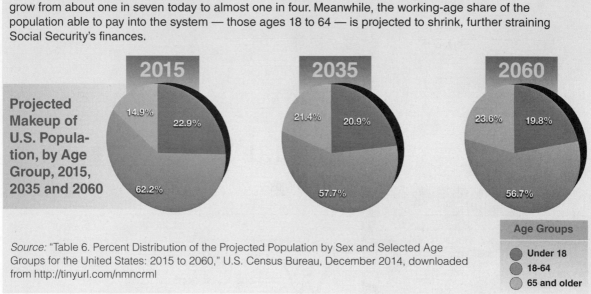

Aging Population Challenges Social Security

Over the next 45 years, the proportion of Americans age 65 or older eligible for Social Security benefits will grow from about one in seven today to almost one in four. Meanwhile, the working-age share of the population able to pay into the system — those ages 18 to 64 — is projected to shrink, further straining Social Security's finances.

Projected Makeup of U.S. Population, by Age Group, 2015, 2035 and 2060

2015
14.9%
22.9%
62.2%

2035
21.4%
20.9%
57.7%

2060
23.6%
19.8%
56.7%

Source: "Table 6. Percent Distribution of the Projected Population by Sex and Selected Age Groups for the United States: 2015 to 2060," U.S. Census Bureau, December 2014, downloaded from http://tinyurl.com/nmncrml

Age Groups
- Under 18
- 18-64
- 65 and older

But policy experts warn that the venerable system is in trouble, mostly due to demographics: An aging population means fewer workers are paying into the system and more retirees demanding benefits. At the same time increased life expectancy means the average retiree receives a monthly check for years longer than when the program was established. The Social Security trust fund currently has a $2.8 trillion balance — or surplus — which comes from payroll taxes and interest on the surplus. Earmarked for paying current and future retirees, the fund will run out of money within a generation, imperiling full retirement benefits for tens of millions of Americans, without congressional action.[2]

"Unless we deal with this crisis, the young people of this country will get poorer, the disparity between young and old, the working middle class and the retired will grow even larger," New Jersey Gov. Chris Christie, who briefly ran for the 2016 Republican presidential nomination, said last year.[3]

The so-called silver tsunami — the huge wave of aging post-World War II Baby Boomers born between 1946 and 1964 that began retiring in 2012 — is straining the system, a stress that will only grow. By 2035, the number of Americans over age 65 will jump from today's 48 million to 79 million.[4] In addition, today's seniors can expect to live, for almost 21 years, on average, after retiring, compared with 14 years in 1940, when Social Security began making regular monthly payments.[5]

Such demographic trends can be devastating to Social Security, a pay-as-you-go system funded by a 12.4 percent payroll tax, half paid by workers and half by employers.[6]* As the nation's population ages, the number of retirees collecting Social Security benefits is rising far more quickly than the number of workers paying taxes to support the system. In 1950, 16 workers paid into the system for every retiree collecting benefits.[7] In the last few years, that ratio is down to 2.8 workers per retiree — and shrinking.[8]

In 2010, the Social Security trust fund for the first time began paying out more than it raised in taxes, drawing down the trust fund surplus to cover the shortfall. At the current rate, the surplus will be depleted in 2034, and Social Security will be able to make just 79 percent of its payments, funded by payroll tax revenues.[9]

---

* The self-employed pay the full 12.4 percent.

Policy experts say it is critical for lawmakers to put the program on sounder fiscal footing as soon as possible. But Congress appears hopelessly split between those who would save money by cutting benefits and those who want to raise taxes to shore up the program. Furthermore, Washington these days has little appetite to change the popular entitlement, known as the "third rail" of politics because any major change likely would provoke furious resistance.

"It's part of the fabric of the country," says Max Richtman, president and CEO of the National Committee to Preserve Social Security and Medicare. "There's a disconnect somewhere between the sentiment of the people on Social Security and members of Congress who want to cut it."

Indeed, polls consistently show broad public support among Republicans and Democrats alike for the program. A 2014 survey by the nonpartisan National Academy of Social Insurance, for example, found that 85 percent of Americans believe that Social Security is more important than ever to ensure that retirees have a dependable income. Most respondents said they were willing to pay higher taxes to keep the system strong.[10]

The Social Security Administration (SSA) also provides benefits to 11 million disabled workers and their dependents through a pair of disability programs called Supplemental Security Income (SSI) and Social Security Disability Insurance (SSDI), which are facing even greater fiscal pressure.[11] In 2015, when the disability trust fund was down had only about a year's worth of cash, Congress took money from the Social Security retirement trust fund to cover the shortfall. But the disability programs are still expected to run out of money early in the next decade.[12]

The two programs combined will have spent about $877 billion in 2015, representing about 24 percent of the total federal budget.[13]

On the presidential trail this year, the candidates have proposed various solutions for fixing Social Security: increasing benefits, raising the retirement age, increasing Social Security taxes on wealthier Americans and privatizing the program. Some have even proposed

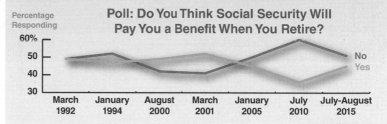

Many Skeptical of Receiving Benefits

About half of nonretired Americans said in 2015 they did not expect to receive Social Security benefits when they stop working, down from 60 percent in 2010, when skepticism about the program's long-term viability peaked, particularly among younger Americans.

Poll: Do You Think Social Security Will Pay You a Benefit When You Retire?

Percentage Responding

Source: Frank Newport, "Many Americans Doubt They Will Get Social Security Benefits," Gallup, Aug. 13, 2015, http://tinyurl.com/jc2xb6h; full results downloaded from link at bottom of page

raising payroll taxes enough to increase benefits for lower income retirees. But they generally have not emphasized the type of all-encompassing approach policy experts say is needed to ensure the long-term fiscal health of the system.

"We have more money going out than we have" coming in, says Munnell. "There is no silver bullet. We need to close that gap. When the political craziness calms down, I hope they do the same thing as last time — name a commission and then Congress takes its recommendations."

Munell was referring to the National Commission on Social Security Reform, which in 1983 issued recommendations later adopted by Congress that put the retirement program on a stronger fiscal footing.

While liberals generally want to retain the Social Security program or even increase benefits, the conservatives worry that it is inordinately expensive.

"Social Security is a major contributor to our current debt problem," says Romina Boccia, deputy director of the Roe Institute for Economic Policy Studies at the conservative Heritage Foundation in Washington. "It's the largest federal program. Twenty-five cents of every dollar the federal government spends is on Social Security — and it is growing."

If the federal budget is ever to be reined in, conservatives say, government must make changes to Social Security and Medicare, the other major federal entitlement program, which provides federal health insurance

Fraud and Waste Sap Social Security Funds

"Every dollar misallocated is a dollar lost for those who truly need it."

The Social Security system pays out hundreds of billions of dollars each year in retirement and disability payments, and some of that money is winding up in the hands of crooks and fraudsters.

Examples abound:

- Millions of Social Security numbers belonging to deceased Americans born more than a century ago remain available for people wanting to fraudulently collect monthly payments.
- Criminals are using fraudulent medical documents to obtain Social Security disability benefits.
- Children are collecting benefits by using Social Security numbers of their deceased parents.

Underscoring the scope of the problem, a report last year by the Social Security Administration's Office of the Inspector General identified about 6.5 million Social Security number holders aged 112 or older — even though just 35 people worldwide were that old. In one case, an individual had recently opened bank accounts by using Social Security numbers for individuals born in 1886 and 1893.[1]

"It is incredible that the Social Security Administration in 2015 does not have the technical sophistication to ensure that people they know to be deceased are actually noted as dead," said Sen. Ron Johnson, R-Wis., who chairs the Senate committee that oversees the Social Security Administration. "This problem has serious consequences."[2]

The report urged the agency to better manage data for "number holders who exceeded maximum reasonable life expectancies and were likely deceased."[3]

Politicians have raised concerns about the extent to which false or stolen Social Security numbers may be costing the government or putting Americans at risk of identity theft.

"Not only do these types of avoidable errors waste millions of taxpayers' dollars annually and expose our citizens to identify theft, but they also undermine confidence in our government," said Sen. Tom Carper, D-Del.[4]

Businessman Donald Trump, the presumptive GOP presidential nominee, has gone so far as to suggest that Social Security's fiscal problems could be largely solved if it cut down on waste, fraud and abuse.[5] But fiscal experts say the notion that reducing those problems would significantly change the finances of the Social Security program is illusory.

"It's absurd to pretend you can fix it by ending fraud," says Maya MacGuineas, president of Committee for a Responsible Federal Budget, a bipartisan think tank in Washington. "You can get rid of every penny of fraud, waste and abuse and would still have the same problems," she adds.

Social Security's disability system is viewed as more vulnerable to fraud than its retirement system because the determination of whether someone qualifies for disability depends on complex factors such as medical records. Earlier this year, a grand jury in Kentucky indicted three people, including a former judge and a disability lawyer, on charges

for senior citizens. Together, Social Security and Medicare represent about 40 percent of the federal budget.

One of the most outspoken critics of Social Security finances is Laurence Kotlikoff, an economics professor at Boston University who has written widely about Social Security benefits. He worries the program is taking money from young workers with no guarantee that it will provide retirement income for them and future generations.

"The system is broken. It's a Ponzi scheme," says Kotlikoff, who would prefer a system in which workers

invest in the stock market. "The sooner we move away from it, the better off our kids will be."

As concern about Social Security grows, here are some questions policy makers and everyday Americans are asking:

Is the Social Security system running out of money?

Ask younger Americans if they ever expect to receive Social Security benefits and most are skeptical. In fact, a recent Gallup Poll found that nearly two-thirds of those

that they defrauded the government of $600 million in disability benefits by submitting false medical documentation.[6]

A report last year by the Social Security inspector general concluded that the Social Security Administration had made $16.8 billion in disability overpayments over the past 10 years ending in 2014. Much of the money went to people who were no longer disabled or were earning too much to be eligible for the program. Some also went to people in prison or who had died.[7] The agency was able to recover $8.1 billion, although it took several years.[8]

Amid growing concerns about Social Security's finances, Congress last year approved stiffer criminal and civil penalties and fines for Social Security fraud. The new law imposed penalties of up to 10 years in prison for individuals in trusted positions, such as doctors or former Social Security Administration employees, and also created a new felony classification, punishable by up to five years in prison and up to $250,000 in fines, for conspiracy to commit Social Security fraud.[9]

But a study this year by the Government Accountability Office warned that the Social Security Administration is failing to focus on cases that could generate more savings. "As a result, it may be missing opportunities to efficiently and effectively use federal resources," the report concluded.[10]

Despite the large overpayments and other issues, Social Security Administration officials maintained that the system has a high degree of accuracy for both retirement and disability payments. "For fiscal year 2013 — the last year for which we have complete data — approximately 99.8 percent of all Social Security payments were free of overpayment, and nearly 99.9 percent were free of underpayment," said Social Security spokesman Mark Hinkle.[11]

But critics said errors are making Social Security's fiscal condition more precarious.

"Every dollar misallocated is a dollar lost for those who truly need it most," said Senate Finance Committee Chairman Orrin Hatch, R-Utah.[12]

— *David Hosansky*

[1] "Numberholders Age 112 or Older Who Did Not Have a Death Entry on the Numident," Office of the Inspector General, Social Security Administration, March 4, 2015, http://tinyurl.com/j6z9e2v.

[2] Josh Hicks, "Millions over 112 have Social Security numbers, and it's not because we're living longer," *The Washington Post*, March 10, 2015, http://tinyurl.com/zwl5f44.

[3] "Numberholders," *op. cit.*

[4] Hicks, *op. cit.*

[5] Michael Tanner, "Trump on 'Waste, Fraud, and Abuse,'" *National Review*, Feb. 17, 2016, http://tinyurl.com/h8ggnu7.

[6] "Retired Judge, Attorney, and Psychologist Indicted in $600 Million Social Security Disability Fraud Scheme," Office of the Inspector General, Social Security Administration, April 5, 2016, http://tinyurl.com/jhz4dsx.

[7] "Overpayments in the Social Security Administration's Disability Programs — A 10-Year Study," June 2015, Office of the Inspector General, Social Security Administration, http://tinyurl.com/jalxet6.

[8] *Ibid.*

[9] Eric Pianin, "Why Social Security's Crackdown on Disability Fraud Is Coming up Short," *The Fiscal Times*, March 14, 2016, http://tinyurl.com/h8pc4je.

[10] "Social Security Disability: SSA Could Increase Savings by Refining Its Selection of Cases for Disability Review," U.S. Government Accountability Office, Feb. 11, 2016, http://tinyurl.com/jy5tzbg.

[11] Stephen Ohlemacher, "Report: Social Security Overpaid Disability Benefits by $17 Billion," *Business Insider*, June 5, 2015, http://tinyurl.com/zswbwmk.

[12] *Ibid.*

29 and younger answered "no" when asked whether Social Security would "be able to pay you a benefit when you retire?"[14]

Demographic changes are costing Social Security billions of dollars every month, leading political leaders to raise alarms about both Social Security and its impact on the federal budget.

"But anyone who tells you that Social Security can stay the way it is is lying," Sen. Marco Rubio, R-Fla., said during a presidential campaign debate earlier this year when he was a candidate. "Social Security will go bankrupt, and it will bankrupt the country with it," he said. "So what it will require is people younger, like myself, people that are 30 years away from retirement, to accept that our Social Security is going to work differently than it did for my parents."[15]

Many experts, however, emphatically reject such dire predictions.

"Absolutely not," says Richtman of the National Committee to Preserve Social Security and Medicare. "The terms that are thrown around — crisis, bankrupt, there's no money there — that's part of the mythology that's being pushed by people who don't care for the program or want to see people take care of themselves. This program is sound. Everybody will get every penny of their benefits."

Both sides agree on the basic contours of the fiscal situation. The Social Security trust fund last year paid out about $84 billion more in benefits than it raised in taxes, and that loss rate is expected to grow as the Baby Boomers continue to retire. By about 2034, the trust fund balance will decline to zero, at which point the payroll taxes collected on workers every month will be enough to pay only 79 percent of benefits to retirees. The exact date that the trust fund will be depleted depends on such factors as economic growth and the life expectancy of retirees, according to the Social Security trustees.[16]

Moreover, those trustees, who have been required since the early days of the program to issue an annual projection of the trust fund's solvency over the next 75 years, estimate that the fund will face a deficit of $10.7 trillion in current dollars over the next three-quarters of a century.[17]

But that may be a relatively optimistic scenario. The Congressional Budget Office says the trust fund most likely will run out of money in 2029.[18] Or it could be depleted years earlier, warns a team of political scientists and demographers at Harvard University and Dartmouth College, partly because the trustees may not be fully taking into account longer life expectancies and other factors that could drain the fund earlier than estimated.[19]

Whatever the exact date, many fiscal experts say the system as currently configured is headed toward insolvency. "It's facing a pending crisis. We cannot pay the promised benefits with the revenues we have," says Michael Tanner, a senior fellow at the libertarian Cato Institute. "It's only going to get deeper and deeper in the red."

But other experts, especially those on the left, say Social Security is generally sound and needs only minor adjustments, such as increasing payroll taxes on wealthier workers.

"No other program has to be perpetually fully funded 75 years into the future that way," says Monique Morrissey, an economist at the Economic Policy Institute, which focuses on the needs of low- and middle-income workers. "To always be in balance over 75 years is very difficult to do, and it doesn't mean the program is a bust if it doesn't attain it."

Morrissey and other Social Security experts also point out that, even in the unlikely event that Congress were to allow the trust fund balance to dwindle to nothing, companies and employees would continue to fund it every month through payroll taxes. Under that scenario, retirees would get about 79 percent of their full benefits, according to estimates by the Social Security trustees.[20]

"Absent a complete and total collapse of the U.S. economy so that no one anywhere is working, Social Security will always have a revenue source of some sort in the future," says Kurt Czarnowski, a former Social Security regional communications director who now works as a consultant advising workers about Social Security benefits. "The question is: Will that revenue source cover 100 percent of the promised benefits?

"With some reasonable changes to close that 21 percent gap — increases on the income side, slowdown on the benefits side — it can remain that solid program that Americans have counted on for 80-plus years," says Czarnowski.

Should Congress cut Social Security benefits to ensure the program's long-term sustainability?

Warren Adamsbaum has never forgotten the day he received his first Social Security check: He had just turned 65 and was eligible for full benefits.

"When I first got it, I remember thinking this is the greatest thing in the world," says the former public relations and advertising vice president for Weight Watchers, who is now 91 and living in Boca Raton, Fla.

But the era of Americans receiving full Social Security benefits at age 65 is gone. Those wanting full benefits now must wait until they're at least 66 or, if born in 1960 or later, 67.

With Americans living longer and Social Security beginning to run out of money, experts wonder whether it is time to raise the full retirement age even further for younger and middle-aged workers. Boccia of the Heritage Foundation, for example, would like to see the retirement age raised gradually to 70 over the next couple of decades.

"You have people living increasingly longer in retirement, which requires increasing taxes to pay for them" unless the retirement age is pushed back, she says.

But advocates for retirees fiercely oppose any increase in the retirement age or cut in benefits. They prefer to balance the trust fund and maintain current benefits — or

Social Security Consumes Growing Share of Budget

The share of the federal budget spent on Social Security has grown from 15 percent in 1966 to about 24 percent today. It is projected to edge up to 25 percent in 2024. Medicare, the federal health insurance program for senior citizens, adds another 17 percent to the federal budget.

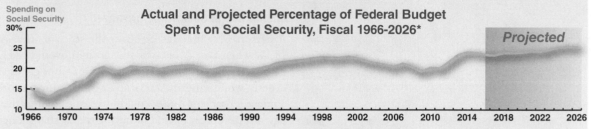

Spending on Social Security

Actual and Projected Percentage of Federal Budget Spent on Social Security, Fiscal 1966-2026*

Projected

x-axis: 1966, 1970, 1974, 1978, 1982, 1986, 1990, 1994, 1998, 2002, 2006, 2010, 2014, 2018, 2022, 2026

y-axis: 10, 15, 20, 25, 30%

* Share of budget projected for 2016-2026

Source: "Historical Budget Data," Congressional Budget Office, March 2016, downloaded from http://tinyurl.com/h6rgsgl; "10-Year Budget Projections," Congressional Budget Office, March 2016, downloaded from http://tinyurl.com/h6rgsgl

even increase them — by raising payroll taxes, especially on wealthier Americans, by raising the cap on how much income is taxed. Under current law, taxable wages are capped at $118,500, so income above that amount is exempt from payroll taxes, known as FICA taxes for the Federal Insurance Contributions Act of 1935.[21]

"Social Security really needs a little more money," says the Economic Policy Institute's Morrissey. "The vast majority of people would be better off even if they were paying slightly more in contributions."

Polls show Americans are more inclined to preserve Social Security by raising taxes than by cutting benefits. For example, a 2014 survey by the National Academy of Social Insurance found that 77 percent of respondents said it's critical to preserve Social Security, even if that meant paying more in taxes. Presented with a range of options for raising taxes or cutting benefits, the respondents preferred to pay higher taxes themselves and to impose higher taxes on the wealthy, rather than raise the retirement age or cut benefits.[22]

Policymakers could adjust benefit formulas to help get Social Security on a more solid fiscal footing. Currently, benefits are based on the highest 35 years of the recipient's wages and are linked to average U.S. wage growth. If they were based on the highest 38 years of earnings (thereby incorporating three years of lower earnings) and

linked to inflation (which tends to rise more slowly than wages), average benefits would be lower.[23]

But liberals say benefits are already stingy, especially for lower-income workers and those — especially women — who dropped out of the workplace for a period of time, usually to focus on family caretaking. And it is unfair to raise the retirement age, they say, because lower-income workers are not living longer like wealthier workers and manual laborers may be physically unable to spend additional years on the job.

"I have a feeling that most of those people who are talking about it can easily work for a few more years," Richtman says. "I bet you don't hear many nurses or factory workers or people doing manual labor advocating a higher retirement age."

But other policy experts say the retirement age can be increased while still protecting workers in physically demanding jobs by, for instance, allowing such laborers to retire sooner or receive disability payments to tide them over until retirement. "Raising the retirement age doesn't have to be regressive," says Maya MacGuineas, president of the bipartisan Committee for a Responsible Federal Budget.

Conservatives view a tax increase as a nonstarter, citing estimates by the Social Security trustees that the payroll tax would have to be raised by 20 percent — from

As exercise and improved medical care help Americans live longer, some experts say major changes must be made in Social Security, such as raising the retirement age or reducing benefits. Others say minor adjustments, such as increasing payroll taxes on wealthier workers, would largely keep the system solvent. Above, older Americans take a water aerobics class.

12.4 percent to about 15 percent — to balance the trust fund without benefit cuts. "You're really inflicting a fair amount of pain at that point," says Cato's Tanner. "People are going to get hit with a substantial tax increase."

As for raising the cap on payroll taxes, that would affect more than just the wealthy, because "$118,500 is really middle class in cities like New York," Tanner says.

Budget experts also questioned whether raising Social Security taxes should take priority over raising taxes for other needs, such as increasing the gasoline tax to pay for infrastructure improvements.

"If we're talking about a tax increase, I think there are more important things we should be spending money on," says Eugene Steuerle, a fellow and the Richard B.

Fischer chair at the Urban Institute. Steuerle and some other experts say Social Security would be best helped through a combination of policy changes, handled in such a way that lower-income people are not adversely affected.

Should Social Security be privatized?

A person who invested $100 in the stock market in 1935, when Social Security was created, would likely have more than $200,000 today.[24] That sort of gain has experts wondering if Americans would enjoy a more affluent retirement if they could invest the amount they pay in FICA taxes instead of having to pay that money into the Social Security trust fund.

"There are much better ways for workers to build toward retirement," says the Heritage Foundation's Boccia. "For income replacement and to ensure a comfortable retirement, I think private retirement savings are much better at accomplishing that."

For decades, conservatives have pressed to partially or completely privatize Social Security by allowing workers to divert some or all of the 12.4 percent FICA tax into specially designed retirement accounts.

They could provide workers with better returns over time, privatization advocates say. The stock market has delivered average earnings of more than 10 percent per year (compounded, including interest) over the last 80 years.[25] The Treasury bonds that the Social Security trust fund invests in generally return much less than half of that.[26]

But experts who support the traditional, conservative approach of Social Security say the stock market is far too unstable to be the only source of retirement income for workers.

"People don't want their benefits to depend on whether Wall Street has a good year or bad year," says Gary Burtless, a senior fellow in economic studies at the liberal Brookings Institution think tank in Washington. "It's very hard for most people on their own to make the calculations and investment choices in setting aside a certain proportion of their current income into a retirement savings account. And Social Security does that very well."

The political debate over privatizing Social Security has cooled since President George W. Bush made it a top priority but could not get Congress to vote on the issue.

His plan would have allowed younger and middle-aged workers to direct a limited portion of the payroll taxes that they and their employers pay into certain stock funds administered by the government.

The stock market crash of 2008, which wreaked havoc on retirement accounts, further dampened interest in privatization. "We've all lived through the Great Recession," says Boston College's Munnell. "That would have been even more of a tragedy if everyone had all their retirement savings in the stock market."

Some experts also argue that while establishing private savings accounts might strengthen overall retirement savings in the long run, it would worsen Social Security's financial condition in the short term. The trust fund would run out of money even more quickly if a portion of the payroll tax were diverted to the market, they say.

"Creating private accounts made a good deal of sense when we had Social Security surpluses," says the Committee for a Responsible Federal Budget's MacGuineas, who supported some privatization proposals in the past. "But the moment for creating them has passed now that Social Security is running deficits."

Still, the idea of putting money into private accounts is enticing to some, such as the Cato Institute's Tanner. He advocates allowing workers younger than 55 to divert up to 6.2 percent of their FICA payroll taxes into their own private retirement accounts, while agreeing to forgo future Social Security benefits. The other 6.2 percent would go into financing the trust fund during a transition period away from the traditional system.

"If we move to a system of personal accounts, we would reduce the future obligations of Social Security substantially, but we have to find a way to cover current retirees," Tanner says. "There is no painless way to do it. But it makes the system better in the long term."

To some extent, the debate over privatization comes down to whether the risk of investing in the market is worth the higher returns. Advocates of Social Security favor the reliability of the current system, which not only provides a check every month but also increases the amount based on inflation. They say this is particularly important as pensions become less common.

"Social Security is that solid, foundation income protection that people can count on being there," says Czarnowski, the consultant. "The changes in the other

A 1935 poster introduces the newly enacted Social Security program to the American public. "We can never insure 100 percent of the population against 100 percent of the hazards and vicissitudes of life," said President Franklin D. Roosevelt, who championed the landmark program. "But we have tried to frame a law which will give some measure of protection to the average citizen and to his family against . . . poverty-ridden old age."

parts of the retirement world these days [such as the loss of pensions] makes that especially important."

Boccia, however, warns that Social Security — like the market — should not be viewed as a guaranteed source of income.

"There's also risk in giving all your money to the government and then expecting the government to take care of you," she says. "There's political risk, and there's risk of fiscal crisis."

CHRONOLOGY

1930s *Social Security is created to combat widespread poverty among the elderly during the Great Depression.*

1935 President Franklin D. Roosevelt signs the Social Security Act, the nation's first major anti-poverty insurance program providing benefits to older Americans.

1939 Ida May Fuller of Ludlow, Vt., becomes the first retiree to receive a monthly Social Security check. Social Security is expanded to provide benefits to workers' survivors.

1940s-1960s *Post-World War II population boom sets the stage for Social Security's future funding shortfall.*

1946 The first year of the Baby Boom starts a demographic bulge that will last for the next 18 years.

1950 Cost-of-living adjustments are applied to Social Security benefits to protect them from inflation. There are 16 workers for every retiree in the United States, more than enough to cover Social Security benefits.

1954 Congress expands Social Security to cover disabled workers who are 50 and older, and disabled adult dependents.

1961 All workers are allowed to receive reduced, early-retirement benefits at age 62.

1965 Medicare, the most far-reaching change to the entitlement system for seniors, becomes law, providing health insurance to millions of Americans age 65 or older.

1970s-1990s *Concern mounts over Social Security's solvency as demographers warn of a coming wave of Baby Boom retirements.*

1972 Social Security's new Supplement Security Income program provides additional benefits to low-income seniors and includes coverage for the blind and disabled — groups previously served by states and localities with federal funding.

1977 To restore the Social Security trust funds' financial soundness, Congress agrees to gradually raise payroll taxes from 9.9 percent to 10.8 percent and increases the maximum earnings subject to those taxes.

1983 Congress authorizes taxation of Social Security benefits, brings federal employees into the system, raises the payroll tax to 12.4 percent and sets in motion a gradual increase — from 65 to 67 — in the age at which retirees can claim full benefits.

1999 The Ticket to Work and Work Incentives Improvement Act provides vocational rehabilitation and employment services to help disability beneficiaries find work.

2000s *Elected officials fail to reach consensus on major changes to Social Security.*

2005 Republican President George W. Bush's proposal to partially privatize Social Security fails to pick up significant support in Congress.

2008 The first Baby Boomers reach age 62, making them eligible for reduced, early-retirement Social Security benefits.

2009 The age at which retirees may receive full Social Security benefits rises to 66 for those born after 1943.

2010 The Social Security trust fund begins to pay out more in benefits than it collects in revenues.

2015 Congress agrees to put money from the Social Security trust fund into the nearly depleted Disability Insurance trust fund, which was estimated to run out of money in 2022. . . . In a sign of the potential scope of fraud, the Social Security Administration's Office of the Inspector General identified about 6.5 million Social Security number holders who were 112 or older — even though just 35 people worldwide were that old.

2027 The retirement age for full Social Security benefits is scheduled to rise to 67 for those born in 1960 or later.

2029-2034 The Social Security trust fund will run out of money in 2029, according to projections by the Congressional Budget Office; the Social Security Administration says it will happen in 2034.

BACKGROUND

Depression Roots

Social Security began during the Depression, but the concept of a public safety net to protect citizens from poverty dates back to the earliest days of the country.

In his pamphlet "Agrarian Justice," written shortly after the Revolutionary War, American patriot Thomas Paine proposed creating a fund, financed through an inheritance tax, to provide a single payment of 15 pounds sterling to citizens reaching age 21 to help them get started in life, and annual payments of 10 pounds sterling to everyone 50 and older to prevent poverty in old age.[27]

Paine's idea never made its way into public policy. Before the Industrial Revolution drew workers from the farms into urban factories, people who could no longer work as a result of injury or old age relied on family for support and care. But the move to cities eroded that safety net, as extended families broke into smaller, "nuclear" households composed of parents and their children. Charities and a patchwork of state welfare programs turned out to be a poor substitute for family-based support.

Only one segment of American society — veterans — enjoyed government-provided income protection. Workers for private companies did not have guaranteed benefits, although some paternalistic companies retained older workers in token jobs at reduced pay. In a few other cases, workers received some form of retirement stipend. More commonly, however, older workers were simply dismissed when they were no longer productive.

In 1882, one of the first formal pension plans for workers was introduced by the Alfred Dolge Co., a builder of pianos and organs. Dolge placed 1 percent of each worker's salary into a pension fund and added 6 percent interest each year. But the plan was largely unsuccessful because it required a worker to spend many years with the company, and the pension disappeared when the company went out of business. Other company pensions also failed to take hold for varying reasons. By 1932, only 5 percent of the elderly were receiving company pensions.[28]

Meanwhile, several factors were combining to undermine the living standards of older Americans: urbanization, the breakdown of the extended family, increasing reliance on wage income for survival and a rapid increase in life expectancy due to improved sanitation and health care. By the 1920s, the country was older and significantly more industrialized, with more people living in cities than on farms for the first time. With no one to care for them and no income, millions of former workers faced the prospect of dying in poverty.

The plight of America's elderly population worsened after the stock market crashed in 1929 and the Great Depression began. Thousands of letters from destitute elderly people poured into Washington. "I'm 72 years old and have no one to take care of me," wrote a woman from South Carolina. A letter that reached the White House from a Virginia woman stated: "I'm a 60-year-old widow greatly in need of medical aid, food and fuel, I pray that you would have pity on me."[29]

President Herbert Hoover (1929-33) asked Americans to volunteer their services and charitable contributions to alleviate the plight of the unemployed and the elderly. But with so many people facing financial hardship nationwide, Hoover's call went largely unanswered, leaving much of the challenge to the states.

By the 1930s, most states had established limited old-age "pensions" for older Americans who met financial need standards. But these programs were implemented unevenly. By 1935, only 3 percent of the elderly were receiving benefits — and the average benefit was just 65 cents per day.[30]

> "I bet you don't hear many nurses or factory workers or people doing manual labor advocating a higher retirement age."
>
> — *Max Richtman,*
> *President and CEO,*
> *National Committee to Preserve Social*
> *Security and Medicare*

Disability Program Faces Financial Challenges

As claims mount, policy experts seek to get recipients back to work.

Patty, 59 years old and taking powerful medication for back pain, has been receiving disability payments from Social Security for five years. But she says she can't make ends meet on her monthly check of slightly more than $1,100.

So, she says, she breaks the rules. Despite chronic pain and rules against earning an additional $1,130 a month or more, she regularly makes herself available to help elderly neighbors with light chores to keep up on her bills.

"I'm not supposed to be working, but I have to make ends meet," says the New York woman, who asked that her last name not be used. "What they give you for disability is really not enough to live off with. . . . My rent is $1,374 so I'm already short, and then you've got your regular living to do."

Some 11 million disabled workers and their dependents get monthly checks under a pair of programs for the disabled called Supplemental Security Income, or SSI (for those with the greatest financial need) and Social Security Disability Insurance (for those who become disabled after having worked for a number of years). The average monthly benefit is $1,165.[1] Even though the programs are designed as a safety net for the permanently disabled, critics say they are instead trapping beneficiaries in near poverty by issuing small checks and prohibiting them from earning much outside income.

"Being on disability might mean that a person has some sort of income but is still homeless or is struggling to afford medication or food or transportation to medical appointments," says Colleen Rivecca, advocacy program lead at St. Anthony's, a nonprofit that provides services to low-income people in San Francisco.

The disability programs are controversial, both because the rules make it difficult for Americans to get into or out of the programs and because of mounting expenses. By some measures, disability programs have become the most important element of the nation's safety net. The federal government spends about $145 billion annually on these programs, more than food stamps ($74 billion) and welfare ($17 billion) combined.[2]

Last year, Congress had to transfer emergency funds into the Disability Insurance trust fund to keep it from running out of money. It did so by increasing the portion of the 12.4 percent payroll tax that goes into the disability trust fund from 1.8 to 2.37 percent for a three-year period.[3] Even so, the fund is in more precarious shape than Social Security's program for the retired and is projected to run out of money by about 2022.

Concerned about beneficiaries remaining in the program indefinitely, Congress in 1999 created the Ticket to Work program to help people with disabilities return to work. But the program has had limited success. The last time it was evaluated in 2013, only about 60,000 people had received support through the program out of several million receiving disability benefits.[4]

As more Americans say they are too disabled to work, critics worry that disability is becoming a substitute for welfare. The number of Americans receiving disability payments has quadrupled since 1970, with more than 2 million additional recipients coming on the rolls in the decade after Congress scaled back traditional welfare payments in 1996.[5] Whereas the leading cause of disability in the early years of the program were heart disease and stroke, more than half the beneficiaries have mental disorders or musculoskeletal diseases, which can often be difficult to prove.[6]

"Over half the people on disability are either anxious or their back hurts," said Sen. Rand Paul, R-Ky. "Join the club. Everybody over 40 has a back pain."[7]

But advocates for the disabled say claims of program abuse are largely exaggerated.

"You will hear examples of someone who's collecting disability benefits and playing golf," says Max Richtman, president and CEO of the National Committee to Preserve Social Security and Medicare. "But the vast majority are not playing golf. They're often bedridden."

Bipartisan consensus seems to be growing on the need to make changes to the disability system. Most important, policy experts agree, is to provide more incentives to get disabled Americans back into the workforce.

"Right now we don't allow partial disability," says Michael Tanner, a senior fellow at the libertarian Cato Institute. "It's almost like a light switch that's on or off. The current system basically forces you out of the workforce. To the degree that Congress can come together on mom and apple pie, I think we may see changes. Even supporters of the system would like to see changes."

Some experts favor an approach that would steer applicants into rehabilitation programs with the goal of eventually moving them back into the workforce. Only if the rehabilitation was unsuccessful — or if an applicant was so disabled that rehabilitation was not worth trying to begin with — would the person become eligible for permanent disability benefits.

"The idea is to make sure that workers have access to the types of support that we believe can help people stay in the labor force even when they have significant medical conditions," says David Stapleton of the Princeton, N.J.-based policy research organization Mathematica Policy Research, who has worked on this type of plan.

"Under the current process, the Social Security Administration can't distinguish in many cases between people who can work with the right support and medical treatment versus those who reasonably cannot work," adds Stapleton, director of Mathematica's Center for Studying Disability Policy. "We should change the rules so the process takes into account the technologies and other things that will allow a person to work despite having a very significant medical problem."

To enable recipients to start earning more income, Congress last year directed the Social Security Administration to test a plan that would reduce monthly benefits by $1 for every $2 of outside earnings that exceed the $1,130 threshold. In contrast, recipients currently lose their entire benefits if their outside earnings exceed the threshold for more than nine months.

Rivecca says such changes could make a major difference for recipients. "They can't survive on the income they have," she says. "Even to make an extra $50 a month can help to buy food."

— *David Hosansky*

Kevin Cook for *The Washington Post* via Getty Images

Patrick McGarvey, 48, of Riegelsville, Pa., says he waited seven years to get approved by the Social Security Administration to receive disability benefits for his debilitating back pain. "I'd much rather be working," he said.

[1] "Social Security Basic Facts," Social Security Administration, http://tinyurl.com/j7nwkff.

[2] The funding estimates come from various sources. For Social Security disability: "A Summary of the 2015 Annual Reports," Social Security Administration, http://tinyurl.com/goa7zg8; for the Supplemental Nutrition Assistance Program, or food stamps: "Supplemental Nutrition Assistance Program Participation and Costs," U.S. Department of Agriculture, May 6, 2016, http://tinyurl.com/o28odbs; and for Temporary Assistance for Needy Families: "Temporary Assistance for Needy Families: Spending and Policy Options," Congressional Budget Office, Jan. 21, 2015, http://tinyurl.com/hotwwl8.

[3] Philip Moeller, "How the Budget Deal Will Change Medicare and Social Security," *Time*, Oct. 30, 2015, http://tinyurl.com/pnjdyv9.

[4] Gina Livermore *et al.*, "Executive Summary of the Seventh Ticket to Work Evaluation Report," Center for Studying Disability Policy, July 30, 2013, http://tinyurl.com/gr95yds.

[5] "Social Security Beneficiary Statistics: Number of beneficiaries receiving benefits on Dec. 31, 1970-2015," Social Security Administration, http://tinyurl.com/hgv5plg.

[6] Steve Contorno, "Rand Paul says most people receive disability for back pain, anxiety," *PolitiFact*, Jan. 16, 2015, http://tinyurl.com/mgo8a8e.

[7] Stephen Ohlemacher, "Report: Social Security Overpaid Disability Benefits by $17 Billion," *Business Insider*, June 5, 2015, http://tinyurl.com/zswbwmk.

Social Security Act

President Franklin D. Roosevelt (1933-45) took office promising to shift the model for federal economic security policy from state-based welfare assistance programs to federal programs similar to the "social insurance" plans prevalent in Europe. First adopted in 1889 in Chancellor Otto von Bismarck's Germany, social insurance plans worked like commercial insurance plans, collecting premiums, or taxes, from a large pool of working-age citizens to pay benefits to those who meet eligibility conditions, such as the disabled and the elderly.

On June 8, 1934, Roosevelt announced his support for a similar approach in the United States and created the Committee on Economic Security to propose a plan. Seeking to placate critics of such an expanded role for the federal government, he said: "This seeking for a greater measure of welfare and happiness does not indicate a change in values. It is rather a return to values lost in the course of our economic development and expansion."[31]

The following year, Congress began debating legislation based on recommendations by the committee. Both chambers passed the Social Security Act by overwhelming margins. On Aug. 14, 1935, Roosevelt signed the new program into law.

It created a social insurance program to pay retired workers a steady income for the rest of their lives. "We can never insure 100 percent of the population against 100 percent of the hazards and vicissitudes of life," Roosevelt said. "But we have tried to frame a law which will give some measure of protection to the average citizen and to his family against the loss of a job and against poverty-ridden old age."[32] The law also included incentives for states to establish unemployment insurance programs, which all of the states had done by 1937.[33]

Although the law had been passed with significant Republican support, it became a major issue in the 1936 presidential election, facing withering attacks from GOP nominee Alf Landon, who denounced it as "unjust, unworkable, stupidly drafted and wastefully financed." He also said that, "to call it social security is a fraud on the working man."[34]

The law also withstood fierce legal challenges from companies, with the Supreme Court in 1937 agreeing with the administration that the new program was constitutional. The landmark ruling would permanently extend the reach of the federal government.[35]

The law provided the basic structure for today's Social Security program, awarding benefits only to covered workers when they retired at age 65. And, unlike the state old-age pension plans, it was funded through a contributory system, in which future beneficiaries contributed to their own retirement though payroll deductions made during their working lives. On Jan. 1, 1937, workers began acquiring credits toward their old-age benefits, and they and their employers began paying FICA taxes. The revenues were placed in a dedicated Social Security trust fund to be used for paying benefits.

For the first three years Social Security paid each beneficiary a small, single, lump-sum payment because early recipients had not paid enough into the system to be vested for monthly benefits. This changed as the trust fund accumulated sufficient revenue. The first retiree to receive a monthly Social Security check was legal secretary Ida May Fuller of Ludlow, Vt., who retired in 1939 at age 65. Because of Social Security's pay-as-you-go financing arrangements, she got a great return. After contributing just $24.75 into the system over three years, Fuller collected $22,888.02 in Social Security benefits before she died in 1975 at the age of 100.[36]

Amendments Passed

In 1939 Congress expanded Social Security, transforming it from a retirement system for workers into a broader family income-security system. The changes added so-called dependent's benefits (payments to the spouse and children under 18 of a retired worker who died) as well as survivors' benefits paid to the family if a covered worker died prematurely. Lawmakers subsequently adopted cost-of-living allowances (COLAs) to make sure benefits kept up with inflation.[37]

President Dwight D. Eisenhower (1953-61) signed laws that gradually expanded the program to cover disabled workers and their dependents. In 1956, Congress reduced from 65 to 62 the age at which women could begin receiving benefits. Women who took benefits earlier would receive smaller monthly checks based on the actuarial notion that they would receive benefits for a longer period of time than if they waited until age 65. The same early-retirement option was extended to men in 1961.[38]

In 1965, building on Roosevelt's vision of a strong governmental role in protecting older Americans from poverty, President Lyndon B. Johnson (1963-69) signed legislation establishing Medicare. By providing health insurance to nearly all Americans age 65 and older, Medicare would become one of the most far-reaching changes in the health and financial security of older Americans.[39]

By the late 1960s, there was growing interest in reducing waste and redundancy by merging state and local welfare programs with the federal Social Security system. The 1972 Social Security Amendments brought three such "adult categories" — the needy aged, blind and disabled — under a single new Social Security program called Supplemental Security Income (SSI). More than 3 million people were shifted from the state welfare rolls to the new federal SSI program.[40]

The 1972 amendments also increased Social Security benefits for elderly widows and widowers, extended Medicare to individuals receiving disability benefits and those with chronic renal disease and increased Social Security benefits for workers who delayed retirement past age 65.[41]

Concerns about Social Security's soundness began to surface in the late 1970s. An economy beset by "stagflation" — inflation and minimal economic growth — and the coming demographic time bomb posed by the Baby Boom Generation fueled predictions that the trust funds would soon be exhausted. To address the potential shortfall, Congress passed the 1977 Social Security Amendments, which gradually increased the payroll tax from 9.9 to its current 12.4 percent rate, increased the maximum earnings subject to Social Security taxes and adjusted the way COLAs and the wage base were calculated.[42]

But within a few years Social Security again faced a serious funding crisis due to rapid growth in benefit expenditures. The crisis prompted President Ronald Reagan (1981-89) to appoint a panel to recommend ways to fix the system, headed by economist Alan Greenspan (who would later become chairman of the Federal Reserve). Based on the group's recommendations, the 1983 amendments made Social Security benefits taxable, brought federal employees into the system and gradually increased the official retirement age from 65 to 66 in 2009, and 67 in 2027. It also raised, over time, the payroll tax for the self-employed from 8.05 percent to its current level of 12.4 percent.[43]

The increased revenues, designed to prepare Social Security for the coming retirement of the Baby Boomers, generated a large surplus that was invested in special, non-tradeable Treasury bonds, with interest credited to Social Security. The surplus was available to the Treasury for the funding of other programs, although it had to be repaid whenever the Social Security commissioner wanted to redeem them.

The surplus has generated debate in recent decades, particularly after Vice President Al Gore in his failed 2000 presidential campaign proposed the creation of a Social Security "lockbox" to protect the program's annual surplus, which at the time amounted to about $150 billion or more. Part of the issue — which has dogged Social Security since it began racking up surpluses in the 1930s — is that the government lacks a ready mechanism to sock away surplus funds to keep them from being used by other programs. With surpluses gradually dwindling away, the issue has faded, although some economists say the surplus indirectly enabled President George W. Bush (2001-09) to pay for such priorities as a 2001 tax cut.[44]

Reagan also oversaw the beginnings of a shift in philosophy on social safety net programs, calling for smaller government and tighter eligibility standards for welfare programs. The Republican-led Congress in 1996 passed legislation that disqualified applicants for Social Security or SSI disability benefits if drug or alcohol addiction contributed to the disability. Congress in 1996 also ended SSI eligibility for most legal, non-citizen immigrants and tightened eligibility standards for disabled children. After public outcry, lawmakers later relaxed some of the new restrictions on non-citizens and children.[45]

President Bill Clinton (1993-2001) signed two other bills aimed at encouraging Social Security beneficiaries to work. The 1999 Ticket to Work and Work Incentives Improvement Act established a new program providing vocational rehabilitation and employment services to help disability beneficiaries find productive work. The 2000 Senior Citizens' Freedom to Work Act allowed workers to receive benefits even if they continued to work past the normal retirement age.[46]

Privatization Debate

Mistrust of large government programs, combined with high returns on stock market investments in the 1990s, created interest in partially or entirely privatizing Social Security. At the beginning of his second term, President

Bush proposed overhauling the program and allowing younger workers to voluntarily divert a portion of their payroll taxes into private accounts.

"Here's why the personal accounts are a better deal," said Bush in his State of the Union address on Feb. 2, 2005. "Your money will grow, over time, at a greater rate than anything the current system can deliver — and your account will provide money for retirement over and above the check you will receive from Social Security. In addition, you'll be able to pass along the money that accumulates in your personal account, if you wish, to your children and/or grandchildren. And best of all, the money in the account is yours, and the government can never take it away."[47]

At the time, Americans were becoming increasingly dependent on tax-deferred 401(k) accounts invested in the stock market. Congress created such accounts in 1978, and they gradually became a cornerstone of the retirement system, especially as companies cut costs by phasing out traditional pensions or, in some cases, were unable to cover promised pension benefits after going bankrupt.[48]

Bush then embarked on a national campaign, traveling around the country to promote the plan. But growing numbers of Americans expressed disquiet with privatization. In March 2005, a survey by the Pew Research Center for the People and the Press showed that only 29 percent of respondents approved of Bush's handling of Social Security.[49] The issue largely faded away without a vote in Congress, as the administration was beset by other issues, such as recovery efforts in New Orleans and the Gulf Coast after Hurricane Katrina struck in August.

By 2008, talk of privatization of Social Security had evaporated, along with public trust in Wall Street investments, in the wake of a mortgage crisis and subsequent stock market crash that cost U.S. households almost $8 trillion in wealth.[50]

Congress instead focused on minor changes to the program. Last fall, with the Disability Insurance trust fund just a year away from running out of money, lawmakers agreed to allow the reallocation of funds from the Social Security trust fund (officially called the Old-Age and Survivors Insurance trust fund). This temporary infusion of cash will keep the disability trust fund solvent until 2022.[51]

Lawmakers also made other changes, including saving money by ending a popular practice known as "file-and-suspend," under which a retiree could file for benefits and then suspend them, enabling them to grow for several more years while still being eligible to collect a spouse's monthly payments.

CURRENT SITUATION
Presidential Politics

In this year's tumultuous presidential race, Republicans and Democrats have staked out vastly different positions on Social Security.

Donald Trump, the GOP front-runner, has repeatedly vowed to protect Social Security and other entitlements. "It's my absolute intention to leave Social Security the way it is," he said during a Republican debate in March. "I want to make our country rich again so we can afford it."[52]

After his opponents dropped out of the race and Trump became the presumptive GOP nominee, however, his campaign seemed to signal an openness to considering cuts to the program. A Trump policy adviser said at a conservative conference in May that "after the administration's been in place, then we will start to take a look at all of the programs, including entitlement programs like Social Security and Medicare."[53]

Several of Trump's political opponents laid out more traditionally conservative positions before dropping out of the race, calling for various approaches to scaling back benefits and, in some cases, partially privatizing the system.

For instance, New Jersey Gov. Christie suggested reducing benefits for those with more than $80,000 in other income and eliminating benefits for anyone making more than $200,000. He also would have raised the age for early retirement from 62 to 64 and for full retirement from 67 to 69. Former Florida Gov. Jeb Bush proposed gradually raising the retirement age to 70, reducing benefits for the wealthiest seniors and allowing recipients who claim early Social Security benefits to earn more without losing benefits. Sen. Ted Cruz of Texas backed partial privatization, raising the eligibility age and reducing benefits.[54]

Perhaps not wanting to alienate the sizable senior voting bloc, all of the candidates stressed that they would not touch benefits for Americans already receiving benefits or those about to retire.

On the Democratic side, the candidates focused on shoring up the program and even expanding it, rather than reducing benefits. Former Secretary of State Hillary

Should Congress raise the full retirement age to 70?

YES

Romina Boccia
RESEARCH FELLOW IN FEDERAL BUDGETARY Affairs and Deputy Director, Roe Institute for Economic Policy Studies, The Heritage Foundation

Written for *CQ Researcher*, June 2016

It makes sense to raise the age at which people can claim full Social Security benefits to 70 in a gradual, predictable manner. The change would treat retirees fairly, strengthen Social Security for current and future generations and protect workers from excessive payroll taxes.

Americans live much longer than they did when Social Security began in 1935, but the retirement age has not kept pace with longer life expectancies. Since 1940, life expectancy at age 65 has risen six years for men and seven for women. Longer lives translate into greater work capacity and potentially greater earnings. Yet, largely because of the availability of Social Security and other age-based retirement benefits, many individuals retire long before they have to. A recent study concluded that average Americans could work 2.5 to 4.2 years longer than they do now.

As it is, more and more Americans are drawing benefits for longer periods. This puts a tremendous — indeed, unsustainable — financial strain on the Social Security system. It also makes our economy less dynamic, as experienced and productive workers leave the workforce prematurely.

Lawmakers should gradually increase the Social Security retirement age, to 70 over the next decade, and future rises should be tied to improvements in life expectancy. The alternative is ever-lengthening benefit payouts requiring ever-increasing taxes to pay for them. Social Security already faces an annual cashflow deficit in the tens of billions. Its trust fund will be completely depleted by 2034, if not sooner.

Social Security was never meant to be workers' sole source of income in retirement. Individuals should continue to have the choice to retire on their own schedule, using their private retirement savings. Lawmakers can help by reducing the program's size and scope to ensure workers don't wind up dependent on government in their old age because excessive taxes left them unable to save adequately during their working years.

Social Security was designed as a safety net to protect individuals too old to work from poverty. Forcing workers to subsidize decades-long retirements of able-bodied, well-to-do retirees is unfair and damaging to the workers. Meanwhile, individuals unable to work until the higher retirement age can apply for Social Security disability.

Increasing the Social Security retirement age to 70 and indexing it to life expectancy can help ensure that benefits will be there for those who truly need them, while protecting workers from undue tax burdens.

NO

Gary Burtless
Senior Fellow, Economic Studies, The Brookings Institution

Written for *CQ Researcher*, June 2016

Social Security faces a serious funding problem. The program takes in too little money to pay all that has been promised to future beneficiaries. Government forecasters predict Social Security's reserve fund will be depleted between 2030 and 2034. There are two basic ways we can eliminate the funding gap: cut benefits or increase contributions. A common proposal is to increase the age at which workers can claim full retirement benefits. For people nearing retirement today, the full retirement age is 66. As a result of a 1983 law, that age will rise to 67 for workers born after 1959.

When policymakers urge us to raise the retirement age, they are proposing to increase the full retirement age beyond 67, possibly to 70, for workers now in their 30s or 40s. This saves money, but it also cuts monthly retirement benefits by the same percentage for every worker, unless workers delay claiming benefits. The policy might seem fair if workers in future generations could all expect to share in gains in life expectancy. However, new research shows that gains in life expectancy have been very unequal, with the biggest improvements among workers who earn top incomes. Life expectancy gains for workers with the lowest incomes have been small or negligible.

If the full retirement age were raised, future retirees with high lifetime earnings can expect to receive some compensation when their monthly benefits are cut. Because they can expect to live longer than today's retirees, they will receive benefits for a longer span of years after 65. For low-wage workers, there is no compensation. Since they are not living longer, their lifetime benefits will fall by the same proportion as their monthly benefits. Thus, "raising the retirement age" is a policy that cuts the lifetime benefits of future low-wage workers by a bigger percentage than it does of future high-wage workers.

The fact that low-wage workers have seen small or negligible gains in life expectancy signals that their health when they are past 60 is no better than that of low-wage workers born 20 or 30 years ago. This suggests their capacity to work past 60 is no better than it was for past generations. A sensible policy for cutting future benefits should therefore preserve current benefit levels for workers who have contributed to Social Security for many years but have earned low wages.

Sen. Elizabeth Warren, D-Mass., and other liberals are pushing to increase Social Security benefits this year. Legislation proposed by Warren would give Social Security recipients and veterans receiving pensions and other benefits a one-time payment of $581 to compensate for the lack of a cost-of-living adjustment in 2016.

Clinton would raise the cap on payroll taxes, thereby taxing higher-income workers. She would also increase benefits for lower-income Americans, especially women who would otherwise qualify for lower benefits because they earned less than their male counterparts or took time off to care for their families.

"We have a lot of women on Social Security, particularly widowed and single women who didn't make a lot of money during their careers. They are impoverished, and they need more help from the Social Security system," she said during a debate last year. "And I will focus — I will focus on helping those people who need it the most."[55]

Sen. Bernie Sanders of Vermont has introduced legislation that would increase benefits by about $65 a month for most recipients, with the greatest increase going to lower-income retirees. Like Clinton, he would raise the payroll tax cap.[56]

Despite the debate on the campaign trail, Social Security has attracted relatively little attention this year in Congress, which is split between those who propose cutting benefits and those who want to raise the payroll tax cap.

Long-term changes aside, liberals are pushing to increase benefits this year. Legislation proposed by Sen. Elizabeth Warren, D-Mass., would give recipients of Social Security retirement and disability benefits, as well

as Americans receiving veterans' benefits, a one-time payment of $581 to compensate for the lack of a cost-of-living adjustment in 2016. With inflation dropping in 2015 due to declining oil and gasoline prices, this year marked just the third time since 1975 that recipients did not receive a cost-of-living increase. However, seniors are disproportionately affected by health care costs, which are rising faster than inflation.

"The 0 percent COLA was calculated partly by figuring in a lower price for gas, but I don't drive very much," said Susan Taylor, a member of the Maryland/DC Alliance for Retired Americans, who attended a March rally to deliver a petition with 800,000 signatures to Senate Majority Leader Mitch McConnell, R-Ky., calling for a vote on the bill. "This one-time emergency payment would help me with what I do spend money on: food, health care expenses, and housing."[57]

However, no legislation addressing Social Security's overall fiscal condition has been introduced this year. That concerns fiscal experts, who say political leaders must start working on the issue well before the trust funds run out of money. They also want to see more balanced proposals that address both major aspects of the issue: how Social Security can better serve retirees and how its long-term finances can be strengthened.

"This is an election where people are talking about a lot of easy things and not grappling with the choices we have to make," says MacGuineas of the Committee for a Responsible Federal Budget. "It's not the policies that have me concerned. It's the politics."

Savings Crisis

Amid growing concerns that American workers are not setting aside enough money to supplement their future Social Security checks, policy experts wonder if there are better ways to encourage retirement savings.

One widely quoted guideline suggests workers should start saving for retirement by age 25, aiming to save three times their annual salary by age 45 and five times their annual salary by age 55.[58] But most Americans fall well short.

A report last year by the U.S. Government Accountability Office found that 52 percent of American households 55 and older have saved nothing for retirement, although half of those households have a pension. Of the older workers with retirement savings, the median amount is just $104,000 per household.[59] And, the median retirement balance in tax-deferred accounts, such as 401(k) plans, is just $3,000 for all working-age households, according to a survey by the National Institute on Retirement Security.[60]

"The magnitude of this crisis is considerably worse than many realize," concluded the National Institute on Retirement Security report.

Some economists worry that many retirees in coming generations will be impoverished, further widening the gap in the United States between rich and poor.[61]

"In America, when we had disability and defined benefit plans, you actually had an equality of retirement period," said Teresa Ghilarducci, a labor economist at the New School for Social Research. "Now the rich can retire, and workers have to work until they die."[62]

The lack of savings in retirement accounts, combined with the fact that fewer American workers have pensions, will make retirees even more dependent on Social Security. But because the program is not designed to cover 100 percent of a retiree's income, retirement experts are discussing ways to encourage workers to save more.

Munnell of Boston College favors the establishment of universal retirement accounts with contributions from both workers and their employers. The current tax deductions on 401(k) accounts would be redirected to help lower-income earners.

"It's fruitless to lecture people that they should put more aside," she says. "The only way people will save is with automatic savings mechanisms. Automatically enroll them into a 401(k), start with 3 percent of their salaries in funds with low fees, and automatically increase their contributions over time."

Ways to encourage workers to save more have also been floated in Congress. Sen. Jeff Merkley, D-Ore., has proposed creating personal savings accounts for all workers without access to a retirement savings plan through their employer. Modeled on the savings plans used by federal workers and members of Congress, it would require employers to set aside 3 percent of a worker's paycheck into an account unless the worker chose to opt out.

"It shouldn't matter whether you work part time or full time, as an employee or as a contractor, or for a huge corporation or a tiny business: Every American worker deserves access to a financially secure retirement," said Merkley.[63]

The plan, however, is opposed by the Federal Retirement Thrift Savings Board, which said it lacks the staff and resources to open and manage millions of accounts by private workers. The measure has failed to get a hearing in the Senate.

Congress appears unlikely to take any significant action on retirement before the November elections, and there is little discussion of sweeping changes even afterward. Conservatives are leery of creating major retirement policies that would impose new requirements on companies to direct salary money into investment accounts or require additional government administration. They say the failure of many workers to invest in private accounts is evidence that the payroll tax should be scaled back or eliminated, with the money being directed into personal market accounts instead of the Social Security trust fund.

"People who would benefit the most from personal accounts are those on the lower end of the scale because they don't have the opportunity to invest in higher-earning accounts," says the Cato Institute's Tanner. "This is a way of getting lower-earning people into those accounts."

But that is a nonstarter for liberals. They say the failure of 401(k) plans to provide retirement security is exactly why the payroll tax should, if anything, be increased and the focus placed on Social Security instead of the stock market.

"401(k)'s have been a disaster," says Morrissey of the Economic Policy Institute. "I don't see why we would want to expand on a disastrous program. We should expand Social Security and be done with it."

With opinions so divided and little impetus for change in Congress, experts warn that many older workers could be facing a lean retirement.

"Americans today face a retirement savings crisis," Ghilarducci and a colleague said this year. "If we don't act, millions will face poverty."[64]

OUTLOOK
Kicking the Can

Policy experts expect little action on Social Security for at least several years.

"I don't think we'll see much happening in the near term," says Boccia of The Heritage Foundation. "The next administration is most likely to tackle the issue in its second term. Social Security is politically very difficult. Whenever anyone suggests any changes to Social Security, no matter how small, special interest groups will work to scare seniors."

"We're waiting until there's a sense of urgency about entitlement reform, and then we'll talk about it again," agrees Tanner of the Cato Institute. "The public right now is not in the mood to change."

However, the longer lawmakers delay, the more limited their options will be and the larger the benefit cuts will have to be to bring the trust fund into balance, experts say.

"The policy options are well-known," says MacGuineas of the Committee for a Responsible Federal Budget. "Every year we wait, it becomes more expensive and it becomes more burdensome, and it jeopardizes people who really rely on the program."

Plus, major policy changes take time to implement, so if lawmakers are up against a tight deadline they will need to opt for a straightforward fix, such as raising the payroll tax rate or increasing the cap on taxable income.

"If you wait until you have to act, then I get my way," says Boston College's Munnell. "Because the only thing you can do fast is raise taxes. You can't suddenly cut benefits."

Indeed, the Social Security disability program may provide an example of this. Last year, when that trust fund was about a year from running out of money, Congress agreed to move around funds to keep it solvent into the 2020s. But lawmakers made no major changes to the program, even though it has faced bipartisan criticism for discouraging recipients from returning to the workforce.

If Congress moves slowly on the retirement trust fund, it may likewise find itself unable to change it. "The closer we come to 2030 or 2034, the more pressure there's going to be on Congress in the short run to protect the benefit level," says Burtless of the Brookings Institution.

Looking further down the road, the long-term demographic trends indicate that the system eventually will become more fiscally stable, because the ratio of workers to retirees should begin to expand again as the Baby Boomer Generation recedes.

"The Baby Boomer Generation is an anomaly," says MacGuineas. "It's a very large problem but once we get through the Baby Boomers, we won't have that structural problem. Social Security is a model that can continue and will continue to be successful."

"One of the strengths of the program for its 80-plus years is its ability to adapt and change as society changes," agrees Czarnowski, the consultant. "I think it will always be there for Americans in some form."

NOTES

1. "Social Security Beneficiary Statistics" (as of Dec. 31, 2015), Social Security Administration, http://tinyurl.com/hgv5plg.

2. "2015 OASDI [Old Age, Survivor, and Disability Insurance] Trustees Report, Overview," Social Security Administration, http://tinyurl.com/hlyz5mf.

3. Matt Arco, "Christie urging Social Security reform with an eye to 2016," NJ.com, April 15, 2015, http://tinyurl.com/zjltdo7.

4. "Social Security Beneficiary Statistics," *op. cit.*

5. "Social Security Basic Facts," Social Security Administration, http://tinyurl.com/j7nwkff.

6. The Center on Budget and Policy Priorities maintains a helpful explainer about the complex financing of the Social Security trust at http://tinyurl.com/nj4htja.

7. "Ratio of Covered Workers to Beneficiaries," Social Security Administration, http://tinyurl.com/jynbvmo.

8. "2015 OASDI Trustees Report, Long-Range Estimates," Social Security Administration, http://tinyurl.com/jmkxusc.

9. "Status of the Social Security and Medicare Programs: A Summary of the 2015 Annual Reports," Social Security Administration, http://tinyurl.com/goa7zg8. More detail about Social Security's financial situation can be found at the "2015 OASDI Trustees Report," *op. cit.*

10. "Public Opinions on Social Security," National Academy of Social Insurance, 2014, http://tinyurl.com/q5sehmp.

11. "Social Security Beneficiary Statistics," Social Security Administration, http://tinyurl.com/hgv5plg.

12. Philip Moeller, "How the Budget Deal Will Change Medicare and Social Security," *Time*, Oct. 30, 2015, http://tinyurl.com/pnjdyv9.

13. The Social Security expenditures can be found at "CBO's 2015 Long-Term Projections for Social Security: Additional Information," http://tinyurl.com/gpjwhsq. The overall figure for the government's budget office comes from the main budget page of the Congressional Budget Office, http://tinyurl.com/zvsl2eh.

14. Frank Newport, "Many Americans doubt they will get Social Security benefits," Gallup, Aug. 13, 2015, http://tinyurl.com/jc2xb6h.

15. "Transcript of Republican debate in Miami, Full Text," CNN, March 15, 2016, http://tinyurl.com/hsaorpq.

16. "2015 OASDI Trustees Report, Overview," *op. cit.*

17. *Ibid.*

18. "CBO's 2015 Long-Term Projections for Social Security: Additional Information," Congressional Budget Office, Dec. 16, 2015, http://tinyurl.com/gpjwhsq.

19. Bill Alpert, "Social Security's Predictions: Off by a $1 Trillion," *Barron's*, May 9, 2015, http://tinyurl.com/ztv6hr3.

20. "2015 OASDI Trustees Report, Overview," *op. cit.*

21. For chart of taxable wages cap over time, see "Benefits Planner: Maximum Taxable Earnings (1937-2016)," Social Security Administration, http://tinyurl.com/zmxstw2.

22. Elisa A. Walker, Virginia P. Reno and Thomas N. Bethell, "Americans Make Hard Choices on Social Security: Survey Highlights," National Academy of Social Insurance, October 2014, http://tinyurl.com/zzgsotu.

23. The Congressional Budget Office summarizes these and other options for reducing Social Security costs at http://tinyurl.com/htvhu6y.

24. Robert Lenzner, "$1 million in stocks invested in 1935 is worth $240 billion today (if you held on)," *Forbes*, Feb. 14, 2013, http://tinyurl.com/z5ozbnw.

25. *Ibid.*

26. "Annual Returns on Stock, T. Bonds and T. Bills: 1928 — Current," New York University Stern School of Business, updated Jan. 5, 2016, http://tinyurl.com/5jhm7. (Note that geometric average, not arithmetic average, determines returns over time.)

27. "Historical Background and Development of Social Security," Social Security Administration, http://tinyurl.com/h2m7wps.

28. *Ibid.*

29. *Ibid.*

30. *Ibid.*

31. *Ibid.*

32. *Ibid.*

33. "Unemployment Insurance," Social Security Administration, http://tinyurl.com/zdpw95t.

34. T. J. Hamilton Jr., "The Social Security Controversy," *Editorial Research Reports*, Oct. 2, 1936, available at *CQ Researcher Archives*.

35. See "Constitutionality of Social Security Act," Social Security Administration, http://tinyurl.com/zxlnw4y.

36. "Historical Background and Development of Social Security," *op. cit.*

37. *Ibid.*

38. *Ibid.*

39. *Ibid.*

40. *Ibid.*

41. *Ibid.*

42. *Ibid.*

43. *Ibid.*

44. The complex question of whether presidents have used the Social Security surplus to fund other priorities is addressed in several articles, including: Linda Qiu, "Did George W. Bush 'borrow' from Social Security to fund the war in Iraq and tax cuts?" *PolitiFact*, Aug. 3, 2015, http://tinyurl.com/og2dg37; and Michael Hilzik, "Disproving the Notion of a Social Security trust fund 'lockbox,'" *Los Angeles Times*, March 8, 2011; http://tinyurl.com/hcw4dwl.

45. "Historical Background and Development of Social Security," *op. cit.*

46. *Ibid.*

47. "Text of President Bush's 2005 State of the Union Address," *The Washington Post*, Feb. 2, 2005, http://tinyurl.com/yz99rlc.

48. "History of 401(k) Plans: An Update," "Facts from EPRI," Employee Benefit Research Institute, updated February 2005, http://tinyurl.com/gmplp5h.

49. "Bush Failing in Social Security Push," Pew Research Center, March 2, 2005, http://tinyurl.com/h37h6po.

50. For background, see the following *CQ Researchers*: Marcia Clemmitt, "Mortgage Crisis," Nov. 2, 2007, pp. 913-936, and Kenneth Jost, "Financial Crisis," May 9, 2008, pp. 409-432; and Henry C. K. Liu, "The Crisis of Wealth Destruction," Roosevelt Institute, April 7, 2010, http://tinyurl.com/hd8sclw.

51. Moeller, *op. cit.*

52. Emily Stephenson, "Trump open to Social Security changes if elected: advisor," Reuters, May 11, 2016, http://tinyurl.com/hxoywvq.

53. *Ibid.*

54. Russ Wiles, "How presidential candidates would change Social Security," *The Arizona Republic*, March 15, 2016, http://tinyurl.com/hwutnaw.

55. Michael Hilzik, "Hillary Clinton got one thing very right about Social Security — but not everything," *Los Angeles Times*, Oct. 14, 2015, http://tinyurl.com/jdr5vs8. "CNN Democratic Debate — Full Transcript," Oct. 13, 2015, http://tinyurl.com/o7zboab.

56. "Strengthen and Expand Social Security," Bernie Sanders Website, http://tinyurl.com/hng5y5z.

57. Nik DeCosta-Klipa, "Petitioners deliver 800,000 signatures to Mitch McConnell in support of Elizabeth Warren's Social Security bill," *The Boston Globe*, March 9, 2016, http://tinyurl.com/z52a69h.

58. Dan Kadlec, "What You Should Save By 35, 45, 55 To Be On Target," *Time*, Sept. 21, 2012, http://tinyurl.com/hvhstkl.

59. "Retirement Security: Most Households Approaching Retirement Have Low Savings," U.S. General Accountability Office, May 12, 2015, http://tinyurl.com/zdp339s.

60. Nari Rhee, "The Retirement Savings Crisis: Is It Worse Than We Think," National Institute on Retirement Security, June 2013, http://tinyurl.com/hk2el3m.

61. For background, see the following *CQ Researchers*: Peter Katel, "Future of the Middle Class," April 8, 2016, pp. 313-336; and Marcia Clemmitt, "Income Inequality," Dec. 3, 2010, pp. 989-1012.

62. Kelley Holland, "Retirement Crisis: The Great 401(k) Experiment Has Failed for Many Americans," CNBC, March 23, 2015, http://tinyurl.com/kew9c9m.

63. "Merkley introduces retirement savings plan," KTVZ, Jan. 28, 2016, http://tinyurl.com/zokksxl.

64. Tony James and Teresa Ghilarducci, "America's looming retirement savings crisis," CNBC, March 15, 2016, http://tinyurl.com/hw4m38n.

BIBLIOGRAPHY
Selected Sources
Books

Altman, Nancy J., and Eric Kingson, *Social Security Works!* **The New Press, 2015.**
The co-directors of a Social Security advocacy organization and former staffers for the 1982 National Commission on Social Security Reform contend that the program is vital and should be expanded.

Eberstadt, Nicholas, *A Nation of Takers: America's Entitlement Epidemic,* **Templeton Press, 2012.**
An economist and demographer with the conservative American Enterprise Institute traces the growth of entitlement spending over the past half-century and contends it has hurt the nation's economy and culture. A rebuttal by William Galston of the liberal Brookings Institution is included.

Kotlikoff, Laurence, Philip Moeller and Paul Solman, *Get What's Yours,* **Simon and Schuster, 2015.**
An economist (Laurence), an expert on retirement, aging and health (Moeller) and a business and economics journalist (Solman) explain the Social Security retirement system and offer ways to maximize benefits. The book finishes with a spirited debate among the

authors about whether Social Security can be sustained over the long term.

Articles

Alpert, Bill, "Social Security's Predictions: Off by a $1 Trillion," *Barron's*, **May 9, 2015, http://tinyurl.com/ztv6hr3.**
Quoting economists and other policy experts, a journalist warns that predictions that the Social Security trust fund will run out of money in 2034 may be overly optimistic.

Holland, Kelley, "Retirement Crisis: The Great 401(k) Experiment Has Failed for Many Americans," CNBC, March 23, 2015, http://tinyurl.com/kew9c9m.
A business journalist explores the history of 401(k) plans and why the tax-deferred accounts have failed to spur many Americans to set aside enough for retirement.

Joffe-Walt, Chana, "Unfit for Work: The Startling Rise of Disability in America," NPR, 2013, http://tinyurl.com/d7u7n8f.
The broadcast series explores why a fast-growing number of Americans are receiving disability insurance and the implications for the nation.

Pianin, Eric, "Harsh New Penalties for Social Security Fraud Are Coming," *The Fiscal Times*, **Oct. 27, 2015, http://tinyurl.com/hemwv69.**
A journalist summarizes some of the biggest recent Social Security fraud cases and Congress' response of tougher criminal and civil penalties.

Turkewitz, Julie, and Juliet Linderman, "The Disability Trap," *The New York Times*, **Oct. 20, 2012, http://tinyurl.com/8hn47ga.**
The authors show how the Social Security system keeps millions of disabled Americans in poverty even as it is supposed to help them.

Wiles, Russ, "How presidential candidates would change Social Security," *The Arizona Republic*, **March 15, 2016, http://tinyurl.com/hwutnaw.**
In a summary of leading presidential candidates' Social Security proposals, Democrats defend the program or favor expansion, while Republicans generally focus on cutting costs.

Reports and Studies

"2015 OASDI Trustees Report," Social Security Administration, 2015, http://tinyurl.com/jx6to4b.
The annual report on Social Security Old Age, Survivor, and Disability Insurance summarizes the programs' finances and warns payments are exceeding revenues.

"Retirement Security: Most Households Approaching Retirement Have Low Savings," U.S. General Accountability Office, May 12, 2015, http://tinyurl.com/ojz8gqf.
The government watchdog agency finds that more than half of American households headed by an adult 55 or older have put away nothing for retirement and the remaining ones have median retirement savings of only $104,000 per household.

"Social Security Policy Options, 2015," Congressional Budget Office, Dec. 15, 2015, http://tinyurl.com/zu3v6hq.
The CBO, which provides Congress with nonpartisan budget analysis, warns of Social Security's negative cash flow and examines 36 policy options that would help its financial condition, though not all would significantly improve its long-term outlook.

"Numberholders Age 112 or Older Who Did Not Have a Death Entry on the Numident," Office of the Inspector General, Social Security Administration, March 4, 2015, http://tinyurl.com/j6z9e2v.
The much-publicized study shows that some 6.5 million Social Security numbers remain active for Americans age 112 or older, highlighting the extent to which such numbers can be used for fraud.

Walker, Elisa A., Virginia P. Reno and Thomas N. Bethell, "Americans Make Hard Choices on Social Security: Report Highlights," National Academy of Social Insurance, October 2014, http://tinyurl.com/zzgsotu.
The authors detail national survey findings that Americans would prefer to pay more in taxes than face cuts in Social Security benefits.

For More Information

Brookings Institution, 1775 Massachusetts Ave., N.W., Washington, DC 20036; 202-797-6000; www.brookings .edu. Think tank that analyzes issues from a centrist perspective; opposes raising the retirement age or cutting Social Security benefits.

Cato Institute, 1000 Massachusetts Ave., N.W., Washington DC 20001; 202-842-0200; www.cato.org. Libertarian think tank that supports allowing workers to divert some payroll taxes into private retirement accounts.

Center for Retirement Research, Boston College, Hovey House, 258 Hammond St., Chestnut Hill, MA 02467; 617-552-1762; www.bc.edu. Research center that studies issues related to Social Security and other sources of retirement income.

Committee for a Responsible Federal Budget, 1900 M St., N.W., Suite 850, Washington, DC 20036; 202-596-3597; www.crfb.org. Nonpartisan think tank that advocates policies to strengthen Social Security finances.

Economic Policy Institute, 1225 I St., N.W., Suite 600, Washington, DC 20005; 202-775-8810; www.epi.org. Liberal think tank that focuses on the economic needs of low- and middle-income workers and opposes privatizing Social Security.

The Heritage Foundation, 214 Massachusetts Ave., N.E., Washington, DC 20002; 202-546-4400. Conservative think tank that favors raising the retirement age to help reduce Social Security costs and advocates transitioning to a system of private retirement accounts.

Mathematica Policy Research, 600 Alexander Park, Princeton, NJ 08453; 609-799-3535; www.mathematica-mpr. com. Research organization formulating proposals to change the Social Security disability program and provide stronger incentives to keep disabled workers employed.

National Committee to Preserve Social Security and Medicare, 10 G St., N.E., Suite 600, Washington, DC 20002; 202-216-0420; www.ncpssm.org. Advocacy group opposing any reduction in Social Security benefits and supporting increased payments to retirees by raising taxes.

Social Security Administration, 6401 Security Blvd., Baltimore, MD 21235; 410-965-3120; www.ssa.gov. Federal agency that administers Social Security.

10

Future of the Middle Class

Peter Katel

Jonah Devorak had been washing dishes and manning the grill at a Cleveland restaurant since he was 16. But his future brightened when he heard about a program at Cuyahoga Community College that trains students for manufacturing jobs. Now he's a full-time machine operator at Swagelok, a maker of high-pressure valves and fittings.

From *CQ Researcher*,
April 8, 2016.

In only one sentence, Sediena Barry summed up her view that the American middle-class dream has evaporated: "Young people were told, 'Get an education and work and you'll get ahead,' and none of us are."[1]

The 34-year-old office equipment installer in Reynoldsburg, Ohio, outside Columbus, spoke to *The New York Times* after voting in the most turbulent presidential primary season in decades.

Vote-seeking politicians in both parties have been pounding on the theme that the middle class is embattled. But they didn't invent the concept of declining economic mobility. A growing number of academic studies, data analyses and scholarly commentary warn that America's middle class is shrinking, its wealth far outpaced by the holdings of the rich and super-rich.

The central theme emerging from most of this work is that after decades of defining itself as an overwhelmingly middle-class country, the United States increasingly is fracturing into a nation of haves and have-nots. Many analysts fear a vision long shared by a majority of Americans is eroding: that hard work will get anyone into the middle class or from the middle class into the top reaches of society.

"The share of the American adult population that is middle income is falling, and rising shares are living in economic tiers above and below the middle," the nonpartisan Pew Research Center stated in an extensive 2015 analysis of income trends in the United States. "The hollowing of the middle has proceeded steadily for four decades, and it may have reached a tipping point."[2]

Many scholars — as well as numerous politicians and voters — trace the challenges facing the middle-class to the loss of good-paying

Manufacturing Jobs Vanish

The number of U.S. manufacturing jobs fell from about 19 million in 1979 to 12 million in 2015, as companies increasingly automated factories or outsourced work to countries with cheaper labor. Once a major source of middle-class income, manufacturing jobs declined most rapidly after 2000 as U.S. manufacturing productivity increased, reducing hours for factory workers, while competition from foreign countries weakened demand for U.S.-produced goods.

(Millions of workers)

**U.S. Manufacturing Employment
(1970-2015 Seasonally Adjusted)**

Source: "Manufacturing: NAICS 31-33" Workforce Statistics, U.S. Bureau of Labor Statistics, accessed March 30, 2016, http://tinyurl.com/mgomng9; "Factors Underlying the Decline in Manufacturing Employment Since 2000," Congressional Budget Office, Dec. 23, 2008, http://tinyurl.com/glhsj6z

manufacturing jobs that defined the post-World War II economic boom but then disappeared as U.S. companies shifted operations overseas or succumbed to foreign competition.

Stephen J. Rose, a research professor at the Center on Education and the Workforce at George Washington University in Washington, says the postwar economic boom continues to shape middle-class expectations, even though the U.S. economy — with its preeminent place in the global economic landscape — has undergone an irrevocable shift.

"We suffer from a political and emotional problem: the 30 glorious years from 1945 to 1975," Rose says. The postwar years were "a period of unbelievable growth," but one followed by the rise of major industrial competition in low-wage countries and the growth of job-killing automation.

"Europe needed us to provide a lot of capital goods to them," he continues. "Unionized and blue-collar workers with low education and fairly low skills were getting fairly good middle-class wages. That was not sustainable. No one wants to say that out loud, but that's the bottom line."

Pew's analysis highlights many of the factors that led to that stark bottom line:

- The share of adults in middle-income households fell from 61 percent of the population in 1971 to 50 percent in 2015. For the first time, they were outnumbered by those in lower- and upper-income tiers. The share of overall household income among middle-income families has declined from 62 percent in 1970 to 43 percent in 2014. On the other hand, wealthy households — representing only about one-fifth of the adult population — earned almost half the nation's household income. In 1970, they held only 29 percent of it.
- The gap between rich and poor has widened. In 2015, 20 percent of American adults were in the lowest-income tier, compared with 16 percent in 1971. On the opposite side, the share of adults in the highest income tier has more than doubled during that period, from 4 percent to 9 percent.[3]

Still, while many economic analysts agree the middle class has suffered setbacks in recent years, not all see such a grim picture.

For instance, Pew's analysis did not include ancillary forms of income, such as employee health care benefits, which other researchers routinely count in assessing middle-class conditions, notes Scott Winship, a policy analyst at the conservative Manhattan Institute for Policy Research, a New York City think tank. When that income source is counted, the middle class is better off than it was three or four decades ago, he says.

"The middle fifth of American households is richer today than in 1979 by at least 35 percent," he says. "That translates to over $10,000 that the middle fifth has today that it didn't have in 1979."

But the wealthy have fared far better in recent decades. Incomes of the top 1 percent grew by 275 percent between 1979 and 2007, according to nonpartisan Congressional Budget Office (CBO) data, as analyzed by the liberal Center on Budget and Policy Priorities.[4]

Winship acknowledges the disparity. The growth in middle-class earnings, he says, "is much smaller than growth at the very top, and smaller than what growth was in the middle in the '50s and '60s, so it's not an unabashedly great story."

Debates about the middle class go beyond disagreements over statistical methods. They also center on the very meaning of "middle class," which can be a self-definition as much as a statistical category.[5]

A few decades ago, the notion was common that all Americans in the middle of the income distribution table shared a middle-class identity. That included blue-collar workers, who enjoyed homeownership, steady, well-paid employment and the possibility that their children would go into even better-paid white-collar work. In today's world, however, an economic — and resulting cultural and political — divide is opening between working-class Americans and those in the middle class.

Scholars say that division shows up most clearly in differences between those with and without college diplomas. "The sharpest class division is between people with four-year college degrees and everybody else," says Andrew J. Cherlin, a sociologist at Johns Hopkins University in Baltimore. "They wait to marry to have kids, their divorce rates are going down. People without degrees marry in much smaller numbers and have a much larger proportion of kids without marriage; you used to see that just among the poor."

That social distinction accompanies significant income differences. The earnings of college-educated workers consistently outpace those without bachelor's degrees. In 2013, according to the latest available statistics, median earnings for those with bachelor's degrees — $48,500 a year — amounted to $18,500 more than the earnings of high school graduates.[6]

But many ordinary Americans do not view a college diploma as a middle-class credential. An overwhelming 89 percent of respondents to a Pew survey this year said the first requirement for being considered middle class is a secure job. Only 30 percent said a college education is a necessity.[7]

Even so, Jacob Hacker, a political scientist at Yale University in New Haven, Conn., says the upper-income tiers of the college-educated middle class also are feeling uncertain about their future. "They're more likely to switch jobs and have to balance work and family, to deal with health care costs, education costs and housing in particular," he says. "Even if they feel relatively secure at the moment, they know they're going to have to put their kids through college, to save to own a home."

That uncertainty is well founded, some experts say. "Incomes are growing more slowly" in the middle class, says Lane Kenworthy, a sociologist at the University of California, San Diego.

And even though the economy is recovering from the housing crash and ensuing 2007-09 recession, the youngest college graduates are still seeing their earnings decrease, according to data compiled by the Economic Policy Institute, a liberal think tank in Washington. Average hourly wages, inflation-adjusted, for college graduates age 21-24 have fallen from $18.41 in 2000 to $17.94 in 2015. What's more, according to a survey by Harvard University's Institute of Politics, 73 percent of current college students expect to have trouble finding a job when they graduate.[8]

As young adults continue to face struggles, they appear to be responding to political messages aimed at middle-class voters. Many young Democrats — including Barry, the office equipment installer in Ohio — have been flocking to Democratic presidential candidate Bernie Sanders, who pledges to "rebuild the American middle class." He has called for curbs on the growing concentration of wealth in the hands of the ultrarich and an end to foreign trade deals that cost American jobs. By mid-March, Sanders had won 1.5 million youth votes in the Democratic presidential primaries and caucuses — more than twice as many as his Democratic competitor, Hillary Clinton.[9]

Clinton and GOP front-runner Donald Trump, along with other Republican candidates, also are campaigning hard on the issue of middle-class economic prospects and income disparities. Clinton now opposes the Trans-Pacific Partnership free trade agreement, citing its

U.S. Income Gap Widening

Median earnings of upper-income households rose to nearly $175,000 in 2014, up 47 percent since 1970 after adjusting for inflation. Earnings of middle- and lower-income households rose 34 percent and 28 percent, respectively, during the period. Incomes of all three groups fell since 2000, but middle- and lower-income households saw larger declines than wealthier ones.

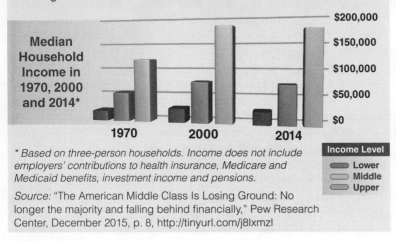

Median Household Income in 1970, 2000 and 2014*

Income Level: Lower, Middle, Upper

* Based on three-person households. Income does not include employers' contributions to health insurance, Medicare and Medicaid benefits, investment income and pensions.

Source: "The American Middle Class Is Losing Ground: No longer the majority and falling behind financially," Pew Research Center, December 2015, p. 8, http://tinyurl.com/j8lxmzl

Does income stagnation mean the middle class is in decline?

In a flood tide of political rhetoric, scholarly books and journalism about the nation's changing economy and the growing disparity in America's wealth distribution, the single most explosive concept for middle-class Americans is the idea that they are an endangered species.

But experts disagree over whether the middle class is shrinking, in large part because the term "middle class" is partly an economic concept and partly a social one. In its recent report, Pew took the economic approach, defining middle-income households as those with income amounting to two-thirds to double the national median. For a three-person household, that works out to about $42,000 to $126,000 a year, in 2014 dollars.[12]

Although Pew used the terms "middle income" and "middle class" interchangeably, the report acknowledged that the terms are not necessarily synonymous. "Being middle class can connote more than income, be it a college education, white-collar work, economic security, owning a home," the report said. "Class could also be . . . a matter of self-identification."[13]

In any case, by Pew's method, the middle class is diminishing — from 61 percent of the adult population in 1971 to 50 percent last year.[14]

Some experts not affiliated with Pew agree that a variety of data support the report's conclusion. "The share of Americans with incomes in what we might call the middle has been decreasing," says Kenworthy of the University of California.

And results from a 2015 Gallup Poll were remarkably similar to Pew's: 51 percent of Americans categorized themselves as middle or upper-middle class — a sharp decline from the 61 percent, on average, who had labeled themselves as such in 2000-08.[15]

That data may not be definitive. The respected General Social Survey, run by NORC at the University of Chicago (and which also asks respondents if they are

potential to harm American workers.[10] And Republican Sen. Ted Cruz of Texas is pitching a 10 percent flat tax as a way to counter a situation in which "Washington pads Wall Street's pockets" through tax loopholes.[11]

Even some experts who view middle-class anxieties as well-founded argue that the political system is capable of resolving them. "The big if is [whether] we can get our political system moving," says Hacker. "Our standard of living encompasses a lot more than income, and I believe we have enormous potential in providing income security, access to high-quality health care" and other things the middle class worries about.

Analysts on the left are more pessimistic, saying growing middle-class discontent reflects a coming to terms with reality. "Your kids are not going to do better than you, and their opportunities, unless they're born into money, are very, very poor," says Alan Nasser, a professor emeritus of political economy at Evergreen State College in Olympia, Wash. "I can't imagine this wouldn't produce a significant change in consciousness."

As economists, politicians and average Americans discuss the future of the middle class, here are some of the questions being debated:

lower class, working class or upper class), shows that the share of Americans describing themselves as middle class has been at roughly its most recently recorded level, 42 percent for 2014, since 1990.

However, Noah Smith, a finance professor at Stony Brook University in New York who analyzed the Gallup data, concluded that the Gallup results appear to show an anxiety rooted in hard financial reality. "Even if your family makes $180,000 a year, well above the national median, it might be hard to think of yourself as upper-middle class if you could be fired at any time, or one medical emergency could send you into bankruptcy."[16]

Different ways of measuring income can lead to different conclusions about the size and condition of the middle class. Using CBO's methodology of including Medicare, investment income and pensions, Winship, of the Manhattan Institute, concluded that middle-class households have grown 35 percent more prosperous since 1979.[17]

Income growth for the middle class "is much smaller than growth at the very top," Winship acknowledges, "and smaller than what growth was for the middle in the '50s and '60s, but we are significantly better off."

Winship argues that those in the middle class have less reason to worry about potential job and benefits losses than they seem to think. "These are real anxieties," he says, but in surveys, "about the same share of people" say they fear dying in airplane crashes or becoming victims of crime or terrorist attacks as say they worry about losing their jobs and benefits.

Kenworthy says income stagnation may be more important than the shrinking size of the middle class. Statistics from the Economic Policy Institute show a near-absence of growth in middle-income earnings between 1979 and 2013, compared with what higher-income earners made. Middle-class wages rose 6 percent during that period, while compensation for highly paid workers jumped 41 percent, the institute found.[18]

"Household income has been going up, but very slowly," Kenworthy says, and that's only because "more and more households have added a second earner."

Still, says Rose of George Washington University, earnings data not only exclude employer-paid benefits, but they also fail to account for smaller household sizes and rising living standards. "We have bigger houses, better cars; we eat out more," he says. "And we're living

longer." Indeed, for the U.S. population overall, life expectancy rose from about 71 years in 1970 to 79 in 2013.[19]

Rose acknowledged that a rising mortality rate among lower-earning Americans in blue-collar jobs reflects a grimmer reality for people who may once have considered themselves, or their parents, as middle class.

"I'm not saying there's no pain and anxiety," he says. "If sons and daughters tried to follow their parents into factories, they were really in bad shape. But people who work in offices, including education and health care, do OK. And what do you see when you're in Albuquerque or Baltimore or Denver? You don't see factories. You see offices and health care and educational facilities."

Experts, such as Cherlin at Johns Hopkins University, also find that wages for those with bachelor's and advanced degrees are falling. "During the '70s, '80s and '90s, the wages of college-educated workers went up," he says, drawing a contrast with today's situation. But data from 2000 to 2014, the most recent figures available, show median annual earnings of male bachelor's degree holders fell — from $67,470 to $60,933. And those with doctorates saw a drop from almost $98,000 in 2000 to about $92,000 in 2014.[20]

Cherlin speculates that bachelor's degrees may have become an inadequate credential for middle-class status. "You have to wonder, as the economy becomes more automated and computerized, whether college graduates will have trouble achieving their economic dreams."

Since the rise of automation in workplaces of all kinds in recent decades, employment in so-called middle-skill jobs — including sales, office and administrative work — has fallen from 60 percent of the workforce in 1979 to 46 percent in 2012.[21]

But fears that highly advanced automation software may eliminate even upper-middle-class jobs that require considerable analytical capabilities — such as financial analysis — are largely unfounded, says David Autor, a Massachusetts Institute of Technology economist considered an authority on automation's effects.

"The pressure of automation on labor forces is likely to be more downward than upward," he says. "More autonomous vehicles, more dexterous robots are doing more labor-intensive tasks. Automation replaces some high-skilled workers, but often complements them as well, as with robots that doctors work with."

Would helping the poor also bolster the middle class?

Overall, the U.S. economy is recovering from the 2007-09 recession, with unemployment falling to 5 percent this year — about half what it was in 2009 at the height of the recession. For those with bachelor's degrees or higher, unemployment was 2.5 percent by the end of 2015, a year in which nearly 2.7 million jobs were created.[22]

But the poverty rate for 2014 is 14.8 percent — representing 46.7 million people — up from 12.2 percent in 2000 and barely changed since 2010.[23]

Given those statistics, many policy experts say focusing too much on the middle class ignores the plight of the poor. "The safety net should be limited to people who are truly indigent, as opposed to being spread around in a way that metastasizes into middle-class entitlements," Arthur Brooks, president of the American Enterprise Institute, a conservative think tank, said during a panel discussion with President Obama last year.

His argument echoed a long-standing conservative view that Medicare and Social Security should be "means-tested" so rich people do not benefit. Liberals say if such programs were means-tested, they would lose their broad public support because they would be seen as anti-poverty programs.[24]

Low-wage workers have been urging local and state governments to raise the minimum wage to $15 an hour, which some say would also push up wages of higher-earning employees, thus expanding the middle class. A growing number of cities and two states — New York and California — have approved or are in the process of enacting such laws.[25]

But debates over whether to focus on helping the poor or the middle class have roiled Democrats in recent years. In late 2014, Democratic Sen. Charles Schumer of New York criticized the Obama administration and liberal Democrats for pushing the Affordable Care Act in 2010, arguing that it benefited mostly the poor because most middle-class Americans have insurance through their jobs. At that time, he said, the Democrats should have "continued to propose middle-class-oriented programs."[26]

Nevertheless, Winship of the Manhattan Institute says government initiatives focusing on the middle class would siphon resources more urgently needed by the poor.

"To focus too much on the perception that the middle class is in decline is bad for poor people," he says, citing a Department of Agriculture survey showing that 20 percent of U.S. households are worried that their food will run out before the end of the month.[27] Programs should focus instead on improving the standard of living and upward mobility of the bottom fifth of the income scale, he says.

But political will is not focused on the poor, says Anthony P. Carnevale, an economist and the director of Georgetown University's Center on Education and the Workforce. "It is morally repulsive, but the poor are not in the game," he says. "They have been disappeared in America. Strengthening the middle class is the mantra."

The most recent major government action directed at poor families, Carnevale says, was the 1996 welfare reform law, which included job training.[28] But its beneficial effects vanished when the job market tightened in the early 2000s. "When there is no surplus, the poor get nothing" because they have no political leverage, he says. "I think that, in the end, doing something for the poor will have to wait until the rest of us are taken care of."

Others, like Rose of George Washington University, say providing more for the middle class is "just too expensive," and no firm data show that the educated middle class needs rescuing. And while median household income for the highly educated may be in the

J. Paul Gorman does computer coding at Bit Source, a tech startup in Pikeville, Ky., on Feb. 1, 2016. The company hired 10 coders recently but said nearly 1,000 people responded to its recent job ads. Many companies now send their coding work to firms overseas.

Most College Grads in Wealthier Households

Four in 10 Americans with bachelor's degrees lived in upper-income households in 2015, and nearly half lived in middle-income households. Most adults who completed high school or some college lived in middle-income households. A majority of those who did not graduate from high school lived in lower-income households.

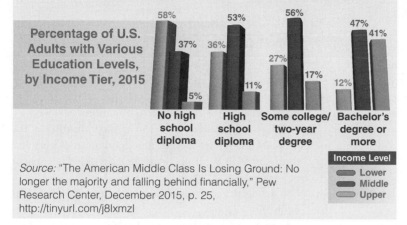

Percentage of U.S. Adults with Various Education Levels, by Income Tier, 2015

	No high school diploma	High school diploma	Some college/ two-year degree	Bachelor's degree or more
Lower	58%	36%	27%	12%
Middle	37%	53%	56%	47%
Upper	5%	11%	17%	41%

Income Level
- Lower
- Middle
- Upper

Source: "The American Middle Class Is Losing Ground: No longer the majority and falling behind financially," Pew Research Center, December 2015, p. 25, http://tinyurl.com/j8lxmzl

$60,000 range, he says, it grows substantially with age. As of 2013, median income for those age 40 or older with an associate's or bachelor's degree was slightly less than $80,000 a year.[29]

Most members of the middle class have periods when they are doing well and times when they are doing less well. Over time, "people who play by the rules can get hurt," Rose says, "but they also can win."

Some experts, including Kenworthy of the University of California, say some programs designed to aid the middle class would also help the poor.

"For example, if we were to put in place a good-quality universal early-education system, along the lines of what Sweden and Denmark do, with some user fee or co-payment," Kenworthy says, would produce "a real increase in living standards" for both poor and for middle-class families.

Early-childhood education is a longtime liberal anti-poverty solution. Advocates cite studies showing that early education improves the earnings of adults who attended as children. Studies in Tulsa, Okla., and Boston calculate that poor children would earn about $3 more for each dollar spent on their early education.[30]

But some conservatives, most recently in Tennessee, cite studies showing that early education makes little difference in the long run.[31]

Can improved education and training protect the middle class?

Statistics show that higher education pays off. Men with bachelor's degrees earn $900,000 more in median lifetime earnings than male high-school graduates, and women $630,000 more. For those with graduate degrees, the differential amounts to $1.5 million for men and $1.1 million for women.[32] Associate's degree holders earn $798 per week — $120 more than high-school graduates.[33]

Questions remain, however, about what type of higher education — and in which fields — best prepares a student for the present and future economic climate. A growing number of experts say a student's training should be geared toward new technological advancements.

"Are your skills a complement to the skills of the computer?" asked Tyler Cowen, a professor of economics at George Mason University in Fairfax, Va. "If [so], your wage and labor market prospects are likely to be cheery."[34]

In his book *Average Is Over*, Cowen warns, "Lacking the right training means being shut out of opportunities like never before." The highest earners, usually those with advanced postsecondary degrees, "are earning much more," he adds. But all science and technology degrees are not automatically valuable, he writes, arguing that a trained marketer likely will do better than, say, an astronomer.[35]

Still, machines may replace a variety of careers. A 2013 study by two technology specialists at the University of Oxford in Britain estimated that 47 percent of all U.S. jobs are at high risk of being replaced by robots or other technologies in the next 20 years.[36]

But while fear of automation builds, others say demand remains high in certain jobs that do not require college or postgraduate degrees. "We might train some high-school graduates for mid-level jobs that are still around and might be growing — medical technicians, who run X-ray machines and medical devices; [and] there are factory jobs that require knowledge of computer-controlled machinery," Cherlin says.

However, the need for such vocational training, much of which can be done at community colleges, poses a policy question. "Do we give up on the dream that every young adult should have a four-year college degree, and pour resources into community colleges?" Cherlin asks. He and others favor a community college-based strategy, on the grounds that not all students will make it through a four-year college, which is also far more expensive.[37]

Winship of the Manhattan Institute rejects the argument that college is becoming unaffordable. "The cost of higher education and increases in student indebtedness have definitely led a lot of people to worry that pathways to the middle class are blocked off," he says, "but that is not reflected in rising graduation rates" at American colleges. Graduation rates at four-year colleges have increased, though modestly, from about 58 percent for those entering in 2000 to 59 percent for those students entering in 2006.[38]

And undergraduates typically accumulate far less debt than graduate students, Winship notes. In 2011-12, the most recent years for which figures are available, 30 percent of bachelor's degree graduates owed no debt, 10 percent owed less than $10,000 and 18 percent owed less than $30,000. By contrast 54 percent of professional, doctoral-level degree graduates owed $120,000 or more.[39]

Worries over debt are "misplaced," Winship says. "People who get a degree and come out with $20,000 to $30,000 in debt — that is not nearly as big a problem as people who drop out and have $10,000 to $20,000 in debt."

But Rose of George Washington University argues that the education issue goes deeper than acquiring diplomas. The dropout rates for students seeking bachelor's degrees reflect the failure of high schools to prepare graduates for college work, he says. "What we're talking about is people who don't have skills" that enable them to succeed in college.

Consequently, he says, the most urgent task is to expand the community college system. "Otherwise we will force more people into the four-year system, in which a small number will find themselves and thrive, and another group will make it through because they're at colleges with very low standards."

And even those like Cowen, who advocate education and training geared specifically toward new technologies

used in today's workplaces, say the educational infrastructure is nowhere near ready for the task.

"That takes a full generation," Cowen says. "It's a slow process. We don't even have teachers trained to do that much training. We're starting, but I wouldn't say we have started in a big way."

BACKGROUND
Early Middle Class

Even before the Civil War, long before the modern emphasis on the United States as a middle-class country, at least one writer was already celebrating the American middle class as the embodiment of national ideals.

"The most valuable class in any community is the middle class — the men of moderate means," poet and journalist Walt Whitman wrote in a Brooklyn newspaper editorial in 1858.[40]

During that era, according to sociologist C. Wright Mills, a scholar of the U.S. class system, "the middle class was so broad a stratum and of such economic weight that even by the standards of the statistician the society as a whole was a middle-class society." Mills counted professionals, self-employed manufacturers and independent farmers as members of the middle class.[41]

But Mills may have painted too romantic a picture, ignoring sharp class differences within the working population, with wage workers on one side and far-better-paid professionals and bosses on the other, according to economics professor Robert J. Gordon of Northwestern University in Evanston, Ill. If middle class in the 1870s meant a household that employed a servant — a standard definition — then the middle class accounted for only 15 percent of households and the rest were working class, writes Gordon.[42]

The period between the 1870s and America's entry into World War I in 1917 was also marked by the excesses of what is known as the Gilded Age, when industrialists such as Andrew Carnegie, John D. Rockefeller and Cornelius Vanderbilt built immense fortunes by monopolizing the steel, oil and shipping industries. Wealth was concentrated at the top of the socioeconomic ladder: By 1917 the top 1 percent of earners received more than 40 percent of the national income. Today, that percentage is even higher, leading many experts to call this America's new gilded age.[43]

Gilded Age excesses gave rise to the Progressive movement of 1900 to 1920. Led by members of the upper class and of the still relatively small professional middle class, the Progressives were outraged at big-business domination of the economy and politics. One of the movement's major champions, President Theodore Roosevelt, railed against the power of the industrial monopolies, or trusts, and used the Sherman Anti-Trust Act to break up the Northern Securities Corp., a holding company of railroads.[44]

Overall, the movement succeeded in imposing regulations on factories that improved worker safety and limited work hours of children and women. But most attempts to impose major curbs on big business failed, given the strength of the interests involved. And when the Progressive era had run its course, by 1920, it was followed by the "Roaring Twenties," when wealth was celebrated and regulation of business weakened.[45]

Government Intervention

The Great Depression, preceded by a catastrophic stock market crash in 1929, ended the hopes and dreams of vast numbers of Americans. Millions of savings accounts were wiped out when more than 10,000 banks failed.[46] By 1933, more than 25 percent of the workforce was unemployed.[47]

After taking office in 1933, President Franklin D. Roosevelt initiated a series of laws and programs known as the New Deal, designed to rescue millions of unemployed Americans devastated by the Depression. New Deal innovations included the Social Security system; legislation authorizing and regulating collective bargaining; and federal employment in public works of all kinds. The Works Progress Administration (WPA) — which sent jobless workers across the country to build and repair bridges, roads, parks and other public facilities — employed 8.5 million Americans during its eight-year existence, which ended in 1943. However, in a political compromise with segregationist Southerners in Congress, African-Americans were excluded from major New Deal programs in the South.[48]

After World War II, the Servicemen's Readjustment Act of 1944 — better known as the GI Bill of Rights — authorized federal benefits, including tuition for college or trade school, low-cost home mortgages and business loans, to 12.4 million veterans — about 78 percent of all those who served.[49] The legislation was designed

A biology class meets at Massasoit Community College in Brockton, Mass. Many jobs that will be in demand in the future, such as medical technician, don't require four-year college degrees, prompting policymakers to ask whether every young adult should have a four-year degree.

to — and did — create a bigger, more financially secure middle class.

"The increasing share of the population with high school diplomas and then college degrees helped pave the way for a transformation from a working-class society before World War II to a middle-class society afterward," Gordon writes, expressing a virtually universal view.[50]

Some 5.6 million veterans attended trade schools or took on-the-job training in fields such as auto and radio repair, accounting, construction trades, cooking, flight training and other work. As a result, the bill expanded the service sector of a diversifying economy.[51]

However, some local administrators, following racist practices common at the time and unwilling to empower African-Americans, denied GI Bill benefits to black veterans. The long-term effect was to severely limit the formation of a black middle class at a time when the white middle class was expanding.[52]

The early postwar period was also marked by an economic boom that made the United States the envy of other countries. The nation's GNP more than doubled from $200 billion in 1940 to more than $500 billion in 1960. The United States had three-quarters of the world's investment capital and two-thirds of its industrial capacity.[53]

Economic Boom

Some of America's postwar economic advantages dated back to war production in a country that, unlike war-ravaged Europe and Asia, suffered no battles on its soil (with the exception of the 1941 Japanese attack on Pearl Harbor).

For instance, thanks in part to the expanded wartime manufacture of tanks and other vehicles, American auto-makers could produce far more cars after the war. They sold 9.1 million cars and trucks in 1954, compared with only 4.7 million in 1941. The vast expansion of the national automobile fleet helped stimulate GDP and income growth. Thanks to the latter, ordinary working families could own more than one car — an advantage previously confined to the wealthy.[54]

Construction of the Interstate Highway System (begun in 1956), which allowed faster and easier ship-ping, accounted for a 31 percent jump in productivity during the 1950s. Northwestern's Gordon writes that 32 of 35 industries benefited from lower costs because of transportation improvements.[55]

Meanwhile, the housing market exploded, in large part because of federally backed mortgages under the GI Bill. By 1955, 57 percent of U.S. households owned a home — up from 41 percent in 1940 — strengthening the connec-tion between homeownership and middle-class status. Middle-class Americans came to view homeownership "as an inalienable right," one scholar has written.[56]

By the mid-1950s, households in the top 1 percent of the income distribution spectrum held about 10 percent of the nation's income — down from nearly 24 percent in 1928, the year before the Great Depression. And dur-ing the period from 1947-79, average overall hourly compensation rose by about 100 percent.[57]

The Reversal

As far back as 1962, sociologist Mills was warning that mostly middle-class office workers — those earning sala-ries rather than hourly wages — were vulnerable in ways that the early 19th-century middle class was not.[58]

By the late 1970s, Gordon and others write, the earn-ings of those in the middle (and bottom) of the earning scale were being held down by the growing practice of outsourcing jobs and increasing automation, which also reduced the number of jobs. These were coupled with a steep decline in labor union power.

By 1981, 26 percent of the cars, 25 percent of the steel and 60 percent of televisions and consumer electronics sold in the United States were imported.[59]

The decline of American manufacturing gave rise to the term Rust Belt to describe the Midwestern region where factories were shutting and well-paying manufacturing jobs were disappearing.[60] Steel industry employment, for instance, declined from more than 1 million in 1970 to 630,000 in 1990.[61]

The 1980s and early '90s also saw the advent of the personal computer age, which would transform office work and communications. Desktop computers came into homes and offices, and users began connecting to networks over phone lines. Email began replacing busi-ness letters. And computers put powerful search and analytical capabilities into millions of hands.

The computer revolution eliminated jobs or enabled them to be moved overseas. With the emergence of the Internet and instantaneous global connections, compa-nies began to shift tasks such as accounting, document search and medical-image interpreting to English-speaking countries where labor was cheaper.

As the Internet rapidly expanded and the benefits of digital technology seemed limitless, a stock market frenzy took hold, with shares in virtually any Internet startup skyrocketing in value. The "dotcom bubble" burst on March 11, 2000. Within a month, the total value of all shares traded on Nasdaq, the main tech stock market, had plummeted by almost $1 trillion.[62]

A recession followed, spurred by further declines in manufacturing. Those in the middle-earnings group took the hardest hit — with 1.3 million job losses in 2001.[63] Although the recession officially ended after eight months, economist Jared Bernstein, later the chief economic adviser to Vice President Joseph Biden, warned in 2003 that the recovery was a jobless one, with 2.1 mil-lion fewer private-sector jobs than existed in 2000.[64]

Worries about labor market changes persisted as tech-nological advances enabled employers in a growing vari-ety of fields to "offshore" services to contractors abroad. Economist Alan S. Blinder of Princeton University, a former vice chairman of the Federal Reserve, estimated in 2006 that offshored service-sector jobs eventually could number two to three times the 14 million manu-facturing jobs that existed at the time.[65]

In the next few years, worries about foreign competi-tion took a back seat to fears over possible collapse of the entire economy, as a plunge in housing prices sparked the 2007-09 recession, in which 8.7 million jobs were

CHRONOLOGY

1760-1920 *Colonial and post-independence middle class make up majority of the non-slave population.*

1760 Seventy percent of free Americans — farmers, craftspeople and professionals — are considered middle class.

1870 As the country industrializes, class distinctions sharpen, with professionals and business owners accounting for 15 percent of U.S. households.

1920 New consumer credit industry enables purchases of appliances and other consumer goods.

1929-1944 *Great Depression devastates U.S.*

1929 Stock market crash precedes a widespread financial system failure.

1933 About one-quarter of the nation's workforce — 15.5 million people — are unemployed as Great Depression reaches bottom. . . . President Franklin D. Roosevelt's New Deal authorizes labor organizing and collective bargaining and spurs massive government employment in public works.

1941 United States enters World War II, begins to expand industrial capacity for vital war materiel.

1944 GI Bill helps pay for college and vocational education and provides home mortgages and business loans for more than 12 million veterans.

1947-1981 *U.S. economy soars; home and car ownership mark middle-class status.*

1947 Average hourly compensation for workers begins steady increase.

1954 U.S. auto industry sells 9.1 million cars, nearly double the 1941 total.

1955 Fifty-seven percent of U.S. households own their homes, up from 41 percent in 1940.

1956 U.S. Interstate Highway System construction begins, leading to declines in shipping costs.

1959 At Moscow debate with Soviet Premier Nikita S. Khrushchev, Vice President Richard Nixon touts products available to U.S. steelworkers.

1962 Columbia University sociologist C. Wright Mills warns that middle-class office workers are losing economic independence that early 19th-century middle class enjoyed.

1981 As effects of globalizing world economy begin to take hold, 26 percent of cars, 25 percent of steel and 60 percent of consumer electronics are imported.

1982-Present *Continuing globalization, outsourcing and digital innovation cause disruptive economic change, sparking intense political debate.*

1982 Personal computers become commercially available.

1990 American steel industry employment falls to 630,000 from more than 1 million in 1970.

1994 Amazon, which will cause huge job losses in retail and other industries, is founded.

2006 Leading economist estimates that up to 42 million service-sector jobs face potential offshoring.

2007-2009 Major recession pushes unemployment rate to 10 percent. . . . Long-term unemployed include educated, skilled workers.

2011 "Occupy Wall Street" movement reflects growing debate over economic disparity in American society.

2013 Economist Thomas Piketty's *Capital in the Twenty-First Century* intensifies debate over fate of middle class.

2015 Pew Research Center concludes the middle-income population is shrinking. . . . Princeton University economists document death rate increase among lesser-educated whites. . . . Young college graduates' hourly pay (inflation-adjusted) is $17.94 an hour, down from $18.41 in 2000.

2016 Presidential primary candidates from both parties attack U.S. trade policy for allegedly eliminating U.S. jobs.

Recession Underscores Black-White Economic Gap

Bulk of African-American wealth tied up in homes.

The brutal recession of 2007-'09 and its aftermath spurred many Americans to talk about class distinction, but the crash and recovery also is a story about race.

Black households lost 40 percent of their wealth, on average, from 2009 to 2011, when recovery from the recession was beginning. During the same period, the median loss among white households (excluding home equity) dwindled to zero.[1]

Much of that disparity stems from the different natures of black wealth and white wealth. The Social Science Research Council, a New York-based organization of academics in sociology and related fields, examined the racial dimensions of the recession and recovery for the American Civil Liberties Union. It noted that black home-owning households depended on the values of their homes for their wealth to a greater extent than whites.

In 2007, home equity accounted for 71 percent of the total wealth of the typical black homeowner. *For white homeowners, home equity made up 51 percent of wealth.[2] That difference partly explains why median wealth — excluding home equity — was $14,200 for blacks and $92,950 for whites in 2007.[3]

Some experts conclude that this gap in resources is due, in part, to a history of housing discrimination, in which many minorities were denied mortgage loans or were required to pay higher loan rates than those charged to whites. A boom in mortgage lending that began in the 1990s eventually triggered the recession, underscoring the legacy of that discrimination, in the view of some experts.[4] A disproportionate percentage of

---

* Home equity is a home's fair-market value minus any debt outstanding on the property.

blacks, as well as Latinos, held "subprime" mortgages, which carried higher interest rates because subprime borrowers were perceived to be at a higher risk of defaulting.[5]

"Before the subprime boom, black borrowers were more likely to be denied loans overall," wrote sociologists Jacob S. Rugh, now an assistant professor at Brigham Young University, and Douglas S. Massey, a professor at Princeton University. "During the boom, minority borrowers' underserved status made them prime targets for subprime lenders who systematically targeted their communities for aggressive marketing campaigns."[6]

Rugh and Massey said data showed that subprime mortgages went disproportionally not only to black and Latino borrowers but also to non-college-educated borrowers.[7]

Among blacks, as among whites, a college degree increasingly is seen as the dividing line between being middle class and working class. Karyn Lacy, a sociology professor at the University of Michigan in Ann Arbor, who wrote a book based on fieldwork in black communities in the Virginia and Maryland suburbs of Washington, D.C., argues that the black lower middle class is more accurately described as working class.[8] Its members earn $30,000 to $49,000 a year in jobs that don't typically require a college degree.

"Most of the rewards associated with a middle-class lifestyle, such as a safe neighborhood, quality public schools or job security are merely wishful thinking for this group," Lacy wrote in 2012.[9]

Overall, African-Americans are poorer than whites, with black median household income at $35,398 in 2014, compared to $60,256 for white non-Hispanics. But 11 percent of black Americans earn $100,000 to $200,000 a year, and 1.6 percent earn $200,000 a year or more — putting both those groups within the upper middle class.[10]

---

lost.[66] Joblessness peaked at 10 percent in October 2009, the highest rate since the Depression.[67]

The housing crash followed a vast expansion of easy mortgage lending, financed largely by investors who bought securities based on mortgage obligations. The

investments failed when homeowners couldn't make their mortgage payments. For the 30 preceding years, administrations and Congress had left financial institutions to mostly supervise themselves, relying on the self-correcting nature of the markets.

Lacy urges that the continuing plight of many black households not lead to an overly generalized conclusion that the entire black middle class has been economically devastated over the past nine years.

Now doing research in Atlanta, Lacy says, "Here you have athletes, entertainers, many not college-educated but rich, as well as very wealthy black business owners. I've interviewed some of these people, and as far as I can tell, their lifestyles have not changed. There is still a black elite middle class that have maintained their status."

Despite black communities' history with subprime mortgages, as well as other institutional barriers, Lacy finds that African-Americans who are lower down on the economic-class hierarchy are more likely to blame themselves than others for obstacles they encounter.[11]

"When lower-middle-class [black] people are not successful, they tend to think, 'I didn't make the sacrifices to go to college,'" Lacy observes. "The feeling is, 'I fell short due to some individual deficiency.'"

Blaming oneself, rather than the system, is consistent with research by other scholars, who have found young African-Americans acknowledging that the conditions they face are somewhat better than those of earlier generations. For a 2014 book, Andrew J. Cherlin, a sociologist at Johns Hopkins University, and colleague Timothy Nelson interviewed men of both races and found more optimism among African-Americans. "I think there are better opportunities now because first of all, the economy's changing," a black interviewee said. "The color barrier is not as harsh as it was back then."[12]

White men, however, were less optimistic. The gap between the races showed up in responses to survey questions about how respondents expect their children to fare. Negative responses among whites increased from 12 percent in 1994 to 15 percent in 2012. But negative responses among blacks declined during the same period, from 17 percent to 14 percent.[13]

Orlando Patterson, a Harvard University sociologist, noted last year that inner-city young blacks with little education and few possibilities tend to subscribe wholeheartedly to the classic American success doctrine. "The most hardened, disconnected youth insisted on attributing their failures to their own shortcomings and refused to blame racism," Patterson wrote.[14]

But members of the black middle and upper-middle classes, Lacy says, tend to blame institutionalized discrimination more than themselves for obstacles they encounter. "The higher you ascend on the class ladder, the more cognizant you are of barriers you have to overcome," she says.

— *Peter Katel*

[1] Sarah Burd-Sharps and Rebecca Rasch, "Impact of the US Housing Crisis on the Racial Wealth Gap Across Generations," Social Science Research Council, June 2015, p. 1, http://tinyurl.com/j6uoc4e.

[2] *Ibid.*, p. 12.

[3] *Ibid.*

[4] For background, see Kenneth Jost, "Housing Discrimination," *CQ Researcher*, Nov. 6, 2015, pp. 937-960.

[5] Jacob S. Rugh and Douglas S. Massey, "Racial Segregation and the American Foreclosure Crisis," *American Sociological Review*, 2010, http://tinyurl.com/jjha3jm.

[6] *Ibid.*, p. 632.

[7] *Ibid.*, p. 633.

[8] Karyn Lacy, *Blue-Chip Black* (2007).

[9] Karyn Lacy, "All's Fair? The Foreclosure Crisis and Middle-Class Black (In)Stability," *American Behavioral Scientist*, November 2012, p. 1568, http://tinyurl.com/gs592e3.

[10] Carmen DeNavas-Walt and Bernadette D. Proctor, "Income and Poverty in the United States: 2014," Current Population Reports, U.S. Census Bureau, September 2015, p. 5, http://tinyurl.com/oskydlu; "African American Income," *BlackDemographics.com*, undated, http://tinyurl.com/h8pt5px.

[11] For background, see Peter Katel, "Racial Conflict," *CQ Researcher*, Jan. 8, 2016, pp. 25-48.

[12] Andrew J. Cherlin, *Labor's Love Lost: The Rise and Fall of the Working-Class Family in America* (2014), pp. 170-171.

[13] *Ibid.*, p. 170.

[14] Orlando Patterson, "The Social and Cultural Matrix of Black Youth," p. 50, in Orlando Patterson, with Ethan Fosse, ed., *The Cultural Matrix: Understanding Black Youth* (2015).

But in 1999, Congress weakened the 1933 Glass-Steagall Act, a major law governing the financial industry. The 1999 action allowed banks to engage in commercial activities, such as insurance and investment banking, which previously had been forbidden. Many experts say weakening Glass-Steagall contributed to the mortgage crisis by allowing banks to become "too big to fail."[68]

"The financial industry itself played a key role in weakening regulatory constraints on institutions,

Rising Death Rates Signal Troubled Middle Class

Some despairing whites turn to alcohol, drugs.

For decades, death rates fell throughout the industrialized world as health habits and medical care improved. Lately, that trend has reversed — but only in one country, the United States, and only for middle-aged whites with a limited education.

From 1999 to 2014, the death rate for non-Latino whites with a high-school education or less shot up by 134.4 per 100,000, a jump of more than 20 percent. In the two decades before the spike, the mortality rate for all white Americans had fallen by nearly 2 percent a year, in line with the average rate of decline in other wealthy countries.[1] The findings emerged from an analysis of Centers for Disease Control and Prevention and Census Bureau data by Princeton University economists Anne Case and her husband, Angus Deaton, last year's winner of the Nobel Prize in economics.

Case and Deaton's alarming study made headlines. The immediate causes of the new trend were as troubling as the rise in death rates itself: drug overdoses, alcoholism, suicide and two illnesses associated with drug or alcohol abuse: chronic liver disease and cirrhosis. Not coincidentally, mortality rose hand in hand with a massive increase in prescriptions for opioid painkillers — chemical cousins of morphine and heroin — and an associated surge in heroin use in predominantly white regions, especially New England.[2]

Andrew Gelman, a professor of political science and statistics at Columbia University, questioned some of the Case-Deaton data analysis. He and a colleague didn't find an increase in the overall death rate for middle-aged whites — though they did find that they were doing worse in mortality than their counterparts in other countries. And those who are facing an increase are not men, Gelman said: "Actually, what we see is an increasing mortality among [white] women aged 52 and younger." That trend, he said, is geographically limited to the South and Midwest.[3] Gelman did not examine the regional discrepancy or any possible reasons for the female death-rate increase that he found in his analysis.

Deaton and Case stood by their analysis. But they acknowledged that some explanation was needed that went beyond specific causes of death. "Ties to economic insecurity are possible," Case and Deaton speculated. "Many of the baby-boom generation are the first to find, in midlife, that they will not be better off than were their parents."[4]

Deaton, who also studies global poverty, told the Council on Foreign Relations, a New York-based foreign-policy think tank, that he sees in the mortality spike the effects of a decline in manufacturing, a byproduct of globalized trade and automation. "These are the people who used to have good factory jobs with on-the-job training," he said. "These are the people who could build good lives for themselves and for their kids. And all of that has gone away."[5]

markets, and products," said the 2011 report of the bipartisan National Commission on the Causes of the Financial and Economic Crisis. In 1999-2008 alone, Wall Street firms spent $2.7 billion lobbying Congress and more than $1 billion on campaign contributions, the panel noted.[69]

The effects of the financial crisis were long-lasting, especially for the middle class.[70] By late 2010, nearly 6.7 million jobless Americans were considered "long-term unemployed." And many of these long-term jobless were skilled workers who had earned middle-class salaries.[71]

Anger over Wall Street firms' role in creating the mortgage crisis prompted the "Occupy Wall Street" movement, which began in New York City and spread nationwide in 2011. The movement claimed to represent the "99 percent" who were losing out to those at the top of the socioeconomic ladder. In fact, the protesters were largely middle class: Eighty percent of active Occupy

But Lane Kenworthy, a sociology professor at the University of California, San Diego, argues that the mortality data do not support that hypothesis. Notably, the death-rate increase was higher before the 2007-'09 recession — when economic conditions worsened — than after it began, he noted in a blog post.[6]

Kenworthy argues that, without a statistical analysis, the opioid boom alone could account for the death-rate increase, though he acknowledges that there could well be some connection to economic dislocation. "It is more likely that since around 1980, there has been a sizable segment of the American population who felt insecure or struggled economically but weren't addicted to pain relievers or heroin, or overdosing or killing themselves intentionally, until there was a change in the distribution of pain relievers," he says. "If all these people were happy with their lives, there might be some increase in addiction, but not enough to change the direction of the mortality rate."

Other scholars squarely defend the Case-Deaton hypothesis, arguing that changes in the class structure could well explain a sense of alienation among middle-aged white workers. The children of fathers whose working-class incomes provided a comfortable, secure existence have seen the economic environment change, says Andrew J. Cherlin, a sociology professor at Johns Hopkins University in Baltimore. And these workers, if they lacked college degrees, weren't prepared for the transformation.

"They thought they could be prosperous like their parents," he says. "College-educated people, I think they are doing just as well. It's the non-college-educated, especially whites, who feel correctly that they are not able to live up to the standards of their parents' generation."

Deaton told the Council on Foreign Relations that anguish could come not only from people's memories of their parents' generation, but also from a view of their own children's future.

"One of the things that would really make you despair in middle age is not only if you were not going to be better off than your parents," said the economist, who grew up in a coal-mining family, "but if you thought your kids were going to be even worse off than you were going to be and if the kids are turning to drugs and all of that too. I think that would make me despair."[7]

— Peter Katel

[1] Anne Case and Angus Deaton, "Rising morbidity and mortality in midlife among white non-Hispanic Americans in the 21st century," *PNAS* (Proceedings of the National Academy of Sciences), Dec. 8, 2015, http://tinyurl.com/j378n6b; Gina Kolata, "Death Rates Rising for Middle-Aged White Americans, Study Finds," *The New York Times*, Nov. 2, 2015, http://tinyurl.com/nrf6d5x.

[2] Katharine Q. Seelye, "Heroin in New England, More Abundant and Deadly," *The New York Times*, July 18, 2013, http://tinyurl.com/h5tygzn; "Here and There with Dave Marash," interview, Sam Quinones, author of *Dreamland*, Feb. 25, 2016, http://tinyurl.com/j63ov6k.

[3] Andrew Gelman, "Is the Death Rate Really Increasing for Middle-Aged White Americans?," *Slate*, Nov. 11, 2015, http://tinyurl.com/h87m3y3. Andrew Gelman and Jonathan Auerbach, "Age-aggregation bias in mortality trends," undated, http://tinyurl.com/jvde4l7; "More Details on Rising Mortality Among Middle-Aged Whites," *The New York Times*, Nov. 6, 2015, http://tinyurl.com/hmautna; "Middle-aged white death trends update: It's all about women in the south," Statistical Modeling, Causal Inference, and Social Science (blog), Jan. 19, 2016, http://tinyurl.com/jx7e5kk.

[4] Case and Deaton, *op. cit.*, p. 4.

[5] "Angus Deaton on Foreign Aid and Inequality," Council on Foreign Relations, Feb. 18, 2016, http://tinyurl.com/hysdpk5.

[6] Lane Kenworthy, "Is economic insecurity to blame for the increase in deaths among middle-aged whites?" blog post, Nov. 5, 2015, http://tinyurl.com/h7fljux.

[7] "Angus Deaton . . .," *op. cit.*; John Kay, "The Great Escape: Health, Wealth and the Origins of Inequality by Angus Deaton (book review)," *Prospect Magazine*, Nov. 14, 2013, http://tinyurl.com/hfrh6cf.

members in the movement's New York heart had bachelor's or graduate degrees. According to a 2012 survey, 29 percent of Occupy activists had lost their jobs in the previous five years, nearly half were professionals and 36 percent had household incomes of at least $100,000.[72]

Although the movement ebbed, it had put the growing disparity in the distribution of the nation's wealth — and the fate of the middle class — squarely on the national agenda. A 2012 Pew survey of self-described middle-class Americans found that 62 percent blamed Congress "a lot" for the mortgage crisis and 54 percent blamed financial institutions.[73]

Debate on the growing income gap — including such largely middle-class issues as student debt — took on still more urgency after the 2014 publication of French economist Thomas Piketty's bestseller *Capital in the Twenty-First Century*. He used income tax data to show that the top 1 percent of Americans had doubled their income over the past 30 years and those in the top 0.1 percent had quadrupled theirs.[74]

By late 2015, the centrist Pew center's report on the shrinking middle-income population prompted even more attention to the widening income gap and its relation to the condition of the middle class.

These conditions were accompanied by a steep drop in the power of unions, which push for higher wages and benefits for workers. By 2015, union membership had dropped from 35 percent of the workforce in the mid-1950s to 11 percent.[75]

Meanwhile, executive pay soared. Between 1997 and 2014, CEO pay increased 997 percent, according to the Economic Policy Institute. And Bloomberg, the business news service, calculated in 2015 that the difference between CEO and worker pay reached as high as 644 to 1 — $7.29 million a year for the McDonald's CEO versus $11,324 a year for the average McDonald's employee.

Reflecting growing public indignation over such disparities, the Securities and Exchange Commission voted last year to require most public companies to report on their CEO-employee pay ratio.[76]

French economist Thomas Piketty intensified the debate on the growing income gap with his bestselling book *Capital in the Twenty-First Century*. Using income tax data, he showed that the top 1 percent of Americans had doubled their income over the past 30 years — and that those in the top 0.1 percent had quadrupled theirs.

CURRENT SITUATION
Student Debt

Experts agree that getting the best education possible is the wisest investment young people can make. But some experts say the deck is stacked against low-income students, effectively making it harder for them to earn what is becoming an essential middle-class credential.

Low-income students are held back by the high cost of four-year degree programs and fear of graduating with an untenable amount of college debt. Total outstanding student debt reached a staggering $1.3 trillion last year, about 11 percent of which was delinquent or in default for at least 90 days. Borrowers owing half of the total have sought to postpone payment.[77]

Definitive explanations for skyrocketing college debt are hard to come by. Experts at the Brookings Institution say tuition increases do not explain all of the ballooning debt: Net tuition — the amount after deducting financial aid — increased 12 percent in 2002-2012, while total student debt increased 77 percent. And enrollment increases are not large enough to explain debt growth, the think tank analysts said.[78]

Brookings researchers Michael Greenstone and Adam Looney said students seem to increasingly be relying on loans to finance higher education, possibly because of the recession's negative impact on family finances.

Recently, the growth in college debt has been slowing. And, counterintuitively, borrowers who default owe less on average than borrowers in good standing, which could reflect lower earnings in some students' post-college careers. The average debt was $22,550 in 2014, while the average debt of those in default was $14,380.[79]

Democratic presidential candidate Sanders vows to end tuition at all public colleges and universities. Clinton has a similar but somewhat more complicated plan, in which students would not pay tuition but their parents would have to pay some college costs.[80]

And President Obama is proposing a plan that would provide free community college tuition for low-income students who attend classes at least half time and maintain at least a 2.5 grade point average. The federal government would pick up 75 percent of the tab and states the remainder.[81]

Low-income students are more likely to earn certificates or associate degrees, which can be completed in fewer years, according to Sandy Baum, a senior fellow at the Urban Institute think tank who specializes in higher education finance, and Martha C. Johnson, a research associate there.[82]

The financial barriers to bachelor's and postgraduate degrees have racial and ethnic, as well as class, dimensions. According to an analysis by Demos, a liberal think tank, 81 percent of black students at public institutions — and 86 percent at private colleges — must borrow money to pay for tuition, compared with 63 percent and 72 percent, respectively, for whites. The same study concluded that middle-class black and Latino students are having the hardest time making student loan payments. For those at the bottom of the middle class, the hardship of college loan payments threatens membership in the middle class.[83]

Because of the high indebtedness rate for black and Latino students, they drop out of college owing money at a far higher rate than white students. Thirty-nine percent of black borrowers drop out, compared with 29 percent of white borrowers.

"And despite bipartisan rhetoric around closing attainment gaps among students of color and low-income students," wrote Mark Huelsman, a senior policy analyst at Demos, referring to the disproportionately low share of minority college students, "we have created a system in which more underrepresented students take on debt and drop out."[84]

Proposed Solutions

Obama's latest proposed budget contains plans designed to boost employment in high-skilled, so-called middle-class jobs.

The budget would provide $75 million for the proposed American Technical Training Fund, which would expand tuition-free job training in fields such as manufacturing, health care and information technology.[85] But it is unlikely the fund will see the light of day. Congressional Republicans, who control both the House and Senate, have announced they won't even hold hearings on Obama's proposed budget.[86]

But another Obama budget proposal — to supplement the wages of displaced manufacturing workers who take lower-paying service jobs by providing them up to $10,000 over two years — conceivably could get Republican support.

"The idea of targeting financial support to people who, especially later in their careers, are choosing between going back to a lower-wage job or potentially ending up on disability or something else — it's a win-win to have them in the workforce," said Oren Cass, a senior fellow at the Manhattan Institute and former domestic policy director for 2012 Republican presidential nominee Mitt Romney.[87]

Obama's plan to shore up the middle class and enlarge gateways to enter it takes a less ambitious approach than that of Sanders, who calls for spending $1 trillion over five years to rebuild roads, bridges, water systems and other infrastructure. "If we are truly serious about reversing the decline of the middle class, we need a major federal jobs program which puts millions of Americans back to work at decent paying jobs," Sanders said last May.[88]

Sanders is dueling Clinton on whose proposals would best help the middle class. She argues that his recommendations, which include expanding Medicare to cover all Americans, would raise middle-class taxes, which she vows not to do. She defines the middle class as individuals earning less than $200,000 a year and couples earning less than $250,000. "We need to give middle class families a break, not a tax increase," said Jake Sullivan, a senior Clinton adviser.[89]

Clinton's definition of middle class has raised considerable criticism among liberal Democrats. "But under Mrs. Clinton's pledge, some of the well off [are] lumped in for receiving a boost," Bryce Covert, economic policy editor at ThinkProgress, a left-of-center news site, wrote in *The New York Times*.[90]

The Tax Policy Center of the Urban Institute and Brookings Institution confirmed that Clinton's proposal would raise taxes on the top 1 percent of earners. Under Sanders' proposal, all income groups would pay some increases, but most would come from the highest earners, the center said.[91]

On the Republican side, Trump has proposed reducing the number of tax brackets to three and eliminating income taxes on individuals making $25,000 a year or less, or couples making $50,000 or less. He called it a "substantial reduction for the middle-income people." However, the Tax Policy Center concluded that Trump's plan would give the biggest breaks to the highest-income households. And the corporate income tax rate would be cut from 35 percent to 15 percent.[92]

Cruz proposed a 10 percent flat tax on income, plus a consumption tax. That would give high-income taxpayers a 29.6 percent tax cut, according to the Tax Policy Center, and a 3.2 percent cut for middle-income households.[93]

For all the attention politicians are devoting to taxes, a bipartisan team of analysts from Brookings has concluded that raising taxes on the wealthy would produce "exceedingly modest" results in reducing income disparities overall.[94]

A less complicated idea is to raise the minimum wage to $15 an hour — more than double the current federal minimum of $7.25 an hour. In early June, Democratic Gov. Jerry Brown of California signed into law the first statewide $15-an-hour minimum, and Gov. Andrew Cuomo of New York, also a Democrat, enacted a $15-an-hour minimum for the New York City metropolitan area and a $12.50 minimum for the rest of the state, where the cost of living is lower.[95]

Both new minimum wages will be phased in, reaching the top level by 2022 in California, and by 2018 in New York City, with the lower wage required elsewhere in the state by 2021.[96]

Before California and New York acted, at least 14 cities and counties had already adopted the $15 minimum.[97] Many experts are unsure how the higher minimum wages will affect other wages. "It's very unclear how that's going to stack up," said Ben Zipperer, an economist at the Washington Center for Equitable Growth, a research and grantmaking organization.[98]

Some advocates argue that raising the minimum to $15 would push other wages further up, expanding the middle class. "A policy that can shore up the middle class will also reduce income inequality and serve as a foundation for job creation," wrote Oren M. Levin-Waldman, a professor of public policy at the Metropolitan College of New York.[99]

Others, like Charles Fay of Rutgers University's School of Management and Labor Relations, say employers instead will just give smaller wage increases across the board. "There's a decreasing increase so that you can maintain equity across the different wage levels," he said.[100]

OUTLOOK
Slower Growth

In a much-discussed new book, economist Gordon of Northwestern University argues that whatever the fate of the middle class, it will not be vastly expanded by a new era of massive economic growth like that triggered by life-transforming innovations in the 1870-1970 era.

Revolutionary changes, such as universal electricity, water and sewer service, paved highways and air travel, are unlikely to be equaled in the foreseeable future, he contends.[101]

"I am not predicting zero growth" in the economy, Gordon says. Citing recent advances in oil and gas drilling and other technological developments, he says, "I'm not saying we are not going to invent anything; there is plenty of room for fracking, 3-D printing, autonomous cars. But each of these innovations is evolutionary rather than revolutionary."

Nasser of Evergreen State College agrees with Gordon. "U.S. long-term growth has always been associated with things like the steam engine, railroads, electricity, automobiles, suburbanization, which transformed the country's whole way of life," says Nasser, author of the forthcoming book *United States of Emergency: American Capitalism and its Crises.* "The more you think about it, the more intuitively improbable it is that any economic system could generate large-scale transformations of that kind ad infinitum."

As for the middle class, Gordon says it will likely be smaller, barring a change in how the fruits of slow growth are distributed. "With the rise of inequality, . . . already slow growth in the income available is being siphoned off into the top 1 percent, leaving less for everyone else to share."

Hacker of Yale says political changes could lay the groundwork for greater economic growth and for ensuring that the middle class shares in whatever growth occurs. For now, "We are not making the kinds of investments we would need to make in order to have growth like we used to have. Are we putting the kind of money we need to in infrastructure, early-childhood education, research and development?" he asks rhetorically.

And as automation requires fewer workers to produce more goods and services, Nasser says, private business won't be motivated to maintain high employment. The solution,

Is the American middle class in permanent decline?

YES Alan Nasser
Professor Emeritus of Political Economy, The Evergreen State College

Written for *CQ Researcher*, April 2016

NO Scott Winship
Fellow, Manhattan Institute

Written for *CQ Researcher*, April 2016

Capitalism does not normally produce a middle class. The middle-class myth is based on the "golden age" of 1949 to 1973. During that period, the income of one breadwinner bought many families a house, an automobile, a plethora of durable goods, higher education for the kids, health care and sufficient savings for retirement. This suggests that hard work earned a desirable standard of living as a reward — namely, the wage — for that work. But the wage of the breadwinner has never been sufficient to enable the benefits touted in the single-breadwinner story.

The "American dream" was achieved by initiating a bubble in consumption, encouraging households to augment their buying power by taking on *increasing* debt. In 1946, the ratio of household debt to disposable income stood at 24 percent, by 1950 at 38 percent, by 1955 at 53 percent, by 1960 at 62 percent, and by 1965 at 72 percent. The stagnation of real wages that began in 1974 pressured households to further increase their debt in order to maintain desirable living standards, pushing the ratio of debt to disposable income to 77 percent by 1979. Then the median wage began, in 1974, a long-term decline persisting to this day. By the mid-1980s, the ratio began a dangerous ascent, from 80 percent in 1985 to 88 percent in 1990 to 95 percent in 1995 to more than 100 percent in 2000 and 138 percent in 2007.

Rising debt was necessary not merely to purchase more consumer "toys," but to meet growing housing, health care, education and child-care costs. With soaring health care costs the leading cause of personal bankruptcy, *mounting* debt was necessary for most workers to stay out of poverty. Middle-class status was bought at the expense of *addiction* to debt.

If "middle class" connotes material security based on income from work, absent unsustainable debt addiction, there has never been an American middle class.

The debt bubble was unsustainable, and it climaxed in the debacle of September 2008, when the housing bubble finally burst. Since then, we have witnessed rising and record inequality and the further hollowing out of middle-income jobs. And automation in both manufacturing and services, more than job outsourcing, has resulted in the fastest-growing jobs being temporary, part-time and low-paying. With economists as distinguished as Paul Krugman, Lawrence Summers and Robert Gordon forecasting secular, or chronic and therefore long-term, stagnation "forever" (in Summers' words), it is unlikely that there will even *appear* to be a middle class.

Is the middle class in permanent decline? It's not even temporarily so. Seven years from the darkest days of the Great Recession, the American economy has almost fully rebounded to the considerable health it previously enjoyed. The unemployment rate is below 5 percent, not far from where it was before the recession started. Median hourly wages are back to their historical peak in 2007. Median annual household income also is nearly at its historic high.

Over the long run, hourly pay has risen in line with productivity growth. Median pay among male workers stagnated during the 1980s and early '90s. But that was a historical adjustment that gradually whittled away the unfair premium that male breadwinners received in earlier decades because married women were discouraged from working. Pay among female workers increased with productivity growth, and since the boom of the 1990s, male and female pay levels both have risen with productivity gains.

Some commentators focus on relatively low labor-force participation rates to argue that the unemployment rate no longer captures the weakness of the labor market. But much of the decline in labor-force participation is due to rising school enrollment and the retirement of baby boomers. And much of the rest of it is voluntary. Fewer than 40 percent of men aged 25 to 54 who are out of the labor force tell government surveyors they want a job, and the rise between 1979 and 2006 in the number of these men who are not interested in work statistically accounts for the entire drop in labor-force participation over that period.

Claims that the middle class has shrunk use a threshold for the middle that rises as the country grows richer. They also conceal the fact that most of the "shrinking" is due to an increase in the share of Americans with enough money that they are better off than the "middle class" as it is defined in these analyses. The Congressional Budget Office, Congress' nonpartisan budget analysts, and other sources show the middle fifth of American households richer by one-third compared with 1979 — by $15,000, according to the CBO.

Finally, economic mobility rates have held steady even as inequality has risen and family disruption increased. While the income growth rates of the mid-20th century have not returned, the American middle class is far richer than its counterpart from that era, and tomorrow's will be richer than today's.

he says, is "direct government employment" in activities such as infrastructure reconstruction and repair. The alternative, he says, is "long-term imposed austerity, with an increase in social disorder, burglaries, robberies, psychological depression [and] disillusion with government."

But Winship of the Manhattan Institute argues that technological innovation promises significantly more growth than Gordon forecasts, while acknowledging that there will be less need for labor. "I see a future where things are going to get quite a bit cheaper," he says. "People won't have to work as long for the same standard of living."

However, he adds, "We do need to be concerned about people at the bottom who have few marketable skills." But that is not to say that there are no possibilities. Workers must "look ahead and think imaginatively about jobs that will be created in the future for even people with relatively few skills."

Journalist James Fallows, who spent three years visiting small cities in overlooked parts of America, writes that many small towns are undergoing "a process of revival and reinvention that has largely if understandably been overlooked in the political and media concentration on the strains of this Second Gilded Age."[102]

He found that many places considered backward and isolated are producing more innovation than the big coastal cities thought to attract talented and innovative young people.[103]

But whatever the future of fly-over country innovation, and regardless of whether Gordon is correct about a lower-growth future, says Kenworthy of the University of California, "we have had pretty decent economic growth since the late 1970s."

If that growth had been evenly distributed, "we would have good income gains for the middle class, so much so that I don't think we'd be having this conversation."

NOTES

1. Quoted in Patrick Healy and Amy Chozick, "Hillary Clinton Wins 4 Races, Rebounding From Michigan Loss," *The New York Times*, March 15, 2016, http://tinyurl.com/j3sn9te.

2. "The American Middle Class Is Losing Ground," Pew Research Center, Dec. 9, 2015, p. 13, http://tinyurl.com/j8lxmzl.

3. *Ibid.*, pp. 4-5.

4. Chad Stone *et al.*, "A Guide to Statistics on Historical Trends in Income Inequality," Center on Budget and Policy Priorities, updated Oct. 26, 2015, http://tinyurl.com/j6pqdue.

5. "The American Middle Class is Losing Ground," *op. cit.*, p. 6.

6. "Annual Earnings of Young Adults," National Center for Education Statistics, U.S. Department of Education, updated May 2015, http://tinyurl.com/nc8vrf6.

7. Anna Brown, "What Americans say it takes to be middle class," Pew Research Center, Feb. 4, 2016, http://tinyurl.com/hszvehw.

8. Alyssa Davis, Will Kimball and Elise Gould, "The Class of 2015: Despite an Improving Economy, Young Grades Still Face an Uphill Climb," Economic Policy Institute, May 27, 2015, pp. 21-22, http://tinyurl.com/hg9wrl3; John Wagner, "Why millennials love Bernie Sanders, and why that may not be enough," *The Washington Post*, Oct. 27, 2015, http://tinyurl.com/jrbu8m8.

9. Quoted in "Democratic town hall: Transcript, video," CNN, Feb. 4, 2016, http://tinyurl.com/hl6qekl; Aaron Blake, "74-year-old Bernie Sanders's remarkable dominance among young voters, in 1 chart," *The Washington Post*, March 17, 2016, http://tinyurl.com/hy8vt43; Wagner, *op. cit.*; John Cassidy, "What Bernie Sanders Has Achieved," *The New Yorker*, March 17, 2016, http://tinyurl.com/jygf2bd.

10. For background, see "U.S. Trade Policy," *CQ Researcher*, Sept. 13, 2013, pp. 765-788.

11. Dan Merica and Eric Bradner, "Hillary Clinton comes out against TPP trade deal," CNN, Oct. 7, 2015, http://tinyurl.com/jpj3u5o; Joseph Lawler, "Cruz pits Wall Street against middle class in new ad," *Washington Examiner*, March 25, 2016, http://tinyurl.com/zyfbwnp.

12. "The American Middle Class is Losing Ground," *op. cit.*

13. *Ibid.*, p. 6.

14. *Ibid.*, p. 5.

15. Frank Newport, "Fewer Americans Identify as Middle Class in Recent Years," Gallup, April 28, 2015, http://tinyurl.com/j69rzsz.

16. Noah Smith, "Decline of the U.S. Middle Class," Bloomberg, March 28, 2016, http://tinyurl.com/zmcxvtd. "Class (subjective class identification), General Social Survey, NORC at University of Chicago, 2014; "Class Identification," GSS Data Explorer, http://tinyurl.com/zt7on2m.

17. "The Distribution of Household Income and Federal Taxes, 2011," Congressional Budget Office, November 2014, pp. 6-7, http://tinyurl.com/zxxkc74. Scott Winship, "Sorry EPI, The Rich Did Not Steal $18,000 from the Middle-Class," The Manhattan Institute, http://tinyurl.com/h4zzfrq.

18. Lawrence Mishel, Elise Gould and Josh Bivens, "Wage Stagnation in Nine Charts," Economic Policy Institute, Jan. 6, 2015, p. 6, http://tinyurl.com/zvtrngt.

19. "Life expectancy at birth, at age 65, at age 75, by sex, race and Hispanic origin: United States, selected years 1900-2013," U.S. Centers for Disease Control and Prevention, updated May 6, 2015, http://tinyurl.com/zlomsln.

20. "Table P-16. Educational Attainment-People 25 Years Old and Over by Median Income and Sex: 1991 to 2014," U.S. Census Bureau, http://tinyurl.com/87hwyqn.

21. David H. Autor, "Why Are There Still So Many Jobs? The History and Future of Workplace Automation," Journal of Economic Perspectives, Summer 2015, p. 14, http://tinyurl.com/zw6hboh.

22. "Unemployment rate," U.S. Bureau of Labor Statistics, March 12, 2016, http://tinyurl.com/3gss8qd; Patricia Cohen, "Robust Hiring in December Caps Solid Year for U.S. Jobs," The New York Times, Jan. 8, 2016, http://tinyurl.com/h757xna.

23. Alemayehu Bishaw, "Poverty: 2000 to 2012," U.S. Census Bureau, September 2013, p. 5, http://tinyurl.com/k9hzfer; "Income and Poverty in the United States: 2014," U.S. Census Bureau, September 2015, pp. 12, 13, http://tinyurl.com/oskydlu.

24. "Remarks by the President in Conversation on Poverty at Georgetown University," The White House, May 12, 2015, http://tinyurl.com/juhj7zf; James Pethokoukis, "Yuval Levin on means testing Medicare and Social Security," American Enterprise Institute, Feb. 20, 2013, http://tinyurl.com/h25fn7o; Dean Baker and Hye Jin Rho, "The Potential Savings to Social Security from Means Testing," Center for Economic and Policy Research, March 2011, pp. 1-2, 13, http://tinyurl.com/h3wjryq.

25. Jesse McKinley and Vivian Yee, "New York Budget Deal With Higher Minimum Wage Is Reached," The New York Times, March 31, 2016, http://tinyurl.com/hfs9op7.

26. Quoted in Sarah Mimms, "Chuck Schumer: Passing Obamacare in 2010 Was a Mistake," The Atlantic, Nov. 25, 2014, http://tinyurl.com/j3p97o6.

27. Alisha Coleman-Jensen et al., "Household Food Security in the United States in 2014," U.S. Department of Agriculture, September 2015, p. 8, http://tinyurl.com/o3fpopl.

28. For background, see "Welfare Reform," CQ Researcher, Aug. 3, 2001, pp. 601-632.

29. Ray Boshara, William R. Emmons and Bryan J. Noeth, "The Demographics of Wealth: How Age, Education and Race Separate Thrives from Strugglers in Today's Economy," Federal Reserve Bank of St. Louis, May 2015, p. 10, http://tinyurl.com/jx5qbs4.

30. Tim J. Bartik, "What the available evidence shows about middle-class benefits of early childhood education," Investing in Kids (blog), Feb. 4, 2014, http://tinyurl.com/zdmphjb.

31. Kevin Huffman, "Democrats love universal pre-K — and don't seem to care that it may not work," The Washington Post, Feb. 4, 2016, http://tinyurl.com/h92ccfq; Cory Turner, "The Tennessee Pre-K Debate: Spinach Vs. Easter Grass," NPR, Sept. 29, 2015, http://tinyurl.com/ospvl7y.

32. "Education and Lifetime Earnings," Office of Retirement Policy, Social Security Administration, November 2015, http://tinyurl.com/j89gymz.

33. "Earnings and unemployment rates by educational attainment," U.S. Bureau of Labor Statistics,

updated March 15, 2016, http://tinyurl.com/ybn8p8p.

34. Tyler Cowen, *Average Is Over: Powering America Beyond the age of the Great Stagnation* (2013), p. 4.

35. *Ibid.*, pp. 3, 21-22.

36. Carl Benedikt Frey and Michael A. Osborne, "The Future of Employment: How Susceptible Are Jobs to Computerisation?" University of Oxford, Sept. 17, 2013, http://tinyurl.com/oj67kae.

37. For background, see David Hosansky, "Community Colleges," *CQ Researcher*, May 1, 2015, pp. 385-408.

38. "Graduation rate from first institution attended for first-time, full-time bachelor's degree-seeking students at 4-year postsecondary institutions," National Center for Education Statistics, undated, http://tinyurl.com/p58rtjk.

39. "Cumulative Debt of Bachelor's Degree Recipients by Sector over Time," Trends in Higher Education, College Board, undated, http://tinyurl.com/h3cye3b; "Cumulative Debt for Undergraduate and Graduate Studies over Time," Trends in Higher Education, College Board, undated, http://tinyurl.com/hujcet4.

40. Quoted in Stuart M. Blumin, *The Emergence of the Middle Class: Social Experience in the American City, 1760-1900* (1989), p. 1.

41. C. Wright Mills, *White Collar: The American Middle Classes* (1951, 2002), p. 6.

42. Robert J. Gordon, *The Rise and Fall of American Growth: The U.S Standard of Living since the Civil War* (2016), Kindle ed.

43. Emmanuel Saez, "Striking it Richer: The Evolution of Top Incomes in the United States," University of California, Berkeley, Sept. 3, 2013, figure 1, http://tinyurl.com/o3vrnwt; Paul Krugman, "Why We're in a New Gilded Age," *New York Review of Books*, May 8, 2014, http://tinyurl.com/zecxnm4.

44. "Progressive Movement," American Political History, Eagleton Institute of Politics, Rutgers University, undated, http://tinyurl.com/nuvbytj; Jacob S. Hacker and Paul Pierson, *Winner-Take-All Politics: How Washington Made the Rich Richer and Turned Its Back on the Middle Class* (2010), pp. 83-87; "Sherman Act," Theodore Roosevelt Center, Dickinson State University, undated, http://tinyurl.com/huyrkcz.

45. *Ibid.*; Gordon, *op. cit.*, Kindle edition.

46. Earl Wysong, Robert Perrucci, David Wright, *The New Class Society: Goodbye American Dream?* (2014), p. 14.

47. Irving Bernstein, "Americans in Depression and War," U.S. Department of Labor, undated, http://tinyurl.com/h2nvt2l.

48. *Ibid.*; John E. Hansan, "The Works Progress Administration," Social Welfare History Project, undated, http://tinyurl.com/zp5mf4c; for background, see Peter Katel, "Racial Conflict," *CQ Researcher*, Jan. 8, 2016, pp. 25-48.

49. Glenn C. Altschuler and Stuart M. Blumin, *The GI Bill: A New Deal for Veterans* (2009), pp. x; 132-134.

50. Gordon, *op. cit.*, Kindle edition.

51. Altschuler and Blumin, *op. cit.*, pp. 152-170.

52. Ira Katznelson, *When Affirmative Action Was White: An Untold History of Racial Inequality in Twentieth-Century America* (2005), p. 11.

53. Wysong *et al.*, *op. cit.*, pp. 15-16; "The Postwar Economy: 1945-1960," United States History, Country Studies, Library of Congress, undated, http://tinyurl.com/h628sam.

54. *Ibid.*, Kindle edition.

55. Gordon, *op. cit.*, Kindle edition.

56. David L. Mason, *From Buildings and Loans to Bail-Outs: A History of the American Savings and Loan Industry, 1831-1995* (2004), p. 145.

57. David Weil, *The Fissured Workplace: Why Work Became So Bad for Many and What Can Be Done to Improve It* (2014), Kindle edition.

58. Mills, *op. cit.*, Kindle edition.

59. Wysong *et al.*, p. 22.

60. Lee E. Ohanian, "Competition and the Decline of the Rust Belt," Federal Reserve Bank of Minneapolis, Dec. 20, 2014, http://tinyurl.com/z85z8oc.

61. Cherlin, Love's Labor Lost, *op. cit.*, p. 122.

62. Ben Geier, "What Did We Learn From the Dotcom Bubble of 2000?" *Time Magazine*, March 12, 2015, http://tinyurl.com/grw7344.

63. David S. Langdon, Terence M. McMenamin and Thomas J. Krolik, "U.S. labor market in 2001: Economy enters a recession," U.S. Bureau of Labor Statistics, Monthly Labor Review, February 2002, p. 19, http://tinyurl.com/jygndg5.

64. Jared Bernstein, "The Jobless Recovery," Economic Policy Institute, March 24, 2003, http://tinyurl.com/gnepwfx.

65. Alan S. Blinder, "Offshoring: The Next Industrial Revolution?" *Foreign Affairs*, March/April 2006, http://tinyurl.com/hgw4ccx.

66. For background, see Marcia Clemmitt, "Mortgage Crisis," *CQ Researcher*, Nov. 2, 2007, pp. 913-936.

67. "The Recession of 2007-2009," U.S. Bureau of Labor Statistics, February 2012, http://tinyurl.com/8tuqc8k.

68. See Jim Zarroli, "Fact Check: Did Glass-Steagall Cause the 2008 Financial Crisis?," NPR, Oct. 14, 2015, http://tinyurl.com/hssxrf2.

69. "The Financial Crisis Inquiry Report," National Commission on the Causes of the Financial and Economic Crisis in the United States, January 2011, p. xviii, http://tinyurl.com/44pkjn3.

70. For background, see Thomas J. Billitteri, "Middle-class Squeeze," *CQ Researcher*, March 6, 2009, pp. 201-224.

71. Nancy Cook, "What the Great Recession Taught Us about Long-Term Unemployment," *The Atlantic*, March 31, 2015, http://tinyurl.com/zjcjatz.

72. Ruth Milkman, Stephanie Luce and Penny Lewis, "Changing the Subject: A Bottom-Up Account of Occupy Wall Street in New York City," Joseph S. Murphy Institute for Worker Education and Labor Studies, City University of New York, 2013, pp. 10-13, 47, http://tinyurl.com/hnjvw3x.

73. For background, see Peter Katel, " 'Occupy' Movement," *CQ Researcher*, Jan. 13, 2012, pp. 25-52; Michael Levitin, "The Triumph of Occupy Wall Street," *The Atlantic*, June 10, 2015, http://tinyurl.com/nohkdr2.

74. Paul Krugman, "Review: 'The Economics of Inequality; by Thomas Piketty," *The New York Times*, Aug. 2, 2015, http://tinyurl.com/qzlm3bc; "The Lost Decade of the Middle Class," Pew Research Center, Aug. 22, 2012, http://tinyurl.com/cqhthqa.

75. Gordon, *op. cit.*, Kindle edition; "Union Members Summary," U.S. Bureau of Labor Statistics, Jan. 28, 2016, http://tinyurl.com/27c4z5; Steven Greenhouse, "Union Membership in U.S. Fell to a 70-Year Low Last Year," *The New York Times*, Jan. 21, 2011, http://tinyurl.com/4kml6ep. For background, see Chuck McCutcheon, "Unions at a Crossroads," *CQ Researcher*, Aug. 7, 2015, pp. 673-696.

76. Peter Eavis, "S.E.C. Approves Rule on C.E.O. Pay Ratio," *The New York Times*, Aug. 5, 2015, http://tinyurl.com/nv4rep5; Dave Michaels, "These U.S. CEOs Make a Lot More Money Than Their Workers," Bloomberg, Aug. 13, 2015, http://tinyurl.com/qapde3u; Lawrence Mishel and Alyssa Davis, "CEO Pay Has Grown 90 Times Faster than Typical Worker Pay Since 1978," Economic Policy Institute, July 1, 2015, http://tinyurl.com/zr6ura7.

77. Janet Lorin, "Borrowers Fall Further Behind on $1.3 Trillion in Student Loans," Bloomberg, Aug. 13, 2015, http://tinyurl.com/jgr66pq.

78. Michael Greenstone and Adam Looney, "Rising Student Debt Burdens: Factors Behind the Phenomenon," Brookings Institution, July 5, 2013, http://tinyurl.com/h2juov2.

79. Sandy Baum and Martha Johnson, "Student Debt: Who Borrows Most? What Lies Ahead?" Urban Institute, April 2015, pp. 1, 7, http://tinyurl.com/glzkcw6.

80. Laura Meckler and Josh Mitchell, "Hillary Clinton Proposes Debt-Free Tuition at Public Colleges," *The Wall Street Journal*, Aug. 10, 2015, http://tinyurl.com/hfr962h; Jordan Weissman, "Bernie Sanders Wants to Make College Tuition Free. Here's Why We Should Take Him Seriously," *Slate*, May 19, 2015, http://tinyurl.com/qguhtua.

81. Greg Jaffe, "Obama announces free community college plan," *The Washington Post*, Jan. 9, 2015, http://tinyurl.com/hsaa7xl.

82. *Ibid.*, p. 13.

83. Mark Huelsman, "The Debt Divide: The Racial and Class Bias Behind the 'New Normal' of Student Borrowing," *Demos*, 2015, p. 8, http://tinyurl.com/jmlgf3t.

84. *Ibid.*, p. 2.

85. "Meeting Our Great Challenges: Opportunity for All," White House, http://tinyurl.com/hc6u4ae; "Fiscal Year 2017 Budget Overview," Office of Management and Budget, undated, http://tinyurl.com/hqf9uaz.

86. Jackie Calmes, "Congressional Republicans Balk at Obama's Budget, Sight Unseen," *The New York Times*, Feb. 8, 2016, http://tinyurl.com/zxxx4cj.

87. Quoted in Noam Scheiber, "Obama Budget Seeks to Ease Economic Fears for U.S. Workers," *The New York Times*, Feb. 9, 2016, http://tinyurl.com/hf2jhql.

88. "Bernie's Announcement," Bernie 2016, May 26, 2015, http://tinyurl.com/nmh5qft.

89. Tami Luhby, "Clinton vs. Sanders: The battle for the middle class," CNN, Jan. 14, 2016, http://tinyurl.com/zqegvh3.

90. Bryce Covert, "$250,000 a Year Is Not Middle Class," *The New York Times*, Dec. 28, 2015, http://tinyurl.com/jl84pdb.

91. Frank Sammartino *et al.*, "An Analysis of Senator Bernie Sanders's Tax Proposals," Tax Policy Center, March 4, 2016, http://tinyurl.com/jlrkr5m; Richard Auxier *et al.*, "An Analysis of Hillary Clinton's Tax Proposals," Tax Policy Center, March 3, 2016, http://tinyurl.com/h94yr4f.

92. Quoted in Matthew Boyle, "Donald Trump: Cut Taxes on Middle Class, End Tax Breaks for Billionaires on Wall Street," *Breitbart*, Sept. 27, 2015, http://tinyurl.com/pufqohw; James Nunns *et al.*, "An Analysis of Donald Trump's Tax Plan," Tax Policy Center, Dec. 22, 2015, http://tinyurl.com/jqbrcyl.

93. Joseph Rosenberg *et al.*, "An Analysis of Ted Cruz' Tax Plan," Tax Policy Center, Feb. 16, 2016, http://tinyurl.com/gtgze2u.

94. William G. Gale, Melissa S. Kearney, Peter R. Orszag, "Would a significant increase in the top income tax rate substantially alter income inequality?" Brookings Institution, September 2015, http://tinyurl.com/nmdkdlp.

95. Edward Krudy, "New York's Cuomo signs two-tier minimum wage law in push for state-wide $15/hour," Reuters, April 4, 2016, http://preview.tinyurl.com/jzx6ug4; John Bacon, "$15 minimum wage coming to New York, Calif.," *USA Today*, April 5, 2016, http://tinyurl.com/huub28r.

96. *Ibid.*

97. "State Minimum Wages/2016 Minimum Wage by State," National Conference of State Legislatures, updated Jan. 1, 2016, http://tinyurl.com/kxlue7a; "14 Cities & States Approved $15 Minimum Wage in 2015," National Employment Law Project, Dec. 21, 2015, http://tinyurl.com/hpjbbxa.

98. Quoted in Noam Scheiber and Ian Lovett, "$15-an-Hour Minimum Wage in California? Plan Has Some Worried," *The New York Times*, March 28, 2016, http://tinyurl.com/j3z2gtm.

99. Oren M. Levin-Waldman, "How Raising the Minimum Wage Would Boost the Middle Class," *Governing*, Feb. 13, 2014, http://tinyurl.com/jmb3k99.

100. Lydia DePillis and Jim Tankersley, "Minimum wage increases haven't grown the middle class. $15 might be different," *The Washington Post*, Aug. 12, 2015, http://tinyurl.com/howtdll.

101. Gordon, *The Rise and Fall of American Growth*, *op. cit.*

102. James Fallows, "How America Is Putting Itself Back Together," *The Atlantic*, March 2016, http://tinyurl.com/h8gykmy.

103. *Ibid.*

BIBLIOGRAPHY
Selected Sources
Books

Cowen, Tyler, *Average is Over: Powering America Beyond the Age of the Great Stagnation*, **Dutton, 2013.**
A George Mason University economist argues that because of technological changes, highly educated and imaginative individuals are becoming more valuable in the job market, but those considered ordinary are less in demand.

Gordon, Robert J., *The Rise and Fall of American Growth: The U.S. Standard of Living Since the Civil War*, **Princeton University Press, 2016.**
In a much-discussed study, a Northwestern University economist contends that the age of inventions that transformed daily life is over for the foreseeable future.

Hacker, Jacob, and Paul Pierson, *Winner-Take-All Politics: How Washington Made the Rich Richer — And Turned Its Back on the Middle Class*, **Simon & Schuster, 2010.**
Political scientists from Yale (Hacker) the University of California, Berkeley (Pierson) effectively predicted the current furor over inequality and the problems facing the middle class.

Lacy, Karyn, *Blue-Chip Black: Race, Class and Status in the New Black Middle Class*, **University of California Press, 2007.**
The African-American middle class — often portrayed as a single bloc — actually is divided by occupation, lifestyle and goals, much like the American middle class in general, a University of Michigan sociologist writes after conducting research in suburban Washington, D.C.

Porter, Katherine, ed., *Broke: How Debt Bankrupts the Middle Class*, **Stanford University Press, 2012.**
A collection of studies presents a picture of middle-class families whose finances are threatened by necessities such as higher education and medical expenses.

Articles

Balz, Dan, "Charting Donald Trump's rise through the decline of the middle class," *The Washington Post*, **Dec. 12, 2015, http://tinyurl.com/jq2km8c.**
A political reporter uses a Pew Research Center report on the decline of the middle class to explain the current Republican presidential frontrunner's appeal.

Ellison, Charles D., "Are We Talking Enough About the Black Middle Class?" *Pacific Standard*, **April 13, 2015, http://tinyurl.com/zu4n85l.**
An African-American political analyst argues that viewing the entire black population as poor fosters biased policies that keep the black middle class from expanding.

Fletcher, Michael A., "Is the American middle class doing better than we think?" *The Washington Post*, **Dec. 18, 2014, http://tinyurl.com/j6xc7bm.**
An economics writer reports on researchers dissenting from conventional wisdom on the condition of the middle class.

Popper, Nathaniel, "The Robots Are Coming for Wall Street," *The New York Times Magazine*, **Feb. 25, 2016, http://tinyurl.com/h35d429.**
The success of new analytical software on Wall Street may spell the end of many high-paying jobs there, a financial journalist reports.

Scheiber, Noam, "Growth in the 'Gig Economy' Fuels Work Force Anxieties," *The New York Times*, **July 12, 2015, http://tinyurl.com/nblwpuj.**
A labor reporter describes the effects of companies' growing use of freelance contractors.

Searcy, Dionne, and Robert Gebeloff, "Middle Class Shrinks Further as More Fall out Instead of Climbing Up," *The New York Times*, **Jan. 25, 2016, http:// tinyurl.com/mubr5at.**
Journalists report that President Obama's most recent proposed budget attempts to extend a hand to middle-income households.

Reports and Studies

"The American Middle Class Is Losing Ground," Pew Research Center, Dec. 9, 2015, http://tinyurl.com/j8lxmzl.
A nonpartisan think tank finds that middle-income Americans are no longer in the majority and the middle class is losing ground financially.

Carnevale, Anthony P., Tamara Jayasundera and Artem Gulish, "Six Million Missing Jobs: The Lingering Pain of the Great Recession," Center on Education and the Workforce, Georgetown University, December 2015, http://tinyurl.com/zhvd5ts.

Researchers conclude that, despite overall economic recovery, the recession of 2007-'09 continues to affect millions of households.

Mishel, Lawrence, Elise Gould and Josh Bivens, "Wage Stagnation in Nine Charts," Economic Policy Institute, Jan. 6, 2015, http://tinyurl.com/zvtrngt.
Researchers at a liberal think tank present data showing that most Americans are not advancing under current economic conditions.

Rose, Stephen, "Beyond the Wage Stagnation Story," Urban Institute, August 2015, http://tinyurl.com/jbxg84j.
A labor economist shows that middle-income wages have increased, though at a lesser rate than for the wealthy.

For More Information

Brookings Institution, 1775 Massachusetts Ave., N.W., Washington, DC 20036; 202-797-6000; www.brookings.edu. Centrist think tank researching income disparities.

Center on Education and the Workforce, Georgetown University, 3300 Whitehaven St., N.W., Suite 3200, Washington, DC 20007; https://cew.georgetown.edu/. Conducts research on the relationship between academic training and career planning.

Manhattan Institute for Policy Research, 52 Vanderbilt Ave., New York, NY 10017; 212-599-7000; www.manhattan-institute.org. Conservative research organization that questions whether the middle class is endangered.

Pew Research Center, 1615 L St., N.W., Washington, DC 20036, 202-419-4300; www.pewresearch.org. Nonpartisan public opinion survey and data-analysis organization studying issues involving the middle class.

Urban Institute, 2100 M St., N.W., Washington, DC 20037; 202-833-7200; www.urban.org. Nonpartisan think tank researching income disparity.

U.S. Bureau of Labor Statistics, 2 Massachusetts Ave., N.E., Washington, DC 20212; 202-691-5200; www.bls.gov. Publishes statistics on earnings.

11

Student Debt

Tom Price

Kristina Michaud, a student at the University of New England College of Osteopathic Medicine, will owe about $150,000 when she finishes her studies. Students with big loan balances usually are seeking graduate degrees, which often lead to high earnings, so they normally can repay their loans. But many undergraduates with lower debt drop out and end up unemployed or in low-paying jobs that make it difficult to pay back their loans.

From *CQ Researcher*,
November 18, 2016.

In seven years and stops at three campuses, Jasmin Johnson has racked up more than $65,000 in student debt, and she's still a year or more away from earning her degree.

She enrolled first at Pine Manor College, a small liberal arts school in Brookline, Mass. Halfway to a degree, she dropped out because she couldn't afford the cost. Next, she entered the University of Massachusetts at Boston but couldn't keep up her studies while working full time to pay her bills. She returned to class this year at Bridgewater State University in Massachusetts while working both a full-time and a part-time job.[1]

There are thousands of working students like Johnson — piling up debt but no degree, despite taking longer than four years to do so. Student debt in the United States has soared to an average of $35,000 for borrowers in the class of 2015. Total student debt this year hit nearly $1.3 trillion — up 350 percent since 2005 — and the ramifications are widespread.[2]

Sixteen percent of student borrowers are more than 361 days late in their loan repayments. Falling behind can leave debtors owing more than they borrowed due to late penalties and accrued interest. Student debt has caused some borrowers to delay buying a house or car or starting a business, and nearly 30 percent of families report feeling stressed by college debt.[3]

Deep concern about student debt — particularly among Millennial voters — thrust the issue into the 2016 presidential campaign. It played a major role in the debate between Democratic hopefuls Hillary Clinton and Bernie Sanders, who both eventually championed free tuition at public colleges. But Republican

College Costs Doubled Since '70s

The cost of tuition, fees and room and board paid by in-state students at private and public four-year institutions more than doubled since the 1971-72 academic year (adjusted for inflation). Costs have risen 12 percent at private universities and 10 percent at public institutions since 2011-12.

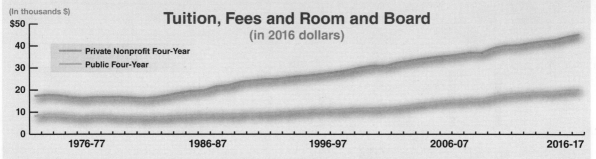

(In thousands $)

Tuition, Fees and Room and Board
(in 2016 dollars)

— Private Nonprofit Four-Year
— Public Four-Year

Source: "Tuition and Fees and Room and Board over Time," College Board, http://tinyurl.com/pg9zc38

Donald Trump's victory in the general election gave more importance to his plan for easing the burden of debt without eliminating tuition, although Trump's proposal runs counter to past GOP positions and may face significant opposition in Congress.

Experts say total student debt has risen in part because more students have attended college in this decade than ever before. In addition, the federal government has expanded eligibility for student loans. While originally loans went only to low-income students and those studying subjects important to national security, now anyone can borrow from the federal government. Many also borrow from private lenders.

Greater numbers of older students, who tend to borrow more than younger students, also are attending college. And students like Johnson who attend college for longer than four years run up more debt. Experts also blame debt-related problems on predatory lenders, unscrupulous debt-collectors and the rapid rise of for-profit colleges, whose students incur more individual debt than those at other types of schools.

But many experts say the biggest cause of rising debt is the steady increase in tuition and fees, which critics variously blame on falling state support for public universities, light faculty workloads and excessive spending on facilities, athletics and administration.

Since the 2007-08 academic year, the average tuition at four-year public universities has risen 28 percent faster than inflation.[4] And during the decade starting in 2004, state per-student support fell by more than 30 percent adjusted for inflation — from $9,529 to $6,505 — according to Sandy Baum, a senior fellow at the Urban Institute think tank in Washington who prepares the College Board's annual study of higher education prices.[5]

"The states are gradually disinvesting from public higher education, and that disinvestment is being shifted to students in the form of larger tuition," says Barmak Nassirian, federal policy director at the American Association of State Colleges and Universities, which represents more than 400 public colleges, universities and higher-education systems.

"State funds that used to be spent on higher education have been gobbled up by tax cuts and spending on health care, for the most part," says Jane Wellman, a policy analyst at the College Futures Foundation, a San Francisco organization that helps low-income Californians go to college, and the founder of the Delta Cost Project, which studies higher education spending.

In 2012, tuition for the first time surpassed state spending in covering public college expenses, according to the U.S. Government Accountability Office.[6] In the 1970s, states paid three-quarters of state colleges' bills; by 2014 states were paying only half, according to the Federal Reserve Bank of Cleveland.[7]

Some analysts say excessive university spending on facilities, athletics and administration is putting upward pressure on tuition rates. For instance, colleges more than doubled the number of administrators between 1987 and 2012, adding 517,636 positions, according to the New England Center for Investigative Reporting and the American Institutes for Research.[8] Administrative salaries also have grown over the years, Baum said.[9] Five public university chief executives earned more than $1 million in 2015, according to a study by *The Chronicle of Higher Education.*[10]

In contrast, full-time faculty members' inflation-adjusted pay has been essentially flat since 1971 — and actually dropped in 14 of those years — according to the American Association of University Professors (AAUP).[11] Overall faculty pay has declined because universities increasingly are hiring lower-paid, part-time teachers, according to Paul Campos a law professor at the University of Colorado, Boulder, who writes a column for the Scripps Howard News Service about political, social and legal issues.[12]

However, all is not doom and gloom. More than 30 percent of recent graduates have no college debt, and most borrowers make their payments on time. "For the vast majority of students, there is no crisis," says Nassirian.

Perhaps counterintuitively, those with the most debt are not the problem. Research shows that big borrowers usually are those obtaining graduate and professional degrees, which tend to lead to high earnings, so they normally can pay off their debt. But many undergraduates with low debt drop out and end up unemployed or in low-paying jobs that make it difficult to pay back their loans.[13]

"The people who get the most education have the lowest levels of default and other measures of financial hardship," says Beth Akers, an economist at the Center on Children and Families at the centrist Brookings Institution think tank in Washington. "That's because education pays off."

And most borrowers manage to repay their loans, Akers says. The median monthly payment is just $193, or 4 percent of borrowers' median monthly income, she says. Jason Delisle, a resident fellow at the conservative American Enterprise Institute think tank in Washington, points out that borrowers with higher debt can cap their payments at 10 percent of their earnings by entering an income-based repayment program.

Scholarships and grants can ease the burden. While tuition and fees at private nonprofit colleges averaged $32,400 in the 2014-15 academic year, students there actually paid less than $15,000 out of pocket after receiving scholarships or grants, said Baum.[14]

Students attending for-profit colleges have the most difficulty managing their debt. Enrollments at such colleges jumped from 111,000 in 1980 to nearly 2 million in 2010 before beginning to decline. And while only 10 to 12 percent of post-secondary students attend such colleges, those students receive a quarter of federal student aid and account for 44 percent of loan defaults, according to A.J. Angulo, an education professor at Winthrop University in Rock Hill, S.C.[15]

Courts and regulatory agencies in recent years have taken action against certain lenders and debt collectors serving student borrowers. In August, for example, Wells Fargo & Co. agreed to pay $3.6 million to settle a Consumer Financial Protection Bureau allegation that the bank illegally processed loan payments in ways that maximized late fees.[16] Collection agencies have paid millions of dollars in fines for harassing student debtors. And last year the federal government said it was canceling contracts with five of 22 collection agencies for "materially inaccurate representations" to borrowers.[17]

Looking at student debt overall, Nassirian says, "If present trends continue, we will get to the crisis point." That's partly because as college costs have risen, average family incomes and the wages working students can earn while enrolled have been relatively stagnant.[18]

And student debt can place a heavier burden on borrowers than other debt. College loans cannot be canceled in bankruptcy except for "undue hardship."[19] Moreover, Social Security payments can be garnished for student loan payments, and debt can follow borrowers to the grave: Lenders can seek reimbursement from a debtor's estate.[20]

As many borrowers struggle to pay off their loans, here are some questions students, graduates, university administrators and government officials are debating:

Should college tuition be free?

Free college tuition — a major point of contention during the Democratic presidential primaries — is unlikely to become federal policy now that Republican Donald Trump has won the presidency and Republicans will continue to control both chambers of Congress. But some advocates will undoubtedly continue the push for free tuition, and Trump has offered a plan designed to ease the burden of student debt.

Most Student Loans Under $50,000

Fewer than one-fifth of the 44 million students who took out loans in 2015 borrowed more than $50,000. Total student loan debt surpassed $1 trillion this year.

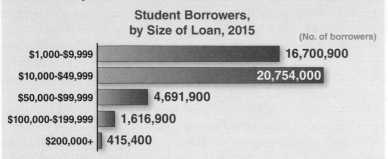

Student Borrowers, by Size of Loan, 2015

(No. of borrowers)

Loan size	Borrowers
$1,000-$9,999	16,700,900
$10,000-$49,999	20,754,000
$50,000-$99,999	4,691,900
$100,000-$199,999	1,616,900
$200,000+	415,400

Source: "2016 Student Loan Update: Distribution of Student Loan Borrowers by Balance," Federal Reserve Bank of New York Consumer Credit Panel, Equifax, http://tinyurl.com/qjqm4dd; "Household Debt and Credit Report: Non-Housing Debt Balance," Federal Reserve Bank of New York, June 30, 2016, http://tinyurl.com/h3tc56b

During their long contest for the Democratic presidential nomination, former Secretary of State Hillary Clinton called the idea of free tuition at public colleges — promoted by her primary opponent, U.S. Sen. Bernie Sanders of Vermont — impractical. But in July, having wrapped up the nomination and won Sanders' endorsement, Clinton released her own plan that would move toward free tuition for in-state students at public colleges.

The aid would have been available immediately for families earning no more than $85,000 a year, a cap that would increase to $125,000 in four years, covering 80 percent of American families.

The federal government would not provide all of the funding. States would help, and students would have been required to contribute by working 10 hours a week. Federal Pell Grants for low-income students would remain available to pay other costs, such as books, fees and room and board. The grants would have been available year-round to help students graduate faster.

Clinton also would have allowed borrowers to save money by refinancing their federal loans at lower interest rates and by cutting interest rates so the government did not collect more from students than it spends administering the loans. Interest rates on new government loans, which have dropped in recent years, now range from

3.76 percent to 6.31 percent, depending on the type of loan. Additional benefits would be offered to borrowers who take public service jobs or otherwise work in the public interest. Repayment for all borrowers could be made as part of federal payroll tax deductions.

The cost of Clinton's plan — estimated at more than $35 billion a year — would be paid by limiting tax deductions for high-income taxpayers and closing Wall Street tax "loopholes," she said.[21]

Sanders argued for free tuition because, he said, "a college degree is the new high school diploma. . . . If our economy is to be strong, we need the best-educated workforce in the world." Some states, including California and New York, offered nearly free tuition in the past, he noted, and public colleges in numerous countries — including Germany, Finland, Denmark, Ireland, Iceland, Norway, Sweden and Mexico — charge no tuition. Germans even provide free tuition for international students, he added.[22]

Trump opposed free tuition. Instead, he proposed easing the burden of student debt by capping monthly repayments at 12.5 percent of a borrower's earnings and forgiving the unpaid balance after 15 years.

Free tuition still has supporters, especially on college campuses. Sara Goldrick-Rab, a professor of higher education policy and sociology at Temple University who studies college affordability, argued that free tuition for all would be better for low- and middle-income students than means-tested aid, which is based on a student's or the student's family's income and wealth. Means-tested aid involves a "massive bureaucracy" that "leaves out both the very poorest, who cannot navigate the system, and squeezes the middle class," who would then be offered only loans, she said.[23]

Some critics challenge the push to get more students to go to college, disputing the notion that a college degree today is the equivalent of a high school degree in the past. "Most jobs — 69 percent in 2010, estimates the Labor Department — don't require a post-high-school degree," wrote nationally syndicated economics columnist Robert Samuelson. "They're truck drivers, store clerks, some technicians."[24]

Others question the practicality of free-tuition proposals. "I don't think the federal government can make college free," says University of Pennsylvania education professor Joni Finney. The state-by-state differences in public-college tuition would require vastly different federal contributions to each state, which would be politically problematic, she says.

Even before Republicans gained control of the White House and retained their congressional majorities on Nov. 8, college-finance experts predicted that Republican leaders in the states would block the kind of federal-state partnership that free-tuition advocates propose. Kevin Carey, director of the education policy program at the centrist New America think tank in Washington, noted that most GOP-run states refused to implement provisions in the Affordable Care Act, a health insurance program that offers federal funding for states to expand Medicaid and establish insurance marketplaces.[25]

A spokesman for Wisconsin Gov. Scott Walker, for instance, said the Republican governor would not buy into Clinton's plan because it would be costly and ineffective.[26] He said it would "put more money into the university system without addressing the very legitimate question about why is tuition going up so much?" Walker has called on the state's colleges to increase professors' teaching workload.[27]

Some criticized Clinton's plan for offering aid to families with six-digit incomes. "Every dollar used to keep tuition low for families who can afford to pay is a dollar that could be used to reduce the living costs or provide other support for students for whom free tuition is not enough," Akers, of the Brookings Institution, says. "It creates large transfers of wealth to people who probably need it the least."

Others warn of unintended consequences. The Georgetown University Center on Education and the Workforce projected that free tuition at public institutions would increase enrollment by between 9 percent and 22 percent. While some enrollees would not have attended college in the past, the center said, others would transfer from private nonprofit schools, cutting attendance at small colleges by between 7 percent and 15 percent. Prestigious private institutions such as the Ivy League schools would not be affected, the study concluded.[28]

Free tuition at public institutions would kill off the weaker, private, unendowed colleges, said Kent John Chabotar, former president of Guilford College, a small liberal-arts school in Greensboro, N.C.[29]

But some experts question how many additional students public colleges would be willing or able to accept. "We assume that selective public institutions will not increase capacity, or will increase it very little," the Georgetown Center on Education's report said. Similarly, many midranked public schools might become more selective rather than expand enrollments significantly, added Anthony Carnevale, director of the Georgetown center.[30]

Donald Hossler, a senior scholar at the Center for Enrollment, Research, Policy, and Practice at the University of Southern California's School of Education, said states probably would not increase spending enough to enable much expansion.[31] As a result, gaining admission to the best public colleges would be even harder, according to the Georgetown study. Less-prepared students, who often are less affluent, would be relegated to lower-tier schools, he said, which would increase inequality, the study concluded.[32]

Do government subsidies contribute to rising tuition?

Some critics contend that increasing government aid to both students and colleges encourages universities to raise their rates because students do not feel the financial pain of the higher tuition.

It's a theory called the "Bennett Hypothesis" after William Bennett, a former secretary of Education and a conservative leader on education issues. While serving as President Ronald Reagan's Education secretary, Bennett wrote in 1987 that federal aid enables colleges "blithely to raise their tuitions, confident that federal loan subsidies would help cushion the increase."[33]

Likewise, free tuition "would encourage every state college to raise its tuition," says the University of Pennsylvania's Finney. "Why not get as much from the federal government as you can?"

"As it did in the housing market," said Veronique de Rugy, a senior research fellow at George Mason University's conservative-leaning Mercatus Center, "free or reduced-price money has artificially inflated the price of a college education."[34] The concurrent increases create

Students at Washington University in St. Louis pull a mock ball and chain representing the nearly $1.3 trillion in outstanding U.S. student debt. Free college tuition — endorsed by Democratic presidential nominee Hillary Clinton — is unlikely to become federal policy now that Republican Donald Trump has won the presidency and Republicans continue to control both chambers of Congress. But Trump has offered a plan designed to ease the burden of student debt.

"a classic upward price spiral," she added. "Subsidies raise prices, leading to higher subsidies, which raise prices even more."[35]

Government aid also contributes to tuition increases by reducing pressure for colleges to contain spending, some critics say. "If you make tuition free, it completely eliminates the incentive to look at the cost side of the equation," says Rick Staisloff, an Annapolis, Md.,-based consultant to educational and other nonprofit institutions whose expertise includes cost containment. "Higher education has not shown a willingness on its own to change the model" of recurring price increases.

Both colleges and students need to have "some skin in the game" or they won't care enough about the cost and quality of education, says Delisle of the American Enterprise Institute. Without economic pressures, "it really lets them off the hook," he says.

Such critics found support in a New York Federal Reserve Bank study published last year and updated this year. Bank researchers compared institutions' price increases with their students' use of grants and loans. As the size of subsidized loans increased, colleges hiked tuition by about 60 percent of the loans' higher value, the bank reported. The researchers found smaller tuition hikes connected to the rising number of Pell Grants and unsubsidized loans. The effects were strongest at opposite ends of the college spectrum — at expensive schools, private schools, two-year colleges and vocational programs.[36]

Others, however, say the situation is more complex than these critics of federal aid believe. "I would concede that federal money has accommodated price increases," says Nassirian of the American Association of State Colleges and Universities. "I just don't think causality is related to the federal money. It created a path of least resistance for some price increases but has not caused them."

The Urban Institute's Baum said empirical evidence shows that "federal grant aid does not explain much about rising prices," except at for-profit schools.[37] For the most part, increased federal aid and tuition simply replaced lower state support at public colleges, said Peter McPherson, president of the Association of Public and Land-Grant Universities.[38]

Gary Fethke, a professor of management science and economics at the University of Iowa, argued in *The Chronicle of Higher Education* in 2012 that with thousands of higher education institutions vying for students, competition helps to keep prices down. "If there were a monopoly provider of education services, it could respond to a government grant per student by increasing the sticker price," he said. "Tuition revenue must rise in response to a reduction in taxpayer support to sustain base-level expenditures." And, he added, because federal subsidies can mitigate state cuts somewhat, they actually "make possible more-modest tuition increases than would otherwise be the case."[39]

Donald Heller, provost and an education professor at the University of San Francisco who reviewed research into the impact of federal aid on tuition, found the studies "ambiguous at best." Some found correlation, while others — even within the same institution — did not.[40] For example, while the recent study by the New York Fed tied aid to tuition increases, other researchers at the Fed in 2012 placed the blame on declining state and local government support.[41]

It's difficult to identify a single cause of price hikes because "higher education institutions are complex, often multibillion-dollar institutions, and numerous factors go into the setting of tuition prices," according to Heller.

Researchers cited factors other than declining state support, he wrote, including the fact that higher education is labor-intensive, with highly skilled and highly compensated employees. Colleges have "complex missions of teaching, research and service" that are difficult to measure and therefore resistant to cost controls.[42]

Are schools doing enough to hold down costs?

Robert Morin worked as a cataloger at the University of New Hampshire's Dimond Library for some 50 years, lived frugally, saved his earnings and died last year with a fortune, $4 million, which he willed to his employer. The university announced in September that $100,000 of the bequest would go to the library — but $1 million would be used to install a video scoreboard in the school's football stadium.[43]

The announcement offers an example of what many critics cite as misplaced priorities that help drive up college charges: expensive athletics programs that receive substantial university subsidies, construction of plush facilities, inefficient use of campus buildings, bloated administrative costs and faculty who don't teach enough.

These critics say schools are engaged in a sports-related "arms race" that drives college spending ever higher. For instance, among universities in the National Collegiate Athletic Association's (NCAA) Football Bowl Subdivision — the top level of football competition — inflation-adjusted football spending per scholarship player jumped 55 percent from 2005 to 2014, according to the Knight Commission on Intercollegiate Athletics. Per-athlete spending on all athletics rose 43 percent, adjusted for inflation, said the commission, which advocates for college sports reform. Meanwhile, academic spending per full-time student at those institutions rose by only 9 percent.[44]

"The Power Five conferences [the wealthiest college sports leagues] are renegotiating television deals, and most of them now have their own TV networks," says Amy Perko, the Knight Commission's executive

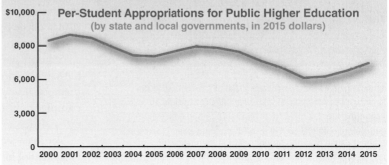

Funding Down for Higher Education

Per-student spending by state and local governments on public higher education fell 20 percent between 2001 and 2015 (adjusted for inflation). The decline has contributed to higher tuition costs, which are partially responsible for rising student debt.

Per-Student Appropriations for Public Higher Education
(by state and local governments, in 2015 dollars)

Source: Urban Institute

director. By selling the rights for networks to show their football games, these schools "are bringing in more revenues than ever before. They're also spending more than ever before" on such things as expensive athletic facilities and high salaries for coaches. (The highest-paid college football coach in 2016 is Jim Harbaugh of the University of Michigan, who makes $9 million in salary and bonuses.[45])

Despite the huge revenues generated by football and basketball television contracts, just 24 athletics programs — all in Power Five conferences — are self-supporting. As a result — at the highest level of competition — university per athlete funds spent on athletics soared 98 percent from 2005 to 2014.[46]

Colleges that don't have access to the same media revenues as schools in the Power Five conferences "in some ways are still trying to keep up with those market leaders" on the playing field, Perko says, creating high institutional subsidies for athletics.

Eastern Michigan University accounting professor Howard Bunsis says that's the case in the Mid American Conference, where Eastern Michigan plays. "I'm a huge sports fan," he says. "It does bring a certain energy to campus, but not at this cost."

Athletic spending at his university increased by nearly two-thirds, from $20 million in 2005 to more than $33 million in 2015, according to a 2016 report Bunsis helped to prepare. But athletic income — from such sources as

Athletic trophies shimmer in the Hall of Champions at the University of Alabama. Opulent facilities at big-time athletic programs are designed to attract recruits and entice alumni to generously support sports programs. Many experts say the biggest cause of rising student debt is the steady increase in tuition and fees, which critics variously blame on falling state support for public universities, light faculty workloads and excessive spending on facilities, athletics and administration.

ticket sales and shared NCAA revenues — dropped from $10 million to $7 million. Increased university subsidies covered the difference.[47]

Critics of university spending also complain about expensive construction projects elsewhere on campus, such as luxury student residences, recreation centers and college presidents' homes.

Conservative commentator Charlie Sykes cited "Taj-Mahal-like facilities," such as Purdue University's $98 million Cordova Recreational Sports Center, which is available for use by all students and features a climbing wall, a vortex pool and a 25-person spa.[48] Experts say schools are responding to the demands of affluent students whose families can afford full tuition and who might become generous donors in the future.

Yale University spent $17 million to upgrade its president's house, and Columbia spent $20 million.[49] University officials say such expenditures are justified because college presidents use their homes for entertaining VIPs and for fundraising.[50]

Whatever their cost, critics say, college facilities tend to be used inefficiently, especially during evenings, weekends and summer. On average, says consultant Staisloff, university facilities sit idle about 70 percent of the time. About $1 billion in facilities at George Washington University go unused for at least a third of the year

because of the traditional academic calendar, said university President Emeritus Stephen Trachtenberg. Thousands of additional students could be enrolled if the facilities were used year-round, he said.[51]

Many faculty — including Bunsis, who heads the school's American Association of University Professors chapter — say "administrative bloat" is a major cause of rising college costs. But others say that oversimplifies the situation.

Staisloff points out that nonfaculty employees work in many essential areas, such as information technology, financial aid and health services. And while some faculty complain about the high number of administrators, other critics say faculty don't work enough hours.

For instance, David Levy, a former chancellor of the New School in New York City, says that while professors at research universities often work long hours because of their research projects, professors at nonresearch schools often work just over one-third as much as other professionals, due to light teaching loads and long summer breaks.

But Michael S. Harris, an associate professor of higher education and director of the Center for Teaching Excellence at Southern Methodist University in Dallas, said faculty workloads are equivalent to other professionals' because "preparation, grading, meeting with students and student correspondence take far more time than the actual hours of instruction."[52]

One report, based on a national survey of 687 faculty members, found that teachers were working 51.4 hours a week when classes were in session and 45.1 at other times.[53] In addition, says Nassirian, of the American Association of State Colleges and Universities, "highly paid research faculty — and there aren't that many people like that — are actually pulling money into the university because they have grant funding from the outside."

At Eastern Michigan University, Bunsis says, "we teach four classes a term, advise students and keep up a research agenda, and that is a 50- to 60-hour-a-week commitment."

Schools are cutting faculty costs by hiring low-paid part-timers, many without benefits, who now teach more than half of all credit hours, says Wellman of the College Futures Foundation. Part-time teachers — called adjunct faculty — on average earn just $16,718 annually per employer and often cobble together several jobs to increase their earnings, according to a survey by the American Association of University Professors.[54]

BACKGROUND
Federal Involvement

Until the mid-19th century, higher education in America was primarily a private affair, although a number of states had established public colleges. The first federal support came in the Morrill Act of 1862, which granted the states more than 100 million acres of federal land to be sold to establish and operate public "land-grant" colleges and universities.

Eight decades later, the federal government began providing financial support to higher-education students through the Servicemen's Readjustment Act, better known as the GI Bill, which offered educational grants and living-expense stipends to World War II veterans.[55] And many jumped at the opportunity: From 1939, before the war, to 1947, two years after its end, college attendance soared by more than 50 percent, from 1.5 million to 2.3 million.[56]

In the 1950s, the Soviet Union launched *Sputnik* — the first satellite to orbit Earth — raising concern about U.S. science education and spurring establishment of the first federal student loans. Authorized by the National Defense Education Act of 1958, the subsidized loans were intended to make the United States more competitive scientifically with the Soviets and to enhance U.S. national defense and diplomacy. They were made available to undergraduate and graduate students who were studying science, engineering and some foreign languages.

President Lyndon B. Johnson's Great Society initiatives greatly expanded federal support for college students. "This nation could never rest," he said, "while the door to knowledge remained closed to any American." The Higher Education Act of 1965 authorized private banks to make government-guaranteed loans available to low- and moderate-income students without regard to their field of study. The government paid the interest on the loans while the low-income students were enrolled in classes, but did not provide a subsidy for moderate-income students.[57]

Seven years later, the federal government began offering grants —- named after the sponsor Democratic Sen. Claiborne Pell of Rhode Island — to students with financial need. Soon a majority of high school graduates were entering college, with the federal government providing grants to a third of full-time undergraduates and loans to nearly half.[58] That same year, Congress established the Student Loan Marketing Association, known as Sallie Mae, a quasi-governmental organization that bought loans from banks so the banks could make more loans.[59]

In 1978, Congress made guaranteed loans available for students at all income levels, and in 1980 the government began guaranteeing loans to parents. The government guaranteed to repay lenders if borrowers defaulted. Government employees serviced and collected the student and parent loans until the 1980s. Then Republican Ronald Reagan's administration began transferring those tasks to private companies. Eventually, private contractors were doing all of that work.

In 1993, with Democrats controlling Congress and the White House, the government created direct federal loans to compete with private lending and allowed lower-income students to make repayments tied to their earnings. Democrats argued that the government saved money by cutting out the middleman and the need for profit.

Two years later Republicans took control of both congressional chambers, however, and moved to eliminate direct federal loans and to privatize Sallie Mae. Championing free enterprise, they argued that banks and other private lenders would do a better job than the government and that Sallie Mae would function more effectively as a private business.

Eventually, in a compromise, Republicans allowed the direct-loan program to continue, and Democrats agreed to privatize Sallie Mae and permit it to lend directly to students. Republican Rep. Howard "Buck" McKeon of California — who later became chairman of the House Education Committee, said privatization was "paving the way to the future of a smaller, less intrusive government."[60]

Student Loan Scandals

Republicans and Democrats continued to battle over the proper balance between government and private lending after Clinton left office.

During Republican George W. Bush's administration, the federal direct loan program shrank, and the now-private Sallie Mae became the country's biggest lender of student loans. The company also came under investigation for alleged improprieties, such as placing its employees in university call centers to speak with students, who thought they were talking with college loan officers, and paying for trips by university financial aid officers.[61]

In 2007, college officials were charged with steering students to preferred private lenders in exchange for kickbacks to officials or their colleges. Several college financial aid officers resigned, and universities and lenders — including Citibank and Sallie Mae — paid financial penalties and agreed to alter their behavior. Sallie Mae agreed to keep its employees out of college financial aid offices and to stop paying the travel expenses of financial aid officers' or for the officers to serve on Sallie Mae advisory boards.[62]

The same year, the newly Democratic-controlled Congress established a loan-forgiveness program for graduates working in public service jobs, and forgave loans by all borrowers after 25 years. Congress also expanded availability of income-based repayment, which limited monthly payments to 15 percent of a borrower's earnings.

In 2010, with President Obama in the White House and his fellow Democrats still running Congress, lawmakers adopted (effective in 2014) legislation to lower income-based payments to 10 percent of earnings and offered debt forgiveness after 20 years. Arguing that removing the profit motive would produce loans more favorable to borrowers, Congress also replaced guaranteed private loans with direct federal lending. Lenders still can make private loans, but without government support.

In 2014, Obama bypassed the then-Republican Congress and issued an executive order to provide loan forgiveness after 10 years for borrowers doing public-service work.[63]

Congress had begun tightening repayment requirements in 1976 by decreeing that bankruptcy courts couldn't discharge education loans for five years after graduation. That period later was lengthened to seven years and then escaping student loans through bankruptcy was made almost impossible in 2005.

When Congress considered easing the requirements in 2009, J. Douglas Cuthbertson — then a lawyer for a trade association of lenders — testified that strict repayment provisions were essential for a healthy student loan program. Borrowers who could easily default on their loans would "enjoy the benefits of their education" and then go into bankruptcy "without ever attempting to repay," he said. That would effectively change the loan into a scholarship and cause lenders to abandon the market, he said.

A scholar of student loans and bankruptcy disputed Cuthbertson's argument. Congress stiffened the requirements because of "perceived abuse of the bankruptcy system, as opposed to any real abuse," said Rafael Pardo, who then was an associate law professor at Seattle University and now is a law professor at Emory University in Atlanta. Cuthbertson then admitted that he didn't have empirical data to support his warnings about abuse.[64]

Rise of For-Profits

For-profit schools — which account for a disproportionate amount of student loan problems — have been around since the country's earliest days, addressing a need for practical training that traditional public and nonprofit institutions often did not offer. Throughout their history, they have been praised for serving students who were ignored by traditional schools and criticized for cheating students by offering subpar education at inflated prices.

Early American colleges provided classical education and looked down upon practical training. That left an opening for for-profit schools to focus on such subjects as surveying, navigation, bookkeeping and even law and medicine. They suffered as traditional institutions eventually began creating curriculums in medicine, law and other professions. But for-profits continued to function by teaching such skills as barbering, cosmetology and stenography.

World War II spurred a jump in the number of for-profit schools — first training workers needed by wartime industries, then admitting returning veterans flush with the GI Bill's education benefits. Another growth spurt followed the 1972 amendments to the Higher Education Act, which made students at for-profit colleges eligible for federal education assistance. Previously such aid could be used only at public and nonprofit institutions.[65]

Enrollment in degree-granting for-profit schools soared between 1980 and 2010, before beginning to decline, but the percentage of their students who

CHRONOLOGY

1944-1976 *Federal government begins offering aid to college students.*

1944 GI Bill grants to World War II veterans spurs college attendance.

1958 Shaken by the 1957 Soviet Union launch of the *Sputnik* satellite, Congress covers 90 percent of the costs of colleges making low-interest loans to students in fields deemed essential to national defense.

1965 Federally guaranteed private loans are made available to low- and moderate-income students. . . . Federal government pays the interest for low-income students until they leave school. . . . Federal employees handle debt collection. . . . More than half of high school graduates now attend post-secondary schools.

1972 Pell Grants are created for needy students. . . . Student Loan Marketing Association (Sallie Mae) is established to purchase loans from lenders so they can make more loans.

1976 Congress bans cancellation of student loans durring bankruptcy proceedings until five years after graduation.

1978-2005 *Federal government expands eligibility for loans and grants.*

1978 All students become eligible for private loans guaranteed by the federal government.

1980 Parents can obtain guaranteed loans for their children.

1981 Republican Ronald Reagan's administration begins to transfer debt collection from the Education Department to private contractors.

1993 Federal government begins lending to students in competition with private lenders. . . . Lower-income students become eligible for repayment plans tied to their earnings.

1997 Sallie Mae starts evolving into a private business that lends directly to students. . . . Middle-class families are allowed to receive tuition tax credits, tax deductions for student loan interest and tax-free college savings

accounts. . . . Two-thirds of high school graduates attend post-secondary educational institutions, the highest proportion ever.

2005 Congress makes student loans almost impossible to escape through bankruptcy.

2007-Present *Scandal rocks private lenders, and federal government moves into direct-lending business.*

2007 Lender-to-college kickbacks and other scandals lead to agreements by Sallie Mae and other lenders to pay financial penalties and end unethical practices. . . . Loan forgiveness is offered to low-income borrowers in public service jobs who have made payments for 10 years and to others who have made payments for 25 years. . . . More borrowers can have repayments tied to their earnings.

2010 Federal government stops guaranteeing private loans.

2012 Tuition for the first time exceeds state aid as a funding source for public colleges.

2014 Borrowers can make repayments at just 10 percent of their earnings, with forgiveness after 20 years. . . . All public service workers get loan forgiveness after 10 years.

2015 Congress rejects President Obama's proposed federal-state program to provide free tuition at two-year community colleges. . . . Sen. Bernie Sanders of Vermont makes free college tuition a key issue in his campaign for the 2016 Democratic presidential nomination. . . . Former Secretary of State Hillary Clinton, Sanders' chief rival, proposes giving federal funds to state colleges that lower tuition so students don't need to borrow.

2016 Total student debt reaches $1.26 billion. Clinton joins Sanders in proposing free college tuition. . . . Obama instructs Labor Department to give community colleges $100 million for education, training and free-tuition programs. . . . Administration moves some debt collection from private companies to federal agencies. . . . Cost of attending public universities has risen 28 percent above inflation since 2007-08 school year. . . . Then-GOP-candidate Donald Trump proposes capping monthly student debt repayments at 12.5 percent of a borrower's earnings and forgiving the unpaid balance after 15 years.

Some Reformers Hail Europe as a Model

But critics say free tuition isn't really free.

Many American education reformers look enviously at Ireland, Sweden, Germany and other European countries that offer free tuition to their citizens — and even to international students who enroll there. They also look longingly at Australia and its handling of student loan payments, where repayment is tied to the borrower's income.

But American critics say "free" tuition comes at a cost: European countries hold down the government's free tuition costs by limiting college admission. What's more, foreign schools are Spartan compared with their American counterparts, offering fewer extracurricular activities and other amenities.

Some research indicates that free tuition can lead students to discount the value of education and not work as hard to succeed at it. "European studies have found that students who pay more in tuition exert greater effort and are more likely to graduate on time," said Chenny Ng, an education policy researcher at Northwestern University.[1] Germany also found that free tuition led students to extend their time in college, with some becoming "eternal students."[2]

The policy remains extremely popular, however. When Germany's high court in 2005 overturned a national law banning tuition, for example, 10 states began assessing students about 500 euros a semester, which would be about $545 today. By the end of 2014, public protest had caused all the assessments to be repealed.[3]

Free tuition in Europe is certainly popular with American and British students, thousands of whom study in continental Europe each year to avoid higher costs at universities in their own countries. With more than 300 European colleges teaching courses in English, U.S. and U.K. students are even attracted to schools that charge tuition, because most cost less than $2,225 a year.[4]

Tuition is free or nominal in some countries because national and state governments pay most of the costs. But European educational institutions — including those that charge tuition — tend to be more bare-boned than in the United States, with more basic campus facilities and few intercollegiate sports, recreational facilities or extracurricular activities.[5]

European students spend little time on campus when not studying because "there is not a lot to do other than classes," said Mirjam Milsch, a German who studied at the New Jersey Institute of Technology and at Fachhochschule Hannover in Germany.[6]

And free tuition, ironically, is no panacea for students wanting to avoid debt, according to the international Organisation for Economic Co-operation and Development (OECD) in Paris. European students borrow to pay for such things as books, supplies, food and housing. Because borrowers repay only a small amount each month, they may take 20 to 30 years to retire the debt, and they don't tend to default.[7]

Cultural reasons help explain why European students borrow. For instance, in Sweden, college students are considered self-supporting adults so their parents are not expected to help pay for their higher education. One study found that only 2 percent of Swedish men were still living with their parents at home after age 30, compared with a quarter in Spain and a third in Italy.[8]

In addition, the cost of living in Sweden is high. As a result, at least seven in 10 Swedish students borrow to pay for schooling, and they accumulate an average debt of about $20,000.[9]

Australia was a pioneer in tying loan repayments to borrowers' incomes, a practice later adopted in the United Kingdom and New Zealand.

"One great benefit of the Australian system is simplicity," said Andrew Norton, higher-education program director of the Grattan Institute, an Australian think tank.[10]

The country has one repayment system, and payments are collected along with taxes, usually as a paycheck deduction. But Australian students can borrow only for education costs, not living expenses, and debt is not forgiven until death. However, repayment doesn't begin until borrowers are earning the equivalent of about $41,500 in U.S. dollars, and then they pay 4 percent of their annual earnings.

The Grattan Institute says the system has one significant flaw: It provides benefits to affluent families that don't need the assistance. For instance, Norton said, many Australian women drop out of the workforce to raise children and often return to take part-time jobs with wages below the repayment threshold. As a result, they can avoid repayment for a substantial period, even if married to a high-income spouse. Denying forgiveness to larger estates would help prevent that, the institute said.[11]

European countries hold down government costs for free tuition by limiting admissions at their higher education institutions. Germany, for instance, begins placing pupils in educational "tracks" by age 10: the Gymnasium (the most advanced school) for academic careers; the Realschule (a secondary school) for other white-collar jobs; and the Hauptschule (a general school) for learning a trade.[12]

In contrast, says Barmak Nassirian, federal policy director at the American Association of State Colleges and Universities in Washington, the United States is "the world leader in access to higher education. Nobody else admits as large a portion of the population."

"We want more people and more kinds of people" to go to college, says Rick Staisloff, a consultant in Annapolis, Md., to educational and other nonprofit institutions who opposes federally supported free tuition because, he says, it would relieve pressure on colleges to control costs.

While a larger proportion of Americans than Europeans may be admitted to postsecondary schools, a bigger percentage of Irish and Norwegian students graduate, according to an OECD report this year. Among Americans ages 25 to 34, the report said, 46.5 percent had earned a postsecondary degree, compared with 52 percent in Ireland and 48.1 percent in Norway. The United States was substantially ahead of Germany's 29.6 percent, marginally ahead of Sweden and Denmark and about 6 percentage points better than Finland and Iceland.

The OECD figures count all postsecondary education, including vocational programs leading to blue-collar jobs.[13]

— *Tom Price*

Ulrich Baumgarten via Getty Images

A student studies at the Free University of Berlin. Germany and several other European countries offer free tuition to citizens — and even to international students.

Samantha North, "British students ditch costly UK for free education in Europe," *The Telegraph*, Jan. 29, 2015, http://tinyurl.com/jlwh2ez; Katie Lobosco, "Americans are moving to Europe for free college degrees," CNN Money, Feb. 23, 2016, http://tinyurl.com/zqzkjgx.

[5] Karin Klein, " 'Free' college in Europe isn't that great a deal," *The Sacramento Bee*, June 27, 2016, http://tinyurl.com/j8ooysj.

[6] Mirjam Milsch, "Contrast College Life in the U.S. Against a Home Country," *U.S. News & World Report*, Aug. 14, 2014, http://tinyurl.com/zac44xb.

[7] Susan Dynarski, "America Can Fix Its Student Loan Crisis. Ask Australia," *The New York Times*, July 9, 2016, http://tinyurl.com/hn46vu4.

[8] Matt Phillips, "The High Price of a Free College Education in Sweden," *The Atlantic*, May 31, 2013, http://tinyurl.com/hlzd2um.

[9] Susan Dynarski, "Why Small Student Debt Can Mean Big Problems," *The New York Times*, Sept. 1, 2015, http://tinyurl.com/o67nsfa.

[10] Beckie Supiano, "What America Can Learn From Australia's Student-Loan System," *The Chronicle of Higher Education*, Jan. 5, 2016, http://tinyurl.com/gnh25q2.

[11] *Ibid.*; Dynarski, "America Can Fix Its Student Loan Crisis," *op. cit.*

[12] Isabelle de Pommereau, "Global education lessons: Germany's respected voc-tech path with Meisters," *The Christian Science Monitor*, Sept. 1, 2013, http://tinyurl.com/kdnzhxt.

[13] "Population with tertiary education," Organisation for Economic Co-operation and Development, 2016, http://tinyurl.com/j5penpc.

[1] Chenny Ng, "Free tuition won't help students," *The Washington Post*, Nov. 13, 2015, http://tinyurl.com/hhl2ppg.

[2] Charles Lane, "College doesn't need to be free," *The Washington Post*, May 21, 2015, http://tinyurl.com/zetauvn.

[3] Sonali Kohli, "The price of free education," *Los Angeles Times*, Nov. 4, 2015, http://tinyurl.com/27dkhbv.

[4] Bernie Sanders, "Make college free for all," *The Washington Post*, Oct. 22, 2015, http://tinyurl.com/zqkjw8w; Cathaleen Chen, "Free college in Europe: An attractive option, but not for everyone," *The Christian Science Monitor*, Feb. 23, 2016, http://tinyurl.com/hakw8ge; and

How College Loans Work

Most are provided by the federal government.

Students and parents face a bewildering array of options when shopping for loans to finance postsecondary education.[1] Potential lenders include federal and state governments as well as banks, credit unions, other private lending companies and schools themselves.

More than 90 percent of outstanding student debt is for federal loans, which are available in a variety of programs and repayment plans, some of which are subsidized.[2] For instance:

- **Perkins Loans** provide up to $5,500 a year for undergraduates ($8,000 for graduate students) from low-income families at 5 percent interest. Colleges administer the loans from a revolving fund replenished by borrowers' repayments and federal support, so the number of such loans available on a campus depends on the balance in a school's fund.
- **Direct Subsidized Loans** are available to undergraduate students with financial need. The loans do not accrue interest — currently at 3.76 percent — until the student leaves school. The annual maximum loan amount varies: $3,500 for freshmen, $4,500 for sophomores and $5,500 for juniors and seniors.
- **Direct Unsubsidized Loans** provide between $5,500 and $20,500 to undergraduate and graduate students, depending on the level of study and whether borrowers are dependent on their parents. Interest is currently 3.76 percent for undergraduates and 5.31 percent for graduate students.

- **Direct PLUS Loans** are available to graduate students and parents of undergrads, currently at 6.31 percent interest. The maximum loan amount depends on the cost of attending the school.

Federal loans offer benefits usually not provided by private lenders. Borrowers don't start repaying the loans until they leave school or fail to carry at least a half-time course load. The government does not conduct credit checks, except for PLUS loans, and a student usually does not need a co-signer to guarantee the loan's repayment. The government will temporarily postpone or lower payments if a borrower has financial hardship.

In addition, federal loans can be forgiven if a school defrauds a borrower, if the borrower dies or is disabled or if a school closes and students cannot transfer their credits — a problem faced by many students who attended shoddy for-profit institutions.[3]

Some or all of a federal loan also can be forgiven if the borrower takes a public-service job.

For instance, a direct loan borrower can get up to $17,500 forgiven after teaching in a low-income school for five straight years. The remaining debt can be forgiven after a borrower makes repayments and works for 10 years in a combination of any government job, any 501 (c)(3) non-profit organization, AmeriCorps, Peace Corps and any non-profit that provides services to the military, emergency management, public safety, law enforcement, public interest law, early childhood education, public health, public education, public libraries, the disabled and the elderly.

borrowed money to pay for the courses rose, from 61.3 percent in the 1995-96 academic year to almost all — 92 percent — in 2007-08.[66] The growth was boosted by the Reagan administration's promotion of privatization in the 1980s, the increasing availability of education aid and aggressive marketing that later caused legal problems for many of the schools.[67]

Some schools ran misleading advertising that claimed to place high percentages of graduates into good jobs. Some sent recruiters to unemployment and welfare lines

to sign up students who would qualify for aid but wouldn't necessarily do well in class. Some had recruiters canvass door-to-door in low-income neighborhoods to seek similar potential enrollees. Many of the recruiters were paid on commission, a violation of federal law. A study of 30 for-profit schools found that they spent an average 17 percent of their revenues on instruction and 23 percent on marketing.

The parent company of the University of Phoenix — the nation's largest for-profit university — paid a $10

Borrowers with multiple federal loans can consolidate them into one to simplify repayment and lower monthly payments by stretching them over up to 30 years. If the loans have different interest rates, they will be averaged to create a new rate.

Borrowers also can choose among income-based repayment plans, which require payments of 10 to 20 percent of the borrower's adjusted gross income above the poverty rate, which for the contiguous 48 states currently is $11,880 annually for an individual, plus about $4,100 for each additional family member. The remaining balance is forgiven after 20 to 25 years, depending on the plan. Borrowers must recertify their income and family size each year. Critics say some borrowers don't enter income-based plans because they think the plans are too complicated.

Except for Perkins loans, interest rates are calculated each July 1 for loans to be made during the following 12 months. The rate is based on the spring rates for the 10-year Treasury note, increased by varying amounts depending on the loan type. The rate then is fixed for the life of the loan.[4] Those borrowers also pay an origination fee — about 1 percent on Direct Loans and about 4.25 percent on PLUS loans. Because of generally lower interest rates and opportunities for lowering monthly payments and having outstanding balances forgiven, most borrowers find federal loans more appealing than those offered by banks or other private-sector lenders. But the federal government restricts how much students and parents can borrow, so private lenders often fill in the gaps.

Interest rates and loan terms vary among private lenders. A study this year by Credible, an online lending marketplace, determined that the average rates at private lenders were 5.37 percent for undergraduates with a co-signer and 7.46 percent for those who did not have a co-signer. Graduate students with a co-signer paid 4.59 percent, while those without paid 6.21.

According to MeasureOne, a market-research and consulting firm, 94 percent of new private undergraduate loans during the 2015-16 academic year had a co-signer, as did 61 percent of loans to graduate students.[5]

Some states offer their own loan programs. For instance, New Jersey — the state with the largest program, with about $2 billion in outstanding loans — has been criticized for its aggressive repayment policies. The program charges higher interest than the federal government and commands repayment by garnishing wages, canceling state income tax refunds, revoking professional licenses and confiscating lottery winnings, all without obtaining court orders. Death does not end demands for repayment from the borrower's estate or from co-signers.

In contrast, Massachusetts — with the second-largest loan portfolio, $1.3 billion — forgives the debt if a borrower becomes disabled or dies. Rather than offering its own loans, Pennsylvania services federal loans provided to its residents.[6]

— *Tom Price*

[1] Unless otherwise noted, information in this section came from "Federal student loans for college or career school are an investment in your future," U.S. Department of Education, http://tinyurl.com/hpb33dj.

[2] Tara Siegel Bernard, "The Many Pitfalls of Private Student Loans," *The New York Times*, Sept. 5, 2015, http://tinyurl.com/ndsuuuf.

[3] For background, see Barbara Mantel, "Career Colleges," *CQ Researcher*, Jan. 7, 2011, pp. 1-24.

[4] Ann Carrns, "Rates on Federal Student Loans Are Falling for This Year," *The New York Times*, June 25, 2016, http://tinyurl.com/zt3td3k.

[5] Ron Lieber, "Co-Signing for a Student? Think First About Yourself," *The New York Times*, Aug. 13, 2016, http://tinyurl.com/zjtmlhd.

[6] Annie Waldman, "Even Death Is No Reprieve From a Student's Debt," *The New York Times*, July 4, 2016, http://tinyurl.com/nu35ujd.

million fine in 2004 for paying commissions. Career Education Corp. in 2013 agreed to a $10 million settlement for publishing greatly inflated placement rates.[68]

The Department of Education announced in September that it would stop recognizing accreditation of for-profit colleges by the Accrediting Council for Independent Colleges and Schools. The council had routinely approved schools that government agencies charged with fraud and mismanagement, the department said. The council is appealing the decision.[69]

Many of the schools' students were the first from lower-income families to seek higher education and did not thoroughly understand what they should expect from the schools and what obligations they were accepting when obtaining loans. Many also held jobs that interfered with the time they needed to keep up their studies.

Some for-profit schools went out of business, leaving students with debt and academic credits that were not transferable to other institutions. For instance, Corinthian Colleges, which served more than 81,000 students at 100 campuses in mostly Western states, filed for Chapter 11 bankruptcy in 2015.[70] As a result of such closings, students often failed to get a degree and found it difficult to find good-paying jobs needed to repay their loans.[71]

Reform Proposals

Obama, in his 2015 State of the Union address, had proposed a federal-state partnership to provide free tuition at two-year community colleges.

His plan would use $6 billion in federal funds each year to pay three-quarters of the cost of making tuition free. States would pay for the rest. Students would have to maintain at least a 2.5 grade-point average and study at least half time to earn credits that would lead to a two-year certificate or could be transferred to a four-year institution. Lower-income students could use Pell Grants to pay other expenses.

Congress rejected Obama's plan, but his administration this year by executive action instructed the Labor Department to make $100 million available to community colleges for education and training, including free-tuition programs.[72]

Addressing complaints about abusive debt collectors, Obama also began an experimental program to have federal employees collect debts and help students cope with their repayment difficulties.

Deanne Loonin, founding director of the National Consumer Law Center's Student Loan Borrower Assistance Project, said all private debt collectors should be replaced. "They are incentivized just to collect money, not to work out ways that might be better for the borrowers," she said.[73]

CURRENT SITUATION

Federal Fixes

As the presidential campaign raced toward its conclusion in October, Donald Trump provided details on his plan to ease the burden of student debt.

Trump said he would roll all public and private loans into an income-based repayment plan that would cap monthly repayments at 12.5 percent of a borrower's earnings, with the unpaid balance forgiven after 15 years. He did not offer a cost estimate. Congressional Republicans in the past have called similar plans fiscally irresponsible.

"Students should not be asked to pay more on the debt than they can afford," Trump said. "And the debt should not be an albatross around their necks for the rest of their lives."

The government could afford the program, he said, because the more-favorable repayment provisions would reduce loan defaults. He said he would free-up funds by cutting federal spending in other areas.

Trump also supported forcing colleges to use more of their endowments to reduce tuition and fees, called for lowering college costs by cutting federal regulations and promised to hold schools accountable for "administrative bloat."[74]

Investors viewed Trump's promises on cutting regulations as a likely boon for private lenders and for-profit colleges. The University of Phoenix, DeVry University and Strayer University — leading for-profit schools — saw their stock prices rise the day after the election. Analysts attributed the gains in part to speculation that Trump will ease the Obama administration's clampdown on the industry.[75]

Sallie Mae's stock jumped 15 percent on the same day. The financial publication *Barron's* linked the increase to the likely failure of free-tuition proposals, which would sustain demand for college loans.[76]

Other Trump reforms proposed at the federal level include allowing borrowers to refinance loans at lower rates, reducing interest rates on federal loans and simplifying the system.

Democratic Sen. Al Franken of Minnesota this year introduced legislation to allow borrowers to refinance federal loans, a proposal that has failed in previous Congresses. "You're able to do that on a car loan," he said. "You're able to do it on a mortgage. You're able to do it on a business loan. You should be able to do it on federal student loans."[77]

But that's a bad idea, says the Brookings Institution's Akers, because "it would create huge transfers to the people who need it the least." Refinancing federal loans at lower rates reduces federal income and transfers money "from taxpayers to borrowers," Akers says. Those with the highest debt — who tend to be well-paid professionals — would get the most relief, she notes. That federal aid should be focused on the needy, she argues.

Similar criticisms are directed at other proposals to reduce costs for both high- and low-income borrowers.

But there is broad agreement about the need for simplification. Many borrowers who would benefit from income-based repayment plans, for example, don't enroll because the process seems too complicated.

"Our current system of income-driven repayment is a hodgepodge of problems that is difficult for students to navigate," Akers says. "People who need it the most are the least able to negotiate the barriers."

One complication for borrowers — having to file new paperwork every year to update earnings information — could be eliminated by tying repayment to the federal income tax system, said the Urban Institute's Baum. There is "broad consensus that borrowers should automatically be placed in [an income-driven] plan and that payments should be made through payroll withholding," she said.[78]

Akers also likes the idea of income sharing, first proposed by Nobel Prize-winning economist Milton Friedman in 1955. In exchange for loans, borrowers agree to pay the lender a percentage of their income for a set period of time. Borrowers with high-paying jobs might end up repaying more than they borrowed. Others would repay less.[79] Akers also proposes consolidating all student aid into one lending program and one grant program, while eliminating educational tax credits and loans to parents.

Controlling Tuition

While the idea of free tuition commanded attention during the presidential campaign, federal and state lawmakers are adopting or considering other measures designed to constrain tuition. And some companies are helping debt-encumbered employees.

At the federal level, lawmakers are examining how high sports spending by colleges is affecting tuition rates. Five House members — three Democrats and two Republicans — have introduced a bill to create a Presidential Commission on Intercollegiate Athletics to study college sports financing, among other matters.

"The NCAA is simply incapable of reforming itself," said Rep. Charlie Dent, R-Pa., one of the sponsors. "It's important for us to have a serious conversation about how all these conferences are going to be able to survive in this new system," he said, referring to new rules adopted by the NCAA in 2014, in which the Power Five conferences were exempted from some requirements, such as limits on expense payments to players, staff sizes and recruiting.[80]

The NCAA last month did, however, increase emphasis on academics in the formula it uses to distribute revenues from its annual "March Madness" basketball championship tournament. Beginning in the 2019-20 academic year, the formula will take into account the proportion of a school's athletes who graduate within six years of enrollment. Currently, a school's share of those revenues depends on its success in the tournament, the number of athletic scholarships it awards and the number of teams it fields.[81]

The Knight Commission is urging that all NCAA distributions to schools be used only for education, health and safety — not for coaching salaries, recruiting and new athletic facilities.[82]

In addition to sports, federal lawmakers are looking at college endowments as a potential source of funds to reduce tuition charges. Rep. Tom Reed, a New York Republican, has proposed, but not yet introduced, legislation requiring colleges with endowments of more than $1 billion to spend a quarter of the funds' annual earnings to reduce tuition. The plan would affect about 90 schools.[83]

"It is a disservice to the next generation of students that colleges continue to stockpile large sums of money that are tax exempt, and for which donors receive tax deductions, while tuition costs continue to rise," Reed said.[84]

Two congressional committees have asked 56 private institutions with endowments greater than $1 billion for information about how they use them. Reed said he hopes Congress will take up the bill next year.[85] However, Finney says, the proposal could be unrealistic because many endowment donors prescribe how the money must be spent, and it is illegal to use restricted funds for other purposes.

In its response to the committees, Harvard said 84 percent of its $37.6 billion endowment — the largest in the country — is restricted. Last year, Harvard spent $1.8 billion from the endowment, including $175 million — less than 10 percent — for financial aid for undergraduates.[86]

At the state level, Virginia state colleges have until mid-2021 to comply with a law that caps how much they can subsidize intercollegiate athletics. The law hits hardest at Power Five universities — the University of Virginia and Virginia Tech — which bring in the most

Should public-college tuition be free?

YES — Morley Winograd
President and CEO, Campaign for Free College Tuition

Written for *CQ Researcher*, November 2016

It's a simple fact that our nation's economic success depends on a highly educated and skilled workforce. In the 20th century, as our growing Industrial Age economy required workers with a high school education, states and communities funded public high schools for both girls and boys to respond to these new demands. Later in the century, Congress enacted the GI Bill of Rights and then the Higher Education Act of 1965 to encourage college enrollment, thereby establishing the educational foundation for our rapidly expanding middle class.

It is only in this century that we have asked a generation — Millennials, born between about 1982 and 2003 — to self-finance the education they need and that our country needs in order to be economically successful. This misguided approach must end before America loses its global competitive edge for good.

Just when a college degree or certificate became a ticket to the middle class, we have made it too expensive for most families to send their kids to college. Since 1973, according to the Center on Budget and Policy Priorities, "average inflation-adjusted public college tuition has increased by 274 percent while median household income has grown by only 7 percent." Students and families took out loans to cover the gap, effectively mortgaging their financial future to try to meet the challenge. The resulting rise in student debt levels is a dangerous warning sign that our country is abandoning its historical commitment to education as a key component of the promise of upward economic mobility.

Only free public college tuition has the power to permanently fix this problem. America has always used government resources to provide sufficient funds to those willing and able to acquire the skills and knowledge they need to be successful. While free public college tuition will require a major investment by government, the return on that investment will pay dividends for decades. The W.E. Upjohn Institute for Employment Research found that the Kalamazoo Promise — the nation's pioneering scholarship program providing a free college education to public high school graduates — has produced a return on investment of 11.3 percent in the first 10 years of its existence.

Now is the time to expand our country's commitment to free universal public education from primary and secondary education to higher education to ensure we have a skilled workforce capable of competing in the 21st-century economy.

NO — Rick Staisloff
Founder, RPKgroup, a Higher-Education consulting firm

Written for *CQ Researcher*, November 2016

The call for free college tuition is in the air. During this past season of campaigning, political candidates competed to offer more and more largess for higher education. And who shouldn't want free tuition? Precisely the colleges that would receive this gift.

Over the past 50-plus years, our national and state policies have focused on how to help students afford an ever costlier degree. Nowhere have we asked the more fundamental question: Why does college cost so much to begin with? It is time to tackle the real issues that increase the cost of college for all students without adding to the quality of their educational experience. Adopting a free-college policy would likely eliminate the momentum of a very nascent movement seeking to lower the cost of a college education.

What would a lower-cost education look like? It would not be one of lower quality. It would require fewer degree programs, appropriately larger class sizes, less research at nonresearch institutions and more streamlined and efficient administrative services. All doable, as demonstrated by best practices at colleges that have been willing to do the basic blocking and tackling involved with reforming education.

Beyond the improvements in the traditional model most of us passed through as students, real cost reductions are achievable from the emergence of innovative delivery models. Competency-based education models, for example, focus on mastery of competencies and not on the length of time needed to learn these skills. Such models show great promise in "bending the cost curve" of higher education.

Rather than write an ever larger, publicly funded check for costly, inefficient education models, colleges and students would be better served by targeted investment in programs that create efficiencies at colleges and support educational innovations until they become sustainable. Use the funding that would go for free college to provide seed money for innovations such as competency-based education and open educational resources, which make educational materials free and accessible. We also should fund shared service models in which institutions can more cost effectively share curriculum, faculty, libraries and materials, as well as administrative services.

If we make college free, we risk devaluing a college education. More to the point, we'll lose any concern over what it costs. That's not good for higher education or the students it serves.

income from such sources as ticket sales and television rights. The schools can obtain no more than 20 percent of their sports budgets from student fees and other non-sports-generated university income.

Schools that play in the NCAA's top-tier Football Bowl Subdivision — but outside the Power Five conferences — can use institutional money for no more than 55 percent of their total athletics budget. The percentage rises as the level of competition diminishes and the opportunity for outside income shrinks. It's 70 percent for schools in the Football Championship Subdivision, the second tier of football competition. It's 92 percent in the lowest tier — Division III institutions that don't play football.

"I don't think this is going to be an anomaly," Wood Selig, athletic director at Old Dominion University in Norfolk, Va., the only school with a 55 percent cap, said about the new Virginia law. "My sense is other states are going to take note."[87]

State lawmakers also are looking into endowment-like reserve funds that public schools are accumulating. For instance, the University of Virginia has built a $2.2 billion fund for "strategic investments," such as technology, laboratories or faculty recruitment, in addition to its $6 billion endowment. In recent years, similar reserve funds have totaled $2.4 billion at the University of Illinois, $2.3 billion at the University of Pittsburgh, $1.7 billion at the University of Michigan and $648 million at the University of Wisconsin.[88]

University officials say the reserves help to stabilize their finances at a time of economic volatility and shrinking and unreliable state aid. High reserves also lead to higher credit ratings, which cut borrowing costs, the officials say.

Democrat J. Chapman Petersen, a member of the Virginia Senate Education Committee, was among legislators who found the practice of retaining high reserves disturbing. If the University of Virginia spent the money, Petersen said, it could refund tuition and hire a personal tutor for all 16,500 undergraduate students.[89]

The university in October announced that it has used $6.8 million from the fund this year to provide financial aid to doctoral and business students as well as law students who take public service positions after graduation. The university's Board of Regents, at its November meeting, discussed other options for using the fund to make the school more affordable.[90]

Some businesses also are offering debt relief as a recruiting incentive. Law school graduates, for instance, currently enter the workforce with an average debt of $185,000 — up from $75,000 a decade ago, according to Mark Kantrowitz, an Illinois-based financial aid adviser. As a result, personnel officers have observed, young recruits find debt relief more attractive than generous retirement benefits.

Benefits can range from $100 a month to $2,000 a year. Companies usually cap the total benefit — up to $10,000 at PricewaterhouseCoopers and Fidelity Investments, and up to $30,000 at the computer graphics company Nvidia.

Six-figure debts dwarf such benefits, however, and just 3 percent of employers currently offer the aid. But it is popular with workers. More than 6,000 of Fidelity's 45,000 employees signed up for the benefit by November, for example, says company spokesperson Alicia Curran Sweeney.[91]

OUTLOOK
Cost-Cutting Challenges

In the coming years, it will be difficult for colleges to shrink students' need to borrow. Schools are expected to have a hard time reducing tuition by cutting costs, and they likely will encounter new challenges that could drive up spending in other areas.

But constantly raising tuition and fees is unsustainable, some experts say, so colleges will face substantial pressure to become more efficient.

One solution is to drop out of top-tier football, as the University of Idaho is doing.[92] Schools unwilling to take that radical step know they must find ways to curtail ever-rising sports costs.

"We've always got to build something bigger and better . . . and I don't think it is sustainable," said Kansas State University President Kirk Schulz. Louisiana State University President F. King Alexander said the Southeastern Conference is "trying to figure out how to slow this spending machine down, [but] we just don't know where this whole thing is going to end up."[93]

Beyond the pressures of competition, legal considerations restrict some attempts to rein in sports spending. For instance, federal antitrust laws prevent the NCAA or athletic conferences from imposing caps on multi-million-dollar salaries for coaches. And some college athletes have gone to court to overturn NCAA rules that prevent them from being paid to play. Athletes also asked the National Labor Relations Board (NLRB) for the right to unionize.

So far, the athletes have lost in court and at the NLRB, but the rulings were convoluted and the disputes are not over.[94]

The board already has supported unionization rights for students who work as teaching or research assistants at private colleges, ruling in August that students at Columbia could bargain with the university as members of the United Auto Workers (UAW). Some states had already allowed public-college students to organize.[95]

A growing number of students and part-time faculty across the country are seeking to join unions, challenging colleges' use of cheap labor to hold down costs, according to UAW Regional Director Julie Kushner.[96] An *Inside Higher Ed* survey released this year found that only 8 percent of college chief academic officers expected to rely less on non-tenure-track faculty in the future, while 27 percent expected to rely more.[97]

Like many employers, colleges will have to pay mounting health care and retirement expenses, says Wellman, the former director of the Delta Cost Project. Such items can be more burdensome in higher education because of "stove-pipe" management: People who hire faculty don't think of those costs because fringe benefits are administered elsewhere, she says.

Beyond specific challenges to cost cutting, higher education institutions remain tough to manage because they lack the kind of "objectively measured" outcomes that businesses rely on to make budget decisions, University of San Francisco Provost Heller said. "This absence of clear, measurable goals hampers universities in their attempts to control costs by closing or shrinking marginal programs," he said. "Instead, new initiatives tend to get layered on top of old ones, thus adding to costs."[98]

Staisloff, the cost-containment consultant, says some colleges are moving to a new management model that holds down spending without diminishing educational quality. Faculty members teach more classes, while others take over such nonteaching duties as grading and advising, he says.

Colleges also need to look at eliminating under-subscribed classes, he says. "Generally we find in almost every university we've studied that 50 percent or more of undergraduate students are in 20 or fewer programs, at institutions with 50, 100 or 150 programs," he says.

Universities could also become more efficient by utilizing facilities during evenings, weekends and summer breaks, Staisloff says. Information technology offers cost-cutting opportunities as well, he says.

"Once you get smart about how you're utilizing your most important asset — your faculty members — you can really increase their efficiency and put millions of dollars back on the table," Staisloff says.

NOTES

1. Neil Swidey, "The college debt crisis, is even worse than you think," *The Boston Globe*, May 22, 2016, http://tinyurl.com/zp8oxxo.

2. Jillian Berman, "Class of 2015 has the most student debt in U.S. history," Market Watch, May 9, 2015, http://tinyurl.com/o4adbnk; Josh Boak, "Why It Matters: Student Debt," The Associated Press, Sept. 5, 2016, http://tinyurl.com/zebsdcr.

3. Jeffrey J. Selingo, "Incomes aren't the only thing not keeping pace with rising tuition. Neither are scholarships," *The Washington Post*, Sept. 16, 2016, http://tinyurl.com/j5cl4ff.

4. Danielle Douglas-Gabriel, "Tuition at public colleges has soared in the past decade, but student fees have risen faster," *The Washington Post*, June 22, 2016, http://tinyurl.com/jxfdh2p.

5. Sandy Baum, "College Endowments, College Prices, and Financial Aid," statement before the Subcommittee on Oversight, U.S. House Ways and Means Committee, Sept. 13, 2016, http://tinyurl.com/jasn6do.

6. "Higher Education: State Funding Trends and Policies on Affordability," U.S. Government Accountability Office, December 2014, http://tinyurl.com/hpdcctf.

7. Danielle Douglas-Gabriel, "Students now pay more of their public university tuition than state governments," *The Washington Post*, Jan. 5, 2015, http://tinyurl.com/jo77ctp.

8. Jon Marcus, "New analysis shows problematic boom in higher ed administrators," The Eye, New England Center for Investigative Reporting, Feb. 6, 2014, http://tinyurl.com/jnyaz6e.

9. Baum, *op. cit.*

10. Also see Dan Bauman, "Bonuses Push More Public-College Leaders Past $1 Million," *The Chronicle of Higher Education*, July 17, 2016, http://tinyurl.com/h62sukk.

11. "Busting the Myths: The Annual Report on the Economic Status of the Profession 2014-15," American Association of University Professors, 2014-15, http://tinyurl.com/z73q6s3; "Higher Education at a Crossroads: The Annual Report on the Economic Status of the Profession, 2015-16," American Association of University Professors, http://tinyurl.com/hqk5dfr.

12. Paul F. Campos, "The Real Reason College Tuition Costs So Much," *The New York Times*, April 4, 2015, http://tinyurl.com/ktho7pk.

13. Susan Dynarski, "Why Students with Smallest Debt Have the Larger Problems," *The New York Times*, Aug. 31, 2015, http://tinyurl.com/o67nsfa; Alan Greenblatt, "Hot Topics: Student Debt" *CQ Researcher*, June 27, 2016.

14. Baum, *op. cit.*

15. A.J. Angulo, *Diploma Mills: How For-Profit Colleges Stiffed Students, Taxpayers, and the American Dream* (2016); Donald E. Heller, "Does Federal Financial Aid Drive Up College Prices?" American Council on Education, April 2013, http://tinyurl.com/nhmuulr.

16. Ann Carrns, "U.S. Puts Private Student Loan Servicers on Notice: Play Nice," *The New York Times*, Aug. 26, 2016, http://tinyurl.com/hnlv7ua.

17. James B. Steele and Lance Williams, "Who Got Rich off the Student Debt Crisis," The Center for Investigative Reporting, June 28, 2016, http://tinyurl.com/hz83bke.

18. Joni E. Finney, "2016 College Affordability Diagnosis National Report," Institute for Research on Higher Education, University of Pennsylvania Graduate School of Education, http://tinyurl.com/j83uq3z.

19. Greenblatt, *op. cit.*

20. Katrina vanden Heuvel, "Free college? We can afford it," *The Washington Post*, May 1, 2012, http://tinyurl.com/guoqhof. Also see Deanna Templeton and Credit.com, "What Happens to Student Loans When You Die?" ABC News, June 23, 2013, http://tinyurl.com/kdtm76v.

21. "Here's what every student and family should expect under Hillary's plan," Hillary for America, http://tinyurl.com/zolgake; "Hillary Clinton's Commitment: A Debt-Free Future for America's Graduates," Hillary for America, http://tinyurl.com/zejyasy; Stephanie Saul and Matt Flegenheimer, "Hillary Clinton Embraces Ideas From Bernie Sanders's College Tuition Plan," *The New York Times*, July 6, 2016, http://tinyurl.com/hn2dple.

22. Bernie Sanders, "Make college free for all," *The Washington Post*, Oct. 22, 2015, http://tinyurl.com/zqkjw8w.

23. Sara Goldrick-Rab, "Make college free," Social Mobility Memos, Brookings Institution, Oct. 16, 2015, http://tinyurl.com/jmpnten.

24. Robert J. Samuelson, "It's time to drop the college-for-all crusade," *The Washington Post*, May 27, 2012, http://tinyurl.com/gw9hq7g.

25. Kevin Carey, "The Trouble With Hillary Clinton's Free Tuition Plan," *The New York Times*, July 19, 2016, http://tinyurl.com/jv4lb4p.

26. Saul and Flegenheimer, *op. cit.*

27. Katie Pavlich, "Scott Walker: Hillary's Education Plan Benefits Her Liberal Academic Friends, Not Students," *Townhall*, Aug. 12, 2015, http://tinyurl.com/zluwyyk; Julie Bosman, "2016 Ambitions Seen in Walker's Push for University Cuts in Wisconsin," *The New York Times*, Feb. 16, 2015, http://tinyurl.com/ofu3f5q.

28. Doug Lederman, "Clinton 'Free' Plan Would Swell College Enrollments," *Inside Higher Ed*, Sept. 2, 2016, http://tinyurl.com/jotz4k9.

29. Scott Carlson and Beckie Supiano, "How Clinton's 'Free College' Could Cause a Cascade of Problems," *The Chronicle of Higher Education*, July 27, 2016, http://tinyurl.com/h3rs2pl.

30. Lederman, *op. cit.*

31. Carlson and Supiano, *op. cit.*

32. Lederman, *op. cit.*

33. David O. Lucca, Taylor Nadauld and Karen Shen, "Credit Supply and the Rise in College Tuition: Evidence from the Expansion in Federal Student Aid Programs," Federal Reserve Bank of New York, July 2015, revised October 2016, http://tinyurl.com/hus2s6c.

34. Veronique De Rugy, "Subsidized loans drive college tuition, student debt to record levels," *The Washington Examiner*, July 12, 2013, http://tinyurl.com/gkpabkl.

35. *Ibid.*

36. Lucca, *op. cit.*

37. Baum, *op. cit.*

38. Robert Kiener, "Future of Public Universities," *CQ Researcher*, Jan. 18, 2013, pp. 53-80.

39. Gary Fethke, "Why Does Tuition Go Up? Because Taxpayer Support Goes Down," *The Chronicle of Higher Education*, April 1, 2012, http://tinyurl.com/zrormv6.

40. Heller, *op. cit.*

41. Rajashri Chakrabarti, Maricar Mabutas and Basit Zafar, "Soaring Tuitions: Are Public Funding Cuts to Blame?" Liberty Street Economics, Federal Reserve Bank of New York, Sept. 19, 2012, http://tinyurl.com/jts43bt.

42. Heller, *op. cit.*

43. Valerie Strauss, "School left $4 million by librarian is spending $100,000 on library — and $1 million on a scoreboard," *The Washington Post*, Sept. 17, 2016, http://tinyurl.com/he64yxh.

44. "Trends In Spending And Institutional Funding," Knight Commission on Intercollegiate Athletics, http://tinyurl.com/zyll53m.

45. Steve Berkowitz, Christopher Schnaars and Sean Dougherty, "NCAA Salaries," *USA Today*, 2016, http://tinyurl.com/m58t4yl.

46. Trends In Spending And Institutional Funding," *op. cit.*

47. Robert Carpenter, Howard Bunsis, Judith Kullberg and Steven Cole, "Moving toward Financial Sustainability: Student & Faculty Report on the University Budget," Eastern Michigan University, 2016.

48. Charlie Sykes, "Hillary Clinton's Bailout for the College-Industrial Complex," Right Wisconsin, Aug. 23, 2016, http://tinyurl.com/jmgdmt2.

49. Stephanie Saul, "N.Y.U. President's Penthouse Gets a Face-Lift Worth $1.1 Million (or More)," *The New York Times*, Dec. 15, 2015, http://tinyurl.com/z52vowl.

50. *Ibid.*

51. Steven Pearlstein, "Four tough things universities should do to rein in costs," *The Washington Post*, Nov. 25, 2015, http://tinyurl.com/znxpomb.

52. Michael S. Harris, "What is the typical teaching load for university faculty?" *Higher Ed Professor*, May 11, 2015, http://tinyurl.com/zlp86lo.

53. Peter James Bentley and Svein Kyvik, "Academic work from a comparative perspective," *Higher Education*, April 2012, http://tinyurl.com/z5um2ex.

54. "Higher Education at a Crossroads: The Annual Report on the Economic Status of the Profession, 2015-16," *op. cit.*

55. Heller, *op. cit.*

56. Tom Price, "Rising College Costs: Should Congress penalize schools that raise fees?" *CQ Researcher*, Dec. 5, 2003, pp. 1013-1044.

57. Marcia Clemmitt, "Student Debt," *CQ Researcher*, Oct. 21, 2011, pp. 877-900; Heller, *op. cit.*; Steele and Williams, *op. cit.*

58. Heller, *op. cit.*

59. Steele and Williams, *op. cit.*

60. Clemmitt, *op. cit.*; Steele and Williams, *op. cit.*

61. *Ibid.*

62. "Attorney General Cuomo Announces Settlement With Sallie Mae Over Its Student Loan Practices," Office of the Attorney General of New York, April 11, 2007, http://tinyurl.com/n4a3wmm.

63. "Student loan fixes that make sense," *The Washington Post*, June 15, 2014, http://tinyurl.com/h45swen.

64. "An Undue Hardship? Discharging Educational Debt in Bankruptcy," hearing before the Commercial and Administrative Law Subcommittee, House Judiciary Committee, Sept. 23, 2009, http://tinyurl.com/nn0drq5.

65. Angulo, *op. cit.*

66. Heller, *op. cit.*; Clemmitt, *op. cit.*

67. Angulo, *op. cit.*

68. *Ibid.*

69. Susan Dynarski, "A Conveyor Belt of Dropouts and Debt at For-Profit Colleges," *The New York Times*, Oct. 28, 2016, http://tinyurl.com/gnld576.

70. Allie Bidwell, "For-Profit Corinthian Colleges Files for Chapter 11 Bankruptcy," *U.S. News & World Report*, May 4, 2015, http://tinyurl.com/z7pmc43.

71. Steele and Williams, *op. cit.*

72. Greenblatt, *op. cit.*; "President Obama's community college proposal doesn't make the grade," *The Washington Post*, Feb. 11, 2015, http://tinyurl.com/zh3nab9.

73. Steele and Williams, *op. cit.*

74. Danielle Douglas-Gabriel, "Trump just laid out a pretty radical student debt plan," *The Washington Post*, Oct. 13, 2016, http://tinyurl.com/zxnj8vo.

75. Amy Scott, "For-profit colleges get a post-election bounce," "Marketplace," Nov. 10, 2016, http://tinyurl.com/jysbjzr.

76. Alex Eule, "Election 2016: And Now for the Winning Stocks," *Barron's*, Nov. 9, 2016, http://tinyurl.com/h9slnxp.

77. Esme Murphy, "Franken Introduces Bill To Allow Refinancing Of Federal Student Loans," CBS Minnesota, Jan. 21, 2016, http://tinyurl.com/grwyktu.

78. Sandy Baum and Martha C. Johnson, "Strengthening Federal Student Aid: An Assessment of Proposals for Reforming Federal Student Loan Repayment and Federal Education Tax Benefits," Urban Institute, Feb. 3, 2016, http://tinyurl.com/gvuxr7c.

79. Beth Akers, "How Income Share Agreements Could Play a Role in Higher Ed Financing," Brookings Institution, Oct. 16, 2014, http://tinyurl.com/hezcsw2.

80. "H.R. 275," Congress.gov, http://tinyurl.com/jprcoyf; Erik Brady, Steve Berkowitz and Jodi Upton, "Can college athletics continue to spend like this?" *USA Today*, April 23, 2016, http://tinyurl.com/zl00umw.

81. Michelle Brutlag Hosick, "DI to distribute revenue based on academics," National Collegiate Athletic Association, Oct. 27, 2016, http://tinyurl.com/h8gzk57; "DI group issues survey on revenue distribution," National Collegiate Athletic Association, May 6, 2016, http://tinyurl.com/zr5947l.

82. "Knight Commission Calls for NCAA To Transform Its Guidelines for March Madness Revenues To Better Support College Athletes and Protect Financial Integrity," Knight Commission on Intercollegiate Athletics, May 10, 2016, http://tinyurl.com/gmtgc6m.

83. Alan Greenblatt, "Hot Topics: Student Debt" *CQ Researcher*, June 27, 2016.

84. Collin Binkley, "Trump off on how colleges use endowments," The Associated Press, Sept. 24, 2016, http://bigstory.ap.org/article/ec43426d2c04489a819eb84254a879cc/ap-fact-check-trump-how-colleges-use-endowments.

85. Rick Seltzer, "Lawmaker With the Idea Higher Ed Leaders Hate," *Inside Higher Ed*, May 12, 2016, http://tinyurl.com/jnf4f69.

86. Drew Gilpin Faust, Harvard University President, letter to Orrin Hatch, Chairman, U.S. Senate Finance Committee; Kevin Brady, Chairman, House Ways and Means Committee; Peter Roskam, Chairman, Ways and Means Subcommittee on Oversight, March 31, 2016, http://tinyurl.com/z8lojq7.

87. "H 1897," Virginia Legislative Information System, 2015, http://tinyurl.com/h7vef43; Erik Brady, Steve Berkowitz and Christopher Schnaars, "2nd-tier schools feeling squeeze," *USA Today*, May 27, 2015, http://tinyurl.com/z2juawc.

88. Nick Anderson, "U-Va. set aside $2.2 billion for 'strategic investments,' " *The Washington Post*, July 13, 2016, http://tinyurl.com/j6j36w6; Nick Anderson, Susan Svrluga and Danielle Douglas-Gabriel, "Lawmakers want to know why U-Va. stockpiled billions but still boosted tuition," *The*

Washington Post, Aug. 25 2016, http://tinyurl.com/zl7e5ce.

89. *Ibid.*

90. T. Rees Shapiro and Danielle Douglas-Gabriel, "U-Va. board is discussing ways to decrease tuition," *The Washington Post*, Nov. 11, 2016, http://tinyurl.com/za5pufk.

91. Elizabeth Olson, "Firms Offering Cash to Help New Lawyers Pay Their Student Debt," *The New York Times*, http://tinyurl.com/gr97obl; Greenblatt, *op. cit.*; Tara Siegel Bernard, "Aid to Repay School Loan Is Coveted Job Benefit," *The New York Times*, March 26, 2016, http://tinyurl.com/hq9lff6.

92. Chuck Staben, "Why We're Leaving the Football Arms Race," *Inside Higher Ed*, April 29, 2016, http://tinyurl.com/jsr3zry.

93. Will Hobson, "At Clemson, football success brings windfall that most schools only dream of," *The Washington Post*, Sept. 21, 2016, http://tinyurl.com/gutsl7o.

94. Joe Nocera, "Ruling Stands, but Status Quo May Yet Collapse," *The New York Times*, Oct. 4, 2016, http://tinyurl.com/h3rysa5.

95. Danielle Douglas-Gabriel, "Labor board ruling on graduate student employment rankles universities, lawmakers," *The Washington Post*, Aug. 24, 2016, http://tinyurl.com/jbpdfua.

96. Kathleen Megan, "UConn Graduate Assistants First To Unionize In State," *The Hartford Courant*, April 18, 2014, http://tinyurl.com/kdx76xk.

97. "Higher Education at a Crossroads: The Economic Value of Tenure and the Security of the Profession," *op. cit.*

98. Heller, *op. cit.*

BIBLIOGRAPHY

Selected Sources

Books

Akers, Beth, and Matthew M. Chingos, *Game of Loans: The Rhetoric and Reality of Student Debt*, Princeton University Press, 2016.
Akers of the Brookings Institution and Chingos of the Urban Institute say public panic about student debt is overblown.

Angulo, A.J., *Diploma Mill$: How For-Profit Colleges Stiffed Students, Taxpayers, and the American Dream*, Johns Hopkins University Press, 2016.
A professor of education and history at Winthrop University in Rock Hill, S.C., says for-profit schools have exploited low-income students and that those schools' students account for a disproportionate number of loan defaults.

Baum, Sandy, *Student Debt: Rhetoric and Realities of Higher Education Financing*, Palgrave Macmillan, 2016.
Many student debt problems stem from bad borrowing choices, says the author, who prepares the College Board's annual report on higher-education prices.

Brada, Josef C., Wojciech Bienkowski and Masaaki Kuboniwa, eds., *International Perspectives on Financing Higher Education*, Palgrave Macmillan, 2015.
Education scholars from around the world describe how various countries pay for higher education.

Articles

Carlson, Scott, and Beckie Supiano, "How Clinton's 'Free College' Could Cause a Cascade of Problems," *The Chronicle of Higher Education*, July 27, 2016, http://tinyurl.com/h3rs2pl.
Free public-school tuition can have unintended consequences, including the possible demise of small private schools, experts say.

Dynarski, Susan, "Why Students With Smallest Debts Have the Larger Problem," *The New York Times*, Sept. 1, 2015, http://tinyurl.com/o67nsfa.
A professor of public policy, education and economics at the University of Michigan explains that student-debt defaults are concentrated among student drop-outs, who tend to have small debts but have more difficulty than graduates paying the loans back.

Goldrick-Rab, Sara, "Make college free," Social Mobility Memos, Brookings Institution, Oct. 16, 2015, http://tinyurl.com/jmpnten.
An expert on college affordability argues that low-income students would benefit from a simple system that makes college free for everyone.

Samuelson, Robert J., "It's time to drop the college-for-all crusade," *The Washington Post*, May 27, 2012, http://tinyurl.com/gw9hq7g.

Encouraging college for everyone ignores the fact that most U.S. jobs do not require higher education, says an economics columnist.

Staben, Chuck, "Why We're Leaving the Football Arms Race," *Inside Higher Ed*, **April 29, 2016, http:// tinyurl.com/jsr3zry.**
The University of Idaho's president says his school decided to drop out of big-time football largely to save money on rising football program costs, which some say add to tuition costs and contribute to higher student debt.

Steele, James B., and Lance Williams, "Who Got Rich Off the Student Debt Crisis," The Center for Investigative Reporting, June 28, 2016, http://tinyurl .com/hz83bke.
Investigative reporters argue that government, lenders and for-profit schools are substantially to blame for the student debt crisis.

Reports and Studies

"Great Jobs, Great Lives: The Relationship Between Student Debt, Experiences and Perceptions of College Worth," Gallup Inc. and Purdue University, 2015, http://tinyurl.com/hj299mt.
An annual survey of college graduates explores graduates' attitudes toward the cost and value of education and how well they are prepared for the job market. Significant numbers say debt caused them to postpone further education, buying a house or car or starting a business.

Baum, Sandy, "College Endowments, College Prices and Financial Aid," statement before the Subcommittee on Oversight, U.S. House Ways and Means Committee, Sept. 13, 2016, http://tinyurl .com/jasn6do.
A researcher who prepares the annual College Board study of tuition costs reviews key issues in college finance, including declining state support and the relationship between rising tuition and federal subsidies.

Harris, Michael S., "What is the typical teaching load for university faculty?" *Higher Ed Professor*, **May 11, 2015, http://tinyurl.com/zlp86lo.**
The director of the Center for Teaching Excellence at Southern Methodist University explores typical faculty workloads.

Heller, Donald E., "Does Federal Financial Aid Drive Up College Prices?" American Council on Education, April 2013, http://tinyurl.com/nhmuulr.
The provost at the University of San Francisco, who is also a professor of education, reviews scores of studies on the impact of federal aid on tuition and finds the studies to be "ambiguous at best."

For More Information

American Association of State Colleges and Universities, 1307 New York Ave., N.W., Fifth Floor, Washington, DC 20005; 202-293-7070; www.aascu.org. Promotes public higher education.

American Association of University Professors, 1133 19th St., N.W., Suite 200, Washington, DC 20036; 202-737-5900; www.aaup.org. Defends academic freedom, advances faculty influence in higher education, defines professional standards.

The College Board, 250 Vesey St., New York, NY 10281; 212-713-8000; www.collegeboard.org. Administers the Scholastic Aptitude Test and the Advanced Placement program and publishes an annual report on the costs of college.

Institute for Research on Higher Education, Graduate School of Education, University of Pennsylvania, 3700 Walnut St., Philadelphia, PA 19104; 215-573-4960; www2 .gse.upenn.edu/irhe. Researches finance in public higher education.

Knight Commission on Intercollegiate Athletics, 200 S. Biscayne Blvd., Miami, FL 33131; 910-551-6809; www .knightcommission.org. Advocates college sports reform.

12

Prescription Drug Costs

Leslie Allen

A scientist analyzes drug samples at a Gilead Sciences laboratory in Foster City, Calif. After an 18-month investigation, the Senate Finance Committee concluded in December that Gilead — in developing the costly new hepatitis C drugs Sovaldi and Harvoni, in part using public funds — "focused on maximizing revenue even as the company's analysis showed a lower price would allow more patients to be treated."

David Paul Morris/Bloomberg via Getty Images

From *CQ Researcher*,
May 20, 2016.

The drug was a lifesaver: For years, a steady supply of Daraprim had kept Reva Jones of Baltimore free from the devastating effects of toxoplasmosis, an infection that can cause brain damage and blindness. The price had risen in recent years, but at $13.50 a pill, it was still an affordable, effective solution for her and thousands of others with immune systems weakened by chemotherapy, HIV infection, organ transplants or other conditions.

Then last September, the medication stopped arriving from Jones' mail-order pharmacy. She and her family learned the price had suddenly skyrocketed, and they suspected the insurance company was refusing to cover it. But before she had time to investigate, Jones' supply ran out.

"She became more and more confused and couldn't walk or bathe or take care of herself," recalls her daughter, Louise. By the time the family got Jones to Johns Hopkins Hospital in Baltimore, she couldn't speak.

Dr. Annie Antar, who led the Hopkins team caring for Jones, soon discovered that besides jacking up the price, drugmaker Turing Pharmaceuticals had also drastically curtailed Daraprim's distribution.[1] "It took almost five days to get a supply," Antar says. When the bottle of 90 pills finally did arrive, it was priced at $67,500, or $750 a pill.[2]

Daraprim (pyrimethamine) is the only treatment approved for toxoplasmosis. Few Americans had even heard of the 62-year-old drug until last August, when Turing acquired the rights to manufacture it from Impax Laboratories, the sole U.S. supplier of Daraprim, and promptly raised the price by 5,000 percent.[3] Since then, the startup and its then-CEO — former hedge fund manager Martin Shkreli (later arrested on fraud charges in an unrelated case) — have been Exhibit A in a growing scandal over alleged price gouging by some drug companies.

Turing's business model represents an extreme example of what many see as excessive profit-seeking and has been widely condemned by other drugmakers, as well as patients and members of Congress. "This is not what we do in the biotech industry," Alnylam Pharmaceuticals' CEO John Maraganore told CNBC. "We're about innovation, patience and 21st-century medicines. We're not about repricing drugs from the 1950s to make a profit."[4]

But the actions of Turing and a few other outliers have shone a spotlight on the much larger issue of skyrocketing costs for both brand and non-brand, or generic, drugs. Between 2013 and 2015 the cost of more than two dozen prescription drugs grew 400 percent or more, and by more than 1,000 percent for a few drugs.[5]

Drug Spending Continues to Climb

Per capita U.S. spending on prescription drugs rose more than 11 percent from 2013 to 2014, the latest year tallied by the U.S. Centers for Medicare and Medicaid (CMS), while inflation grew less than 1 percent during that period. The agency projected a 7 percent increase in 2015 and average growth of about 5 percent annually over the next nine years. Spending slowed in the 2000s because many drug patents expired and generic prices and drug purchases fell during the 2007-09 recession. Spending then declined in 2010 and 2012 as Americans increasingly relied on generic medications.

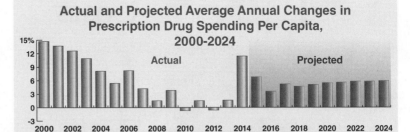

Actual and Projected Average Annual Changes in Prescription Drug Spending Per Capita, 2000-2024

Sources: Rabah Kamal and Gary Claxton, "Recent trends in prescription drug spending, and what to look out for in coming years," Kaiser Family Foundation, Dec. 9, 2015, http://tinyurl.com/zjlsmsr; "What are the recent and forecasted trends in prescription drug spending?" Kaiser Family Foundation, http://tinyurl.com/hgf8mmv; Marilyn Werber Serafini, "National Health Spending Grew Slowly In 2010," *Kaiser Health News*, Jan. 9, 2012, http://tinyurl.com/h34llv2; inflation figure from U.S. Bureau of Labor Statistics, http://tinyurl.com/zjp4mte

But the price surge is not a new phenomenon: Before moderating somewhat during the 2007-09 recession, prices for 416 brand-name drugs rose anywhere from 100 percent to, in some cases, more than 1,000 percent between 2000 and 2008, according to a report by the Government Accountability Office (GAO).[6] Since 2008, brand-name drug prices have risen 164 percent overall.[7]

By 2018, total prescription drug spending is projected to rise to $535 billion, representing 16.8 percent of annual health care costs — up from 7 percent in the 1990s — most of it due to rising drug prices.[8]

Some modern drugs — many developed through taxpayer subsidized research — provide enormous benefits and sometimes even cures. But the rising prices raise fundamental questions about the current system's sustainability, because they are straining federal and state health care budgets and raising out-of-pocket costs for both the insured and uninsured.[9]

More basically, experts are beginning to question whether the free-market model of drug pricing conflicts with medical ethics, especially if companies are earning what society sees as unreasonably high profits on products that patients need to survive.

For example, the latest drug for leukemia, a blood cancer, runs $768,000 a year, and the critical cystic fibrosis drug Kalydeco up to $373,000.[10] The annual cost of the newest lung cancer drug is $168,000 and the cancer drug Revlimid about $150,000.[11] Prices also have risen steeply even for older brand-name drugs, such as the leukemia drug Gleevec, which listed at $26,400 a year when it was introduced in 2001; it now costs more than $120,000, wholesale.[12]

In justifying the price increases, manufacturers cite enormous research and development (R&D) costs, along with the high risk that the drugs won't make it through the years-long process of gaining Food and Drug Administration (FDA) approval. Only 12 percent of drugs tested on people ever make it to market, according to the Pharmaceutical Research and Manufacturers of America (PhRMA), the industry's main trade association. And drugmakers point out that discounts and rebates lower the effective cost to patients, most of whom have insurance to help cover costs. Publicly traded companies also cite pressure from shareholders to keep earnings high.

But critics of industry pricing practices say companies are seeking unreasonably high profits and criticize drugmakers' free-flowing marketing budgets, up sharply since the government allowed direct-to-consumer drug advertising in 1997. Critics also say the industry's R&D expense estimates are too high. In addition, many experts question who should profit, through patents and licensing, from new blockbuster medicines developed with public money.

Two such blockbusters are the costly new hepatitis C drugs Sovaldi and Harvoni. After an 18-month investigation, the Senate Finance Committee concluded in December that the developer of the two drugs, Gilead Sciences, pursued a strategy "focused on maximizing revenue even as the company's analysis showed a lower price would allow more patients to be treated."[13] Under a never-used federal provision, the government can withdraw the exclusive marketing rights awarded to drug companies if they have unreasonably priced their products.

Exacerbating the drug pricing situation — and contrary to normal market forces — price tags on some generics have risen steeply as well. Typically, prices for such non-brand versions of patent-expired drugs decline over time as competitors emerge. Yet, from 2013 to 2015, the common antibiotic tetracycline, for instance, rose 7,567 percent, while the cost of the antidepressant amitriptyline climbed 2,475 percent.[14]

Experts blame the rising cost of generics on manufacturing problems, drug shortages and, primarily, industry consolidation, resulting in fewer suppliers to meet growing demand.[15]

"In some corners of the generic industry, prices are rising by eye-popping numbers, and there's no magic as to why: low competition," says Aaron Kesselheim, an associate professor of medicine at Harvard Medical School who studies prescription drug costs, availability and regulation. "When competition breaks down, companies can raise prices, and natural monopolies occur. It's not illegal."

Still, recent price hikes for decades-old drugs have sparked widespread outrage. Last December, during a Senate Special Committee on Aging hearing on the issue, senators from both parties directed their ire at Turing and another small company, Valeant Pharmaceuticals International, which has steeply increased the price of several older drugs, including critically important heart medications.[16]

Critics allege that Turing intentionally restricted access to Daraprim so the company, the drug's sole manufacturer, could keep prices high and prevent a potential competitor from obtaining enough of the drug to create a generic version.[17] In a statement, Turing said it is committed to ensuring access to Daraprim for any patient who needs it by lowering the price.[18]

Reva Jones' daughter Louise blames the long delays in obtaining the drug for her mother's slower-than-expected recovery. Years ago, when her mother had first developed symptoms of the infection, prompt treatment with Daraprim had allowed a speedy recovery, she says. "But this time it's different."

"I love my mother, and this makes me so angry," says Louise, who once donated a kidney to her. "I think this is all about greed."

Americans also pay significantly more than consumers in other countries for the same drugs.[19] Daraprim costs less than a dollar per pill in the United Kingdom.[20] In India, more than a dozen drugmakers manufacture and sell generic versions of the drug for as low as 4 cents per pill.[21] Unlike other countries, which have universal health care systems that directly or indirectly regulate and subsidize drug prices, the United States mainly leaves drug pricing to market forces.[22]

But Americans' traditional advocacy of free markets and wariness of government involvement increasingly are bumping up against calls for action, with a majority of Americans now citing drug prices as their top health concern, according to polling by the nonpartisan Henry J. Kaiser Family Foundation.[23]

Experts suggest a variety of measures to deal with high drug prices, including requiring more transparency about how drugmakers set prices; lifting a federal ban on

Medicare's Share of Drug Bill Soars

Medicare covered 29 cents of every dollar spent on prescription drugs in 2014, up from less than 2 cents in 2004. Health-policy experts attribute the increase in part to implementation of a Medicare prescription drug benefit in 2006. The share of spending covered by private insurers shrank from 49 cents to 43 cents.

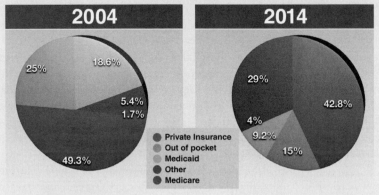

Percentage of U.S. Prescription Drug Spending by Source, 2004 and 2014

2004
- 25%
- 18.6%
- 5.4%
- 1.7%
- 49.3%

2014
- 29%
- 42.8%
- 4%
- 9.2%
- 15%

Legend:
- Private Insurance
- Out of pocket
- Medicaid
- Other
- Medicare

Sources: "Table 16, Retail Prescription Drugs Expenditures," National Health Expenditures tables, Centers for Medicare & Medicaid Services, updated Dec. 3, 2015, http://tinyurl.com/zp7vbz7; "Visualizing Health Policy: Recent Trends in Prescription Drug Costs," Kaiser Family Foundation, April 5, 2016, http://tinyurl.com/hoc35s4

Medicare negotiating with drugmakers for discounted prices; and allowing the importation of lower-cost drugs from abroad. Some medical experts, insurers and others favor excluding coverage of high-priced drugs if lower-priced alternatives exist.

As patients, physicians, drugmakers, ethicists and lawmakers discuss skyrocketing drug prices, here are some of the questions they are debating:

Do high development costs justify soaring drug prices?

One of the most contentious areas of debate surrounding drug pricing is the high cost of research and development — inventing and testing a new drug and shepherding it to the market through the FDA approval process.

Drugmakers say high R&D costs justify rising prices, while critics want more disclosure about those costs. The industry says it needs to cover past costs, for both drugs that get approval and those that fail; critics say the revenue

from a new drug should pay only for the cost of developing that product.

Both the industry and its critics agree the FDA approval process is challenging. Clinical trials alone take six or seven years of the average 10-year drug-development process, according to PhRMA, the big industry trade group, and compounds that make it to market represent a tiny fraction of the "thousands and sometimes millions" that are screened during the early phases of investigation.[24]

But experts disagree on the extent to which research and development costs contribute to rising drug prices. PhRMA and drug company representatives say it costs about $2.6 billion to steer the average drug to market, according to figures from a 2014 study by the Tufts Center for the Study of Drug Development, which is heavily funded by the pharmaceutical industry.[25] The figure was nearly $1 billion higher than a 2012 estimate by the London-based Office of Health Economics, which receives drug industry funding as well.[26] The $2.6 billion figure also reflects, with adjustments for inflation, a 145 percent increase over the Tufts Center's own 2003 estimate of $802 million. A systematic review in 2010 of studies of drug R&D costs found estimates ranging from $161 million to $1.8 billion per successful drug.[27]

The Tufts research looked at 106 new drugs tested in humans between 1995 and 2007, but it did not disclose the particular drugs, the drugmakers or the data supporting the findings.[28]

"Those data are secret, and no one else gets to really see or verify them," said Aaron Carroll, a professor of pediatrics at Indiana University who writes on health policy.[29]

Carroll and other skeptics of the Tufts estimate question the study's methodology. For example, they say, the Tufts researchers assigned $1.2 billion — almost half their total R&D estimate — to opportunity costs: the returns investors might otherwise have earned in non-drug-related

Andrew Burton/Getty Images

WHY PUT
$ BILLION
IN PROFITS OVER
CHILDREN'S LIVES?
#ASKPHARMA

VISIT AFAIRSHOT.ORG FOR MORE INFORMATION

Doctors Without Borders employees and volunteers protest at Pfizer headquarters in New York City on April 23, 2015, against the drugmaker's high vaccine prices in developing nations. Drug manufacturers say rising research and development costs force them to raise prices, but critics blame excessive profit-seeking and marketing budgets. A majority of Americans say keeping drugs affordable should be the top national health care priority, and all three remaining presidential candidates have promised relief.

investments while a drug was in development. Critics say those hypothetical returns are unrealistically high and point out that research is the backbone of the drug business.[30]

Of the remaining $1.4 billion, several factors accounted for the big jump in R&D estimates, according to Joseph A. DiMasi, the Tufts study's lead author: "Clinical trials are becoming more complex," he says. There is also more testing against comparable existing drugs, DiMasi says, and medical cost inflation.

Increasingly complex approval procedures are responsible for "a substantial increase in clinical failure rates," which contributes to a large share of the increase in costs, DiMasi says. Fewer than 12 percent of new drugs make it to market now, compared with 21.5 percent in the earlier study.[31]

Critics of the study note that many new cancer drugs are eligible for expedited clinical trials, which helps lower development costs. Companies also receive special tax credits that cover half of the cost of clinical trials, they say, further reducing development costs.[32]

These critics point out that, directly or indirectly, American taxpayers are the single largest investor in the pharmaceutical industry. The government subsidizes the development of many new drugs twice: by providing tax credits to help cover the cost of clinical trials and by funding research at drug research centers across the country through the National Institutes of Health, whose proposed 2017 budget is $33.1 billion.[33]

According to one recent analysis, more than half of the groundbreaking drugs developed in recent decades originated in publicly funded research centers.[34] Another recent study said "public-sector research has had a more immediate effect on improving public health than was previously realized."[35]

The Tufts study did not address the role of public funding of basic research in the development of new drugs. It looked only at "entirely private-sector research costs," DiMasi says.

Fueled by the Senate's investigation into Gilead's pricing strategy for its new hepatitis C drugs, industry critics increasingly are challenging companies' R&D estimates. "We've learned that drugmakers don't base their prices on recouping R&D, but rather on the pricing scheme that will maximize their bottom lines," says John Rother, president and CEO of the National Coalition on Health Care, a nonpartisan alliance of consumer groups, labor unions, medical societies and other groups that advocate for increased affordability, transparency and other reforms in the health care system.

Drug industry representatives also justify the high prices by noting the cost-cutting and lifesaving importance of new drugs, such as the hepatitis C drugs.

"Curing hepatitis C not only dramatically improves patients' lives but has the potential to save the U.S. health care system as much as $9 billion per year by preventing expensive hospitalizations and avoiding thousands of liver transplants that routinely cost over $500,000 each," PhRMA's then-President and CEO John Castellani said in 2014.[36]

Should patent rights be changed?

FDA approval signals a new drug's safety and evidence of effectiveness, but not its therapeutic or monetary value compared with other drugs for the same condition.

When it approves a drug, the FDA gives the manufacturer exclusive rights to market the drug for a period of time, usually five years. During that period, the drug is protected by law from competing brand-name products or low-priced generics, so pharmaceutical companies are free to set prices as high as the market will bear.[37]

Most spending on brand-name prescription drugs, which represent only about one-fifth of all prescription drugs, occurs during these exclusivity periods.[38]

The exclusivity period may be longer or shorter depending on the circumstances of approval and the drug. For example, under the Affordable Care Act (ACA) of 2010, complex drugs known as biologics, made from living cells, are protected from competition for 12 years because of their lengthier development periods and higher associated costs.[39]

But some critics argue that some new drugs, such as so-called follow-on drugs — introduced after a comparable drug has gained FDA approval, and often nicknamed "me-too" drugs — involve little innovation and do not justify a lengthy exclusivity period. "A drug which provides little or no incremental value over existing products gets the same ability to charge a monopoly price for an extended period of time as a lifesaving breakthrough," according to Alfred Engelberg, founder of the Engelberg Center for Health Care Reform at the Brookings Institution, a centrist think tank in Washington.[40]

Tufts' DiMasi and other researchers say follow-on drugs deserve exclusivity because they may offer more treatment options and keep prices down by enhancing competition.[41]

But several studies have found that the pricing of these drugs defies conventional economic theory, which holds that competition should bring down prices. Newer drugs often cost considerably more than comparable but slightly older ones, and their prices remain high.[42]

U.S. patent law also influences drug pricing by allowing drug companies to file for a patent, valid for 20 years, during which time other companies cannot make, use or sell the drug. Drug patent exclusivity periods may or may not run concurrently with FDA-granted exclusivity periods.[43]

However, in a practice known as "evergreening," or "product-hopping," drug companies whose patents are about to expire can receive new patents by slightly tweaking the drugs' makeup, thus renewing the drug's exclusivity period and keeping lower-priced generic versions from entering the market.

"There is a consistently low threshold for granting patents," Harvard's Kesselheim says. "Many are not innovative at all but, instead, [are] high-cost and low value."

"Pay-for delay," another controversial practice in drug patenting, occurs when branded drugmakers pay potential generic competitors to delay introduction of lower-priced products. The Federal Trade Commission (FTC), which identified 29 potential pay-for-delay deals in 2013 worth $4.3 billion, has sued several drugmakers over the practice.[44] That same year the Supreme Court said pay-for-delay agreements may violate antitrust rules, although it did not address whether the agreements were unlawful.[45]

The patent process also affects drug prices by creating so-called lost drugs. These are created when drugmakers, early in the development process, patent thousands of drug compounds, some of which they ultimately will discard, says Benjamin Roin, an assistant professor at the Massachusetts Institute of Technology's Sloan School of Management. "Discarded compounds could be valuable drugs in the future, but when later research reveals this potential, companies can't patent the drugs because they're no longer new," he says.

Roin proposes giving drugmakers lengthier exclusivity periods so they will have more incentive to develop drugs from these discarded patented compounds. But Boston University law professor Kevin Outterson has recommended government funding to develop such unpatentable lost drugs.[46]

Under the so-called Bayh-Dole Act of 1980, the federal government gives academic and nonprofit research centers the right to patent drugs developed based on federally funded basic research. Those institutions can then license or sell the patents to pharmaceutical companies. But the law also allows government agencies to take over those patents to ensure the public pays reasonable prices for drugs developed with government funding.[47] Those "march-in" rights have never been enforced, however.

Some critics suggest bypassing the patenting process altogether, particularly if public funding or a billionaire philanthropist's donation, for example, subsidized clinical trials that led to one or two breakthrough drugs.

"Imagine if a major new cancer drug was available for less than $1,000 a year when the drugs being developed through the patent system were selling for $150,000 or more," says economist Dean Baker, co-director of the liberal Washington-based Center for Economic and Policy Research, who has written extensively on drug research financing. "That would really be a shock to the industry."

Majority Backs Stiffer Price Rules

About three-fifths of American adults say the government needs to do more to regulate prescription drug prices, while a fifth say the government uses a proper level of regulation.

Percentage of U.S. Adults with Views on Prescription Drug Price Regulation*

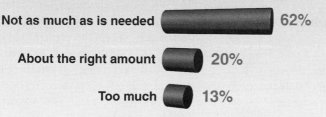

Not as much as is needed — 62%

About the right amount — 20%

Too much — 13%

* Data exclude refused or "don't know" responses.

Source: Bianca DiJulio, Jamie Firth and Mollyann Brodie, "Kaiser Health Tracking Poll: October 2015," Oct. 28, 2015, http://tinyurl.com/h6zlze5

Should the United States adopt cost-containing measures used in other industrialized countries?

Overall, Americans pay significantly more for prescription drugs than citizens of other countries — more than twice as much as in most other developed nations and more than three times as much as citizens in Denmark, New Zealand and Israel.[48] For the 20 top-selling drugs, Americans pay an average of three times as much as British consumers.[49]

Patients in other countries usually receive prescription drugs covered by universal health insurance programs subsidized by taxpayers. In the United States, where income taxes are much lower, public insurance programs are available only to senior citizens, low-income Americans, people with disabilities, veterans and active U.S. military personnel. More than half of Americans rely on private insurance plans, which have little bargaining clout with big pharmaceutical companies.[50]

And a variety of regulations constrain big public plans in the United States. For instance, the Veterans Health Administration and the Medicaid program for low-income Americans can limit the prices they pay to drug companies. But in a compromise involving drug manufacturers and other parties, Congress prohibited Medicare from negotiating lower group prices for its Part D prescription drug insurance program, which

lawmakers created in 2003 and now covers 70 million older Americans.

According to federal and academic data, if Medicare Part D benefited from the same discounts as the Veterans Administration, for instance, the government would save $16 billion a year.[51]

Governments in other countries use a variety of strategies to keep drug prices down, including negotiating with drugmakers. They also guide coverage and pricing decisions for new drugs by relying on "reference pricing" — grouping drugs with the same or similar therapeutic effect into classes. For example, Advil, Motrin and other ibuprofen-based drugs might be grouped into a single class. The reference price then becomes the standard price insurers will cover, usually based on the lowest-priced product or an average of all the products in a class.[52] Makers of competing drugs may charge more or less, but patients pay out-of-pocket for any costs above the reference price.[53]

In a systematic review of 16 studies of reference pricing published between 2002 and 2011 in six countries, researchers concluded that the policy reduced drug prices by up to 24 percent and reduced expenses for both patients and insurers. The review also found that reference pricing did not result in more doctor visits or hospital stays.[54]

Critics of reference pricing contend that it has stifled innovation in the pharmaceutical industries in other developed countries, mainly by reducing money available for R&D. And a literature review for the nonprofit Institute of Medicine — part of the National Academies of Sciences — concluded that a similar outcome could be expected if pricing controls were instituted in the United States.[55]

But others believe that reference pricing would not stifle innovation. According to Austin Frakt, a health economist with Boston University and the Veterans Administration, "Such a drug might be placed in a new class and therefore could be priced high."[56]

Congress has defeated repeated efforts by Democrats to legislate drug price caps and to authorize Medicare to negotiate discounted prices.[57]

"These issues come up again and again," says conservative economist Douglas Holtz-Eakin, former director of the nonpartisan Congressional Budget Office under Republican President George W. Bush. "The last thing I would want to see is Congress getting involved. It's not good for anyone," Holtz-Eakin said. Instead he would streamline the FDA to cut the cost of getting prescription drugs approved.

In 2003 Holtz-Eakin developed cost estimates for the Medicare Part D prescription drug benefit. Originally projected to cost $122.88 billion a year by 2012, actual costs for the program in 2012 were $55 billion. Holtz-Eakin in 2014 called Part D "the best-functioning federal entitlement program, one that actually provides the benefits promised at a low cost."[58]

Almost two-thirds of Americans say the government should act to lower drug prices, according to a 2015 poll by the Kaiser Family Foundation.[59]

For many medical experts, the issue comes down to the relative value of available drugs — how different drugs for the same conditions compare in terms of therapeutic value and cost.

"Americans at the same time are getting tremendously ripped off with drugs and also getting tremendous value, and we almost never know when we're getting ripped off and when we're getting real value," said Steven Pearson, a lecturer at Harvard Medical School.[60]

To help answer that question, Pearson founded the nonprofit Institute for Clinical and Economic Review in Boston, which reviews the clinical and cost effectiveness and other potential benefits of new drugs, along with projected budget impacts of the drugs at their list prices. The information yields a "value-based price benchmark" that, he says, insurers are beginning to use to help them decide reasonable prices for reimbursing patients.

PhRMA, the drug industry lobbying group, says the concept "is based on untested, short-term budget-impact thresholds that do not reflect overall health care value and are biased against new innovative medicines."[61]

Other efforts are underway to include value-based information on new drugs, especially for ultra-expensive new cancer drugs. The Memorial Sloan Kettering Cancer Center in New York City has introduced an interactive online tool, the Drug Abacus, which describes the attributes of 54 new cancer drugs and offers comparisons within classes. The American Society of Clinical Oncology also has published value-based comparative data on cancer drugs.[62]

Doctors at Sloan Kettering touched off a national debate about drug pricing in 2012, when they wrote an op-ed for *The New York Times* detailing the center's refusal to recommend a new cancer drug they said was no more effective than existing drugs but was twice as expensive. "In most industries something that offers no advantage over its competitors and yet sells for twice the price would never even get on the market," the doctors wrote. "But that is not how things work for drugs."[63]

Sloan Kettering's action prompted similar objections from other doctors. Last July more than 100 oncologists from around the country called for new regulations to control soaring cancer-drug prices.[64]

Several insurance companies and pharmacy benefit managers — which administer drug programs for groups of plans — are striking "value-based" deals with manufacturers. In May, health insurer Cigna Corp. announced that makers of new cholesterol drugs will provide discounts if the drugs do not work as well as expected.[65]

Medical experts generally agree that new perspectives on drug pricing will take hold slowly. "America doesn't do things in one fell swoop," Pearson says. "But we're not using our resources wisely, and maybe we are ready to have this conversation."

BACKGROUND
"Patent" Medicines

The tension between commerce and societal perceptions of ethical practice is a long-standing theme in American drug manufacturing and pricing. During most of the 19th century, few people believed in the effectiveness of drugs, which came to be known as patent medicines.

"If all the medicines in the world were thrown into the sea, it would be all the better for mankind and all the worse for the fishes," the eminent physician Oliver Wendell Holmes Sr., father of the Supreme Court justice, famously remarked in 1842.[66]

At the time, practitioners, who often prepared their own remedies, were facing stiffening competition from companies that concocted nostrums containing secret ingredients whose curative powers manufacturers promoted relentlessly in newspapers, health guides and advice columns. Supporting these patent medicines were robust advertising budgets that formed the financial backbone of many newspapers. Other papers got their start as one-page sheets created by nostrum makers to tout their products.[67]

These patent medicines were not protected by patents as defined by current law, which would have required the makers to disclose the products' formulas. Rather, "patent" was a term denoting the formula's secrecy; technically, patent medicines were "proprietary" products with copyright-protected trademarks.[68] But those secret formulas often included opium, cocaine and other highly addictive ingredients that ensured continued sales.[69]

Nostrum makers also cast a wide net across disease categories to protect their profits. William "Old Bill" Rockefeller, father of Standard Oil founder John D. Rockefeller hawked bottled "Nujol" as a cancer cure — and later, as a cure for constipation, cholera, bronchitis and various other complaints.[70]

The "ethical" sector of the industry, which disclosed its drug formulas and marketed only to physicians, argued that patenting drugs was quackery.[71] Since its founding in 1847, the American Medical Association (AMA) asserted that all drug formulas, along with other medical knowledge, should be made public.[72]

In 1881, patent medicine manufacturers formed their own trade group, the Proprietary Association of America. By 1902, nearly one-fourth of New York City physicians were prescribing patent medicines, and the AMA could not persuade medical journals to stop running ads for them.[73]

During the early 1900s, several forces combined to shift power in the drug industry. Muckraking journalists detailed the outright fraud perpetrated by the patent medicine companies, often with lethal results for unsuspecting Americans. And Progressive-era activists crusaded for change.

In 1906 Congress passed the Pure Food and Drug Act, which made it illegal to misrepresent the ingredients in foods or medicines.[74] But the law did not require manufacturers to verify claims about their products' effectiveness or safety. Before long, nostrum makers were again making outrageous claims.[75]

Meanwhile, though, the AMA began setting standards for drugs and testing them in its own laboratory. It also formulated strict rules on newspaper advertising of nostrums, with which many newspapers complied despite the loss of revenue.[76]

Zane Pauley of Whitmore Lake, Mich., holds up a list of prescription drugs he plans to buy in Canada. By the mid-1990s busloads of older Americans were making highly publicized buying trips to Canada and Mexico, where drug prices were much lower than in the United States. In 2003 Congress narrowly voted to create the Medicare Part D prescription program but barred Medicare from negotiating drug prices.

Bill Pugliano/Getty Images

The goal was to keep information about nostrums from consumers "and re-channel drug purchasing through physicians," Princeton University sociologist Paul Starr wrote in *The Social Transformation of American Medicine*.[77] Still, the FDA, created in 1931, did not establish rules for labeling certain drugs "by prescription only" until 1938.[78]

The Food, Drug, and Cosmetic Act of 1938 required drugmakers to demonstrate their products' safety before marketing them. While previous food and drug legislation had focused on the food supply, this law for the first time focused on scientifically based drugs. It passed in the wake of a national tragedy: More than 100 people, mostly children, had died after taking a sulfa-based antibiotic that contained a solvent used in antifreeze.

Prescription-only sales, which took decision-making out of the hands of consumers, allowed drugmakers to cut their advertising budgets and focus their marketing efforts on physicians.[79]

Few science-based drugs, and even fewer therapeutically effective ones, came on the market during the first half of the 20th century. Of those that did, by far the most significant were antibiotics, wonder drugs that could speedily cure until-then deadly infections. Penicillin, isolated in 1929, was the first of them. During World War II, the government developed techniques for its mass production, making penicillin the most common treatment for battlefield injuries.[80] After the war, the government licensed generic penicillin to several firms, which competed fiercely for market share. As a result, the price of a pound of penicillin fell from $3,995 to $282 between 1945 and 1950.[81]

Something similar happened after Selman Waksman, a New Jersey soil scientist, developed the first of a new class of antibiotics from bacteria-killing microbes found in soil. Streptomycin, the first effective treatment for tuberculosis, earned Waksman the Nobel Prize. Ultimately, the drug was licensed to several companies and sold generically; its price plummeted, just as penicillin's had.[82]

Drug companies realized that to profit from new miracle drugs, they had to adopt a new business model: They quickly developed a host of new antibiotics, similar to streptomycin and penicillin, patented them and refused to license them to other companies. Then they marketed these so-called me-too drugs as new and improved versions of the generic originals.[83] The companies dispatched representatives, called detail men, to personally explain to doctors why their new antibiotic was superior to its competitors. During the 1950s, the main antibiotic-producing drugmakers spent more than half of their advertising budget on detailing.[84]

With so many similar antibiotics jostling for market share, prices would be expected to drop. Instead, they soared, largely because detail men were able to keep physicians interested in new products.

Similarly, when whole new classes of drugs — antidepressants, antacids, blood-pressure medicines and others — were introduced in the 1950s, other firms rushed in with copycat drugs, marketed as new and improved, and sold them at the higher prices.[85] In defiance of textbook economic principles, prices remained high.

Between late 1959 and 1963, the powerful Sen. Estes Kefauver, D-Tenn., chairman of the Senate Antitrust and Monopoly Subcommittee, shifted the panel's focus from attacking organized crime to the drug industry's profit margins, advertising practices and patent law abuses.[86] In one hearing, a former research director for a major drugmaker admitted that a desire for copycat drugs that "promise no utility" drove more than half of his company's research.[87]

Kefauver wanted legislation to rein in such abuses, but the 1962 amendments to the Pure Food and Drug Act required only that drugmakers seeking new drug approvals provide substantial evidence of effectiveness and safety, based on sound studies.[88]

The issue had surfaced amid a tragedy in which European babies were born with missing or shrunken limbs to mothers who had taken a common sedative containing the drug thalidomide during pregnancy. The same thing did not occur in the United States because a courageous FDA medical officer, Frances Oldham Kelsey, had stalled approval of the drug.[89]

Patent Puzzles

The first major era of drug discovery ended in the mid-1960s. In the 1970s, as discoveries in genetic engineering led to the creation of new drugs, the biotechnology revolution in medicine began gaining steam.[90] Meanwhile, new medical challenges and old regulatory ones defined the drug pricing landscape.

Researchers increasingly began focusing on chronic diseases — heart disease, cancer, stroke, diabetes and dementia — that had become the leading causes of death as Americans began living longer.[91] At the same time, health insurance coverage for medicines grew in the 1970s, leading to greater consumer demand for more drugs.[92]

Aided by a post-World War II surge in government-funded drug research, scientists promised new cures.[93] But lawmakers and the public began to question who should profit, through control of patents and licensing, from new medicines developed with public funds. Before the 1980s, the government argued mostly that it — and the public — should. However, for various reasons there had been little commercialization of government-owned inventions.[94]

In 1980, Sens. Birch Bayh, D-Ind., and Robert Dole, R-Kan., co-sponsored legislation to spur commercialization of government-funded inventions of various kinds, including medicines. The law allowed universities and labs that invented products and drugs to patent them. Those facilities in turn could commercialize their discoveries, license them to drugmakers or sell them to pharmaceutical companies.[95]

CHRONOLOGY

1850s-1905 *The heyday of patent medicines ushers in widespread, unregulated advertising.*

1905 *Collier's* magazine publishes an exposé of patent medicines by Samuel Hopkins Adams, one of several muckraking journalists crusading against deception in the business.

1906-1959 *Congress regulates drugs and investigates drug companies' wrongdoing.*

1906 Pure Food and Drug Act makes it illegal to misrepresent ingredients in foods or medicines.

1938 Food, Drug and Cosmetic Act bans false therapeutic claims in pharmaceutical labeling.

1951 Durham-Humphrey Amendment defines over-the-counter and prescription-only drugs.

1958 A Federal Trade Commission investigation into antibiotic pricing finds overwhelming evidence of companies fixing prices and reaping unreasonable profits.

1959 Testimony begins at Senate Antitrust and Monopoly Subcommittee hearings led by Estes Kefauver, D-Tenn. Over four years, the hearings expose profit-seeking at the expense of safety and effectiveness within drug industry.

1980-1984 *Biotechnology revolution and other innovations send new-drug prices higher.*

1980 Bayh-Dole Act allows universities and laboratories conducting government-funded research to patent their inventions, but allows government to withdraw inventors' intellectual property rights if they price the drugs unreasonably high.

1983 Orphan Drug Act offers incentives to encourage drugmakers to develop treatments for rare diseases.

1984 Hatch-Waxman Act establishes a pathway for streamlined FDA approval for generic drugs.

1987-Present *High and sharply rising drug prices prompt calls for reform.*

1987 FDA approves AZT as the first drug to treat HIV infection. AIDS activists and others protest for years over the drug's high price.

1993 Republicans and the health care industry join to stop President Bill Clinton's proposed Health Security Act, which, among other things, calls for a federal advisory body to evaluate new drug prices.

1994 To help drugmakers, Uruguay Round Agreements Act extends patent protection from 17 years to 20 years from the date the manufacturer first file a patent application.

1997 FDA allows drug companies to advertise their products directly to consumers. . . . FDA Modernization Act allows pharmaceutical companies to advertise "off-label" uses.

2000 Maine passes a law that would trigger price controls if drug makers did not lower prices in the state. Companies challenge the law in court.

2003 The Medicare Prescription Drug, Improvement and Modernization Act provides a prescription drug benefit for senior citizens but bars Medicare from negotiating with pharmaceutical companies for discounted drug prices. . . . U.S. Supreme Court lifts injunction blocking Maine from implementing its prescription drug program but leaves the program vulnerable to further legal challenges.

2010 Patient Protection and Affordable Care Act includes prescription drug coverage as an "essential benefit" insurers must offer.

2013 Supreme Court rules that "pay-for-delay" deals, in which drugmakers pay rivals to keep cheaper generic versions of brand-name drugs off the market, may violate antitrust rules. . . . Gilead Sciences introduces Sovaldi and Harvoni (2014), treatments for hepatitis C, at $1,000 a pill.

2015 The average price of existing brand-name drugs rises by 16.2 percent during the year, up 98 percent since 2011.

2016 Several states introduce bills requiring drugmakers to disclose data on pricing decisions.

Drug Ads Cause Headaches for Physicians

Critics, manufacturers differ on whether TV commercials help consumers.

In one TV commercial, a middle-aged couple contentedly strolls on a beach, waves lapping at their feet, as a voiceover extols the benefits of an unnamed drug. A Web address flashes across the screen.

Flick the remote, and an action-filled ad features a giant, helmet-clad big toe charging down the gridiron. "Tackle it!" the narrator exhorts, as the crowd roars approval for the toenail-fungus drug Jublia. The ad, which ran during the 2015 Super Bowl after singer Katy Perry's halftime performance, did not mention that a course of treatment costs thousands of dollars and that studies have found it cures the fungus in fewer than 20 percent of cases.[1]

Ads for costly brand-name prescription drugs promise relief for whatever ails Americans. Besides the United States, only New Zealand allows so-called direct-to-consumer advertising for prescription drugs, which the U.S. Food and Drug Administration (FDA) greenlighted in 1997.

Pharmaceutical companies are spending more than ever on drug ads, prompting physicians' groups and some members of Congress to call for restrictions on such advertising due to concerns that the ads are driving up demand for expensive drugs. In 2015, drug-ad spending on TV and in other media reached $5.2 billion, up more than 60 percent over the previous four years.[2] Between 2014 and 2015 alone, the amount rose by nearly $1 billion. A quarter of last year's total was spent on ads for just five high-priced drugs, used to treat common conditions such as arthritis, muscle pain and erectile dysfunction.[3] Drugmakers spent more than $100 million each on 16 drugs in 2015 — including $117 million on Jublia, the toenail-fungus fighter.

This year, total spending on drug ads will be even higher, according to drug industry market reports.[4] The lion's share of the money goes to television "spots" but also to newspaper, magazine and radio ads. Drug advertising on social media, not included in the totals, is on the upswing as well.

Critics such as the American Medical Association (AMA), the nation's largest physicians' group, say drug ads drive up prices by redirecting patients away from more reasonably priced, and often more appropriate, medicines. In November 2015, the AMA voted in favor of a ban on direct-to-consumer advertising of prescription drugs. But the vote was largely symbolic, because any such ban would require Congress to pass a bill — an unlikely event.[5] In addition, any legislation would face constitutional challenges based on First Amendment protections for commercial speech.

Nevertheless, Democratic members of Congress have become involved. In March, Sen. Al Franken, D-Minn., introduced a bill to eliminate a corporate tax deduction drugmakers take for the money they spend on advertising.

Pharmaceutical companies "have been spending billions of advertising dollars trying to encourage Americans to buy the most expensive drugs — even when cheaper, equally effective drugs are on the market," Franken said.[6] Democratic presidential front-runner Hillary Clinton also has called for ending tax breaks for prescription drug advertising.[7] Presumptive Republican nominee Donald Trump's health care plan does not address the issue.[8]

In February, Rep. Rosa DeLauro, D-Conn., introduced legislation that would impose a three-year moratorium on advertising new prescription drugs. DeLauro said, among other things, that new drugs have a higher risk of unidentified side effects.[9]

As of May, neither bill had a Republican co-sponsor, and, with the GOP in control of both chambers, neither was likely to move forward.

The law, which applied to government-funded inventions, drew harsh assessments. Adm. Hyman Rickover, commander of the U.S. nuclear submarine fleet, predicted that it would help large companies and hurt small businesses in many industries. Sen. Russell B. Long, D-La., asked why U.S. taxpayers should "pay twice: first for the research and development and then through monopoly prices." The law did allow the government to seize a drug patent if the owner did not charge reasonable prices or use the invention to "alleviate health or safety needs."[96]

But even with the incentives provided by the Bayh-Dole Act, few drug companies were interested in using government-funded research to develop treatments for

In general, the FDA cannot require drugmakers to submit ads for review before they air, although drugmakers often seek guidance from the agency before releasing an ad. The FDA demands that newly released ads be pulled if it believes they violate the law by misrepresenting data or otherwise violating the law. The FDA is investigating whether many ads — including those that feature cartoon characters — distract consumers from understanding the risks associated with some drugs.[10]

Under current FDA regulations, ads are not required to provide information about a drug's cost, effectiveness or alternatives. Companies, however, must disclose all potential side effects, although they can avoid disclosing side effects or risks by not naming the drug being advertised and by directing viewers to a website instead.[11]

Drug companies oppose any additional limits on advertising. Pharmaceutical Research and Manufacturers of America (PhRMA), the drugmakers' trade group, said on its website that advertising "brings patients into their doctors' offices and starts important doctor-patient conversations about health that might otherwise not take place."[12]

The ads also push patients to manage chronic conditions in a responsible and timely way, by reminding them about the drugs' availability, PhRMA said.[13]

About half of respondents to a 2015 Kaiser Family Foundation poll said prescription drug ads generally were helpful, although fewer than half said the ads did a good job of explaining drugs' benefits and potential side effects. Nearly three in 10 said they had talked to a doctor about a particular drug because of an ad they had seen or heard. At the same time, almost nine in 10 of those interviewed wanted the FDA to review drug ads for accuracy before they are broadcast. And a large majority of those interviewed said the affordability of prescription drugs for serious conditions should be the government's top health care priority.[14]

Brad Shapiro, a University of Chicago economist and drug marketing researcher, summed up the pros and cons of drug advertising. "If they are truly sick people, then the ad did a good thing by getting them to their physician," he told the *Deseret News*. "If they are hypochondriacs who will pester their physicians into giving them unnecessary treatment, then the ads are a bad thing."[15]

— *Leslie Allen*

[1] Elisabeth Rosenthal, "Ask Your Doctor if This Ad Is Right for You," *The New York Times*, Feb. 27, 2016, http://tinyurl.com/hzrjbwp.

[2] Rebecca Robbins, "Drug Makers Now Spend $5 Billion a Year on Advertising. Here's What That Buys," *STAT*, March 9, 2016, http://tinyurl.com/jfcxpoe.

[3] *Ibid.*

[4] *Ibid.*

[5] Ed Silverman, "Why doctors' call to ban drug advertising is a dead end," *STAT*, Dec. 8, 2015. http://tinyurl.com/z7xvmd8.

[6] Al Franken, "Sen. Franken Presses to End Marketing Tax Breaks for Rx Drug Companies," press release, U.S. Senate, March 3, 2016, http://tinyurl.com/zgq4fmu.

[7] "Factsheets: Hillary Clinton's Plan to Lower Prescription Drug Costs," Hillary for America, 2016, http://tinyurl.com/zr7vvpo.

[8] "Healthcare reform to make America great again," Donald J. Trump for President, http://tinyurl.com/z6xmsyo.

[9] Ed Silverman, "Lawmaker Seeks Moratorium on Consumer Drug Ads," *STAT*, Feb. 22, 2016, http://tinyurl.com/z948h38.

[10] Ed Silverman, "FDA Wants to Know Whether Animated Ads Distort Drug Risks," *STAT*, March 2, 2016, http://tinyurl.com/z6dguqm/.

[11] Rosenthal, *op. cit.*

[12] "Direct to Consumer Pharmaceutical Advertising," PhRMA, http://tinyurl.com/zotjsqj.

[13] Robbins, *op. cit.*

[14] Bianca DiJulio, Jamie Firth and Mollyann Brodie, "Kaiser Health Tracking Poll: October 2015," The Henry J. Kaiser Family Foundation, Oct 28, 2015, http://tinyurl.com/h6zlze5.

[15] Chandra Johnson, "Do prescription drug ads help or hurt consumers seeking relief?" *Deseret News*, April 10, 2016, http://tinyurl.com/jke8kms.

certain rare diseases. Such treatments were called "orphan drugs" because the development process was costly and the patients too few to justify the investment.

Soon after Bayh-Dole became law Congress again used intellectual property rights, this time to address the lack of development of orphan drugs.[97] The Orphan Drug Act of 1983, along with federal grants and tax credits for clinical trials, gave drugmakers a longer period — seven years — of market exclusivity. The new law led to a surge in orphan drugs, which now constitute nearly one-fourth of all new biologic drugs on the market.

Fueling the surge, ironically, was more widespread use: Once approved for a rare disease, these drugs can be prescribed to a much wider population for "off-label," or

Drug-Vial Waste Costs Billions

"This is a calculated way of increasing revenue."

In February, Lena Haddad, 53, visited a doctor's office in Bethesda, Md., to receive her weekly dose of Velcade, an injectable cancer medication for multiple myeloma and lymphoma. After opening the $1,034 vial of the drug and drawing Haddad's full dose, her nurse discarded the rest of the medicine — about half the vial, or roughly $500 worth of Velcade.[1]

"You can't use the remainder for the patient the next time she comes in or use it on another patient, so it has to be discarded as waste," the nurse said.[2]

Centers for Disease Control and Prevention (CDC) guidelines say single-use vials should be used only for a single patient and open vials should not be stored for future use. The guidelines say using opened vials on multiple patients could contaminate the vials and spread infection.[3]

Care providers can share some vials among multiple patients within six hours after opening them, but only if handled by specialized pharmacies, according to the nonprofit U.S. Pharmacopoeia Convention, which creates global public health care standards.[4]

Some medical researchers say that in packaging injectable cancer medicine in large, single-size vials, drugmakers are driving up health care costs by forcing hospitals and physicians to pay for medicine they must discard — costs they then pass on to patients, insurers or Medicare and Medicaid.

Drugmakers defend their production methods, saying they work with regulators to make sure packaging meets the needs of a diverse patient population. An official from Takeda Pharmaceuticals, which makes Velcade, said the company "worked closely" with the Food and Drug Administration (FDA) to ensure that vials provide enough medicine for patients of "almost any size."[5]

Public and private health insurers will spend at least $2.8 billion paying for unused injectable cancer medications

in 2016, according to a study by researchers at Memorial Sloan Kettering Cancer Center and the University of Chicago, published in the *British Medical Journal* in March. That figure includes $1 billion or more in markup costs added by hospitals and physician's offices for the medicine.[6]

Reacting to the study, Democratic Sens. Jeanne Shaheen of New Hampshire and Amy Klobuchar of Minnesota urged FDA Commissioner Robert Califf to explore ways to reduce waste and help companies find more cost-efficient ways to offer cancer medications. "Families fighting cancer should not have to worry about being able to afford the next dose of medication," they wrote.[7]

The FDA said it will respond directly to the senators about their letter.

In reviewing vial sizes, the agency focuses "on safety, not cost," an FDA spokesman said in a statement, because the agency is not authorized to consider cost. It does not mandate specific vial sizes, but vial-volume guidelines published last June urge manufacturers to supply slightly more medicine in vials than is indicated on the label to ensure sufficient dosages. However, the guidelines also say single-dose vials should "not contain a significant volume beyond what would be considered a usual or maximum dose" for the product or be so small that providers must use multiple vials to administer a typical dose. If a proposed vial size does not meet those specifications, the agency can ask the manufacturer to justify its proposal or change the vial size.[8]

The authors of the March study were highly critical of drug manufacturers. Under the U.S. health care system, they wrote, drug makers have an incentive to sell more medication than is necessary and providers have a profit incentive to buy more medication because they can mark up the cost and send the bill to patients or insurers.[9]

other uses. Highly subsidized medicines also are the most costly drugs on the market today.[98]

Responding to very high prices for such brand-name, patented drugs, Rep. Henry Waxman, a California Democrat who had sponsored the Orphan Drug Act, teamed in 1984 with Republican Sen. Orrin Hatch of Utah to pass the 1984 Drug Price

Competition and Patent Term Restoration Act, known as the Hatch-Waxman Act. It streamlined the FDA approval process for generic drugs after patents on brand-name equivalents expire. The law removed the requirement for new clinical trials — and paved the way for the rapid growth of generic drugs in the prescription drug industry.[99]

Dr. Leonard Saltz, a co-author of the study and chairman of a Sloan Kettering committee that determines which drugs the hospital will stock in its pharmacy, says he has watched for years as some drug makers raised cancer medication prices and volumes. For example, he says, Merck used to offer 50-milligram vials of its skin and lung cancer drug Keytruda. But after introducing 100-milligram vials in February 2015, the company stopped providing the smaller vials in the United States.[10]

"We don't think this is an accident," Saltz says. "We think this is, in most cases, a calculated way of increasing revenue that is not in patients' or society's best interest."

Merck still offers Keytruda in 50-milligram vials in Europe, where regulators wield more influence in setting health care prices than U.S. regulators, Saltz says.

Merck changed its U.S. vial size to make it easier for care providers to administer the medication to patients, the company said in a statement. The 50-milligram dose came in powdered form that needed to be mixed into a solution; the 100-milligram dose did not require mixing.

"Changing the vial size requires manufacturing changes, stability testing and regulatory approval even if patient dosing does not change," the company said in a statement.

A typical patient needs 140 milligrams of Keytruda, according to the March study. So the new, larger vial size effectively guarantees that care providers will waste, on average, 60 milligrams of the drug by needing to use two 100-milligram vials, based on calculations from the study.[11] Merck says it is conducting clinical trials for a 200-milligram dose.

Some manufacturers of high-cost medications offer a variety of vial selections that help reduce waste, Saltz says. For example, Teva Pharmaceutical Industries offers four sizes of its drug Treanda, a treatment for non-Hodgkins lymphoma and a type of leukemia, and Genentech offers two sizes of its breast cancer medication Kadcyla.[12]

Saltz says drug companies could help reduce waste by offering more multiple-dose vials that preserve medication over time and are designed to treat multiple patients, more single-dose options or buyback programs for medical providers.[13] In buyback programs, hospitals and doctors could bill manufacturers for unused medicine, and the drug makers could give the providers credit or reimburse them.

"The buyback would not be . . . unfairly onerous to companies" and would give them an incentive to create vial sizes "that allow for minimization of waste," Saltz says. If companies created just "one additional vial size," he says, it could "make a billion dollars of waste go away per year."[14]

— *Ethan McLeod*

[1] Gardiner Harris, "Waste in Cancer Drugs Costs $3 Billion a Year, a Study Says," *The New York Times*, March 1, 2016, http://tinyurl.com/j4exqn7.

[2] *Ibid.*

[3] "Questions about Single-dose/Single-use Vials," Centers for Disease Control and Prevention, updated Feb. 9, 2011, http://tinyurl.com/gnm6gxa.

[4] Claudia C. Okeke, "USP Chapter <797> Update on Recent Revisions," United States Pharmacopoeia, May 20, 2008, http://tinyurl.com/jng86k7; Peter B. Bach *et al.*, "Overspending driven by oversized single dose vials of cancer drugs," *British Medical Journal*, March 1, 2016, http://tinyurl.com/zwduj4p.

[5] Harris, *op. cit.*

[6] Bach *et al.*, *op. cit.*

[7] "Following Release of New Report, Klobuchar and Shaheen Urge the Food and Drug Administration to Examine the Dosage Size of Cancer Fighting Drugs," press release, Sen. Amy Klobuchar, U.S. Senate, March 2, 2016, http://tinyurl.com/j4a74zv.

[8] "Allowable Excess Volume and Labeled Vial Fill Size in Injectable Drug and Biological Products," Food and Drug Administration, June 2015, p. 4, http://tinyurl.com/j2g5yyh.

[9] Bach *et al.*, *op. cit.*

[10] *Ibid.*

[11] *Ibid.*

[12] *Ibid.*

[13] For information on multi-use vials, see "Questions about Multi-dose vials," Centers for Disease Control and Prevention, updated Feb. 9, 2011, http://tinyurl.com/l6e39yq.

[14] See table 3 in Bach *et al.*, *op. cit.*

Seeking Alternatives

Under the Hatch-Waxman Act generics dominated the prescription drug market for decades. At the same time, major advances in biotechnology and molecular biology, coupled with abundant public and private funding, allowed pharmaceutical companies to bring many important, new drugs to market.[100]

Drugs that helped control the ravages of the human immunodeficiency virus (HIV), which causes AIDS, were especially prominent. The virus was discovered in 1983, and the first drug to treat it, zidovudine (AZT), was approved by the FDA in 1987; for years it remained the only drug for HIV.[101] Yet, the death rate from AIDS remained stubbornly high, as did the price of AZT.

In 1991, prodded by AIDS activists' years-long outrage over drug costs, the National Institutes of Health (NIH), whose scientists had played important roles in the drug's discovery, took the unprecedented step of licensing AZT to a generic manufacturer, which brought down the price.[102]

Other important new drugs were coming onto the market with astonishing price tags. To focus on the issue, the Democratic-controlled Congress held hearings in 1991 on the high price of Taxol, a cancer drug made from the Pacific Yew tree that had been developed with public funding.[103]

Me-too drugs in the same therapeutic classes often quickly joined the new drugs. In 1994, FDA Commissioner David Kessler and a group of agency drug reviewers wrote that of 127 new drugs approved between 1989 and 1993, the majority were "virtually indistinguishable" from their competitors. Most were in widespread use, by millions of people, for common conditions such as mild pain and high blood pressure. "Victory in these therapeutic-class wars can mean millions of dollars for a drug company," the authors wrote.[104]

"Each patient is unique," PhRMA countered. "Physicians and patients benefit from a variety of medicines available to treat each ailment."[105]

Either way, the early 1990s saw drug prices, along with overall health care costs, rise by double-digit rates annually, despite efforts to slow the rise.[106]

President Bill Clinton's proposed Health Security Act of 1993 called for a federal advisory body to evaluate new drug prices; it also suggested giving the secretary of Health and Human Services the authority to exclude overpriced drugs from Medicare coverage. The measure was defeated after steep opposition from the pharmaceutical industry and health insurance companies opposed to universal coverage and government oversight.[107]

Taking matters into their own hands, Americans looked abroad for cheaper brand-name drugs. By the mid-1990s busloads of senior citizens from border states made highly publicized buying trips to Canada and Mexico, where prices were much lower than in the United States. PhRMA said the trips would ultimately "force U.S. consumers to pay more for research and development."[108]

Discontent with the status quo around the country finally led Congress to narrowly pass the 2003 Medicare Prescription Drug, Improvement, and Modernization Act, which created the Medicare Part D prescription program. But at the same time, it barred Medicare from negotiating drug prices, and large gaps in cost coverage remained for senior citizens.[109] The law also banned the importation of drugs from Canada and Europe.

The controversial 2010 Patient Protection and Affordable Care Act (ACA), commonly known as Obamacare because of the law's strong advocacy by President Obama, included prescription drug coverage as one of the 10 "essential benefits" health plans must offer. Under the ACA, state Medicaid programs for low-income people also must provide drug benefits.[110]

CURRENT SITUATION
Price Controls

In recent polling, 72 percent of Americans say prescription drug prices are unreasonable, and 86 percent say pharmaceutical companies should be forced to release information on how they set their drug prices.[111]

The industry maintains that this information is proprietary. But some experts say the ACA, which required drugmakers to disclose how much they pay doctors and hospitals for meals and other services, established a precedent for requiring drug companies to disclose proprietary information about pricing decisions.[112] Some research links the size of such payments to providers' prescribing patterns for a company's drugs.[113]

President Obama favors increased drug pricing transparency: His proposed 2017 federal budget would make drug companies reveal their research, development and marketing costs. The administration wants to eventually use the data to negotiate lower drug prices for Medicare recipients.[114]

Around the country, lawmakers are pushing for more transparency on drug pricing. At least 11 states are considering bills that would require drugmakers to disclose their actual costs and data on pricing decisions. In California, a transparency bill was withdrawn, under pressure from drug companies and other opponents, in the state Legislature in January.[115]

Although the bills differ, many feature provisions that would kick in only above certain pricing levels. Companion bills in Virginia's House and Senate, for example, would require drugmakers to disclose cost data for every drug whose wholesale price is $10,000 per treatment course or above. The data — including R&D, marketing, price increases, financial assistance programs and other information — would be available online.[116]

Under a Massachusetts bill — one of the toughest in the country — the state Health Policy Commission every year would formulate a list of widely prescribed critical drugs. Pharmaceutical companies would be required to disclose development and marketing costs as well as data on public funding for each drug; how much it costs in other countries; and other detailed information. The commission would identify drugs whose pricing would imperil the state's public health program budgets and overall medical spending. Taking such factors into account, the commission could then set a "maximum allowable price" for certain prescription drugs.[117]

Using similar language, Democratic New York Gov. Andrew Cuomo in January called for the state health department to develop "a list of critical prescription drugs for which there is a significant public interest in ensuring rational pricing." The health department could then set a "ceiling price" for the drugs after evaluating their value.[118] A spokesman for Cuomo said setting ceiling prices for certain critical drugs could save the state at least $6 million in the next fiscal year.[119]

Health insurers, hospitals and their trade groups support efforts to increase transparency in drug pricing. "With pharmacy costs as one of the biggest drivers of health care costs overall, consumers need and deserve basic pricing information," Paul Macielak, head of the New York Health Plan Association, which represents insurers, said in a statement.[120]

But drugmakers and their trade groups — especially PhRMA — vigorously oppose such bills. "Not only will implementing price controls have a very negative impact on innovation and send a signal that risk taking will not be rewarded, but also the so-called 'transparency' information called for in the proposals would be virtually impossible to achieve because it does not include the cost of failures inherent in the search for new treatments and cures," said Priscilla VanderVeer, a PhRMA spokeswoman.[121]

After California's drug pricing transparency bill failed for the second time in January, the state approved a ballot initiative that would require state-run health programs to pay no more for drugs than the discounted rate paid by the U.S. Department of Veterans Affairs (VA), which receives a 24 percent discount on drugs. Although Californians won't vote on the initiative until November, PhRMA and many drug companies already have spent more than $49 million to fight it.[122]

In Ohio, consumer activists got a similar initiative on the November ballot, but PhRMA filed suit in March to block it, alleging that false addresses and illegal alterations invalidated many of the signatures.[123]

Sticker Shock

The controversy over the high price of new hepatitis C drugs is helping to galvanize the push for state- and national-level action to rein in drug prices. Sovaldi came onto the market in late 2013, and its manufacturer, Gilead Sciences, introduced Harvoni in 2014. By year's end, the two drugs had nearly become the world's best-selling drugs, earning $12.4 billion for Gilead, more than it paid for the small company that developed the drugs.[124]

A number of factors are keeping these drugs in the public eye. For one, they are remarkably effective against hepatitis C, a virus that over time destroys the liver and can lead to cancer. "The previous treatment worked less than half the time and was toxic and absolutely fraught with medical complications," says James Hamilton, a physician and liver specialist at Johns Hopkins University. By comparison, "this treatment is shockingly easy — with a 95 percent or higher cure rate, including those with advanced disease — and no problems. Most patients are ecstatic."

Hepatitis C is also a common infection, afflicting more than 3 million Americans. Finally, and critically, the new drugs are extremely costly, with a list price of $84,000 to $94,500 for a 12-week treatment course.

"There has never been this expensive a drug for this common a condition," says Steve Miller, the chief medical officer at the nation's largest pharmacy benefit manager, Express Scripts, which administers prescription drug benefits for insurance companies and employers. A newer drug, Viekira Pak from a competitor, is priced at $83,000.[125]

The manufacturers say that through rebates, discounting and generous assistance programs for low-income patients, the actual price of these drugs is much lower.[126] Further, they point out, most patients have insurance that covers most of the cost.

Regardless, high demand and high prices are taxing health insurance plans and straining the budgets of state Medicaid programs and prison systems.

In January, Massachusetts Attorney General Maura Healey urged Gilead to adjust its pricing strategy for the drugs and threatened legal action over potentially unlawful trade practices if it didn't. She pointed out that the company sells the medicines for $4 a pill in India and $10 in Egypt, and noted that Massachusetts is facing a class-action suit seeking more access to treatment in state prisons, where the hepatitis C infection rate is 17 times higher than in the general population.[127]

State-run Medicaid programs for low-income and disabled persons are severely restricting access to the drugs, according to a study of 2,000 patients.[128]

Congress Debates

After the 18-month investigation into Gilead's pricing strategy for its hepatitis C drugs, U.S. senators excoriated the company, saying it had placed profits ahead of patients. And several drug company executives faced withering questioning before other recent Senate and House committee hearings.

In January, 51 Democratic members of the House recommended that guidelines be developed to enable federal agencies to "bring relief from out-of-control drug pricing" by using the "march-in" provisions of the 1980 Bayh-Dole Act — which allow the government to withdraw the exclusive marketing rights awarded to drug companies if they have unreasonably priced their products. The lawmakers said up to a quarter of important new drugs have received public funding during the development stage.[129]

But in early April, NIH Director Francis Collins told the Senate Appropriations Labor and Health Subcommittee that under the law, march-in rights don't "really appear to be designed to be utilized in a fashion where the price is the obstacle. If we begin to march in in a very broad way about drug pricing," drug companies may lose interest in working with the NIH to develop new treatments.[130]

Despite the public outcry over skyrocketing prices, Congress has been reluctant to legislate solutions in recent years. "Between 2005 and 2014 alone, bill titles mentioning prescription drugs decreased by 76 percent, more steadily than bills with titles referencing health insurance," said academic researchers. That downward trend continues in the current congressional session.[131]

Democratic presidential candidates, whose party has long been critical of the drug industry, hope to reverse this trend if elected. Hillary Clinton and Bernie Sanders say they would legalize the importation of prescription drugs from Canada; limit out-of-pocket costs; encourage more competition and ban "pay-for-delay" agreements that block or slow the introduction of generic drugs. Both also support allowing Medicare to negotiate drug prices with drugmakers — which even presumptive GOP nominee Donald Trump has endorsed, breaking with Republican policy.[132]

OUTLOOK
Good News, Bad News

Many drug price watchers foresee a good news-bad news scenario over the next several years.

"We're going to get a lot of great new drugs," says Pearson of the Institute for Clinical and Economic Review.

Miller, of Express Scripts, says, "I'm incredibly excited about where the science is going." He is optimistic, among other things, about the possibility of more effective Alzheimer's disease treatments. "There are already 70 million people over the age of 55 who'd love to prevent Alzheimer's in themselves," he says.

The bad news, Miller says, is that any groundbreaking drug for this devastating disease or other common conditions such as diabetes will almost certainly carry a high price tag.

When that happens, the budget strains created now by new hepatitis C drugs will seem modest in comparison, experts predict. And as the prices of other drugs — new and old, branded and generic — continue their steady rise, experts ask whether policy changes will occur to help make prescription drugs more affordable in the United States.

Peter Arno, director of Health Policy Research at the Political Economy Research Institute at the University of Massachusetts, says he is hopeful. "Change is in the wind," he says. "The path we are on is untenable. But the public has to get behind it."

Several experts agree the issue of high drug prices has more staying power with the public now than at other

AT ISSUE

Should Medicare be allowed to negotiate drug prices?

YES

Peter S. Arno
Senior Fellow and Director of Health Policy Research, Political Economy Research Institute, University of Massachusetts, Amherst, and

Michael H. Davis
Professor of Law, Cleveland State University

Written for *CQ Researcher*, May 2016

Bending the health care cost curve in the right direction will require new mechanisms to control drug prices. Drug spending in the United States increased 12 percent in 2014, faster than nearly every other health care spending component and the highest rate in more than a decade. Overall, Medicare spending grew 5.5 percent, but drug spending grew 16.9 percent, hardly a sustainable rate.

Medicare is the largest purchaser of drugs, with 39 million individuals enrolled in Part D plans that help pay for prescriptions. Yet a recent study by Marc-André Gagnon and Sidney Wolfe reported that the program pays 73 percent more than Medicaid and 80 percent more than the Veterans Administration for brand-name drugs. Both agencies negotiate with drug companies for price discounts.

The Medicare Drug, Improvement, and Modernization Act of 2003 created prescription drug coverage through the Medicare Part D program but specifically prohibited Medicare from negotiating lower prices for drugs. Calls to change this have gone unheeded. Some opponents to negotiating Medicare drug prices fall back on hackneyed arguments that the pharmaceutical industry has used for years whenever the issue has come up: that negotiation would stymie innovation and limit access to medications. Others question whether the government could successfully negotiate lower prices. But these arguments assume the government cannot change and enforce laws to ensure the necessary leverage for negotiating reasonable prices. The arguments also violate the principle that prices should — and, in fact, must — be subject to the free market when a patent expires.

To pretend that negotiation will discourage progress violates every economic rule we know. Negotiation is how two parties reach a mutually advantageous compromise. Plus, we know that excess monopoly profits, from which Big Pharma [the Pharmaceutical Research and Manufacturers of America] has "suffered" for decades, do not lead to greater research but rather to higher dividends and greater market concentration through acquisition of competitors, a guarantee of even more inflated prices.

Monopoly drug pricing, particularly in the Medicare program, can only be called corporate welfare. The American public has had enough. A national survey conducted by the Kaiser Family Foundation in August 2015 reported that 83 percent believe the government should directly negotiate drug prices for Medicare beneficiaries. This is a step long overdue.

NO

Douglas Holtz-Eakin
President, American Action Forum; Former Director, Congressional Budget Office

Written for *CQ Researcher*, May 2016

Presidential candidates and members of Congress often recommend having the government negotiate for drug discounts on behalf of the Medicare program. Most recently, presumptive GOP presidential nominee Donald Trump joined Vermont Sen. Bernie Sanders and Democratic front-runner Hillary Clinton in supporting negotiations.

The typical proposal is to allow the secretary of Health and Human Services (HHS) to negotiate with prescription drug manufacturers on behalf of the Medicare Part D program — something banned by the so-called "noninterference" clause in the 2003 Medicare Modernization Act. This idea is hardly new. It arose during discussions over passage of the law, and the Congressional Budget Office, Congress' nonpartisan budget analysis agency, noted at the time that getting rid of the noninterference provision would have a negligible impact.

This is hardly surprising. Drug companies negotiate annually with prescription drug insurance plans. Those plans go into the negotiations with some strong leverage: a formulary, or list of drugs offering the greatest overall value, that can be used to favor a drug company's products and millions of customers who could be delivered to the drug company or, faced with too high a price, its competitors. Adding HHS to the mix does not change that leverage. Here's how such a negotiation would go:

HHS Secretary: I'd like a discount on your prescription drugs.

Drug Manufacturer: What do you have to offer?

HHS Secretary: I can guarantee millions of senior citizens as customers; shouldn't I get a discount?

Drug Manufacturer: What is your formulary like?

HHS Secretary: I don't have one. We can't discriminate.

Drug Manufacturer: Sorry, the prescription drug plans have already guaranteed us the customer base, promised to treat our drugs favorably in the formulary, and we've given them the discounts. What else have you got?

HHS Secretary: Uh, a used copy of healthcare.gov?

Drug Manufacturer: We are done here.

The private-sector prescription drug plans already have all available market-based leverage. Of course, the government can do one thing that the private sector can't: impose price controls. Thus, many suspect that a call to repeal the noninterference clause is really just a stalking horse for price controls. Price-fixing never works, will hurt innovation and restrict the availability of valuable therapies.

Medicare Part D is not broken. It is the best-functioning entitlement program, and adding secretarial negotiation would be far from fixing it.

times in recent years. Others are pessimistic. "Even though 75 percent of Americans believe drug costs are a major health care issue, I don't foresee any major overhauls," says Harvard's Kesselheim. "The political power of the industry is too strong and the system is not amenable. Every time there has been an attempt, it has been undercut."

He and others suggest that smaller-scale reforms, especially those that do not depend on government action, could go forward. Nonprofit organizations that evaluate drugs' effectiveness or cost compared with others in their therapeutic class will continue to grow in importance, most experts believe.

Such value-based assessments likely will play an increasingly important role in controlling costs, as insurance companies, hospital systems, pharmacy benefit managers and others decide which drugs to offer their patients. In addition, drugs known as biosimilars, which are like generic versions of high-priced biologics, will become common alternatives to higher-priced prescription biologics, Miller predicts.

Almost everyone involved in this policy debate agrees, though, that difficult conversations lie ahead on ethical and economic issues. "It's very complicated," says Tricia Neuman, a senior vice president of the Kaiser Family Foundation, which researches health care issues. "Value is a relative thing. If you are sick you want the best possible drug that may or may not work. Who decides value?"

An even bigger question, Pearson says, is, "How much do we as a society want to spend on health care?"

NOTES

1. James Surowiecki, "Taking on the Drug Profiteers," *The New Yorker*, Oct. 10, 2015, http://tinyurl.com/qy7s4at.

2. Leah Dickstein, Rachel Kruzan and Annie Antar, "What happens when a company hikes the cost of crucial medicine by 5,000%," *USA Today*, Dec. 27, 2015, http://tinyurl.com/z6mc7hh.

3. Andrew Pollack, "Drug goes from $13.50 a tablet to $750, overnight," *The New York Times*, Sept. 20, 2015, http://tinyurl.com/p2lhfvq.

4. Matthew Belvedere, "Biotech CEO blasts Turing over 5000% price hike," CNBC, Sept. 23, 2015, http://tinyurl.com/npdofv6.

5. "Hedge Funds Attack American Health Care," *HedgePapers No. 22*, Sept. 30, 2015, http://tinyurl.com/gw9xhur.

6. "Brand Name Prescription Drug Pricing: Lack of Therapeutically Equivalent Drugs and Limited Competition May Contribute to Extraordinary Price Increases," U.S. Government Accountability Office, December 2009, http://tinyurl.com/ydyv23j.

7. "Express Scripts Drug Trend Report 2015," Express Scripts, http://tinyurl.com/jsh9v9z.

8. Stephanie Armour, "U.S. Prescription drug spending is on the rise," *The Wall Street Journal*, March 8, 2016, http://tinyurl.com/h4phtlz.

9. "ASPE Issue Brief: Observations on Trends in Prescription Drug Pricing," U.S. Department of Health and Human Services, March 8, 2016.

10. John Fauber, "Kalydeco: A Price Too High to Pay?" *MedPage Today*, Oct. 2, 2013, http://tinyurl.com/lau2yws.

11. Andrew Pollack, "Drug Prices Soar, Prompting Calls for Justification," *The New York Times*, July 23, 2015, http://tinyurl.com/nr8uhcc.

12. Carolyn Y. Johnson, "This drug is defying a rare form of leukemia — and it keeps getting pricier," *The Washington Post*, March 9, 2016, http://tinyurl.com/z392jqm.

13. "The Price of Sovaldi and its Impact on the U.S. Health Care System, Executive Summary," Senate Committee on Finance, December 2015, http://tinyurl.com/hh6hof3.

14. Priyanka Dayal McCluskey, "As competition wanes, prices for generics skyrocket," *The Boston Globe*, Nov. 6, 2015, http://tinyurl.com/pb9ueam.

15. Government Accountability Office, December 2009, *op. cit.*

16. Andrew Pollack, "Senators Condemn Big Price Increases for Drugs," *The New York Times*, Dec. 9, 2015, http://tinyurl.com/p45kvmq.

17. Surowiecki, *op. cit.*, Dec. 9, 2015.

18. Pollack, *op. cit.*, Dec. 9, 2015.

19. Ben Hirschler, "Exclusive: Transatlantic divide: how U.S. pays three times more for drugs," Reuters, Oct. 12, 2015, http://tinyurl.com/h2a8kdt.

20. Surowiecki, *op. cit.*, Oct. 10, 2015.

21. Karthick Arvinth, "Daraprim: Generic version of drug costs less than £0.07 in India," *International Business Times*, Sept. 25, 2015, http://tinyurl.com/hrcscr8.

22. *Ibid.*

23. Bianca DiJulio, Jamie Firth and Mollyann Brodie, "Kaiser Health Tracking Poll: October 2015," The Henry J. Kaiser Family Foundation, Oct. 28, 2015, http://tinyurl.com/h6zlze5.

24. "Biopharmaceutical Research & Development: The Process Behind New Medicines," PhRMA, 2015, http://tinyurl.com/nm7d727.

25. "Briefing: Cost of Developing a New Drug," Tufts Center for the Study of Drug Development, http://tinyurl.com/q5kn8wn.

26. Jorge Mestre-Ferrandiz, "The R&D Cost of a New Medicine," Office of Health Economics, University College London, Jan. 29, 2013, http://tinyurl.com/jr7a58n.

27. Aaron E. Carroll, "$2.6 Billion to Develop a Drug? New Estimate Makes Questionable Assumptions," *The New York Times*, Nov. 18, 2014, http://tinyurl.com/z2wmj6w.

28. Jerry Avorn, "The $2.6 Billion Pill — Methodologic and Policy Considerations," *The New England Journal of Medicine*, May 14, 2015, http://tinyurl.com/jlsfhal.

29. Carroll, *op. cit.*

30. *Ibid.*

31. Joseph A. DiMasi, Henry G. Grabowski and Ronald W. Hansen, "The cost of drug development," *The New England Journal of Medicine*, May 14, 2015, http://tinyurl.com/z6rv467.

32. James Love, "KEI comment on the new Tufts Study on Drug Development Costs," *Knowledge Ecology International*, Nov. 14, 2014, http://tinyurl.com/z3a9npb.

33. Office of Budget, National Institutes of Health, http://tinyurl.com/z5m3d6x.

34. Aaron Kesselheim *et al.*, "The roles of academia, rare diseases, and repurposing in the development of the most transformative drugs," *Health Affairs*, 2015, pp. 286-293, http://tinyurl.com/jgwz374.

35. Ashley J. Stevens *et al.*, "The Role of Public-Sector Research in the Discovery of Drugs and Vaccines," *The New England Journal of Medicine*, Feb. 10, 2011, http://tinyurl.com/6q6ytj7.

36. "Castellani Statement on Prescription Drug Costs," PhRMA, May 29, 2014, http://tinyurl.com/zn6bugr.

37. Topher Spiro, Maura Calsyn and Thomas Huelskoetter, "Enough Is Enough: The Time Has Come to Address Sky-High Drug Prices," Center for American Progress, September 2015, http://tinyurl.com/z89oscw.

38. *Ibid.*

39. Alexander Gaffney, "FDA Sets Policy for Granting New Biologic Medicines Extensive Market Exclusivity," Regulatory Affairs Professionals Society, Aug. 4, 2014, http://tinyurl.com/gnoo7ra.

40. Alfred Engelberg, "How Government Policy Promotes High Drug Prices," *Health Affairs Blog*, Oct. 29, 2015, http://tinyurl.com/j57rffb.

41. J. DiMasi J and C. Paquette, "The Economics of Follow-on Drug Research and Development Trends in Entry Rates and the Timing of Development," *Pharmacoeconomics 22* (Suppl. 2), 2004, pp. 1-14, http://tinyurl.com/gsh3vdn.

42. Aidan Hollis, "Me-too drugs: is there a problem?" World Health Organization, 2004, http://tinyurl.com/zx7wnb8.

43. "Patents and Exclusivity," *FDA/CDER SBIA Chronicles*, U.S. Food and Drug Administration, May 9, 2015, http://tinyurl.com/j5fllfl.

44. "FTC Staff Issues FY 2013 Report on Branded Drug Firms' Patent Settlements with Generic Competitors," U.S. Federal Trade Commission, Dec. 22, 2014, http://tinyurl.com/llns59r.

45. Edward Wyatt, "Supreme Court Lets Regulators Sue Over Generic Drug Deals," *The New York Times*, June 17, 2013, http://tinyurl.com/z7s5dsw.

46. Kevin Outterson, "Death from the Public Domain?" *Texas Law Review*, 2010, pp. 45-55, http://tinyurl.com/zbq4k6e.

47. Peter Arno and Michael Davis, "Paying Twice for the Same Drugs," *The Washington Post*, March 27, 2002, http://tinyurl.com/jrxmalw.

48. Marc-André Gagnon and Sidney Wolfe, "Mirror, Mirror on the Wall: Medicare Part D pays needlessly high brand-name drug prices compared with other OECD countries and with U.S. government programs," Carleton University and Public Citizen, July 23, 2015, http://tinyurl.com/jbs3t6d.

49. Hirschler, *op. cit.* See also Tim Smedley, "Patent wars: has India taken on Big Pharma and won?" *The Guardian*, May 14, 2013, http://tinyurl.com/hu8uydx; and David Squires and Chloe Anderson, "U.S. health care from a global perspective: Spending, Use of Services, Prices, and Health in 13 Countries," The Commonwealth Fund, October 2015.

50. "Health Insurance Coverage of the Total Population 2014," The Henry J. Kaiser Family Foundation, 2014, http://tinyurl.com/j928v8m.

51. Gagnon and Wolfe, *op. cit.*

52. Austin Frakt, "To Reduce the Cost of Drugs, Look to Europe," *The New York Times*, Oct. 19, 2015, http://tinyurl.com/npgho7p.

53. *Ibid.*

54. Joy Li-Yueh Lee *et al.*, "A Systematic Review of Reference Pricing: Implications for US Prescription Drug Spending," *The American Journal of Managed Care*, Nov. 16, 2012, http://tinyurl.com/zc5h3gs.

55. Luke Steward, "The Impact of Regulation on Innovation in the United States: A Cross-Industry Literature Review," Information Technology & Innovation Foundation, June 2010, http://tinyurl.com/oo5qsf2.

56. *Ibid.* Also see Frakt, *op. cit.*

57. "Pharmaceutical Pricing: Lessons from Abroad," *op. cit.*

58. Douglas Holtz-Eakin and Christopher Holt, "How CMS Is Trying to Wreck the Virtues of Medicare Part D," *National Review*, Feb. 2, 2014, http://tinyurl.com/j73glan.

59. DiJulio, Firth and Brodie, *op. cit.*

60. "Drug Pricing: Public Health Implications," The Forum at Harvard T.H. Chan School of Public Health, Oct. 23, 2015, http://tinyurl.com/gssejga.

61. Robert Weisman, "Boston watchdog takes aim at rising drug prices," *The Boston Globe*, Sept. 13, 2015, http://tinyurl.com/h2fpwdr.

62. Steven D. Pearson, "A U.S. approach to value-based drug assessment," *MedNous*, November/December 2015, http://tinyurl.com/j77ybrr.

63. Peter B. Bach, Leonard B. Saltz and Robert E. Wittes, "In Cancer Care, Cost Matters," *The New York Times*, Oct. 14, 2012, http://tinyurl.com/9x342el.

64. Jeanne Whalen, "Doctors Object to High Cancer-Drug Prices," *The Wall Street Journal*, July 23, 2015, http://tinyurl.com/nfg2cfe.

65. Peter Loftus and Anna Wilde Mathews, "Health Insurers Push to Tie Prices to Outcomes," *The Wall Street Journal*, May 11, 2016, http://tinyurl.com/hwwsudb.

66. Quoted in Stan Finkelstein and Peter Temin, *Reasonable Rx: Solving the Drug Price Crisis* (2008), pp. 21-22.

67. Paul Starr, *The Social Transformation of American Medicine* (1982), p. 127.

68. Starr, *op. cit.*

69. *Ibid.*

70. Loker, *op. cit.*

71. Joseph M. Gabriel, *Medical Monopoly: Intellectual Property Rights and the Origins of the Modern Pharmaceutical Industry* (2014), pp. 2-3.

72. *Ibid.*

73. Starr, *op. cit.*

74. Finkelstein and Temin, *op. cit.*, p. 42.

75. Starr, *op. cit.*

76. *Ibid.*

77. *Ibid.*, p. 133.

78. Finkelstein and Temin, *op. cit.*, p. 21.

79. *Ibid.*, pp. 40-41.

80. *Ibid.*, p. 41.

81. Merrill Goozner, *The $800 Million Pill: The Truth Behind the Cost of New Drugs* (2004), p. 211.

82. *Ibid.*, p. 212.

83. *Ibid.*

84. Finkelstein and Temin, *op. cit.*, p. 42.

85. Goozner, *op. cit.*, p. 212

86. Gabriel, *op. cit.*, p. 247.

87. Goozner, *op. cit.*, p. 214.

88. *Ibid.*; Michelle Meadows, "Promoting Safe and Effective Drugs for 100 Years," *FDA Consumer*, The Centennial Edition, January-February 2006, http://tinyurl.com/zw34c9l.

89. Goozner, *op. cit.*, p. 214.

90. For background, see Melinda Wenner, "20 New Biotech Breakthroughs that Will Change Medicine," *Popular Mechanics*, Dec. 17, 2009, http://tinyurl.com/jq28h2b.

91. Goozner, *op. cit.*, p. 215.

92. Finkelstein and Temin, *op. cit.*, p. 29.

93. Goozner, *op. cit.*

94. Michael Henry Davis and Peter Arno, "Why Don't We Enforce Existing Drug Price Controls? The Unrecognized and Unenforced Reasonable Pricing Requirements Imposed upon Patents Deriving in Whole or in Part from Federally-Funded Research," *75 Tulane Law Review 631*, 2001, http://tinyurl.com/je938dy.

95. Goozner, *op. cit.*, p. 127.

96. *Ibid.*

97. *Ibid.*

98. Aaron Kesselheim, "Using Market-Exclusivity Incentives to Promote Pharmaceutical Innovation," *The New England Journal of Medicine*, Nov. 4, 2010, http://tinyurl.com/j28xqln.

99. "History of Federal Regulation: 1902 — Present," *FDA Review*, http://tinyurl.com/hmhjrtx.

100. Finkelstein and Temin, *op. cit.*, pp. 108-109.

101. Goozner, *op. cit.*, p. 88.

102. *Ibid.*, pp. 216-217, pp. 123-124.

103. *Ibid.*

104. *Ibid.*

105. *Ibid.*, p. 217.

106. *Ibid.*

107. "Pharmaceutical Pricing: Lessons from Abroad," *op. cit.*; W. K. Mariner, "Patients' rights to care under Clinton's Health Security Act: the structure of reform," *American Journal of Public Health*,

August 1994, pp. 1330-1335, http://tinyurl.com/h25ke9w.

108. Finkelstein and Temin, *op. cit.*, pp. 78-79.

109. *Ibid.*

110. "Closing the Coverage Gap — Medicare Prescription Drugs Are Becoming More Affordable," Centers for Medicare and Medicaid Services, http://tinyurl.com/j7zw8no.

111. DiJulio, Firth and Brodie, *op. cit.*

112. Ed Silverman, "With Drug Costs Rising, It's Time for Pharma Companies to Open Their Books," *STAT*, Feb. 16, 2016, http://tinyurl.com/jz2j3zk.

113. Charles Ornstein, Ryann Grochowski Jones and Mike Tigas, "Now There's Proof: Docs Who Get Company Cash Tend to Prescribe More Brand-Name Meds," *ProPublica*, March 17, 2016, http://tinyurl.com/zevmunp.

114. *Ibid.*

115. Michael Ollove, "High Drug Prices Prompt Demands for Transparency," *Stateline*, March 7, 2016, http://tinyurl.com/jxrarzu.

116. Ed Silverman, "Virginia the Latest State to Push Drug Pricing Transparency Bill," *STAT*, Feb. 2, 2016, http://tinyurl.com/z7ww2hn.

117. "Bill S.1048: An Act to promote transparency and cost control of pharmaceutical drug prices," 189th General Court of the Commonwealth of Massachusetts, http://tinyurl.com/zbl7a5r.

118. "2016-2017 New York State Executive Budget: Health and Mental Hygiene: Article VII Legislation," http://tinyurl.com/zvvebwq.

119. Ed Silverman, "New York Governor Andrew Cuomo Seeks to Cap Some Drug Prices," *STAT*, Jan. 22, 2016, http://tinyurl.com/zbjevdp.

120. Statement by Paul Macielak, President & CEO, "New York Health Plan Association Response to State of the State/Budget Proposal," Health Plan Association, Jan. 13, 2016, http://tinyurl.com/zlb9h3k.

121. Quoted in Dan Goldberg, "Cuomo Enters National Debate With Proposal to Cap Drug Prices," *Politico*, Jan. 20, 2016, http://tinyurl.com/zqyu5f4.

122. Ed Silverman, "Pharma Goes to Court in Ohio to Stop Drug Pricing Ballot Initiative," *STAT*, March 1, 2016, http://tinyurl.com/hzw5kdq.

123. Ned Pagliarulo, "PhRMA Sues to Challenge Ohio Ballot Initiative Limiting Drug Prices," *BioPharmaDive*, March 1, 2016, http://tinyurl.com/zt9xzxp.

124. Andrew Pollack, "Sales of Sovaldi, New Gilead Hepatitis C Drug, Soar to $10.3 Billion," *The New York Times*, Feb. 3, 2015, http://tinyurl.com/kckn7w4.

125. *Ibid.*

126. *Ibid.*

127. Maura Healey, letter to John C. Martin, Chairman and Chief Executive Officer, Gilead Sciences, Inc., Jan. 22, 2016, http://tinyurl.com/hj8tj34.

128. Zachary Tracer and Caroline Chen, "New York said to probe insurers over hepatitis C drugs," Bloomberg.com, March 2, 2016, http://tinyurl.com/gth49ea.

129. James Love, "51 members of Congress have asked the NIH to use March-In rights to rein in high drug prices," *Knowledge Ecology International*, Jan. 11, 2016, http://tinyurl.com/h4esxr9; Ed Silverman, "NIH Asked to Fight Price Gouging by Overriding Drug Patents," *STAT*, Jan. 11, 2016, http://tinyurl.com/heeogom.

130. Jeannie Baumann, "NIH Pulls Back on Using Bayh-Dole for Drug Pricing," Bloomberg BNA, April 8, 2016, http://tinyurl.com/zlvktsg.

131. Philip Rocco, Walid Gellad and Julie Donohue, "How Much Does Congress Care About Drug Prices? Less Than It Should," *Health Affairs Blog*, Jan. 13, 2016, http://tinyurl.com/jl3lngs.

132. *Ibid.* Also see Glenn Kessler, "Trump's truly absurd claim he would save $300 billion a year on prescription drugs," *The Washington Post*, Feb. 18, 2016, http://tinyurl.com/zbrdzby.

BIBLIOGRAPHY
Selected Sources
Books

Avorn, Jerry, *Powerful Medicines: The Benefits, Risks, and Costs of Prescription Drugs*, **Alfred A. Knopf, 2004.**

A professor of medicine at Harvard Medical School examines issues surrounding drug costs in this 10th printing of his book.

Danzon, Patricia M., and Sean Nicholson, eds., *The Oxford Handbook of the Economics of the Biopharmaceutical Industry*, **Oxford University Press, 2012.**

A reference book examines the economics of the pharmaceutical industry, with 18 articles by leading academic health economists.

Gabriel, Joseph A., *Medical Monopoly: Intellectual Property Rights and the Origins of the Modern Pharmaceutical Industry*, **The University of Chicago Press, 2014.**

An associate professor of behavioral sciences and social medicine at Florida State University chronicles the pharmaceutical industry through the lens of intellectual property policies that help determine drug costs.

Goozner, Merrill, *The $800 Million Pill: The Truth Behind the Cost of New Drugs*, **University of California Press, 2005.**

A journalist and editorial director of *Modern Healthcare* argues that Americans pay twice for most important prescription drugs: first by funding research that leads to their creation with taxpayer dollars, and second, by paying skyrocketing prices for those drugs to pharmaceutical companies.

Greene, Jeremy A., *Generic: The Unbranding of Modern Medicine*, **Johns Hopkins University Press, 2014.**

An associate professor of medicine and the history of medicine at Johns Hopkins University discusses the growth of generic drugs (which have risen from 10 percent of drug prescriptions in 1960 to almost 80 percent in 2010) and considers the cost implications of such growth.

Articles

Anderson, Richard, "Pharmaceutical industry gets high on fat profits," BBC News, Nov. 6, 2014, http://tinyurl.com/q4v9qus.

A reporter shows that average profit margins for drug companies in 2013 approached 20 percent, with one company, Pfizer, achieving a 42 percent profit margin.

Bach, Peter B., Leonard B. Saltz and Robert E. Wittesoct, "In Cancer Care, Cost Matters," *The New York Times*, Oct. 14, 2012, http://tinyurl.com/8cfhekv.
Three specialists at New York's renowned Memorial Sloan-Kettering Cancer Center explain why they decided not to offer patients an expensive new drug, saying that it was no better than a similar drug used to treat advanced colon cancer.

Pollack, Andrew, "Drug Makers Sidestep Barriers on Pricing," *The New York Times*, Oct. 19, 2015, http://tinyurl.com/of2678b.
A reporter documents the rise of specialty pharmacies that help drug makers avoid insurers' and pharmacists' efforts to switch patients to lower-priced generic drugs or to over-the-counter versions of expensive branded drugs.

Rockoff, Jonathan D., "How Pfizer Set the Cost of Its New Drug at $9,850 a Month," *The Wall Street Journal*, Dec. 9, 2015, http://tinyurl.com/p9tj397.
A reporter investigates what he describes as a secretive and arcane world of drug pricing as he follows a company's lead-up to unveiling a new breast cancer drug.

Reports and Studies

"2015 Biopharmaceutical Research Industry Profile," Pharmaceutical Research and Manufacturers of America, April 2015, http://tinyurl.com/zvys3d7.
The pharmaceutical companies' main trade group provides an annual overview of innovation in the industry.

"The Price of Sovaldi and its Impact on the U.S. Health Care System," Committee on Finance, United States Senate, December 2015, http://tinyurl.com/jzw86d3.
After an 18-month investigation, a Senate committee disputes a drug company's contention that it developed its groundbreaking $1,000-a-pill hepatitis C drug to treat the largest possible number of patients. Instead, the panel concluded, the company focused primarily on maximizing profits.

"What the U.S. Can Learn about Drug Pricing from Australia, the U.K. and Germany," Kaiser Permanente Institute for Health Policy, May 20, 2015, http://tinyurl.com/z4wcmcv.
A hospital network's research arm compares what it calls "unsustainable" drug pricing in the United States with other nations' policies that keep prices down.

Spiro, Topher, Maura Calsyn, and Thomas Huelskoetter, "Enough Is Enough: The Time Has Come to Address Sky-High Drug Prices," Center for American Progress, September 2015, http://tinyurl.com/oh6mhjw.
Researchers at a liberal think tank explore the life cycle of a prescription drug and discuss pricing issues.

Video

"Drug Pricing: Public Health Implications," Harvard T.H. Chan School of Public Health, Oct. 23, 2015, http://tinyurl.com/gssejga.
A panel of physicians and policy experts discusses why drug costs are so high and what policy changes could ensure that patients can afford high-value drugs.

FOR MORE INFORMATION

AARP Public Policy Institute, 601 E St., N.W., Washington, DC 20049; 202-434-3840; www.aarp.org/ppi. Conducts research on price trends for prescription drugs.

FiercePharma, 275 Grove St., Suite 2-130, Newton, MA 02466; 617-219-8300; www.fiercepharma.com. Online news service focusing on the drug industry.

Kaiser Family Foundation, 2400 Sand Hill Rd., Menlo Park, CA 94025; 650-854-9400; www.kff.org. Nonprofit focusing on health issues with a news service offering nonpartisan research, data, journalism and other information.

Knowledge Ecology International, 1621 Connecticut Ave., N.W., Suite 500, Washington, DC 20009; 202-332-2670; http://keionline.org/a2m. A nonprofit whose Access to Medical Technologies program examines prescription drug issues.

National Coalition on Health Care, 1825 K St., N.W., Suite 411, Washington, DC 20006; 202-638-7151; www.nchc.org. Nonprofit, nonpartisan coalition of about 80 organizations working for more transparency in drug pricing.

Pharmaceutical Research and Manufacturers of America, 950 F St., N.W., Suite 300, Washington, DC 20004; 202-835-3400; www.phrma.org. Pharmaceutical industry's main trade group.

13

Opioid Crisis

Peter Katel

To kick his addiction to prescription opioids, Kelly Pierce of Bradenton, Fla., has been in treatment since 2009 at Operation PAR, a Bradenton methadone clinic where he also works. Methadone proponents say the drug allows addicts to live productive lives. Critics argue that it perpetuates addiction.

From *CQ Researcher*, October 7, 2016.

Tiffany Tompkins/McClatchy DC/TNS via Getty Images

Gary Henson said the news came late in the evening. It was April 22, 2015, and Henson's wife answered a knock on the door to find two police officers. They told the Hensons that their oldest son, Garrett, 20, had been found dead in his apartment in Basalt, Colo., earlier that day. The cause of death, according to Gary Henson, was "an accidental overdose of a lethal combination of sedatives and opioids — just one week after leaving [drug] rehab."

For the Hensons, the news was "life-shattering." Three months earlier, when Garrett was still in rehab, father and son had gone skiing in Aspen. "We had a nice dinner with one of his friends who was also in recovery," Gary Henson recalled. "I felt hopeful. We discussed what he would do after rehab. We made plans for his stepsister to come live with him in the summer." Instead, Garrett relapsed and overdosed.[1]

Garrett Henson's death was part of what experts are calling a national opioid crisis — a torrent of prescription painkillers, black-market synthetic versions and heroin — that caused nearly 250,000 fatalities between 2000 and 2014 (the most recent figures available). Overall, the federal Substance Abuse and Mental Health Services Administration estimates that nearly 2.5 million people suffer from "use disorder" (a term that includes addiction) involving prescription opioids and heroin.[2]

Abuse of opioid painkillers and heroin has been spreading throughout the U.S. population, from inner-city youths, jobless rural residents and high school students to wealthy suburbanites, young professionals and pop stars.

Painkillers Cause More Deaths Than Heroin

About 1.8 times more people died from prescription painkillers than heroin in 2014, the most recent year for which data are available. Over the past 15 years, 189,917 Americans have died from prescription painkillers and 54,672 from heroin.

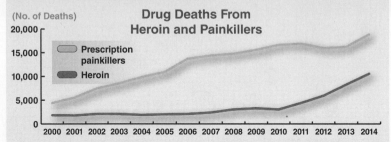

(No. of Deaths)

Drug Deaths From Heroin and Painkillers

Source: "Number and age-adjusted rates of drug-poisoning deaths involving opioid analgesics and heroin: United States, 2000-2014," Centers for Disease Control and Prevention, March 2016, p. 2, http://tinyurl.com/ot5454u

More adults use prescription painkillers than cigarettes, smokeless tobacco or cigars combined, according to a federal Substance Abuse and Mental Health Services Administration report released in September.[3] Forty-four percent of respondents in an April Kaiser Family Foundation poll said they knew someone who had been addicted to prescription painkillers.[4]

In September, two graphic symbols of the crisis circulated widely: a video of a woman passed out from an overdose in a Family Dollar Store in Lawrence, Mass., with her 2-year-old trying to wake her up; and a photo of a 4-year-old boy in a car in East Liverpool, Ohio, with his grandmother and the driver passed out in the front seat from heroin overdoses.[5]

Fatalities have continued to rise in the past two years. In Massachusetts, there were 1,379 confirmed deaths from opioid-related overdoses last year — and the number of overdoses rose 41 percent from 2013 to 2014. In Kentucky, fentanyl — a synthetic opioid that is 50 to 100 times more potent than morphine — was a factor in 420 fatal overdoses in 2015, more than triple the previous year's level.[6]

Overdoses are so dangerous because opioids link chemically to the part of the brain that controls respiration. Someone who takes too much may stop breathing.[7]

The epidemic has alarmed the federal government. In July, President Obama signed the Comprehensive Addiction and Recovery Act, a bipartisan law designed to encourage expansion of treatment programs and to develop alternatives to opioid painkillers. "I have heard from too many families across the country whose lives have been shattered by this epidemic," Obama declared.[8]

The law — the first major legislation in 40 years dealing with addiction — calls for spending more than $180 million annually to address the opioid problem.[9] Authorities are also trying to stop "doctor shopping," in which patients go from doctor to doctor to obtain prescriptions for painkillers. To curb the practice, some states are strengthening electronic databases known as Prescription Drug Monitoring Programs, with California the latest of 30 states to require physicians to check the database before prescribing opioids or other restricted drugs.[10]

Experts see some progress in the fight against opioid painkiller abuse. After peaking in 2012, the number of prescriptions written for opioids declined 12 percent between 2013 and 2015, according to IMS Health, a market research company. Symphony Health Solutions, a data company that studies the pharmaceutical industry, found an 18 percent drop in that period.[11]

"Deaths are up, but consumption has plateaued and come down a bit since 2012-2013," says Dr. Andrew Kolodny, chief medical officer of Phoenix House, a New York-based network of addiction treatment centers.

But Kolodny and many other experts say that considerable challenges remain, and debate is fierce over how to proceed. A number of policy experts are promoting a "harm reduction" approach, such as opening "safe injection sites" where addicts can safely shoot up under medical supervision. The Obama administration is effectively endorsing this strategy of keeping addicts as healthy as possible by touting the efforts of the advocacy group Harm Reduction Coalition. Harm reduction also helps addicts manage their addictions by giving them limited doses of certain opioids without getting high or suffering withdrawal symptoms.[12]

But critics say the harm-reduction approach can amount to simply helping drug addicts get drugs. The goal of treatment, they say, should be ending addiction and that stigmatizing drug users can be effective.

"The idea that the drug addict isn't responsible for using drugs is completely wrong," says Dr. Robert DuPont of Rockville, Md., who served as the first director of the National Institute on Drug Abuse in 1973. "Yes, you've got a disease, but I don't think an alcoholic is not responsible for his drinking when he runs over a 5-year-old. Stigma is bad when applied to recovery but positive when it's applied to drug use. I don't want to have a tolerance for that."

While the opioid epidemic has worsened in recent years, opioids themselves are not new. The original opioids were derived from the opium poppy, a flower grown in Asia and Mexico. These included heroin, which is illegal. Synthetic opioids, such as oxycodone and fentanyl, are manufactured both legally and illegally.

Two factors contributed to the spread. One was a growing recognition in the 1990s that doctors needed to do more to help patients manage their pain. The other was the belief that a new type of opioid could be safely prescribed without becoming addictive. In 1996, Purdue Pharma, the developer and manufacturer of OxyContin — a formulation of oxycodone — told doctors the drug would carry little addiction risk for those using it for chronic pain because its time-release form would limit how much entered the bloodstream at a given time.[13]

So-called "pill mill" doctors concerned solely with making money wrote thousands of oxycodone prescriptions. By 2014, 4.3 million Americans were taking prescription painkillers each month without medical authorization.[14]

Also contributing to the opioid crisis is the ease with which users can obtain heroin. A network of heroin dealers based in the Mexican coastal state of Nayarit devised a marketing scheme that feeds on the growing appetite for the drug in white communities in medium-sized U.S. cities and suburbs. In the Nayarit system, according to author Sam Quinones, who interviewed dealers, police and customers, users can simply pick up the phone to order heroin and have it delivered to their door or in parking lots.[15]

Not everyone who takes prescription opioids becomes addicted. Scientists define drug addiction as a brain illness characterized by an obsession with a drug and the inability to quit taking it even if the user knows it is causing harm. The condition is partly genetic, in much the way diabetes and high blood pressure are.[16]

Opioids' effects vary depending on the individual, but they range from a sense of well-being to drowsiness and mental confusion. For non-addicts, a common reaction is, " 'It made me nauseous; who would ever get addicted to this junk?' " says Dr. Brian Johnson, an addiction specialist at State University of New York's (SUNY) Upstate Medical University in Syracuse, N.Y. But those who misuse opioids may say, " 'Oh, God, this feels great.' "And they become dependent on or addicted to the opioid.[17]

Addiction develops in about 8 percent of patients who take opioids for non-cancer chronic pain, according to an article in The New England Journal of Medicine. Researchers have traced one underlying cause to differences in the brain. "Recent studies have shown that the molecular mechanisms underlying addiction are distinct from those responsible for tolerance and physical dependence," the article said.[18]

The combination of widely available prescription opioids and order-by-phone heroin hit critical mass in middle-class areas of the Northeast and Southeast roughly as the 2016 presidential campaign got under way. When parents spoke out last year at candidate forums and other events, the epidemic hit the national radar, forcing candidates to confront the issue. "If they [candidates] didn't get it before they started campaigning," said Tim Soucy, director of the Manchester, N.H., health department, "they certainly get it now."[19]

As experts, politicians and others debate opioid addiction, here are some of the questions being asked:

Are authorities getting the opioid epidemic under control?

Those fighting the opioid crisis believe they have taken one step forward and one step back. Prescriptions for painkillers have dropped three years in a row, but fatal overdoses from prescribed and unprescribed opioids are still rising. One reason for the increase: a growing supply of illegally produced fentanyl and the even more powerful carfentanil, which was developed as an elephant tranquilizer.[20]

On the positive side, some experts say, was last summer's passage of the Comprehensive Addiction and Recovery Act, which authorizes the National Institutes of

Change in Heroin Use Soars

Heroin use more than doubled among non-Hispanic whites (to 3 percent of that population segment) and among adults ages 18-25 (to more than 7 percent of that group) between 2002-04 and 2011-13. Helping to drive the increases was a flood of cheap heroin from Mexico.

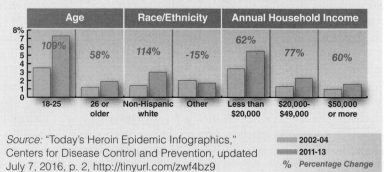

Change in Heroin Use by Age, Race, Income

Source: "Today's Heroin Epidemic Infographics," Centers for Disease Control and Prevention, updated July 7, 2016, p. 2, http://tinyurl.com/zwf4bz9

Health to accelerate research on developing non-opioid painkillers. The act also creates or codifies programs that award grants to states for addiction treatment. One such program is medication-assisted treatment, in which addicts are prescribed methadone or buprenorphine, opioids that dull addiction craving but generally don't produce a high. The law also allows nurse practitioners and physician assistants to prescribe buprenorphine.[21]

Experts and politicians say the law is important because it recognizes that recovery is a long-term process and that addicts suffer from an illness. "This bill is not just about reversing overdoses," Republican Sen. Rob Portman of Ohio — a state hard-hit by the epidemic — wrote on his website. "It's about helping people put their lives back together."[22]

But Democrats complain the law is inadequately funded. They wanted Congress to allocate $920 million total for the initiatives, but Republicans argued that funding should be appropriated annually, in accordance with congressional procedures. "That's how the system works here," Portman said when the bill passed the Senate without the $920 million provision. Sen. Charles Schumer, D-N.Y., said proper funding was essential. He called the law "something that appears real on the surface but has no substance."[23]

Also on the plus side, experts say, was the CDC's issuance in March of an opioid-prescribing guideline, which advises physicians to limit most opioid prescriptions for pain to three days. The guideline also urges caution in prescribing opioids to adolescents, who run a higher risk of addiction.[24]

Grants authorized by the Comprehensive Addiction and Recovery Act include awards to improve or expand the Prescription Drug Monitoring Program, electronic databases used in every state except Missouri.[25]

Taken together, the various measures represent a major turnaround from the regulatory and medical climate of the 1990s and early 2000s, in which prescribed opioids flooded the market.

Gary Mendell, who started the nonprofit drug policy group Shatterproof after his son committed suicide while struggling with drug addiction, says the Comprehensive Addiction and Recovery Act and CDC guideline will narrow the opioid pipeline. But he adds this is only a start; he wants to see the addiction rate cut in half over the next 20 years, as doctors become more cautious in prescribing opioids.

Mendell says his son's struggle with drugs began with Xanax, a non-opioid anti-anxiety medication. He cites data from the CDC calculating that medical opioid sales quadrupled in 1999-2010, with enough prescribed to medicate every American adult with a standard pain treatment dose every four hours for a month. By 2012, the number of prescriptions increased to about 259 million. "I don't think you could find someone who would disagree." Mendell says, "that the whole epidemic is driven by a four-time increase in opioid prescriptions."[26]

David Courtwright, a history professor at the University of North Florida in Jacksonville and a specialist in opioid addictio n history, says that those calling for cautious opioid prescribing are knocking on an open door. "I think it's already the case that the medical profession has collectively awakened to the fact that we have a problem," he says.

But excessive opioid prescribing is only one engine of the epidemic, Courtwright says. "We've got massive importation of Mexican heroin, and more recently Mexican heroin spiked with fentanyl," he says. Given the vast supply, Courtwright says he is "guardedly pessimistic" that the United States can curb the epidemic.

Another opioid historian, Eric C. Schneider of the University of Pennsylvania, says historical patterns indicate that the opioid wave will weaken largely on its own. "We may be at a crest, but we will inevitably get to a trough," he says, calling the medical profession's moves an important recognition of responsibility.

Schneider acknowledges that the heroin supply is growing even as prescribed opioids diminish. "But the evidence from past heroin waves suggests that while at one point in time you might have a fairly significant population of people using, the population of people severely addicted is going to be smaller," he says.

One of the most pessimistic experts is former National Institute on Drug Abuse director DuPont, who has been active in drug policy since the 1970s. He argues that the widespread availability of opioids — especially heroin and illegally produced synthetics — remains a significant problem. "The real big issue here is that the supply has dramatically changed — the quality of drugs, the accessibility, the marketing," he says. "It's like the effect of Amazon on retail sales."

Moreover, DuPont argues that the opioid epidemic can't be isolated from the drug boom in general. He cites a U.S. Department of Health and Human Services study that concludes that about 80 percent of heroin users had first used non-prescribed opioids and other illegal drugs, including marijuana and cocaine.[27]

"The reality is that people using heroin are largely people who've been using drugs for a long period of time," he says. "The heroin problem is not just about heroin; the opioid problem is not just about [non-heroin] opioids."

Should opioids be used to treat addiction?

When doctors prescribe medication to treat opioid addiction, the drugs themselves are often opioids.

Essentially, methadone and buprenorphine activate the same brain "receptors" as opioids but lessen drug craving and related behavior because the brain absorbs them more slowly. (Another class of treatment drugs

A heroin user in New London, Conn., prepares to inject himself on March 23. Addiction to opioids, including heroin, has spread throughout the United States, from inner cities to suburbia to rural areas, and afflicted every demographic group — rich and poor, minority and white, young and old. Heroin use has risen especially sharply among adults ages 18 to 25 and non-Hispanic whites.

blocks the receptors and prevents the feel-good effects that addicts seek.)[28] Many experts endorse the strategy, but others consider it a disturbing contradiction.

The leading medications are methadone, which has been used in addiction treatment since the early 1960s, and buprenorphine, sold as Suboxone. Dr. Nora Volkow, director of the National Institute on Drug Abuse and an authority on addiction, called the latter drug "effective . . . in significantly reducing opiate drug abuse and cravings."[29]

Opioids are also called "agonists." Others are "antagonists" — drugs that block the effects of opioids. The latter includes naltrexone, marketed as Vivitrol.

In 2014 testimony to the Senate Caucus on International Narcotics Control, Volkow called the antagonists especially effective. "When administered in the context of an addiction treatment program, [the medications] can effectively maintain abstinence from other opioids and reduce harmful behavior."[30]

But addiction-recovery programs and law enforcement officials say abstinence is necessary to beat addiction. "I have heard recently from judges in some pretty big courts that 'we are not in the business of substituting one addiction for another,'" says Harlan Matusow, a project director at the National Development & Research Institutes, a think tank in New York City that specializes in drug use studies.

With funding from the National Institute on Drug Abuse, Matusow is updating a 2013 survey that found that only one-third of a nationwide sample of drug courts — which divert nonviolent drug offenders into treatment programs instead of jail — accepted medication therapy for defendants who had been using opioids. But 40 percent allowed continuation of medication for those who already were receiving the treatment.[31]

Medication-assisted treatment has the backing of the federal health establishment. In 2015 a federal rule prohibited drug courts that receive grants from the Substance Abuse and Mental Health Services Administration from ordering defendants to quit taking the medications.[32]

In promoting medication treatment, some specialists say patients who have stopped opioid use run a high risk of overdosing if they relapse because they have lost a physical tolerance for the drug — but not the craving. If they give in to the craving, a dose of opioids could kill them.[33]

Medication treatment experts acknowledge this strategy is no silver bullet. A recent study by experts from Integrated Substance Abuse Programs at the University of California, Los Angeles, found that 43 percent of patients treated with buprenorphine and 32 percent with methadone were illicitly using opioids after treatment.[34]

Johnson, of SUNY Upstate Medical University, says those results point to the inadequacy of medication treatment. "People use drugs for a reason," he says. "It's not random — people have emotional issues, and opioids get rid of them."

Johnson, who also is a psychiatry professor, runs a recovery program that offers therapy aimed at resolving addicts' underlying psychological problems, but no buprenorphine or other opioid medication. While such medications "alter the nature of the use of opioids," he says, heroin users often are using other drugs that the medications do not affect.

Mark Parrino, president of the New York City-based American Association for the Treatment of Opioid Dependence — which began as an organization of methadone treatment centers — argues that many medication treatment critics don't acknowledge the weaknesses of the abstinence-based approach.

"The true goal of treating a chronic recurring disorder is getting that person to an abstinent state," he says.

Counseling and other services can work, Parrino continues. "But what happens when [an addict] can't do it? A certain number of addicted people will not be able to be abstinent for any period of time, and they run the risk of relapse."

Given the power of addiction, Parrino says drug court judges, child protective services workers or correctional institution employees should not require a drug user to abstain. "I think that's a faulty premise not borne out by reality," he says.

But the Denver-based National Association of Addiction Treatment Providers includes medication treatment providers and those who oppose using opioids in treatment. Marvin Ventrell, the organization's executive director, says, "I always feel I'm arguing one thing to one camp and another to the other: To the physical-based treatment people, 'You also have to help the individual psychological and spiritual dimensions.' To the spiritual-treatment people, 'You have to allow people to use [medication-assisted treatment].' "

Ventrell supports drugs to treat opioid addiction but says it is just "a component of treatment" that varies depending on the individual.

Kevin Sabet, director of the Drug Policy Institute at the University of Florida College of Medicine and a former Obama administration drug policy official, argues that much of the treatment method debate bypasses a key issue: "getting people to realize they have a problem in the first place," he says. "Most people with a drug problem don't realize they have one."

Sabet adds, "For some people, medication is important and necessary; for others, it is inadequate. Everybody has a different path."

Are doctors properly trained in pain management?

U.S. Surgeon General Vivek Murthy said he wants to turn the page on the training that doctors began receiving in pain management 20 to 30 years ago.

"I came across a training document from the early 1990s that was directed at nurses and doctors," he said. "And one of the lines stood out to me clearly. It said, 'If your patient is concerned that they may develop dependence on opioids, you can safely reassure them that addiction to opioids is very rare in patients who have pain.' "[35]

That advice predated the 1996 launch of OxyContin by Purdue Pharmaceuticals, which was accompanied by a marketing campaign that told doctors the drug was appropriate for long-term treatment of chronic pain. One study estimated that the condition was undertreated in up to 80 percent of patients.[36]

Opioids' power to end or diminish pain is unquestioned when a patient has an immediate need, or over the longer term in treating cancer-related pain. But it's another question whether opioids work over the long term for non-cancer conditions.

The CDC, in its new guideline, concludes that pain-relieving effects may wear off for longtime users. "There is weak evidence that patients who are able to continue opioid therapy for at least six months can experience clinically significant pain relief," the CDC said.[37]

The Purdue marketing campaign was not the only encouragement physicians received to prescribe opioids for pain. Starting in the 1990s, medical authorities also told doctors to assign the same importance to pain as they did to the vital signs — pulse rate, temperature, respiration rate and blood pressure. The "fifth vital sign" classification became standard, in part because the Veterans Administration adopted it in 1998.[38]

The requirement for doctors to evaluate pain as a vital sign added a new layer to the interplay between patients' need for pain relief and their addiction potential. It also added to the possibility that a patient might sell prescribed pills or give them to a friend or relative; sometimes the pills were stolen.

In June, the American Medical Association (AMA) called for the Joint Commission, the major hospital-accrediting organization, to drop the "fifth vital sign" classification because of the opioid crisis. The association also urged that patient-satisfaction surveys drop questions about pain management. The commission denied that it had endorsed the vital sign categorization of pain, and it noted that opioid prescriptions were increasing before the commission adopted its pain assessment standards.[39]

By taking those steps, the AMA was echoing some drug policy advocates' demands. "The adaptation of pain as a vital sign is aligned with the beginning of our current

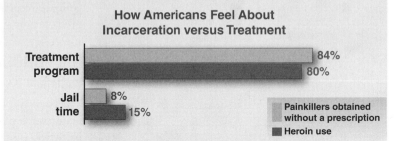

Most Favor Treatment Over Jail

Large majorities of Americans favor treatment over incarceration, both for those possessing small amounts of opioid painkillers illegally and those using heroin.

How Americans Feel About Incarceration versus Treatment

Treatment program	84%
	80%
Jail time	8%
	15%

Painkillers obtained without a prescription
Heroin use

Source: "Americans' Attitudes About Prescription Painkiller Abuse," Harvard T.H. Chan School of Public Health, March 2016, p. 2, http://tinyurl.com/gsq4evk

epidemic," said Robert Brandt, founder of Robby's Voice, a drug education nonprofit in Medina, Ohio, named after Brandt's son, who died of a heroin overdose. Robby received prescription opioids when his wisdom teeth were extracted. "Pain is the only subjective vital sign, and that subjectivity is exploited by those who continue to abuse prescription medications," Brandt said.[40]

But Dr. Lynn Webster, a pain doctor in Salt Lake City, calls the AMA move a mistake. "Asking people about their pain has been interpreted as meaning that if there is pain, you give them an opioid," he says. "But why wouldn't we ask people about their pain?"

To some extent, the CDC has bypassed the "fifth vital sign" issue by recommending stringent safeguards designed to take pain seriously without automatically relying on opioids. Webster, however, argues the guideline could promote an inflexible approach that could harm patients — for instance, the recommended three-day limit on opioid use for acute pain. Although Webster and others agree with the CDC that exercise and psychological techniques may work better for chronic pain than opioids, insurance companies, he says, won't pay for the extended treatment those approaches require.[41] "We have defaulted to using opioids," Webster says. "It is quick, easy, cheap and wrong in many instances."

An insurance industry leader, Cigna Corp. President and CEO David Cordani, wrote that his company has committed to reducing its clients' opioid use by

House Speaker Paul Ryan, R-Wis., flanked by lawmakers, signs the Comprehensive Addiction and Recovery Act on July 14, 2016. The first major legislation in 40 years dealing with addiction, the law calls for spending more than $180 million annually to address the opioid problem. Although Democrats supported the bill, they wanted Congress to fully fund the legislation by allocating $920 million, but Republicans argued that funding should be appropriated annually.

25 percent over the next three years. And he said the company is researching how to cover lifetime treatment of substance use disorder.[42]

Mendell of Shatterproof agrees with Webster that insurance limits are a problem, but he calls the CDC guideline a much-needed return to past caution on opioids. "If physicians follow these 12 recommendations, then pills will be prescribed a lot more appropriately," he says.

The CDC guideline also will be valuable in educating patients, Mendell says, as doctors tell them why prescribing opioids for more than 10 days could put them at risk for addiction. "If I were president of the United States, I would issue an executive order that every doctor in the country had to receive a course on the guideline by September 1, and not be allowed to prescribe narcotics until they take the course," he says.

But DuPont, the National Institute on Drug Abuse's former director, warns against overestimating the guideline's effect: "Physician training is a good idea, but what [doctors] need to know is that some patients lie."

He tells of a drug-addict acquaintance who obtained the opioid Dilaudid from a drug-dealing friend. The friend had gotten the prescription from a pain doctor, who thought he was a legitimate pain sufferer. Another acquaintance had a problematic-seeming back X-ray that she took from doctor to doctor. "That was all she needed, and a good story," DuPont says. "How is a smart doctor going to recognize that? You tell me. There's no way to overcome the problem entirely."

BACKGROUND
Battlefield Disease

The Civil War (1861-65) saw the beginnings of the first major wave of opioid addiction. Massive numbers of battlefield casualties and illnesses — including diarrhea, dysentery and malaria — arising from unsanitary field conditions left military doctors with few alternatives to the potent pain relieving properties of opium and its derivatives.

Historian Courtwright of the University of North Florida wrote that Union forces alone consumed almost 10 million opium pills and more than 2.8 million ounces of various opium preparations. (The hypodermic syringe became available in the United States in 1856 but was not in wide use.)[43]

After the war, veterans made up a substantial segment of the nation's addict population. But most addicts in late-19th- and early-20th-century America were women whose doctors had prescribed opioids, which were the treatment of choice for gynecological problems.[44]

Morphine also became the common remedy for alcoholism-related delirium tremens; tuberculosis and other respiratory illnesses; dysentery; rheumatism; and syphilis. But as leading doctors recognized the dangers of addiction, they warned against widespread prescribing of opioids.

Partly because of that pressure, and because of the development of vaccines and of non-opioid painkillers, most states and some towns and cities enacted laws limiting the sale of opium-based drugs (and cocaine) to customers with prescriptions.[45]

Opium Dens

In the late 1800s and early 20th century, municipal and state officials attempted to prohibit some narcotic use. The period also saw passage of the first major federal drug-control legislation.

Initial laws focused on opium, the original opioid. Chinese immigrants who smoked the drug, which had been popular in their country since the 1600s, brought it to the United States. Smokers congregated in opium parlors in the Chinatowns that sprang up in San Francisco and elsewhere in the West starting around 1850.[46]

In the 1870s, some white Americans — mostly prostitutes, gamblers and others considered apart from respectable society — took up opium smoking. In 1909 Congress passed the Smoking Opium Exclusion Act, which banned importation of opium into the United States for nonmedical purposes. By 1915, 27 states had passed laws designed to shut down opium-smoking locales.

But opioids processed into more refined forms — morphine and heroin — became available. The latter went on the market in 1898 as a cough suppressant. Physicians soon learned that users could become addicted, so they limited prescriptions. However, illicit heroin caught on among former opium smokers and thrill-seekers. Some of them also began using cocaine, a drug originally prescribed as an anti-depressant and used as an anesthetic.[47]

As recreational drug use increased, American officials sought to pass more far-reaching anti-drug legislation. They stepped up efforts after the U.S. takeover of the Philippines in 1898 made America a power in Asia, where the opium trade had long been established. Officials concluded that if they wanted other countries to sign on to an international crackdown, they would have to demonstrate their own drug-control efforts. That step was required, in fact, under an international treaty that the United States and 33 other nations had signed by 1912.[48]

Drug-control advocates began working to ban all non-medicinal narcotics use. After resolving disputes with pharmaceutical makers and druggists, Congress passed the Harrison Act of 1914, the first federal law to regulate opioids and other drugs. The law did not explicitly make narcotics illegal for non-medical purposes. Instead, it required doctors and pharmacists to register with the Treasury Department, pay a tax on narcotics sales and keep records of narcotics prescriptions.[49]

But some of those involved in writing the bill argued that the government now could directly regulate sales of narcotics. Other lawmakers countered that only

An opium den operates in New York City's Chinatown in 1925. Chinese immigrants brought opium to the United States in the mid-19th century. In 1909 the Smoking Opium Exclusion Act banned importation of opium into the country for nonmedical purposes. By 1915, 27 states had passed laws designed to shut down opium-smoking facilities.

Bettmann/Contributor via Getty Images

states had the power to prohibit such actions as barring physicians from prescribing opioids for non-medicinal purposes.

In 1919, the U.S. Supreme Court, by upholding criminal cases against doctors and a pharmacist, ruled that the Harrison Act was a valid federal drug-enforcement law. In two decisions that year, the court said doctors and pharmacists could not provide morphine to known addicts to enable them to manage their addictions.

David F. Musto, a physician and pioneering drug historian, said the two decisions reflected a national mood that had taken hold during World War I (1914-18) that alcohol and drugs sapped the national will. By 1918, states had ratified an amendment to the Constitution banning all alcoholic beverages. Prohibition took effect in 1919.[50]

Heroin Takes Off

In the 1920s, New York City became the national center for the new and growing heroin trade, which was fed by transatlantic networks that smuggled the drug from Asia through Europe. Heroin addiction was considered a serious enough problem that Congress in 1929 ordered the establishment of special prisons designed to cure addiction. The first of these "narcotic farms" opened in Lexington, Ky., in 1935.[51]

Congress in 1930 created a special drug law enforcement agency — the Federal Bureau of Narcotics. It was separate from the division that enforced the widely unpopular and ineffective alcohol prohibition that was in effect from 1919 to 1933.

World War II interrupted transatlantic heroin smuggling. Heroin from Mexico, where opium poppies also grow in mountainous regions, did not fully meet the East Coast supply gap. But the drug entered Southern California in such quantities that heroin became common in working-class Mexican-American neighborhoods.[52]

The postwar period also saw a major cultural trend in which jazz musicians took up heroin, making it a badge of hipness in some circles. Formative figures in American music who became addicts included Charlie Parker, Billie Holiday, Ray Charles and Miles Davis. Four New York jazz nightclubs lost their licenses in 1945 because drug dealers were doing business there.[53]

In the 1950s and '60s heroin became a mass-market product in black and Latino city neighborhoods. "Heroin had just about taken over Harlem," author Claude Brown wrote in the early 1950s. "Every time I went uptown, somebody else was hooked."

The people most exposed to heroin trafficking — young blacks and Latinos — had the highest risk for trying the drug and becoming addicts. At the same time, steady job opportunities for that population dried up as manufacturing jobs moved away. In their absence, more people turned to pushing heroin.[54]

The epidemic persisted into the '60s and '70s, prompting some community leaders and politicians to demand what some critics deemed a heavy-handed law enforcement response. The 1973 "Rockefeller drug law," named for then-Republican New York Gov. Nelson Rockefeller, was the result. It imposed mandatory sentences of 15 years to life for selling drugs.[55]

But another approach to addiction began before law enforcement became more heavily involved. A New York-based team of physicians and scientists in 1963 began testing a synthetic opioid, methadone, as a cure for heroin addiction. Methadone reduced drug cravings, was long acting and didn't produce the euphoria of heroin. Early results were promising, with a six-week

treatment enabling a small group of addicts to resume productive lives without returning to heroin.[56]

As word spread that methadone was effective, politicians responded. New York City opened a free methadone clinic in 1969, and city jails offered the drug to any prisoner suffering heroin withdrawal. Washington, D.C., followed suit, and Illinois had opened 15 methadone treatment sites by 1970.[57]

The federal government turned to methadone treatment as well to help returning Vietnam vets who had used heroin in the field. With federal aid, the number of methadone treatment centers nationwide increased from 16 in 1969 to 926 in 1974, serving about 74,000 patients. President Richard M. Nixon called methadone "the best available answer" to the heroin plague.[58]

The late '60s and the '70s saw heroin use among some of the young whites who had taken to marijuana and psychedelics such as LSD. That trend reached into well-to-do suburban enclaves, shattering the view of heroin as only the drug of poor, urban minorities.

In the overwhelmingly white New York suburbs of Long Island, heroin and methadone use accounted for about 45 fatal overdoses in 1972. And during the same period, the high-income, virtually entirely white Detroit suburb of Grosse Pointe, had a heroin-use rate of about 4 percent of the adolescent population — double the national rate.[59]

Overdose deaths of white celebrities underscored heroin's power to cross racial lines. Singer Janis Joplin, a white blues singer who became a 1960s superstar, died of a heroin overdose in 1970.[60]

Addiction by Prescription

Heroin remained a presence during the final decades of the 20th century, even as the use of other drugs boomed.

In the 1980s, cocaine was the nation's main drug of concern. From 1980 to 1985, supplies of the drug increased so much that the price decreased by one-third. And in a cheap, highly addictive and physiologically devastating form — crack — the drug swept through predominantly minority city neighborhoods, sparking addiction as well as crime. Rival drug gangs fought over territory, and crack addicts committed robberies and thefts to feed their habits.[61]

Slightly later, beginning in the 1990s, another highly destructive stimulant — methamphetamine — ravaged

CHRONOLOGY

1865-1914 *Prescriptions prompt first wave of opioid addiction.*

1865 As Civil War ends, addictions swell due to morphine use during the war.

1881 California passes first state law to shut down opium dens serving mainly immigrant Chinese smokers.

1898 Newly developed heroin goes on sale as cough suppressant.

1914 Congress passes first federal drug law, requiring doctors and pharmacists to keep narcotics-dispensing records.

1919-1940s *U.S. Supreme Court affirms federal power to prohibit opioid use.*

1919 High court says U.S. government can block doctors and pharmacists from providing morphine to addicts.

1920s New York City gangster Arnold Rothstein develops international heroin smuggling networks.

1929 Congress creates "narcotic farms," special prisons designed to cure addiction.

1930 Congress establishes Federal Bureau of Narcotics, the first drug enforcement agency.

1941 World War II cuts off transatlantic heroin smuggling, but major new source develops in Mexico.

1950s-1980s *Heroin spreads in poor black and Latino urban neighborhoods.*

1950s Enormous heroin addiction wave hits Harlem, New York City's major black community.

1963 Physician-scientist team in New York City begins testing heroin addiction-curing potential of synthetic opioid methadone.

1969 New York City opens free methadone clinic for heroin addicts.

1972 In an early sign of heroin's popularity across racial and class lines, heroin and methadone overdoses kill 45 in middle-class suburbs.

1985 Cocaine abuse eclipses heroin.

1990s-Present *Heroin returns as major threat, propelled in part by growth in opioid prescriptions.*

1994 Kurt Cobain, founder of rock band Nirvana, commits suicide after struggling with heroin addiction.

1996 Purdue Pharmaceuticals launches OxyContin, a time-released form of the synthetic opioid oxycodone; the company tells doctors that time-release formula lessens addiction potential.

2003 Nonmedical use of opioid painkillers soars, with more than 2 million adults a year starting use without prescriptions.

2007 Purdue pleads guilty to felony fraudulent marketing, and three executives to misdemeanors; company is fined $634.5 million.

2013 Number of opioid prescriptions increases to 207 million, from 76 million in 1991.

2014 Democratic Vermont Gov. Peter Shumlin cites 250 percent increase in heroin addiction treatment cases in his state since 2000.

2015 Voters confront candidates in Republican and Democratic presidential primaries with demands for solutions to epidemic.

2016 Centers for Disease Control and Prevention issues guideline to Limit opioid prescriptions (March). . . . Pop star Prince dies from fentanyl overdose (April). . . . Drug Enforcement Administration reports that heroin and fentanyl supply is high, and prices are down (June). . . . U.S. Surgeon General urges physicians to screen patients for opioid-use disorder and follow CDC guideline (August). . . . An even more powerful synthetic opioid, carfentanil, causes surge of fatal overdoses in Ohio, Indiana, West Virginia and Kentucky (September).

Rural County Struggles With Heroin

"What you hear is, 'Addiction is my inheritance.' "

Nestled between the tourist haunts of Santa Fe and Taos in the high desert and canyons of northern New Mexico, Rio Arriba County inspired painter Georgia O'Keeffe and photographer Ansel Adams to create some of their best-known works. But for decades, Rio Arriba also has had a sadder reputation, as a hotbed of heroin addiction and overdose deaths.

"I graduated high school in '93; I saw a lot of my friends start on heroin," says Ambrose Baros, director of Hoy ("Today") Recovery center in the hamlet of Velarde. "Before that, it was marijuana and alcohol and [psychedelic] mushrooms. All of a sudden heroin came, and it just exploded."

Rio Arriba's crisis centering on heroin and, more recently, prescription opioids long predates the epidemic now raising national concern. "We had this problem for years and years and nobody paid any attention," says Dr. Leslie Hayes, a physician who treats addicts by prescribing Suboxone at El Centro Family Health, a federally funded network of clinics. Suboxone (buprenorphine) is a synthetic opioid which, because of its long duration and less intense effect, is used to treat opioid addicts.

Younger residents may point to the 1990s as the crisis takeoff point, but heroin was well entrenched in Rio Arriba by then. As a border state, New Mexico in the '60s was one of the first stops for a then-new and expanding supply of Mexican-produced heroin. Within the state, the drug traveled from Albuquerque up the Rio Grande Valley to predominantly Hispanic counties, especially sprawling Rio Arriba ("Up River," in Spanish), which stretches to the Colorado border and is larger than Connecticut.[1]

And even before then, old-timers in the county told anthropologist Angela Garcia of Stanford University, when residents headed to Denver or Los Angeles for work in the '50s, some returned with heroin habits as well as supply connections. Garcia has written a book about addiction and recovery efforts in the county.[2]

By 2014 Rio Arriba suffered 110.2 opioid overdose fatalities per 100,000 population, more than seven times the national rate and the main reason New Mexico ranked second nationally that year, behind West Virginia. In 2015, Rio Arriba's death rate decreased to 81.4 per 100,000.[3]

No single explanation accounts for opioids' grip on Rio Arriba. Garcia has explored theories centered on toxic family patterns, poverty and a history of dispossession in the county, settled by Spanish conquerors in the 17th century and 71 percent Hispanic today.

"One of the main stories I was hearing was of having lost a sense of cultural integrity," she says. "This is a region where people were supposed to inherit, and everything they were to inherit is mostly gone," she says, referring to the loss of land inherited from 17th-century land grants by the Spanish crown and the later Mexican government. These (which conveyed land on which Indians had lived for centuries) were largely lost in the 1900s to what one historian calls "sharp-eyed American lawyers and their associates."[4]

Today, Garcia says, "What you hear is, 'Addiction is my inheritance.' "

Rio Arriba is poor, with average annual per capita income of $20,253, well below the national average of $28,889, but not far below the New Mexico statewide average. Many of its

rural regions and cities in the West and Midwest. The hit TV series "Breaking Bad," set in Albuquerque, N.M., centered on the methamphetamine trade.[62]

But heroin never went away. The deaths of two prominent musicians underlined that addiction to it remained a major problem. Singer and guitarist Kurt Cobain, founder of the influential band Nirvana, struggled with heroin addiction before killing himself in 1994, and Grateful Dead co-founder and lead guitarist Jerry Garcia died of a heart attack in 1995 after years of heroin addiction.[63]

To be sure, heroin was among the least-used drugs in the 1990s, ranking far below marijuana, cocaine and hallucinogens, according to an annual U.S. Health and Human Services Department survey. But the 2002 survey also found the number of first-time heroin users increasing to more than 100,000 each year between 1995 and 2001 — the highest level since the late 1970s.

The survey also noted the early stage of the painkiller boom. Use of pain medication increased steadily, from 8.7 percent of the population ages 18 to 25 in 1990 to

small communities are hard to reach, and even the county seat of Española has relatively few treatment services, considering the scale of demand. The county's health and human services director, Lauren Reichelt, told the Santa Fe *New Mexican* that the county's recovery service has a waiting list, perhaps in part because Medicaid now covers addiction treatment.[5] In this setting, people with emotional or psychological problems readily turn to addictive drugs — what many call *medicina*, Garcia says.

Addicts include Rio Arriba's success stories. The county government's young spokesman, Carlos Trujillo, whom some saw as a likely future congressman, quit his job last year after he was found passed out in a car with fresh needle marks on his arms. "It's prevalent," he told *The New Mexican*. "For every person that law enforcement puts away, five more will pop up. That's just the reality of the situation."[6]

Trujillo's family tried to help him overcome his addiction. But family bonds don't always work that way. Garcia, during her work at a recovery clinic as part of her book research, interviewed subjects who included a mother-daughter pair of addicts; the daughter later died of an overdose.

"It becomes a bond — your mother is sleeping beside you and she's in withdrawal, and all you want to do is to take away her pain," she says. "Heroin comes into a household and it becomes a key element of what keeps people together; they begin sharing drugs, they become addicted together."

Physician Hayes agrees that family ties are strong. "But that doesn't mean they are functional family ties," she says. "In cases where family members are violent, or are substance abusers, family ties can be problematic."

Finding an explanation for heroin abuse matters less to Hayes than dealing with its consequences. "We're diagnosing really, really late," she says. "We're not diagnosing heroin addicts until they come in with overdoses and injection abscesses. We have to do a lot more around prevention, finding out a way to support families and do outreach to teens."

Meanwhile, a relatively recent trend is making Rio Arriba's addiction crisis even worse. Hayes is now seeing about one-quarter of her heroin addict patients also using methamphetamine, which is physically even more debilitating than heroin. "I've been in Española for 20 years; I've been prescribing Suboxone for 10 years," she says. "People keep asking, 'Have you made a difference in the community?' I've made a big difference for individuals, but as far as the community as a whole, I don't feel so."

— Peter Katel

[1] John C. Ball, "Two Patterns of Narcotic Drug Addiction in the United States," *Journal of Criminal Law and Criminology*, June 1965, p. 209, http://tinyurl.com/jy3jq52; Stephen J. Kunitz, *Regional Cultures and Mortality in America* (2014), pp. 262-264; "Rio Arriba County, New Mexico (NM)," City-Data.com, http://tinyurl.com/zvqmtdw; "State Area Measurements and Internal Point Coordinates," U.S. Census Bureau, 2010, http://tinyurl.com/zj2ktba.

[2] Angela Garcia, *The Pastoral Clinic* (2010).

[3] "Number and age-adjusted rates of drug overdose deaths by state, US 2014," Centers for Disease Control and Prevention, updated, May 2, 2016, http://tinyurl.com/glwgfje; Rose A. Rudd *et al.*, "Increase in Drug and Opioid Overdose Deaths 2000-2014," Centers for Disease Control and Prevention, Jan. 1, 2016, http://tinyurl.com/huhmjbn; "Overdose Deaths Decline in Nearly Two-Thirds of New Mexico's 33 Counties," New Mexico Department of Health, Sept. 20, 2016, http://tinyurl.com/zypcobg.

[4] Marc Simmons, *New Mexico: An Interpretive History* (1988), pp. 183-185.

[5] Daniel J. Chacón and Phaedra Haywood, "Descent into heroin addiction derails political up-and-comer's career," *The New Mexican*, Oct. 10, 2015, http://tinyurl.com/h9kyny4.

[6] *Ibid.*

22.1 percent in 2002. And 13.5 percent of those who had used the drugs in the past — 1.5 million — were classified as having a dependence on the pain relievers.[64]

By 2014, 1.9 million people were reported to suffer from a "use disorder" for painkillers, and 600,000 for heroin.[65]

The 1996 launch of OxyContin was the major event behind the trend. The drug provided a time-released dose of oxycodone, a synthetic opioid first produced in 1916 by Purdue Pharma. The firm undertook an intensive OxyContin marketing program for doctors — including funding more than 20,000 educational sessions advocating long-term use of the drug for chronic, non-cancer pain.

Purdue claimed that the addiction potential was minimal because the measured, time-release formula wouldn't get patients high or leave them craving for more. Abbott Laboratories, a larger firm that marketed OxyContin in 1996-2002, was instrumental in helping Purdue push OxyContin sales revenue from $49 million

Opioids a Scourge of the Middle Class

Heroin "does not only grip those who are born into poverty."

Greg Williams' struggles with addiction surfaced when he began drinking alcohol at age 12. The suburban Connecticut youth soon moved to marijuana and prescription drugs, developing a strong OxyContin addiction by age 17. Williams' road to recovery began only after a near-fatal car accident in the summer of 2001.

"I don't remember much of it, but my face hit the dashboard, and I knocked out a bunch of teeth. I was on a lot of drugs," says Williams, now 32, who was the lone passenger in the car. He says he and the driver "left the scene of the accident and the police called my family saying, 'We found your son's car; we don't know where your son is, but it's totaled and there's blood on the inside.' They found me in the center of town trying to sell drugs, with missing teeth and blood all over myself, just totally out of my mind."

Williams has not been alone in struggling with opioids. Those fighting addiction to painkillers or heroin are not only from the inner city but also from middle-class and upper-class suburbs.

Many middle-class addicts do not survive. In a 2014 speech that helped bring the opioid crisis to national attention, Democratic Vermont Gov. Peter Shumlin cited Will Gates, a private-school graduate, molecular genetics major at the University of Vermont and championship skier, who died at 21 in 2009 after overdosing on heroin.

"Heroin is a drug that does not only grip those who are born into poverty," Shumlin said. "We must address it as a public health crisis, providing treatment and support, rather than simply doling out punishment, claiming victory and moving onto our next conviction."[1]

Williams, now co-founder and executive vice president of the nonprofit organization Facing Addiction, says he wants to change the stigma surrounding addiction, including the perception that it affects mainly the poor. Although heroin addicts in the 1960s and '70s were predominantly minority males, recent users have been people who were introduced to opioids through prescription drugs, and nearly 90 percent of those who began using heroin in the last decade were white.[2]

"They started using words at 17 with me like alcoholic and addict, and I had this visual of what that looked like, and that was a homeless person on the streets of New York City, you know, and that wasn't my experience," Williams says. "The language that we use in our media and our culture around this issue often creates this sense of, 'Well, that's not me.'"

Williams also says he wants to alter the approach to treatment — to encourage addicts to seek help and people to intervene with addicted friends or family — instead "of waiting until [addiction] gets bad enough."

The group with the largest increase in heroin use between 2002 and 2013 had annual household incomes below $50,000, according to the latest analysis. But the number of heroin users earning at least $50,000 a year increased by 60 percent between 2002 and 2013, according to an analysis of data published by the Centers for Disease Control and Prevention. And the population sector with private health insurance — often a badge of middle-class status — registered a heroin use growth rate of 62.5 percent, somewhat higher than the 59.5 percent growth rate of the cohort with no health coverage.[3]

Eric C. Schneider, assistant dean and associate director for academic affairs at the University of Pennsylvania and author of a history of 20th-century heroin use, argues that social class and race have led to a major shift in attitudes. "If

in 1996 to $1.6 billion by 2002, according to court records from a lawsuit against the two firms by the state of West Virginia. Abbott and Purdue denied wrongdoing but settled the lawsuit, which alleged deceptive marketing, with a $10 million payment to the state. Purdue settled a similar lawsuit last year by Kentucky with a $24 million payment. The company has said it is working hard to combat opioid abuse.[66]

Purdue's sales campaign prompted doctors to widely prescribe OxyContin and other opioid painkillers. Addicts and experimental users immediately figured out a way around the time-release formula — they crushed the pills

somebody's next-door neighbor has a problem with prescription drugs, we are inclined to view that sympathetically," he says. "The fact that the [opioid] wave involves white people surely makes a difference."

David T. Courtwright, a professor of history at the University of North Florida in Jacksonville who wrote a history of opioids in America, adds that class may ultimately matter more than race. "A 19-year-old who steals hydrocodone from his mother's medicine cabinet and grinds up the pills and snorts them is [seen as] no more sympathetic than the black kid who uses drugs in the inner city," he says.

The methamphetamine epidemic of the 1990s and 2000s, which persists today and is most prevalent in poor, rural states, has not aroused great sympathy for users even though a majority of them have been white, says Michael Javen Fortner, academic director of urban studies at City University of New York, who has written about law-and-order sentiment in the black community during the heroin wave of the 1950s and '60s.[4] Noting a strong association between meth addiction and robbery, as users seek to maintain their addictions, Fortner says that "when drug addiction becomes a serious threat to the property and lives of people, whether white or black," they begin calling for punishment.

Past heroin epidemics in low-income minority communities did produce crime waves, but debate and discussion about today's opioid wave is notable for its focus on treatment and on not stigmatizing addicts.

Angela Garcia, an anthropology professor at Stanford University who has studied opioid addiction in poor, rural New Mexico, says the spread of addiction in well-to-do communities is forcing the young and comfortable to acknowledge some realities. "I have students write anonymously about all the drugs they've taken and whether they have overdosed," Garcia says. "I am always shocked."

— *Anika Reed*

Author provided

Recovering opioid addict Greg Williams, co-founder and executive vice president of the nonprofit group Facing Addiction, wants to change the stigma surrounding addiction.

[1] "Gov. Shumlin's 2014 State of the State Address," Office of Gov. Peter Shumlin, Jan. 8, 2014, http://tinyurl.com/z7qxctf.

[2] "The Changing Face of Heroin Use in the United States: A Retrospective Analysis of the Past 50 Years," *JAMA Psychiatry*, July 2014, http://tinyurl.com/hej94hr.

[3] Theodore J. Cicero *et al.*, "Vital Signs: Demographic and Substance Use Trends Among Heroin Users — United States, 2002-2013," Centers for Disease Control and Prevention, July 10, 2015, http://tinyurl.com/jxbhc4c.

[4] "The Meth Epidemic — Frequently Asked Questions," "Frontline," PBS, 2006, http://tinyurl.com/398a6uo; "2015 — National Drug Threat Assessment Summary," Drug Enforcement Administration, October 2015, pp. 45-53, http://tinyurl.com/zvh7s53; Michael Javen Fortner, *Black Silent Majority: The Rockefeller Drug Laws and the Politics of Punishment* (2015).

into powder, then injected or snorted it. (Purdue reformulated the pill in 2010 to make that impossible.) Opioid addiction numbers soared. Thousands of users whose prescriptions ran out turned to heroin, which was cheaper and easier to obtain. Nationwide, from 1999 to the mid-2000s, more than 2 million adults a year began using prescription opioids for non-medical reasons, and the rate for young-adult opioid abuse tripled between 1990 and 2003.[67]

In 2007, the U.S. attorney for western Virginia, where opioid use was rampant, charged Purdue with fraudulent marketing because of its claim that the addiction potential was low. The company pleaded guilty to one felony count of "misbranding." Three company executives pleaded guilty to misdemeanor charges of the same offense. No one went to prison, and the company paid a $634.5 million fine.[68]

Meanwhile, the Mexican heroin dealers from Nayarit state were expanding their order-by-phone system throughout the West and mid-Atlantic. Some of them deliberately set up operations in areas with high levels of OxyContin addiction, such as central and southern Ohio.[69]

News coverage of the OxyContin trend in the early 2000s focused on the drug's popularity in poor regions, and on the flourishing "pill mills" in some states — including Florida and Virginia.[70]

But 10 years later, the opioid crisis had leapt beyond chronically depressed regions and into New England and Midwestern states with large middle-class populations. In 2014, Vermont Gov. Peter Shumlin, a Democrat, made national headlines by devoting his entire annual State of the State speech to the heroin epidemic, calling it an "immediate health crisis" that grew out of a boom in opioid prescriptions. Since 2000, Shumlin said, the number of people treated for heroin addiction had risen 250 percent. "We must do for this disease what we do for cancer, diabetes, heart and other chronic illness: First, aim for prevention," he said. Shumlin noted that opioid addiction no longer was linked exclusively to poverty.[71]

By the following year, the beginning of the presidential primary races made clear that opioid addiction had become a major issue among middle-class voters in New England, who were raising it before all candidates in both parties.

In April, shortly before Democrat Hillary Clinton clinched the presidential nomination, she backed a proposal by Democratic Sen. Joe Manchin of opioid-ravaged West Virginia to impose a 1-cent tax on prescription opioids to pay for drug treatment.[72]

Republican nominee Donald Trump pledged, without specifics, to fund treatment as well as prevention. He also said he would "cut off the [drug] source, build a wall" on the Mexican border.[73]

CURRENT SITUATION
State, Industry Actions

Vermont, whose governor played a key role in drawing national attention to the opioid epidemic, is — along with other states — adopting measures designed to begin reversing the crisis. Under a law enacted in June, the state health commissioner is drawing up regulations to limit the number of opioid painkillers that doctors and dentists can prescribe for pain cases, depending on the kinds of conditions. An aide to Gov. Shumlin said the regulation would allow up to a five-day supply for some acute pain cases.[74]

The rules would also require that prescriptions for nalaxone — the anti-overdose drug — accompany opioid prescriptions for patients who take benzodiazepenes, anti-anxiety drugs such as Clonazapam and Xanax. These drugs can multiply opioids' effects, making overdoses more likely.

Nalaxone was at the heart of the earliest state law growing out of the opioid epidemic. New Mexico, which has a long-standing heroin problem, enacted a law in 2001 that allowed non-physicians, including family members and police, to administer the drug, and granted them immunity from civil lawsuits if they were unsuccessful.[75]

Forty-seven other states and Washington, D.C., now have similar laws. (Montana, Wyoming and Kansas are the exceptions.) Separately, 37 states and Washington, D.C., have "Good Samaritan" laws that provide protection from arrest and prosecution for people who report overdoses, as well as for the person overdosing.[76]

As in Vermont, the most recent laws place limits on opioid prescriptions. Connecticut last May set a seven-day limit on new opioid prescriptions for adults, and prohibited them for minors. Chronic and cancer pain, as well as end-of-life cases, are excepted.[77]

On the pharmaceutical industry side, Pfizer, the world's second-largest drug company, reached an agreement with the city of Chicago, which had sued five other firms for alleged misleading marketing of opioids. The company agreed to include in promotional material a statement that opioid painkillers carry serious addiction risk. And Pfizer also agreed to state that there is no solid evidence of opioids' effectiveness past 12 weeks.[78]

Purdue Pharma, meanwhile, whose OxyContin containers already include warnings on the dangers of addiction, reports on its website that it has alerted federal and state law enforcement to evidence of large-scale diversion of OxyContin to "pill mills." "We have robust programs designed to ensure that Purdue is compliant with the Controlled Substances Act," the company says, referring to the major federal drug-control law, "and have at all times complied with the law."[79]

Powerful Synthetics

The extraordinarily potent synthetic opioid carfentanil — designed as a sedative for elephants and other large animals — is blamed for a surge of fatal overdoses in the Midwest. Those have come as China and the Obama administration have begun separate crackdowns on the export of this laboratory product, which contains no opium.

In early September, the administration announced that China had agreed to block exports of fentanyl, which was designed for use in anesthesia and in patch form for chronic pain. It now is being trafficked on the U.S. black market, sometimes in the guise of heroin or prescription opioids, or mixed in with genuine heroin.[80]

Complicating matters, the synthetics are increasingly being sold in small towns and midsized cities, where police have less experience with opioids and have fewer resources than their counterparts in the big cities where heroin was traditionally centered. "It's hard to imagine how it could have gotten worse than the heroin we were dealing with," said Brad Schimel, the Wisconsin attorney general. But "the fentanyl has taken this to a new level."[81]

Fentanyl played a part in more than 9,600 fatal overdoses since 2013 in about 12 states that test for fentanyl overdoses, according to a Wall Street Journal analysis. On a smaller level, in Ohio's Cuyahoga County, where Cleveland is located, there were more than twice as many fatal overdoses from fentanyl (24) as from heroin (11) in August.[82]

Authorities in a region centered on Cincinnati sought to cope with the effects of carfentanil, which was blamed for more than 200 overdoses in August and September.[83]

Carfentanil is a chemical cousin of fentanyl. According to the Drug Enforcement Administration, carfentanil is rated 10,000 times more powerful than morphine (from which heroin is derived) and 100 times more potent than fentanyl.[84]

In Hamilton County, Cincinnati police and sheriff's officers now carry overdose medication, including Narcan, for themselves as well as victims because carfentanil can be dangerous to someone who touches or accidentally inhales it. Rescue personnel report that one dose of nalaxone hasn't been enough to revive some overdose

Christopher Morris/Cortis via Getty Images

A city-sanctioned "safe injection site" has operated in Vancouver, British Columbia, across the border from Seattle, for the past 13 years. After the facility opened, the fatal opioid overdose rate in the neighborhood decreased by 35 percent between 2001 and 2005, according to The Lancet, a leading British medical journal. Similar safe injection programs are underway in several Western European countries.

victims, who need two to five doses to prevent death. "Our antidote, our Narcan, is ineffective," said Sheriff Jim Neil. "It was meant for heroin. It wasn't meant for fentanyl or carfentanil."

Drug users aren't necessarily aware they are taking fentanyl or an equally or more potent chemical cousin, authorities say, because those drugs are often laced in heroin.[85]

"Safe Injection Sites"

Some cities are considering giving drug users a safe, clean alternative to alleys and shabby rooms to shoot up.

In Seattle, a county task force of health providers, police and social service agencies is recommending opening two injection sites to cope with a heroin plague that can be seen in the used needles commonly found in streets and alleys.[86]

"One of the driving ideas behind this is creating a safe space where we can get people the medical, prevention and treatment services already provided elsewhere," said Brad Finegood, assistant director of the King County Behavioral Health and Recovery Division and co-chairman of the King County Heroin Crisis Task Force, which made the proposal.[87]

Are "safe injection sites" a valid response to the opioid epidemic?

YES   Gary Mendell
Founder and CEO, Shatterproof

Written for *CQ Researcher*, October 2016

There is no single way to end the addiction crisis that has ravaged so many communities. It requires an "all hands on deck" approach — we need to do more to prevent addiction and more to help people seeking treatment. And we must do more to save the lives of people in the throes of addiction.

Recognizing that addiction is a disease, not a character flaw, is one way to do that. These are our sons and daughters, brothers and sisters, mothers and fathers. We as a country must do everything we can to save them.

That is why I support supervised injection sites. They allow people struggling with addiction to be as safe as possible. Doctors are on hand to help in the case of overdose. Drug counselors can talk about treatment options. Heroin users have the opportunity to get clean needles.

Critics make a simple argument — that supervised injection sites make it easier to use drugs. It may sound good, but the evidence proves otherwise. One major study from the European Monitoring Center for Drugs and Drug Addiction found no evidence that these sites lead to increased drug use. Instead, they lead to fewer overdoses, improved public safety and easier access to treatment.

The sites already exist in several cities around the world, including Sydney, Vancouver and Amsterdam. The Associated Press reported that at a center in Sydney, no patient has died in the past 15 years. In Vancouver, *The New York Times* said, fatal overdoses fell by 9 percent and about one-third of visitors requested referral to a detox program. And now the mayor of Ithaca, N.Y., is hoping to make his city the first in the United States to approve a supervised injection site. California, Massachusetts and Washington state also are examining the issue.

Let me be clear: No one thinks this should be the primary way we fight addiction. A supervised injection site is not an alternative to a treatment center. But it can keep alive those suffering from addiction. Maybe that will be for just another day, but that could be all it takes for that person to ask for help and start treatment.

More than 30,000 people are dying every year from opioid addiction. We must be willing to try anything and everything to reduce this devastation, because those people leave behind 30,000 families. They deserve nothing less.

NO   Dr. Brian Johnson
Professor, Psychiatry and Anesthesia, Upstate Medical University, State University of New York; Director, Addiction Medicine

Written for *CQ Researcher*, October 2016

There is a tradition of the taxpayers supporting the medical costs of the addictive drug industry. Of course, it started with tobacco. By 1670, half the men in England used tobacco every day. George Washington and Thomas Jefferson were great American heroes, but in early America they also were typical drug dealers. They used slaves to grow tobacco.

By the 20th century and beyond, the tobacco industry was profiting from the billions of dollars in sales to millions of American smokers who were dying by the thousands annually.

Today, children who use cigarettes before the age of 15 are 80 times more likely to use illicit drugs. We pay all of the medical costs for the industry, in contrast with how we treat any other entrepreneur. If a Ford Motor truck causes expectable deaths because the truck is dangerous, Ford pays, not taxpayers.

Safe injection sites are yet another proposal that would have the government subsidize the addictive drug industry. The addictive drug problem will not be solved by spending more money to hire people for the dismal job of watching unfortunates who have been taken over by drug dealers inject the product.

The customers still are more likely to use the drug dealer's bathroom than to delay gratification until they can bring the illicit opioids to the safe injection site. Imagine how neighbors will feel when street-based drug dealers surround the injection sites.

Instead, the obvious solution to the addictive drug problem is for the government to sell the drugs at State Addictive Drug (SAD) Centers. All addictive drugs, including tobacco, could be produced and marketed by the government. A brief course would be required to obtain the picture ID needed to purchase each drug, giving people a chance to think through what they are doing.

Sales would recoup most of the expenses of providing medical care for the victims of the drug. We could advertise, "Citizens of New York, we would like to control your brain by having you buy our drugs." Treatment could be made constantly available, paid for by the customers when they purchase their addictive drugs. Addictive drug sales would nosedive.

Let's see the proposal for "safe injection sites" for what it is — just another way to help dealers sell their drugs in the guise of being "safe."

King County Executive Dow Constantine endorsed the proposal, while Seattle Mayor Ed Murray offered qualified support. Murray said he would support opening the sites if they could be run "in a way that reduces the negative impacts" on neighborhoods.[88]

One site would be in the city, the other in the surrounding county. If they open, they would be the first such places in the United States. But an official injection site has operated across the nearby Canadian border in Vancouver, British Columbia, for the past 13 years. In an article in *The Lancet*, the leading British medical journal, a group of experts studied the fatal overdose rate in two periods: Jan. 1, 2001, to Sept. 20, 2003, before the site was opened, and Sept. 21, 2003, to Dec. 31, 2005, the better part of its first two years of operation. The conclusion: The fatal overdose rate decreased by 35 percent between 2001 and 2005. Similar programs are underway in several Western European countries.[89]

Other U.S. cities and states — San Francisco; Ithaca, N.Y.; Maryland; New York state and California — are debating using safe injection sites.

Opponents can barely contain their outrage at the idea. "We would not think of treating alcoholics by saying they should have three glasses of wine instead of 10," says Sabet of the University of Florida.

Sabet has visited the Vancouver site and says it is not an encouraging model. "I see a city that has barely any [addiction] treatment, where they've had a heroin crisis for 20 years, and their solution is 12 stainless-steel desks where people can inject heroin," he says.

Supporters insist that the need to save lives is more important than debating the correct approach to treating addiction. "One hundred and twenty-five people will die in America today from opioid overdose, will die in the streets or will die in their homes, or will die in gas station bathrooms," Ithaca Mayor Svante Myrick told reporters in February. Myrick's father was a heroin addict.[90]

The Ithaca idea has run into serious opposition. Beth Hurney of the Prevention Network, a county treatment-referral agency, said an injection center could become a drug trafficking center.[91]

Drug policy expert DuPont argues that the proposed sites help addicts maintain their addictions, thereby sabotaging the goal of getting then into treatment. "I understand they like it," he says of addicts. "They're helpless."

Parrino of the American Association for the Treatment of Opioid Dependence acknowledges that safe injection sites will not alone persuade an addict to seek treatment. "If I were to design those programs, I would have some really good people there, who can develop trust and engage people," he says. "Then I'd have people from treatment programs showing up. You need a coordinated model."

OUTLOOK
A Better Place?

Experts disagree on how soon the opioid crisis might end.

Pain physician Webster of Salt Lake City says history tells him that a light is at the end of the opioid crisis tunnel. "All epidemics have cycles," he says.

Webster, who has given up private practice for research, is working with pharmaceutical companies on non-addictive painkillers. In 20 years, he says, "we'll be in a better place in prevalence of opioid addiction, and in a better place for people with pain."

But drug policy veteran DuPont points to the ease of production of synthetic opioids as a reason to temper optimism. "The users are really quite eager to try other chemicals," he says. "They don't have a lot of brand loyalty to heroin; there are hundreds, perhaps thousands of chemicals that have these effects on [the brain's] opioid receptors."

DuPont does expect that the present epidemic will lead to advances. "We're going to get a lot smarter, we're going to save a lot of lives," he says. "But we're not going to end the problem of drugs. Nothing is a silver bullet. When a person is addicted to drugs, they've got a lifetime problem. The culture needs to learn that."

Angela Garcia, an anthropology professor at Stanford University who has studied opioid addiction, laments that people "want silver bullets" instead of trying to understand the complexity of addiction.

She says her research in Rio Arriba County, N.M., underscores the importance of providing good health care. Without that, she says, "people will take what is on hand. What is on hand there has been this drug, which of course creates its own pain and suffering."

Sabet of the University of Florida argues that developments will depend on the lessons people draw from this epidemic. One lesson he sees is that the addiction-as-disease model is inadequate. "It's not exactly like heart disease," he says. "Heart disease didn't make someone lie to their mother or steal from their grandmother."

If this epidemic doesn't teach that addiction is a long-term condition, he says, "in 30 years, they'll be overprescribing opioids or another class of drugs because they've forgotten they had this epidemic."

A mother in a Washington, D.C., suburb, whose son has been cycling in out of treatment for nearly 10 years for an opioid habit that became a heroin addiction, argues that one way of ensuring a better future would be to follow the example of public-interest activists and lawyers who took on cigarette smoking and drunk driving.

In the last half century, the number of smokers has declined by half, a drop attributed in part to Drug Abuse Resistance Education (DARE) programs in elementary schools.[92] Similarly, the number of U.S. drunk-driving deaths has fallen by half since Mothers Against Drunk Driving (MADD) was founded in 1980.[93]

"I think if you shone a similar spotlight on the overprescription and overproduction of opioid pain drugs, the result could be what it was with cigarettes," she says. "Smoking really got cut back. Younger people understood, 'Hey, it isn't cool.' "

NOTES

1. Gary Mendell and Gary Henson, "Fathers Join Forces To Fight Addiction Epidemic After Losing Sons To Drug-Related Causes," *The Huffington Post*, June 17, 2016, http://tinyurl.com/zhacn38; "Man found dead in his Basalt apartment," *The Aspen Times*, April 24, 2015, http://tinyurl.com/jdn3sdo.

2. "Substance Use Disorders," Substance Abuse and Mental Health Services Administration, updated Oct. 27, 2015, http://tinyurl.com/j8svq29; "Number and age-adjust rates of drug-poisoning deaths involving opioid analgesics and heroin: United States, 2000-2014," Centers for Disease Control and Prevention, undated, http://tinyurl.com/ot5454u.

4. "Most Americans Say Federal and State Governments Are Not Doing to Combat Prescripton Painkiller and Heroin Abuse; Large Majorities Believe Wide Range of Strategies Would be Effective," Henry J. Kaiser Family Foundation, May 3, 2016, http://tinyurl.com/guxvzee.

3. Christopher Ingraham, "Prescription painkillers are more widely used than tobacco, new federal study finds," *The Washington Post*, Sept. 20, 2016, http://tinyurl.com/zjokke8.

5. Casey Ross, "Behind the photo: How heroin took over an Ohio town," STAT, Sept. 21, 2016, http://tinyurl.com/zczlsm4; Katharine Q. Seelye, "Addicted Parents Get Their Fix, Even With Children Watching," *The New York Times*, Sept. 27, 2016, http://tinyurl.com/zcgxbyy.

6. "Mass. Statistics Show Opioid Overdose Deaths Continue To Rise," WBUR.org, May 2, 2016, http://tinyurl.com/hdpuaz; Beth Warren, "Drug that killed Prince tied to Ky death surge," *Louisville Courier-Journal*, June 14, 2016, http://tinyurl.com/jgbkamy.

7. Rose A. Rudd *et al.*, "Increases in Drug and Opioid Overdose Deaths — United States, 2000-2014," Centers for Disease Control and Prevention, Jan. 1, 2016, http://tinyurl.com/zultgc7. "Information sheet on opioid overdose," World Health Organization, November 2014, http://tinyurl.com/hmkc3gy.

8. "Statement by the President on the Comprehensive Addiction and Recovery Act of 2016," The White House, July 22, 2016, http://tinyurl.com/gp5y5w7.

9. "Comprehensive Addiction and Recovery Act (CARA)," Community Anti-Drug Coalitions of America, http://tinyurl.com/gumfwxx.

10. Christine Vestal, "States Require Opioid Prescribers to Check for 'Doctor Shopping,' " Stateline, Pew Charitable Trusts, May 9, 2016, http://tinyurl.com/zdaseog; Patrick McGreevy, " 'Doctor shopping' targeted in new law signed by Gov. Brown to curb epidemic of opioid overdose deaths," *Los Angeles Times*, Sept. 27, 2016, http://tinyurl.com/jejgqjq.

11. Abby Goodnough and Sabrina Tavernise, "Opioid Prescriptions Drop for First Time in Two Decades," *The New York Times*, May 20, 2016, http://tinyurl.com/zdyweun.

12. "Fact Sheet: Obama Administration Announces Public and Private Sector Efforts to Address Prescription Drug Abuse and Heroin Use," The White House, Oct. 21, 2015, http://tinyurl.com/z5msmxs; "Principles of Harm Reduction," Harm Reduction Coalition, undated, http://tinyurl.com/lfbmras.

13. Art Van Zee, "The Promotion and Marketing of OxyContin: Commercial Triumph, Public Health Tragedy," *American Journal of Public Health*, February 2009, http://tinyurl.com/cf6n5u2; Celine Gounder, "Who Is Responsible for the Pain-Pill Epidemic," *The New Yorker*, Nov. 8, 2013, http://tinyurl.com/z65pssd. "Prescription Opioids," Substance Abuse and Mental Health Services Administration, updated Feb. 23, 2016, www.samhsa.gov/atod/opioids.

14. Andrew Kolodny *et al.*, "The Prescription Opioid and Heroin Crisis: A Public Health Approach to an Epidemic of Addiction," Annual Review of Public Health, Jan. 12, 2015, p. 563, http://tinyurl.com/zd878cp; Nora D. Volkow, testimony, "America's Addiction to Opioids: Heroin and Prescription Drug Abuse," National Institute on Drug Abuse, May 14, 2014, http://tinyurl.com/zzvjhme.

15. Sam Quinones, *Dreamland: The True Tale of America's Opiate Epidemic* (2016), pp. 40-67.

16. Nora D. Volkow and A. Thomas McLellan, "Opioid Abuse in Chronic Pain — Misconceptions and Mitigation Strategies," *The New England Journal of Medicine*, March 31, 2016, pp. 1256-1257, http://tinyurl.com/j9mytay.

17. "Information sheet on opioid overdose," World Health Organization, November 2014, http://tinyurl.com/hmkc3gy; *ibid.*, Volkow and McLellan, *op. cit.*, p. 1259.

18. *Ibid.*, Volkow and McLellan, "Opioid Abuse in Chronic Pain."

19. Seema Mehta, "New Hampshire heroin crisis leads presidential candidates to tackle drug abuse," *Los Angeles Times*, Dec. 20, 2015, http://tinyurl.com/j43dyys.

20. Goodnough and Tavernise, *op. cit.*

21. "Summary of the House-Senate Conference Report on S. 524, the Comprehensive Addiction and Recovery Act," House Committee on Energy and Commerce, undated, http://tinyurl.com/zvjt9wh.

22. Rob Portman, "Help is On the Way in Fight Against Addiction," Office of U.S. Sen. Rob Portman, July 15, 2016, http://tinyurl.com/hgqgejf.

23. Deirdre Shesgreen, "Congress approves anti-addiction bill as funding fight continues," *USA Today*, July 13, 2016, http://tinyurl.com/z2yq2gz; "Statement by the President," *op. cit.*

24. "CDC Guideline for Prescribing Opioids for Chronic Pain — United States, 2016," U.S. Centers for Disease Control and Prevention, March 18, 2016, http://tinyurl.com/zcc5x4q.

25. Vestal, *op. cit.*; "S.524: Comprehensive Addiction and Recovery Act of 2016," GovTrack, July 14, 2016, http://tinyurl.com/zmym9c7.

26. Silvia Mathews Burwell, "It's Time to Act to Reduce Opioid Related Injuries and Deaths," U.S. Health and Human Services Department, March 26, 2015, http://tinyurl.com/z5w5czy. "Vital Signs: Overdoses of Prescription Opioid Pain Relievers — United States, 1999-2008," Centers for Disease Control and Prevention, Nov. 4, 2011, http://tinyurl.com/jzbhtvu. "Vital Signs: Opioid Painkiller Prescribing," Centers for Disease Control and Prevention, July 2014, http://tinyurl.com/l8h2per.

27. Pradip K. Muhuri, Joseph C. Gfroerer and M. Christine Davies, "Associations of Nonmedical Pain Reliever Use and Initiation of Heroin Use in the United States," Substance Abuse and Mental Health Services Administration, August 2013, http://tinyurl.com/jgqmsok.

28. Volkow, "America's Addiction to Opioids," *op. cit.*

29. *Ibid.*

30. *Ibid.*

31. Harlan Matusow *et al.*, "Medication Assisted Treatment in US Drug Courts: Results from a Nationwide Survey of Availability, Barriers and Attitudes," *Journal of Substance Abuse Treatment*, May 2013, http://tinyurl.com/gtjcgs3.

32. Alison Knopf, "SAMHSA bans drug court grantees from ordering participants off MAT," *Alcoholism Drug Abuse Weekly*, Feb. 16, 2015, http://tinyurl.com/zegby9m.

33. John Strang *et al.*, "Loss of tolerance and overdose mortality after inpatient opiate detoxification: follow up study," *British Medical Journal*, May 3, 2003, http://tinyurl.com/jeqcgpb.

34. Hser Yi *et al.*, "Long-term outcomes after randomization to buprenorphine/naloxone versus methadone in a multi-site trial," *Addiction*, April 2016, http://tinyurl.com/jy9ond2.

35. Joanne Kenen, "Surgeon General uses bully pulpit to combat opioid crisis," *Politico*, April 8, 2016, http://tinyurl.com/zz2ov5r.

36. Richard A. Mularski *et al.*, "Measuring Pain as the 5th Vital Sign Does Not Improve Quality of Pain Management," *Journal of General Internal Medicine*, Jan. 12, 2006, p. 607, http://tinyurl.com/z3u2lqn.

37. "CDC Guideline for Prescribing Opioids for Chronic Pain," *op. cit.*

38. Mularski *et al.*, *op. cit.*, p. 607.

39. "AMA calls for comprehensive pain care, removal of 'pain as the fifth sign,' " American Medical Association, June 23, 2016, http://tinyurl.com/gq9kjlc; "Joint Commission Statement on Pain Management," Joint Commission, April 18, 2016, http://tinyurl.com/zudaj3u.

40. Robert Brandt testimony, Senate Homeland Security and Governmental Affairs Committee, April 22, 2016, http://tinyurl.com/h2duytv.

41. "CDC guideline," *op. cit.*

42. David Cordani, "How the insurance industry can fight substance use disorders," *The Washington Post*, July 6, 2016, http://tinyurl.com/gng6v8f.

43. David T. Courtwright, *Dark Paradise: A History of Opiate Addiction in America* (2001), Kindle edition.

44. *Ibid.*

45. *Ibid.*

46. *Ibid.*

47. *Ibid.*

48. David F. Musto, *The American Disease: Origins of Narcotics Control* (1999), Kindle edition.

49. Courtwright, *op. cit.*

50. *Ibid.*, Kindle edition.

51. Musto, *op. cit.*, Kindle edition.

52. Eric C. Schneider, *Smack: Heroin and the American City* (2008), pp. 31, 75-84.

53. *Ibid.*, pp. 24-34.

54. *Ibid.*, pp. 100-105; *Claude Brown, Manchild in the Promised Land* (1965), p. 187.

55. For background, see Peter Katel, "Prisoner Reentry," *CQ Researcher*, Dec. 4, 2009, pp. 1005-1028.

56. Schneider, *op. cit.*, pp. 165-168.

57. *Ibid.*, pp. 165-168.

58. *Ibid.*, p. 171.

59. *Ibid.*, pp. 156-158.

60. George Gent, "Death of Janis Joplin Attributed to Accidental Heroin Overdose," *The New York Times*, Oct. 6, 1970, http://tinyurl.com/huwewm8.

61. Schneider, *op. cit.*, pp. 192-195.

62. Dylan Matthews, "Here's what 'Breaking Bad' gets right, and wrong, about the meth business," *The Washington Post*, Aug. 15, 2013, http://tinyurl.com/zk4mb6a.

63. Neil Strauss, "Kurt Cobain's Downward Spiral: The Last Days of Nirvana's Leader," *Rolling Stone*, June 2, 1994, http://tinyurl.com/bpybb7l; Mikal Gilmore, "Jerry Garcia: 1942-1995," *Rolling Stone*, Sept. 21, 1995, http://tinyurl.com/gouyz6s.

64. "Results from the 2002 National Survey on Drug Use and Health: National Findings," Substance Abuse and Mental Health Services Administration, U.S. Health and Human Services Department, September 2003, pp. 45, 56, http://tinyurl.com/jx5cuoy.

65. "Behavioral Health Trends in the United States: Results from the 2014 National Survey on Drug use and Health," Substance Abuse and Mental Health Services Administration, U.S. Health and Human Services Department, September 2015, pp. 26-27, http://tinyurl.com/jd2cctm.

66. Quinones, *op. cit.*, pp. 124-127; Kolodny *et al.*, *op. cit.*, "Setting the Record Straight on our Anti-Diversion Programs," Purdue Pharma, undated, http://tinyurl.com/gozca65.

67. John Mendelson *et al.*, "Addiction to Prescription Opioids: Characteristics of the Emerging Epidemic and Treatment with Buprenorphine," *Experimental and Clinical Psycho-pharmacology*, October 2008, p. 1, http://tinyurl.com/godvdqx; David Armstrong, "Secret trove reveals bold 'crusade' to make OxyContin a blockbuster," STAT, Sept. 22, 2016, http://tinyurl.com/jtsgut4.

68. Quinones, *op. cit.*, pp. 264-268.

69. *Ibid.*, pp. 193-195.

70. Barry Meier, "OxyContin Prescribers Face Charges in Fatal Overdoses," *The New York Times*, Jan. 19, 2002, http://tinyurl.com/jb3j72u; Andrew Donohue, "US VA: 'Oxys' become new Drug of Choice in S.W. Virginia," *Roanoke Times*, Aug. 16, 2000, http://tinyurl.com/z8ofxsu.

71. 2014 State of the State Speech, Office of Vermont Gov. Peter Shumlin, Jan. 8, 2014, http://tinyurl.com/z7qxctf.

72. Dan Merica, "Clinton backs Manchin plan to tax opioids," CNN, May 3, 2016, http://tinyurl.com/zyw8cbh.

73. Dylan Scott, "Donald Trump's plan for heroin addiction: Build a wall — and offer some treatment," STAT, Aug. 1, 2016, http://tinyurl.com/zjxe6t5.

74. Neal P. Goswami, "New rules unveiled for opioid providers," *Rutland Herald*, Sept. 28, 2016, http://tinyurl.com/zfrljl2.

75. Clifford Rees, "Naloxone: The New Mexico Experience," Network for Public Health Law, Aug. 13, 2014, http://tinyurl.com/zuh67nm.

76. "Drug Overdose Immunity and Good Samaritan Laws," National Conference of State Legislatures, Aug. 1, 2016, http://tinyurl.com/pr299r6.

77. "Finding Solutions to the Prescription Opioid and Heroin Crisis: A Road Map," National Governors Association, 2016, p. 33, http://tinyurl.com/z6blh7b.

78. Ed Silverman, "Pfizer agrees to opioid marketing deal to escape a lawsuit by Chicago," STAT, July 6, 2016, http://tinyurl.com/zys3je8.

79. "Setting the Record Straight on our Anti-Diversion Programs," *op. cit.*

80. "Statement by National Security Council Spokesperson Ned Price on U.S.-China Enhanced Control Measures for Fentanyl," The White House, Sept. 3, 2016, http://tinyurl.com/zdwl9uw.

81. Jeanne Whalen, "For Small-Town Cops, Opioid Scourge Hits Home," *The Wall Street Journal*, Sept. 28, 2016, http://tinyurl.com/h7byjw4.

82. Adam Ferrise, "August is deadliest month for heroin, fentanyl overdoses in Cuyahoga County history," Cleveland.com, Sept. 8, 2016, http://tinyurl.com/j95qocs; Jon Kamp, "U.S., China Reach Agreement to Stem U.S.-Bound Flow of Fentanyl," *The Wall Street Journal*, Sept. 3, 2016, http://tinyurl.com/gv82uy3.

83. Jack Healy, "Drug Linked to Ohio Overdoses Can Kill in Doses Smaller Than a Snowflake," *The New York Times*, Sept. 5, 2016, http://tinyurl.com/jre2ar8.

84. *Ibid.*; "Drug Fact Sheets: Fentanyl," Drug Enforcement Administration, undated, http://tinyurl.com/zl8y9ke.

85. *Ibid.*, Jay Weaver and David Ovalle, "The China Pipeline: The deadly toll of synthetic drugs in South Florida," *The Miami Herald*, Sept. 26, 2015, http://tinyurl.com/gtfo4w3.

86. Vernal Coleman, "Open 'safe places' in Seattle, King County for heroin use, task force says," *The Seattle Times*, Sept. 15, 2016, http://tinyurl.com/hf7zmyr.

87. Quoted in *ibid.*; "King County Heroin Crisis Task Force recommends 2 injection sites," KIRO 7, Sept. 15, 2016, http://tinyurl.com/gqerxzm.

88. Coleman, *op. cit.*

89. Brandon D. L. Marshall *et al.*, "Reduction in overdose mortality after the opening of North America's first medically supervised safer injecting facility: a retrospective population-based study," *The Lancet*, April 18, 2011, http://tinyurl.com/3ef8qoo.

90. Afeef Nessouli, "Upstate N.Y. mayor proposes nation's first drug injection centers," CNN, Feb. 25, 2016, http://tinyurl.com/ho6dwxv.

91. James T. Mulder, "Should Ithaca provide safe place to shoot heroin? Addiction experts divided," Syracuse.com, Feb. 24, 2016, http://tinyurl.com/zexophp.

92. Jesse Rifkin, "Why Cigarette Use Is At Record Lows and Dropping," *The Huffington Post*, updated March 30, 2015, http://tinyurl.com/oyuudf5.

93. "Drunk Driving Deaths 1982-2014," Mothers Against Drunk Driving, http://tinyurl.com/njr5fkd.

BIBLIOGRAPHY

Selected Sources

Books

Courtwright, David T., *Dark Paradise: A History of Opiate Addiction in America*, **Harvard University Press, 2001.**
A University of North Florida historian examines the past waves and troughs of opioid addiction.

Garcia, Angela, *The Pastoral Clinic: Addiction and Dispossession along the Rio Grande*, **University of California Press, 2010.**
After conducting research in a heroin recovery clinic, a Stanford University anthropologist examines a northern New Mexico county's deeply embedded heroin culture.

Quinones, Sam, *Dreamland: The True Tale of America's Opiate Epidemic*, **Bloomsbury Press, 2016.**
A Los Angeles Times correspondent explores the origins of the prescription opioid epidemic and describes innovations in heroin trafficking that made the drug far more accessible outside major cities.

Szalavitz, Maia, *Unbroken Brain: A Revolutionary New Way of Understanding Addiction*, **St. Martin's Press, 2016.**
A prolific writer on addiction-related topics argues for a nonpunitive approach to addiction recovery.

Articles

Ahmed, Azam, "Drug That Killed Prince Is Making Mexican Cartels Richer, U.S. Says," *The New York Times*, **June 9, 2016, http://tinyurl.com/jyjcc4x.**
Drug gangs are producing and trafficking in fentanyl.

Bennett, Brian, "Democrats aren't the only tourists flocking to Philadelphia. So are heroin addicts," *Los Angeles Times*, **July 23, 2016, http://tinyurl.com/hvznf65.**
Philadelphia is a heroin-trafficking hub for the Northeast, a national security correspondent reports.

Chacón, Daniel J., and Phaedra Haywood, "Descent into heroin addiction derails political up-and-comer's career," *The New Mexican*, **Oct. 10, 2015, http://tinyurl.com/h9kyny4.**
A Santa Fe, N.M., newspaper chronicles a talented young man's struggle to overcome heroin.

Davidson, Joe, "Is DEA a bad guy in opioid addiction fight?" *The Washington Post*, **June 23, 2016, http://tinyurl.com/j62w6gq.**
An Illinois senator accuses the Drug Enforcement Administration of allowing a vast increase in opioid prescribing.

Galofaro, Claire, "4 Hours in Huntington: how the heroin epidemic choked a city," The Associated Press, **Sept. 4, 2016, http://tinyurl.com/h8jeujw.**
In one of the centers of the opioid epidemic, a journalist reports on the experiences of emergency responders handling a steady stream of overdoses.

Goodnough, Abby, "Finding Good Pain Treatment Is Hard. If You're Not White, It's Even Harder," *The New York Times*, **Aug. 9, 2016, http://tinyurl.com/hg5jcht.**
The over-prescribing of opioids for pain helped cause the largely white opioid epidemic, but some doctors may view African-Americans as more likely to abuse drugs, so they prescribe far fewer opioids to black patients, researchers say.

Jula, Megan, "How Staten Island's Drug Problem Made It a Target for Poaching Patients," *The New York Times*, **Aug. 23, 2016, http://tinyurl.com/j3a6ayq.**
A New York City borough hard hit by the opioid epidemic is a hunting ground for competing recovery programs.

Ryan, Harriet, Scott Glover and Lisa Girion, "How black-market OxyContin spurred a town's descent into crime, addiction and heartbreak," *Los Angeles Times*, **July 10, 2016, http://tinyurl.com/zseoxbk.**
An investigative team unravels the tale of a massive trafficking operation that prompted one city's opioid crisis.

Reports and Studies

"National Heroin Threat Assessment Summary," U.S. Drug Enforcement Administration, June 2016, http://tinyurl.com/h8w8e4x.
The law enforcement agency compiles facts and figures showing major new supplies of heroin and fentanyl.

Bagalman, Erin, *et al.*, "Prescription Drug Abuse," Congressional Research Service, Feb. 23, 2016, http://tinyurl.com/hu3wano.
Congress' nonpartisan research arm details efforts to curb the diversion of prescribed opioids for nonmedical use.

Rosenblum, Andrew, *et al.*, "Opioids and the Treatment of Chronic Pain: Controversies, Current Status, and Future Directions," National Institutes of Health, October 2008, http://tinyurl.com/l4a225e.
The epidemic has become big news in recent years, but in this 8-year-old report, specialists already were examining the controversies surrounding opioids.

Volkow, Nora D., "America's Addiction to Opioids: Heroin and Prescription Drug Abuse," National Institute on Drug Abuse, May 14, 2014, http://tinyurl.com/zzvjhme.
In Senate testimony, the government's top addiction specialist reports on the medical aspects of the crisis and approaches toward solving it.

For More Information

American Academy of Pain Medicine, 8735 W. Higgins Rd., Chicago, IL 60631; 847-375-6477; www.painmed.org. Organization of doctors specializing in treating pain that provides information on non-opioid pain treatment.

American Association for the Treatment of Opioid Dependence, 225 Varick St., New York, NY 10014; 212-566-5555; www.aatod.org. Supports use of certain opioid drugs to treat addiction.

Facing Addiction, 100 Mill Plain Road, Danbury, CT 06811; 203-733-8326; www.facingaddiction.org. Aims to unite families affected by substance abuse.

National Association of Addiction Treatment Providers, 1120 Lincoln St., Denver, CO 80203; 888-574-1008; www.naatp.org. Represents treatment providers.

Shatterproof, 101 Merritt 7 Corporate Park, Norwalk, CT 06851; 800-597-2557; www.shatterproof.org. Advocates limiting the number of opioid prescriptions.

U.S. Centers for Disease Control and Prevention, 1600 Clifton Rd., Atlanta, GA 30329; 800-232-4636; www.cdc.gov/drugoverdose/epidemic/index.html. Federal agency that conducts research on opioids and their abuse.

14

Vaccine Controversies

Jane Fullerton Lemons

Celebrity vaccine skeptics, including actors Jim Carrey and Jenny McCarthy, who has an autistic son, have helped anti-vaccine activists garner attention. Although the scientific community backs vaccines as effective and safe, skeptics worry about injuries vaccines can cause and say mandatory policies violate parents' right to decide for themselves about vaccinating their children.

AP Photo/Jose Luis Magana

From *CQ Researcher*, February 19, 2016.

When Facebook co-founder Mark Zuckerberg took his infant daughter, Max, to the doctor for a check-up in January, he posted a cute picture with this comment: "Doctor's visit — time for vaccines!"[1]

The post ignited a social media firestorm over the high-tech billionaire's decision to vaccinate his daughter and his public advocacy on the issue.[2] It generated more than 3.4 million "likes" and was shared more than 36,000 times, with comments that reflected all sides of the vaccine safety issue. Zuckerberg, whose wife is a pediatrician, has more than 49 million followers on Facebook.[3]

The more than 79,000 commenters ranged from being supportive ("Thank you for doing what's right and also for showing everyone else that it's the right thing to do as well") to critical ("I am sorry to see you unnecessarily putting your kid at risk by responding to faux science and propaganda") to concerned about individual rights ("I'm for informed consent for any medical procedure, no matter how small the risk").

Hailed by the scientific community as one of history's most successful breakthroughs, virtually eradicating once-dreaded diseases, vaccines have come under fire from a small but ardent group of skeptics who have long questioned the safety and necessity of inoculations. They continue to express concerns about whether vaccines are linked to adverse reactions and illnesses, and some adhere to the notion — widely discredited in scientific circles — that vaccines can cause autism.

Although the vast majority of Americans continue to vaccinate their children, studies have found that as many as 1 in 10 parents

Most States Allow Vaccination Exemptions

Beginning this July, 47 states and the District of Columbia will allow religious exemptions from requirements that children receive certain childhood vaccines before attending public school. Eighteen of those states also will allow exemptions for philosophical reasons. California, Mississippi and West Virginia allow no exemptions.

States that Allow Childhood Vaccine Exemptions, as of July 2016

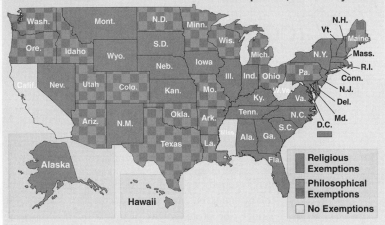

Religious Exemptions
Philosophical Exemptions
No Exemptions

Source: "States with Religious and Philosophical Exemptions from School Immunization Requirements," National Conference of State Legislatures, Jan. 21, 2016, http://tinyurl.com/mhxgt6w

2000. Recorded cases of whooping cough, which hit a low in 1975, have been increasing as well.[5]

Those outbreaks illustrate how vulnerable people still are to infectious diseases, says Amy Pisani, executive director of Every Child By Two, a vaccine advocacy organization. The immunization effort has, in some ways, been a victim of its own success because many of today's parents have never experienced the infectious diseases that vaccines keep at bay.

"Just keeping up those immunization rates, even though we don't see the diseases, is important because the diseases are still out there," Pisani says. "We're just doing such a great job vaccinating that they're not circulating as much as they used to be. So we have to just stay diligent."

Some parents object to the rising number of shots their infants are being given. Today, the CDC recommends that children receive vaccines for 10 diseases — plus the flu vaccine — by age 6, which can mean up to 37 separate shots. That compares to five vaccines for the same age group in 1995.[6]

The federal government does not mandate vaccination, but all 50 states and the District of Columbia require certain immunizations for children entering public schools. Every state allows exemptions for medical reasons. And all but California, Mississippi and West Virginia allow for exemptions based on religious or philosophical reasons.[7]

Most U.S. children still get their vaccinations. According to the most recent CDC numbers, among children ages 19 months through 35 months, more than 90 percent were vaccinated for measles-mumps-rubella (MMR), polio, hepatitis B and varicella (chicken pox). The percentage of children who do not receive any vaccinations was less than 1 percent.[8]

At the same time, polls consistently show that the public strongly favors vaccines: 83 percent believe vaccines are safe, although some groups are more skeptical

are delaying or forgoing some or all recommended vaccines for their children.[4]

As scientists have sought to quell those controversies, particularly the one surrounding vaccines and autism, attention among the skeptical has turned to individual rights. With an increasing number of vaccines recommended for children, coupled with mandates for students — and sometimes health care workers — to get vaccinated, opponents worry their rights are being eroded.

Those fears, propelled by high-profile opponents and heated online discussions, have translated into lower vaccination rates in some places. Meanwhile, growing outbreaks of certain communicable diseases, such as measles and pertussis (whooping cough), have led to medical and legislative efforts to increase vaccination rates.

In 2014, 23 measles outbreaks occurred in 27 states, according to the federal Centers for Disease Control and Prevention (CDC) — causing the highest number of cases since the disease had supposedly been eliminated in

than others, according to the Pew Research Center. Younger adults are more likely to say vaccines are not safe and that parents should have the right to decide whether to vaccinate their children.[9]

The Pew poll was conducted shortly after a measles outbreak began in December 2014, caused by a single visitor to Disneyland in Anaheim, Calif., whose infection led to 141 cases in seven states plus Canada and Mexico — an outbreak fueled by immunization rates as low as 50 percent in some areas.[10]

A study of the Disneyland outbreak found that "substandard vaccination compliance" led to the measles outbreak. To prevent the spread of measles and maintain what scientists call "herd immunity" — vaccinating a large percentage of people to prevent the spread of a disease — vaccination rates need to be between 96 percent and 99 percent.[11]

One of those at risk was 6-year-old Rhett Krawitt, who has leukemia and, as a result, can't be vaccinated for measles. His family called for schools in Marin County, Calif., to ban students who haven't been vaccinated. More than 6 percent of kindergartners there had personal-belief exemptions allowing them to bypass state laws requiring vaccinations — nearly three times the statewide average of 2.5 percent.[12]

"If you choose not to immunize your own child and your own child dies because they get measles, OK, that's your responsibility, that's your choice," said Rhett's father, Carl Krawitt. "But if your child gets sick and gets my child sick and my child dies, then . . . your action has harmed my child."[13]

In the wake of the outbreak, Democratic Gov. Jerry Brown signed one of the nation's strictest vaccine laws, making California the third state to bar religious and other personal-belief exemptions for schoolchildren.[14]

Vaccines work by exposing individuals safely to a germ, such as from a particular virus, so their immune system can produce antibodies to fend off a particular virus.[15] Research is continuing into ways to improve existing vaccines and expand underused ones such as the vaccine against human papillomavirus (HPV). Scientists are also seeking vaccines for newer diseases such as the Zika virus, which is suspected of causing birth defects, and Ebola, which is often fatal.

Despite scientific certainty about the safety and effectiveness of vaccination, some Americans still doubt the benefits of vaccines and remain concerned about the government's role in advocating and mandating immunizations. They also distrust the pharmaceutical industry, which has been exempted by Congress from liability for harms caused by vaccines.[16]

One ardent foe is Barbara Loe Fisher, who became worried about vaccine safety when her 2-year-old son suffered a convulsion and collapsed within hours of a routine diphtheria-pertussis-tetanus (DPT) vaccination. He was left with multiple learning disabilities and attention deficit disorder. She joined with other parents in 1982 to create the National Vaccine Information Center (NVIC), which advocates for vaccine safety and informed consent.[17]

It's informed consent — the right to choose immunization — that Fisher particularly advocates.[18]

"Vaccines should be available for anyone who wants to use them, [and] we should have high standards for proof of safety and effectiveness of these products," Fisher says. But the bottom line, she says, is that people should be able to make their own choices. "I defend without compromise the ethical principle of informed consent in medical risk-taking. At our peril do we abandon that ethical principle."

Those who remain skeptical of vaccines have garnered attention in part because of high-profile support from Hollywood celebrities, such as actors Jim Carrey and Jenny McCarthy, who has an autistic son, and environmental activist Robert F. Kennedy Jr., who has questioned the roles of the government and pharmaceutical industry in ensuring the safety of vaccine ingredients.[19]

Opposition is not limited to the United States.[20] Countries ranging from Australia and Canada to France and Saudia Arabia have dealt with issues surrounding their vaccine policies.[21]

"There is opposition to vaccine, I think, in every country around the world," said Dr. Alan Hinman, a public health scientist with the Task Force for Global Health, an international charity affiliated with Emory University.[22]

As advocates and critics debate vaccines, here are some of the questions being asked:

Are vaccines safe?

Those who hesitate to get vaccines cite a number of concerns, but many boil down to safety.

Studies indicate that parents who delay or refuse vaccination are significantly less likely to believe that vaccines are safe or necessary to protect children's health.[23]

Specifically, these parents fear vaccines could have serious side effects, question the vaccines' effectiveness and worry children get too many shots at one time or could develop autism. They also are more distrustful of the medical community than those who vaccinate.[24] According to the CDC, any vaccine can cause side effects. With that in mind, Congress created the National Vaccine Injury Compensation Program to provide damages to victims while shielding manufacturers from liability in order to maintain a steady vaccine supply.[25]

Studies have found some consistent demographic trends among those who refuse to vaccinate their children.[26] Compared with under-vaccinated children, "the unvaccinated children were more likely to be male, to be white, to belong to households with higher income, to have a married mother with a college education and to live with four or more children," according to a study published in *The New England Journal of Medicine*.[27]

"Other studies have shown that children who are unvaccinated are likely to belong to families that intentionally refuse vaccines," the study added, "whereas children who are undervaccinated are likely to have missed some vaccinations because of factors related to the health care system or sociodemographic characteristics."

Many of these parents also tend to trust their own online research or the experiences of others more than they trust research conducted by the scientific and medical communities.[28]

Vaccination Support Rises After Measles Outbreak

Eighty-seven percent of U.S. adults surveyed in February 2015 said commonly administered childhood vaccines are safe or very safe, up from 77 percent seven months earlier. Support for vaccinations increased after a measles outbreak began in December 2014 in Anaheim, Calif., and spread to seven U.S. states, Canada and Mexico.

Percentage of U.S. Adults Who Say Common Vaccines Are Safe or Very Safe, 2014 Versus 2015

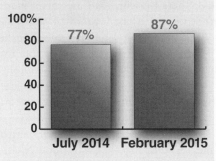

Source: Amy Norton, "More Americans Embracing Vaccines: HealthDay/Harris Poll," Harris Poll, March 12, 2015, http://tinyurl.com/zzqzzlu

"Right now," said Jacklyn Smoot, a California mother trying to decide whether to vaccinate her baby, "the people telling their personal stories influence me more. I feel like the data could be flawed for one reason or another, but I feel like someone's story, because they've gone through something, and they don't want other people to go through it, I feel like I trust that more."[29]

Many of these parents are clustered in certain cities or towns, which can lead to pockets with lower immunization rates. In one study, researchers identified five statistically significant clusters of underimmunization among preschoolers in 13 Northern California counties.[30]

Much of the skepticism started in 1998 with a now-discredited report in the British weekly medical journal *Lancet* that cited the measles-mumps-rubella (MMR) vaccine as a potential cause of autism. The journal retracted the study in February 2010, and the lead author, Andrew Wakefield, lost his medical license.[31] In retracting Wakefield's work, Dr. Fiona Godlee, editor in chief of the *British Medical Journal*, said "the MMR scare was based not on bad science but on a deliberate fraud" and that such "clear evidence of falsification of data should now close the door on this damaging vaccine scare."

But concerns about a link between vaccines and autism have lingered.[32]

"Unfortunately, one thing we've learned is that it's far easier to scare people than it is to reassure them, and once a specific fear has been raised it will take on a life of its own — almost like a virus," said Seth Mnookin, an assistant professor of science writing at the Massachusetts Institute of Technology.[33]

Another concern focused on the use of thimerosal — a mercury-containing preservative used in vaccines since the 1930s — in some childhood vaccines. Although studies have shown thimerosal to be safe and to have no links to autism, it has not been used in childhood vaccines since 2001 as a result of concerns raised by parents.[34]

In addition, some parents who generally support vaccination contend young children receive too many shots too soon, so they advocate delaying or spreading out the immunization schedule.[35]

Some of them are abiding by recommendations outlined by Dr. Bob Sears, a California pediatrician who advocates giving parents the option to follow a delayed inoculation schedule.[36] "I created my alternative vaccine schedule that allows parents to go ahead and vaccinate, simply in a more gradual manner," Sears said. "And I find a lot of worried parents who otherwise would refuse vaccines altogether are very happy to go ahead and vaccinate if they're doing it in a way that they feel safer about."[37]

A study by the Institute of Medicine, a division of the National Academies of Sciences, Engineering and Medicine, examined the current vaccine schedule. It concluded the schedule results in fewer illnesses, deaths and hospital stays, and that new vaccines are evaluated before the federal Advisory Committee for Immunization Practices adds them to the schedule.[38]

"However, the elements of the schedule — the number, frequency, timing, order and age at which vaccines are given — are not well-defined in existing research and should be improved," the report found.[39]

The medical community as a whole, however, doesn't support delaying or skipping any of the shots outlined on the CDC schedule.[40] Various studies have found no problems based on the current immunization schedule.[41]

"We don't advocate for spread-out schedules because they leave children vulnerable," said Dr. Deborah Lehman, associate director of pediatric infectious diseases at Cedars-Sinai Medical Center in Los Angeles. "The schedule is set up the way it is because it's been tested on tens of thousands of children. If you make up your own schedule, you are flying by the seat of your pants."[42]

Some pediatricians refuse to treat patients who are not up-to-date on their vaccines because most parents want to be sure they won't expose their children to disease simply by taking them to the doctor's office.[43]

"We decided that the patients who are not vaccinated are presenting a clear and present danger," said Dr. Charles Goodman, a California pediatrician. "It just wasn't fair for a small number of patients to put those many patients, who either couldn't be vaccinated because they're too young or had a weakened immune system, at risk."[44]

Should parents be required to vaccinate their children?

The issue of how to balance the rights of the individual with the larger public good lies at the center of debate over health laws, including mandatory vaccines.[45]

The Supreme Court has twice upheld the government's right to require immunizations:

- In 1905, the court held that mandating smallpox vaccination was a reasonable exercise of the state's police power under the 14th Amendment to the U.S. Constitution.[46]
- In *Zucht v. King*, the court ruled in 1922 that children could be barred from attending school if they didn't get their vaccinations.[47]

The judicial system also recognizes *parens patriae*, the doctrine under which the court protects the interests of a juvenile.[48]

Under that principle, the Supreme Court said in 1944 that "neither rights of religion nor rights of parenthood are beyond limitation," and the government can restrict a parent's rights in order to safeguard a child's well-being.[49]

If the issue involved individuals making a choice that only affected themselves, such as whether to take antibiotics or undergo chemotherapy, the debate would be different, says Paul Offit, a pediatrician who heads the Vaccine Education Center at the Children's Hospital of Philadelphia.

"Is it your right as a parent in this country to expose your child to a potentially fatal infection? I think the answer to that question is no," Offit says. "We talk endlessly about parents' rights. How about children's rights? There's not a year that goes by at our hospital where we don't see a child suffer and die from a vaccine-preventable disease."

Offit compares immunization mandates to child carseat and seat-belt laws, which require parents to use them for their children's protection. "Frankly, this is a civil-rights issue, and the civil rights are those of the child," he says.

Similar views come from a range of voices on the ideological spectrum, from the liberal Center for American Progress to the libertarian Cato Institute to the conservative American Ideas Institute.[50]

"Vaccination is communitarianism in its purest, laboratory form," wrote conservative columnist Michael Gerson. "The choices of citizens are restricted for a clearly (even mathematically) defined social good."[51]

But for those skeptical of vaccines, the issue of individual liberty is crucial.[52]

"The question isn't whether to vaccinate or not to vaccinate. The question is whether parents should have the right to make an informed medical decision for their child's health," said Shannon Kroner and Tim Donnelly, backers of a referendum to overturn California's new law banning most immunization exemptions. (The effort failed to get enough signatures to put the question on the ballot.)[53]

Fisher, of the National Vaccine Information Center, uses words like oppression and tyranny when she talks about vaccine mandates. She sees vaccination as a civil-rights issue, encompassing freedom of thought, speech and religion. "You have people who feel that they are oppressed, that they are losing their ability to protect their children," she says.

Fisher cites efforts in California and elsewhere to restrict religious or philosophical exemptions to school vaccine requirements. Given the well-defined legal precedent that allows the state to impose mandates for children, opponents have focused on maintaining these exemptions.[54]

"A system that will not bend will break," Fisher says. "You cannot oppress the people, when they believe their lives and their health are on the line, with a policy that's so inflexible that they cannot protect themselves or their children from harm. You cannot expect anything but resistance to that kind of oppressive policy."

That sentiment echoes comments Sen. Rand Paul, R-Ky., made during the early days of the presidential campaign last year when he was still a candidate. Paul, an ophthalmologist who holds libertarian views, said most vaccines should be voluntary, and he called mandates government overreach.[55]

But that view contrasts with the position of another libertarian, who says that while the rights of the state are limited, so are the rights of the parents.

"Parents have agency over their children, but it's not unlimited," says Michael Tanner, a senior fellow at the Cato Institute. "They just have a certain agency over them because children aren't able to exercise their own decisions."

"In the end," Tanner says, "I favor these mandatory vaccine laws, but they don't make me comfortable because it is a little bit gray, and it is an area where you are granting the state certain rights of intervention to override individual choice, and I want a pretty high bar for that."

A study by Indiana University researchers tried to determine whether the concept of "benefit to others" — in the form of the herd immunity needed to prevent the spread of disease — influences parents' decisions about immunization.[56]

What they found was the need for more study. "There appears to be some parental willingness to immunize children for the benefit of others, but its relative importance as a motivator is largely unknown," the Indiana University team wrote.[57]

Does the pharmaceutical industry have too much influence over vaccination policy?

The distrust of government expressed by those opposed to mandatory immunization extends to the pharmaceutical companies that produce the vaccines. Numerous opinion polls show Americans don't hold drug manufacturers in high regard, in large part because they see drug prices as too high and industry profits as too big.[58]

A Kaiser Family Foundation poll, for instance, found fewer than half held a favorable opinion of pharmaceutical companies — below doctors, food manufacturers, banks, airlines and health insurance companies. Only oil companies ranked lower in public opinion.[59]

"You have real animosities about pharmaceutical companies making massive profits," said Mark Largent, a historian at Michigan State University who wrote *Vaccine: The Debate in Modern America.*[60]

Vaccination skeptics say government researchers and regulators push for new vaccines, and industry happily supplies them. Because of the many ties between them, everyone profits, according to industry critics. They often cite the case of Julie Gerberding, who resigned as CDC director in 2009 to become president of drug manufacturer Merck's vaccine division.[61]

Several federal agencies are involved in vaccine research and regulation. At the Department of Health and Human Services (HHS), the National Vaccine Program Office coordinates vaccine-related activities, and the Food and Drug Administration (FDA) is responsible for regulating vaccines and other biologics. Also involved in vaccine activities are the National Institutes of Health, the CDC and the Health Resources and Services Administration, all of which are within HHS.[62]

The FDA's Vaccines and Related Biological Products Advisory Committee recommends whether new vaccines are safe and effective. The CDC's Advisory Committee on Immunization Practices recommends which vaccines should be included on the national Childhood Immunization Schedule, the list that states follow in requiring certain vaccines as a prerequisite for school admission.[63]

Critics — including, but not limited to, vaccine skeptics — have long questioned the revolving-door relationships between these public agencies, the drug manufacturers they regulate and the medical research community.[64]

Dr. Marcia Angell, the former editor-in-chief of *The New England Journal of Medicine*, traces the rise of the pharmaceutical industry's influence to the early 1980s, when changes in tax and patent laws altered the relationships between the drug manufacturers, private researchers and government institutions. The result was a research atmosphere that enabled more players to cash in, said Angell, author of *The Truth About the Drug Companies: How They Deceive Us and What to Do About It.*

Since then, "the pharmaceutical industry has moved very far from its original high purpose of discovering and producing useful new drugs," Angell said. "Now primarily a marketing machine to sell drugs of dubious benefit, this industry uses its wealth and power to co-opt every institution that might stand in its way, including the U.S. Congress, the FDA, academic medical centers and the medical profession itself."[65]

According to several studies, the pharmaceutical industry's influence also can be found in medical journals, where medical professionals rely on objective data to make decisions about prescription drugs and vaccines.[66]

Fisher, of the NVIC, points to a study about industry influence that was published in the *British Medical Journal.*[67]

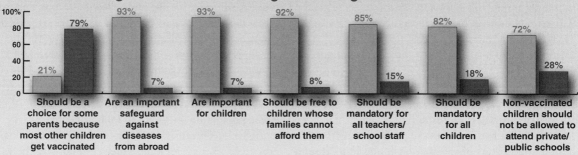

Most Adults See Vaccinations as Important Safeguard

More than nine in 10 U.S. adults agree that vaccines are important to fight diseases from abroad and that families unable to afford vaccines for their children should not have to pay for them. One-fifth believe that because most children get vaccinated, parents should be free to decide whether to vaccinate their own children. Yet 85 percent agree that vaccinations should be required of teachers and other school personnel, and 72 percent say non-vaccinated students should not be permitted to attend school.

Percentage of U.S. Adults Who Agree or Disagree That Vaccinations . . .

Category	Agree	Disagree
Should be a choice for some parents because most other children get vaccinated	21%	79%
Are an important safeguard against diseases from abroad	93%	7%
Are important for children	93%	7%
Should be free to children whose families cannot afford them	92%	8%
Should be mandatory for all teachers/school staff	85%	15%
Should be mandatory for all children	82%	18%
Non-vaccinated children should not be allowed to attend private/public schools	72%	28%

Source: Amy Norton, "More Americans Embracing Vaccines: HealthDay/Harris Poll," Harris Poll, March 12, 2015, http://tinyurl.com/zzqzzlu

"The public voices that are questioning the system, that want reform of the system, have a legitimate argument," she says. "They have been marginalized and demonized by special interest groups who don't want to truly consider the legitimate questions that have arisen."

Kennedy, the environmental activist, is one of the industry's harshest critics. His celebrity status and political connections have helped him gain attention for his argument that thimerosal can be linked to childhood neurological disorders, including autism. He also contends pharmaceutical profits, not medical progress, are behind the increasing number of vaccines children are required to get.[68]

He outlined his theories in a 2005 article, called "Deadly Immunity," published in *Rolling Stone* and *Salon* magazines. But both publications soon backtracked. *Rolling Stone* issued corrections, while *Salon* retracted the purported exposé.[69]

Other critics, such as Fisher's group, note that in the early 1980s, the pharmaceutical companies were so powerful that they threatened to stop producing vaccines unless Congress passed a law exempting them from liability for harms caused by their products. At the time Americans were suing drug companies for problems allegedly caused by vaccines, particularly those for whooping cough and polio.[70] Congress in 1986 created the National Vaccine Injury Compensation Program, which set up a federal fund to compensate victims who claim they were harmed by vaccines.

In addition to questions about conflicts of interest, drug manufacturers face criticism over their profits and how expensive vaccines are.[71]

Vaccines were once considered something of a stepchild in the manufacturing industry because they cost more to produce than conventional drugs. Now, however, they can be a profitable product. The average cost to fully vaccinate a child with private insurance to the age of 18 increased from $100 in 1986 to $2,192 in 2014.[72]

The result has been that previous concerns about low prices driving manufacturers out of the market and leading to shortages have been replaced by new concerns about high prices, particularly in developing countries with an acute need for vaccines.[73]

On the other hand, a recent study examining the economic ramifications of vaccination found that "from a societal perspective, every dollar spent ultimately saves at least 10 dollars."[74]

Because of vaccination, the study estimated, U.S. children born in 2009 would have 20 million fewer cases of vaccine-preventable diseases and 42,000 fewer early deaths related to those diseases during their lifetimes. That means with an investment of $7.5 billion, the routine immunization schedule would save $76 billion in direct and indirect costs, resulting in a net savings of $69 billion.

The pharmaceutical industry also notes how expensive and complicated it is to develop a vaccine. Sally Beatty, a spokeswoman for Pfizer, said it can take five years and $600 million to build a lab where a vaccine is manufactured, and that another two years are needed to produce just one vaccine batch.[75]

BACKGROUND
Early Vaccinations

The use of vaccines to prevent disease dates to early times, when the first inoculations were done in China in the 11th century. While immunizations have saved millions of lives, especially in the past 200 years, they've also been controversial from the beginning.[76]

In 1661, when Chinese Emperor Fu-lin died of smallpox, his third son became Emperor K'ang. The boy had already survived a case of smallpox, and he eventually supported inoculation in its earliest known form. Called variation, the process involved deliberate infection with smallpox using dried scabs or fluid from the pustules; it usually resulted in a milder form of the disease that would leave the person immune, although it also could lead to death. The emperor immunized his children, but not without facing some criticism.[77]

For hundreds of years, diseases such as smallpox, measles, whooping cough and yellow fever took their toll across the globe. When European colonists came to the Americas, they brought those diseases with them. Smallpox is believed to have arrived in Mexico in 1520 on a Spanish ship sailing from Cuba, carried by an infected African slave. Ultimately those diseases spread throughout the Americas, killing some 95 percent of the native population — up to 20 million people.[78]

In 1694, Queen Mary II of England died of smallpox. In 1713, measles killed three children and the wife of Cotton Mather, a prominent Boston clergyman who became an inoculation advocate. Eight years later, when a smallpox outbreak in Boston left 844 people dead, Mather promoted variolation but was widely criticized for it. At one point, a primitive grenade was thrown through a window of his house, with this note attached: "Cotton Mather, you dog, dam you. I'll inoculate you with this, with a pox to you."[79]

In 1782, King George III of England lost a son who died after receiving the smallpox variolation.

Benjamin Franklin also lost a son to smallpox. Rumors abounded that he died from failed variolation, rather than the disease itself, which Franklin denied. In his autobiography, Franklin wrote about the death, discussing the kind of parental quandary that resonates today.

"In 1736 I lost one of my sons, a fine boy of four years old, by the small-pox, taken in the common way," he wrote. "I long regretted . . . that I had not given it to him by inoculation. This I mention for the sake of parents, who omit that operation on the supposition that they should never forgive themselves if a child died under it; my example showing that the regret may be the same either way, and that therefore the safer should be chosen."[80]

Franklin wasn't alone. Dr. Howard Markel, a historian of medicine, wrote that "John Adams was inoculated in 1764. Twelve years later, while he was in Philadelphia declaring American independence, his wife and children were inoculated as an epidemic raged in Boston. Gen. George Washington ordered his soldiers to be inoculated in 1777 because more men were falling to smallpox than to Redcoat muskets."[81]

Discovery of Vaccines

At about the same time the founders were building a new nation, British physician Edward Jenner was revolutionizing medicine by ushering in the era of vaccination with his discovery in 1796 that infection with cowpox could protect a person from smallpox, and its use quickly spread.[82]

Key among the scientists working in the 19th century was Louis Pasteur, a French chemist and microbiologist who developed vaccines for anthrax and rabies. Work also began on finding vaccines for such diseases as diphtheria, rubella, tuberculosis, cholera and typhoid fever.

In the 20th century, researchers began to focus on finding a vaccine for polio. In 1953, American medical researcher Dr. Jonas Salk injected himself, his wife and their three sons with his experimental poliovirus vaccine. Soon after, large-scale trials were underway, and by 1955, public vaccination began.

While Salk's vaccine used a "killed" form of the virus, another American researcher, Dr. Albert Sabin, developed an oral polio vaccine that used a live version of the virus, which became commercially available in 1961. The live vaccine largely replaced Salk's earlier version in the United States until 1999. Neither Salk nor Sabin patented his vaccine, donating the rights as gifts to humanity.[83]

During the same time period the race was on for a polio vaccine, American microbiologist Maurice Hilleman began work that resulted in creating or improving more than 25 other vaccines, including nine of those now routinely recommended for children. At his death in 2005, other researchers credited him with having saved more lives than any other scientist in the 20th century.[84]

But opposition to vaccines began even before they were fully developed. After Jenner developed the smallpox vaccine, it was met with suspicion and mistrust. Some objected that it was administered by piercing the skin, while others did not like that the vaccine came from an animal. Other skeptics had a general distrust of medicine. And many opposed the vaccine because they believed it violated their personal liberty.[85]

When Britain implemented laws between 1840 and 1853 making vaccination compulsory, almost immediately anti-vaccination leagues challenged them as a violation of civil liberty.

One article characterized the "vaccination monster" with this vivid description: "A mighty and horrible monster, with the horns of a bull, the hind of a horse, the jaws of a krakin, the teeth and claws of a tyger, the tail of a cow, all the evils of Pandora's box in his belly, plague, pestilence, leprosy, purple blotches, foetid ulcers, and filthy running sores covering his body."[86]

In 1879, the Anti-Vaccination Society of America was founded. Two other leagues, the New England Anti-Compulsory Vaccination League and the Anti-Vaccination League of New York City, soon followed.

In 1898, the British vaccination law was amended to allow exemptions to the smallpox mandate for parents, based on conscience, which introduced the concept of "conscientious objector" into English law.[87]

American medical researcher Albert Sabin developed an oral polio vaccine that became commercially available in 1961, largely replacing a vaccine developed by another American, Jonas Salk, that was dispensed by injection. By 1979 the last U.S. cases of polio had occurred among unvaccinated persons.

The federal government's role in vaccine policy is extensive, particularly in the development of guidelines for when to administer specific vaccines — and when not to — and to which populations.[88]

Its role in public health matters stems from the U.S. Constitution's Commerce Clause, which states that Congress shall have the power "[t]o regulate Commerce with foreign Nations, and among the several States." In certain situations, this has applied to vaccines, such as requirements that military personal and immigrants be vaccinated.[89]

The federal role is more limited when it comes to requiring vaccines: It does not mandate the use of any childhood vaccines; it only provides recommendations. Generally, the decision to mandate a vaccine falls to state and local governments, where the authority to enact laws for protecting public health derives from the state's general police powers.

When it comes to communicable disease outbreaks, these powers may include the enactment of mandatory vaccination laws. Massachusetts was the first, in 1809, when it passed a smallpox vaccination law. In 1827, Boston became the first city to require vaccination against smallpox for public school students, and the law was expanded to the entire state in 1855.[90]

The other 49 states and the District of Columbia eventually passed laws requiring mandatory vaccinations for children entering school, with varying exemptions. Many states also have laws providing for mandatory vaccinations during a public health emergency or the outbreak of a communicable disease.

Modern Fears

In 1955, just weeks after the Salk polio vaccine became available for widespread use, a production error led to one of the worst pharmaceutical disasters in U.S. history, causing some vaccines from Cutter Laboratories to be tainted with live polio virus. Ten people died while more than 150 others were paralyzed.[91]

Public trust in official reassurances about vaccine safety eroded again in 1976, when people contracted Guillain-Barre syndrome after receiving a vaccination for the H1N1 influenza, known as swine flu. Health officials had predicted an epidemic, which never materialized, but it prompted massive immunizations. The episode triggered a public backlash against flu vaccination, embarrassed the federal government and cost the CDC director his job.[92]

In the mid-1970s, controversy over the safety of the DTP vaccine erupted in Europe, Asia, Australia and North America. In the United States, a television documentary about the dangers of the vaccine spurred a flurry of lawsuits against manufacturers. It also prompted vaccine critic Fisher to join with other parents in forming what would become the advocacy group NVIC. In 1985, she published *DTP: A Shot in the Dark*, a book detailing the impact the vaccine had on her son's life.[93]

Since then, the DPT vaccine has been replaced with a formulation that does not produce the same adverse reactions.[94]

During the Persian Gulf War in the early 1990s, controversy surrounded the military's program to vaccinate troops for anthrax in anticipation of potential biological attacks. Critics questioned its safety, contending the

CHRONOLOGY

1800s *Smallpox vaccinations become widespread.*

1809 Massachusetts is first jurisdiction to mandate smallpox vaccination.

1898 Britain allows conscience exemptions to its smallpox vaccination mandate.

1900s-1940s *Vaccines are licensed for rabies, pertussis, influenza, diphtheria and typhoid fever. Immunization opposition continues.*

1905 Supreme Court upholds state law mandating smallpox vaccinations.

1922 Supreme Court declares unvaccinated children can be kept out of school.

1949 The last case of smallpox in the United States is reported.

1950s-1970s *Vaccine development continues with focus on polio and measles. Modern school immunization policies developed.*

1952 Worst recorded polio epidemic in U.S. history occurs.

1955 Polio vaccine developed by Dr. Jonas Salk becomes available.

1955 Production error at Cutter Laboratories causes deaths and paralysis from tainted polio vaccine, one of the worst pharmaceutical disasters in U.S. history.

1961 Dr. Albert Sabin develops oral polio vaccine.

1962 Vaccination Assistance Act allows for mass immunizations.

1963 Measles vaccine licensed.

1976 Public trust in vaccine safety erodes when people contract Guillain-Barre syndrome after receiving the swine flu vaccination.

1977 Federal government undertakes the Childhood Immunization Initiative with a goal of achieving 90 percent vaccination levels.

1979 The last U.S. cases of polio occur among unvaccinated persons.

1980s-1990s *Concern about vaccine safety increases.*

1980 World Health Organization declares smallpox eradicated.

1986 National Childhood Vaccine Injury Act reduces vaccine manufacturers' liability over vaccine injuries.

1988 Vaccine Injury Compensation Program provides alternative to civil litigation.

1996 Parental concerns about the DPT (diphtheria-pertussis-tetanus) vaccine lead to different formulation.

1998 British medical journal *Lancet* publishes study by Dr. Andrew Wakefield linking the MMR (measles-mumps-rubella) vaccine to autism, fueling anti-vaccination sentiment.

2000s *The number of parents not vaccinating their children grows, leading to outbreaks of diseases such as measles and pertussis.*

2000 Measles declared no longer endemic in the United States.

2001 After complaints from parents, thimerosal is removed from childhood vaccines, but it continues to be used in flu vaccines.

2004 Wakefield study discredited over fraudulent research.

2010 Britain's General Medical Council rules that Wakefield engaged in professional misconduct; *Lancet* retracts his paper; Wakefield subsequently loses his medical license.

2014 Measles outbreak at Disneyland raises awareness about the number of unvaccinated people.

2015 California becomes third state to eliminate religious or philosophical vaccination exemptions from school vaccination mandates.

Vaccine Compensation Program Faulted

It has been "astonishingly slow and surprisingly combative."

When Tarah Gramza's daughter was diagnosed with an autoimmune disorder, the last thing on the Phoenix nurse's mind was the human papillomavirus (HPV) immunization her teenager had received more than a year earlier. But then Gramza found research linking the disorder to the vaccine.

"I did not think in a million years it would have been a vaccine," Gramza said.[1]

Now she finds herself in a legal battle to win compensation from the National Vaccine Injury Compensation Program, a federal program designed to provide efficient and fair support to vaccine victims. But congressional researchers, vaccine skeptics and some legal observers say the nearly 30-year-old program has failed to live up to its mission.[2]

The compensation process has evolved since 1902, when Congress passed the U.S. Biologics Control Act, the first measure designed to regulate vaccines. After that, product-liability laws were passed throughout the 20th century, allowing individuals who claimed they had been harmed by vaccines to sue the manufacturer or the physician.[3]

In 1955, that process was tested by lawsuits arising from a disaster in which, just weeks after the polio vaccine became available, some tainted lots caused by a Cutter Laboratories production error led to 10 deaths and more than 150 cases of paralysis. A key lawsuit stemming from the incident had a lasting effect on liability law.[4]

Lawsuits against drug makers increased in the 1970s and '80s, with many cases related to the diphtheria-pertussis-tetanus (DPT) vaccine. Facing mounting legal fees and large jury awards, many pharmaceutical companies stopped vaccine production, and health officials worried that a shortage would develop.[5]

In 1986, Congress stepped in, passing the National Vaccine Injury Compensation Act, which led to the creation of the National Vaccine Injury Program. While recognizing that vaccines occasionally cause harm, lawmakers sought to find a balance between ensuring a steady supply of vaccines and providing a financial remedy to those injured. The program's no-fault compensation plan capped damage awards for pain and suffering.[6]

But those who have studied the system say only half that equation has worked. By shielding manufacturers from liability, the program has ensured that vaccines remain available to the public. But according to an Associated Press investigation, the program has failed to keep its promise of "quickly and generously" compensating those harmed by vaccines because the process often takes years, has a high standard of proof and has led to the very courtroom litigation it sought to avoid.[7]

A report by the Government Accountability Office (GAO), the independent watchdog agency of Congress, found similar problems. A 2014 GAO study into vaccine injury claims found an "adversarial environment" in which more than half of the 9,800 claims filed since 1999 took several years to resolve.[8]

Here's how the vaccine compensation process works:[9]

- An individual, parent or legal guardian can file a claim for an injury that lasted more than six months after the vaccine was given, resulted in a hospital stay and surgery or led to death. Claims must be filed with the U.S. Court of Federal Claims, commonly known as vaccine court.[10]
- Compensation varies, depending on the injury, and can include as much as $250,000 for pain and suffering, lost earnings, legal fees and/or a reasonable amount for past and future care. For a death, the payout is capped at $250,000.
- Under a statute of limitations, claims must be filed within three years for an injury or two years for a death.

vaccine, with a history of manufacturing problems, may have led to the mysterious ailments known as Gulf War syndrome that afflicted many veterans, although the Defense Department countered with studies supporting the vaccine's safety.[95]

Parents' concerns also surrounded the use in vaccines of thimerosal — a form of mercury known as ethylmercury that had been used as a preservative for decades. Since 2001, childhood vaccines in the United States have contained no thimerosal, or only trace

Sixteen vaccines currently are covered under the program, although people can petition to have their cases reviewed if another vaccine is involved.

- The Court of Federal Claims makes the final decision regarding claims, compensation and the amount of the award.

To win a claim, petitioners must prove they received a vaccine and developed a condition included on the government's vaccine injury table, which lists the vaccines and the associated illness, disability or injury covered. They don't have to prove the immunization caused their condition.[11]

But if the injury is not listed in the table, the burden of proof is higher. Some critics contend it is too high, especially in cases where the harm is clear but the scientific evidence is not. The Associated Press investigation found many claims fall into such a gray area. The science is clear on only nine of 144 vaccine-injury combinations that a vaccine could cause the illness.

According to Department of Health and Human Services (HHS) data, more than 16,729 claims have been filed since 1988. Of those, 9,915 were dismissed and 4,482 received compensation from the $3.3 billion paid out over the program's lifetime.[12]

When Stanford University law professor Nora Freeman Engstrom examined how well the injury compensation program had fared as an alternative to traditional litigation, she found the system wanting.

"The results are discouraging," Engstrom said. "Despite initial optimism in Congress and beyond that such a fund could resolve claims efficiently and amicably, in operation the program has been astonishingly slow and surprisingly combative."[13]

But those who defend the vaccine compensation program say that while the system has room for improvement, it has helped ensure a steady availability of vaccines, and it has made it easier for vaccine victims to get compensation.

Going through the regular courts is "much harder" for those seeking compensation, said Dorit Rubinstein Reiss, a University of California, Hastings, law professor, because they would have to prove the vaccine is defective,

and they would have to prove a link between the injury and the vaccine.[14]

— Jane Fullerton Lemons

[1] Jessica Boehm, "Vaccine injury funds climbs, patients struggle to get payment," *The Arizona Republic*, May 23, 2015, http://tinyurl.com/nntph72.

[2] "National Vaccine Injury Compensation Program," Department of Health and Human Services, undated, http://tinyurl.com/mkwh7m8.

[3] "Vaccine Injury Compensation Programs," History of Vaccines, http://tinyurl.com/nbp56c4.

[4] Sabin Russell, "When polio vaccine backfired / Tainted batches killed 10 and paralyzed 164," *San Francisco Chronicle*, April 25, 2005, http://tinyurl.com/heydzca.

[5] "Vaccine Injury Compensation Programs," *op. cit.*

[6] Sarah A. Lister *et al.*, "Selected Federal Compensation Programs for Physical Injury or Death," Congressional Research Service, March 2007, http://tinyurl.com/zdrll4d.

[7] Mitch Weiss, Justin Pritchard and Troy Thibodeaux, "AP Impact: 'Vaccine court' keeps claimants waiting," *Salon*, Nov. 17, 2014, http://tinyurl.com/zk4f6e8.

[8] "Vaccine Injury Compensation: Most Claims Took Multiple Years and Many Were Settled through Negotiation," Government Accountability Office, Nov. 21, 2014, http://tinyurl.com/mql68yz.

[9] "How to File a Claim," National Vaccine Injury Compensation Program, Health Resources and Services Administration, Department of Health and Human Services, http://tinyurl.com/c3glfzl.

[10] "Vaccine Claims/Office of Special Masters," U.S. Court of Federal Claims, http://tinyurl.com/dm7fnt.

[11] "Vaccine Injury Table," National Vaccine Injury Compensation Program, Health Resources and Services Administration, http://tinyurl.com/6sxm3mb.

[12] "Data and Statistics," *Montly Statistics Report*, National Vaccine Injury Compensation Program, updated Feb. 3, 2016, http://tinyurl.com/jpswrg2.

[13] Clifton B. Parker, "Federal program for vaccine-injured children is failing, Stanford scholar says," *Stanford News*, July 6, 2015, http://tinyurl.com/jrrwe4q.

[14] Dorit Rubinstein Reiss, " 'A Dose of Reality' Does Not Support Abolishing VICP," *Shot of Prevention*, Aug. 11, 2015, http://tinyurl.com/zdc6na3. Also see http://tinyurl.com/hwyn7do.

amounts, although flu vaccines continue to contain thimerosal.[96]

In 1998, the MMR vaccine came under scrutiny after British gastroenterologist Wakefield linked the routinely recommended shot to the rising incidence of autism.

In 2004, the study was called into question amid reports of fraudulent research and conflicts of interest. In 2010, Britain's General Medical Council ruled that Wakefield was guilty of misconduct, and *The Lancet* formally retracted the paper. In May

Vaccination Mandates for Adults on the Rise

"More should be done to protect the most vulnerable populations."

It's not just schoolchildren who have to roll up their sleeves. Many adults do, too. In California, a new law requires daycare workers to be vaccinated for measles, whooping cough and influenza by Sept. 1, although exemptions for religious and other reasons are allowed.[1] They join soldiers, hospital workers and other adults required to be immunized against many common communicable diseases.

"Public health officials have been sounding the alarm that more should be done to protect the most vulnerable populations such as children and seniors," said Democratic state Sen. Tony Mendoza, in explaining his sponsorship of the California measure.

That rationale has led an increasing number of health care facilities to require their employees to be immunized for various diseases.[2] In 2013, Rhode Island became the first state to mandate flu shots for health care workers, although 17 states have laws related to flu shots for adults, such as requiring hospitals to offer vaccination.[3]

The Centers for Disease Control and Prevention (CDC) recommends health care workers be vaccinated to reduce the chance they will get or spread vaccine-preventable diseases.[4] The CDC estimates that more than 200,000 people are hospitalized from seasonal flu-related complications annually, although cases vary. Between 1976 and 2006, the number of deaths attributed annually to the flu ranged from 3,000 to 49,000.[5]

Vaccination reduces the flu risk by 50 percent to 60 percent, according to the CDC.[6]

But the issue of mandatory vaccination raises questions about whose rights come first — those of health care workers or of their patients.[7]

When Virginia Mason Hospital in Seattle began requiring its employees to receive an annual flu shot in 2005, the staff vaccination rate went from 54 percent to 98 percent, although the nurses' union successfully challenged the policy.[8] More than 500 facilities have followed suit with exemptions for medical, philosophical and religious reasons.[9]

CDC data show that vaccination rates are higher when immunization is required or recommended. For the early part of the 2014-15 flu season, vaccination coverage among health care workers averaged 64.3 percent. The coverage increased to 85.8 percent among workers whose employers required the flu vaccine and 68.4 percent for those where vaccination was recommended.[10]

In 2010, Children's Hospital of Philadelphia began requiring all employees to get the flu vaccine after two young patients on chemotherapy died after becoming infected with influenza from health care workers. "It's not your inalienable right to not get a vaccine if you're helping care for vulnerable patients," said Dr. Paul Offit, director of the hospital's Vaccine Education Center. These two patients "died from getting the flu at the hospital."[11]

But nine Children's Hospital workers, five of whom belonged to a local health care workers union, refused the flu shot and were fired.[12] In 2012, an Indiana hospital fired eight workers for refusing to be vaccinated. At least 15 hospital workers in four states were fired in early 2013 as well.[13]

A number of organized labor groups, including National Nurses United, oppose mandatory flu shots. They contend hospitals should take other measures, such as hand washing and sanitizing of surfaces, which can help curb the spread of influenza.[14]

"I work at a hospital that currently has a seasonal flu mandatory vaccine policy, and I know from experience that this kind of punitive policy only fosters resentment on the part of the bedside caregivers," said Rajini Raj, a registered nurse who works at the MedStar Washington Hospital Center in Washington, D.C. She and others who oppose mandates point out the vaccine is not wholly effective.[15]

But others say workers' individual rights should not come before public health and the medical tenet to "do no harm."[16]

"It is in the highest tradition of the healing professions to set aside our own self-interests and preferences in the moral imperative to best protect and care for our

2010, Wakefield was banned from practicing medicine in Britain.[97]

An analysis of these long-running vaccine controversies by Dr. Jeffrey P. Baker, a Duke University pediatrician

and medical historian, noted how the two sides approach the controversy from opposite angles: Physicians and public health leaders turn to the scientific process and research reports, while vaccine opponents reject these

patients — even if it means accepting some level of self-harm (real or imagined)," wrote Dr. Gregory A. Poland, a vaccine researcher at the Mayo Clinic and editor-in-chief of the journal *Vaccine*.[17]

Those in the U.S. military constitute another group of adults who face mandatory vaccinations. Military regulations require U.S. troops to be immunized against a number of diseases, including diphtheria and yellow fever. These inoculations begin when soldiers enter into service. Depending on their specialties or locations of deployment, troops may be required to get other vaccinations as well. Courts have upheld the legality of the military's mandatory vaccination orders.[18]

— Jane Fullerton Lemons

Dr. Thomas Frieden, director of the Centers for Disease Control and Prevention, receives a flu shot following a Sept. 18, 2014, news conference in which he stressed the importance of flu vaccinations for adults.

[1] Rong-Gong Lin II and Rosanna Xia, "Vaccines required for daycare workers under new California law," *Los Angeles Times*, Oct. 13, 2015, http://tinyurl.com/z9kl9cs.

[2] "Requirements & Laws," Centers for Disease Control and Prevention, Jan. 25, 2016, http://tinyurl.com/z3rlqca; "Healthcare Personnel and Immunization," Immunization Action Coalition, Sept. 20, 2013, http://tinyurl.com/gweb2ax.

[3] "HEALTH Adopts Regulations to Require Flu Shots for Healthcare Workers in Rhode Island," press release, Rhode Island Department of Health, Oct. 5, 2012, http://tinyurl.com/8ao8q6j; "Menu of State Hospital Influenza Vaccination Laws," Public Health Law, Centers for Disease Control and Prevention, Nov. 23, 2015, http://tinyurl.com/zphs3us.

[4] "Recommended Vaccines for Healthcare Workers," Centers for Disease Control and Prevention, April 15, 2014, http://tinyurl.com/hvah352.

[5] "Seasonal Influenza Q&A," Centers for Disease Control and Prevention, Sept. 18, 2015, http://tinyurl.com/z6pud4l.

[6] "Vaccine Effectiveness — How Well Does the Flu Vaccine Work?" Centers for Disease Control and Prevention, Dec. 21, 2015, http://tinyurl.com/26ozkb.

[7] Daniel Goodman and Christopher Webster, "The Mandatory Vaccination of Health Care Workers," *Law Practice Today*, April 2011, http://tinyurl.com/h72asxl; Robert I. Field, "Mandatory Vaccination of Health Care Workers: Whose Rights Should Come First?" *Pharmacy and Therapeutics*, November 2009, http://tinyurl.com/gn4h8yg.

[8] John Tozzi, "Can Your Boss Make You Get Vaccinated?" Bloomberg Business, Jan. 22, 2015, http://tinyurl.com/h2tdypu; Lisa Schnirring, "First hospital to mandate flu vaccination reports on challenges, success," Center for Infectious Disease Research and Policy, Aug. 3, 2010, http://tinyurl.com/ja8krgh.

[9] "Influenza Vaccination Honor Roll," Immunization Action Coalition, Dec. 10, 2015, http://tinyurl.com/nbhag2d.

[10] "Influenza Vaccination Information for Health Care Workers," Centers for Disease Control and Prevention, Sept. 17, 2015, http://tinyurl.com/qj9ke4u.

[11] Marcia Stone, Vaccine Coverage: Individual rights versus the Common Good," Microbe Magazine, September 2011, http://tinyurl.com/h8b75en; Janice Lloyd, "Mandatory flu shots opposed by some health care workers," *USA Today*, Jan. 16, 2013, http://tinyurl.com/j5y72vk.

[12] Stone, *op. cit.*

[13] Brad Tuttle, "Workers Are Being Fired for Refusing to Get Flu Shots," *Money*, Nov. 5, 2015, http://tinyurl.com/hcmfxvk.

[14] Genevieve M. Clavreul, "Should the Flu Shot be Mandatory for Nurses?" *Working Nurse*, undated, http://tinyurl.com/mye3ntu.

[15] "Largest National Nurses Union Opposes Mandatory Flu Vaccination as Condition of Employment," press release, National Nurses United, Feb. 8, 2012, http://tinyurl.com/zhguk3d.

[16] J. J. M. van Delden *et al.*, "The ethics of mandatory vaccination against influenza for health care workers," *Vaccine*, Aug. 21, 2008, http://tinyurl.com/htnqbet.

[17] Gregory A. Poland, "Mandating influenza vaccination for health care workers: Putting patients and professional ethics over personal preference," *Vaccine*, July 13, 2010, http://tinyurl.com/zx69uca.

[18] Jared P. Cole and Kathleen S. Swendiman, "Mandatory Vaccinations: Precedent and Current Laws," Congressional Research Service, May 21, 2014, http://tinyurl.com/j7n6ag4.

studies, charging that the data have been manipulated for political reasons.[98]

"A polarized debate both draws upon and contributes to polarized understandings of history," Baker wrote. As a result, participants "judged the same data using different sets of assumptions, each shaped by history. Articulating and sharing these narratives represent a first step toward transcending the powerful boundaries shaping today's vaccine controversies."

CURRENT SITUATION

State Legislation

As California prepares to begin enforcing its new law tightening restrictions on vaccine exemptions later this year, other states will be considering vaccine-related proposals. Congress, meanwhile, continues work on a bill containing funding for critical health care research and regulation that could affect vaccine policy.

Between 2009 and 2012, lawmakers in 18 states introduced 36 bills involving vaccine exemptions, 31 of which would have made opting out of shots easier, according to the National Conference of State Legislatures. None of those 31 bills passed.[99]

In 2015, following the Disneyland measles outbreak, six states — California, Connecticut, Illinois, South Dakota, Vermont and West Virginia — passed legislation related to exemptions, all but one of which tightened requirements. California removed both personal and religious exemptions, while Vermont removed its philosophical exemption.[100] Several other states also considered legislation in 2015 dealing with exemptions.

This year, states will consider related issues:

- In Washington, a bill that would eliminate the state's personal belief exemption is awaiting a floor vote in the House after being passed out of committee last year.
- In Pennsylvania, a similar bill, introduced in 2015, to eliminate the philosophical exemption awaits committee action.
- In South Dakota, a Senate committee approved a measure in January to require sixth-graders to get a meningococcal vaccine.
- In Hawaii, lawmakers killed a bill in February designed to speed up the state's process for adopting federal vaccination guidelines, after residents spoke out against vaccines.[101]

Emory University researchers studied the correlation between state exemption laws and vaccination rates and found that exemptions for nonmedical reasons increased at a heightened rate from 2005 to 2011.[102]

"Since school immunization requirements play a major role in controlling vaccine-preventable diseases in the United States, studies like this underscore the need for states to examine their current exemption policies," said Saad B. Omer, the study's lead author.[103]

The National Vaccine Information Center monitors state legislative activity involving vaccine-related issues, including bills already filed for 2016.[104] Dawn Richardson, the NVIC's advocacy director, said that state legislatures last year experienced "an unprecedented flood of bills backed by the pharmaceutical and medical trade industries to restrict or remove personal-belief vaccine exemptions, expand electronic vaccine tracking systems and require more vaccines for children in school and adults in the workplace."

Congressional Vote

On Capitol Hill, the House in July passed a massive health care bill — the 21st Century Cures Act — that would increase funding for the National Institutes of Health and streamline the process for approving drugs, including vaccines, and other medical devices.[105]

Rather than vote on the entire measure, the Senate plans to break it into a series of smaller bills this year.[106]

Despite its overwhelming bipartisan vote, 344-77, the House bill has drawn mixed reviews. And it may be an issue where those on different sides of the vaccine debate are in agreement.[107]

Fisher of NVIC worries that the bill, aimed at speeding up the drug-approval process, "seriously compromises the integrity of the FDA drug and vaccine licensing process." She added, in an interview with *CQ Researcher*, "We can't allow these standards to be lowered anymore."[108]

Fisher isn't alone in her concerns. Former FDA Commissioner David Kessler joined with leaders of the HIV/AIDS community to urge Congress to reject the bill. The legislation "could substantially lower the standards for approval of many medical products, potentially placing patients at unnecessary risk of injury or death," they wrote in a *New York Times* op-ed.[109]

Other critics have cited provisions of the bill that would allow researchers to rely on "clinical experience" rather than clinical trials in evaluating the safety and efficacy of new drugs. That "smacks of being a payoff to pharmaceutical companies," wrote Dr. David Gorski, a Michigan surgical oncologist.[110]

House Energy and Commerce Chairman Fred Upton, R-Mich., and Rep. Diana DeGette, D-Colo. led the push for the bill, which they said will bring the nation's health care system into the 21st century, invest in science and medical innovation, incorporate the patient perspective and modernize clinical trials to deliver better, faster cures.[111]

"Every family is impacted by disease; they just are," Upton said. "My wife has lupus, my dad has diabetes, my mom's a cancer survivor. And I'm no different than anyone else."[112]

During the peak of the Disneyland measles outbreak, lawmakers from both parties stressed vaccines' importance.[113]

The Senate Health, Education, Labor and Pensions Committee heard top immunization officials testify about vaccine-preventable diseases. Members emphasized the safety of and need for inoculations while questioning assertions that vaccines can harm children.[114]

"Too many parents are turning away from sound science," said committee Chairman Lamar Alexander, R-Tenn. "Sound science is this: Vaccines save lives."

The hearing came just as a pair of Republican presidential candidates — New Jersey Gov. Chris Christie and Sen. Paul — drew criticism for saying parents should decide whether to vaccinate their children. Paul, a member of the committee, did not attend the hearing.

The topic resurfaced in a September 2015 Republican debate, with comments by several candidates including front-runner Donald Trump, who has linked vaccines to autism, despite scientific evidence to the contrary. He favors smaller doses over a longer period of time, saying the number of vaccinations "looks just like it's meant for a horse, not for a child."[115]

HPV Vaccine

Currently, only three jurisdictions mandate the HPV vaccine. Virginia and the District of Columbia require it for girls entering the sixth grade, while Rhode Island requires it for seventh-grade girls and boys. All three allow broad exemptions for the vaccine.[116]

As of February, at least nine states have proposed HPV-related legislation for the 2015-16 sessions, but only Hawaii has a bill that would mandate use of the vaccine.[117]

HPV is the most common sexually transmitted disease in the United States. Every year, more than 27,000 cases of HPV-caused cancer occur in women and men, according to the CDC, HPV is linked to virtually all cervical cancer. In 2012, the most recent year statistics are available, cervical cancer was diagnosed in more than 12,000 cases, and more than 4,000 patients died.[118] The CDC recommends the vaccine, a series of three shots, for preteen boys and girls at age 11 or 12 so they are protected before ever being exposed to the virus.[119]

When the vaccine received approval in 2006, some states moved quickly to make inoculations mandatory for school attendance. But reactions to an aggressive lobbying campaign by vaccine manufacturer Merck, coupled with safety concerns, stalled efforts to mandate the shots in many states. Conservative groups joined the opposition, saying the vaccine would encourage inappropriate sexual activity and override parental autonomy.[120]

As a result, HPV vaccine coverage remains lower than for other teen immunizations, according to the CDC. Four out of 10 adolescent girls and six out of 10 adolescent boys have not started the HPV vaccine series.[121]

A study showing implementation of the HPV vaccine has lagged behind other new vaccines indicated that early efforts to mandate its use may have backfired. Despite the issues surrounding it, the HPV vaccine "should not be viewed or treated differently than other routinely recommended vaccines," the study said.[122]

OUTLOOK
Pipeline Expanding

As vaccine development continues, research is encompassing not only infectious diseases but also chronic conditions. But with new viruses such as Zika and Ebola cropping up, finding a way to prevent the spread of disease remains the central mission.

For the scientific and medical communities, such research represents continued progress. Dr. Candice Robinson, a medical officer with CDC's Immunization Services Division, says recent developments encompass vaccinations for traditional childhood illnesses and emerging infectious diseases.

"There have been some new vaccines coming down the pipeline, and there's been lots of innovation in terms of Ebola virus vaccines or Zika virus vaccines," Robinson says.

According to the World Health Organization (WHO), vaccines for the Zika virus might be ready for large trials in about 18 months. Possible vaccines at the most advanced stage include one from the National Institutes

Should children have to be vaccinated to attend school?

YES

Amy Pisani
Executive Director, Every Child By Two
Written for *CQ Researcher*, February 2016

When parents enroll their children in day care or kindergarten, they should feel secure knowing their little ones will be safe from preventable infectious diseases. Every Child By Two's co-founders, former first lady Rosalynn Carter and former Arkansas first lady Betty Bumpers, were instrumental in helping to pass laws in every state requiring proof of immunization for school attendance. States passed these laws to protect all children from deadly and debilitating vaccine-preventable diseases.

Massachusetts enacted the first school vaccination requirement in 1809 to prevent smallpox transmission. Today, all 50 states have legislation requiring vaccines for students. In 1905, the Supreme Court upheld the constitutionality of mandatory vaccination. Unfortunately, these laws have been eroded over the years, as states have expanded exemptions from immunization requirements. Although exemptions vary from state to state, all states grant exemptions to children for medical reasons such as allergies. All states, other than Mississippi and West Virginia, grant religious exemptions, while 20 states allow philosophical exemptions for those who object to immunizations because of personal, moral or other beliefs. (California and Vermont will no longer allow these exemptions as of July.)

Continued outbreaks of diseases, including measles, mumps, pertussis and influenza, are jeopardizing public health, prompting state legislators to re-evaluate the wisdom of allowing non-medical exemptions. One study found that children exempt from vaccination requirements were more than 35 times more likely to contract measles and nearly six times more likely to contract pertussis than vaccinated children. In a 2006 study, states with loose exemption policies had approximately 50 percent more whooping cough cases than stricter states.

As executive director of Every Child By Two, I have traveled to dozens of states and as far as Africa. We strive to ensure that all children have access to life-saving vaccines and help initiate and implement policies that remove financial and other barriers. I have come to know many families who have lost children to vaccine-preventable diseases and individuals who have survived these diseases but are left with lifelong, debilitating illnesses. These families are a reminder that the United States cannot let its guard down, as diseases know no borders.

While vaccines are not 100 percent effective, families should feel confident in knowing that their children are surrounded by a high percentage of vaccinated classmates and personnel. "Herd immunity" — vaccinating large numbers of people — is the final barrier to deadly diseases.

NO

Barbara Loe Fisher
President, National Vaccine Information Center
Written for *CQ Researcher*, February 2016

Parents have the right to exercise freedom of conscience and informed consent to medical risk-taking on behalf of their children, and children have the civil right to a school education. Vaccine risks are not being borne equally by all, and vaccine laws that do not include flexible medical, religious and conscientious-belief exemptions are oppressive, inhumane and in violation of civil and human rights.

Vaccines are pharmaceutical products that carry a risk of injury or death. There are genetic, biological and environmental high-risk factors that make some people more susceptible to vaccine harm than others, a fact Congress acknowledged in 1986 in the National Childhood Vaccine Injury Act when it shielded vaccine manufacturers from civil liability. The National Academy of Sciences' Institute of Medicine states that often doctors cannot predict who will be injured because of long-standing gaps in vaccine science knowledge. Yet there are almost no federal exemptions for vaccination, which is one reason more than $3 billion has been paid to vaccine-injured children and adults under the 1986 law.

Like the freedoms of speech and the press, the legal right to exercise freedom of conscience and religious belief is embodied in the Constitution. Internationally, these freedoms are considered basic human rights belonging to all people. In addition, the legal right to informed consent to medical risk-taking is the centerpiece of the ethical practice of modern medicine.

Although the Supreme Court in 1905 affirmed the authority of state legislatures to require smallpox vaccination during "an epidemic of disease," the court warned that vaccine mandates should not go beyond "what was reasonably required for the safety of the public" because excessive mandates could lead to "injustice, oppression or absurd consequence" or be "cruel and inhuman to the last degree." A century later, the mandate for one dose of smallpox vaccine has been replaced by a federal directive that children get 69 doses of 16 vaccines starting on the day of birth, with 49 doses of 14 vaccines given by age 6. State legislatures have mandated multiple doses of at least 10 of these vaccines for children, but many are for diseases that, unlike smallpox, do not have a high complication and mortality rate, are not widespread or are not transmitted in a public setting.

Hundreds of new vaccines are being developed, and many will be mandated. Vaccine mandates lacking informed-consent protections should be repealed.

of Health and another from India-based Bharat Biotech, said Marie-Paule Kieny, WHO's assistant director-general for health systems and innovation.[123]

In recent years, the pharmaceutical industry had more than 270 vaccines in development. These potential vaccines were either in human clinical trials or under review by the Food and Drug Administration. They included 137 for infectious diseases, 99 for cancer, 15 for allergies and 10 for neurological disorders.[124]

Arthur Allen, a journalist and author of *Vaccine: The Controversial Story of Medicine's Greatest Lifesaver*, believes the charged atmosphere around vaccines is changing, due in large part to the discrediting of the Wakefield study linking vaccines to autism, and that bodes well for continued developments.

"The autism link was such a powerful idea," says Allen, whose book looked at the history of vaccine controversies. "Now that that has really been laid to rest, we're sort of back at the general [anti-vaccination] background noise level which is always going to be there."

Pisani, of Every Child By Two, also believes the tone is different. She and others on both sides of the issue say that everyone wants to do the right thing for their children. "People now are having civil conversations," she says.

When it comes to research, Pisani says vaccines under development for childhood illnesses, such as respiratory syncytial virus, or RSV, would be game changers. "Everybody knows someone whose child had RSV, so that's going to be a huge lifesaver," she says.

But NVIC's Fisher worries mandates could accompany all these new vaccines. "You're seeing hundreds of new vaccines being developed that are on the horizon that are going to be added to the federal recommended schedule within a system . . . that's very oppressive," because it limits the exemptions available for parents.

Those skeptical about vaccines also see the number of vaccines under development as evidence of the pharmaceutical industry's continued drive for profits. Vaccine safety advocate Kennedy said such research is aimed at "boosting vaccine revenues to $100 billion by 2025."[125]

Kennedy cited market research showing while vaccines represent only 2 percent to 3 percent of global drug sales, "the growth rate in this market has been extraordinary. This segment has grown at a high rate of 10 to 15 percent annually as compared to the overall pharmaceutical industry, which grows at 5 to 7 percent per year."[126]

Vaccines are currently under development for the following diseases:

- Zika virus, which is spread to people through mosquito bites. The World Health Organization (WHO) has declared an international public health emergency in connection with the outbreak of this virus in more than 30 countries.[127]
- Ebola, which spreads through human-to-human transmission. Clinical trials for a vaccine are underway.[128]
- Malaria, caused by parasites transmitted to people through the bites of infected mosquitoes. Several potential vaccines are undergoing clinical trial.[129]
- Dengue fever, also spread to people through mosquito bites. Trials for a vaccine are underway in Brazil.[130]
- HIV/AIDS, which can be transmitted via the exchange of body fluids from infected individuals. WHO said there are "a number of very encouraging leads" in the search for a vaccine.[131]

In addition to infectious diseases, scientists see vaccines as a way to prevent chronic diseases such as cancer and Alzheimer's.

"The growing cost of caring for an aging population, where noninfectious conditions like dementia will be increasingly common in older people, has added a new dimension to the search for new vaccines," wrote Gary Finnegan, editor of *Vaccines Today.*[132]

Continued vaccine research remains necessary because "infectious diseases still extract an extraordinary toll on humans," wrote Dr. Gary J. Nabel in *The New England Journal of Medicine.* While old vaccines need updating, and new ones are being developed, he said, the key is making them available, particularly in developing countries where more than 1.5 million children die from vaccine-preventable diseases each year.[133]

NOTES

1. Mark Zuckerberg, Facebook post, Jan. 8, 2016, http://tinyurl.com/hozeeq4.
2. Yanan Wang, "Mark Zuckerberg gets his baby vaccinated. Anti-vaxxers go nuts," *The Washington Post*, Jan. 11, 2016, http://tinyurl.com/jjuqbm6.

3. Ian Sherr, "Zuckerberg injects himself into the vaccine controversy with his newborn," *CNet*, Jan. 12, 2016, http://tinyurl.com/je4nd5n.

4. Amanda F. Dempsey *et al.*, "Alternative Vaccination Schedule Preferences Among Parents of Young Children," *Pediatrics*, September 2011, http://tinyurl.com/823wnaj.

5. "Measles Cases and Outbreaks," Centers for Disease Control and Prevention, http://tinyurl.com/kyxc6pz; "Pertussis (Whooping Cough)," Centers for Disease Control and Prevention, Feb. 10, 2016, http://tinyurl.com/jgyxmet.

6. "Vaccine History: Developments by Year," Children's Hospital of Philadelphia, Nov. 19, 2014, http://tinyurl.com/j9dqjfg; "Vaccine and Immunizations," Centers for Disease Control and Prevention, Feb. 11, 2016, http://tinyurl.com/gom37ve.

7. "Immunizations Policy Issues Overview," National Conference of State Legislatures, Jan. 12, 2015, http://tinyurl.com/zuyztg5.

8. "National, State, and Selected Local Area Vaccination Coverage Among Children Aged 19-35 Months — United States, 2014," "Morbidity and Mortality Weekly Report," Centers for Disease Control and Prevention, Aug. 28, 2015, http://tinyurl.com/zfcy8dz.

9. "83% Say Measles Vaccine Is Safe for Healthy Children," Pew Research Center, Feb. 9, 2015, http://tinyurl.com/morpgjh.

10. Karen Kaplan, "Vaccine refusal helped fuel Disneyland measles outbreak, study says," *Los Angeles Times*, March 16, 2015, http://tinyurl.com/q6p9hxm.

11. M.S. Majumder *et al.*, "Substandard Vaccination Compliance and the 2015 Measles Outbreak," *JAMA Pediatrics*, May 2015, http://tinyurl.com/pvvmzu4.

12. Tamar Lewin, "Sick Child's Father Seeks Vaccination Requirement in California," *The New York Times*, Jan. 28, 2015, http://tinyurl.com/myfcqy9.

13. Lisa Aliferis, "To Protect His Son, A Father Asks School To Bar Unvaccinated Children," NPR, updated Jan. 28, 2015, http://tinyurl.com/hoxdyxu.

14. Phil Willon and Melanie Mason, "California Gov. Jerry Brown signs new vaccination law, one of nation's toughest," *Los Angeles Times*, June 30, 2015, http://tinyurl.com/oksmrx5.

15. "Why Are Childhood Vaccines So Important? Centers for Disease Control and Prevention, May 19, 2014, http://tinyurl.com/ck5g854.

16. Laura Parker, "The Anti-Vaccine Generation: How Movement Against Shots Got Its Start," *National Geographic*, Feb. 6, 2015, http://tinyurl.com/kmjdn8d; Seth Mnookin, "Talking to Vaccine Resisters," *The New Yorker*, Feb. 4, 2015, http://tinyurl.com/od2gbjy.

17. National Vaccine Information Center, http://tinyurl.com/5wtjae.

18. Barbara Loe Fisher, "The Moral Right to Conscientious, Philosophical and Personal Belief Exemption to Vaccination," National Vaccine Information Center, 2015, http://tinyurl.com/he5tl5q.

19. Jeffrey Kluger, "Meet the Heroes and Villains of Vaccine History," *Time*, July 29, 2015, http://tinyurl.com/o9wusv7; Phil Plait, "Robert F. Kennedy Jr.: Anti-Vaxxer," *Bad Astronomy* blog, *Slate*, June 5, 2013, http://tinyurl.com/zfzor96.

20. "Addressing Vaccine Hesitancy," World Health Organization, Nov. 16, 2015, http://tinyurl.com/hn86evz; "Global Immunization," Children's Hospital of Philadelphia, Vaccine Education Center, http://tinyurl.com/z7mj4uh.

21. Amy Nordrum, "California Measles Outbreak Highlights Global Clash Between Anti-Vaccine Parents And Governments," *International Business Times*, Feb. 5, 2015, http://tinyurl.com/zeckms3.

22. Teresa Welsh, "Anti-Vaccine Movements Not Unique to the U.S.," *U.S. News & World Report*, Feb. 18, 2015, http://tinyurl.com/pxoyq8l.

23. Philip J. Smith *et al.*, "Parental Delay or Refusal of Vaccine Doses, Childhood Vaccination Coverage at 24 Months of Age, and the Health Belief Model," *Public Health Reports*, 2011, http://tinyurl.com/z4ejjfs.

24. Josh Levs, "The unvaccinated, by the numbers," CNN, Feb. 4, 2015, http://tinyurl.com/o48veen.

25. "Possible Side-effects from Vaccines," Vaccines and Immunizations, Centers for Disease Control and Prevention, http://tinyurl.com/bn59fl.

26. Mariam Siddiqui, Daniel A. Salmon and Saad B. Omer, "Epidemiology of Vaccine Hesitancy in the United States," *Human Vaccines & Immunotherapeutics*, Nov. 18, 2013, http://tinyurl.com/zpwy8an; Yang *et al.*, *op. cit.*

27. Saad B. Omer *et al.*, "Vaccine Refusal, Mandatory Immunization, and the Risks of Vaccine-Preventable Diseases," *The New England Journal of Medicine*, May 7, 2009, http://tinyurl.com/hdohgcz.

28. Lenny Grant *et al.*, "Vaccination Persuasion Online: A Qualitative Study of Two Provaccine and Two Vaccine-Skeptical Websites," *Journal of Medical Internet Research*, May 29, 2015, http://tinyurl.com/j35xvk7.

29. Vanessa Wamsley, "The Psychology of Anti-Vaxers: How Story Trumps Science," *The Atlantic*, Oct. 19, 2014, http://tinyurl.com/msvf8ku.

30. Tracy A. Lieu *et al.*, "Geographic Clusters in Underimmunization and Vaccine Refusal," *Pediatrics*, February 2015, http://tinyurl.com/hbs2qxy.

31. "BMJ declares MMR study 'an elaborate fraud' — Autism claims likened to "Piltdown Man" hoax," press release, *British Medical Journal*, June 26, 2012, http://tinyurl.com/omu52zt. For more information, see Sarah Glazer, "Understanding Autism," *CQ Researcher*, Aug. 1, 2014, pp. 649-672.

32. "Beyond the Autism/Vaccine Hypothesis: What Parents Need to Know about Autism Research," Autism Science Foundation, undated, http://tinyurl.com/z9ts9j5.

33. "Q&A: Seth Mnookin on vaccination and public health," *MIT News*, Feb. 27, 2015, http://tinyurl.com/jxfv2nr.

34. "Thimerosal in Vaccines," Centers for Disease Control and Prevention, http://tinyurl.com/25499vu. Also see Kathy Koch, "Vaccine Controversies," *CQ Researcher*, Aug. 25, 2000, pp. 641-672.

35. Julia Belluz, "The vaccine delayers," *Vox*, March 2, 2015, http://tinyurl.com/njcbubc.

36. "Vaccines," Ask Dr. Sears, http://tinyurl.com/z9qp5gz; Paloma Esquivel, "Vaccination controversy swirls around O.C.'s 'Dr. Bob,' " *Los Angeles Times*, Sept. 6, 2014, http://tinyurl.com/jc5tbnz.

37. Priyanka Boghani, "Dr. Robert W. Sears: Why Partial Vaccinations May Be an Answer," "Frontline," March 23, 2015, http://tinyurl.com/zdyhe7f.

38. Institute of Medicine, "The Childhood Immunization Schedule and Safety: Stakeholder Concerns, Scientific Evidence, and Future Studies," The National Academies Press, Jan. 16, 2013, http://tinyurl.com/no369fp.

39. "IOM Report Details Strategy for Monitoring Safety of Childhood Immunization Schedule," press release, National Academies Press, Jan. 16, 2013, http://tinyurl.com/aeccu8t.

40. Tara Haelle, "An Alternative Vaccination Schedule Actually Presents More Risks Than Benefits," NPR, updated Sept. 18, 2015, http://tinyurl.com/glawlb6.

41. Simon J. Hambidge *et al.*, "Timely Versus Delayed Early Childhood Vaccination and Seizures," *Pediatrics*, May 2014, http://tinyurl.com/zl4z7tk.

42. Gary Baum, "Hollywood's Vaccine Wars: L.A.'s 'Entitled' Westsiders Behind City's Epidemic," *The Hollywood Reporter*, Sept. 10, 2014, http://tinyurl.com/o28tyax.

43. Steve Hendrix, "Parents with doubts about vaccinations face backlash from pediatricians, peers," *The Washington Post*, Feb. 3, 2015, http://tinyurl.com/hbzj4yf.

44. Brittny Mejia, "Doctors turning away unvaccinated children," *Los Angeles Times*, Feb. 10, 2015, http://tinyurl.com/ztycqdz.

45. Lawrence O. Gostin, "Public Health," The Hastings Center, http://tinyurl.com/hgw63oj;*From Birth to Death and Bench to Clinic: The Hastings Center Bioethics Briefing Book for Journalists, Policymakers, and Campaigns* (2008).

46. *Jacobson v. Massachusetts*, 197 US 11 — Supreme Court 1905, http://tinyurl.com/h6yedr7.

47. *Zucht v. King*, 260 US 174 — Supreme Court 1922, http://tinyurl.com/hqgvhuc.

48. "English Legal Glossary," National Center for State Courts, undated, http://tinyurl.com/zho8k5p.

49. *Prince v. Massachusetts*, 321 US 158 — Supreme Court 1944, http://tinyurl.com/h96as69.

50. Marina Olson, "Should the Government Mandate Vaccinations?" *The American Conservative*, Sept. 30, 2013, http://tinyurl.com/hmjdvye.

51. Michael Gerson, "Vaccines and what we owe to our neighbors," *The Washington Post*, Feb. 2, 2015, http://tinyurl.com/z2uom4h.

52. Patrick McGreevy, "Opponents of new California vaccination law begin referendum drive," *Los Angeles Times*, July 15, 2015, http://tinyurl.com/o7dducu.

53. "Let Californians decide about vaccinations: Shannon Kroner and Tim Donnelly," *Los Angeles Daily News*, Aug. 3, 2015, http://tinyurl.com/h6laukd.

54. Dawn Richardson, "The Fallout from California SB277: What Happens Next?" National Vaccine Information Center, Aug. 5, 2015, http://tinyurl.com/jn5kn3o.

55. Elise Viebeck, "Rand Paul: Parents 'own' children, not the state," *The Hill*, Feb. 2, 2015, http://tinyurl.com/ku4wkue.

56. Roxanne Palmer, "Do Parents Weigh The Common Good In Vaccine Choices?" *International Business Times*, Sept. 5, 2012, http://tinyurl.com/h6e8gj5.

57. Maheen Quadri-Sheriff *et al.*, "The Role of Herd Immunity in Parents' Decision to Vaccinate Children: A Systematic Review," *Pediatrics*, August 2012, http://tinyurl.com/j4jxyjn.

58. Jim Norman, "Americans' Views of Pharmaceutical Industry Take a Tumble," Gallup Poll, Sept. 14, 2015, http://tinyurl.com/zzr2aqg.

59. Bianca DiJulio, Jamie Firth and Mollyann Brodie, "Kaiser Health Tracking Poll: August 2015," Henry J. Kaiser Family Foundation, Aug. 20, 2015, http://tinyurl.com/hf96pdw.

60. Baum, *op. cit.*

61. "Former CDC head lands vaccine job at Merck," Reuters, Dec. 21, 2009, http://tinyurl.com/h2j3aek.

62. Susan Thaul, "Vaccine Policy Issues," Congressional Research Service, updated May 19, 2005, http://tinyurl.com/zuxr9yw.

63. "Vaccines and Related Biological Products Advisory Committee," Food and Drug Administration, updated Jan. 29, 2016, http://tinyurl.com/z46fhxp.

64. David Willman, "Stealth Merger: Drug Companies and Government Medical Research," *Los Angeles Times*, Dec. 7, 2003, http://tinyurl.com/66ql78v.

65. Marcia Angell, "The Truth About the Drug Companies," *The New York Review of Books*, July 15, 2004, http://tinyurl.com/hrdofun.

66. John Yaphe *et al.*, "The association between funding by commercial interests and study outcome in randomized controlled drug trials," *Family Practice*, July 9, 2001, http://tinyurl.com/j3xxx7o.

67. "Vaccine Studies: Under the Influence of Pharma," National Vaccine Information Center, Feb. 12, 2009, http://tinyurl.com/jttntf5.

68. Robert F. Kennedy Jr. "Mercury & Vaccines," undated, http://tinyurl.com/zf3by23; Keith Kloor, "Robert Kennedy Jr.'s belief in autism-vaccine connection, and its political peril," *The Washington Post*, July 18, 2014, http://tinyurl.com/o6wbwhg.

69. Robert F. Kennedy Jr., "Deadly Immunity," *Rolling Stone*, Feb. 9, 2011, http://tinyurl.com/gsokt3t; Kerry Lauerman, "Correcting our record," *Salon*, Jan. 16, 2011, http://tinyurl.com/op3j6p8.

70. "No Pharma Liability? No Vaccine Mandates," National Vaccine Information Center, March 2, 2011, http://tinyurl.com/zokcqa7.

71. Richard Anderson, "Pharmaceutical industry gets high on fat profits," BBC News, Nov. 6, 2014, http://tinyurl.com/q4v9qus.

72. Elisabeth Rosenthal, "The Price of Prevention: Vaccine Costs Are Soaring," *The New York Times*, July 2, 2014, http://tinyurl.com/kkxsplw.

73. Bourree Lam, "Vaccines Are Profitable, So What?" *The Atlantic*, Feb. 10, 2015, http://tinyurl.com/nhwk98y.

74. Fangjun Zhou *et al.*, "Economic Evaluation of the Routine Childhood Immunization Program in the United States, 2009," *Pediatrics*, April 2014, http://tinyurl.com/qbtn8pb.

75. Rosenthal, *op. cit.*

76. Alexandra Minna Stern and Howard Markel, "The History Of Vaccines And Immunization: Familiar Patterns, New Challenges," *Health Affairs*, May 2005, http://tinyurl.com/6n4evnj.

77. *The History of Vaccines, ibid.*; "Variolation," U.S. National Library of Medicine, http://tinyurl.com/ozra83w.

78. "The Story Of . . . Smallpox — and other Deadly Eurasian Germs," "Guns, Germs and Steel," PBS, 2005, http://tinyurl.com/btqozjz.

79. "1721: Boston Smallpox Epidemic," *The History of Vaccines*, http://tinyurl.com/235bs3y.

80. M. Best, A. Katamba and D. Neuhauser, "Making the right decision: Benjamin Franklin's son dies of smallpox in 1736," *Quality & Safety in Health Care*, December 2007, http://tinyurl.com/mv6aqnw.

81. Howard Markel, "Life, Liberty and the Pursuit of Vaccines," *The New York Times*, Feb. 28, 2011, http://tinyurl.com/gmrdxlz.

82. "Vaccine Timeline," Immunization Action Coalition, undated, http://tinyurl.com/69qgqy7.

83. "Whatever Happened to Polio," Smithsonian National Museum of American History, http://tinyurl.com/bxe8vcv.

84. Richard Conniff, "A Forgotten Pioneer of Vaccines," *The New York Times*, May 6, 2013, http://tinyurl.com/j4k76vu.

85. Elizabeth Earl, "The Victorian Anti-Vaccination Movement," *The Atlantic*, July 15, 2015, http://tinyurl.com/pvfdxev.

86. Robert M. Wolfe and Lisa K. Sharp, "Anti-vaccinationists past and present," *British Medical Journal*, Aug. 24, 2002, http://tinyurl.com/7x8sc2d.

87. Daniel A. Salmon *et al.*, "Compulsory vaccination and conscientious or philosophical exemptions: past, present, and future," *The Lancet*, Feb. 4, 2006, http://tinyurl.com/jsktekj; *The History of Vaccines, op. cit.*

88. Matthew B. Barry and Jared P. Cole, "The Measles: Background and Federal Role in Vaccine Policy," Congressional Research Service, Feb. 9, 2015, http://tinyurl.com/ha45gyx.

89. Jared P. Cole and Kathleen S. Swendiman, "Mandatory Vaccinations: Precedent and Current Laws," Congressional Research Service, May 21, 2014, http://tinyurl.com/j7n6ag4.

90. *Ibid.*

91. Sabin Russell, "When polio vaccine backfired/ Tainted batches killed 10 and paralyzed 164," *The San Francisco Chronicle*, April 25, 2005, http://tinyurl.com/heydzca.

92. Shari Roan, "Swine flu 'debacle' of 1976 is recalled," *Los Angeles Times*, April 27, 2009, http://tinyurl.com/nxq2d5.

93. "About National Vaccine Information Center," National Vaccine Information Center, Biography, Barbara Loe Fisher, http://tinyurl.com/z4y7ab2.

94. "Pertussis Vaccination: Use of Acellular Pertussis Vaccines Among Infants and Young Children Recommendations of the Advisory Committee on Immunization Practices (ACIP)," Centers for Disease Control and Prevention, March 28, 1997, http://tinyurl.com/29uhx2k.

95. Salynn Boyles, "Controversy Surrounds Anthrax Vaccine," *WebMD Health News*, Nov. 8, 2001, http://tinyurl.com/zkstfgn.

96. "Thimerosal and Childhood Vaccines: What You Should Know," Minnesota Department of Health, http://tinyurl.com/hfawy82; "Thimerosal in Vaccines," Centers for Disease Control and Prevention, July 2005, http://tinyurl.com/6qy7je3; "Thimerosal in Vaccines," Food and Drug Administration, http://tinyurl.com/mqyfkd.

97. "BMJ declares MMR study . . .," *op. cit.*

98. Jeffrey P. Baker, "Mercury, Vaccines, and Autism: One Controversy, Three Histories," *American Journal of Public Health* (2008), http://tinyurl.com/pqkexls.

99. "Calling the Shots," *State Legislatures Magazine*, Feb. 1, 2015, http://tinyurl.com/hgn42l2.

100. Michael Specter, "Vermont Says No to the Anti-Vaccine Movement," *The New Yorker*, May 29, 2015, http://tinyurl.com/nseb756.

101. Rachel LaCorte, "Bill to tighten vaccine exemptions draws dozens of foes," *The Seattle Times*, Feb. 19, 2015, http://tinyurl.com/zo8prgv.

102. "Vaccination Policies and Rates of Exemption from Immunization, 2005-2011," *The New England Journal of Medicine*, Sept. 20, 2012, http://tinyurl.com/zwqd2n3.

103. Saad B. Omer *et al.*, "School immunizations: Study shows accelerated increase of non-medical vaccine exemptions," Emory News Center, Sept. 19, 2012, http://tinyurl.com/z54u6rr.

104. Dawn Richardson "The Stand Against Forced Vaccination Across the States and the NVIC Advocacy Portal," National Vaccine Information Center, Jan. 19, 2016, http://tinyurl.com/guuuo9a.

105. Jennifer Steinhauer and Sabrina Tavernise, "Bipartisan Partnership Produces a Health Bill That Passes the House," *The New York Times*, July 10, 2015, http://tinyurl.com/j4rkj2q.

106. Sarah Ferris, "Senate to break up House-passed 'cures' bill," *The Hill*, Jan. 19, 2016, http://tinyurl.com/hdz7l9x.

107. Julia Belluz, "This new bill would add $9 billion for medical research. Here are 5 reasons critics are terrified," *Vox*, July 14, 2015, http://tinyurl.com/jv4thvz.

108. "Here Comes the 21st Century Cures Act: Say Goodbye to Vaccine Safety Science," National Vaccine Information Center, July 21, 2015, http://tinyurl.com/prkud2c.

109. Gregg Gonsalves, Mark Harrington and David A. Kessler, "Don't Weaken the F.D.A.'s Drug Approval Process," *The New York Times*, June 11, 2015, http://tinyurl.com/zylwyft.

110. David Gorski, "The 21st Century Cures Act: The (Somewhat) Good, The (Mostly) Bad, and The (Very) Ugly," *Science-Based Medicine* blog, Aug. 10, 2015, http://tinyurl.com/z7tp8o6.

111. "House Approves 21st Century Cures Act," House Energy and Commerce Committee, July 10, 2015, http://tinyurl.com/z3rc6xj.

112. Steinhauer and Tavernise, *op. cit.*

113. Peter Sullivan, "Senators: Science settled on vaccines," *The Hill*, Feb. 10, 2015, http://tinyurl.com/ndcowex.

114. "The Reemergence of Vaccine-Preventable Diseases: Exploring the Public Health Successes and Challenges," Senate Committee on Health, Education, Labor and Pensions, Feb. 10, 2015, http://tinyurl.com/jcahj8x.

115. Michael E. Miller, "The GOP's dangerous 'debate' on vaccines and autism," *The Washington Post*, Sept. 17, 2015, http://tinyurl.com/glvj84z.

116. "HPV Mandates for Children in Secondary Schools," Immunization Action Coalition, http://tinyurl.com/zhd6uje.

117. HPV Vaccine Policies," blog, National Conference of State Legislatures, undated, http://tinyurl.com/m7v89p4.

118. "Human Papillomavirus (HPV)," Centers for Disease Control and Prevention, http://tinyurl.com/zlb63tt.

119. "HPV Vaccines: Vaccinating Your Preteen or Teen," Centers for Disease Control and Prevention, http://tinyurl.com/jbn6gxa.

120. "The HPV Vaccine: Access and Use in the U.S.," The Henry J. Kaiser Family Foundation, Sept. 3, 2015, http://tinyurl.com/jwusm67.

121. "Teen Vaccination Coverage," Centers for Disease Control and Prevention, July 30, 2015, http://tinyurl.com/zj8779h.

122. Jason L. Schwartz and Laurel A. Easterling, "State Vaccination Requirements for HPV and Other Vaccines for Adolescents, 1990-2015," *JAMA*, July 14, 2015, http://tinyurl.com/jbaqwmt.

123. Brian Blackstone, "WHO Says Possible Zika Vaccines at Least 18 Months Away From Broad Trials," *The Wall Street Journal*, Feb. 12, 2016, http://tinyurl.com/zgzt4jd.

124. "Medicines in Development: Vaccines," press release, Pharmaceutical Research and Manufacturers of America, Sept. 11, 2013, http://tinyurl.com/hz22kyp.

125. Robert F. Kennedy Jr., "Vaccines, government & Big Pharma's dirty money," *WND*, July 17, 2015, http://tinyurl.com/j7hbeyg.

126. "Global Vaccine Market Pipeline Analysis," *Research and Markets*, January 2014, http://tinyurl.com/jncptre.

127. Noemie Bisserbe and Betsy McKay, "Drug Industry Starts Race to Develop Zika Vaccine," *The Wall Street Journal*, Feb. 2, 2016, http://tinyurl.com/zg48eur.; "All Countries and Territories with Active Zika Virus Transmission," Centers for Disease Control and Prevention, Feb. 5, 2016, http://tinyurl.com/z7q6l43.

128. "Ebola vaccines, therapies, and diagnostics," World Health Organization, Oct. 6, 2015, http://tinyurl.com/k5deeg4.

129. "Malaria vaccine technology roadmap," World Health Organization, November 2013, http://tinyurl.com/z9b5y27.

130. "Dengue Vaccine Enters Phase 3 Trial in Brazil," National Institute of Allergy and Infectious Diseases, Jan. 14, 2016, http://tinyurl.com/z3z5zym.

131. "HIV/AIDS," World Health Organization, Jan. 27, 2014, http://tinyurl.com/gl66v5w.

132. Gary Finnegan, "The future of vaccines," *The Blog, Vaccines Today*, March 27, 2014, http://tinyurl.com/ny4mjdu.

133. Gary J. Nabel, "Designing Tomorrow's Vaccines," *The New England Journal of Medicine*, Feb. 7, 2013, http://tinyurl.com/juaqym9.

BIBLIOGRAPHY
Selected Sources
Books

Donvan, John, and Caren Zucker, *In a Different Key: The Story of Autism*, **Crown Publishers, 2016.**
Two television journalists examine the history and politics of autism, including a look at concerns about the purported link between autism and vaccines.

Mnookin, Seth, *The Panic Virus: The True Story Behind the Vaccine-Autism Controversy*, **Simon & Schuster, 2012.**
A professor of science writing at the Massachusetts Institute of Technology examines the ramifications of a discredited 1998 study linking vaccinations to autism.

Offit, Paul A., *Deadly Choices: How the Anti-Vaccine Movement Threatens Us All*, **Basic Books, 2012.**
A pediatrician who heads the Vaccine Education Center at Children's Hospital of Philadelphia contends that the decision by some parents not to vaccinate their children endangers everyone.

Sears, Robert, *The Vaccine Book: Making the Right Decision for Your Child*, **Little, Brown, 2007.**
A California pediatrician makes the case for an alternate immunization schedule for young children that has become popular with many vaccine skeptics.

Articles

Barbash, Fred, "The saddest story Roald Dahl ever wrote — about his daughter's death from measles — is worth reading today," *The Washington Post*, **Feb. 2, 2015, http://tinyurl.com/mv7m4xw.**
A journalist recounts the story of how children's book author Roald Dahl lost his 7-year-old daughter to measles.

Earl, Elizabeth, "The Victorian Anti-Vaccination Movement," *The Atlantic*, **July 15, 2015, http://tinyurl.com/pvfdxev.**
Current vaccine controversies are similar to 19th-century protests against mandatory vaccinations.

Kloor, Keith, "Robert Kennedy Jr.'s belief in autism-vaccine connection, and its political peril," *The Washington Post*, **July 18, 2014, http://tinyurl.com/o6wbwhg.**
A science writer examines Robert F. Kennedy Jr.'s continued belief in the link between autism and vaccines and how he has become a leading vaccine skeptic.

Omer, Saad B., Walter A. Orenstein and Jeffrey P. Koplan, "Go Big and Go Fast — Vaccine Refusal and Disease Eradication," *New England Journal of Medicine*, **April 11, 2013, http://tinyurl.com/z5mkhbo.**
A trio of Emory University doctors outlines obstacles to vaccination and how the medical community can work to overcome them.

Parker, Laura, "The Anti-Vaccine Generation: How Movement Against Shots Got Its Start," *National Geographic*, **Feb. 6, 2015, http://tinyurl.com/kmjdn8d.**

In a 50-year period, childhood vaccinations went from representing breakthrough science to a topic of public policy debate.

Reports and Studies

"The Childhood Immunization Schedule and Safety: Stakeholder Concerns, Scientific Evidence, and Future Studies," Institute of Medicine, The National Academies Press, Jan. 16, 2013, http://tinyurl.com/no369fp.
The Institute of Medicine, a component of the National Academy of Sciences, conducts a comprehensive review into the safety of the childhood immunization schedule.

"The State of the National Vaccine Plan — 2014," Department of Health and Human Services, 2015, http://tinyurl.com/qfdalmm.
The federal health agency provides its annual update on the department's work toward meeting its goals of high nationwide vaccination levels.

"Vaccine Injury Compensation: Most Claims Took Multiple Years and Many Were Settled through Negotiation," Government Accountability Office, Nov. 21, 2014, http://tinyurl.com/mql68yz.

The independent watchdog agency of Congress examines the agency overseeing vaccine injury claims and found numerous problems with the process.

Cole, Jared P., and Kathleen S. Swendiman, "Mandatory Vaccinations: Precedent and Current Laws," Congressional Research Service, May 21, 2014, http://tinyurl.com/j7n6ag4.
A report by Congress' independent research arm examines past and present laws concerning vaccination.

Documentaries

Palfreman, Jon, and Kate McMahon, "The Vaccine War," PBS/Frontline, March 24, 2015, http://tinyurl.com/p5znqab.
A pair of Oregon filmmakers examines the science and politics of vaccine safety in this multi-part documentary, with interviews and segments from all sides.

Pemberton, Sonya, "Vaccines — Calling the Shots," PBS/NOVA, Aug. 26, 2015, http://tinyurl.com/hz9hl5u.
An Australian journalist produces a television documentary that tracks global epidemics, explores the science behind vaccines and airs the views of parents wrestling with vaccine-related questions and concerns.

FOR MORE INFORMATION

American Academy of Pediatrics, 141 Northwest Point Blvd., Elk Grove Village, IL 60007; 847-434-4000; www.aap.org/en-us/Pages/Contact.aspx. Association of pediatricians concerned with the health of children, adolescents and young adults.

Centers for Disease Control and Prevention, 1600 Clifton Rd., Atlanta, GA 30333; 404-639-3311; www.cdc.gov. Federal agency responsible for preventing disease, injury and disability. Makes recommendations for vaccinations.

Every Child By Two, 1233 20th St., N.W., Suite 403, Washington, DC 20036; 202-783-7034; www.ecbt.org. National nonprofit co-founded by former first lady Rosalyn Carter and former Arkansas first lady Betty Bumpers that advocates for timely immunizations to reduce vaccine-preventable diseases among people of all ages.

Food and Drug Administration, 10903 New Hampshire Ave., Silver Spring, MD 20993; 1-888-463-6332; www.fda.gov/. Federal agency responsible for regulating drugs, biological products, medical devices, food and cosmetics.

Generation Rescue, 13636 Ventura Blvd., #259, Sherman Oaks, CA 91423; 877-982-8847; www.generationrescue.org/. National organization founded by parents that provides information about autism. Actress Jenny McCarthy is president.

National Institutes of Health, 10 Center Dr., Bethesda, MD 20892; 301-496-4000; www.nih.gov/. Agency of the federal Department of Health and Human Services that serves as the focal point for medical research in the United States.

National Vaccine Information Center, 204 Mill St., Suite B1, Vienna, VA 22180; 703-938-0342; www.909shot.com. Advocates safety and informed-consent in the mass-vaccination system.

World Health Organization, Avenue Appia 20m 1211, Geneva, 27, Switzerland; 41-22-791-2111; www.who.int/en/. Coordinates global public health efforts.

15

Closing Guantanamo

Patrick Marshall

Military police bring a Taliban prisoner to Camp X-Ray, the first detention facility at Guantanamo Bay, in 2002. The small compound of tents and open-air cages was replaced soon after it opened by Camp Delta, which includes several camps for detainees of varying risks, recreation rooms, a soccer area, a hospital and courtroom facilities.

From *CQ Researcher,*
September 30, 2016.

When the Islamic State (ISIS) executes captives, it forces them to wear orange jumpsuits nearly identical to those worn by suspected terrorists held at the U.S. military prison at Guantanamo Bay, Cuba.[1]

Critics of the controversial facility say it is a reviled worldwide symbol of inhumane treatment and a recruiting tool for terrorists. ISIS, they say, uses the orange jumpsuits to invoke Guantanamo and incite its followers.[2]

The critics have an important ally. President Obama, along with many Democrats and some top military officials, say the prison not only fails to advance national security but also undermines it.

"Guantanamo harms our partnerships with allies and other countries whose cooperation we need against terrorism," Obama said in February. "When I talk to other world leaders, they bring up the fact that Guantanamo is not resolved."[3]

In one of his first acts as president, Obama issued an executive order to close the prison, part of a 45-square-mile naval base at Cuba's southeastern end.[4] But almost eight years later, as Obama's second term winds down, the prison remains open because of a bitter standoff between the White House and the Republican-controlled Congress.

Republicans — and some Democrats — oppose closure, arguing that Guantanamo inmates would pose a security risk if transferred to prisons on U.S. soil or to other countries. Some prominent Republicans also accuse Obama of failing to work with them on finding a workable alternative to the prison.

Guantanamo Base Has 113-Year History

The U.S. military base at Guantanamo Bay sits on 45 square miles of land leased from Cuba in 1903 as a Navy coal-fueling station. The base, which shares a 17-mile border with Cuba, now includes military housing, schools, stores and recreational areas, as well as support facilities for the Department of Homeland Security. Guantanamo's prison facilities have housed suspected terrorists since 2002. President Obama has sought to shut the prison since taking office in 2009, but Republicans and some Democrats have resisted.

Source: Commander, Navy Installations Command, "Naval Station Guantanamo Bay," http://tinyurl.com/gmq5jul; "Guantanamo Bay Naval Station Fast Facts," CNN, Aug. 19, 2016, http://tinyurl.com/pywr4de

The presidential election is unlikely to resolve the stalemate. Democratic nominee Hillary Clinton has vowed to close the Guantanamo prison, while Republican nominee Donald Trump has promised to keep it open and "load it up with some bad dudes."[5] Trump also promised earlier this year to use waterboarding and other interrogation methods regarded as torture on terrorism suspects, but later said he would follow international law, which outlaws torture.[6]

With Congress and the White House at loggerheads, the prison remains in limbo. The Obama administration has stopped sending new terrorism suspects to Guantanamo and is steadily reducing the prison population. Detainees deemed not dangerous by a review panel are being transferred to other countries, with the largest numbers being sent to Afghanistan, Saudi Arabia and

Pakistan. In August, the Pentagon announced the largest single transfer during the Obama years: 15 prisoners to the United Arab Emirates (UAE).

Of the roughly 780 people who have been held at the prison since it opened in 2002, 710 have been transferred to other countries, nine detainees have died while in custody and 61 remain.[7] Of those sent to other countries, 214 are known or suspected to have returned to terrorist or insurgent activities.[8]

Naureen Shah, Amnesty International USA's director of national security and human rights, said the recent transfers to the UAE were a "powerful sign that President Obama is serious about closing Guantanamo before he leaves office."[9] But Rep. Ed Royce, a California Republican who chairs the House Foreign Affairs Committee, called the transferred detainees "hardened terrorists" who should have remained at Guantanamo.[10]

The American public is divided on closing the prison. According to a CNN/ORC International survey conducted at the end of February, 56 percent of respondents opposed Obama's efforts to close the prison, and 40 percent backed the idea.[11] The division is sharply along party lines, with 83 percent of those identifying as Republicans opposed to shutting down the prison compared with 63 percent of Democrats who supported closure.

Public opinion has shifted significantly since 2009, when a CNN/ORC poll found that 51 percent of respondents favored closing the prison.[12]

When the detention center opened in January 2002, prisoners were first held in Camp X-Ray, a small compound of tents and open-air cages. By April 2002, Camp Delta — which includes six "camps" to house detainees of varying security risk, as well as recreation rooms, soccer areas, hospital and courtroom facilities — was opened and Camp X-Ray was closed.[13]

Despite the improvements, attorneys for detainees say prisoners have suffered abuse — including cold cells, isolation and sleep deprivation — as well as the use of torture during interrogations. The government has not acknowledged the extent and duration of torture in interrogations, including waterboarding. But according to a report released by the Senate Select Committee on Intelligence in April 2014, the CIA employed "enhanced interrogation techniques" at a secret detention site at Guantanamo.[14]

Critics on the left, as well as a few on the right, say Obama should have moved to close the prison during his first two years in office, when Democrats controlled both chambers of Congress and had more political leverage against Republican opponents.

"They blew it," says Charles "Cully" Stimson, deputy assistant secretary of Defense for detainee affairs in President George W. Bush's administration who is now manager of the national security law program at the conservative Heritage Foundation think tank in Washington. "They blew the opportunity to close it in a responsible way in 2009, and then they lost both the House and Senate."

Since then, with Republicans controlling one or both chambers, "President Obama has been unwilling to stand up to Congress," says J. Wells Dixon, a senior staff attorney at the Center for Constitutional Rights, a Washington-based human rights advocacy group that backs the prison's closure.

Obama himself has expressed reservations about not acting sooner. When a seventh-grade student in Cleveland asked him last March what advice he would give himself if he could start his presidency over, Obama replied, "I think I would have closed Guantanamo on the first day." As the issue became a political hot potato in Congress, he said, "the path of least resistance was just to leave it open."[15]

After winning control of the House in the 2010 midterm elections, Republicans banned using federal funds to transfer Guantanamo detainees to the United States for any reason. An additional provision barred the Pentagon from using federal funds to build or modify any facility for Guantanamo detainees anywhere but at Guantanamo.[16]

Supporters of the provisions, which remain in force, generally cite security as their primary concern.

"President Obama's determination to move some of the world's most dangerous terrorists to U.S. soil is inexplicable and unacceptable," House Intelligence Committee Chairman Devin Nunes, R-Calif., said after Obama asked Congress to remove the provisions last February.[17]

But it is not just Republicans who oppose housing Guantanamo detainees on the mainland. Some Democrats do too, even when they support closing the prison. Sen. Michael Bennet, D-Colo., approves bringing the detainees to the states but opposes an administration proposal to convert a high security prison in Colorado into a detention facility for Guantanamo detainees. "I've voted to close the prison, but I believe military detainees should be held in military prisons," Bennet said. "Colorado does not have that type of facility. This plan [of Obama's] has done nothing to change my mind."[18]

At the same time, however, some experts note that many high-level terrorists have long been imprisoned on U.S. soil without incident. As of April 2016, 443 convicted terrorists were in federal prisons in the continental United States, far more than the 61 detainees at Guantanamo.[19]

One implication of Congress' ban on bringing detainees to U.S. soil is that they cannot be tried in federal courts. Instead, they must face Guantanamo-based military commissions — tribunals of military officers used to prosecute detainees captured in the fight against terrorism.[20] However, Thomas Pickering, a former U.S. ambassador to the United Nations, says those commissions have proven "woefully inadequate" because of questions about fairness and the slowness of deliberations. Only eight prisoners have been convicted by military commissions, and four of those convictions were overturned on appeal. In contrast, hundreds of terrorists have been convicted in federal courts.[21]

With political gridlock over Guantanamo continuing, Obama has pushed for changes in the military commissions that would speed up deliberations. But that idea has drawn heavy criticism from congressional Republicans, as well as some human rights groups, because of fears it would compromise the quality of the proceedings.

As experts and policy makers consider closing Guantanamo prison, here are some of the questions they are asking:

Afghanistan Takes the Most Detainees

The United States has transferred about 710 Guantanamo Bay detainees to 59 countries since the prison opened in 2002. The largest number of prisoners transferred — about a third of the total — has gone to Afghanistan and Saudi Arabia. Sixty-one inmates remain at Guantanamo.

(No. of Guantanamo Inmates Transferred)

Top 10 Transfer Countries

Afghanistan	Saudi Arabia	Pakistan	Yemen	United Arab Emirates	Oman	Algeria	Britain	Morocco	Kuwait
203	134	63	22	21	20	17	15	13	12

Source: "The Guantánamo Docket: Transfer Countries," *The New York Times,* http://tinyurl.com/jgw765m

Is keeping Guantanamo open helping to fuel global terrorism?

Obama is not alone in arguing that the detention facility at Guantanamo incites terrorists abroad.

"Guantanamo continues to be a potent symbol of American injustice worldwide," says Alberto Mora, former general counsel of the Navy and a senior fellow at Harvard University's Carr Center for Human Rights. He says the history of human rights violations at Guantanamo is a "strategic gift that has been provided to our adversaries in terms of messaging and recruiting."

Rep. Jackie Speier, D-Calif., a member of the House Armed Services Committee, called the prison "an injurious symbol" that to many people represents "a manifestation of lawless abuse" and "fuels twisted ideological propaganda."[22]

That abuse, critics of the prison say, refers to the treatment inmates received in the facility's early years and to the imprisoning of detainees without charges. For example, only seven of the 61 remaining detainees at Guantanamo Bay have been charged with a crime, leaving the others in legal limbo. Such treatment contributes to Guantanamo's bad reputation and inflames radical elements in the Mideast and elsewhere, Speier and others say.

Other experts and politicians, however, say the prison has little or no impact on the activities of terrorists.

Rep. Vicky Hartzler, R-Mo., another House Armed Services member, said the same terrorist groups were targeting Americans before the Guantanamo prison was opened. The Taliban, for example, had established its regime in Afghanistan in 1996 and al Qaeda had bombed the *USS Cole* in 2000 as well as carried out the Sept. 11 attacks on New York City and Washington a year later, she noted.

"Indeed, it was because of the death and destruction caused by these terrorists that [Guantanamo] came into being," Hartzler said.[23]

David B. Rivkin Jr., a senior fellow at the Foundation for Defense of Democracies, a Washington, think tank focusing on national security, argues Guantanamo does not motivate terrorist groups. "The notion that the existence of Guantanamo is somehow radicalizing people and causing them to engage in attacks is just ridiculous," says Rivkin.

Sen. Tom Cotton, R-Ark., an Iraq War veteran who is hawkish on national security matters, went even further. The prison should be kept open, he said, and those who want to close it on the grounds that it is inciting terrorists are playing politics.

"They don't attack us for what we do [at Guantanamo]; they attack us for who we are" as a nation, Cotton said of terrorists. "To say that [closing the facility] is a security decision based on propaganda value that our enemies get from it is a pretext to justify a political decision."[24]

No one believes closing Guantanamo would lead terrorists to renounce their ideology. Nevertheless, says Mora, such a move would give terrorist groups one less recruiting tool. He pointed to Abu Ghraib prison in Iraq, formerly run by the U.S. military, where photos of tortured inmates sparked a worldwide uproar — and led to the prison's closure — after they were published in 2004.[25] The United States transferred control of the prison in 2006 back to Iraq's government, which closed it eight years later.[26]

Terrorists' use of Abu Ghraib as a symbol "has declined markedly since the United States stopped using it, while the use of Guantanamo by them as a symbol appears to be fairly constant," Mora says. "If we moved out of Guantanamo, I think it's going to be less useful as a new, hottest symbol; it would have less relevancy."

Other experts say that while closure of Guantanamo's detention facilities might not have a direct impact on terrorist groups, it likely would improve relations with allies in the fight against those groups.

"Until the facility is closed, it will continue to be seen by the world as our attempt to avoid the rule of law," Rep. Adam Smith of Washington state, the House Armed Services Committee's top Democrat, said at a 2013 Senate Judiciary Committee hearing. "In addition, it undermines our national security because our allies are less likely to share valuable intelligence with us and hesitate to send their detainees to the United States without a guarantee they won't be sent to Guantanamo Bay."[27]

The State Department's special envoy for Guantanamo closure, Lee S. Wolosky, echoed that view. He noted that critics of Guantanamo have ranged from Pope Francis to the Organization of American States, an international group that promotes democracy in the Americas.[28] The pope, in a 2014 speech, criticized countries that use torture and imprison suspects without trial.[29] The Vatican later offered to help the United States find a way to close the Guantanamo prison.[30]

Is a new international convention needed on the detention and trial of terrorism suspects?

Some experts say Guantanamo has become contentious in large part because the detention and trials of some detainees fall in gray areas of federal and international law.

The U.S. government classifies Guantanamo detainees as "unlawful enemy combatants." The International Committee of the Red Cross, which promotes adherence to the Geneva Conventions governing treatment of prisoners of war, said that while those conventions do not contain the term "unlawful combatant," they still cover the concept. Specifically, "if civilians directly engage in hostilities, they are considered 'unlawful' or 'unprivileged' combatants or belligerents," according to a 2011 Red Cross policy document, and may be prosecuted under the domestic laws of the government that detains them.[31]

Indeed, when the George W. Bush administration launched operations against al Qaeda and the Taliban in Afghanistan in 2001, it took the legal position that captured members of those groups were not entitled to

President Obama pledges on Feb. 23, 2016, to continue his efforts to relocate the terrorism suspects being held at Guantanamo Bay and close the controversial facility. Republicans, and some Democrats, have opposed closing the prison. Flanking Obama are Vice President Joe Biden, left, and Defense Secretary Ashton Carter.

prisoner-of-war status under the Geneva Conventions. In the case of al Qaeda, this determination was made because the organization was not a state party to the Geneva Conventions.

The Taliban's situation was more complicated: It was a functioning government in 2001 and thus was covered under the Geneva Conventions, according to the Bush administration, but it said captured Taliban combatants were disqualified for POW (prisoner of war) status on other grounds.[32] Bush administration press secretary Ari Fleischer declined to specify those grounds but said the Geneva Conventions, adopted in 1949, do "not cover every situation in which people may be captured or detained by military forces, as we see in Afghanistan today."[33]

Bush promised in 2002 that even though the United States was not classifying Guantanamo detainees as POWs, it would treat them humanely and "in a manner consistent with the principles" of the Geneva Conventions, but only "to the extent appropriate and consistent with military necessity."[34]

However, it soon became clear, according to some experts, that the government did not want to subject many of the detainees to domestic U.S. law, as would be expected under the general practices of international law.

As a U.S. military base on another country's soil, "Guantanamo was specifically chosen by the Bush administration because it was thought to be entirely outside the law, domestic and international law," says Dixon of the Center for Constitutional Rights. "The core purpose of Guantanamo was to avoid any legal constraints on the Bush administration in its treatment of detainees."

Shortly after the first detainees arrived at Guantanamo, Dixon's organization sued the Bush administration, challenging the idea that Guantanamo was beyond the reach of federal laws. In 2004, the Supreme Court determined that U.S. federal courts have jurisdiction over Guantanamo detention facilities.[35]

According to Boston University law professor Susan M. Akram, the Supreme Court repeatedly has held that both U.S. and international laws apply to the Guantanamo detainees; that they cannot be held indefinitely without trial; that constitutional habeas corpus protections allowing people to report their unlawful detention before a court apply to the detainees; and that the U.S. government tribunals to determine their status were unconstitutional and violated the Geneva Conventions.[36]

"Yet Congress and the executive branch have, through policy and legislation, strenuously avoided implementation of these decisions," Akram told an interviewer. She noted that other countries and the United Nations repeatedly have criticized the United States over its interpretation of the laws of war as they apply to the detainees.

"There has been deep and perhaps irreparable damage done to the bedrock norms of international humanitarian law and international human rights law, not just by Guantanamo, but the entire paradigm of the U.S. engagement of its so-called war on terror," Akram said.[37]

Pickering, the former U.N. ambassador, acknowledges that it is unclear how international law applies to organizations such as al Qaeda and the Islamic State. It might make sense, he says, to treat them as prisoners of war when they are captured. "But treating them as non-prisoners of war — that is, as armed civilian combatants — because it allows us to do more seriously nasty things to them doesn't seem to me to be easy to reconcile with this gray area," he says.

As a result, some experts have called for developing a new international consensus for dealing with so-called nonstate combatants.

Peter Mansoor, a retired Army colonel and a professor of military history at Ohio State University, says doing so might require writing an entirely new set of Geneva Conventions. Because fighting nonstate combatants instead of other nations' armies is "becoming the norm," says Mansoor, "we're going to have to create international laws to deal with those kinds of groups."

Others argue that current international law, including but not limited to the Geneva Conventions, is adequate for dealing with the Islamic State and al Qaeda.

Rivkin, of the Foundation for the Defense of Democracies, notes that modern international law long has dealt with conflicts involving nonstate combatants, including pirates and mercenaries. "The rules are perfectly sound and valid," he says.

Dixon contends that the absence of precedent or a clear body of law is not what has created confusion. Instead, he says, the U.S. government has chosen to "cherry pick" from the rules of war, denying detainees prisoner-of-war status but not applying domestic laws.

"The [Obama] administration's only borrowing those rules selectively and always to the detriment of the detainees," Dixon says. "The administration wants to have its cake and eat it too" by saying it wants to close the prison while continuing Bush administration policies.

Should the United States continue sending Guantanamo detainees to other countries?

So far this year, the Obama administration has transferred 46 detainees to their home country or to another nation willing to accept them, bringing the total during the president's two terms to 185.[38]

Even more detainees were transferred during the presidency of George W. Bush. Between 2002 and Jan. 22, 2009, the Bush administration transferred 532 of the approximately 780 Guantanamo detainees to other countries, according to the Office of the Director of National Intelligence.[39]

Critics in Congress, however, worry that some of the transferees have returned to the fight and killed Americans. News outlets reported in June that at least 12 transferred detainees had been involved in attacks against allied forces in Afghanistan that resulted in the deaths of about six Americans.[40]

According to American officials who spoke to a *Washington Post* reporter on condition of anonymity, a former Guantanamo detainee who was transferred to Libya in 2007 — only to be released by that country the following year — was likely involved in the Sept. 11, 2012, attack on the American embassy compound in Benghazi that killed U.S. Ambassador J. Christopher Stevens and three other Americans.[41]

"The administration is releasing dangerous terrorists to countries that can't control them," said Royce, the House Foreign Affairs chairman. "The president should halt detainee transfers immediately and be honest with the American people."[42]

Royce also said "many countries just aren't up to the job" of detaining or keeping tabs on ex-Guantanamo inmates. A diplomatic agreement with the United States for such purposes "isn't worth the paper it is written on if a country doesn't have the resources or training to keep committed terrorists from returning to the battlefield," he added.[43]

Obama administration officials, however, say the most problematic detainees were transferred to Afghanistan, Saudi Arabia and elsewhere during the Bush administration. According to the Office of the Director of National Intelligence, 185 detainees, or nearly 35 percent of the total that the Bush administration transferred, are confirmed or suspected of having returned to the fight. Meanwhile, 19 — or 13 percent of the total — of those the Obama administration transferred are confirmed or suspected of renewing terrorist or insurgent activity.[44]

That lower figure is "testament to the rigorous, interagency approach the [Obama] administration has taken to both approving detainees for transfer and to negotiating and vetting . . . detainee transfer frameworks," said the State Department's Wolosky in July.[45]

But others say Obama's transferees are more recent than those transferred by the Bush administration and could still return to the fight. "Only time will tell how

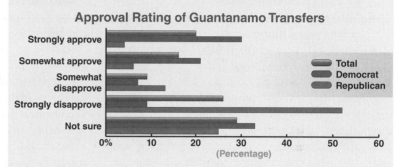

Americans Divided on Guantanamo Transfers

Americans were divided largely along party lines on the transfers of 15 Guantanamo Bay prisoners to the United Arab Emirates in mid-August — the largest single detainee release during the Obama presidency. Republicans overwhelmingly disapproved of the transfers, while a slim majority of Democrats approved. A significant minority from both parties said they were unsure how they felt about the transfers.

Approval Rating of Guantanamo Transfers

Note: Independent, Other and Not Sure of political affiliation not shown.

Source: "Guantanamo Bay results," YouGov, Aug. 16, 2016, http://tinyurl.com/hnqfgph

many of the prisoners Obama released will eventually return to the business of terror and jihad," wrote Arthur Herman, a senior fellow at the Hudson Institute, a conservative think tank in Washington.[46]

Stimson, the former Bush official now at the Heritage Foundation, contends that the number of detainees released by the Obama administration who have returned to combat is "creeping up" compared with the Bush era. "It takes between two to four years to pop up on that list once you've been transferred," he says. "You don't know when they're back to their old ways until they get caught again."

Many of the procedures for screening inmates for potential transfer and ensuring that other countries could guarantee transferees would not affect security was in response to legislation that Congress passed shortly after Obama took office.

Beginning in 2010, with each year's National Defense Authorization Act, which establishes the annual budget and goals for the Defense Department, Congress has set the conditions for transferring detainees. The 2011 law said that for a transfer to occur, the secretary of Defense has to certify to Congress that the destination country or entity:

- Must not be a state sponsor of terror or a terrorist organization.
- Must maintain control over the facility where the detainee will be transferred.
- Must not face security threats likely to affect its ability to control the detainee.
- Must agree to take steps to ensure the detainee doesn't pose a future threat.
- Must agree to share information about the detainee with the United States.[47]

Obama expressed disapproval of the restrictions, calling them an infringement on executive power because they interfere with the president's ability to make foreign policy and national security determinations about whether and under what circumstances transfers should occur.[48] Since then, however, the White House has not challenged Congress' authority in setting those restrictions.

Some in Congress are pressing for even tighter restrictions. In June, the House approved an amendment to the defense policy bill that would prevent the transfer of Guantanamo detainees to any country.

Democrats objected to the proposal as unconstitutional. "What it says is, even if you find that an individual is innocent, even if you factually find out he's guilty of no terrorism, he didn't fight against us, he's not a prisoner of war, he's guilty of nothing, he must stay in jail forever," Rep. Jerry Nadler, D-N.Y., said.[49]

As of September, the legislation was languishing in the Senate, and the White House had already recommended that the president veto the bill because it, among other things, places restrictions on planning for the transfer of detainees to U.S. prisons.

BACKGROUND
Early Military Tribunals

The question of how to treat illegal combatants — including rebels, terrorists, spies, saboteurs and mercenaries — has been answered in different ways throughout U.S. history. But from the beginning, if the military captured an individual, it generally detained and — in some but not all cases — tried the suspected offender.

The Continental Congress in 1775 adopted Articles of War based on Britain's military code that included provisions for courts-martial. The code, however, did not mention illegal combatants. And in the only section that referred to civilians, the code said non-soldiers who served with the army "are to be subject to the articles, rules, and regulations of the continental army."[50]

In 1778, a board of officers investigated whether Thomas Shanks, a former American soldier, had spied for the British. It voted for his conviction and execution, and Shanks was hanged the following day.[51]

During the War of 1812, Gen. Andrew Jackson put New Orleans under martial law as the city awaited a British attack and continued it even after he had defeated the enemy in the Battle of New Orleans in January 1815. When Louis Louallier, a private citizen, published a newspaper article arguing that civilians accused of a crime should be heard before a civil judge, not military tribunals, Jackson arrested him. The general accused Louallier of inciting mutiny and "disaffection" in the army. Louallier eventually was acquitted at his court-martial, in part because his civilian status gave the military court no jurisdiction.[52]

Jackson again convened a military tribunal in 1818 to try two British citizens, Alexander Arbuthnot and Robert Christy Ambrister, who were charged with encouraging Creek Indians to wage war against the United States. Arbuthnot also was charged with being a spy. Both were convicted, though Arbuthnot was found not guilty on the spying charge, and executed. The House Committee on Military Affairs later criticized Jackson, saying it found no law authorizing a military trial for the allegations made against the two men.[53] It said the lone exception was the spying charge on which Arbuthnot was found not guilty.

During the Mexican-American War (1846-48), Gen. Winfield Scott issued an order creating two types of military tribunals. One was "military commissions" trying both soldiers and civilians for acts not covered by courts-martial, including murder, robbery, theft and vandalism. The other tribunal was for violations of the laws of war.[54]

Scott sought congressional approval, but Congress did not respond and those rules remained in effect.[55]

During the Civil War, military commissions were used more frequently. As early as April 1861, President

Abraham Lincoln issued a proclamation suspending writs of habeas corpus — petitions incarcerated people under arrest can file to force the government to justify before a judge their jailing. In 1862, Gen. Henry Halleck, commander of the Union army in Missouri, convened commissions to try civilians for crimes that were not covered by the laws of war. And in 1863, Lincoln issued what became known as the Lieber Code, making military commissions the appropriate forum for trying cases that the Articles of War did not cover.[56] The military commissions were used to try thousands of people, especially in border states where the Union sought to exercise its authority.

After the Civil War, the only significant use of military tribunals to try civilians until World War II was during the U.S. occupation of the Philippines from 1899 to 1902.

During World War II, two military tribunals attracted widespread public attention. In 1942, a military commission was convened to try eight German civilians who surreptitiously entered the United States on U-boats and planned sabotage. Two of the group's leaders tipped off the FBI to the plot, and the bureau planned to charge the Germans in federal court.

But President Franklin D. Roosevelt's administration did not want it publicly revealed that one suspect had turned himself in and fingered the others. It also did not want to broadcast the ease with which U-boats had reached the U.S. mainland undetected.[57]

Roosevelt also wanted to use a military commission because it could impose harsher penalties; the maximum sentence for sabotage in civilian courts was 30 years in prison.[58] After the military commission completed its work, all of the Germans were executed except for the two leaders.

Another high-profile use of a military commission was the International Military Tribunal held by Allied forces in Nuremberg, Germany, at the end of World War II. In addition to trying high-level Nazi officials for war crimes, the tribunal prosecuted civilians for domestic crimes.[59]

First Detainees Arrive

One week after the Sept. 11 attacks on the World Trade Center in New York and the Pentagon in Virginia, Congress passed a joint resolution authorizing the president to use "all necessary and appropriate force" against

Younis Abdurrahman Chekkouri was sent back to Morocco, his home country, in 2015, after being held at Guantanamo for more than 13 years. Of the roughly 780 people who have been held at the facility since it opened, 710 have been transferred to other countries and nine have died; 61 detainees remain. Of the prisoners transferred out of Guantanamo, some 214 are known or suspected to have returned to terrorist or insurgent activities.

terrorists.[60] This Authorization for Use of Military Force (AUMF) gave the president the power to imprison suspects at Guantanamo and, in some cases, have them tried.

Two months after the attacks, President Bush issued a military order creating military commissions to try non-U.S. citizens who were past or current Qaeda members. Bush said applying the normal principles of civilian law was impractical.[61]

The first detainees arrived at the Guantanamo facility in January 2002. Because Guantanamo is in Cuba — on land perpetually leased from that country under a 1903 agreement — it was beyond U.S. courts' jurisdiction, wrote Allan A. Ryan, an attorney who teaches the law of war at the Boston College Law School and Harvard University. "This was a critical concern to those in the president's inner circle, because they had no intention of creating a conventional prisoner-of-war camp, operated in accordance with international law under the constraints of humane treatment imposed by the Geneva Conventions and monitored by the International Committee of the Red Cross," Ryan wrote.[62]

The Bush administration justified the Guantanamo prison on security grounds. In 2009, Dick Cheney — who had been Bush's vice president — said the prisoners left at Guantanamo were "the worst of the worst." He also said that without a place to hold detainees, "the only other option is to kill them, and we don't operate that way."[63]

Ryan, however, disputed that the "worst of the worst" were sent to Guantanamo. Instead, Ryan wrote, they were sent to CIA-operated "black sites" in secret locations in Europe and Asia and subjected to years of "enhanced interrogations" that critics said amounted to torture. "Those sent to Guantanamo were for show," Ryan said.[64]

New Yorker reporter Connie Bruck found that most detainees were not terrorist leaders but lower-level foot soldiers. Local warlords turned over many of them to the U.S. military for a bounty of as much as $25,000 per prisoner.[65]

Some of the Bush administration's critics also disputed its reasons for using military commissions for the relatively few Guantanamo detainees who were actually charged with crimes. An analyst for the Congressional Research Service, Congress' research arm, noted that federal courts were used in the past to try suspected terrorists for war-related offenses, including suspected Palestinian Liberation Organization members accused in the 1985 hijacking of an ocean liner; a group accused in the 1993 bombing of the World Trade Center; the suspects in the bombings of two U.S. embassies in Africa in 1998; and al Qaeda's attack on the *USS Cole* in 2000.[66]

"There is historical precedent for using federal courts to try those accused of terrorism or war related offenses, including some that might under some circumstances be characterized as 'violations of the law or war,' " wrote legislative attorney Jennifer K. Elsea in a report to Congress.[67]

In fact, when Bush's attorney general, John Ashcroft, learned that the president planned to employ military commissions he was enraged, according to Karen J. Greenberg, director of the Center on National Security at Fordham University. "The attorney general immediately went to the White House to argue that the federal courts for the appropriate venue for trials of foreign terrorists," she wrote. "Ashcroft had precedent on his side."[68]

In a series of rulings between 2002 and 2008, however, the Supreme Court made it clear that Guantanamo was not beyond the reach of U.S. laws. In 2004, the court held in *Rasul v. Bush* that federal courts have jurisdiction over Guantanamo and that the detainees could challenge their detention in federal court.[69] Congress responded in 2005 by passing the Detainee Treatment Act, which aimed to restrict detainees' access to federal courts for habeas corpus appeals.[70]

The next year, the Supreme Court ruled in *Hamdan v. Rumsfeld* that the military commissions to try detainees in place of the federal courts were procedurally flawed and violated the Geneva Conventions.[71] Congress responded by passing the Military Commissions Act of 2006, which authorized military commission trials.[72]

According to Dixon of the Center for Constitutional Rights, Congress was essentially using the Military Commission Act to say, "No, we really mean it. We're taking away jurisdiction of the federal courts over Guantanamo."

The Supreme Court again disagreed. In 2008, it ruled in *Boumediene v. Bush* that Congress could not restrict individuals' right to habeas corpus appeals.[73] The key part of the *Boumediene* decision, says Dixon, is that the right to habeas corpus "is a right that is rooted in and guaranteed by the Constitution, which means that Congress cannot take away that right. So that settled that issue."

Obama versus Congress

Upon taking office in 2009, Obama instructed military prosecutors to suspend proceedings in the Guantanamo Bay military commission for 120 days.[74] Two days later, he issued an executive order to close the Guantanamo detention facility within a year.

Four months later, however, Obama announced that the military commissions would resume with expanded legal protections. Obama administration officials said the decision to proceed with military commissions resulted partly from concerns that some federal prosecutions might fail because the interrogation techniques used at Guantanamo tainted the evidence against the detainees.[75]

Among the expanded protections, Obama directed that the secondhand recounting of a conversation, or "hearsay," and information obtained through cruel interrogation methods, such as waterboarding, no longer would be admitted as evidence.[76]

C H R O N O L O G Y

1815-1959 *Military commissions come into use. U.S. takes possession of Guantanamo Bay, Cuba.*

1815-1818 Gen. Andrew Jackson employs military commissions to try British and U.S. civilians during and after the War of 1812.

1846-1848 Gen. Winfield Scott orders the creation of two types of military tribunals during the Mexican-American War.

1903 U.S. leases Guantanamo Bay site from Cuba.

1934 Future Cuban president Fulgencio Batista co-signs a provision stipulating that the lease can't be ended without mutual consent.

1942 President Roosevelt uses a military commission to try eight German civilians accused of planning sabotage.

1945 The Allied Powers convene the International Military Tribunal at Nuremberg to try both soldiers and civilians for war crimes as well as certain domestic crimes not covered by the laws of war.

1959 Communist revolutionary Fidel Castro overthrows Batista. The Castro government subsequently demands return of the Guantanamo base.

2001-2002 *Bush administration brings terrorism suspects to Guantanamo.*

2001 Congress authorizes the president to use "all necessary and appropriate force" against those responsible for the Sept. 11 terrorist attacks and those who aid terrorists. . . . President George W. Bush signs executive order creating military tribunals for the trials of those captured in the war against al Qaeda and the Taliban.

2002 First 20 detainees arrive at the newly opened Guantanamo detention facility. For the first few months they are housed in cages that leave them exposed to the elements.

2004-2008 *Military commission trials proceed amid legal fights.*

2004 Supreme Court rules in *Rasul v. Bush* that federal courts have jurisdiction over Guantanamo and that detainees can challenge their detention in federal court.

2005 Bush signs Detainee Treatment Act, which aims to restrict the access of detainees to federal courts.

2006 Supreme Court rules in *Hamdan v. Rumsfeld* that the military commissions to try detainees in place of the federal courts violate the Geneva Conventions governing the treatment of prisoners of war. . . . Congress passes Military Commission Act, authorizing trials by military commissions.

2008 Supreme Court rules in *Boumediene v. Bush* that the right to habeas corpus is rooted in the Constitution, and Congress cannot restrict it.

2009-Present *Obama and Congress battle over closing Guantanamo.*

2009 On his first day in office, President Obama suspends the Guantanamo military commissions for 120 days, and two days later issues an executive order to close the detention facility within a year. Four months later, he announces resumption of the commissions with expanded legal protections. . . . Congress restricts president's ability to transfer detainees to other countries.

2011 Congress further restricts transfer of Guantanamo detainees, requiring the Defense secretary to certify to Congress that a receiving country is not a designated state sponsor of terrorism and not facing a threat likely to affect its ability to maintain control over a transferred detainee. . . . Obama issues executive order creating review boards to assess whether detainees should be transferred to other countries.

2015 Congress includes provisions in the annual defense bill putting restrictions on transfers of any of the 112 remaining detainees to the United States, making it impossible for detainees to be tried in federal court.

2016 Pentagon announces largest-ever transfer of detainees — 15 prisoners sent to the United Arab Emirates. House Republicans respond by passing a bill that would temporarily block detainee transfers to other countries until stricter requirements are fashioned. The bill's future in the Senate is uncertain. . . . Additional transfers reduce Guantanamo inmate count to 61.

Conditions at Guantanamo Still Mostly a Mystery

Officials cite improvements, but government blocks outside access.

When the first 20 suspected al Qaeda and Taliban members arrived at Guantanamo Bay in January 2002, they were kept in open-air steel-and-wire pens, described by some journalists as "dog cages," while guard dogs were housed in air-conditioned kennels. Each detainee was given one bucket for water and another as a toilet. Some detainees complained of torture, including Mehdi Ghezali, a Swedish citizen and the son of an Algerian-born immigrant, and six British nationals who later sought compensation from the British government for the treatment they received while in American custody in Afghanistan and at Guantanamo Bay.[1]

While the Department of Defense hurried to expand and improve the jail space at the military outpost, then Secretary of Defense Donald H. Rumsfeld defended the choice of Guantanamo Bay as "the least worst place we could have selected."[2]

Conditions at the prison have improved significantly since those early days, according to retired Gen. John Kelly, who ran the prison from 2012 to January 2016. There are now air-conditioned cell blocks and even recreational facilities, and the prison population has fallen from nearly 700 in 2002 to 61 in September. "The facilities they live in today are pretty good," he said. "Again, I wouldn't want to be a detainee, but if you got to be a detainee somewhere, Gitmo is the place to be."[3]

Karen J. Greenberg, director of the Center on National Security at Fordham University Law School, said in 2013 that conditions had improved markedly, especially since President Obama took office in 2009. "As recently as this past fall," she wrote in 2013, "as many as 130 Guantánamo detainees were living in communal areas, many with access to Skype, television and a football pitch [soccer field]. This more relaxed policy was based on the premise that creature comforts could compensate for the lack of hope and due

process afforded to the detainees."[4] Charges have yet to be filed against most of the prisoners.

Greenberg also noted, however, that many of these comforts were temporarily taken away after detainees began a wave of hunger strikes in February 2013. "The recent turn toward feeding tubes, individual cells and violence between detainees and guards has made Guantanamo more like a dungeon, its inmates tormented by lives without resolution or release," Greenberg wrote.

According to some reports, more than half of the 166 detainees at Guantanamo in 2013 were on hunger strikes.[5] After guards discovered homemade weapons, detainees were assigned to individual cells with heavy steel doors.[6]

By 2015, military officials said the majority of detainees were once again living in communal areas and had extensive opportunities to read, exercise and watch TV.[7]

Still, a clampdown on information about the detention facility imposed by the Defense Department in 2013 means that the public remains largely in the dark about current conditions at Guantanamo, analysts and legal experts say. Indeed, in December 2013, the Pentagon announced that it no longer would inform the media about prisoners' hunger strikes. "The release of this information serves no operational purpose and detracts from the more important issues, which are the welfare of detainees and the safety and security of our troops," said Navy Cmdr. John Filostrat, a spokesman for the military's Joint Task Force Guantanamo.[8]

The Obama administration also has continued to refuse to let the United Nations special rapporteur for torture speak with detainees, a policy initiated in 2004 by the George W. Bush administration.

David B. Rivkin, senior fellow at the Foundation for Defense of Democracies, a think tank in Washington that focuses on national security issues, echoes Kelly about current conditions. "I can tell you that, objectively speaking, the Guantanamo detention facility is the best-run prison facility I've ever seen, and I have visited a number of federal and state penitentiaries," Rivkin says. "If I were unfortunate enough to be detained, I'd rather be detained in Guantanamo than just about anywhere else."

Still, some experts say it remains impossible to verify those assertions. Joseph Hickman, a former Army National Guardsman who worked at the detention facility, told reporters in 2015 that Guantanamo no longer was the "cruel place" he saw when he arrived in 2006. He added, however, that the limited access provided to the media and others made it hard to tell that story. "If [the military] would be more transparent with what they're doing, it would make things a lot easier," he said.[9]

At a March meeting of the U.N. Human Rights Council, U.S. Ambassador to the U.N. Keith Harper was peppered with questions about the U.S. refusal to let the U.N. torture investigator onto the base. His response: "We are continuing to have a dialogue with the special rapporteur. It is the hope that we will have an agreement on terms."[10]

The administration's stance puzzles Alberto Mora, a former general counsel of the U.S. Navy. "I don't understand what the rationale [for denial] is," says Mora. "Why one would wish to erode the capability of United Nations in that respect is something that puzzles me."

The United Nations and the Organization for Security and Co-operation in Europe, in an open letter in January 2016, urged the United States to promptly close the detention facility and that failure to do so could encourage other countries to engage in similar behaviors. "The United States must clean up its own house — impunity only generates more abuses as States do not feel compelled to stop engaging in illegal practices," the letter said.[11]

— *Patrick Marshall*

The Guantanamo Bay naval base includes a detention facility that now holds 61 terrorism suspects.

[2] Katharine Q. Seelye, "U.S. to Hold Taliban Detainees in 'the Least Worst Place,' " *The New York Times*, Dec. 28, 2001, http://tinyurl.com/z8qlose.

[3] "The Case for Closing — And Keeping Open — Guantanamo," Weekend Edition Sunday, NPR, March 6, 2016, http://tinyurl.com/h6lufum; "Gitmo upgrades as prison enters5th year," NBC News, Jan. 11, 2006, http://tinyurl.com/hpjnvl3.

[4] Karen J. Greenberg, "Five Myths about Guantanamo Bay," *The Guardian*, May 7, 2013, http://tinyurl.com/gwk24an.

[5] Chris Lawrence and Matt Smith, "Daily life at Guantanamo: Hunger strikes, sprays of filth," CNN, May 17, 2013, http://tinyurl.com/h3ramsw.

[6] *Ibid.*

[7] Tyler Pager and Paige Leskin, "Military: Gitmo detainees not treated like in early days," *USA Today*, March 16, 2015, http://tinyurl.com/zjan64r; Pager and Leskin, *op. cit.*

[8] "Guantanamo detainees' hunger strikes will no longer be disclosed by U.S. military," The Associated Press, *The Washington Post*, Dec. 4, 2013, http://tinyurl.com/jlvm554.

[9] Pager and Leskin, *op. cit.*

[10] Stephanie Nebehay, "U.N. torture envoy appeals again for visits to U.S. prisons, Reuters, March 8, 2016, http://tinyurl.com/zw57hhb.

[11] "Guantánamo Bay, 14 years on — Rights experts urge the US to end impunity and close the detention facility," Office of the United Nations High Commissioner for Human Rights, Jan. 11, 2016, http://tinyurl.com/hhdkxtb.

[1] "Swede says he was tortured in Guantanamo," *The Irish Times*, July 14, 2004, http://tinyurl.com/hj9wlgp; Fran Yeoman, "Blair knew of Guantanamo torture in 2002, lawyers claim," *The Independent*, Sept. 28, 2010.

U.S. Navy/MCS 2nd Class Kegan E. Kay

Lawmakers Spar Over Military Force

Some argue new measures are needed to detain ISIS fighters.

One week after hijackers crashed jetliners into the World Trade Center and the Pentagon, Congress authorized the use of military force against "nations, organizations or persons" responsible for the Sept. 11, 2001, attacks.[1] This Authorization for Use of Military Force (AUMF) also permitted action against those who had helped the attackers.[2]

Congress in the past has passed formal authorizations for the use of military force — which are generally more limited in scope than a declaration of war — at least 10 times since 1798. But experts continue to debate whether presidents need to secure such authorizations before sending troops into combat. Earlier presidents, including George W. Bush, have taken the position that getting congressional approval is beneficial because it strengthens their hand, but is not required.[3]

Related questions on executive power deal with the use of Guantanamo Bay as a prison and the current fight against the Islamic State (also known as ISIS and ISIL). Many legal experts agree that the 2001 AUMF does permit the detention of the 61 prisoners remaining at Guantanamo. But some say it's unclear whether current U.S. military operations — most notably against ISIS — fall under that authority because the AUMF only authorized actions against those responsible for the 9/11 attacks and those who harbored them. ISIS did not exist in 2001.

Among the critics is Democratic vice presidential candidate Tim Kaine, who said in April that the current law "does not provide a legal justification" for fighting the Islamic State.

Kaine, a U.S. senator from Virginia, also said the law gives the executive branch too much power to wage hostilities because only Congress can formally declare war.

Kaine charged that the Obama administration and Congress have "basically come up with a war doctrine that says 'wherever and whenever,' as long as the president feels it's a good idea — without Congress even needing to do anything about it."[4]

But Charles Stimson, deputy assistant secretary of Defense for detainee affairs under Bush, dismisses the view that the AUMF doesn't cover ISIS and other enemies. The Islamic State is "a natural inheritor of al Qaeda, it grew out of al Qaeda," Stimson says, and a new authorization-of-force is unnecessary.

At the same time, though, Stimson says he's unsure whether the 2001 authorization would cover the potential detention of Islamic State prisoners at Guantanamo. (None are there now.) He says the president and Congress should cooperate to pass a law dealing with ISIS.

"The further you get away from the 9/11 attacks, and the further you get away from the narrow class of individuals who fell under the 2001 AUMF, the more tenuous the connection is as a legal matter," he says.

President Obama maintains that he has the authority to fight ISIS under existing laws. Nevertheless, in February 2015, he urged Congress to pass legislation authorizing the use of military force against the terrorist group. Obama submitted a draft for a new AUMF that was more limited than the 2001 version and included, among other restrictions, a three-year limit on the use of ground forces.[5]

The decision to resume military commissions infuriated civil rights groups, who accused Obama of going back on his word to close Guantanamo. "These military commissions are inherently illegitimate, unconstitutional and incapable of delivering outcomes we can trust," said Anthony D. Romero, executive director of the American Civil Liberties Union.[77]

Beginning in 2009, Congress began imposing restrictions on Obama's ability to transfer detainees to other countries even though the Bush administration had been doing the same thing. A bill that year to fund the military and other agencies required the president to notify Congress 15 days before a transfer. Congress also instructed Obama to include a classified report that contains an analysis of the risk the transfer may present to U.S. security, as well as the terms of agreement with the receiving country, including any financial assistance.[78]

In 2011, in the National Defense Appropriations Act, Congress placed even more restrictions on transfers in the annual military spending bill.[79]

Congressional Republicans declined to move forward with Obama's draft or any other legislation in that area. House Speaker Paul Ryan, R-Wis., said the president "has the authority right now" to fight the Islamic State under the existing authorization.[6]

Sen. Robert Menendez, D-N.J., said Republicans oppose an authorization that is more narrowly defined than the earlier version.

"The big debate here is between a universe, mostly Republicans, that wants to basically say, 'Here you go [Mr. President], you have the wherewithal to do anything you need' — you know, an open-ended authorization — and Democrats who don't want to see another Iraq or another Afghanistan in terms of an open-ended military [engagement]; they want to tailor it more," said Menendez, a former chairman of the influential Senate Foreign Relations Committee.[7]

Actually, it seems those Republicans are saying just what Menendez says. They're not against a new authorization but they don't want it to be more limiting than the current one.

Some legal experts say policymakers should refrain from legislating special authorizations. Jennifer Daskal and Stephen I. Vladeck, professors at the American University Washington School of Law, said such measures "perpetuate war at a time when we should be seeking to end it."

Daskal and Vladeck argued that the government already has numerous counterterrorism tools at its disposal, including law enforcement and intelligence gathering. They said those tools "provide a much more strategically sound (and legally justifiable) means of addressing the terrorist threat."[8]

— Patrick Marshall

Democratic vice presidential candidate Tim Kaine said in April that the Authorization for Use of Military Force "does not provide a legal justification" for fighting the Islamic State.

[3] David M. Ackerman and Richard F. Grimmett, "Declarations of War and Authorizations for the Use of Military Force: Historical Background and Legal Implications," Congressional Research Service, updated Jan. 14, 2003, http://tinyurl.com/jjwbfnk.

[4] Susan Jones, "Sen. Tim Kaine: 'We Have Made a Complete Hash of the . . . Doctrines of War,' " CNSNews.com, April 29, 2016, http://tinyurl.com/hgrdose.

[5] "Authorization for the Use of United States Armed Forces in connection with the Islamic State of Iraq and the Levant," Letter from the President to the Congress of the United States, Feb. 11, 2015, http://tinyurl.com/qz8227v.

[6] Rebecca Nelson and Sarah Mimms, "Why the White House Wants an AUMF, and Why It's Not Going to Happen," *The Atlantic*, Dec. 8, 2015, http://tinyurl.com/zbckg7n.

[7] *Ibid.*

[8] Jennifer Daskal and Stephen I. Vladeck, "After the AUMF," *Harvard National Security Journal*, Jan. 22, 2014, http://tinyurl.com/hwmn2wb.

[1] "Public Law 107-40-Authorization for Use of Military Force," U.S. Government Printing Office, 2001, http://tinyurl.com/ha8kvlw.

[2] *Ibid.*

Obama issued an executive order in 2011 that created a process to periodically review the executive branch's use of its detention authority.[80] Critics saw the move as the administration's abandonment of its plans to close the detention facility.

"It is virtually impossible to imagine how one closes Guantanamo in light of this executive order," said the ACLU's Romero. "In a little over two years, the Obama administration has done a complete about-face."[81]

Romero and other critics were further upset when Obama signed the National Defense Authorization Act of 2012, which allowed the government to detain any individuals suspected of involvement with the Sept. 11 attacks "until the end of the hostilities."[82]

Obama had threatened to veto the bill over those provisions but ended up signing it into law because of the legislation's overall merits.

"By signing this defense spending bill, President Obama will go down in history as the president who enshrined indefinite detention without trial in U.S. law," Kenneth Roth, executive director of Human Rights Watch, said in a statement.[83]

In late 2015, Obama again reluctantly signed that year's defense authorization bill, despite provisions he considered objectionable, that restricted transfers of any of the 112 remaining detainees to the United States or a foreign country.

Despite these restrictions, the Obama administration submitted a nine-page plan to Congress for closing the detention facility at Guantanamo that included transferring some detainees to the United States for potential trial.[84]

But congressional Republicans declared the proposal dead on arrival. Sen. Pat Roberts, R-Kan., posted a video on Twitter showing him crumpling the proposal and throwing it in the trash. "This is what I think of the president's plan to send terrorists to the United States," he said.[85]

CURRENT SITUATION

Civilian or Military Courts?

In April, the Obama administration proposed a series of changes to the military commissions aimed at speeding up deliberations while lowering costs. Its proposals included allowing judges to conduct pretrial hearings by videoconference; permitting civilian government lawyers to represent defendants; and allowing the primary judge to appoint a secondary judge to hear some motions, a provision aimed at reducing delays, particularly given the distances judges must travel to Cuba.[86]

Brig. Gen. John Baker, the chief defense lawyer in the military commissions system, criticized the proposed overhaul, calling it an "unfair and unconstitutional" attempt to change the rules "in the middle of the game" because the changes would "deny these individuals the right to be present in the courtroom."[87]

Dixon, of the Center for Constitutional Rights and an advocate for detainees, agrees. "Why would the administration try to change the rules of the game in order to favor the prosecution instead of bringing these men into the United States to face criminal trials in federal court?" Dixon asks. "It makes no sense from a legal perspective, and it makes no sense from a policy perspective."

Cmdr. Gary Ross, a Pentagon spokesman, disagrees with such criticisms, saying the proposals were "narrowly tailored to allow for better management, flexibility and accountability." For example, he said, videoconferencing reduces the need for all necessary participants to travel to Cuba every time an issue is discussed, while allowing civilian government lawyers to represent detainees helps solve the problem of turnover caused by periodic redeployments of military personnel.[88]

Another ongoing — and hotly debated — issue is whether military commissions or federal courts are the better forums for trying detainees.

While the Obama administration now reluctantly favors military commissions over the federal courts — both because of concerns that federal courts may disallow evidence gathered through the interrogation techniques employed at Guantanamo and by the congressional ban on bringing detainees to the mainland — civil rights groups argue that the federal courts are more efficient and more just than the military commissions.

"The military commissions are by and large an abject failure," Dixon says. "More detainees have died at Guantanamo than have been convicted by a military commission."

One of the problems with the commissions, some critics say, is that they have tried to adjudicate crimes that are not considered violations of the international law of war.*

"In 2016 we're still litigating the question of what charges can be brought in a military commission," Dixon says.

In 2012, a federal appeals court overturned the conviction of a Guantanamo detainee — Salim Ahmed Hamdan, a former driver and bodyguard for Osama bin Laden, the Qaeda leader who was killed by U.S. Special Forces in 2011. Hamdan had been accused of providing "material support" for terrorism, but the court said there was no such crime under the international law of war.[89]

Prosecutors and defenders alike are awaiting a crucial ruling by the U.S. Court of Appeals for the D.C. Circuit, which is considering whether conspiracy charges are appropriate for the military commissions to hear. In June 2015, in a 2-1 opinion, the court overturned the 2008 conviction on conspiracy charges of a Guantanamo detainee, Ali Hamza al-Bahlul, on the grounds that while

---

* The international law of war, a set of rules that seeks to limit the effects of armed conflict, is drawn from three sources: treaties, custom and generally accepted principles. The Geneva Con-ventions are in the first category.

AT ISSUE

Should the Guantanamo detention facility be closed?

YES
Alberto J. Mora
Senior Fellow, Carr Center for Human Rights Policy, Harvard University

Excerpted from testimony before the House Subcommittee on National Security, May 24, 2016

The national security interests of the United States would be advanced by permanently closing the Guantanamo detention facility and transferring the detainees there either to a detention facility or facilities in the United States or, if appropriate, to third countries.

While one can understand the reasons why Guantanamo was initially chosen as a detention facility for high-level detainees captured in the war on terror, those reasons no longer apply, circumstances have changed, better alternatives have emerged, and the high costs of Guantanamo are now fully visible and should be regarded as untenable. To keep the Guantanamo detention facility open today would be contrary to our nation's financial, administrative, military, foreign policy and national security interests. Other than for reasons of inertia, there is no need to keep the facility open — but there are pressing reasons to close it. . . .

I believe it should be closed for five reasons. . . . First, Guantanamo is no longer outside the jurisdiction of U.S. federal courts and thus there is no significant legal advantage to holding detainees in Guantanamo vis-à-vis federal detention facilities in the United States. . . .

Second, the financial costs and personnel burdens of maintaining detainees at Guantanamo are extravagantly wasteful in comparison with other alternatives. Guantanamo is incredibly costly from both a financial and personnel perspective — and unnecessarily so. Financially, Guantanamo costs the U.S. taxpayer $445 million a year, or about $5.56 million per detainee annually. The cost to house prisoners in maximum-security prisons, by contrast, is about $78,000 per prisoner. . . .

Third, given the availability of U.S.-based civilian alternatives, by closing Guantanamo the military personnel now serving as guards there could be reassigned to higher-priority duties. . . .

Fourth, because the federal prison system has demonstrated that it can successfully and safely hold terrorists as dangerous as any of those as Guantanamo, closing Guantanamo and transferring the detainees to the United States would not appreciably add to the current level of risk. . . .

Fifth, and most importantly, the foreign policy and national security costs of maintaining Guantanamo as a detention facility are too high and outweigh any benefit it provides. Guantanamo has damaged us with our friends and has constituted a strategic gift to our enemies. It is not an overstatement to say that the Guantanamo has seriously undermined our national security and contributed to a loss of American lives overseas.

NO
Retired Navy Cmdr. Kirk S. Lippold
Former Commander, USS Cole

Excerpted from testimony before the House Subcommittee on National Security, May 24, 2016

The utility that was envisioned for Guantanamo Bay as an intelligence facility has been cast side for political expediency. The failure to use Guantanamo Bay has made the U.S. less safe and more vulnerable, since we no longer have a facility with its unique capabilities to leverage the intelligence advantage that our nation could possess with its use.

In fact, the United States has given up a critical strategic advantage in surrendering to the political expediency to close Guantanamo Bay while failing to give due consideration to how we can replace it with a facility under U.S. control that can be guaranteed to remain operational for the duration of the ongoing conflict. For this reason and more, keeping Guantanamo Bay open is more important now than ever before in the war effort. . . .

Guantanamo Bay has the facilities and capabilities necessary to be the crown jewel in the intelligence effort to defeat transnational terrorist groups like al Qaeda and the Islamic State. Several years ago, the Department of Defense spent over $325 million to build a state-of-the-art headquarters and intelligence fusion center on Guantanamo Bay. It was specifically designed to take the real-time intelligence gleaned from interrogation of detainees, then integrate and construct a robust and capable intelligence picture of their worldwide tactics, techniques and procedures.

Every intelligence agency in the U.S. government could use the facility to protect and defend the United States against attack. Unfortunately, this facility goes virtually unused because of the political decision to attempt to close the detention facility.

Guantanamo Bay is not used as a recruiting tool for terrorist organizations. While Guantanamo Bay is occasionally cited in terrorist propaganda, over the past few years the intelligence community assessed its impact as almost negligible. While many who want Guantanamo Bay closed use the pictures of orange jumpsuits and pictures of detainees from Guantanamo Bay as proof that it is a recruiting tool, the facts do not support this contention. . . .

Keeping the detention facility at Guantanamo Bay open is in the best interest of the United States and the American people. The threat of ongoing terrorist operations against the United States militates that as a nation we should continue using the facilities that have already been built there and expand their use to ensure that another terrorist attack is not carried out against the United States.

Republican Sen. John McCain of Arizona, center, chairman of the Armed Services Committee, and Sens. Kelly Ayotte R-N.H., and Lindsey Graham, R-S.C., hold a news conference on Feb. 24, 2016, to criticize President Obama's latest plan to close the military prison at Guantanamo Bay, calling it "jibberish." Obama has blamed his inability to shut down the prison on Congress, saying it has "repeatedly imposed restrictions aimed at preventing us from closing this facility."

conspiracy is a domestic crime, it is not recognized as a crime under the international law of war.[90]

Standards of Evidence

Civil rights groups have also criticized the military commissions for employing inadequate standards for evidence and allowing hearsay and evidence gathered through coercion.

"Although statements obtained through torture or cruel, inhuman, or degrading treatment are technically inadmissible in the military commissions, there's a significant loophole, because the commissions employ looser evidentiary standards than federal courts," says Ashley Gorski, a staff attorney with the American Civil Liberties Union's National Security Project. "These looser standards permit the introduction of evidence that was obtained through coercion, and government secrecy limits the ability of defense attorneys to show that a statement should be excluded."

Gorski says that even when interrogators stop torturing a detainee, later statements are suspect. "There are grave concerns about the extent to which an individual who has been tortured can then subsequently make statements to interrogators that are voluntary," she says.

But Pentagon spokeswoman Valerie Henderson says "slight procedural differences make military commissions the better forum for certain cases."

For example, Henderson says, using federal courts can be inappropriate in some cases because of rules regarding Miranda warnings and hearsay evidence. The Miranda warnings stem from the controversial but now largely accepted 1966 decision in *Miranda v. Arizona* that required police to advise suspects of their rights, including the right to remain silent, before any custodial interrogation — that is, any interrogation during which the suspect is not free to leave.[91]

"Requiring soldiers to give Miranda warnings to enemy forces they have captured is impractical and dangerous," she says. "Similarly, strict hearsay rules — which were not part of the trial of war criminals at Nuremberg and are unknown to many respected justice systems — may not afford either the prosecution or the defense sufficient flexibility to submit the best available evidence from genuine zones of armed conflict."

Some experts argue that both federal courts and military commissions are needed to accommodate the variety of prosecutions and that the former works more swiftly than the latter. The Heritage Foundation's Stimson says if the cases still pending in the military commissions — totaling seven as of September — had been in federal courts, "the trials would be over" because the federal system is able to dispose of cases more swiftly than military commissions.

Federal courts are the best place to deal with terrorism, and they "have done a good job" in that area, says Peter Margulies, a law professor at Rhode Island's Roger Williams University who specializes in national security law. "Would I want to see everyone tried in military commissions? God forbid," he says. "But is there a role in a small number of cases? Yes," such as cases requiring secrecy.

But some civil libertarians disagree. "The military commissions have continued to exist in large measure to prevent public disclosures about the CIA torture program," says Dixon.

Mora, the former Navy general counsel, says the perception surrounding commissions is that they are less interested in judging the defendants' guilt or innocence and more about how much weight to give allegations of torture. "It is pretty clear that they have failed," he says.

Blame Game

The stare-down between the White House and Congress over the Guantanamo prison's future continues. Obama, in introducing his latest plan to close the detention facility in February, put the blame squarely on Congress for the failure to do so. Noting that after he was elected in 2008 "the public was scared into thinking that, well, if we close it, somehow we'll be less safe," he added that since that time, "Congress has repeatedly imposed restrictions aimed at preventing us from closing this facility."[92]

Some civil rights groups, however, say that while Congress bears much of the responsibility, the president ultimately is responsible for the intractable situation.

"Congress is never going to work with the president on closing Guantanamo, so I blame President Obama," says Dixon of the Center for Constitutional Rights. "There are number of things that the president could be doing, that he should be doing, but that he has been unwilling to do."

For example, Dixon notes that the Supreme Court has ruled that federal courts could order transfers. That means, Dixon says, Obama could simply ask a judge to order the transfers of detainees who have already been cleared by the Periodic Review Board — 20 currently are eligible.*[93]

Stimson, however, blames both sides. "Congress has done nothing to pass a law to work with the administration, nor has the administration worked much with Congress, despite repeated promises to do so, to draft a workable long-term detainment policy," he says. Referring to the "Peanuts" comic strip, he says, "It has been this sort of Charlie Brown with Lucy and the football scenario. Sometimes the Republicans are Lucy, sometimes the Democrats are Lucy, but Gitmo is the football. It's just a political hot potato, to mix metaphors."

Other conservatives say the United States should be sending even more prisoners to Guantanamo. "In my opinion, the only problem of Guantanamo Bay is there are too many empty beds and cells there right now," said Cotton, the senator from Arkansas. "We should be sending more terrorists there for further interrogation to keep this country safe. As far as I'm concerned, every last one

* The Periodic Review Board consists of senior officials from the departments of Defense, Home-land Security, Justice and State; the Joint Staff; and the Office of the Director of National Intelligence. It reviews whether continued detention of a detainee remains necessary.

of them can rot in hell, but as long as they don't do that, then they can rot in Guantanamo Bay!"[94]

Sen. Ted Cruz, R-Texas, agrees. "Don't shut down Gitmo — expand it, and let's have some new terrorists there," he said in February.[95]

While the debate continues, experts advocating a tough approach to national security warn that current policies are hamstringing U.S. forces and hurting their efforts to gather intelligence.

Stimson says that when U.S. troops encounter people in battle zones who could be of use in the terrorism fight, they are turning them over to other nations instead of interrogating them. "What is happening is that when our Special Forces . . . come upon a high-value target who we would like to chat with for a long time in a lawful way, we're not doing that," he says. "We're turning them over to surrogates, and that has all sorts of . . . potential negative consequences."

Rivkin of the Foundation for Defense of Democracies points to a related problem. "We're not detaining anybody, so we are relying on third parties — Saudis or Egyptians or whatever — to detain people," he says. "So there are a bunch of people with the blood of American troops on their hands walking around today because we had no place to bring them. That's a crazy way to fight a war."

OUTLOOK
Finding an End Game

As with many other issues, the fate of the Guantanamo Bay detention facility will likely depend on the general election in November. "As with all things, a new administration, new members of Congress, I think an overall resetting of some key relationships could matter," says Kathleen Hicks, director of the International Security Program at the Center for Strategic and International Studies, a Washington think tank.

"If you get a Democratic president and a Democratic Congress, I think we can begin to think more seriously about completely closing Gitmo," says Margulies of Roger Williams University.

Any other outcome than a Democratic sweep, however, is likely to have uncertain consequences for Guantanamo detainees.

"If Trump is the president, it's anybody's guess," says the Heritage Foundation's Stimson. "I have no way of predicting what he is going to do or say next."

Trump said in February that he would make more, not less, use of Guantanamo Bay's detention facilities. "We're going to load it up with some bad dudes, believe me — we're going to load it up," he said at a rally.[96]

Trump went even further in August when he told a reporter that he was "fine" with prosecuting U.S. citizens at Guantanamo, an act that would be illegal under current law.[97]

Clinton has come out strongly in favor of closing the detention facilities. In a statement issued in February, she said she wanted to "finally close the door on this chapter of our history." Noting that she had also supported the prison's closure as a senator and as secretary of State, she said that "closing Guantanamo would be a sign of strength and resolve."[98]

With respect to the military commissions, "I don't see any political will for addressing the issues at the military commissions," says James G. Connell III, a defense attorney at the Military Commissions Defense Organization, a unit of the Defense Department's Office of Military Commissions. "I believe the military commissions experiment will continue until a political leader has the strength and insight to declare it a failure."

Regardless of the election outcome, experts are doubtful about the potential for reaching an international consensus on how to deal with captured nonstate combatants.

"I don't think there's consensus, and forging that takes quite a bit of time," says Dru Brenner-Beck, president of the National Institute for Military Justice, a Washington-based advocacy group focused on military justice. "I don't think you're going to see any agreed-upon 'go back to the drawing board' again on the Geneva Conventions."

But Dixon, of the Center for Constitutional Rights, says a general international consensus exists — it's just that the United States disagrees with it.

"When it comes to the laws of war, the United States is now an outlier, and not just in the detention context, but also when it comes to targeted killings, drones and the use of force," he says. "That has dangerous repercussions, not only for the United States but for also for the development of international humanitarian law."

As a practical matter, some experts warn that, regardless of legal considerations, continuing to hold detainees at Guantanamo may not be a wise move.

Noting that the current conflicts may have no formal end, Mora said that continuing to hold prisoners "creates a position in which we're caught uncomfortably holding people indefinitely without any possibility of release," he says. "That should make Americans uncomfortable."

Former diplomat Pickering agrees. "There's nothing that says you have to detain prisoners of war until the end of the war," he says.

NOTES

1. "U.S. official: "No coincidence" Islamic State victims in Guantanamo-like jumpsuits," Reuters, Yahoo News, Feb. 5, 2015, http://tinyurl.com/gpkyq6d.

2. "Testimony of Brian P. McKeon," Senate Committee on Armed Services, Feb, 5, 2015, http://tinyurl.com/hu6h7ff.

3. "Remarks by the President on Plan to Close the Prison at Guantanamo Bay," the White House, Feb. 23, 2016, http://tinyurl.com/h5smemv.

4. "Welcome to Naval Station Guantanamo Bay," U.S. Navy, http://tinyurl.com/gmq5jul.

5. S. A. Miller, "Clinton backs GITMO closure, hedges on bringing detainees to S.C.," *The Washington Times*, Feb. 23, 2016, http://tinyurl.com/hgfndov; "Trump: Load Guantanamo Bay Up with 'Bad Dudes,' " YouTube, Feb. 23, 2016, http://tinyurl.com/gpnsvtj.

6. Damian Paletta and Nick Timiraos, "Trump Reverses His Stance on Torture," *The Wall Street Journal*, March 4, 2016, http://tinyurl.com/jhabfhk.

7. "The Guantanamo Docket," *The New York Times*, http://tinyurl.com/zm7bl3p.

8. "Summary of the Reengagement of Detainees Formerly Held at Guantanamo Bay," Office of the Director of National Intelligence, http://tinyurl.com/jkxa8ms.

9. "15 Guantanamo Bay prisoners held without charge transferred to UAE," The Associated Press, *Chicago Tribune*, Aug. 15, 2016, http://tinyurl.com/zg7po2f.

10. *Ibid.*

11. Tom LoBianco, "CNN/ORC poll: Americans oppose plan to close Guantanamo Bay prison," CNN, March 4, 2016, http://tinyurl.com/h8mh524.

12. CNN/ORC poll, Jan. 12-15, 2009, http://tinyurl.com/l75kjv.

13. "Guantanamo Bay — Camp Delta," GlobalSecurity.org, http://tinyurl.com/8050.

14. "Committee Study of the Central Intelligence Agency's Detention and Interrogation Program, Senate Select Committee on Intelligence, April 3, 2014, p. 16, http://tinyurl.com/jd8kuop.

15. Connie Bruck, "Why Obama Has Failed to Close Guantanamo," *The New Yorker*, Aug. 1, 2016, http://tinyurl.com/z8zueed.

16. H.R. 6523 — Ike Skeleton National Authorization Act For Fiscal Year 2011, Congress.gov, Jan. 1, 2011, http://tinyurl.com/hjnwyye.

17. Missy Ryan and Adam Goldman, "Obama asks lawmakers to lift obstacles to closing prison at Guantanamo Bay," *The Washington Post*, Feb. 23, 2016, http://tinyurl.com/h82dj6k.

18. Karoun Demirjian, "Top Republicans slam Obama's plan to close Guantanamo," *The Washington Post,* Feb. 23, 2016, http://tinyurl.com/z7gamxc.

19. Hannah Fairfield and Tim Wallace, "The Terrorists in U.S. Prisons," *The New York Times*, April 7, 2016, http://tinyurl.com/jd4hvlk.

20. For background, see Kenneth Jost, "Prosecuting Terrorists," *CQ Researcher*, March 12, 2010, pp. 217-240.

21. "Up to Speed," Pacific Council on International Policy, February 2016, p. 12, http://tinyurl.com/js4wv9g.

22. Statement of Rep. Jackie Speier, Armed Services Committee Subcommittee on Oversight and Investigations hearing, Feb. 12, 2015, http://tinyurl.com/jznzmpe.

23. Statement of Rep. Vicky Hartzler, Armed Services Committee Subcommittee on Oversight and Investigations hearing, Feb. 12, 2015, http://tinyurl.com/jznzmpe.

24. David Weigel, "Tom Cotton on the Guantanamo Terrorists Who Can 'Rot in Hell,' " Bloomberg Politics, Feb. 5, 2015, http://tinyurl.com/kva2gkj.

25. See Peter Katel and Kenneth Jost, "Treatment of Detainees," *CQ Researcher*, Aug. 25, 2006, pp. 673-696.

26. Duraid Adnan and Tim Arango, "Iraq Shuts Down the Abu Ghraib Prison, Citing Security Concerns," *The New York Times*, April 15, 2014, http://tinyurl.com/hzpxjvt.

27. Statement of Rep. Adam Smith, "Closing Guantanamo: The National Security, Fiscal, and Human Rights Implications," Senate Judiciary Subcommittee on the Constitution, Civil Rights, and Human Rights, July 24, 2013, http://tinyurl.com/jf2wb9j.

28. Statement of Lee S. Wolosky, House Foreign Affairs Committee hearing, July 7, 2016, http://tinyurl.com/zgofty4.

29. "Address of Pope Francis to the Delegates of the International Association of Penal Law," the Vatican, Oct. 23, 2014, http://tinyurl.com/kls86w3.

30. "Pope Francis offers US help in closing Guantanamo," AFP, Dec. 15, 2014, http://tinyurl.com/zauqmp8.

31. "The relevance of IHL in the context of terrorism," International Committee of the Red Cross, Jan. 1, 2011, http://tinyurl.com/hgykaqh.

32. The Third Geneva Convention stipulates that to qualify for POW status, captured combatants must, among other things, have "a fixed distinctive sign recognizable at a distance," have been carrying arms openly and have conducted operations in accordance with the laws and customs of war. See "Convention (III) relative to the treatment of prisoners of war," International Committee of the Red Cross, http://tinyurl.com/hgmrju8.

33. Richard A. Serrano, "U.S. Will Apply Geneva Rules to Taliban Fighters," *Los Angeles Times*, Feb. 8, 2002, http://tinyurl.com/h9gss54.

34. George W. Bush, "Fact Sheet: Status of Detainees at Guantanamo," Feb. 7, 2002; online by Gerhard Peters and John T. Woolley, The American Presidency Project, http://tinyurl.com/hgk6295.

35. *Rasul et al. v. Bush*, President of the United States, June 28, 2004, http://tinyurl.com/jnx8g8y.

36. Susan Seligson, "Guantanamo: The Legal Mess Behind the Ethical Mess," *BU Today*, May 28, 2013, http://tinyurl.com/zvpvdwl.

37. *Ibid.*

38. "The Guantanamo Docket," *op. cit.*

39. Office of the Director of National Intelligence, *op. cit.*

40. Adam Goldman and Missy Ryan, "At least 12 released Guantanamo detainees implicated in attacks on Americans," *The Washington Post*, June 8, 2016, http://tinyurl.com/j4pcp2c.

41. Adam Goldman, "Former Guantanamo detainee implicated in Benghazi Attack," *The Washington Post*, Jan. 7, 2014, http://tinyurl.com/hfp7a6r. Also see Kenneth Jost, "Unrest in the Arab World," *CQ Researcher*, Feb. 1, 2013, pp. 105-132.

42. Goldman and Ryan, *op. cit.*

43. Statement of Rep. Edward R. Royce, House Foreign Affairs Committee hearing, July 7, 2016, http://tinyurl.com/joxaxsq.

44. Office of the Director of National Intelligence, *op. cit.*

45. Statement of Lee S. Wolosky, *op. cit.*

46. Arthur Herman, "Why Hasn't Obama Closed Gitmo?" *Commentary Magazine*, March 23, 2015, http://tinyurl.com/hjtfl6x.

47. Public Law 111-383, 111th Congress, Jan. 7, 2011, http://tinyurl.com/hvc8jkw.

48. Jennifer K. Elsea and Michael John Garcia, "Wartime Detention Provisions in Recent Defense Authorization Legislation," Congressional Research Service, March 12, 2016, p. 31, http://tinyurl.com/hbdvmrz.

49. Karoun Demirjian, "House Votes to block Guantanamo detainee transfers, even to other countries," *The Washington Post*, June 16, 2016, http://tinyurl.com/jpqvzmm.

50. Journals of the Continental Congress, June 30, 1775, Library of Congress, http://tinyurl.com/jbyqchl.

51. "To George Washington from a Board of General Officers, Founders Online, National Archives, June 2, 1778, http://tinyurl.com/gm3tkb6.

52. Louis Fisher, "Military Tribunals: Historical Patterns and Lessons," Congressional Research Service, July 9, 2004, p. 8, http://tinyurl.com/jbal5av.

53. *Ibid.*, p. 9.

54. Military Commissions History, Office of Military Commissions, http://tinyurl.com/j66hrjd.

55. Fisher, *op. cit.*, p. 12.

56. Military Commissions History, *op. cit.*

57. Fisher, *op. cit.*, p. 37.

58. *Ibid.*

59. Military Commissions History, *op. cit.*

60. Joint Resolution, Authorization to Use Military Force Against Terrorists, Public Law 107–40 107th Congress, Sept. 18, 2001, http://tinyurl.com/jgoyhty.

61. "Detention, Treatment, and Trial of Certain Non-Citizens in the War Against Terrorism," the White House, Nov. 13, 2001, http://tinyurl.com/zqrvck5.

62. Allan A. Ryan, *The 9/11 Terror Cases: Constitutional Challenges in the War Against Al-Qaeda* (2015), p. 3.

63. "Cheney: Gitmo holds 'worst of the worst,' " NBC News, http://tinyurl.com/znha9hd.

64. Ryan, *op. cit.*, p. 8.

65. Bruck, *op. cit.*

66. Jennifer K. Elsea, "Comparison of Rights in Military Commission Trials and Trials in Federal Criminal Court," Congressional Research Service, March 21, 2014, p. 7, http://tinyurl.com/hr5sf3c.

67. *Ibid.*

68. Karen J. Greenberg, *Rogue Justice: The Making of the Security State* (2016), p. 47.

69. *Rasul v. Bush*, *op. cit.*

70. Josh White, "Impact of Detainee Act Debated in Court," *The Washington Post*, March 23, 2006, http://tinyurl.com/jrrp67s.

71. *Hamdan v. Rumsfeld*, 2006, Supreme Court of the United States, http://tinyurl.com/j5yk4z8.

72. Military Commissions Act of 2006, Oct. 17, 2006, http://tinyurl.com/zsabt92.

73. *Boumediene v. Bush*, 2007, Supreme Court of the United States, http://tinyurl.com/jsx28hy.

74. Peter Finn, "Obama Seeks Halt to Legal Proceedings at Guantanamo," *The Washington Post*, Jan. 21, 2009, http://tinyurl.com/9cu67o.

75. William Glaberson, "Obama to Keep Tribunals; Stance Angers Some Backers," *The New York Times*, May 15, 2009, http://tinyurl.com/owb8v6.

76. "Obama resurrects military trials for terror suspects," CNN, May 15, 2009, http://tinyurl.com/zjz7kk5.

77. *Ibid.*

78. Michael John Garcia *et al.*, "Closing the Guantanamo Detention Center: Legal Issues," Congressional Research Service, May 30, 2013, http://tinyurl.com/ppozmpb.

79. *Ibid.*

80. "Executive Order: Periodic Review of Individuals Detained at Guantanamo Bay Naval Station Pursuant to the Authorization for Use of Military Force," the White House, March 7, 2011, http://tinyurl.com/jv2a58x.

81. Peter Finn and Anne E. Kornblut, "Obama creates indefinite detention system for prisoners at Guantanamo Bay," *The Washington Post*, March 7, 2011, http://tinyurl.com/j4dxkqp.

82. National Defense Authorization Act for Fiscal Year 2012, http://tinyurl.com/hfnu7fx.

83. "US: Refusal to Veto Detainee Bill a Historic Tragedy for Rights," Human Rights Watch, Dec. 14, 2011, http://tinyurl.com/jpz5fxp.

84. "Plan for Closing the Guantanamo Bay Detention Facility," the White House, 2016, http://tinyurl.com/zym6zaa.

85. Jordan Fabian and Kristina Wong, "President's last-ditch Gitmo plan falls flat," *The Hill*, Feb.23, 2016, http://tinyurl.com/zulmtl8.

86. Charlie Savage, "Obama administration seeks flexibility for Guantanamo trials," *The New York Times*, April 21, 2016, http://tinyurl.com/hvv9z6d.

87. *Ibid.*

88. *Ibid.*

89. John H. Cushman Jr., "Appeals Court Overturns Terrorism Conviction of Bin Laden's Driver," *The New York Times*, Oct. 16, 2012, http://tinyurl.com/hydleav.

90. Julian Hattem, "Court overturns military commission ruling on Gitmo detainee," *The Hill*, June 12, 2015, http://tinyurl.com/zubx6aw.

91. For background, see Kenneth Jost, "Police Misconduct," *CQ Researcher*, April 6, 2012, pp. 301-324.

92. "Remarks by the President on Plan to Close the Prison at Guantanamo Bay," the White House, Feb. 23, 2016, http://tinyurl.com/h5smemv.

93. "The Guantanamo Docket," *op. cit.*

94. Weigel, *op. cit.*

95. Karoun Demirjian, "Top Republicans slam Obama's plan to close Guantanamo," *The Washington Post*, Feb. 23, 2016, http://tinyurl.com/z7gamxc.

96. Dan Bloom, "President Donald Trump would reopen Guantanamo Bay and 'load it up with bad dudes,' " *The Mirror*, Feb. 24, 2016, http://tinyurl.com/h6ha5kw.

97. Charlie Savage, "Donald Trump 'fine' with prosecuting U.S. citizens at Guantanamo," *The New York Times*, Aug. 13, 2016, http://tinyurl.com/ztg969k.

98. "Statement from Hillary Clinton on Guantanamo Bay," http://tinyurl.com/j5zm64y.

BIBLIOGRAPHY

Selected Sources

Books

Greenberg, Karen J., *Rogue Justice: The Making of the Security State*, Crown Publishers, 2016.
The director of the Center on National Security at Fordham University's School of Law argues that the U.S. "war on terror" has led to an assault on the rule of law.

Rosenberg, Carol, *Guantánamo Bay: The Pentagon's Alcatraz of the Caribbean*, Herald Books, 2016.
A *Miami Herald* reporter who has covered Guantanamo Bay since the detention facility opened in 2002 offers her perspective on the people and policies that have resulted in what she describes as the first U.S. military enterprise without an exit strategy since the Vietnam War.

Said, Wadie E., *Crimes of Terror: The Legal and Political Implications of Federal Terrorism Prosecutions*, Oxford University Press, 2015.

A University of South Carolina law professor explains what he sees as the growing tendency of the U.S. government to categorize individuals as terrorism suspects and to withhold longstanding constitutional protections from them.

Articles

Bruck, Connie, "Why Obama Has Failed to Close Guantánamo," *The New Yorker*, Aug. 1, 2016, http://tinyurl.com/z8zueed.
A journalist argues that President Obama's administration has missed opportunities to fulfill his pledge of closing the prison.

Herman, Arthur, "Why Hasn't Obama Closed Gitmo?" *Commentary*, March 23, 2015, http://tinyurl.com/hjtfl6x.
A senior fellow at the conservative Hudson Institute think tank examines the conflicts between Obama and Congress over closing Guantanamo and says the president must "see the sense of keeping Gitmo open."

Nelson, Rebecca and Sarah Mimms, "Why the White House Wants an AUMF, and Why It's Not Going to Happen," *The Atlantic*, Dec. 8, 2015, http://tinyurl.com/zbckg7n.
Two journalists explore the politics behind the debate over whether Congress should pass a new authorization to use military force to deal with the threat of the Islamic State.

Demirjian, Karoun, "Top Republicans slam Obama's plan to close Guantánamo," *The Washington Post*, Feb. 23, 2016, http://tinyurl.com/z7gamxc.
A reporter chronicles Republican opposition to Obama's plan to close Guantanamo, which includes bringing some detainees to the U.S. mainland despite congressional prohibitions.

Gillin, Joel, "Obama Isn't Ready to Give Up His Broad War Powers," *The New Republic*, Feb. 12, 2015, http://tinyurl.com/hebx5l7.
A writer for the liberal magazine finds fault with Obama's approach of asking Congress to authorize military force to defeat the Islamic State.

Rosenberg, Carol, "A Look at Guantánamo Bay prison, then and now," *The Miami Herald*, Jan. 11, 2015, http://tinyurl.com/q7cgu56.
A reporter who has covered the Guantanamo detention facility since it opened describes how conditions for prisoners have changed over 15 years. The article includes a video.

Ryan, Missy, "The Guantánamo quagmire: Still no trial in sight for 9/11 suspects," *The Washington Post*, Sept. 6, 2016, http://tinyurl.com/hytamsw.
A reporter describes the obstacles to putting Guantanamo detainees on trial.

Reports and Studies

"Up to Speed," Pacific Council on International Policy, February 2016, http://tinyurl.com/js4wv9g.
A Los Angeles-based think tank examines delays in the trials of detainees before the military commissions at Guantanamo and recommends putting federal judges in charge.

Elsea, Jennifer K., "Comparison of Rights in Military Commission Trials and Trials in Federal Criminal Court," Congressional Research Service, March 21, 2014, http://tinyurl.com/hr5sf3c.
A report by the research arm of Congress compares the rights afforded to defendants in military commission trials and those tried in federal courts.

Elsea, Jennifer K., and Michael John Garcia, "Wartime Detention Provisions in Recent Defense Authorization Legislation," Congressional Research Service, March 14, 2016, http://tinyurl.com/hbdvmrz.
Two research analysts detail the congressional limitations on the transfer of Guantanamo Bay prisoners to the custody of other countries.

On the Web

"Guantánamo," *The Miami Herald*, http://tinyurl.com/oyx2od6.
A newspaper website provides background articles on Guantanamo detainees.

"The Guantánamo Docket," *The New York Times*, http://tinyurl.com/6h8xka.
A newspaper website provides documents and research on Guantanamo detainees.

For More Information

American Civil Liberties Union, 125 Broad St., 18th Floor, New York, NY 10004; 212-284-7387; www.aclu.org. National organization focused on defending constitutional rights and liberties.

Center for Constitutional Rights, 666 Broadway, 7th Floor, New York, NY 10012; 212-614-6464; www.ccrjustice .org. Policy group focused on protecting rights outlined in the Constitution and the United Nations Universal Declaration of Human Rights.

Center for Strategic and International Studies, 1800 K St., N.W., Washington, DC 20006; 202-887-0200; www .csis.org. Centrist think tank that offers bipartisan proposals on U.S. security issues.

Foundation for the Defense of Democracies, P.O. Box 33249, Washington, DC 20033; 202-207-0190; www. defenddemocracy.org. Think tank focusing on foreign policy and national security.

Heritage Foundation, 214 Massachusetts Ave., N.E., Washington, DC 20002; 202-546-4400; www.heritage.org. Conservative public policy think tank.

Human Rights First, 805 15th St., N.W., Suite 900, Washington, DC 20005; 202-547-5692; www.humanrights first.org/. Advocacy group focusing on human rights and the rule of law.

National Institute of Military Justice, 4801 Massachusetts Ave., N.W., Washington, DC 20016; 202-274-4322; www .nimj.org. Military lawyers' organization focusing on the military justice system.

U.S. Office of Military Commissions, 4800 Mark Center Dr., Suite 11F09-02, Alexandria, VA 22350; www.mc.mil/ home.aspx. Department of Defense office responsible for conducting trials of Guantanamo detainees.

16 Protecting the Power Grid

Kevin Begos

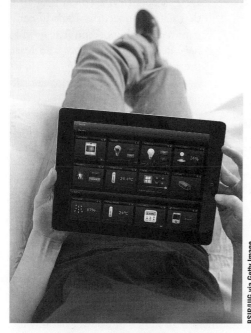

The use of home automation technology, such as handheld devices that can be used to control household systems, is making it harder to secure the nation's power grid, experts say. Some devices have security flaws, potentially enabling foreign governments, criminals and others to gain access to power plant computer systems.

From *CQ Researcher,*
November 11, 2016.

The number is eye-opening — 3.8 million. That's how many times in an eight-week period last year that hackers infiltrated the computer systems of a consortium of small utilities known as the Nebraska Municipal Power Pool. The intrusions ranged from reconnaissance probes to attempts to plant viruses. "I was surprised and concerned to see the high number and severity of threats hitting our network on a daily basis," said Bob Selzer, director of retail utility services at Nebraska Municipal.[1]

The network serves 200 communities in six Midwestern and Rocky Mountain states. Some of the member utilities have fewer than 1,000 customers and employ only one part-time IT worker, making the network an inviting target for hackers.[2]

Nebraska Municipal is far from alone in its vulnerability. The U.S. power grid's vast size and aging equipment make the system highly susceptible to both cyber and physical attacks on its transformers, substations and power lines by saboteurs or terrorists, officials say.[3]

"We basically built a system on quicksand," says Joe Weiss, a partner at Applied Control Systems, a San Francisco company that analyzes and consults on security issues, and "it's sinking."

Many top intelligence officials and independent experts say foreign governments, criminals and lone hackers increasingly are targeting the power grid in the United States and elsewhere, but it is difficult to trace or identify the individuals responsible, and no comprehensive tally of attacks exists. Unlike attacks from suicide bombers, planes or missiles, the identity, location or even motives of cyberattackers can be hard to verify.

Power Grid and Energy Sector Targeted

Cyberattackers targeted the energy sector at higher rates than other critical U.S. infrastructure in 2014. Of the 245 cyber incidents reported, 32 percent occurred in the energy sector, which includes electricity, petroleum and natural gas. The second-highest was critical manufacturing, with 27 percent.

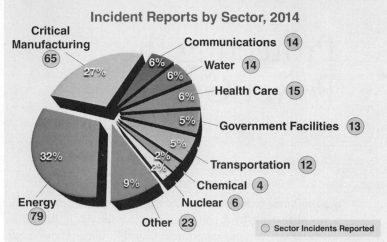

Incident Reports by Sector, 2014

Critical Manufacturing 65 — 27%
Communications 14 — 6%
Water 14 — 6%
Health Care 15 — 6%
Government Facilities 13 — 5%
Transportation 12 — 5%
Chemical 4 — 2%
Nuclear 6 — 2%
Other 23 — 9%
Energy 79 — 32%

○ Sector Incidents Reported

Notes: Incident reports involve cybersecurity threats or attacks made against the computer control systems of critical infrastructure. These reports were filed with the U.S. Industrial Control Systems Cyber Emergency Response Team (ICS-CERT), an agency within the Department of Homeland Security. The data are not comprehensive and understate the number of cyber incidents; security officials believe the actual numbers are far higher.

Source: "ICS-CERT Year in Review," Industrial Control Systems Cyber Emergency Response Team, 2014, p. 6, http://tinyurl.com/gv73ozo

The growing use of a computerized "smart grid," where sensors replace human meter readers to gather data and communicate digitally with a utility's operations center, adds to the challenges. "As we become more interconnected, and we start having iPads on the operations floor, we've created a connectivity-based environment" that can be disrupted without needing to create sophisticated computer viruses or code, says Robert Lee, a former Air Force cybersecurity officer who co-founded Dragos Security, a consulting firm that sells cybersecurity tools to companies and others. "You just need to have access to the system and learn the system," he says.

In a worst-case scenario, coordinated attacks on the U.S. electrical grid could cause massive economic losses and perhaps widespread illness or death.

But that level of attack — the equivalent of an act of war — is unlikely, many analysts say. They note the grid is sprawling and has no single command center controlling it. Divided into three major sections — Eastern, Western and Texas, along with smaller interconnected regional sections — the grid consists of more than 300,000 miles of transmission lines that carry power from 9,200 generating stations to homes and businesses. To knock out power nationwide, a hostile nation or group would have to target specific regions and mount numerous coordinated attacks throughout the United States.

"Yes, there is a risk to the electric grid from a cyberattack, but that threat is nowhere near the levels of fear, uncertainty and doubt being peddled by policymakers, threat-reduction firms and cyberwar hawks," a contributor to *Foreign Policy* wrote, adding that squirrels have historically caused more damage to power lines (by gnawing through them) than cyberattacks.[6]

"Energy firms and public utilities in many nations have had their networks compromised" by cyberattacks from foreign states, Adm. Michael S. Rogers, director of the National Security Agency (NSA) and commander of the U.S. Cyber Command, told a congressional committee in September 2015.[4]

At another congressional hearing in November 2014, Rogers said attackers who get inside computer systems could "tell power turbines to go offline and stop generating power." Not only that, Rogers said, but the threat extends beyond hostile nation-states: "We're going to be dealing with groups, with individuals . . . with a capability that is relatively inexpensive and so easy to acquire, very unlike the nuclear kind of model."[5]

Nevertheless, the private sector and the U.S. military are devoting significant resources to defend against or respond to attacks. Several research firms estimate that U.S. utilities will spend more than $7 billion on security between 2013 and 2020. Companies such as Microsoft and IBM are promising improved security in their products, and smaller security firms are developing software designed to help utility companies find vulnerabilities in their computer systems.[7]

"These are serious threats," says Scott Aaronson, executive director of security and business continuity for the Edison Electric Institute, a group in Washington that represents major electric companies that provide power to 220 million people in all 50 states. "We are constantly evolving and learning from experiences. It is about constantly improving your security, your reliability and your [ability]" to survive an attack.

According to surveys, a majority of experts and the public agree with Aaronson that the threat should be taken seriously. In a January 2016 poll, 84 percent of cybersecurity professionals believed there was a high or medium likelihood of a cybersecurity attack occurring this year that would be serious enough to disrupt critical U.S. infrastructure such as the electric grid. And a Gallup Poll in February found that 73 percent of American adults feel that cyberterrorism — the use of computers to cause disruption or fear in society — will be a critical threat to the nation's vital interests over the next 10 years.[8]

Securing the U.S. power grid against a cyber or physical attack will not be easy because of its size, age and decentralized organizational structure — about 90 percent of the grid is privately owned. And "much of the infrastructure which serves the U.S. power grid is aging . . . with power transformers averaging over 40 years of age, and 70 percent of transmission lines being 25 years old or older," Richard Campbell, an energy policy specialist at the nonpartisan Congressional Research Service, told a congressional committee in April.[9]

M. Granger Morgan, a Carnegie Mellon University professor of engineering who is an expert on the electrical system, said, "We've known we had an issue for a long time and have been very slow to do anything about it."[10]

"The utilities don't have a good handle on [the cyber threat] in my opinion — but they're getting there," says Lee.

Then-House Intelligence Committee Chairman Mike Rogers, R-Mich., said in 2014 that the electric industry and most other critical infrastructure providers "are doing their best to better secure their networks, but if they get attacked by an adversary with the resources and capabilities of a nation-state like China, it certainly isn't a fair fight."[11]

In response to the cyber threat against the power grid and other sectors, President Obama in February announced the Cybersecurity National Action Plan to help government agencies, businesses and the public prevent and respond to attacks. The initiative includes $19 billion in the fiscal 2017 budget for cybersecurity, but critics say the plan does not go far enough. "As a nation, we are spending more on cybersecurity today than at any time in our history, while simultaneously continuing to witness an increasing number of successful cyberattacks and breaches," said Ron Ross, a fellow at the National Institute of Standards and Technology, a federal laboratory, who has more than 30 years of computer security experience.[12]

The U.S. military has created a Cyber Command, training thousands of personnel to conduct both defensive and offensive operations against hackers, and the Department of Energy (DOE) and federal agencies are providing technical support to the power industry.

Hackers and saboteurs don't pose the only threats to the power grid. Massive electromagnetic pulses (EMP) from solar flares or the detonation of a high-altitude nuclear bomb can also cause massive outages.

Chris Currie, director of emergency management and national preparedness issues at the Government Accountability Office (GAO) in Atlanta, told Congress last May that either one "could have a significant impact on the nation's electric grid as well as other infrastructure sectors that depend on electricity. . . . The impact of these events could lead to power outages over broad geographic areas for extended durations."[13]

In a separate report, the GAO found that the Department of Homeland Security recognizes that "space weather and power grid failure are significant risk events, [which] pose great risk to the security of the nation."[14]

Peter Vincent Pry, executive director of the Task Force on National and Homeland Security, a privately funded

Experts See Possibility of Cyberattack

Eighty-four percent of cybersecurity professionals said in January they believed there would be a high or medium likelihood of a cybersecurity attack in the United States this year that would disrupt critical infrastructure. The country's critical infrastructure includes the electrical grid and water supply systems.

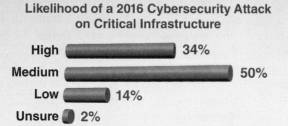

Likelihood of a 2016 Cybersecurity Attack on Critical Infrastructure

High — 34%
Medium — 50%
Low — 14%
Unsure — 2%

Source: "January 2016 Cybersecurity Snapshot US Results," ISACA, January 2016, http://tinyurl.com/zz9bwbo

effort backed by members of Congress, says the country isn't prepared for EMP damage or coordinated cyberattacks. "These things are always characterized as 1 percent [probability] until they happen," he says, noting that "military doctrine and exercises by Russia, China, North Korea and Iran for cyberwarfare include sabotage and EMP attack."

As security officials, the electric industry and politicians debate the threats facing the power grid, here are some of the questions they are asking:

Is the U.S. power grid vulnerable to major attack?

Inadequately protected power plants. Snipers opening fire on transformers. Hackers breaching computer control systems. Nation-states attacking the grid. Security professionals say the list of vulnerabilities is long and worrisome. Yet skeptics caution that most saboteurs, hackers and terrorists lack the ability to cause widespread damage.

Lee of Dragos Security says the worst-case scenario — a combined physical and cyberattack on the grid — would be very difficult to pull off. "The combined cyber-physical attack is way more complex than folks believe, but if it were achieved . . . it would cause significant challenges," Lee says. "So it's realistic enough" to prepare for, and some countries are very worried about it, he says, but "unlikely enough to feel comfortable" about the actual risk of such attacks.

Aaronson of the Edison Electric Institute said "there are a lot of threats to the grid . . . from squirrels to nation-states. And frankly, there have been more blackouts as a result of squirrels than there are from nation-states."[15]

A 2015 report from the Department of Energy found that large transformers, which convert a power plant's electricity to a higher voltage for long-distance transmission and can weigh hundreds of tons, are among the parts of the grid most vulnerable to attacks from saboteurs. The report also found that transmission lines have high vulnerability to physical attacks, and that electric substations and control centers are vulnerable to both physical and cyberattacks.[16] While the United States has "never experienced simultaneous failures of multiple high-voltage transformers," the report said, such attacks could disrupt electric services over a large area.

A confidential Federal Energy Regulatory Commission (FERC) report went even further, suggesting that carefully coordinated attacks using rifles or explosives on just nine key substations in various regions could cause an extended blackout over large areas.[17]

In April 2013, an attack on the Metcalf electric substation near San Jose, Calif., raised alarms among industry experts. The attackers cut phone cables in the early-morning hours, then fired about 100 shots at the substation, knocking 17 transformers offline and causing millions of dollars in damage. The FBI is still investigating, but no arrests have been made. Jon Wellinghoff, a former FERC chairman, said it was "the most significant incident of domestic terrorism involving the grid that has ever occurred" and that "what keeps me awake at night is a physical attack that could take down the grid."[18] But despite the precision of the Metcalf attack, power companies avoided blackouts by re-routing transmissions and getting electricity from other plants.

A 2016 audit of the Western Area Power Administration, which serves 15 states in the central and western United States, also found significant vulnerabilities. "Western had not placed sufficient emphasis on physical security," the Department of Energy said. It "lacked specific policies and procedures for maintaining security equipment, controlling access keys, implementing risk assessment recommendations and conducting performance tests."[19] Western officials agreed to increase security but wondered where funding would come from, "based on how little the regions had spent on physical security in the past."

Cost is an important issue in grid security because power companies must seek approval, generally from public utility commissions, for new infrastructure or rate increases. And experts disagree over the best way to secure electricity infrastructure; debates over the likelihood of major attacks complicate funding requests.

Aaronson says the industry relies on a "defense-in-depth" strategy to protect the grid that involves close coordination among industry and government partners and mandatory regulations for cyber and physical security. The industry, he says, also conducts training exercises; one example was "Grid Ex III" in 2015, where participants practiced responding to combined cyber- and physical attacks. And 54 utilities are participating in programs to maintain and share spare transformers and other vital equipment in the event of a major attack, according to the institute.[20]

However, the Energy Department said that as of 2015, inventory under the transformer program was "not large enough . . . to respond to a large, coordinated attack."[21] Replacing large transformers can take months or even more than a year.

In September, an unknown attacker fired three shots into a Utah transformer, knocking out power for about eight hours to 13,000 people in two counties. "Just from the looks of it, it looked more criminal than vandalism because they knew exactly where to shoot it, and they shot it multiple times in the same spot," said Neal Brown, a spokesman for Garkane Energy Cooperative, whose equipment was damaged. A portable transformer temporarily replaced the damaged unit, and the rural cooperative offered a $50,000 reward for information leading to an arrest and conviction.[22]

Ben Miller, a Dragos partner and former top cyber security coordinator for the Electricity Information Sharing and Analysis Center, a government-industry effort, says it's unlikely that snipers could wreak widespread havoc — and law enforcement would have more than the electric grid to worry about if attackers did possess such capabilities.

"[A] half-dozen teams of well-trained snipers have a lot more targets than the electric grid," he says. "If you have a hypothetical small army in position, then you could come up with any daydream scenario including storming the White House."

Is the U.S. power grid vulnerable to major failure from natural disasters?

Power companies have long had to wrestle with floods, hurricanes and earthquakes, but experts say climate change is making natural disasters even more frequent and dangerous.

Secretary of Energy Ernest Moniz told members of Congress that "we are seeing a rise in extreme weather events that are projected to increase in frequency and intensity. These events have regional and at times national-scale impacts on our energy infrastructures."

Billion-dollar weather events have risen dramatically in the past 15 years, he said, and if sea levels reach predicted levels by 2030, "the number of electricity substations in the Gulf of Mexico exposed to storm surge from Category 1 hurricanes could increase from 255 to 337; by 2050 the number would rise to roughly 400."[23]

A 2015 report from the DOE found that climate change and higher temperatures could reduce hydropower in the West because of smaller snowpacks, increase electricity demand almost everywhere as temperatures rise and damage electric grid infrastructure through increased floods, storms and wildfires.[24]

And then there is the threat of geomagnetic solar storms (GMDs) — sudden eruptions emanating from the sun that send powerful waves of magnetic pulses toward Earth. Such storms can produce electrical surges in the grid, leading to blackouts. For many government agencies, this threat is serious; but for some research scientists, the probability of a solar storm devastating the grid is low.[25]

A 2012 report from the National Intelligence Council called solar storms one of eight potential "Black Swan" events that could have worldwide effects on the power grid and other infrastructure. Major solar storms "could knock out satellites, the electric grid and many sensitive electronic devices, [and] until 'cures' are implemented,

[they] will pose a large-scale threat to the world's social and economic fabric."[26]

Scientists agree the so-called 1859 Carrington Event was the largest observed solar superstorm, but such events are "difficult to study, their rates of occurrence are difficult to estimate, and prediction of a specific future event is virtually impossible," according to a 2012 paper by Pete Riley, vice president and senior research scientist at Predictive Science, a San Diego research company.[27] The Carrington Event, named after a British scientist who studied it, destroyed undersea telegraphic cables and caused fires in telegraph stations and lines on several continents.[28]

The solar storms that caused a blackout in the Canadian province of Quebec in 1989 were much weaker than the Carrington Event. The National Academies of Sciences said that if a Carrington Event occurred today, it could cause massive blackouts and major damage to many electrical transformers and systems.[29]

The United States is especially vulnerable to such storms because the number of high-voltage transmission lines in the country has grown dramatically since 1960. Those lines "turned power grids into giant antennas for geomagnetically induced currents," according to NASA scientists. The surge of power could then reach substations and damage large transformers.

But NASA is working on a new system called Solar Shield that aims to help the electric industry avoid some of the worst effects of a solar storm. The experimental system would "zero in on specific transformers and predict which of them are going to be hit hardest by a space weather event," said Antti Pulkkinen, a scientist at NASA's Goddard Space Flight Center who is studying solar storms. Satellite data would help NASA predict when a solar storm would hit Earth, and utilities could temporarily disconnect at-risk transformers from the grid.[30]

Riley put the probability of a major solar storm over the next decade at about 12 percent, although he cautioned that this is just a loose estimate because of the many variables.

George H. Baker, a professor emeritus of applied science in the James Madison University science department, told Congress that the Department of Defense started protecting critical systems from naturally occurring GMDs and nuclear-bomb-generated EMPs in the 1960s, but that civilian power equipment "remain unprotected."[31]

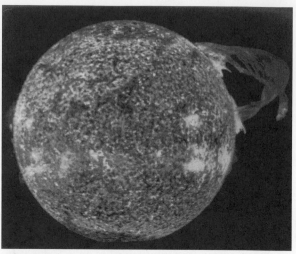

SSPL/Getty Images

Hackers, saboteurs or the detonation of a high-altitude nuclear bomb may not pose the only threats to the power grid. Massive electromagnetic pulses (EMPs) from solar flares can also cause major power outages. This huge solar flare, one of the most spectacular ever recorded, was photographed aboard the Skylab space station in December 1973.

Some experts call for widespread installation of protective devices, said Bridgette Bourge, senior principal, legislative affairs, at the National Rural Electric Cooperative Association. But "there is no consensus on precisely what measures should be taken, the unintended effects they might have on the system, how much such an effort would cost, or how successful such efforts would be in limiting impacts," she said.[32]

The Electric Power Research Institute, founded after a 1965 blackout that darkened the entire city of New York, is researching ways the industry can plan for or recover from severe solar storms. "I bristle at the assertion that the industry is moving too slowly on this," said the Edison Electric Institute's Aaronson. "Instead, we are moving deliberately to ensure the reliability of the electric grid."[33]

FERC has proposed new reliability standards, which the industry would have to meet to ensure its equipment operates during and after a solar storm.[34]

But FERC Commissioner Cheryl LaFleur said the work has been difficult "because we are working on a reliability threat that is not fully understood and as to which actual data are not readily and consistently available." The proposed rules include vulnerability assessments, installation of blocking devices and training.[35]

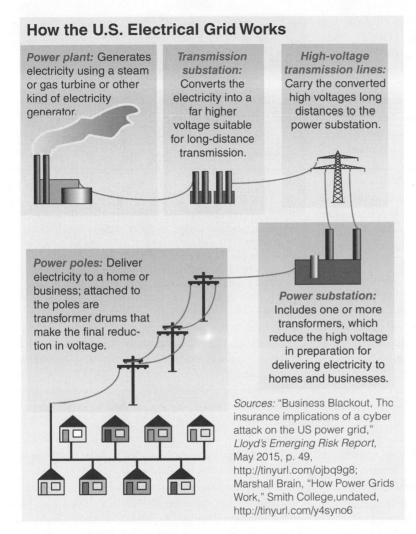

How the U.S. Electrical Grid Works

Power plant: Generates electricity using a steam or gas turbine or other kind of electricity generator.

Transmission substation: Converts the electricity into a far higher voltage suitable for long-distance transmission.

High-voltage transmission lines: Carry the converted high voltages long distances to the power substation.

Power poles: Deliver electricity to a home or business; attached to the poles are transformer drums that make the final reduction in voltage.

Power substation: Includes one or more transformers, which reduce the high voltage in preparation for delivering electricity to homes and businesses.

Sources: "Business Blackout, The insurance implications of a cyber attack on the US power grid," Lloyd's Emerging Risk Report, May 2015, p. 49, http://tinyurl.com/ojbq9g8; Marshall Brain, "How Power Grids Work," Smith College,undated, http://tinyurl.com/y4syno6

Should the primary responsibility for protecting the power grid lie with industry?

Government officials, the electric industry and security experts disagree over who is responsible for protecting the power grid from cyber and physical attacks.

Because most of the grid is privately owned, some say private industry should take the lead. "I don't think it's a government issue to fix," says Lee of Dragos Security. "Although there are a lot of passionate people [in government] and a lot of folks doing some good work, the government doesn't have any better insight — actually has worse insight" — than some private-sector security firms.

Others agree security is the electric industry's responsibility but say the industry hasn't acted strongly enough. "The electric industry is the problem. That is why we haven't made a lot of progress," says Pry of the Task Force on National and Homeland Security. Industry lobbyists have resisted proposed legislation and rules for increased security, he says, adding that government regulators don't have the kind of authority over the electric industry that, for instance, the Federal Aviation Administration has over private airlines.

But many people say the job is so big and complicated that both industry and government must work together to solve it. "Protecting America's core infrastructure [including the grid] requires commitment and actions by all stakeholders," said Sen. Ron Johnson, R-Wis. "The government and the private sector play key roles, but neither can ensure critical infrastructure protection alone."[36]

Others say numerous sectors beyond the electric industry must help improve reliability and security. "In a future where electric cars may connect to a Smart Grid . . ., securing the grid will require the attention not only of utility companies but also of consumers and the manufacturers of the car and its components," said the Center for the Study of the Presidency & Congress, a nonprofit in Washington that studies leadership. The center also called for "combining the resources of the private sector, the technical know-how of national labs and technology companies and the capabilities of government" to improve grid security.[37]

Federal officials have asked Silicon Valley companies to help create flexible, highly local systems that can connect to the broader grid, says Avi Gopstein, the smart-grid program manager for the National Institute of Standards and Technology.

Other solutions could come from the financial and insurance industries, according to the Center for the Study of the Presidency & Congress. "For example, the insurance underwriting process can serve as an opportunity to evaluate vulnerabilities, share information about threats and encourage best practices" to mitigate risk, the center said.[38]

Lee agrees that the military, government and industry need to share information, given that many threats originate overseas. But he says too much of the discussion is centered on cyberweapons.

"We've heard so much about cyber 9/11 and cyber Pearl Harbor" — surprise cyberattacks that could cause massive damage. "And none of that was actually the point," Lee says. "The entire point is, what technical people do we have that can adapt to a situation? I would say that your best [cyberdefenses] are your people."

Some politicians agree the government needs to work more efficiently with the electric and other key industries. "I can't tell you how many companies come to me and say, 'I can't even get in the door, I can't get access, I can't talk to the right person in the department,' " said Rep. Michael McCaul, R-Texas, chairman of the House Committee on Homeland Security.[39]

The Obama administration's National Cyber Incident Response Plan, a draft of which was released in late September and will be finalized in 2017 or later, seeks to improve communication among the various players and formulate a nationwide approach on how to respond to cyberattacks against the grid and other infrastructure. McCaul called the draft an "important step forward in clarifying the lead federal agencies and their roles and responsibilities for . . . responding to domestic cyberattacks."[40]

Suzanne Spaulding, an undersecretary at the Department of Homeland Security, said the department is seeking better ways to work with industry, as well as small businesses. "We are never going to solve the cybersecurity challenge that we confront today until we really take a holistic management approach to it," she said.[41]

Miller of Dragos Security says government agencies are "trying to help the sector, but at this point they're still trying to get self-organized on even knowing what the next step is" after a cyberattack.

But Robert Dix, a vice president at the IT company Juniper Networks, says the government is looking at cyberattacks from the wrong perspective. "The effort was to impose a FEMA-style model," similar to how the government responds to natural disasters. Cyberattacks "are

The National Security Agency's GenCyber program aims to train a new generation of IT security workers and teachers. In 2016, the agency held more than 100 free summer camps in 35 states, compared with 18 the year before. Nonprofit organizations and K-12 school systems are starting to host events. Above, middle school students in the GenCyber program visit the Spy Museum in Washington, D.C., last summer.

not the same," he says, because the first responder to a cyberattack is the private sector and not the government, unlike when a hurricane strikes.

"It's evidence of the lack of clarity and understanding by some of our government partners, as to how cyber works. They keep using the analogy of a fire. It's just not the same. A fire is localized," Dix says, but cyberattacks aren't. He says government agencies must be much more open to collaboration with industry.

Miller agrees that government and industry need to work together on cybersecurity but says there may be some fundamental limits. "At the end of the day, the government doesn't have visibility into what's going on in the private industry side," he says. "And industry doesn't know what's going on on the government side" as far as classified intelligence.

"So without those two linkages — and I'm not sure if there will ever be that sort of open collaboration between industry and government — the industry will know maybe they got attacks, but they won't know why or by who," he says.

BACKGROUND
Early Grid

In the 1870s an invention began to appear in cities, factories and homes around the world: electric lighting.[42]

Inventors, investors and business people across the globe were excited about the potential for electricity to replace the costly and at times dangerous natural gas that provided lighting in that era.

"Electricity promises to come to the rescue, and it will be welcomed with alacrity, if it can do what is claimed for it," *The New York Times* said in 1878, in an article about Thomas Edison's invention of an improved lightbulb.[43]

In the early years, individuals could purchase kits from Edison and other companies to electrify homes, businesses or small communities. As the technology evolved over the next two decades, "the remarkable capacity of electricity to produce good light gave way to the more awe-inspiring possibility of electric power" to run other devices in the home and in factories, cultural anthropologist Gretchen Bakke of Canada's McGill University noted.[44]

However, the power industry had to resolve a major technical question first, the resolution of which laid the groundwork for the modern, long-distance electric grid. Edison controlled patents and systems that used direct current (DC), which runs in one direction.[45] Rival inventor George Westinghouse, based in Pittsburgh, believed alternating current (AC) was superior, because it can change direction and was better suited to long-distance transmission. Westinghouse won out, and in 1896 an AC generating plant powered by Niagara Falls started sending electricity to Buffalo, 22 miles away.[46]

Even at that early stage of electric use, some people saw security issues. In 1903 one of the world's first hackers disrupted a London demonstration of wireless long-range communication. As a crowd waited for the test to begin, a projection lantern began to make rhythmic noises. A man named Nevil Maskelyne was sending his own wireless electromagnetic pulses into the theater, in Morse code. The word "rats" was repeated many times, then a mocking message directed at the scientist behind the demonstration. Maskelyne confessed to the hack a few days later in a newspaper letter, saying he did it to reveal the security flaws of the wireless method.[47] His point was that anyone could listen in to — or interrupt — a wireless transmission.

But the public and businesses embraced electricity. Cities, towns, factories and even streetcar companies began to install their own power-generating systems throughout the nation, mostly around cities. By 1913

New Yorkers leave Manhattan via the Brooklyn Bridge during the largest blackout in U.S. history on Aug. 14, 2003. Sagging power lines that brushed against trees in Ohio triggered the outage, leaving 50 million people in the Northeast without power for two days or longer. Thirty-eight years earlier, overloaded transmission lines caused a power failure that blacked out more than 80,000 square miles in the Northeastern United States, including New York City, for up to 13 hours.

Jonathan Fickies/Getty Images

about 200,000 Chicago homes had electricity, up from 5,000 in 1902.[48] During that era 70 percent of the electricity generated in the United States came from privately owned plants, and municipal power plants provided the remainder. But a major change was in the works.

"Within 20 years the eight largest utility holding companies in the United States controlled three-quarters of the electricity market," Bakke said. "Remarkably disparate interests, including advocates of municipal power networks, of public power projects, and even electricity cooperatives, were all convinced by the 1920s that the monopoly was the best way to manage the manufacture and sale of electric power."[49]

Large power companies such as Consolidated Edison, General Electric and Southern California Edison began to dominate the industry, but they still operated somewhat independently, at least as far as electricity production and transmission. Then in 1932, after controversies over utility practices, Democratic presidential candidate Franklin D. Roosevelt proposed regulating electric companies. "Electricity is no longer a luxury. It is a definite necessity," Roosevelt said.[50]

As president, Roosevelt did more than regulate power companies. He created powerful government-owned competitors that built their own regional grids serving primarily underserved rural areas. The Tennessee Valley Authority was created in 1933, and in 1936 the Rural Electrification Act was passed to help bring power to other rural areas.[51]

The First Crisis

For almost 60 years the U.S. power industry had seen nearly continuous growth. Then in September 1938, the Great New England Hurricane struck Long Island and other parts of the Eastern Seaboard and showed how quickly a storm could destroy large parts of the system. About 700 people died, almost 9,000 homes and other buildings were destroyed and a wind gust of 186 mph was recorded in Massachusetts.[52] Trees downed about 20,000 miles of power lines, one-third of New England lost telephone service and major rail lines between New York City and Boston were out of service for seven to 14 days.[53]

But the 1938 hurricane and related floods were natural events, and the damage was so widespread that the electric industry didn't come in for specific criticism.[54] Soon afterward, however, with the threat of world war looming, Roosevelt began planning a national power grid — a plan that went unrealized for many years.

"Power Grid Plans Told to President," *The New York Times* reported in March 1940. "Long-range plans [are] looking to the creation of a national electric power grid system connecting strategic munitions and manufacturing centers to implement national defense preparations . . . [and] to create a flexible transmission system capable of throwing the power reserves of one area into the productive capacity of another in event of a national emergency."[55]

The electric power industry grew bigger, more complicated and more connected in the first two decades after World War II. Nuclear generating plants came online, and major companies began automating operations with Supervisory Control and Data Acquisition (SCADA) systems.[56]

For decades human operators had needed to manipulate switches, levers or knobs to turn things on or off. SCADA systems began to handle those functions automatically. By the late 1960s many electric power companies had computerized their systems to boost efficiency and lower operating costs. Those same devices would later become pathways for casual or malicious hackers to enter the grid.

The power grid suffered occasional power blackouts during the 1950s and early '60s, but nothing to make the public question the fundamental way electricity was delivered.[57] That changed after the Northeast Blackout of 1965. On Nov. 9, a faulty relay on a transmission line in Ontario, Canada, started a power surge that cascaded through parts of nine states and almost all of New York City, triggering automatic shutdowns along the way.[58] About 25 million people over 80,000 square miles lost power, and newspapers devoted pages of coverage to the crisis, although most power was restored in hours or by the next day.

"The lights and power went out first at 5:17 p.m. Nobody could tell why for hours afterward," said one story. "Within four minutes the line of darkness had plunged across Massachusetts all the way to Boston. It was like a pattern of falling dominoes — darkness sped southward through Connecticut, northward into Vermont, New Hampshire, Maine and Canada."[59]

"Railroads halted. Traffic was jammed. Airplanes found themselves circling, unable to land," the story added, and hundreds of thousands of people were trapped in the New York subway system. Yet the public took it mostly in stride, with volunteers sometimes helping direct traffic. Politicians began seeking answers, and one headline read, "A Nationwide Grid Termed Solution."[60]

The North American Electric Reliability Council was formed in 1968 with the aim of ensuring reliable grid operations, yet solutions proved elusive. On July 14, 1977, lightning strikes and grid overloads caused another huge blackout in New York City, but unlike in 1965 chaos ensued, even though power was restored the next day. Authorities reported widespread looting, more than 3,400 arrests, 558 injured police officers, and millions of dollars in property damage and losses.[61]

As personal computers became available in the late 1970s and early '80s, a new threat to the power grid emerged: hacking. In 1983 the FBI caught a group of young hackers who had broken into computer systems at the Los Alamos National Laboratories and other institutions. Some were teenagers, others in their early 20s.

"We were really just looking around and playing games on these systems; we didn't want to harm anything," Timothy Winslow said later. Three of the

CHRONOLOGY

1870s-1900s *Inventors experiment with new ways to generate light and power from electricity.*

1882 Thomas Edison's first power plant begins operating in New York City, using direct current (DC).

1886 George Westinghouse perfects an alternating current system (AC), creating the possibility of long-distance electric transmission. Westinghouse and Edison compete for market share, and AC wins acceptance.

1896 A Niagara Falls, N.Y., plant transmits electricity over high-voltage lines to Buffalo, 20 miles away.

1903 A demonstration in London of wireless technology is disrupted when a hacker sends electromagnetic pulses into the theater to demonstrate security flaws.

1907 About 8 percent of American homes have electricity, and most power is generated by privately owned plants.

1920s-1940s *Large utility companies begin to dominate the marketplace.*

1928 The Federal Trade Commission begins to investigate power industry monopolies.

1933 President Franklin D. Roosevelt seeks national regulation of electric utilities, and Congress passes the Public Utility Holding Act in 1935. . . . The federal government creates the Tennessee Valley Authority to generate electricity.

1938 The Great New England Hurricane downs more than 20,000 miles of power lines, creating widespread blackouts.

1950s-1980s *The electric industry begins to use computers to manage power.*

1965 Overloaded transmission lines cause a power failure that blacks out more than 80,000 square miles across the Northeastern United States, including New York City, for up to 13 hours. The crisis inspires new calls for a national electric grid.

1989 Solar storm causes power failures throughout the Canadian province of Quebec.

1990s-2000s *Personal electronic devices and renewable energy enter the grid.*

1992 Energy Policy Act increases competition between electric companies. The law gives the Federal Energy Regulatory Commission authority over mandatory reliability standards.

1996 President Bill Clinton creates the Commission on Critical Infrastructure Protection, which lists the power grid as a vital national infrastructure.

1997 The National Security Agency conducts a war game code-named "Eligible Receiver," featuring simulated cyberattacks on military targets and the power grid in eight major cities, including Los Angeles and Chicago.

2003 Sagging power lines hit trees in Ohio triggering power failures and causing the largest blackout in U.S. history, leaving 50 million people in the Northeast without power for two days or longer.

2010s-Present *Government and industry struggle to manage increasing cyberattacks on the power grid.*

2010 U.S. Cyber Command begins operating as a new branch of the military.

2013 Snipers damage a Pacific Gas & Electric substation in California.

2014 Justice Department files criminal charges against five Chinese military hackers accused of stealing information from the U.S. nuclear power and solar industries.

2015 A cyberattack on Ukraine's power grid is attributed to Russian hackers.

2016 President Obama releases a draft Cybersecurity National Action Plan to guide federal and industry responses to major attacks against the grid and other targets (February). . . . An attacker fires three shots into a Utah transformer, knocking out power for about eight hours to 13,000 people (September).

Major Attack on Power Grid Could Be Devastating

Worst-case scenario includes health crisis, billions in economic losses.

What would happen if a coordinated cyberattack knocked out 50 key electric generators in the Northeast?

International insurer Lloyd's of London pondered the consequences: 93 million Americans would be without power, its 2015 report said. If the outage lasted two to three weeks, it continued, the failure of health and safety systems would lead to "a rise in mortality rates . . .; a decline in trade as ports shut down; disruption to water supplies as electric pumps fail; and chaos to transport networks as infrastructure collapses."[1]

Such an attack is improbable but "technologically possible," Lloyd's said, and the worst-case scenario could darken New York and other major cities, causing estimated economic losses of $243 billion — and more than $1 trillion for an attack that took out 100 generators.

A 2012 report from the National Research Council, a division of the National Academies of Sciences, Engineering and Medicine, said a carefully planned attack could deny power to large regions of the country for weeks or even months, leading to turmoil, widespread public fear and an image of helplessness that would play into the hands of adversaries.[2] And an attack during periods of extreme heat or cold could result in hundreds or thousands of deaths, the report said.

Experts say coordinated attacks on the grid could unfold in many different ways.

"[What] does it look like when the American power grid goes down and we try to bring it back up?" asks Robert Lee, co-founder of Dragos Security, a software and consulting company for the power industry and a former Air Force cyberwarfare operations officer. "There's all these questions that we can create models around, but we don't really know."

Power companies are preparing for all kinds of attacks or damage to the grid, says Scott Aaronson, executive director of security for the Edison Electric Institute, a major industry group. "We have always as an industry understood that we are operating critical infrastructure . . . that's critical to the life, health and safety of Americans," he says. "Within those first 24 or 48 hours, you may simply not know whether it was a cyber or a physical attack. But you do know that there was [a power outage] that we need to restore."

Power companies have long shared crews that repair downed power lines after major storms, he says, and now the industry has plans to share cyber computer experts who could help respond to or defend against attacks.

The Lloyd's report said many secondary effects from an attack or disaster could be devastating, too. People could be hurt in riots, or get sick from spoiled food or water when waste treatment facilities fail and pollute waterways.[3]

---

hackers were charged and later sentenced to probation and modest fines in a plea deal.[62]

Politicians and security professionals began to warn that a computer could be used much like "a gun, a knife or a forger's pen," and urged new laws against hacking.[63] In 1987 President Ronald Reagan signed the Computer Security Act, giving authority over security for non-military government computers to the National Institute for Standards and Technology. But the legislation didn't solve security concerns.

In March 1989 another unforeseen event highlighted the electric grid's vulnerability. Huge explosions on the sun with the power of thousands of nuclear bombs sent waves of magnetic energy toward Earth at 1 million mph.[64] Experts later determined that the magnetic currents found a weak spot in Quebec's electrical grid and in less than 2 minutes caused a 12-hour blackout in the entire province. Utilities in New York state and New England also had problems but were able to manage them.[65]

Difficulties in securing prescriptions, caring for the elderly or poor emergency response could "all contribute to a higher death rate in periods of power outage," Lloyd's said.[4]

Alan Crane, who directed the National Research Council report, said it is "the multiple attacks [on key infrastructures] that have the really scary consequences. Living without electricity is one thing. Living without water is something else."[5]

A commission established by Congress in 2001 to study the threats to the grid from electromagnetic pulses (EMP) said in a 2008 report that "should the electrical power system be lost for any substantial period of time . . . the consequences are likely to be catastrophic to civilian society. Machines will stop; transportation and communication will be severely restricted; heating, cooling and lighting will cease; food and water supplies will be interrupted; and many people may die."[6]

An EMP attack caused by the high-altitude detonation of a nuclear weapon could lead to nationwide damage to the grid and computer systems. A one-year nationwide blackout, the commission estimated, "could kill up to 9 of 10 Americans through starvation, disease and societal collapse."[7]

To head off such a scary outcome, the commission recommended close coordination between government and the power industry. "Government is responsible for protecting the society and its infrastructure, including the electric power system," from a nuclear attack, the report said. But if an enemy did succeed in detonating a bomb high over the United States, both the government and industry must be ready with national and regional plans to rapidly restore power, including the stockpiling of spare parts and expanding the availability of emergency power supplies.[8]

— Kevin Begos

A Tesla electric car recharges at a home in Los Angeles. A massive power failure could have dire consequences for civilians, experts say, including disrupted transportation, communication and food supplies.

Citizen of the Planet/Education Images/UIG via Getty Images

[1] "Business Blackout: The insurance implications of a cyber attack on the US power grid," *Lloyd's Emerging Risk Report*, 2015, http://tinyurl.com/hxdn3zh.

[2] "Terrorism and the Electric Power Delivery System," National Research Council, November 2012, http://tinyurl.com/zd6w9xd.

[3] "Business Blackout," *op. cit.*

[4] *Ibid.*

[5] Brian Wingfield and Jeff Bliss, "Thousands Seen Dying if Terrorists Attack U.S. Power Grid," Bloomberg, Nov. 14, 2012, http://tinyurl.com/huxyfq2.

[6] John Foster Jr. *et al.*, "Report of the Commission to Assess the Threat to the United States from Electromagnetic Pulse (EMP) Attack," Congressional EMP Commission, April 2008, p. 18, http://tinyurl.com/5v8vt2.

[7] Peter Pry, statement before the House Subcommittee on National Security, House Oversight and Government Reform Committee, May 13, 2015, http://tinyurl.com/zuqtawa.

[8] Foster Jr. *et al.*, *op. cit.*, pp. 53-56.

Deregulation

Congress passed the Energy Policy Act in 1992, seeking to increase competition among electric companies. The law encouraged new types of power generation, including renewables. It also enabled more companies to sell wholesale power, essentially bringing free-market competition to the grid.[66]

In 1996, President Bill Clinton signed an executive order creating the Commission on Critical Infrastructure Protection, which listed the power grid as a vital national system.[67]

During the 1990s, the U.S. military was detecting frequent hacks of its networks, and in 1997 the National Security Agency staged a war game code-named "Eligible Receiver." It featured simulated coordinated attacks on military targets and the power grid in eight major cities, including Los Angeles, Chicago and Tampa, Fla.[68] A briefing after the exercise, which successfully accessed numerous military computers, suggested that "the Defense Department was completely unprepared [for] and defenseless [against] a cyberattack."[69]

Renewable Energy Could Endanger Grid

"Lightly protected systems could . . . be all too easily infiltrated."

The future is arriving for the electric industry in the United States, with wind and solar power gaining in popularity and usage.

But industry and policy experts say this progress carries a risk: The renewable energy systems are just as susceptible to cyberattacks as traditional generators of power. And their vulnerability has security analysts worried because these new sources of power are connected to the electric grid and thus offer hackers a backdoor way into the main networks. Solar users, for example, sell their excess electricity to the power grid and rely on it as a backup supplier of electricity.

The expanding use of renewable energy is "part of the continual evolution of the grid, but there is a bit of a paradox here," says Scott Aaronson, executive director of security and business continuity at the Edison Electric Institute, an industry group in Washington that represents major electric companies. On the one hand, wind and solar are climate-friendly power sources that diversify and strengthen the U.S. energy supply. Yet they offer additional targets for hackers and another way for them to disrupt the power grid, he says.

Security flaws are already turning up in some renewable energy systems. Frederic Bret-Mounet, an information security officer at McKesson, a San Francisco IT company,

reported that he was able to hack into the solar energy system for his California home over a weekend because of flaws in the software. Then he realized it was possible to shut down safety controls and access other systems in thousands of homes because they were linked by cloud-based computing.

"I could have installed spying software that would have had visibility into their home networks, seeing their emails and everything they did online," Bret-Mounet said.[1]

Because California aims to get 50 percent of its electricity from renewable sources by 2030, he said, "these lightly protected systems could then be all too easily infiltrated, possibly with catastrophic effects on the state's power grid."

The Manhattan Institute, a free-market think tank in New York City, agrees that the nation's turn to renewable energy is making the power grid more susceptible to cyberattacks. In a June report, it urged the industry to slow the turn to wind and solar "until adequate cybersecurity features are available and incorporated."[2]

But Jon Wellinghoff, the former head of the Federal Energy Regulatory Commission, said growth in renewable sources such as rooftop solar panels might actually improve overall grid security. Utilities tend to "invest in security and improvements surrounding the plants they control as opposed to valuing the sort of investments consumers

In January 2000 Clinton announced a National Plan for Information Systems Protection.[70] It noted that the United States depends more on computer networks than any other nation, and that attacks "could crash electrical power grids, telephone networks, transportation systems, and financial institutions." Clinton directed that a plan to protect the nation's computer systems take effect by December 2000 and be fully operational by May 2003.

The plan didn't meet those timelines, partly because the power grid is largely privately owned and operated. "The president and Congress can order federal networks to be secured, [but] they cannot and should not dictate solutions for private-sector systems," Clinton adviser Richard Clarke said.[71]

More warnings about the grid's vulnerability followed the Sept. 11, 2001, terrorist attacks on the World Trade Center in New York and the Pentagon in Northern Virginia.

But hacking continued. In August 2003, the biggest blackout in American history left 50 million people in the Northeast without power for up to two days. Regulators reported that sagging power lines brushing trees had caused transmission lines in Ohio to divert power to other areas. An alarm system failed, and a rolling series of overloads resulted.[72] Investigators later blamed human errors and equipment failures and called for stronger, enforceable industry standards.

A month after the blackout, FBI Executive Assistant Director Larry A. Mefford told Congress that while there

would make," he said. And, Wellinghoff said, "it is basically impossible to hack 10 million solar power systems."[3]

Another researcher reported that hackers could access electric-car charging stations and prevent their use, and perhaps even enter the grid and cause damage. "Essentially a charging station is a computer on the street. And it is not just a computer on the street, but it is also a network on the street," said Ofer Shezaf, a security expert at HP ArcSight, a security company in Sunnyvale, Calif., owned by Hewlett-Packard. Multiple charging stations are grid-connected to manage power access and distribution, so "if somebody finds a way to confuse the smart-car charging system, the denial of service can not only hit charging cars but also the electricity system."[4]

Suzanne Lightman, a senior information security adviser at the National Institute of Standards and Technology (NIST), a physical science laboratory that is part of the Department of Commerce, says electric cars are an example of a bigger shift in the electric grid.

"We see crossover with domains that previously had nothing to do with each other," she says. For example, auto manufacturers never had to consider the impact of their vehicles on the grid before electric cars came along. NIST, Lightman says, is working with cloud-computing providers and other IT sectors on security enhancements.

— Kevin Begos

High-voltage transmission lines pass through a wind farm near Ellsworth, Kan. As wind and solar power gain in popularity, experts warn that renewable energy sources are just as susceptible to cyberattacks as traditional power sources.

AP Photo/Charlie Riedel

---

[1] Elizabeth Weise, "Solar panels, vacation Wi-Fi at risk for hacking," *USA Today*, Aug. 2, 2016, http://tinyurl.com/j2ha7aa.

[2] Mark P. Mills, "Exposed: How America's Electric Grids Are Becoming Greener, Smarter — and More Vulnerable," The Manhattan Institute, June 2016, http://tinyurl.com/jqvphod.

[3] Chip Register, "Former FERC Chief Jon Wellinghoff Speaks Out on Grid Security and Distributed Generation," *Renewable Energy World*, Feb. 9, 2015, http://tinyurl.com/zqm3h23.

[4] Loek Essers, "Hackers could start abusing electric car chargers to cripple the grid, researcher says," *Computerworld*, April 11, 2013, http://tinyurl.com/zztowjf.

---

was no evidence of sabotage, "terrorists could choose a variety of means to attack the electrical power grids . . . ranging from blowing up power wire pylons to [carrying out] major attacks against conventional or nuclear power plants." Al Qaida and other terrorist groups, Mefford said, had considered targeting energy facilities.[73]

Growing Threats

More than 40 years after the 1965 Northeast blackout, officials were still warning about power grid vulnerabilities. In 2009 a former Department of Homeland Security official said Chinese and Russian hackers had attempted to map the electrical grid and that their cyber intrusions were growing. But officials also noted a paradox: China relies on U.S. consumers to buy many of its products, so in theory it shouldn't want to disrupt the American power supply and harm the American economy.[74]

Russian and Chinese officials denied they were behind the intrusions. "These are pure speculations," said Yevgeniy Khorishko, a spokesman at the Russian Embassy in Washington. "Russia has nothing to do with the cyberattacks on the U.S. infrastructure."[75]

In 2010 reports began to emerge that a sophisticated cyberattack had targeted specialized machines used in Iran's nuclear program in what experts call the first successful major cyberattack on a nation's power system. Nearly 1,000 centrifuges were destroyed. Several news

Win McNamee/Getty Images

Adm. Michael S. Rogers, director of the National Security Agency and commander of the U.S. Cyber Command, testifies before a congressional committee in September 2015. "Energy firms and public utilities in many nations have had their networks compromised" by cyberattacks from foreign states, he said.

reports, citing anonymous intelligence sources, said the cyberattack was a joint U.S.-Israeli operation that began during the George W. Bush administration. Iran blamed the United States and Israel for the attacks, but those nations did not officially respond.[76]

Other incidents caused alarm, too. In 2013 snipers opened fire on the Pacific Gas & Electric substation in Metcalf, Calif. A former Federal Energy Regulatory Commission chairman said it was the United States' "most significant incident of domestic terrorism involving the grid." A former PG&E official said it was a "well-thought-out, well-planned" attack that targeted specific parts of the substation, which housed key transformers for the region.[77]

In 2014 the Justice Department for the first time filed criminal charges against specific Chinese military hackers accused of stealing information from U.S. nuclear power, solar and other industries. They also were accused of transmitting computer code "with the intent to cause damage."[78] Since they do not live in the United States, however, they have never been arrested.

About a dozen times in the last decade, according to The Associated Press, "sophisticated foreign hackers have gained enough remote access to control" power grid networks in the United States. Unknown hackers in 2013 and possibly earlier entered the systems of Calpine Corp.,

a utility that operates in 18 states, and took "detailed engineering drawings of networks and power stations from New York to California — 71 in all — showing the precise location of devices that communicate with gas turbines, boilers and other crucial equipment."[79]

Homeland Security Deputy Secretary Alejandro Mayorkas said the country was "not where we need to be" on grid security, and The Associated Press article summarized the core problem: "Many of the substations and equipment that move power across the U.S. are decrepit and were never built with network security in mind."[80]

CURRENT SITUATION
More Coordination

The Obama administration is moving on several fronts to protect the grid and other essential infrastructure.

In July, Obama signed a presidential directive as part of the National Cyber Incident Response Plan, outlining which federal agencies will respond to cyberattacks on the grid or other key infrastructure. The Department of Justice will lead investigations, while the Department of Homeland Security will provide guidance and help the target "find the bad actor on its system [and] repair its system" and try to prevent the incident from spreading.[81] In September, Obama appointed retired Gen. Gregory J. Touhill to be the federal government's first chief information security officer; Touhill's job, according to the White House, is "to drive cybersecurity policy, planning and implementation across the federal government."[82]

But some private-sector experts said the presidential directive left too many questions unanswered. "I don't see how that's really going to work," said French Caldwell, a senior executive at MetricStream, an IT and security company. "There's no real clear organizational changes, [and] the establishment of sort of an emergency response capability, it seems like that's very ad hoc."[83]

Some members of Congress are proposing a retroactive approach. In June, Sens. Susan Collins, R-Maine, Martin Heinrich, D-N.M., and two other members of the U.S. Senate Intelligence Committee introduced The Securing Energy Infrastructure Act, aiming to protect the grid by replacing "key devices like computer-connected operating systems that are vulnerable to cyberattacks" with old-fashioned human-operated systems.[84]

Is the electrical grid vulnerable to a major attack?

YES

Peter Vincent Pry
Executive Director, Task Force on National and Homeland Security

Written for *CQ Researcher*, November 2016

The electric grid is vulnerable to attack from several vectors that could inflict a protracted nationwide blackout — lasting months or years — and kill millions of Americans from starvation and societal collapse.

The congressional EMP Commission and the congressional Strategic Posture Commission both concluded independently that terrorists or rogue states — armed with a single nuclear weapon — could use a missile, aircraft or balloon to make a high-altitude electromagnetic pulse (EMP) attack that would destroy the electric grid. The EMP Commission warns, because all life-sustaining critical infrastructures depend upon electricity, that a nationwide blackout lasting one year could kill 90 percent of the population.

North Korea's KMS-3 and KMS-4 satellites orbit the United States on a trajectory optimized to evade missile defenses and, if they are nuclear-armed, generate an EMP covering North America.

Adm. Michael Rogers, director of the National Security Agency and the U.S. Cyber Command, testified before Congress on Nov. 20, 2014, that China or Russia could launch a cyberattack that would black out the U.S. grid for more than a year.

The U.S. Federal Energy Regulatory Commission found that attackers using rifles or explosives against nine key transformer substations could black out the U.S. grid for 18 months. Terrorists caused nationwide blackouts in Yemen (2014) and Pakistan (2015).

The EMP Commission, NASA and the National Academies of Sciences warn that a natural EMP catastrophe from a solar superstorm, such as the 1859 Carrington Event, is inevitable. Such a storm would black out electric grids worldwide and put the lives of billions at risk.

In 2008, the EMP Commission made recommendations to shield the grid from all these threats by protecting against the worst one — a nuclear EMP attack. The protections in place for an EMP attack would also mitigate the impact from solar storms, sabotage, cyberattacks and severe weather. Among the commission's recommendations were installing surge arrestors and other devices that protect transformers and generators.

Yet little or nothing is being done. Why?

The North American Electric Reliability Corp. and the electric power industry lobby to defeat any initiative to protect the electric grid, producing "junk science" studies that minimize or dismiss threats.

Unfortunately, because policymakers and the press are largely scientific illiterates, they don't know who to believe, and so nothing is being done.

NO

Scott Aaronson
Executive Director, Edison Electric Institute

Written for *CQ Researcher*, November 2016

It's not surprising that the energy grid is a target for adversaries of the United States. Electric companies take their responsibility to protect our nation's most critical infrastructure very seriously, as we know that threats to the grid can impact the life, health and safety of all Americans.

To that end, the industry employs a "defense-in-depth" strategy that includes rigorous, mandatory and enforceable reliability regulations for cyber and physical security; close coordination among industry and government partners; and resilience efforts that include preparations to respond to, and recover from, any incident that affects grid operations.

While electric companies are best equipped to protect their systems, it is the government that has the intelligence-gathering capabilities and law enforcement responsibilities the industry needs to make informed decisions about security. In other words, industry and government must work together to protect critical infrastructure that is largely owned by the private sector.

The president's National Infrastructure Advisory Council views the CEO-led Electricity Subsector Coordinating Council — the principal liaison between leadership in the federal government and the electric power sector — as a model for how critical infrastructure sectors can partner most effectively with senior government officials to improve security, deploy resources and enhance preparedness.

Together, industry and government continue to develop a suite of technologies to enable near real-time sharing of cyber threat data. Through the newly developed Cyber Mutual Assistance program, the industry now has the ability to leverage cyber expertise from across the sector in response to cyber incidents.

Electric companies also hold exercises on emergency situations. Since November 2015, the industry has participated in five national-level exercises, including the GridEx III, which brought together more than 360 organizations and 4,400 participants from industry and state and federal agencies.

There are always ways to improve, and our industry will continue to invest billions in our infrastructure to further strengthen the security and resiliency of the grid. For instance, we are now leading an effort with the communications and financial services sectors to develop a Strategic Infrastructure Coordinating Council that will identify mutual priorities, conduct joint exercises and share information more effectively.

We will continue to work with our government and partners to ensure that our communities have a reliable electricity supply and our nation's most critical infrastructure is protected.

The Edison Electric Institute's Aaronson sees "some cases where we can operate manually" but says there are no simple or single answers to the multiple threats the industry faces.

Pry of the Task Force on National and Homeland Security says several states, including Florida, Maine and Texas, have moved to protect their shares of the grid beyond any federal requirements by calling for companies to institute stronger protections against cyber and other attacks.

Industry Priorities

Liz Dalton, a principal deputy assistant secretary at the Department of Energy, says the department is "pressing the cybersecurity component of all the work we've been funding." DOE has awarded $3.4 billion in grants to help the electric industry accelerate new technologies to make the grid more reliable, and all those projects have a security component.

Dalton says the department also has an office that works on security with Silicon Valley companies that make software or products that tie into the grid.

Aaronson says the power grid faces so many potential threats that "one of the things that we have to focus on is not preventing or defending against every incident, but looking at ways to more effectively respond [to] and recover" from any problems that do arise.

The industry is ranging widely for ideas on how to protect the grid, Aaronson says, such as the visit to the Sandia National Laboratories in New Mexico that electric company CEOs made this year. The industry hopes to apply lessons the government has learned protecting nuclear assets to the electric sector, he says.

Lee, a security expert who worked on Air Force cyber programs, says inaccurate assessments have sometimes led discussions on grid security astray. "Folks have made it sound super easy to take down the power grid for longer, and it's just not. But they've also made it sound very difficult to take down the power for a couple of days, which it's not," Lee says. "So right in the middle somewhere is where we live."

Knocking power out nationwide for a long term would take nation-state resources and years of planning, he says. But statewide attacks are more feasible, Lee continues. "How long could you take off Florida? Well, you could take off Florida from the power grid for like six

months without a whole hell of a lot of effort. And that's where people start realizing, maybe we've got bigger issues than we thought," he says.

Aaronson and other industry executives dispute the idea that sections of the grid could be taken down for an extended period of time, short of all-out war. "I disagree with the premise that we would be in a situation where we would have to deal with a months-long outage," Aaronson said, noting that even after major outages such as the 2003 Northeast blackout, most power was restored in days.[85]

But a major cyber or physical attack on the grid could include other targets, Lee says. "If we're talking about a wartime scenario, it's multiple attacks in multiple dimensions, and it's also the attackers sticking around" to try to take out the grid and other key systems that rely on technology.

For example, in March, hackers unleashed a virus against Southern California hospitals that encrypted medical data so doctors and staff couldn't access it. The hackers demanded payment to unlock the information, but the hospital said it solved the problem without doing so.[86] Then in April, a cyberattack on the Newark Police Department in New Jersey forced authorities to use a backup system for emergency calls for three days.[87] In October, the Obama administration officially said the Russian government was behind the recent hacking of the Democratic National Committee and other U.S. political organizations.[88]

Yukiya Amano, director general of the International Atomic Energy Agency, disclosed in October that cyberattackers targeted a nuclear power plant two or three years ago. He declined to say where the attack took place. "This actually happened and it caused some problems," Amano said, adding while the plant did not have to shut down, it "needed to take some precautionary measures."[89]

"This issue of cyberattacks on nuclear-related facilities or activities should be taken very seriously. We never know if we know everything or if it's the tip of the iceberg," Amano said.

Some analysts say the focus on cyberattacks or natural events misses another key threat. "The foreign cyber threat is not just about computer viruses and hacking," says Pry of the Task Force on National and Homeland Security: Russia, China, North Korea and Iran are preparing for cyberwar.

Booming Security Business

After the Nebraska Municipal Power Pool installed special devices to monitor unauthorized access, it recorded nearly 4 million attempts over eight weeks, including viruses, malware and reconnaissance by hackers. The N-Sentinel devices monitor computer network traffic, rank the incursions by seriousness of threat and alert administrators to those needing the most urgent attention.[90]

But some say spending large amounts of money on security isn't necessarily the answer. "The real problem isn't money but mindset," said Arthur Herman, a senior fellow at the Hudson Institute, a conservative Washington, D.C., think tank that researches domestic and foreign policy. "In cyberwar terms, we've been pouring money and resources into a World War I-style, trench-warfare defensive strategy, while cyberattackers large and small" practice fast, flexible blitzkrieg-style attacks.[91]

Ross of the National Institute of Standards and Technology said in recent testimony before a presidential commission that "our fundamental cybersecurity problems today can be summed up in three words — *too much complexity*," because more software and hardware give adversaries more things to attack. Industry and government, he said, need to work on multiyear projects to develop a national strategy for a new, secure infrastructure system.[92]

Ted Koppel, the former network television newscaster who wrote a book about electric grid vulnerabilities, says part of the challenge is that many politicians and government security experts have "a dozen different alligators nipping at their rear end," such as the Islamic State or other traditional terrorist threats. "And here you come along and say, 'Well, there's a very real danger that the electric power grid can be taken down.' It's just not at the top of their list."

OUTLOOK

Rogue States

With the threat from cyberattack or natural disasters expected to grow in the next few years, some experts say various forces could help inspire change.

Suzanne Lightman, a senior information security adviser at the National Institute of Standards and Technology, says there is a "difference between securing what we see coming in the future and securing what already exists," and that experts are working on both current grid issues and future ones.

Republican President-elect Donald Trump agrees that aggressive action is needed. "We have to get very, very tough on cyber and cyberwarfare. It is — it is a huge problem," Trump said during the first presidential debate.[93]

National Security Agency chief Rogers told Congress that "the states that we watch most closely in cyberspace remain Russia, China, Iran and North Korea. Russia has very capable cyber operators who can and do work with speed, precision and stealth. Russia is also home to a substantial segment of the world's most sophisticated cyber criminals."[94]

The U.S. military is enlarging both offensive and defensive cyber budgets, and Secretary of Defense Ash Carter projects spending almost $35 billion in those areas over the next five years. Projects include training ranges for cybercombat and developing tools and infrastructure for offensive cyber operations.[95]

Gopstein, the institute's smart-grid program manager, says that in the past most computers didn't have powerful enough processors to incorporate good cybersecurity. That is changing, and the electric grid will be significantly different as a result, he says. "Computational capability has increased so dramatically and come down in price so significantly" that computer power doesn't limit security anymore, he says. In theory, Gopstein says, both the grid and IT in general should have much stronger security.

But security expert Weiss of Applied Control Systems says investors, not politicians or the energy industry, will inspire radical changes. "Once Wall Street and the insurance companies start realizing how big a risk they have, things are going to change. And it isn't the government that's going to do it. It's going to be people that have their money at risk," he says. "We live in the biggest glass house of all. We are the most dependent of almost any country in the world on automation and computers," and that translates into financial risk.

The National Security Agency's GenCyber program aims to train a new generation of IT security workers and teachers. In 2016 the agency planned 133 free summer camps in 35 states, compared with 18 the year before. Nonprofit organizations and K-12 school systems are also starting to host events.

"Cyber threats are real, constant and always changing," said Tina Ladabouche, NSA's GenCyber program manager. "We are committed to helping the nation enhance cybersecurity education — providing opportunities for both teachers and students to learn more about an issue that affects all of us and will continue to do so in the future."[96] The agency plans to expand the program to 200 camps by 2020.

But some experts say cyberattacks will just become another aspect of modern life. "There may be a perception that if only government or companies paid more attention these attacks could be thwarted," said Pradeep Khosla, a cybersecurity expert and the chancellor of the University of California, San Diego. "In my mind, this perception is both incorrect and dangerous as it provides a false sense of security. I believe there is no notion of a 100 percent cyber-secure system."[97]

Pry of the Task Force on National and Homeland Security says that Russia, China, Iran and other hostile nations will keep expanding their cyber abilities, partially because such programs are cheaper than building high-tech planes or ships.

Regardless of what the United States' adversaries do, he adds, one threat will always lurk over the horizon: the sun and the major electromagnetic storms that it can cause. "There's no negotiating with the sun," Pry says.

NOTES

1 "N-Dimension Used by NMPP Energy to Protect Joint Action Agency against Cybersecurity Threats," *BusinessWire*, March 17, 2015, http://tinyurl.com/hslmwpa.

2. Jeff St. John, "Finding the Hidden Cyber Threats in the Power Grid," *GreenTech Media*, April 1, 2015, http://tinyurl.com/hmj45l3.

3. Rebecca Smith, "How America Could Go Dark," *The Wall Street Journal*, July 14, 2016, http://tinyurl.com/gtw2crt.

4. Adm. Michael Rogers, statement before the House Committee on Armed Services, Sept. 30, 2015, http://tinyurl.com/zhnr76p.

5. Adm. Michael Rogers, "Cybersecurity Threats: The Way Forward," testimony before the House Select Intelligence Committee, Nov. 20, 2014, http://tinyurl.com/hy2e23k.

6. @Cybersquirrel1, "The Threat to America's Electrical Grid is Much Bigger Than You Can Possibly Imagine. But It's Not Russian hackers you should be worried about," *Foreign Policy*, July 31, 2016, http://tinyurl.com/jmb8daw.

7. Jeff St. John, "Report: US Smart Grid Cybersecurity Spending to Reach $7.25B by 2020," *GreenTech Media*, April 17, 2013, http://tinyurl.com/jzrdy2b; "What is the Smart Grid?" smartgrid.gov (undated), http://tinyurl.com/zoh3gpk.

8. "January 2016 Cybersecurity Snapshot US Results," ISACA, January 2016, http://tinyurl.com/zz9bwbo; Justin McCarthy, "Americans Cite Cyberterrorism Among Top Three Threats to U.S.," Gallup Poll, Feb. 10, 2016, http://tinyurl.com/hc5zzj2.

9. Richard Campbell, "Blackout! Are we Prepared to Manage the Aftermath of a Cyber-Attack or Other Failure of the Electrical Grid?" testimony before the House Committee on Transportation and Infrastructure, April 11, 2016, http://tinyurl.com/hywzs9z.

10. Rebecca Smith, "How America Could Go Dark," *The Wall Street Journal*, July 14, 2016, http://tinyurl.com/gtw2crt.

11. Rep. Mike Rogers, R-Mich., "House Intelligence Committee Open Hearing on Advanced Cyber Threats Facing Our Nation Chairman Rogers Opening Statement," Nov. 20, 2014, http://tinyurl.com/zehfxxr.

12. "Fact Sheet: Cybersecurity National Action Plan," The White House, Feb. 9, 2016, http://tinyurl.com/hgdzfw6; Ron Ross, testimony before the Commission on Enhancing National Cybersecurity, 2016, http://tinyurl.com/j8zcuw4.

13. Chris Currie, testimony before the House Subcommittee on Oversight and Management Efficiency, Committee on Homeland Security, May 17, 2016, http://tinyurl.com/zeucdok.

14. "Critical Infrastructure Protection," U.S. Government Accountability Office, April 25, 2016, http://tinyurl.com/z6org7p.

15. "The Grid," Full Measure, Oct. 30, 2016, http://tinyurl.com/hqrlk75.

16. "Quadrennial Energy Review First Installment: Transforming U.S. Energy Infrastructures in a Time

of Rapid Change," Department of Energy, April 2015, http://tinyurl.com/z4mhfpm.

17. Paul W. Parfomak, "Physical Security of the U.S. Power Grid: High-Voltage Transformer Substations," Congressional Research Service, June 17, 2014, http://tinyurl.com/h56thzv.

18. Rebecca Smith, "Assault on California Power Station Raises Alarm on Potential for Terrorism," *The Wall Street Journal*, Feb. 5, 2014, http://tinyurl.com/oe55uc7.

19. "Followup on Western Area Power Administration's Critical Asset Protection," audit report, Department of Energy, April 2016, http://tinyurl.com/goo4u2n.

20. "Spare Transformers," information page, the Edison Electric Institute, undated, http://tinyurl.com/h59z27y.

21. "Quadrennial Energy Review First Installment," *op. cit.*

22. Pat Reavy, "Power company offers rare $50K reward for information on vandalism," *Deseret News*, Sept. 29, 2016, http://tinyurl.com/ze46pss.

23. Ernest Moniz, Testimony Before the Senate Committee on Energy & Natural Resources, Seattle, Washington, Aug. 15, 2016, http://tinyurl.com/zx86g65.

24. "Climate Change and the U.S. Energy Sector," Department of Energy, October 2015, http://tinyurl.com/nb55cfk.

25. "What are solar storms and how do they affect the Earth?" NASA, undated, http://tinyurl.com/2tgzfp.

26. "Global Trends 2030: Alternate Worlds," National Intelligence Council, December 2012, http://tinyurl.com/z3hvdct.

27. Pete Riley, "On the probability of occurrence of extreme space weather events," Space Weather, Feb. 23, 2012, http://tinyurl.com/gwydtt3.

28. Peter Pry, "The EMP Threat: The State of Preparedness Against the Threat of a Electromagnetic Pulse (EMP) Event," statement before the Subcommittee on National Security, May 13, 2015, http://tinyurl.com/gksnkyf.

29. "Solar Shield, Protecting the North American Power Grid," NASA, Oct. 26, 2010, http://tinyurl.com/ju2229r.

30. *Ibid.*

31. George H. Baker, "The EMP Threat: The State of Preparedness against the Threat of an Electromagnetic Pulse (EMP) Event," testimony to the House Committee on National Security, May 13, 2015, http://tinyurl.com/zz55euy.

32. Bridgette Bourge, testimony to the Committee on Homeland Security and Governmental Affairs, July 22, 2015, http://tinyurl.com/gkqetpp.

33. Jenni Bergal, "States Work to Protect Electric Grid," Pew Charitable Trusts, Feb. 27, 2015, http://tinyurl.com/oevjakx.

34. "2014 Status of EPRI Geomagnetic Disturbance Research and Future Plans," Electric Power Research Institute, Nov. 10, 2014, http://tinyurl.com/znnkuer.

35. Rich Heidorn Jr., "FERC Takes Next Step on GMD Standard," *RTO Insider*, May 18, 2015, http://tinyurl.com/hynd4dk.

36. Ron Johnson, "Assessing the Security of Critical Infrastructure: Threats, Vulnerabilities, and Solutions," opening statement, Senate Committee on Homeland Security and Governmental Affairs, May 18, 2016, http://tinyurl.com/jznk3og.

37. "Securing the U.S. Electrical Grid," Center for the Study of the Presidency and Congress, October 2014, http://tinyurl.com/zyqwt3e.

38. *Ibid.*

39. Meredith Somers, "Texas lawmakers call for DHS to strengthen industry friendship, finalize cyber plans," Federal News Radio, Sept. 16, 2016, http://tinyurl.com/h2c99mk.

40. Peter Behr, "White House Moves to Finish National Cyberattack Recovery Plan," *E&E News*, July 27, 2016, http://tinyurl.com/zd6ho3a; "National Cyber Incident Response Plan," draft, U.S. Computer Emergency Readiness Team, Sept. 30, 2016, http://tinyurl.com/zuwu3xa.

41. Somers, *op. cit.*

42. "The History of Electrification," Edison Tech Center, undated, http://tinyurl.com/nrcvkng.

43. "The Electric Light," *The New York Times*, Oct. 30, 1878, http://tinyurl.com/zzhp7v7.

44. Gretchen Bakke, *The Grid: The Fraying Wires Between Americans and Our Energy Future,* Bloomsbury Publishing (2016), Kindle Location 711.

45. "The War of the Currents: AC vs. DC Power," Energy.gov, Nov. 18, 2014, http://tinyurl.com/p87flex.

46. "Gilbert King, "Edison vs. Westinghouse: A Shocking Rivalry," Smithsonian.com, Oct. 11, 2011, http://tinyurl.com/nqeq6qt; Bakke, *op. cit.*

47. Paul Marks, "Dot-dash-diss: The gentleman hacker's 1903 lulz," *New Scientist,* Dec. 20, 2011, http://tinyurl.com/hwg6u8u.

48. Bakke, *op. cit.*

49. *Ibid.*

50. For background see Jennifer Weeks, "Modernizing the Grid," *CQ Researcher,* Feb. 19, 2010, pp. 145-168.

51. Weeks, *op. cit.*

52. "The Great New England Hurricane of 1938," National Weather Service, http://tinyurl.com/zyx245t.

53. Patricia Grossi, "The 1938 Great New England Hurricane, Looking to the Past to Understand Today's Risk," Risk Management Solutions, 2008, http://tinyurl.com/jgcxoyj.

54. Warren Moscow, "Floods Add Peril to New England," *The New York Times,* Sept. 23, 1938, http://tinyurl.com/jc62uqs.

55. "Power Grid Plans Told to President," *The New York Times,* March 26, 1940, http://tinyurl.com/zymbynf.

56. Jerry Russell, "A Brief History of SCADA/EMS," personal website, undated, http://tinyurl.com/h9ubdsf.

57. Bakke, *op. cit.*

58. "Northeast Is Hit by Blackout," *The Learning Network, The New York Times,* Nov. 9, 2011, http://tinyurl.com/me62drq.

59. Peter Kihss, "Snarl at Rush Hour Spreads Into 9 States," *The New York Times,* Nov. 10, 1965, http://tinyurl.com/jhbtq4h.

60. Gene Smith, "A Nationwide Grid Termed Solution," *The New York Times,* Nov. 10, 1965, http://tinyurl.com/zw6dwmw.

61. Owen Moritz, "Looters prey on city during the blackout of 1977," *Daily News,* reprinted July 12, 2015, http://tinyurl.com/zfyp4e6.

62. Timothy Winslow, "I hacked into a nuclear facility in the '80s. You're welcome," CNN, May 3, 2016, http://tinyurl.com/pfwon8n.

63. "Timeline: The U.S. Government and Cybersecurity," *The Washington Post,* May 16, 2003, http://tinyurl.com/55lodj.

64. Sten Odenwald, "The Day the Sun Brought Darkness," NASA, March 13, 2009, http://tinyurl.com/czs6wa.

65. *Ibid.*

66. "Summary of the Energy Policy Act," U.S. Environmental Protection Agency, http://tinyurl.com/zxordbu.

67. "Timeline: The U.S. Government and Cybersecurity," *op. cit.*

68. Fred Kaplan, "Inside 'Eligible Receiver,'" *Slate,* March 7, 2016, http://tinyurl.com/z6o85rl.

69. *Ibid.*

70. "National Plan For Information Systems Protection," Executive Summary, http://tinyurl.com/zkpp5yt; President William Clinton, "Remarks on the National Plan for Information Systems Protection and an Exchange With Reporters," Jan. 7, 2000, http://tinyurl.com/zc5ga3r.

71. "Defending America's Cyberspace," The White House, Jan. 7, 2000, http://tinyurl.com/j3weqqt.

72. J.R. Minkel, "The 2003 Northeast Blackout — Five Years Later," *Scientific American,* Aug. 13, 2008, http://tinyurl.com/h3h84aw.

73. Larry A. Mefford, "Testimony Before the Subcommittee on Cybersecurity, Science, and Research and Development," FBI, Sept. 4, 2003, http://tinyurl.com/zzfv2x7.

74. Siobhan Gorman, "Electricity Grid in U.S. Penetrated By Spies," *The Wall Street Journal,* April 8, 2009, http://tinyurl.com/z8yzly2.

75. Gorman, op. cit.

76. Ellen Nakashima and Joby Warrick, "Stuxnet was work of U.S. and Israeli experts, officials say," *The Washington Post,* June 2, 2012, http://tinyurl.com/hyes4rx.

77. Steve Johnson, "Experts: sniper attack on PG&E site points to power grid's vulnerability to terrorism," *The Mercury News*, Feb. 5, 2014 (updated Aug. 12, 2016), http://tinyurl.com/he985hl.

78. "U.S. Charges Five Chinese Military Hackers for Cyber Espionage," press release, Department of Justice, May 19, 2014, http://tinyurl.com/jnlyrlt.

79. Garance Burke and Jonathan Fahey, "US power grid vulnerable to foreign hacks," The Associated Press, Dec. 21, 2015, http://tinyurl.com/hdwh6sa.

80. *Ibid.*

81. Homeland Security Secretary Jeh C. Johnson, statement Regarding PPD-41, Cyber Incident Coordination, July 26, 2016, http://tinyurl.com/j4yzt9b.

82. Dustin Volz, "White House names retired Air Force general as first cyber security chief," Reuters, Sept. 9, 2016, http://tinyurl.com/jkvjby6; "Announcing the First Federal Chief Information Security Officer," The White House, Sept. 8, 2016, http://tinyurl.com/zll5eeu.

83. Jory Heckman, "White House cyber response plan raises further questions," Federal News Radio, Aug. 19, 2016, http://tinyurl.com/gteneo3.

84. "Collins, King, Risch, Heinrich Introduce Legislation to Protect Electric Grid from Cyber-Attacks," press release, website of Sen. Susan Collins, June 6, 2016, http://tinyurl.com/hmx7dwx.

85. Bill Loveless, "An attack on the grid? Power execs push back on Koppel claims," *USA Today*, June 5, 2016, http://tinyurl.com/gp2kcdb.

86. W.J. Hennigan and Brian Bennett, "Criminal hackers now target hospitals, police stations and schools," *Los Angeles Times*, April 8, 2016, http://tinyurl.com/j4erxhc.

87. Andrew Blake, "Newark police forced to go offline after cyberattack: report," *The Washington Times*, April 18, 2016, http://tinyurl.com/jsspfau.

88. Ellen Nakashima, "U.S. government officially accuses Russia of hacking campaign to interfere with elections," *The Washington Post*, Oct. 7, 2016, http://tinyurl.com/gq7hmkf.

89. "IAEA Chief: Nuclear Power Plant Was Disrupted by Cyber Attack," Reuters, Oct. 10, 2016, http://tinyurl.com/hk2h4t2.

90. Jeff St. John, "Finding the Hidden Cyber Threats in the Power Grid," GreenTech Media, April 1, 2015, http://tinyurl.com/hdy8xwk.

91. Arthur Herman, "Wanted: A Real National Cyber Action Plan," *National Review*, Feb. 11, 2016, http://tinyurl.com/zblj9yc.

92. Ross testimony, *op. cit.*

93. Presidential debate transcript, *The New York Times*, Sept. 27, 2016, http://tinyurl.com/zoa4n6m.

94. Michael Rogers, statement before the Senate Armed Services Committee, April 5, 2016, http://tinyurl.com/zefdwdz.

95. "Remarks by Secretary Carter on the Budget at the Economic Club of Washington, D.C.," U.S. Department of Defense, Feb. 2, 2016, http://tinyurl.com/hj3vfmg.

96. "NSA GenCyber Camps Triple In Offerings," press release, National Security Agency, May 18, 2016, http://tinyurl.com/z5v8alu.

97. Gary Robbins, "Public yawns at threat of cyber crime," *The San Diego Union-Tribune*, Sept. 5, 2016, http://tinyurl.com/zfre269.

BIBLIOGRAPHY
Selected Sources
Books

Bakke, Gretchen, *The Grid: The Fraying Wires Between Americans and Our Energy Future*, Bloomsbury USA, 2016.
A cultural anthropologist explores how the electric grid has shaped American society and examines the rise of renewable energy and the dramatic changes it is causing.

Chen, Thomas, *Cyberterrorism After Stuxnet*, U.S. Army War College, 2014.
A professor of engineering and internet security examines the cyberterrorism threat before and after Stuxnet, the cyberattack on Iran's nuclear program.

Koppel, Ted, *Lights Out: A Cyberattack, A Nation Unprepared, Surviving the Aftermath*, Crown, 2015.
The former host of the ABC news show "Nightline" investigates the threat of a major cyberattack on the nation's power grid.

Schewe, Phillip F., *The Grid: A Journey Through the Heart of Our Electrified World*, Joseph Henry Press, 2007.

A physicist examines the history of the electric grid, including widespread blackouts.

Articles

Burke, Garance, and Jonathan Fahey, "AP Investigation: US power grid vulnerable to foreign hacks," The Associated Press, Dec. 21, 2015, http://tinyurl.com/gph2rpb.

An Associated Press investigation finds that sophisticated foreign hackers have gained access to the U.S. power grid more than a dozen times over the past decade.

Gertz, Bill, "FBI warns of cyber threat to electric grid," Fox News, *Washington Free Beacon*, April 11, 2016, http://tinyurl.com/gsttjpb.

The FBI and the Department of Homeland Security begin a nationwide program to warn power companies about threats to the electric grid.

Gorman, Siobhan, "NSA Director Warns of 'Dramatic' Cyberattack in Next Decade," *The Wall Street Journal*, Nov. 20, 2014, http://tinyurl.com/z8mzqxv.

The director of the National Security Agency warns about cyber threats to networks that run critical U.S. infrastructure.

Perez, Evan, "U.S. official blames Russia for power grid attack in Ukraine," CNN, Feb. 11, 2016, http://tinyurl.com/gn9nyor.

In a case closely studied by U.S. intelligence officials, Russia was possibly behind a cyberattack on Ukraine's power grid.

Robbins, Gary, "Public yawns at threat of cyber crime," *The San Diego Union-Tribune*, Sept. 5, 2016, http://tinyurl.com/zfre269.

Most members of the public aren't alarmed by news of possible cyberattacks, experts say.

Smith, Rebecca, "U.S. Risks National Blackout From Small-Scale Attack," *The Wall Street Journal*, March 12, 2014, http://tinyurl.com/qdlfwsf.

A study finds that coordinated attacks on the nation's three major electric grids could derail the entire power network.

Reports and Studies

"Analysis of the Cyber Attack on the Ukrainian Power Grid," Electricity Information Sharing and Analysis Center, March 18, 2016, http://tinyurl.com/gnfmx69.

Researchers analyze the December 2015 cyberattacks on the Ukrainian electric systems and discuss the lessons for the U.S. electric industry.

"Attribution, Delayed Attribution and Covert Cyber-Attack: Under What Conditions Should the United States Publicly Acknowledge Responsibility for Cyber Operations?" Naval Postgraduate School, March 2014, http://tinyurl.com/hau9vdd.

A military historian examines the reasons a nation-state would publicly acknowledge its role in a cyberoperation against the grid and other targets.

"Business Blackout, The insurance implications of a cyber attack on the US power grid," *Lloyd's Emerging Risk Report*, July 6, 2015, http://tinyurl.com/hxdn3zh.

An international insurance company looks at the implications of major cyberattacks on the U.S. electric grid.

"Securing the U.S. Electrical Grid," Center for the Study of the Presidency and Congress, March 2014, http://tinyurl.com/zyqwt3e.

A nonpartisan think tank in Washington examines short- and long-term prospects for securing the electrical grid and makes policy recommendations.

"The Smart Grid and Cybersecurity — Regulatory Policy and Issues," Congressional Research Service, 2011, http://tinyurl.com/hptetqf.

A study by Congress' research division explores possible cyber vulnerabilities in smart-grid technology and considers related federal policies.

"World War C: Understanding Nation-State Motives Behind Today's Advanced Cyber Attacks," *FireEye*, 2014, http://tinyurl.com/jqhexkr.

A private security firm describes government-run cyberattacks, using examples from around the world.

For More Information

Edison Electric Institute, 701 Pennsylvania Ave., N.W., Washington, DC 20004-2696; 202-508-5000; www.eei.org/. Represents investor-owned U.S. electric companies serving 220 million people nationwide.

Federal Energy Regulatory Commission, 888 First St., N.E., Washington, DC 20426; 1-866-208-3372; www.ferc .gov. Federal agency that oversees the interstate sale and transmission of electricity, natural gas and oil.

North American Electric Reliability Corp., 1325 G St., N.W., Suite 600, Washington, DC 20005; 202-400-3000; www.nerc.com. Not-for-profit corporation that works to ensure the reliability of the power system in North America.

U.S. Cyber Command, National Security Agency, 4409 Llewellyn Ave., Fort Meade, MD 20755; 301-677-2300; https://www.stratcom.mil/factsheets/2/Cyber_Command/. Guards military information networks, supports combat missions around the world and defends the nation against cyberattacks.

U.S. Office of Electricity Delivery and Energy Reliability, Department of Energy, 1000 Independence Ave., S.W., Washington, DC 20585; 202-586-1411; http://energy.gov/ oe/office-electricity-delivery-and-energy-reliability. Promotes modernizing the electric grid and improving the system's reliability.